HENRY BRADSHAW SOCIETY

founded in the Year of Our Lord 1890
for the editing of Rare Liturgical Texts

VOLUME CXVI

ISSUED TO MEMBERS FOR THE YEAR 2005
AND
PUBLISHED FOR THE SOCIETY
BY
THE BOYDELL PRESS

HENRY BRADSHAW SOCIETY

for the editing of rare liturgical texts

Enquiries concerning membership of the Society should be addressed to the Hon. General Secretary, D. F. L. Chadd, School of Art History & Music, University of East Anglia, Norwich NR4 7TJ.

THE SACRAMENTARY OF RATOLDUS

(Paris, Bibliothèque nationale de France, lat. 12052)

Edited by

Nicholas Orchard

LONDON
2005

First published for the Henry Bradshaw Society 2005
by The Boydell Press
an imprint of Boydell & Brewer Ltd
PO Box 9, Woodbridge, Suffolk IP12 3DF, UK
and of Boydell & Brewer Inc,
668 Mt. Hope Avenue, Rochester, NY 14620, USA
website: www.boydellandbrewer.com

ISBN 1 870252 22 5

ISSN 0144–0241

A CIP catalogue record for this book is available
from the British Library

This publication is printed on acid-free paper

Printed in Great Britain by
Cromwell Press Trowbridge Wiltshire

CONTENTS

PUBLICATION SECRETARY'S PREFACE

Ratoldus, abbot of Corbie from about 972 until his death in 986, gave his name to the remarkable and complex liturgical book, now Paris, Bibliothèque nationale de France, lat. 12052, which was written under his supervision by three scribes whose writing has been dated to the third or fourth quarter of the tenth century. Although it is known as the Sacramentary of Ratoldus, the codex is actually a combined sacramentary and pontifical, a rare species, of which only four other complete examples survive (an edition of one of these, Oxford, Bodleian Library, Bodley 579, better known as the 'Leofric Missal', Nicholas Orchard has only lately toiled over for the Society, vols CXIII–CXIV). Precisely which bishop or archbishop was to have been the recipient of the book is a fact now past recovery, as is the reason why it may never have reached that intended recipient, or was sent straight back to Corbie again upon receipt (where additions were made quite soon after its completion, and on into the eleventh century). Yet what can be established with some certainty is the often surprising range of sources for the materials that were drawn together on Ratoldus's behalf, by scribes who seem at times to have found the complex knitting they were required to do almost beyond them. The sacramentary draws on one which started out at Saint-Denis in Paris, but then acquired later accretions successively reflecting the interests of Dol in Brittany, Orléans, and Saint-Vaast. Such a journey can be pieced together from evidence offered by the calendar and the masses included in the sanctoral, but also from the often tangled web of affiliations with other already localised liturgical books. The pontifical tells an equally intriguing story, and one with the utmost importance for students of the liturgy of Anglo-Saxon England, since it drew upon a pontifical from Canterbury, just possibly taken to the continent by Oswald, nephew of Archbishop Oda of Canterbury (941–58). The Canterbury material in the pontifical offers precious earlier testimony to texts otherwise found only in eleventh-century English liturgical books, notably the 'Second English Coronation Order', of which this manuscript preserves the oldest continental copy. Substantial excerpts from the pontifical in particular were already available in print by the start of the eighteenth century. Almost as complex as the textual archaeology of the Sacramentary of Ratoldus is the tale of its journey into print in full for the first time, since the present project has passed through the hands of four scholars, including a former President and a Vice-President of the Henry Bradshaw Society. The fascinating twists and turns of both its modern fate and its tenth-century creation are here set out with admirable clarity and exhaustive detail by Nicholas Orchard, whose edition of the Sacramentary of Ratoldus the Society takes great pleasure in publishing as vol. CXVI for the year 2005.

Rosalind Love,
for the Publications Committee
April 2005

PREFACE

Twice in the latter half of the twentieth century, Paris, Bibliothèque nationale de France, lat. 12052, the sacramentary of Ratoldus, abbot of Corbie (d. 986), almost found its way into print. Initially its editor was to have been Louis Brou, monk of Quarr Abbey, Vice-President of the Henry Bradshaw Society, and a liturgist of enormous erudition. He is perhaps best known now for his editions of the Mozarabic antiphoner, the Psalter Collects, and Ordinal of Saint-Vaast, though there is much, much more.[1] So far as one can tell, Brou carried the work of producing the edition of *Ratoldus* some way forward. With Christopher Hohler's assistance, a microfilm was acquired; photographs were printed up (by the Photographic Department of the Courtauld Institute of Art, where Hohler was then based); and a transcript and typescript prepared in turn from those. The lengthy and arduous business of typing up the text fell to John (J. B. L.) Tolhurst, president of the Society. But Brou, alas, did not live to see the project through, and the work seems to have passed thereafter to Derek Turner and J. Longuet des Diguères.[2] If progress was actually made – Turner did signal publically in 1971 that things were underway – their efforts unfortunately never came to fruition either and Brou's photos and typescript were eventually deposited with the Henry Bradshaw Society, along with a folder of correspondence. I am grateful to Michael Lapidge for making this material available to me, and to the Society for permission to publish extracts. Monique Cohen of the Bibliothèque nationale de France kindly granted me access to the manuscript, and I should also like to thank Ron Baxter, Richard Gameson, David Ganz, Helen Gittos, Christopher Jones, Sarah Keefer, Peter Kidd, Rosalind Love, the staffs of the British Library, the Bodleian Library, and numerous others for their help and advice. All errors are my own.

---

[1] See Dom Henry Ashworth's short obituary notice in *EL* 75 (1961), 356–61.
[2] Indicated by D. H. Turner, *The Claudius Pontificals*, HBS 97 (London, 1971), p. xxxi, note 1.

ABBREVIATIONS

ASE	*Anglo-Saxon England*
CCSL	Corpus Christianorum series Latina (Turnhout)
CLLA	K. Gamber, *Codices Latini Liturgici Antiquiores*, Spicilegia Friburgensis Subsidia, 2nd ed. (Fribourg, 1969), and Supplement (1988)
DACL	*Dictionnaire d'archéologie chrétienne et de liturgie*, ed. F. Cabrol and H. Leclercq, 30 vols in 15 (Paris, 1907–53)
Delisle, 'Mémoire'	L. V. Delisle, 'Mémoire sur d'anciens sacramentaires', *Mémoires de l'Academie des inscriptions et belles-lettres* 32.i (Paris, 1886)
Deshusses, *Le sacramentaire grégorien*	*Le sacramentaire grégorien*, ed. J. Deshusses, 3 vols, Spicilegium Friburgense 16, 24 and 28, 2nd ed. (Fribourg, 1979–85)
Duine, *Inventaire*	F. Duine, *Inventaire liturgique de l'hagiographie bretonne*, La Bretagne et les pays celtiques 16 (Paris, 1922)
EL	*Ephemerides Liturgicae*
HBS	Henry Bradshaw Society Publications (London)
Hohler, 'Some service-books'	C. Hohler, 'Some service-books of the Anglo-Saxon Church', in *Tenth Century Studies*, ed. D. Parsons (Leicester, 1975), pp. 60–83, and 217–27
JTS	*Journal of Theological Studies*
Leroquais, *Les pontificaux*	V. Leroquais, *Les pontificaux manuscrits*, 4 vols (Paris, 1937)
Leroquais, *Les sacramentaires*	V. Leroquais, *Les sacramentaires et les missels manuscrits*, 4 vols (Paris, 1924)
Martène, *AER*	E. Martène, *De antiquis ecclesiae ritibus*, 2nd ed. (Antwerp, 1736–48)
Martimort, *La documentation liturgique*	A. G. Martimort, *La documentation liturgique de dom Edmond Martène*, Studi e Testi 279 (Vatican City, 1978)

Ménard, *Liber sacramentorum*	H. Ménard, *Diui Gregorii papae huius nominis primi, cognomento magni liber sacramentorum* (Paris, 1642), reprinted in PL 78, cols 25–240
Ménard, *Notae*	H. Ménard, *Notae et obseruationes in librum sacramentorum Sancti Gregorii Magni Papae I* (Paris, 1641), reprinted in PL 78, cols 263–602
MGH	Monumenta Germaniae Historica
SS	Scriptores
Netzer, *L'introduction*	V. Netzer, *L'introduction de la messe romaine sous les carolingiens* (Paris, 1910)
OR	*Les ordines romani du haut moyen âge*, ed. M. Andrieu, 5 vols, Spicilegium Sacrum Lovaniense 11, 23, 24 , 28 and 29 (Louvain, 1931–61)
PL	Patrologia Latina, ed. J. P. Migne, 221 vols (Paris, 1844–64)
Quentin, *Les martyrologes*	H. Quentin, *Les martyrologes historiques du moyen âge* (Paris, 1908)
Rasmussen, *Les pontificaux*	N. K. Rasmussen (and M. Haverals), *Les pontificaux manuscrits du haut moyen âge, genèse du livre de l'évêque*, Spicilegium Sacrum Lovaniense 49 (Paris, 1998)
RB	*Revue Bénédictine*
RGP	*Le pontificale Romano-Germanique du dixième siècle*, ed. C. Vogel and R. Elze, 3 vols, Studi e Testi 226, 227 and 269 (Vatican City, 1963–72)

INTRODUCTION

Paris, Bibliothèque nationale de France, lat. 12052, the sacramentary of Ratoldus, abbot of Corbie, takes its name from an entry added over an erasure in the calendar on 15 March:

> Abbatis domni stat mentio sancta Ratoldi
> Istum qui fecit scribere quippe librum
>
> Blessed mention is here made of Dom Ratoldus, abbot
> who caused the present volume to be written

It is not possible to determine what stood underneath. Facts about Ratoldus are hard to come by. He became abbot of Corbie c. 972, oversaw the return of lands appropriated during the 940s, attended several councils, and died in 986. His abbacy was evidently a good one. For not only was the anniversary of his death commemorated at the order of Maingaudus, his successor, with a splendid meal (*optimam refectionem*) at the church of Saint-Quentin-de-Tourmont, but obituary notices were entered in a mid-tenth-century calendar from Corbie, now in St Petersburg, though the entry is out by one day (14 Mar.); and in the original portions (fols 4–16) of a twelfth-century Corbie martyrology now Paris, Bibliothèque nationale de France, lat. 12410. There is also a record at the end of a late-eighth-century copy of the Acts of the Apostles, an addition of the late tenth century, of the versified inscription on his tomb.[1]

---

[1] The St Petersburg book was first described by K. Gillert, 'Lateinische Handschriften in St Petersburg', *Neues Archiv der Gesellschaft für ältere deutsche Geschichtskunde*, Fünfter Band, Drittes Heft 5 (1880), 243–65, at 255. Its calendar is printed by A. Staerck, *Les manuscrits latins conservés a la bibliothèque impériale de Saint-Petersbourg*, 2 vols (St Petersburg, 1910) I, 205–13, but unfortunately later additions are not always signalled properly in his printed text. For the inscription, see E. Dummler, 'Aus Handschriften', *Neues Archiv* 5 (1880), 621–36, at 622, with D. Ganz, *Corbie in the Carolingian Renaissance*, Beihefte der Francia 20 (Sigmaringen, 1990), p. 146. The martyrology is ed. L. d'Achery, *Spicilegium sive Collectio veterum aliquot scriptorum qui in Galliae bibliothecis detulerant*, 2nd ed., 3 vols (Paris, 1723) II, 1–23, and discussed briefly in *DACL* 3.ii, cols 2929–30. On the relevant Corbie charters, see L. Levillain, *Examen critique des chartes mérovingiennes et caroliniennes d'abbaye de Corbie* (Paris, 1902),

Assuming that the Corbie scribe who added the lines to BNF lat. 12052's calendar was not simply inventing the connexion, and there is no reason to believe that he was, the question naturally arising is: why, precisely, did Ratoldus have the volume made? For his own use, the community's, or for another purpose entirely? The first two can be ruled out immediately. BNF lat. 12052 is a bishop's or archbishop's book. Episcopal benedictions appear in the mass formularies throughout, and an extensive series of pontifical *ordines* are provided at relevant junctures too. Not only that. As Christopher Hohler indicated in 1975, the book as we have it today is evidently the result of a careful working together of the contents of two quite separate sets of texts: a sacramentary from Saint-Denis that had been successively brought into line with the liturgical 'use' of the cathedral of Dol in Brittany, the abbey church of Saint-Symphorien at Orléans, and Saint-Vaast's at Arras; and a pontifical drawn up at Canterbury in the tenth century. The effect, as one might expect, was the creation of a book according to the formal 'use' of nowhere. But *Ratoldus* can hardly have been produced as a sort of speculative venture. The manner in which the pontifical was worked into the sacramentary and augmented with purely continental texts tends to suggest that the book was intended for actual use by some northern French bishop, perhaps even archbishop.

Ratoldus's role in all this is likely therefore to have been that of 'supervisor', gathering together the materials from which BNF lat. 12052 was to be created, that is to say the sacramentary and English pontifical, and ensuring that the complex task of turning at least two sets of text into one went smoothly – all perfectly within the meaning of the words *istum qui fecit scribere quippe librum*: and the book was obviously important enough for Ratoldus's part to be mentioned. Something, however, seems to have gone wrong, and instead of finding its way into the hands of its prospective owner, BNF lat. 12052 either remained at, or was passed back to Corbie, where it was added to in pretty quick order. The ex-libris inscription on fol. A recto shows that it remained at Corbie in later centuries.

pp. 193, 303–4, nos 41–2, printed from Paris, Bibliothèque nationale de France, lat. 13908, the late-tenth-century copy of the Statutes of Adalhard. BNF lat. 13908 also contains a note (fol. 25v) stating that Ratoldus arranged for dole to be distributed on the feast of St Matthew in honour of the return of the village of Dompierre. Françoise Gasparri, 'Le *scriptorium* de Corbie', *Scrittura e civiltà* 15 (1991), 289–305, notes (at 301) that 'A la fin du Xe siècle l'abbé Ratoldus commanda plusieurs livres.' I have failed to find any references to other books, however.

In 1638, however, circumstances changed, and *Ratoldus* was transferred along with many other volumes from the abbey's library to the
library of the Congregation of Saint-Maur at Saint-Germain-des-Près,
where it was first given the shelfmark '587', then, after a rearrangement
of the collection in the late seventeenth or early eighteenth century,
'287'. On folio B recto we have the inscription *Sancti Germani a Pratis*,
and lower down, *287, olim 587*. Shelved to its left for a time was the
so-called 'Missale sancti Eligii' (no. 286), a mid-ninth-century
sacramentary also from Corbie, now Paris, Bibliothèque nationale de
France, lat. 12051; and to its right (no. 288), a late-tenth- or early-eleventh-century sacramentary from the abbey of Saint-Méen in Brittany,
now Paris, Bibliothèque nationale de France, lat. 11589, a book closely
related to *Ratoldus* from a textual standpoint, as we shall see. One can
get an idea of the splendour of Saint-Germain's situation and the position of its library from the engraving of 1683 published by Achille
Peigné-Delacourt in the *Monasticon Gallicanum*.[2]

Finally, in 1795–6, six or so years after the foundation's suppression,
Ratoldus passed to the Bibliothèque Nationale (recast as the
Bibliothèque nationale de France in 1994), where it was catalogued in
the 1860s by Léopold Delisle as MS latin 12052, the shelfmark it bears
today.[3]

2 On the manuscripts of Corbie at Saint-Germain, see L. V. Delisle, *Le Cabinet des
Manuscrits de la Bibliothèque Nationale*, 3 vols in 4 (Paris, 1868–81) II, 40–58, 139–41,
and for BNF lat. 12052, III.i, 274, with III.ii, plate XXXI.2, which reproduces by
heliogravure part of the preface in the order for the consecration of a priest (fol. 92r). For
the engraving, *Monasticon Gallicanum. Collection de 168 planches de vues
topographiques représentant les monastères de l'ordre de Saint-Benoît, Congrégation de
Saint-Maur*, ed. A. Peigné-Delacourt (Paris, 1871), plate 74, which is reproduced by M.
Ultee, *The Abbey of St Germain des Près in the Seventeenth Century* (New Haven, 1981),
frontispiece.
3 See L. V. Delisle, *Inventaire des manuscrits latins conservés à la Bibliothèque
Nationale sous les numéros 8823–18613*, 5 parts (Paris, 1863–71) II, 34, with H. Omont,
*Concordance des numéros anciens et des numéros actuels des manuscrits latins de la
Bibliothèque Nationale* (Paris, 1903), pp. 86, 186.

HISTORY OF THE MANUSCRIPT IN PRINT

Thanks principally to the pioneering efforts of several generations of Maurists, almost all of Saint-Germain, *Ratoldus* has been exceedingly fortunate in print. Taking things in chronological order:

1641–2: an extensive series of excerpts published by Dom Hughes (sometimes Nicolas-Hughes) Ménard in the form of notes to his edition of the book that he (wrongly) took to be the most complete copy of the Gregorian Sacramentary to have come down to us, that is to say, Paris, Bibliothèque nationale de France, lat. 12051, the 'Missale S. Eligii'. The parts he published in full are: the *ordo missae*; the coronation order; the hymn *Tellus ac aethra* with its notation, both text and music engraved in facsimile; the mass for the translation of St Martin; the *ordo defunctorum*; the litany attached to the forms for the ordination of church officers; and the order for the visitation of the sick. A number of other *ordines* were given in complete or partial synopsis, notably those for Holy Week, the dedication of a church, Ash Wednesday and Maundy Thursday, and the ordinations of church officers, particularly the bishop.[4] Believing *Ratoldus* to be of the use of Corbie, Ménard generally only recorded the prayers of its temporal and sanctoral when they differed from the ones assigned in BNF lat. 12051.

1655: the forms for the election and consecration of a bishop given in full by Dom Jean Morinus, a priest of the Oratory at Paris, in his *Commentarius de Sacris Ecclesiae Ordinationibus*.[5] Morinus also made several observations about the book as a whole, something that Ménard had eschewed. He noted first that the couplet on 15 March appeared to

---

[4] Ménard, *Liber sacramentorum*, 259–66, 278–85; *Notae*, esp. 76–7, 86–7, 91, 131–2, 169, 188–208, 221, 231–2, 262–4, 271, 284, 290–302, 308–9, 313–14, 336–9. Ménard's extracts (later reprinted in PL 78) proved to be of enduring value. See, for instance, D. Giorgio, *De liturgia Romani pontificis in solemni celebratione missarum*, 3 vols (Rome, 1744) III, 18–19, 136, 146, 183–4, 212, with J. A. Jungmann, *The Mass of the Roman Rite. Its Origins and Development* (Missarum Sollemnia), transl. F. A. Brunner, 2 vols (New York, 1950) I, 92, 202 n.3, 272 n.4, 278 n.11, 281 n.30, 291 n.3, 312 notes 3 and 8, 325 n.26; II, 12 n.62, 74 n.23, 78 n.11, 79 n.15, 163 n.21, 260 n.7, 266 n.35, 295 n.13, 296 n.15, 320 n.47, 323 n.12, 324 n.16, 333 n.5, 336 n.22, 345 notes 9 and 11, 346 n.14, 387 n.99, 438 n.7.

[5] J. Morinus, *Commentarius de sacris ecclesiae ordinationibus*, 1st ed. (Paris, 1655), pars II, 299–308. A second edition appeared at Antwerp in 1695 (pp. 243–52).

be an addition 'by another hand, and in a different ink' (*sed alia manu, alioque atramento*); and second, drew attention to the fact that 'Albion' was twice mentioned in the coronation order. For Morinus, the mention of 'Albion' could mean only one thing, namely that order had been assembled and copied out (along with the rest of the book) at some point during the lifetime of Louis IV d'Outremer, who had returned from exile at Aethelstan's court in 936 to accept the crown of France, dying in 955; and with a view to explaining how one observation related to the other, Morinus ingeniously went on to suggest that the book had been written at Corbie before 955, doubtless at the instigation of Ratoldus who was not, at the time, abbot. For whatever reason, the inscription had been added later: *Videtur tamen esse nonnihil uetustior, aut saltem Ratoldum abbatis dignitate diu potitum esse, et statim a dignitate adepta librum hunc describi curasse.*

1688: the mass in honour of St Samson (28 July) printed as an appendix to the life of the saint in Luc d'Achéry and Jean Mabillon's *Acta Sanctorum ordinis Sancti Benedicti*. D'Achéry and Mabillon also referred to *Ratoldus*'s calendar in their editions of the lives of saints connected with Arras.[6]

1681: three short passages of text presented by Mabillon in engraved facsimile: the rustic capitals of the title page of the sacramentary (fol. 44r); the Memento of the living in the Canon of the Mass (fol. 46v); and the inscription naming Ratoldus in the calendar (fol. 36r). Mabillon's only comment of any real note was that the scribe of the manuscript sometimes represented the dipthong *ae* as *e* caudata, and sometimes spelled it out.[7]

1706: having reprinted the *ordo missae* and the order for the coronation of the king and queen a few years earlier (1700), Dom Edmond Martène publishes BNF lat. 12052's mass in honour of St Benedict (21 Mar.) for the first time in his *Tractatus de antiqua Ecclesie disciplina in diuinis celebrandis officiis.*[8]

---

6 L. d'Achéry and J. Mabillon, *Acta Sanctorum ordinis sancti Benedicti in saeculorum classes distributa,* 7 vols in 9 (Paris, 1668–85) I (*Saeculum I*), 185–6, 472, for the mass for St Samson, and for the entry in the calendar relating to St Hadulf. The mass was reprinted in *Acta Sanctorum Julii* VI, ed. J. B. Sollerius, J. Pinius, G. Cuperus and P. Boschius (Antwerp, 1729), p. 597.

7 J. Mabillon, *De re diplomatica libri VI*, 2 vols (Paris, 1681–1704) I, 366–7, Tab. XII, no. 2.

8 E. Martène, *Tractatus de antiqua Ecclesie disciplina in diuinis celebrandis officiis*

1717: an edition of the calendar printed by Doms Martène and Ursinus Durand, the latter a member of the Congregation of Saint-Maur at Marmoutiers, in their *Thesaurus novus anecdotum*.[9] All in all the text they gave (entries and days of the month only) was accurate and clearly laid out. Later additions to the calendar were indicated in italics. By some misfortune, however, *quippe* became *beatum* in the inscription mentioning Ratoldus. As far as the calendar's textual history was concerned, Martène and Durand had absolutely no doubt: it was a copy of a calendar from the abbey of Saint-Vaast at Arras, with St Vedastus's name in capitals, and entries for the saint's two translations (one with an octave), for the feast of the dedication of the abbey, and for other bishops of Saint-Vaast's. The entries relating to Corbie, all in black ink, were later but still old.[10]

Also to be classed as 'early report', are the short comments on the book included by Dom Pierre Grenier (d. 1789) in his two volume history of Corbie, a work that only found its way into print in 1910.[11] Although Grenier seems to have relied heavily on the observations of Martène, Durand and Morinus, he did have two of his own to contribute: first, that the feasts connectable with Saint-Vaast's had not only been written in capitals, they were in vermillion too; second, that two other Corbie books appeared, in certain respects, to be related: Corbie MS 53, now Amiens, Bibliothèque municipale 155, an early-eleventh-century missal (though he called it a psalter), which he took to have an *ordo missae* similar to *Ratoldus*'s; and Saint-Germain MS 288, now BNF lat. 11589, which he took to be similar on a more general level.[12] Of the two propositions, only the second is really sustainable, though as we shall see BNF lat. 11589 has no connexion with Corbie whatsoever.

(Lyon, 1706), p. 527. For editions of the other two sets of texts, see his *De antiquis ecclesie ritibus*, 1st ed. (Rouen, 1700–2), Bk I, cap. iv, art. xii, ordo 9, and Bk II, cap. x, ordo 4, with Martimort, *La documentation liturgique*, p. 97, no. 106.

[9] E. Martène and U. Durand, *Thesaurus novus anecdotum*, 5 vols (Paris, 1717) III, cols 1593–1604.

[10] *Ibid.*, col. 1547.

[11] The manuscript draft was long accessible, however, as BNF, Collection dom Grenier, vols 32 and 47. Levillain, *Examen critique*, p. xii, says, a trifle tartly perhaps: 'Dom Grenier, le dernier venu des historiens de Corbie, a largement mis à profit les travaux des ses davanciers et a fait une lourde et ennuyeuse compilation qu'il rédigea deux fois presque entièrement sans que la seconde rédaction apportât des reseignements nouveaux ou des vues personelles.'

[12] P. Grenier, *Histoire de la ville et du comte de Corbie (des origines a 1400)*, 2 vols (Paris, 1910) I, 214–15, 218.

At any rate, by the second decade of the eighteenth century substantial sections of the pontifical embodied in BNF lat. 12052 had been put into print: and that is more or less how the position remained until 1888, the year in which Léopold Delisle, keeper of the Department of Manuscripts in the Bibliothèque Nationale, published in his *Mémoire d'ancien sacramentaires*, extracts from the Canon of the Mass, and the calendar complete with its columns of Golden Numbers and signicative letters, elements that Martène and Durand had omitted. Investigation showed, moreover, that the series of gradings supplied by a later hand were pretty much the same as those added to the tenth-century Corbie calendar preserved in St Petersburg, National Library of Russia, Q. v. I. 56. Delisle's views on *Ratoldus*'s provenance were straightforward enough: it was a sacramentary of Saint-Vaast that had soon found its way to Corbie: 'Sacramentaire des abbayes de Saint-Vast et Corbie'. He set out his reasoning briefly and clearly:[13]

> Il semble donc que le livre ait été copié par le soins de l'abbé Ratold, abbé de Corbie, dont la mort est rapportée au 15 mars 986. Il faut toutefois observer que le distique a été ajouté après coup sur un passage gratté, et que toutes les mentions du calendrier particulièrement relatives au monastère de Corbie y ont été introduites après coup. D'autre part, il est bon de fair observer que Saint Riquier et Saint Vast sont les seuls saints dont les fêtes aient été marqués en capitales rouges par le copiste.

He then printed a short list of the feasts in view, and moved to conclude:

> Il me semble évident que le sacramentaire était primitivement destiné à l'abbaye de Saint-Vast d'Arras; Ratold l'aura sans doute acquis pour l'offrir à l'église de Corbie, en y faisant ajouter certains détails propres à cette abbaye, notamment la messe de saint Précors, qu'on trouve sur le folio 41.

Delisle's hypothesis naturally found a wide measure of acceptance. It was endorsed:

(i) by Victor Netzer, who did great service in publishing a more extensive description of the manuscript's contents and a series of illustrative extracts, notably: a complete synopsis of the forms for the election of a bishop; the text of one of the prayers for ordeal; the litany; the order for Holy Saturday; the preface of the mass for St Samson; a synopsis of the

---

13 Delisle, 'Mémoire', 189–90, 345–60.

order for Maundy Thursday, Good Friday, and Holy Saturday; the verses for vesting from the Order of the Mass; the coronation order; and the chant from the mass for the visitation of the sick.[14] Although Netzer found *Ratoldus* 'le plus curieux <sacramentaire> de tous ceux que nous avons analysés', he too did not say whether he thought it strange that a book purportedly from Saint-Vaast's and Corbie should have an extensive pontifical embedded in it.

(ii) by André Wilmart in the entry he provided on the liturgical manuscripts of Corbie for the great *Dictionnaire d'archéologie chretienne et de liturgie*, edited by Henri Leclerq.[15] Again the contention was that *Ratoldus* had found its way from Saint-Vaast's to Corbie, where additions had been made, 'fairly close in time to the main text'. The only 'personal' comment of note added by Wilmart was that the structure of the calendar, so far as he could judge, generally ran in line with shortened Hieronymian martyrologies (Hieronymian breviates), but he did not indicate which he had consulted.

(iii) perhaps most important of all, by Victor Leroquais, who described *Ratoldus* as 'Sacramentaire de Saint-Vaast d'Arras à l'usage de Corbie, s. Xe siècle, 2e moitié', supplying in his usual fashion a list of the non-Gregorian saints' masses encompassed in the book's sanctoral. His notes on the palaeography, however, revealed for the first time (in print, anyway) that the material relating to Corbie in the body of the volume, namely the prayers in honour of St Praecordius, whose relics were possessed by the community, and the *Memento* naming St Peter, patron of the house, were actually in a gathering that had been added later (fols 41–46).[16]

Aside from the placing of a question mark over Ratoldus's part in the making of the sacramentary, one finds little advance on the position in the useful short account of the manuscript provided by Charles Samaran and Robert Marichal in their catalogue of datable manuscripts in the

---

[14] Netzer, *L'introduction*, esp. pp. 110–22, 252–78, 358. His method of indicating the presence of formulae by incipits alone has sometimes led subsequent scholars astray. See for instance, L. Gjerløw, *Adoratio Crucis* (Oslo, 1961), p. 15, on the prayers for Good Friday (nos 911–13). I am grateful to Sarah Keefer for drawing this point to my attention.
[15] 'Corbie (Manuscrits liturgiques de)', *DACL* 3.ii, cols 2930–1, on the calendar, and cols 2838–40, on the contents of the sacramentary.
[16] Leroquais, *Les sacramentaires*, I, 79–81.

Bibliothèque Nationale.[17] We will return to palaeographical and codicological matters in due course.

Fortunately Delisle's *Mémoire* had the effect of sparking off interest outside France too. A series of letters from Edmund Bishop, late in life, to Armitage Robinson, then Dean of Wells Cathedral, shows that Bishop at least had thought long and hard about aspects of the book that only Morinus and Martène had really given any expression to. Since the letters are of considerable interest it may be useful to print excerpts here.[18] 1–3 September 1916, from Downside:

> I had this MS in hand in 1895 but satisfying myself that it was no good attempting seriously to *aborder* these late 10th century MS until I cleared up the 'Amiens text' or St. Amand – St. Denis problem of the late years of saec. IX, *noted* nothing in detail from it.

The 'Amiens text' must either be the text preserved in Paris, Bibliothèque nationale de France, lat. 12050, a sacramentary compiled for use at Corbie at the request of Hilmerad, bishop of Amiens (849–71) by the priest Rodradus in 853, on the occasion of his ordination; or in Paris, Bibliothèque nationale de France, lat. 9432, an early-tenth-century sacramentary perhaps prepared for use at the cathedral itself.[19] The 'St. Amand – St. Denis problem' no doubt centred on the question of where the texts embodied in Paris, Bibliothèque nationale de France, lat. 2290, a late-ninth-century sacramentary from Saint-Denis, and Paris, Bibliothèque nationale de France, lat. 2291, a sacramentary probably written for Gozlinus, bishop of Paris (884–886), were originally compiled. Both are members of a group of books probably produced at

---

[17] C. Samaran and R. Marichal, *Catalogue des manuscrits en écriture latin portant des indications de date, de lieu ou de copiste*, 7 vols in 14 (Paris, 1959–85) III.i, 645, who endorse the argument for a Saint-Vaast 'provenance' expressed in summary by Denis Escudier, 'Le scriptorium de Saint-Vaast d'Arras des origines au XIIe siècle. Contribution à l'étude des notations neumatiques du nord de la France', *Bibliothèque de l'Ecole des Chartes* 129, Position des thèses (1971), 27–48, esp. 31–2.

[18] I have used the typescripts owned by the HBS. I owe my knowledge of them to the kindness of Michael Lapidge. On Bishop, see N. Abercrombie, *The Life and Work of Edmund Bishop* (London, 1959). For a short account of Armitage Robinson's life and work, see F. C. Burkitt's obituary in *JTS* 34 (1933), 225–31.

[19] On *Rodradus*, see E. Bishop, 'On some early MSS of the *Gregorianum*', in his *Liturgica Historica* (Oxford, 1916), pp. 62–76, at 67, with Delisle, 'Mémoire', pp. 122–26, and Ganz, *Corbie*, p. 57. The text is ed. Deshusses, *Le sacramentaire grégorien*, under the siglum 'Q'. *CLLA*, no. 742. For a description of BNF lat. 9432, see Leroquais, *Les sacramentaires*, I, 38–43. *CLLA*, no. 920.

Saint-Amand for export.[20] The second letter was sent from Barnstaple on 26 November 1916:

> Since the words 'istum . . . scribere fecit . . . librum' are on an erasure, the presumption is that some other words written at St. Vast stood there with quite another sense, – nothing about the origin of the book being due to Ratoldus. – The assertion that (*sic*) the cause or origin of the book being due to Ratoldus was a later idea foisted into (?it) after it had changed hands and had passed from St. Vast (for which monastery only, as is clear from the feasts of that saint in it, it could only properly serve) to Corbie. – Therefore it may be plausibly contended that the statement in the distich which we now read in the volume, that Ratoldus is the 'begetter of the book' is not true.
>
> But I don't think this is at all a necessary conclusion. R., who had not good scribes at Corbie, could very well have *ordered* a Missal from St. Vast which had; and the presence of the St. Vast feasts in it only means that the St. Vast scribe copied a MS of his own monastery, leaving the Corbie people to alter it to suit their own needs themselves.

We do not know what Robinson's reply was. But on the 7th of December, again from Barnstaple, Bishop wrote:

> And a first remark suggests itself at once – the mass Ordo is that of a bishop – nothing much in that, only I would observe that here we find for the first time that sort of 'worship' which so marked a feature of the later mediaeval and of the modern mass function. <Some matter intervening.> *Now it might be said that* – evidently this highly individualistic book was ordered by some bishop, and not by an abbot, whether of Corbie or any other monastery; and that the distich on an erasure is substituted for an original distich stating that such and such a bishop 'istum . . . fecit scribere quippe librum' . . . I doubt if the conclusion – which would exclude Ratoldus, St. Vast and Corbie altogether – would be 'a right judgement'. . . If the distich had been written in the beginning, or in an important place, of the book, as say Hildoard's inscription in the Cambrai MS. of *Greg* . . . or Rodradus's . . . well! – à la bonne heure.[21] – But . . . it occurs in the calendar, and . . . squeezed in

[20] See below, pp. lxv–lxvii.

[21] The copy of the Hadrianic Gregorian sacramentary made for Hildoard, bishop of Cambrai (790–816 × 817) at some point close to the year 812 is now Cambrai, Médiathèque municipale 164. *CLLA*, no. 720. For the text of the colophon, see Deshusses, *Le sacramentaire grégorien*, I, 348.

between Id. Mar. (which is blank) and XVII kal. Apr. – I should be rather inclined to say this: that *someone* (whether the original scribe or not *non liquet*, but 'I' should say not) scribbled in here, a blank space, a couple of verses, – such jottings are common enough; and then someone else, thinking these verses in-signifi-cant, borrowed the idea of scribbling in something here but substi-tuted for the in-significant lines two that were significant and recorded a useful fact that he knew of.

The alternative (on the supposition the original lines recorded that some bishop had this book written) would be this, that the writer deliberately wrote a false statement, in 'honour' we may suppose of his abbot; and (as I understand from Delisle, p. 345, note 1, that the 'additions' to the calendar 'ne sont guère plus recentes que la transcription du corps du calendrier', and he makes no exception for the distich) that at a time when everyone must know he was telling a – *terradiddle*. –

In my belief, or reading of things, the distich records an actual fact, – that Ratoldus did cause 'this book' to be written. We come back then on *its highly individualistic character*. Are we to attribute this to the St. Vast scribe, or (and) some of his friends inspiring him? I think this not a reasonable supposition. With a book to be written *ordered* by the Abbot of Corbie I cannot believe that a St. Vast scribe left to himself would have produced anything but a sacramentary of a current type, or would have ventured on what I might almost call a 'freak' compilation.

I am disposed to think that the traces of English connexion found in the Coronation Order are due to Ratoldus and Corbie, not to a St. Vast scribe. –

And, so far, the Sacramentary of Ratoldus may be said to give countenance, if not credit, to the statement . . . unexpected and wholly singular as it is, as to some relations between Ethelwold and Corbie.

Bishop, in his inimitable fashion, makes the essential points: first, that BNF lat. 12052 is a bishop's book; second, that it can hardly have been compiled for use at Saint-Vaast's; and third, that the inscription stating that the book had been copied at Ratoldus's order is highly unlikely to be 'wrong'.

Little else on the origins and character of BNF lat. 12052 seems to have found its way into print in the first half of the twentieth century, though it is perhaps worth recording in passing that thanks to the efforts of François Duine and Paul Ward new editions of its masses for St Samson and SS Samson and Paternus, and its coronation order, came out in 1922 and 1942, respectively.[22] We shall return to these in due course.

In 1975, however, Christopher Hohler advanced a view differing in almost all respects from those that had gone before. In essence, it was that the sacramentary underlying BNF lat. 12052 had not only begun life at Saint-Denis, but that it had passed to at least one other house – Saint-Symphorien's at Orléans – before finding its way eventually to Saint-Vaast's and Corbie. Somewhere along the way an English pontifical containing a version of the so-called English coronation order had been worked in.[23] But Hohler's view seems not to have been one he had recently formed. For in 1962 Derek Turner was already reporting a provisional version in an article on a late-tenth-century sacramentary from Noyon once owned by Sir Thomas Phillipps.[24] Having noted that *Ratoldus* was one of the earliest surviving books to contain a mass for St Vedastus (6 Feb.) but that the text of the sacramentary as a whole did 'not seem, as has been suggested, to be from St Vaast, Arras', Turner went on to add at the end of a lengthy footnote that:

> 'Ratoldus' goes against the tradition of prayers at Vedast's Mass, and has *Deus qui nos deuota* on Oct. 1 instead of Feb. 6. I am indebted to Christopher Hohler for the following suggested itinerary for the text of 'Ratoldus': Paris-St. Symphorian, Orleans-Arras-Corbie, with a possible English stage as well.

Two letters shed further light on the genesis of Hohler's thinking. The first is to Jeremy Myers, Keeper of Western Manuscripts at the Bodleian Library:[25]

3 Dec 1966
Long Crendon Manor

Dear Jeremy,

I certainly could not convince you by speech about the Coronation Service, but will try to set it out, assuming you know Bouman.[26] I do it from memory and may make mistakes.

---

[22] Duine, *Inventaire*, pp. 20–23.
[23] Hohler, 'Some service-books', pp. 65–69.
[24] D. H. Turner, 'A 10th–11th century Noyon sacramentary', *Studia Patristica* 5, *Texte und Untersuchungen zur Geschichte der altchristlichen Literatur* 80, ed. F. L. Cross (Berlin, 1962), 143–51, at 145, note 1.
[25] Published by kind permission of the Bodleian Library.
[26] C. A. Bouman, *Sacring and Crowning*, Bidragen van het Instituut voor middeleeuwe Geschiedenis der Rijks-Universiteit te Utrecht 30 (Groningen, Djakarta, 1957).

1) The so called Edgar Ordo is in the Sacramentary of Ratoldus. This, as it stands, is a single continuous text with numbered formularies and I do not doubt that it was copied (as is stated in the calendar) for Ratoldus abbot of Corbie. The calendar, however, is that of S. Vaast, Arras, which is no doubt where R. found the book (of which) he thought it worthwhile to have a copy made. The book, however, was not compiled in the first place for S. Vaast since the masses for S. Vaast are wrong. I forget the details, but how S. Vaast used the available proper masses is known both from earlier and later books: and in this book, say, the proper for the Translation is used for the Deposition, the proper for the octave of the Translation is used for the Translation, and the proper for the Deposition for the Octave of the Translation – or something of the kind. This should mean that Ratoldus' scribe, not being a monk of S. Vaast and finding the three masses on a flyleaf, inserted them at what he hoped were the right places, and got it wrong. We can therefore forget about Corbie and S. Vaast and try to see what sort of a book had found its way to S. Vaast and received additions there. This was a particularly good fused Gregorian with a full set of masses for the principal S. Denis saints (Denis and companions and Cucuphas) and also the Gallican masses, clumsily adapted, for S. Symphorian and S. Samson of Dol; an extraordinary and unique mass for S. Cuthbert (I think the one embodying a text only otherwise found in the Bangor antiphoner); and a unique mass for S. Samson and S. Paternus jointly. This can only mean one thing, and one thing only: the refugee clergy of Dol, who, fleeing from the Normans, reached Orleans via Paris, collecting en route the body of S. Paternus of Avranches, were established in the church of S. Symphorian at Orleans. There, as we know from a relic-docquet found in a shrine at Milton Abbas and copied by William of Malmesbury, they were in touch with Athelstan and sold him some of their relics. The group of S. Denis masses is, rather unexpectedly, best attested in books, notably Breton ones, from the province of Tours and I consider the *sacramentary* was ready apart from the Symphorian and joint Samson and Paternus masses before the chapter of Dol took to its heels. But it is conceivable that they picked it up in Paris en route, or indeed that they adopted it after arrival in Orleans.

The *pontifical* embodied in Ratoldus' book was in my view English: at any rate it agrees with the kind of pontifical current in England (most of whose contents must of course be of ultimate continental origin, I admit) notably in including the mysterious episcopal blessing for S. Andrew's day in which the saint is called 'patronus peculiaris'. If this text *is* English, the choice is Hexham, Rochester, and Wells, of which Wells is far the most likely.

The question is then: when did this English type pontifical get fused with the sacramentary?

2) The Edgar-ordo was edited with variants in the E.H.R. by an American.[27] In most copies the ruler is called, I think, Rex Anglorum: in Ratoldus he is Rex Francorum in one place, I cannot remember if in both: in the Sicilian (!) copy he is Rex Anglosaxonum et Merciorum. The last must be right: it is Athelstan's style, not Edgar's.

This ordo became the basis of the coronation service of the king of France, against the entire Carolingian tradition, so far as we know anything about it. Why? Well, I should assert that it is because Louis d'Outremer's following took it with them from England and used it for his coronation at Laon.

In other words, the Edgar ordo is Athelstan's and the pontifical embodied in Ratoldus' text is English and was embodied some time in the 930s – I should think in England but the details of this need thought.

3) The Edgar-ordo is an expansion of the Leofric ordo, which is *not* (as Schramm said) in a secondary hand in the Bodleian book: and Ker is prepared to say Leofric hand A is 9th/10th.[28] In other words, this formulary should have existed in Alfred's time. Of the various formularies assigned now to Hincmar of Reims the only one with which it shares a text is the coronation of Judith (of Wessex) on her marriage to Charles the Bald. On the theory which Sir Arthur Evans used to describe as the view that everything that matters was invented in Potsdam, this might be taken to prove that Leofric depends on Hincmar.[29] I should say it should be obvious

---

[27] P. L. Ward, 'An early version of the Anglo-Saxon coronation ceremony', *English Historical Review* 57 (1942), 345–61.

[28] The 'Leofric Missal', an early-tenth-century sacramentary written by a scribe from Arras or Cambrai for use in England, probably at Canterbury, later owned by Leofric, bishop of Exeter (1050–72). For Ker's comment, see his *Catalogue of Manuscripts containing Anglo-Saxon* (Oxford, 1957), pp. 378–9, no. 315.

[29] Sir Arthur Evans (1851–1941), excavator of the Palace of Knossos on Crete. Hohler had presumably heard a good deal about Sir Arthur from Joan Evans, Sir Arthur's younger sister and eventual biographer: J. Evans, *Time and Chance: The Story of Arthur Evans and his Forebears* (London, 1943). Dame Joan was a noted authority on the architecture of the Cluniac order (and much else besides), lecturing periodically at the Courtauld Institute during Hohler's time. Under her general editorship, Hohler contributed an essay to *The Flowering of the Middle Ages* (London, 1966).

to anyone except a German that Hincmar took over an English text.

Obviously to establish this to general satisfaction is impossible till we have a complete edition of the Sacramentary of Ratoldus. Dom Louis Brou made a transcript and the H.B.S. should one day publish it. And as I have always pressed for this edition, got the film for L.B, can't really 'snitch' the most interesting features of the text from the eventual edition, I have confined myself to saying it in letters and miscellaneous obiter dicta. But I am pretty sure I am right.

Yours ever, Christopher Hohler

The gist of what Hohler says about the coronation order also figures, albeit in an expanded form, in the introduction to Turner's edition of the so-called 'Claudius Pontificals'.[30] A short note written at some point in 1971 from 20 Portman Square, the former home of the Courtauld Institute of Art, indicates that the two were in touch fairly regularly:

Dear Derek,

My hunch was right! There is NO mass on 1st October in the Table of Contents in Ratoldus: the combined mass for SS Samson and Pair is also absent: and Cuthbert is bishop, but not saint. The book is Dol, the mass of S. Symphorian must have been altered at Orléans, and it needs closer comparison than I have undertaken with 'Winchcomb' (Cluniac secret for S. Bartholomew, cf. S. Vaast book – clearly in spite of L.B. almost pure Cluny – calendared in L'Ordinaire de S. Vaast;[31] printed missal of Cluny; ditto Braga (I think); your ms. Nevers sacr., and Sens:[32] this secret is not in Ratoldus or the others) S. Méen and BN Lat. 2297.[33] There is some sort of S. Denis book circulating in Prov. Tours behind the lot. The Votives are interesting too: I will return your Deshusses.

'Winchcomb' is discussed at cautious length in the Millénaire

---

[30] Turner, *The Claudius Pontificals*, p. xxxiii.

[31] L. Brou, *The Monastic Ordinal of St Vedast's Abbey, Arras*, 2 vols, HBS 86–7 (1955–6) I, 73–89.

[32] It is not clear which book Hohler had in mind. Perhaps, mistakenly, he meant London, British Library, Harley 2991–2, a sacramentary from St Columba, Sens, prepared for the use of the bishop of Nevers in the early tenth century, which has among a set of prefatory additions (BL Harley 2991, fol. 2r), a mass for St Anianus of Orléans (17 Nov.), but nothing of St Symphorian.

[33] On these books, see below, pp. lxi–lxiii.

du M. S. Michel.[34] I withdraw: it cannot, I fear, be Fleury, at least not straight Fleury and Winchcomb: but S. Florent de Saumur won't make any sense.
Must stop. Many thanks for lunch.

Yours ever, Christopher

Work by five others also deserves mention. In 1973 Michael Richter demonstrated that the profession of faith embodied in *Ratoldus*'s order for the consecration of a bishop corresponded, quite remarkably, almost word for word with a profession known to have been adopted for the consecration of Herewine, bishop of Lichfield, 814 × 816; and Richter further proposed that the consecratory order embodied in *Ratoldus*, taken as a whole, generally resembled that of the 'Leofric Missal'.[35] However, Saint-Vaast's, in his eyes, was still the most likely 'provenance', in spite of the fact that he held, in company with the Turner, the coronation order to be associable with Aethelstan.

Equally important is the analysis of *Ratoldus*'s episcopal blessings provided by Andrew Prescott in his article on the splendid benedictional written for Aethelwold, bishop of Winchester (963–84), by the scribe Godeman in the early 970s.[36] Prescott made three fundamental points. First, that the blessings in *Ratoldus* came from two distinct sources: an English benedictional akin to *Aethelwold*, and a benedictional akin to the one embodied in Reims, Bibliothèque municipale, 214, a late-tenth-century sacramentary written for the abbey of Saint-Thierry at Reims. Second, that the formulae in *Ratoldus* are sometimes peculiarly arranged. Third, that the English benedictional, and by association the English pontifical with which it travelled, was likely to have been compiled in the mid tenth century, not in the 930s, as Hohler seems tentatively to have supposed.

Also of great value is Richard Jackson's critical edition of the text of all the known continental copies of the so-called 'Second English Order'. Although Jackson did not concern himself particularly with the question of how the *ordo* had found its way into *Ratoldus*, he was able to

---

[34] D. Gremont and L. Donnat, 'Fleury, le Mont Saint-Michel et l'Angleterre à la fin du Xe et au début du XIe siècle à propos du manuscrit d'Orléans no. 127 (105)', *Millénaire monastique de Mont Saint-Michel*, ed. J. Laporte *et al.*, 4 vols (Paris, 1966–7) I, 751–93.
[35] *Canterbury Professions*, ed. M. Richter, Canterbury and York Society 67 (London, 1973), esp. pp. xli–xliii, xlviii–liii.
[36] A. Prescott, 'The text of the benedictional of St Æthelwold', in *Bishop Æthelwold: His Career and Influence*, ed. B. Yorke (Woodbridge, 1988), pp. 119–47, esp. 135–44.

demonstrate not only that its text differed at points from the related texts embodied in later continental books, and that most later versions of the order descend, so far as can be judged, from post-Conquest models.[37] The English pontifical underlying *Ratoldus* only seems to have been influential in limited respects.

Finally, we have Christopher Jones's ground-breaking work on *Ratoldus*'s extensive order for Maundy Thursday, and Sarah Keefer's on the order for Good Friday.[38]

THE CONSTITUENT PARTS OF *RATOLDUS*

In view of the fact that the elements embodied in *Ratoldus* are so unusual, it may be useful to provide, by way of introduction, a sort of reasoned analysis of contents. More will be said on particular points in due course.

The Sacramentary

As Hohler indicated, the text clearly began life at Saint-Denis. We have three masses for St Denis and his companions (nos. 1840–49, 1858–60); a mass for St Cucuphas of Barcelona (nos. 1558–60), whose relics had been acquired by the abbey in the ninth century; the Saint-Denis baptismal order and *ordo defunctorum* (nos. 2239–85); and the remains of the original Saint-Denis order for the dedication of a church (nos 2–5, perhaps more). However, the text transmitted is by no means 'pure', for later accretions show that the sacramentary found its way into the hands of the canons of Dol who had fled, during the Viking invasions of the 920s, to Paris, then Orléans. We not only have two masses for St Samson (28 July), patron of Dol, the first of which also names

---

[37] R. A. Jackson, *Ordines coronationis Franciae. Texts and ordines for the Coronation of Frankish and French Kings and Queens in the Middle Ages*, 2 vols (Philadelphia, 1995–2000) I, 168–200, though it appears that Jackson thought that Hohler had suggested that the order stemmed originally from Saint-Denis.

[38] C. Jones, 'The chrism mass in later Anglo-Saxon England', in *Ritual and Belief*, ed. H. Gittos and B. A. Bedingfield (forthcoming), and S. Keefer, 'The Veneration of the Cross synaxis in Anglo-Saxon England', *ibid.*

St Paternus of Avranches, whose relics the community possessed for a time, the second, a rather clumsy reworking of forms normally used in Brittany on both vigil and feast (nos. 1566–72); but we have a highly distinctive patronal mass (nos 1678–80), not to be found elsewhere, for St Symphorian (28 Aug.), patron of the church of Saint-Symphorien at Orléans, the church given over to the community by Hugh the Great, Duke of France and Count of Paris (d. 956). Hugh, it should be said, also seems to have been responsible for finding quarters for the canons – either in the church of St Bartholomew in the Cité, or possibly the church of St George on the right bank – when they first arrived in Paris.[39]

As for the twin questions of where and when the canons came by their Saint-Denis sacramentary, Paris seems much more likely than Dol, for the mention of St Paternus in the secondary mass for St Samson need not necessarily suggest, *pace* Hohler, that the canons went anywhere near Avranches. For one thing, the community of Dol seems by the 920s to have had relics of their own, and even though these are known to have been sent to Aethelstan, along with those of St Scupilio, the devotion must have lived on. For another, further relics might easily have been acquired when the canons met the refugee community of Avranches, whose patron St Paternus was, en route for Paris (not at Avranches itself). Perhaps most suggestive, however, is the character of the underlying Saint-Denis book. A date earlier than the mid tenth century would be extremely surprising, as we shall see.

Last in line we have the material proper to Saint-Vaast, not only the calendar (no. 202), as Morinus indicated, but highly distinctive masses for the deposition and 'translation' of St Vedastus, patron of the house (nos. 430–34, 1827–31), all likely to have been introduced, in my view, as BNF lat. 12052, that is to say the manuscript as we have it today, was being made, and presumably not at Saint-Vaast's itself. For the prayers

---

[39] See H. Guillotel, 'L'exode du clerge breton devant les invasions scandinaves', *Mémoires de la Société d'Histoire et d'Archéologie de Bretagne* 59 (1982), 269–315, esp. 292–300, with A. Terroine and L. Fossier, *Chartes et Documents de l'Abbaye de Saint-Magloire*, 3 vols (Turnhout, 1976–98) I, 512–15, 532–3 (maps). For the relics of St Paternus, see the letter of *c.* 926–7 from Radbodus, prior of the Dol community, to Aethelstan, ed. D. Whitelock, M. Brett and C. N. L. Brooke, *Councils and Synods with other documents relating to the English Church I, A.D. 871–1204*, 2 vols (Oxford, 1981) I, 38–40, no. 9. For Hugh's gift, see *Gallia Christiana*, ed. D. de Sainte-Marthe *et al.*, 13 vols (Paris, 1715–1865) VIII, 1573, with l'Abbé Surcin, *La paroisse de Saint-Paterne dans le passé et dans le présent* (Orléans, 1894), pp. 13–14, and Cottineau, *Répertoire*, II, 2143–4 for the churches in Orléans.

provided for the deposition of St Vedastus, as Hohler saw, are only correct for the octave, a feast unnoticed in the sanctoral, and the feast of the translation, quite without parallel, is called the *natale*, which it is plainly not – pretty clear indications that book was neither drawn up for use at Saint-Vaast's, nor written by anyone connected with the house. That additions were later made at Corbie merely means that the monks of Corbie decided to make use of the sacramentary, not that it was made for use at Arras. As is so often the case, 'place of production' clearly need not be 'place of use'. One only needs look to Paris, Bibliothèque nationale de France, lat. 9436, a sacramentary certainly written at Saint-Vaast's (for the abbot of Saint-Denis), to find proof of that.[40] BNF lat. 12052, as has already indicated, is arranged for the use of a bishop or archbishop. Further work on the palaeography will probably do much to help resolve the question of where Ratoldus had the manuscript produced – whether at Corbie itself, a major centre nearby (the abbey of Saint-Amand, for instance), or perhaps even a house in the vicinity of Saint-Vaast's.

The Pontifical

The material extracted from the English pontifical may be classed under twelve main headings. It contained:

(i) an order for the consecration of a church (substantially nos. 2–97).

(ii) an order for the election and consecration of a bishop (nos. 98–128).

(iii) prayers for the consigning of an archbishop's pallium (nos. 129–131).

(iv) forms for the coronation of a king and queen (nos. 132–175).

(v) miscellaneous blessings of objects (nos. 176–192).

(vi) a mass for St Cuthbert (nos. 459–463).

(vii) a penitential order for Ash Wednesday (nos. 495–512).

(viii) orders for the consecration of church officers (nos. 566–653).

---

[40] For descriptions of the book, see Leroquais, *Les sacramentaires*, I, 142–46, and Robertson, *Service Books*, pp. 387–91.

(ix) three blessings for Palm Sunday (nos. 808–812).

(x) a suite of *ordines* for Holy Week (nos. 836–881, 908–916, 1012–1017, 1047, 1056, 1063), and the underlying structure of the Ordinary of the Mass, given as an order for Easter Sunday (nos. 1068–1129).

(xi) an order for the visitation of the sick (nos. 2194–2214).

(xii) an extensive benedictional. The blessings are now to be found distributed among the masses of the sanctoral, temporal and votives of the sacramentary.

Although the book to which Ratoldus had access was, in a number of respects, rather eccentrically arranged, its text, as we shall see, evidently ran in parallel for long stretches with the early-eleventh-century pontifical generally known as 'Claudius I', a book copied for Wulfstan I, bishop of Worcester (1002–16), from a model prepared in Bishop Oswald's time, that is to say the last third of the tenth century. As one might expect, there are points of contact with other books too, principally: the 'Lanalet Pontifical', the 'Sidney Sussex Pontifical' (which is also associable with Oswald), and with several pontificals from Canterbury.[41] Indeed, a Canterbury origin seems almost certain, the link with Worcester no doubt reflecting the closeness of Oswald to Archbishop Oda (941–58): nephew and uncle.[42] Here and there, however, a number of purely English texts appear side-by-side in *Ratoldus* with material extracted some early copy of the Roman-German Pontifical, a type of book, or rather 'compilation', prepared at Mainz *c.* 950. By and large the 'adding-in' seems to have been done in England.

As for the attendant benedictional (its blessings now dispersed throughout the sacramentary), that, as Andrew Prescott has demonstrated, plainly stood somewhere in between, and very possibly behind, the splendid benedictional drawn up for Aethelwold, bishop of Winchester (963–84), early in the 970s; *Lanalet*; and *Claudius*. However, the texts embodied in *Ratoldus*, most of which ultimately descend, as in other English books (*Claudius* especially), from Cambrai and Reims, appear to have been rather clumsily handled.

Quite how Ratoldus came by such a pontifical (and benedictional) is

---

[41] See below, pp. xcviii–ciii.
[42] See A. Wareham, 'St Oswald's family and kin', in *St Oswald of Worcester. Life and Influence*, ed. N. Brooks and C. Cubitt (Leicester, 1996), 46–63.

difficult to say for certain. Perhaps it was acquired specially; it may even have been dispatched to the continent with Oswald. But what does seem clear is that both appearance and content were greatly admired, the book's *ordines* for the consecration of church officers and the coronation of a king and queen, particularly so. Further work in continental libraries will doubtless add a good deal more to the picture.

PALAEOGRAPHY AND CODICOLOGY OF THE MANUSCRIPT

Binding: clean modern calf on boards. A separate folder containing the old (sixteenth-century?) parchment wrapper is stored with the manuscript.[43]

Dimensions: 283 parchment leaves of *c.* 320 × 260mm. There are no apparent signs of trimming. Written space measures *c.* 210 × 135mm. *Ratoldus* is a surprisingly bulky book, the layout of its pages highly reminiscent of the luxury volumes produced at Saint-Amand in the second half of the ninth century.[44] Generous margins presumably intended both for 'display' (to set off the main text block), and to serve when necessary as convenient 'homes' for any additions that future owners might feel in need of.

---

[43] Leroquais, *Les sacramentaires*, I, 81, describes the old binding as: relieure parchemin sur carton.

[44] Reims, Bibliothèque municipale 213, the sacramentary written at Saint-Amand *c.* 870 for use at the abbey of Saint-Thierry, Reims, for instance, measures 340 × 260mm and has a written space of approximately 215 × 160mm. Unfortunately no reproductions of the full mis-en-page of the major Saint-Amand sacramentaries seem yet to have been published. However, for illustrations showing the text block of Reims BM 213 and St Petersburg, National Library of Russia, Q. v. I. 41, the sacramentary written for Raginelmus, bishop of Noyon-Tournai, in the early 860s, see *Trésors de la Bibliothèque Municipale de Reims. I. Manuscrits*, ed. M. de Lemps (Reims, 1978), no. 10; and A. Staerck, *Les manuscrits latins conservés a la bibliothèque impériale de Saint-Petersbourg*, 2 vols (St Petersburg, 1910) I, plate XVII. Books such as Cambrai MM 164, the copy of the Hadrianic Gregorian sacramentary prepared at some point close to the year 812 for Hildoard, bishop of Cambrai (790 – 816 × 817), and London, British Library, Loans 36/9 (formerly Phillipps 3340), an early-tenth-century sacramentary from Noyon, both exceptionally tall and narrow, have little space in their margins for anything except signes de renvoi.

1</

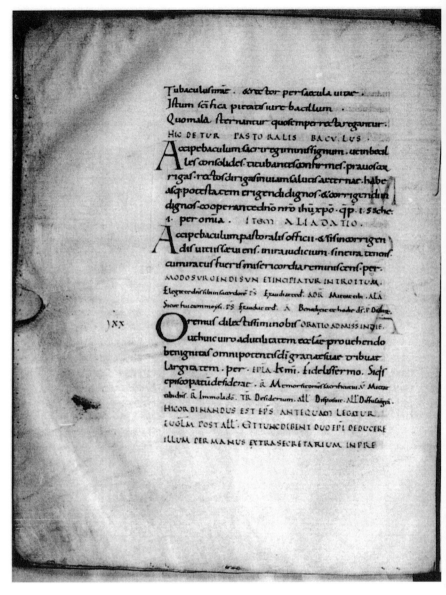

Paris, Bibliothèque nationale de France, lat. 12052, fol. 16v

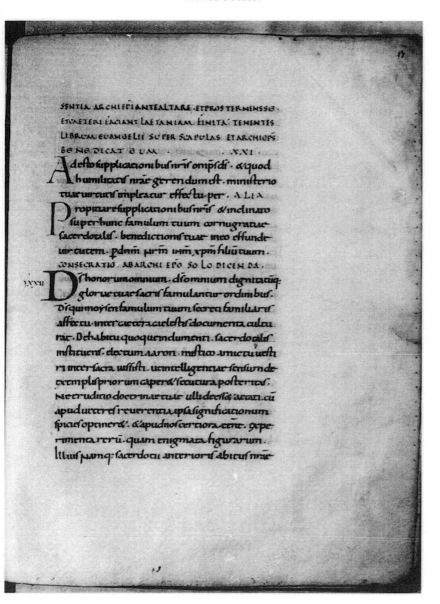

Paris, Bibliothèque nationale de France, lat. 12052, fol. 17r

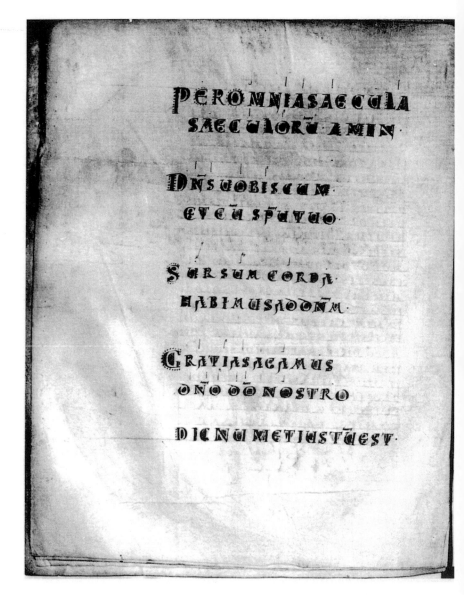

Paris, Bibliothèque nationale de France, lat. 12052, fol. 44v

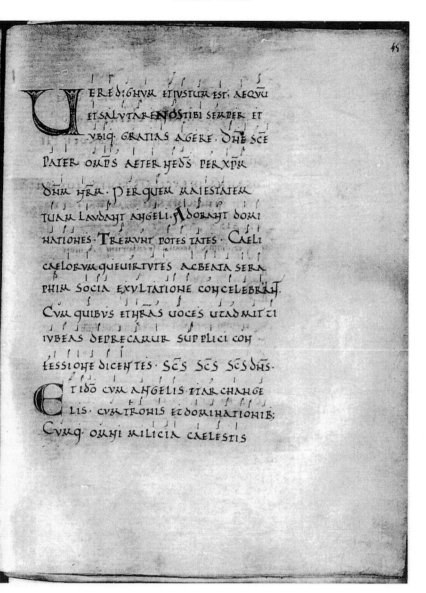

Paris, Bibliothèque nationale de France, lat. 12052, fol. 45r

Foliation: the first seven leaves are lettered A to G, and the remaining 276 numbered 1 to 156 and 158 to 277. Nothing is lost in between.

Additional leaves (unnumbered): preceding the manuscript proper, one paper leaf containing a seventeenth- or eighteenth-century inscription:

> Hic continetur Sacramentale S. Gregorii, id est Liber Sacramentorum seu Missale et Kalendarium: ante annum 986 scriptum jubente Ratoldo Corbeiensi Abbati; tempore Caroli Calvi Imperatorii. In fine subditur pars Sermonis S. Fulgentii Episcopi de Nativitate Domini.

At the end of the volume, another paper leaf. Between this and fol. 277, two fragments from the old parchment wrapper, also unnumbered, are bound in.

Marks of ownership: on fol. Ar, in a sixteenth-century hand, the inscription: *Ex Libris Corbeiensis Monasterii. Anno 986 editus est iste Codex, uide (?) . . . ex (?) Calendario die 15 Martii.*[45] A large capital 'I' stands below. At the head of fol. C^r in a sixteenth- or seventeenth-century hand: *Sancti Germani a Pratis* (the monastery of Saint-Germain-des-Pres in Paris). In the right margin *No. 286, olim 587*; and in the lower margin: *587.*

Collation: a singleton (fol. A); I^8 (fols Br – 2v); II–VI^8 (fols 3r–34v); VII^6 (fols 35r–40v, the calendar); VII^6 (fols 41r–46v, added at Corbie); VIII^8 (fols 47r–51v, the first three leaves of the gathering excised, stubs visible); IX–XX^8 (fols 52r–155v); XXI^8 (fols 156r–164v, due to faulty numeration); XXII–XXXV^8 (fols 165r–276v); finally a singleton (fol. 277).

Ruling: in hardpoint throughout, generally 25 lines to a page. Laid out with much care. Main bounding lines never stretch the whole height or width of the page:

---

[45] Next to the entry on fol. 36r, a more or less contemporary hand notes: *Hic fuit* (?) *26 abbas huius loci qui obiit anno domini 986 idus Martii.*

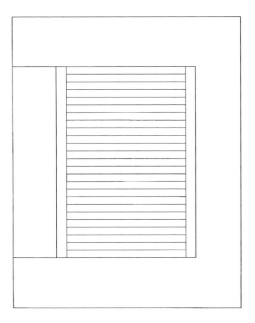

Pricking is visible in top, bottom and outer margins throughout.

Scribes: the original portions of the manuscript were written by three scribes, all using light brown ink, in fairly expert forms of caroline minuscule:

Scribe 1. The main scribe. Wrote the greater part of the book in a small, even hand. Provided his own musical notation. Presumably knowing that the text of the sacramentary was a long one, he did what he could to save space at the beginning, leaving few gaps between words and writing smaller than usual. He supplied his own superscriptions, rubric and formula numbers in the orange ink/paint used for the minor initials.

Scribe 2. Immediately identifiable by the broad and looping bowl of his letter 'g'. His writing is slightly larger (and more rounded) than that of Scribe 1. He wrote 67r lines 14–25; 68r lines 14–25; 86r lines 14–25; 117r lines 13–23; 124r lines 1–7; 132v line 14–133r; 181v lines 4–25; 184v lines 1–21; 188r, 212r lines 1–6. He also supplied the alternative prayer for Holy Saturday (no. 2*) in the right margin of fol. 138r, and very possibly the calendar (fols 35–41) in a much smaller hand. The calendar is certainly not the work of Scribes 1 or 3.

Scribe 3. Small and compact; rather 'dispersed'. Letter 'g' a squashed figure of eight; an exceedingly high point employed at the end of sentences. He wrote folios 131v lines 1–15; 134r line 15–135v; 140v lines 1–15; 149r line 5–149v line 10; 154r lines 8–25; 154v lines 2–9; 155v lines 10–20; 156r lines 15–23; 159v lines 15–25; 213r–214r; 250r lines 19–25. In the majority of these stints he provided his own superscriptions, which are considerably larger than the ones provided by Scribe 1, and necessary rubric, all generally speaking in the orange ink used for the initials. Now and again, however, the colour seems slightly deeper.

In view of the expertise of their writing, the scriptorium to which these scribes belonged was obviously a good one. Their work has so far not been identified in another manuscript. However, in general terms, the style of writing practised is similar to that of the main scribe of:

Reims, Bibliothèque municipale 214: a sacramentary written for use at the abbey of Saint-Thierry at Reims at some point close to the year 975.[46] Masses are provided in the sanctoral for the feasts of saints Remigius (13 Jan., 30 Sept., 1 Oct.); Theodericus, patron of the house (1 July); Nicasius (23 July, 14 Dec.); Timothy and Apollinaris (23 Aug.), patrons of the abbey nearby; Sixtus, Sinicius and Nivardus (1 Sept.); and Basolus (15 Oct.); in the baptismal litany on fols 44v–46v the names of SS Theodoricus and Theodulfus are in capitals; a mass *in honore sanctorum Theodorici et Theodulfi*, signalled on fol. 4v, appears among the votives on fol. 132; and the *missa pro ipsa familia* on fol. 144v has a collect also naming the saints. However, the mass provided on fol. 71v for the elevation of St Theodericus, an event which took place on 11 December 976, is an addition by another hand.[47] As we shall see, substantial parts of the book's main text were copied from a model from Reims cathedral.

---

[46] The volume measures 295 × 255mm, and its text block, which contains between 29 and 33 lines per page, rather more, therefore, than *Ratoldus*, *c.* 205 × 270mm.

[47] See Leroquais, *Les sacramentaires*, I, 91–94; and *Trésors de la Bibliothèque Municipale de Reims*, ed. de Lemps, no. 14, which reproduces a small (though fairly unrepresentative) passage of writing. The litany is printed by Delisle, 'Mémoire', 369–71. For the sacramentary in context, see J. Deshusses, 'Sur quelques anciens livres liturgiques de Saint-Thierry: les etapes d'une transformation de la liturgie', in *Saint-Thierry, une abbaye du VIe au XXe siècle*, ed. M. Bur (Saint-Thierry, 1979), 133–45. However, it has to be said that the book is not, as he claims, related in any way to the so-called 'Leofric Missal'. Nor does he seem to find it strange that texts proper to a bishop are provided throughout, in particular an extensive series of episcopal benedictions and an order for the dedication of a church. Mitred abbots, that is to say, abbots who had been granted certain episcopal rights, were never allowed, no matter how grand their pretensions, to dedicate churches.

For *Ratoldus*, a date in the third or fourth quarter of the tenth century is therefore substantiable on palaeographical grounds alone. Further work will doubtless throw light on the matter of where its scribes were working.

Chant

Original musical notation occurs at four principal points in the manuscript: on fols 116r–116v, in the proper preface for Maundy Thursday (no. 856); on fol. 120v, in the hymn *Tellus ac aethra* (no. 878); on fols 136r–137r in the Exultet preface (nos 1018–1019); and on fols 141v–142r, in the proper preface for Holy Saturday (no. 1060). To call it 'incontestably' of Saint-Vaast, as Denis Escudier has done, would seem to be taking matters a little too far. For, as even the briefest of glances will show, the notation provided in the short late-tenth- or early-eleventh-century tonary from the house now preserved in Cambridge, Trinity College Library 939 (II), diverges in several important respects, not least its general aspect, from that of *Ratoldus*. Unfortunately, therefore, it is difficult to determine at present whether *Ratoldus*'s chant is genuinely 'local', that is to say definitely of Arras, or whether it is simply imitative or derivative.[48] That the principal scribe (Scribe 1) made a colossal muddle of working the masses for St Vedastus, Saint-Vaast's patron, into the main text of the sacramentary lends weight to the feeling (expressed by Hohler) that the men charged with producing it had no first-hand experience of Artesian practice.[49]

[48] See Susan Rankin's entry on the manuscript in *Cambridge Music Manuscripts 900–1700*, ed. I. Fenlon (Cambridge, 1982), pp. 10–13, no. 3 and plate, with D. Escudier, 'La notation musicale de Saint-Vaast d'Arras. Étude d'une particularité graphique', in *Musicologie médiévale. Notations et Séquences*, ed. M. Huglo (Paris, 1987), 107–120, esp. 120.

[49] See below, pp. lxxxiv–lxxxv. Note too that the scribe, having made some mistake in transcribing the text of the collect for the translation (no. 1827), had to erase what he had written and supply St Vedastus's name over the erasure. Perhaps he was used to commemorating SS Remigius, Germanus and Bavo on 1 October too. See for instance, Deshusses, *Le sacramentaire grégorien*, II, 325–6, nos 3617–21.

Decoration

Although there is no major decoration to speak of, something was evidently planned to accompany the text of the order for the dedication of a church: fols Gv and 1r were left unwritten, presumably to receive, on the analogy of a number of English pontificals, a representation of the alphabet traced on the ground by the dedicating bishop, and a full-page miniature of some part of the ceremony.[50]

Minor initials, normally two or three lines high, were supplied in two campaigns, the first extending from the beginnning of the book to fol. 221r, the second from fol. 221v to the end. Different sets of colours were employed in each: in the first, a light, bright green alternates with the orange that was used throughout the book for superscriptions, rubric and formula numbers. In the second, however, the initials are for the most part alternately dark brown (pen-drawn) and red or reddish-orange, the only exceptions being fol. 253r and fols 260v–261r, where a sort of chalky green briefly reappears.

Clearly, in view of the ubiquity of the orange, the first set of initials must be 'original', either having been added as the book was being written or shortly thereafter. The second set, on the other hand, looks like a later addition, presumably supplied at Corbie, for the unusual canted form of the letter 'A' that occurs on fols 237v, 245v and 252r is only found elsewhere in the manuscript on fol. 45v, a page written by a scribe we shall come to in a moment (Scribe vi). Unfortunately there is no way of telling how much time elapsed between the two campaigns.

Additions at Corbie

Eleven scribes, listed below in order of appearance, added material either on spaces originally left blank, or on the gathering (fols 41–46) newly supplied when *Ratoldus* came to be disbound (assuming, of course, it had ever been fully bound up to begin with) in the late tenth or early eleventh century:

[50] See for instance, *The Benedictional of Archbishop Robert*, ed. H. A. Wilson, HBS 24 (London, 1902), plate V; *Pontificale Lanaletense*, ed. G. H. Doble, HBS 74 (London, 1937), plates 1 and 2; and *The Benedictional of St Aethelwold*, ed. in facs. A. Prescott (London, 2000), fol. 118v.

Scribe i. Late-tenth- or early-eleventh-century. Folios 33v line 19–34v, spaces originally left blank: a mass for the dedication of a church and a mass for the invention of St Stephen (nos 193–201). The scribe's writing (in dark brown ink) is similar in general aspect to that of Scribe vi.

Scribe ii. Early- or perhaps mid-eleventh-century. A mass for St Praecordius (nos 203–206), fol. 41r, written in dark brown ink.

Scribe iii. Early- to mid-twelfth-century. A nuptial mass (nos 207–210), fols 41v–42r. The scribe's writing is large and attractive in appearance. His rustic capitals, in the normal tenth- and eleventh-century Corbie manner, are highly decorative, though somewhat disorderly. Dark brown ink.

Scribe iv. Early- to mid-eleventh-century. A formula for blessing of candles on the feast of the Purification of the Virgin (no. 211), fols 42v–43r, written every other line in a large and amply spaced hand. Mid brown ink. Folio 43v is blank.

Scribe v. Late-tenth- or early-eleventh-century. On fol. 44r, the right hand leaf of the central opening of the new Corbie gathering, a title page for the sacramentary (no. 212) evenly written in orangy-red rustic capitals.

Scribe vi. Late-tenth- or early-eleventh-century. Replacements for texts that were lost when the first three leaves of gathering XI of *Ratoldus* were very expertly cut away. On fol. 44v, we have the introduction to the proper preface in dark brown display capitals (no. 213) flecked with red; on fols 45r–45v line 7, the proper preface, the termination *Et ideo* (for use on christological feasts), and the *Sanctus* (nos 214–215) in finer brown rustic capitals, with a competent pen-drawn initial 'V'; and a second proper preface, with introduction, termination, and *Sanctus* (nos 216–218) on fols 45v line 8–46r line 16.[51] The texts supplied were all written on every other line. Some change of plan seems to have occurred as this part of the gathering was being prepared, however. Underneath the last lines of fol. 45r and throughout fol. 45v, that is to say under the termination of the proper preface, the *Sanctus* and *Per omnia* (nos 215–216), the remains of some other text written in red, but rather hastily erased,

---

[51] Fol. 45r is reproduced in *Le codex 903 de la Bibliothèque nationale de Paris (XIe siècle). Graduel de Saint-Yrieix*, Paléographie musicale 13, ed. Dom André Mocquereau (Tournai, 1925), p. 76 (fig. 4). The text of the christological termination *Et ideo* is first set out in full in BNF lat. 12050, the mid-ninth-century sacramentary from Corbie, ed. Deshusses, *Le sacramentaire grégorien*, I, 687, no. 1*.

are clearly visible. In all likelihood, the prayer in question was the *Te igitur*, which normally follows the proper preface and first few words of the *Sanctus* in early sacramentaries.[52] Scribe vi appears to have been a man of some importance. Not only was he responsible for adding a good number of hagiographical additions to *Ratoldus*'s calendar, but, as Samaran and Marichal have noted, he also supplied a new proper preface and *Sanctus* on fol. 5v of BNF lat. 12051, the so-called 'Missale Sancti Eligii', a splendid ninth-century sacramentary possibly written for Odo, bishop of Beauvais (861–81), who had been a monk at, and abbot of, Corbie.[53] In general aspect, Scribe vi's hand resembles that of the scribe who added at some point in the period 986–1013 a list of abbots of Corbie to the principal Corbie copy of Adalhard's Statutes.[54]

Scribe vii. Late-tenth- or early-eleventh-century. Provided the text of the *Te igitur*, *Memento* and *Communicantes* (nos 219–221) on fols 46r line 17–47v. The first lines of the *Te igitur* on fol. 46r are in orangy-red ink. Minor initials are dotted around with red. The scribe added a further *Memento* (no. 1*) in the left margin of fol. 47v, and the names Eutropia, Agna and Cecilia to the *Nobis quoque* on fol. 48r.

Scribe viii. Probably mid- to late-eleventh-century. A mass for St Mary Magdalene (nos 3*–5*) in the right hand margin of fol. 192r, written in a rather spiky and cramped hand; a mass for St Nicholas (nos 6*–8*) in the margin of fol. 235r. The scribe used dark black ink. Minor initials in red.

Scribe ix. Mid- to late-eleventh-century. A mass for the fifth Sunday before Christmas (nos 9*–12*) in the left margin of fol. 235v, rather shakily written in dark black ink. Minor initials in red.

Scribe viii. A second stint. A relic mass (nos 15*–17*) in the right margin of fol. 243r, and a mass invoking the Holy Spirit (nos 18*–20*) in the right margin of fol. 247r.

---

[52] See Deshusses, *Le sacramentaire grégorien*, I, 86–7, nos 3–5.

[53] Samaran and Marichal, *Catalogue des manuscrits en écriture latin*, III.i, 645. BNF lat. 12051, fol. 5v, is reproduced by S. Rankin, 'Neumatic notations in Anglo-Saxon England', in *Musicologie médiévale*, ed. Huglo, 129–44, plate XVIII.

[54] Paris, Bibliothèque nationale de France, lat. 13908, fol. 27v. The list, as originally written, ran from Theofridus up to and including Ratoldus. The names of Maingaudus, Ratoldus's successor (who died in 1013), and the two abbots who followed him, Hubertus and Ricardus, were written by a later scribe. Further additions were made by others.

Scribe x. Mid- to late-eleventh-century. In the margin of fol. 254r, a mass for someone lying sick (nos 21*–23*). Written in dark black ink. Minor initials in shiny red. The scribe's hand is similar to that of Odolricus, the Corbie monk who wrote Paris, Bibliothèque nationale de France, lat. 12297, books V to VIII of Paschasius Radbertus's *Expositio in Matthaeum.*[55]

Scribe xi. Late-tenth- or early-eleventh-century. A mass for a priest or abbot (nos 2323–2330), a mass, attributed to St Augustine, for the living and dead (nos 2331–2333), and a mass for the dead (nos 2334–2337) added on fols 275r line 17–276v, originally left blank. Initials in red. At least three items copied appear to be 'Saint-Denis', or perhaps more broadly, 'Parisian' propers. The first is the prayer *Suscipe sancta trinitas deus hanc oblationem* (no. 2327) , which only otherwise occurs in Paris, Bibliothèque nationale de France, lat. 2290, a mid- to late-ninth-century sacramentary from Saint-Denis. The second and third, also in the mass for a dead abbot or priest, are the readings from the Apocalypse (XIV, 13–14) and John (V, 21–24), which only otherwise occur together in Paris, Bibliothèque nationale de France, lat. 2291, a sacramentary written for Gozlinus, when bishop of Paris (884–86).[56] Scribe xi presumably was either doing the last of the copying from the underlying Saint-Denis model, in other words completing the writing of the main text, which had been left unfinished; or he was merely adding material that had found its way to Corbie from Saint-Denis by another route.

Also provided at Corbie during the course of the late tenth and eleventh century were: (i) a number of texts relative to the Ordinary of the Mass (nos i–xii) on fol. Av, a singleton; (ii) a series of entries in the calendar on fols 35r–40v; (iii) improved readings, sometimes over erasures in the main text, sometimes in the book's margins; and (iv) an extract from a sermon of St Fulgentius (no. 2338) also on a single sheet (fol. 277r–v). The text of the sermon ends incomplete.

It is important to note too that a 'corrector', possibly at Corbie, erased a supplementary text that had been supplied in the upper left margin of fol. 137v for use in the clause beginning *Precamur* at the end of the Exultet preface (no. 1019). Normally, in its most compact form, the *Precamur* reads:[57]

---

55 See Samaran and Marichal, *Catalogue des manuscrits*, III.ii, plate CCXXXVIb.
56 See Deshusses, *Le sacramentaire grégorien*, II, 232, no. 3069; III, 299–300, no. 504. On the two sacramentaries, see below, pp. lxv–lxvii.
57 Ed. Deshusses, *Le sacramentaire grégorien*, I, 362–3, no. 1022c.

> Precamur ergo te domine, ut nos famulos tuos omnem clerum et deuotissimum populum, una cum patre nostro papa ill., quiete temporum concessa, in his paschalibus gaudiis conseruare digneris.

The name of the pope, and if need be those of the king, queen, abbot or bishop, were left for the celebrant to supply. But for some communities, such 'neutrality' evidently proved inconvenient, and specifics were consequently worked in. In the main text of Verona, Biblioteca capitolare 87, a sacramentary written for Wolfgang, bishop of Regensburg in 993 or 994, we have: *una cum papa nostro ill. et gloriosissimo rege nostro OTTONE necnon et uenerabili antistite nostro UUOLFKANGO*; and in Munich, Bayerische Staatsbibliothek, Clm 6425, a collection of *ordines* compiled for Egilbert, bishop of Freising (1006–39): *antistite nostro Egilberto* (in gold) *cum omni congregatione sanctae mariae.*[58]

One therefore suspects that the text given in *Ratoldus*'s margins was, in some important respect, unsuitable for use at Corbie. Could it have carried the name of the man for whom the book was originally made?

In view of the book's complex nature, it will be best to deal with its constituent parts separately: index and calendar first; the sacramentary; and last, the material descending from the English pontifical. Elements not securely attributable either to sacramentary or pontifical will be signalled as clearly as possible.

THE TABLE OF CONTENTS (no. 1)

The arrangement is admirably straightforward: the table of contents simply lists the 434 items (sections of text) that were destined to be marked off with Roman capitals in the body of the book. For anyone new to the sacramentary, it will have been a real boon. One can not only see at a glance, for instance, where material from the pontifical is set out, but whether such and such a saint's day figures in the sanctoral. On

---

[58] *Das Sakramentar-Pontifikale des Bischofs Wolfgang von Regensburg (Verona, Bibl. Cap., Cod. LXXXVII)*, ed. K. Gamber and S. Rehle, Textus patristici et liturgici 15 (Regensburg, 1985), p. 399, no. 2478; and *OR*, V, 270–71.

a general level, precursors are not hard to find, the principal examples being:

Reims, Bibliothèque municipale 8 (fols 1–2): the so-called 'Index of Saint-Thierry', the fragmentary remains of a table of contents originally drawn up for a sacramentary similar to the so-called 'Old' or 'Vatican Gelasian Sacramentary'. Probably written in the last third of the eighth century.[59] At the abbey of Saint-Thierry, Reims, by the tenth century.

Paris, Bibliothèque nationale de France, lat. 12048: the so-called 'Sacramentary of Gellone', a sacramentary-cum-pontifical prepared for Hildoard, bishop of Cambrai (d. 816 × 817), that found its way to Gellone soon thereafter. Although the text is marked off in numbered sections, a proper table of contents seems only to have been provided for the book's benedictional.[60]

Trent, Castel del Buonconsiglio 1590: the famous early- to mid-ninth-century sacramentary of Trent, a book that preserves more or less intact the text of a pre-Hadrianic Gregorian Sacramentary. Has a full table of contents. Numbering in Roman numerals throughout.[61]

The Supplement drawn up, probably by Benedict of Aniane, for the Hadrianic Gregorian Sacramentary.[62] Benedict may have taken his

---

[59] Ed. A. Wilmart, 'L'index liturgique de Saint-Thierry', *RB* 30 (1913), 437–50, and L. C. Mohlberg, *Liber Sacramentorum Romani aecclesiae ordinis anni circuli*, Rerum ecclesiasticarum Documenta, Series maior, Fontes 4 (Rome, 1960), 267–75. *CLLA*, no. 601. On the Vatican Gelasian Sacramentary, which has section numbers throughout, but no table, see below, pp. lxxiii–lxxiv.

[60] See *Liber Sacramentorum Gellonensis*, ed. A. Dumas and J. Deshusses, 2 vols, CCSL 159 and 159A (Turnhout, 1981) I, 262–4, no. 1986.

[61] *Sacramentarium Tridentinum*, ed. F. dell'Oro and H. Rogger, Monumenta liturgica ecclesiae Tridentinae saeculo XIII antiquiora 2A (Trent, 1985), pp. 75–82. Two hundred and ten sections are marked off in the main text, and a further eighty-eight in the 'supplement'. Several fragments of pre-Hadrianic southern German sacramentaries also have numbered sections. See *CLLA*, no. 719*. On 'Hadrianic' systems, see W. H. Frere, 'The Carolingian Gregorianum: its sections and their numbering', *JTS* 18 (1916), 47–55.

[62] Ed. Deshusses, *Le sacramentaire grégorien*, I, 351–9 (following the famous *Hucusque* prologue). For the ascription to Benedict, see J. Deshusses, 'Le "Supplement" au sacramentaire grégorien: Alcuin ou saint Benoît d'Aniane?', *Archiv für Liturgiewissenschaft* 9 (1965), 48–71. The case against Benedict made by Philippe Bernard, 'Benoît d'Aniane est-il l'auteur de l'avertissement "Hucusque" et du Supplément au sacramentaire "Hadrianum"?', *Studi medievali*, 3rd series, 39.i (1998), 1–120, is unconvincing as it stands. A number of the (major) objections he raises were in any case raised, succinctly, by Achille Triacca in 1973, reviewing Deshusses: 'In margine al "Sacramentario Gregoriano" recentemente edito', *EL* 87 (1973), 415–334, esp. 426–8. The

lead from some 'pre-Hadrianic' book, perhaps something akin to the one now embodied in *Trent*.

As for books closer in date to *Ratoldus*, the most relevant are:

Angers, Bibliothèque municipale 80: a late-tenth- or early-eleventh-century pontifical from a cathedral in the province of Tours, probably Angers itself.[63] The table on fols 1–6, which is incomplete, contains sixty-five items.

Cologne, Dombibliothek 141: a pontifical written in the mid eleventh century at the abbey of Saint-Vaast either for Gerardus I (*c.* 1013–48) or Liutbertus (*c.* 1049–76), successive bishops of Cambrai.[64] After 1093, when Arras once more became a separate diocese, the book seems to have passed back. The table of contents begins, as in *Ratoldus*, with a short introduction: *In nomine domini. Incipit liber episcopalis. Capitula sequentis libri.* Fifty items are listed in the

stark facts about the 'Supplement' are that copies were being made by 840; that it contains a number of formulae not recorded in sources that are earlier from a palaeographical standpoint; and that Hildoard's sacramentary, Cambrai MM 164, which was probably written *c.* 811–12, does not have it. There is not a shred of evidence to suggest that the 'Supplement' existed in Charlemagne's time; and on a quite unrelated tack, it is clearly a matter of some importance, *pace* Bernard, that the name *Hludovvicus* (Louis) appears in varying combinations of prayers for a king in the copies of the 'Supplement' made at Arles (*c.* 840), Rheinau (*c.* 850–900) and Beauvais (*c.* 870–900). It is comparatively rare to find references of this sort in liturgical texts. That Louis the Pious is probably not meant in all three cases (though he is certainly intended at Arles), as Deshusses thought, is merely a side issue. Questions surrounding the Supplement's date are well handled by J. Decreaux, *Le sacramentaire de Marmoutier* (Autun 19 bis), 2 vols, Studi di Antichitá Cristiana 38–39 (Vatican City, 1985) I, 219–34, though it can hardly be said, despite what he and Deshusses assert, that the *Concordia regularum*, in terms of style, has anything much in common with the *Hucusque* and *Hunc codicem* prologues on the one hand, and Helisachar's letter on the other. It is also somewhat alarming to find that with a magician's flourish Decreaux attempts to pull a 'new' *Hadrianum* (his so-called 'Gregorian Sacramentary of 810') out of the hat. Once again, the number of possible Carolingian archetypes of the 'Gregorian Sacramentary' is limited to two (one *Hadrianum* and one *pre-Hadrianum*). But to judge from even a small proportion of the books that have come down to us, a far greater number of texts, all 'authoritative' in their own right (though some more than others), were evidently in circulation in the late eighth and early ninth centuries. A thorough re-appraisal of the types of variant readings preserved in the classes of text delineated by Deshusses (for instance, the pre-Hadrianic 'Alcuinian/English' text at Tours; the *Hadrianum* itself; and the so-called corrections of Aniane) is desperately needed.

[63] See Leroquais, *Les pontificaux*, I, 25–32, with Rasmussen, *Les pontificaux*, pp. 401–4.

[64] See *OR*, I, 108–14, with *Glaube und Wissen im Mittelalter. Katalogbuch zur Ausstellung, Erzbischöfliches Diozesanmuseum, Köln, 7. August bis 15. November, 1998*, ed. J. Plotzek (Munich, 1998), pp. 405–14, no. 84 (with numerous plates). A full set of digital pictures of the book is available at http://www.ceec.uni-koeln.de. Also see below, pp. cxxxv–cxxxvi, cxli.

table and numbered in red in the book's margins.[65] The extensive *ordines* embodied throughout descend on the one hand from the so-called 'Romano-German Pontifical', and on the other, from earlier books from Arras and Cambrai, in particular Cambrai, Mediathèque municipale 162–3, a late-ninth- century sacramentary in two volumes, probably from Saint-Vaast's; and Cambrai, Mediathèque municipale 164, the copy of the Hadrianic Gregorian sacramentary prepared at some point close to the year 812 for Hildoard, bishop of Cambrai (790–816 × 817).[66] The benedictional of the Cologne pontifical is intimately related to that of Paris, Bibliothèque nationale de France, lat. 13313, an eleventh-century pontifical from Trier later adjusted for use at Cambrai. Neither, *pace* Dom Laporte, are related to *Ratoldus*.[67]

It should not be forgotten that English pontificals also have similar systems of numeration. But *Ratoldus* differs from all the books mentioned above in two main respects: first in the sheer scale of the numbering, which is not to be paralleled until well into the thirteenth-century; second, in the apparent arbitrariness with which the numbering itself was sometimes carried out. The short prayers accompanying acts of tradition in the order provided for the consecration of a bishop are sections unto themselves, for instance, whereas the complex series of scrutinies preceding the Baptismal Order are not covered at all: and there are other anomalies, as Hohler indicated, the most serious of which would seem to be the absence of entries for the 'secondary' set of

[65] The table is printed by J. Hartzheim, *Catalogus historicus-criticus codicum MSS Bibliothecae Ecclesiae Metropolitanae Coloniensis* (Cologne, 1752), pp. 112–13.
[66] The original portions of Cambrai MM 162–3 and 164 are ed. Deshusses, *Le sacramentaire grégorien*, under the sigla 'S' and 'A'. *CLLA*, nos 720 and 761. Also see N. A. Orchard, 'The ninth and tenth-century additions to Cambrai, Médiathèque municipale, 164', *RB*, forthcoming.
[67] The two benedictionals are based on the benedictional compiled as a supplement to the *Hadrianum* by Benedict of Aniane, but have a number of 'extras', the most important of which are the Sangallian blessings *Deus qui filii sui domini nostri* for the vigil of Christmas, and *Omnipotens deus qui te populi sui uoluit esse*, ed. E. Moeller, *Corpus Benedictionum Pontificalium*, 4 vols, CCSL 162, 162A–C (Turnhout, 1980–81) I, no. 925, and II, no. 1667. For a brief account of the benedictional of BNF lat. 13313, see Moeller, *Corpus*, III, 62. See further below, p. cxxxvi. The hypothetical family of 'Saint-Vaast' benedictionals envisaged by J. Laporte, 'Quelques particularités du recueil des "Benedictiones Pontificales" de Durand de Mende', in *Mélanges en l'honneur de Monseigneur Andrieu*, ed. M. Nédoncelle and C. Vogel (Strasbourg, 1956), 279–86, esp. 282, is analysed and expertly dismantled by Prescott, 'The text of the benedictional of St Aethelwold', 125–34.

formulae for St Samson's day (nos 1569–72), and the October translation of St Vedastus (nos 1828–31).

What appears to have sent the compiler astray in both cases was the nature of his model: for neither of the two saints' masses can have appeared in the underlying sacramentary's main text. The mass for St Samson, an early addition, presumably came in on loose leaves, since the prayers in their original form will have been too long for even the most generously proportioned of margins; and the masses provided for St Vedastus, doubtless appeared on the scribe's desk in much the same way. In effect the compiler of the index simply overlooked things that had been 'slipped in'.[68] That an entry should have been given in the table for the 'first' mass for St Samson (and Paternus), also an Orléans 'latecomer', is no doubt due to the fact that the prayers in question, being short, were marginal additions, jotted in at the relevant point in the model's sanctoral. Clearly there were limits, on the one hand, to the amount of material that could be accommodated in margins, and on the other, to the number of times that fresh copies of long books could be made.

Before we move on, it is worth pointing out too that Roman numerals were not always supplied consistently. The forms for the ordination of a deacon (nos 614–618), a section belonging to the pontifical, properly speaking, were never marked out as section CXI, nor the Saturday of the third full week in Lent (nos 726–730), to take an example from the sacramentary, as CXXXV.[69] Perhaps more alarming is the fact that four listed items do not appear at all:

CCCCXIII. Oratio ad portam ciuitatis.	CCCCXV. Oratio ad sponsas benedicendas.
CCCCXIIII. Missa pro infirmis.	CCCCXVI. Benedictio uestium uirginum uel uiduę.

The text of the sacramentary moves quietly from no. CCCCXII, the *oratio in caminata* (no. 2193), to no. CCCCXVII, the *ordo unctionis* (no. 2194). Both numbers are given. Text and table were evidently compiled, at times, without direct reference to each other.

---

[68] See below, pp. lxxxiv–lxxxvi. Also not indexed were the masses for the Saturday before Quadragesima Sunday (nos 528–30) and the forms for Pascha Annotinum (nos 1202–1205).

[69] Seventeen numbers were never supplied: XI, XIII, LXVIII, LXX, LXXII, XCVIII, CXI, CXXXV, CLIIII, CLII, CLXII, CLXXXVI, CLXXXVII, CCVI, CCXLI, CCCX and CCCLXXV.

THE CALENDAR (no. 202)

Ratoldus's calendar-martyrology, the *martyrologium siue compotum* of the table of contents, is, as numerous scholars have observed, clearly of Saint-Vaast, Arras, but with additions relating to Corbie.[70] The principal Artesian feasts encompassed are:

5 Febr.	Et uigilia sancti VEDASTI EPISCOPI.
6 Febr.	DEPOSITIO SANCTI VEDASTI.
21 Febr.	Dedicatio ecclesie sancti VEDASTI.
12 Mar.	Depositio sancti uinditiani atrebatensis episcopi.
19 May	Atrebas, depositio sancti hadulfi episcopi.
4 June	Translatio sancti VEDASTI in cripta.
1 Oct.	Nobiliaco monasterio translatio sancti uedasti.
2 Oct.	Atrebatis depositio sancti scupilionis presbiteri.
8 Oct.	OCTAVAE SANCTI VEDASTI.
19 Oct.	Depositio sancti amati confessoris.
9 Nov.	Et sancti ragnulfi martiris.

All but two appear in the (fully liturgical) Saint-Vaast calendars of later centuries: the translation of St Vedastus's relics on 4 June, which evidently marks one of the mid-ninth-century translations mentioned in the short book of miracles complied by Ulmar, prepositus of Saint-Vaast's, in the late ninth century; and the deposition of St Scupilio.[71] These, presumably, simply fell out of fashion. Indeed, it may

---

[70] A. Borst, *Der karolingische Reichskalendar und seine Überlieferung bis ins 12. Jahrhundert*, 3 vols, MGH Libri Memoriales (Hanover, 2001) I, 87, mistakenly assigns the calendar (which he calls 'Kalendarium Corbiense' [siglum a.14]) to Cambrai. Borst's monumental work must be used with care, for his analyses of manuscripts, texts and 'traditions' often fall short of the mark. His tabulations, however, are exceptionally useful.

[71] Ulmar's accounts are ed. O. Holder Egger, *Monumenta Vedastina Minora*, MGH SS 15.i (Hanover, 1887), pp. 399–402. St Scupilio is recorded as being a helper of St Vedastus in Jonas's Life. See the *Vita S. Vedasti*, ed. B. Krusch, MGH rer. Meroving. 3 (Hanover, 1896), 399–412, with Brou, 'L'ancien office de Saint Vaast, évêque d'Arras', *Etudes grégoriennes* 4 (1961), 7–42, at 37, note 1. The later calendars from Saint-Vaast that I have consulted are those of Arras, Bibliothèque municipale, 230, the thirteenth-century ordinal, ed. Brou, *The Monastic Ordinal* I, 105–116; Arras, Bibliothèque municipale 444, a thirteenth-century missal; Arras, Bibliothèque municipale 725, a late-thirteenth-century breviary; and Arras, Bibliothèque municipale 729, an early-fourteenth-century breviary in two volumes. Calendars from the cathedral, such as those of Arras, Bibliothèque municipale 297 and 303, two fourteenth-century missals, are distinctively different. Photographs of the texts concerned are available in the Conway Library of the Courtauld Institute of Art.

even be that ideas about what was actually being commemorated in June were already hazy when *Ratoldus* was written. For according to Ulmar, the translation of the saint's relics into the abbey's crypt for safekeeping during Viking raids took place on 2 July (*vi nonas Julii*) 852. It was the return of the relics to their original position in the upper church that took place on 4 June (*ii nonas iunii*) 853. The entry in the calendar, properly speaking, should therefore read *ex crypta* not *in*.

A further peculiarity is the presence of an entry for the deposition of St Amatus, bishop of Sens, presumably at Douai in 870, on 19 October, the day set aside in later centuries at Cambrai for the commemoration of the (alleged) translation of his relics to Cambrai under Bishop Gerardus II (1076–92) in 1078.[72] As *Ratoldus* is clearly not a late-eleventh-century book one can only suppose that the Cambrai communities, as a matter of convenience, simply 'borrowed' the 19 October for their translation.

But the situation is an odd one, for the community of Saint-Amé at Douai apparently treated the day as the one on which the saint (its patron) was ordained, and 13 September as the one on which, although it is not expressly described as such, he was deposed. Quite how this tangle arose is difficult to say, but it must have come about long after Ratoldus's time. For as long as St Amatus was venerated on 19 October there could be no doubt that he was the bishop of Sens, rather than the abbot of Remiremont, who by a great misfortune also happened to be remembered on 13 September. The monks of Saint-Vaast's continued to venerate the saint in October (and in copes) well into the fourteenth century.[73]

The only 'local' feasts not encompassed in *Ratoldus* that one might otherwise have expected to find are the translation of St Hadulfus,

---

[72] No instances of entries for the feast of the translation of St Amatus on 19 October in calendars or sanctoralia of books from Cambrai are recorded by V. Leroquais, *Les breviaires manuscrits*, 6 vols (Paris, 1934), or *idem*, *Les sacramentaires*. However, photographs indicate that the calendar of Cambrai, Médiathèque municipale, 233, a late-thirteenth-century missal from Saint-Autbert's at Cambrai, has entries for the deposition of the saint on 13 September and the translation in October, and Arras BM 303, the fourteenth-century missal from Arras Cathedral, an entry for the translation alone. The matter needs to be investigated further, since proper offices (and masses) are generally speaking far more abundant for the feast in October.

[73] See the calendar of Lille, Bibliothèque municipale 23, a late-thirteenth-century missal, described by Leroquais, *Les sacramentaires*, II, 148. For Saint-Vaast's in the thirteenth century, see for instance, the calendar ed. Brou, *The Monastic Ordinal*, I, 114, and for the office, II, 21–2.

second abbot of Saint-Vaast's (710–29), whose relics were apparently moved into the main abbatial church from the collegiate church of Saint-Pierre on 31 August (the year is not known) by Engrannus, bishop of Cambrai (d. *c.* 960), a former monk of Corbie; and the *relatio sancti Vedasti*, which commemorates (according to eleventh-century accounts) the return of St Vedastus's relics from a period of safekeeping at Beauvais in the 880s.[74] At any rate, both are fixtures in the thirteenth- and fourteenth-century texts that have come down to us from Arras, cathedral and abbey; but it is likely that *Ratoldus* represents a state of affairs before these feasts became popular.

The rest of the calendar-martyrology may be dealt with more briefly. There are a substantial number of entries for saints venerated at houses in northern France generally, and Picardy particularly:

Amiens: Salvius, bishop (11 Jan.); Firmin II (1 Sept.); and Firmin I (25 Sept.).

Auxy-les-Moines: Silvinus (15 Febr.).

Beauvais: Lucian, Maximus and Julianus (8 Jan. and 16 Oct.), Justus (18 Oct.).

Blangy: Bertha (4 July).

Cambrai: Autbertus (13 Dec.), Gaugericus (11 Aug.).

Liège: Lambert (17 Sept.), Hubert (3 Nov.)

Maastricht: Servatius (13 May).

Maubeuge: Aldegundis (30 Jan.).

Nivelles: Gertrude (17 Mar.).

Noyon: Eligius (1 Dec.).

Peronne: Furseus (16 Jan.).

Reims: Remigius (13 Jan.), and the translation with SS Germanus, Bavo and Piat (1 Oct.); Timothy and Apollinaris (23 Aug.); Nicasius and Eutropia (14 Dec.).

---

[74] See the *Gesta Episcopum Cameracensium*, compiled in the time of Bishop Gerardus I (*c.* 1013–48), ed. L. C. Bethmann, MGH SS 7 (Hanover, 1846), 393–938, at 414–15 and 433 (Bk I, caps 35 and 85–7). *Ratoldus*'s calendar provides the earliest surviving evidence for St Hadulfus's 'deposition' on 19 May. Clearly if no cult had grown up around the saint before the tenth century, it is just possible that this 'deposition' actually relates to Engrannus's actions: technically St Hadulfus's relics were 'deposed' by him at Saint-Vaast's, not 'translated'. The 'translation' recorded in later Arras calendars on 31 August (Arras BM 444, for instance) might therefore refer to a later (post tenth-century) event. For the proper office of the translation embodied in Arras, Bibliothèque municipale 465, a fourteenth-century breviary from Saint-Vaast's, see the Cantus database at: http://www.publish.uwo.ca/~cantus. No life of the saint survives.

Saint-Amand: Amand (6 Febr.), his translation and the dedication of the basilica (26 Oct.).
Saint-Bertin: Bertin (5 Sept.).
Saint-Josse-sur-Mer: Judoc (13 Dec.).
Saint-Omer: Audomarus (9 Sept.), Winnoc (6 Nov.).
Saint-Quentin: invention of the relics of St Quentin (23 June), main feast (31 Oct.).
Saint-Riquier: Richarius, in capitals (26 Apr.).
Saint-Trond: Trudo (23 Nov.).
Saint-Wandrille: Wandregisilis (22 July).
Saint-Valéry: Valericus (1 Apr.; and translation, 12 Dec.).
Tournus: Philibert (20 Aug.).
Valenciennes: Salvius (26 June).

Houses in the great German provinces are well represented too. But the region providing the greatest number of entries, Picardy and the Pas-de-Calais aside, is western central France; and it seems fairly clear from the presence of the feasts of no less than four bishops of Auxerre, SS Amator (1 May), Ursus (30 July), German (31 July), Fraternus (29 Sept.), along with those of the deacon St Corchodomus (4 May), the lector St Iuuinianus (5 May), the priest St Marsus (4 Oct.), and others, that the monk, or even abbot of Arras who compiled *Ratoldus*'s calendar had access to an Auxerrois recension either of the martyrology of Florus of Lyon, or of Ado of Vienne.[75]

Additions at Corbie

As Delisle indicated, *Ratoldus* and St Petersburg, National Library of Russia, Q. v. I. 56, a late-ninth or early-tenth-century calendar from Arras Cathedral that later found its way to Corbie, are in certain respects twins. Both came to Corbie from houses in Arras; and both have a number of later additions in common, in particular a distinctive series of gradings, probably of the thirteenth century: *M.*, *R. iiii*, *R. nouem*, and *R. xii.*, standing for the number of lessons, or rather responses to

[75] Note also the presence of entries for the rare feasts of St Gregory, bishop of Langres (6 Jan.), and Stephen, bishop of Lyon (13 Feb.). Entries for the feasts of Annanias and companions (24 Apr.), Iosue (1 Sept.), Moses (4 Sept.), amd Zacharias (6 Sept.) descend ultimately from Florus's martyrology. See Quentin, *Les martyrologes*, p. 349.

lessons, assigned at matins on the days in question, a simple *Memoria*, *Responsoria iii*, *Responsoria nouem*, and *Responsoria xii*.[76]

The principal additions to *Ratoldus* are:

17 Jan.	Et depositio sancti antonii monachii.
1 Febr.	Depositio sancti precordii confessoris.
3 Febr.	Natalis sanctę uualdetrudę uirginis.
7 Febr.	VERIS INITIVM habet dies xci.
10 Febr.	Et translatio sancte gertrudis.
11 Febr.	Lugduno desiderii episcopi.
15 Febr.	Diabolus retrorsum a domino captus recessit.
24 Febr.	Hic fit bissextus.
8 Mar.	Prima incensio lune paschalis.
10 Mar.	Translatio sancti uiti ad nouam corbeiam.
13 Mar.	In attica miluus apparet.
14 Mar.	Post istum locum non potest esse quadragesima.
15 Mar.	Abbatis domni stat mentio sancta Ratoldi. Istum qui fecit scribere quippe librum.
17 Mar.	Adam et eua seducti sunt. Et translatio corporis sanctę bathildis reginę.
22 Mar.	Primum pascha, et sedes epactarum.
24 Mar.	Concurrentium locus.
25 Mar.	Adam plasmatus est et cunctis animantibus nomina inposuit.
1 Apr.	Liganau monasterio depositio sancti uualarici confessoris.
27 Apr.	Obiit Odo.
28 Apr.	Et sancti christophori martyris.
9 May	ESTATIS INITIVM habet dies xci.
14 May	QVADRAGISIMA ANTE FESTVM SANCTI iohannis.
16 May	Ambianensis ciuitate depositio sancti honorati episcopi.
5 June	Corbeia translatio sancti precordii confessoris.
13 June	Vltimum pentecostes.

---

[76] Delisle, 'Mémoire', 345–60, 392–6. The calendar, which originally formed part of a volume of miscellaneous treatises from Arras (now St Petersburg, National Library of Russia, Q. v. I. 34 and Q. v. II. 5), is ed. A. Staerck, *Les manuscrits latins conservés a la bibliothèque impériale de Saint-Petersbourg*, 2 vols (St Petersburg, 1910) I, 205–212, with a plate of the page for December. For a good general account of the manuscripts and some of the texts concerned, see Andrieu, *OR*, I, 319–21 and 348–51. Attempts to date the book (as originally constituted) *c*. 825 or 855–78 on the basis of computistical entries accompanying the calendar are unconvincing. The series of years running from 826 to 854 entered on the page for December are plainly late-tenth-century Corbie additions. The tables for 855–78, which follow the calendar, if not added at Corbie (I have not seen the page in question), were doubtless copied from the model.

22 June	Nola ciuitate natale sancti paulini episcopi et confessoris.
1 July	Natale sancti carilephi presbiteri.
15 July	Corbeia monasterio exceptio reliquiarum sancti dion<is>ii.
20 July	Corbeiae monasterio dedicatio sancti stephani martyris.
24 July	In Tiro ciuitate natale sancte christine uirginis.
28 July	Corbeia dedicatio sancti petri apostoli.
7 Aug.	Transfiguratio domini. Autumni initium habet dies xci.
19 Aug.	Hierusolimis apparatio sanctę crucis.
21 Aug.	Consecratio sanctę gertrudis uirginis.
25 Aug.	Natalis sancti genesii martiris.
26 Aug.	Natalis sancti eleutherii episcopi.
20 Sept.	Eleuatio corporis sancti amandi.
23 Oct.	Restitutio corporis sancti amandi episcopi.
7 Nov.	Hiemis initium habet dies xcii.
14 Nov.	QVADRAGINTA ANTE NATALEM DOMINI.
15 Dec.	Aurelianis depositio Maximi episcopi.

Entries of note are those for St Precordius, whose relics were translated into the abbey church on 5 June 940, and for whom a proper mass was added to the book *c*. 1000; the dedications of the basilicas of St Stephen and St Peter; the translation of St Vitus's relics to 'New Corbie' or Corvey in Saxony, founded from Corbie *c*. 815; the obituary of Odo, the former abbot of the house who became bishop of Beauvais (861–81); and the feasts of saints venerated nearby, notably those relating to St Gertrude, patron of Nivelles.

Naturally, varying numbers of these are to be found in the Corbie martyrologies that have come down to us.[77] Paris, Bibliothèque nationale de France, lat. 12260, a shortened Hieronymian martyrology in Maudramnus script of the last quarter of the eighth century gives:[78]

30 Jan.	Cala monasterio depositio Baldechildis reginae. Corbeia monasterio dedicatio basilicae sancti Iohannis euangelistae.
28 July	Corbeia monasterio dedicatio basilicae sancti Petri apostoli.
20 Sept.	Corbeia monasterio dedicatio basilicae Albini et Marcellini.
9 Oct.	Corbeia monasterio depositio Theodredi abbatis.

Bathildis and Theodredus were the founders of the house. Paris, Bibliothèque nationale de France, lat. 17767, the martyrology written by

---

[77] For a useful list of indicative feasts, see Wilmart, *DACL* 3.ii, cols 2926–7.
[78] Ed. Martène and Durand, *Thesaurus novus anecdotum*, III, 1571–88. Also see Ganz, *Corbie*, pp. 134–5.

the scribe Nevelo in the eleventh century, gives in addition to those just mentioned:[79]

16 Jan.   Arelate depositio sancti Honorati episcopi et confessoris.
9 Feb.   In Parrona natalis Fursei confessoris.
15 Mar.   Obiit Ratoldus Abbas bonae memoriae.
1 Apr.   <L>iganau monasterio depositio beati Vualerici confessoris.
23 May   In nola ciuitate natalis sancti paulini episcopi et confessoris.
25 May   Corbeia monasterio translatio corporis sancti Gentiani.
5 June   Corbeia translatio corporis sancti Praecordii confessoris.
1 July   Cinomannico Anisola monasterio depositio sancti Karilefi presbyteri et confessoris.
15 July   Corbeia monasterio exceptio reliquiarium sancti dionysii et sociorum eius.

The only feast that ought to have been added to *Ratoldus* is that of the translation of St Gentian, whose relics were brought to the abbey on 5 May 893 under the guidance of Otger, bishop of Amiens (*c.* 893–928).[80] But the Corbie annotator may have felt that the notice of the deposition (11 Dec.), which names SS Fuscian and Victoricus, fellow martyrs, sufficed: the feast, in any case, was not one of those registered at Corbie in *St Petersburg*. The feasts that were added to the original text of *St Petersburg* are:

5 Jan.   Et natale sancti simeonis qui columna stetit.
13 Jan.   Depositio sancti remigii episcopi.
16 Jan.   Fursei.
1 Feb.   Natale sancti precordii.
6 Feb.   Et depositio sancti amandi.
14 Mar.   Obitus Ratoldi.
3 May   Et inuentio sancte crucis.
30 May   Cenobio centule sanctorum confessorum caydoci adriani madelgisli.
5 June   Translatio sancti precordii confessoris.
8 June   Et sancti gildardi.
14 June   Rufini et Valerii (of Bazoches).
27 June   Obiit hildebrandi custos.

[79] Ed. d'Achery, *Spicilegium*, II, 1–23. See Quentin, *Les martyrologes*, pp. 677–9.
[80] For the collect of the proper mass for the translation added to BNF lat. 12051 in the early eleventh century, see Delisle, 'Mémoire', 177.

15 July	Exceptio reliquiarum sancti dionisii cum sociis.
20 July	Corbeia dedicatio sancti stephani. Margaretae.
28 July	Corbeia dedicatio sancti petri.
2 Aug.	Sancti petri ad uincula.
18 Aug.	Et sancti martini pape.
24 Aug.	Et depositio audoeni episcopi.
1 Sept.	Natale sancti firmini.
8 Sept.	Et natiuitas sancta maria.
9 Sept.	Et depositio sancti audomari episcopi.
14 Sept.	Et natale sanctorum corneli et cipriani.
1 Oct.	Et translatio sancti uedasti et natale sancti piatone et sancti germani episcopi.
23 Oct.	Natale sancti gratiani martyris. (shepherd of Picardy, Coulombes).
1 Nov.	siue omnium sanctorum. Cenobio centule depositio sancti VIGORIS episcopi et confessoris.
11 Nov.	Et depositio sancti martini episcopi.
23 Nov.	Et sancti columbani.
29 Nov.	Et natale sancti saturnini et sancti crisanti.
11 Dec.	Gentiani.

As far as the provenance of the original parts of *St Petersburg* is concerned, Arras is clearly in view, as Delisle suggested, since an entry is provided on 2 January for the *dedicatio ecclesie sancte marie atrebatensis*. This is the former cathedral of St Mary, which was probably still served by a small community in the tenth century: and we can tell that the day given in *St Petersburg* is the right one because an entry for the feast, cast in precisely the same terms, figured, before erasure, in the calendar of Cambrai, Mediathèque municipale 75, a mid-eleventh-century gradual from Arras. An entry also survives, this time intact, in the calendar of Paris, Bibliothèque Saint-Geneviève 126, a mid-twelfth-century missal from Saint-Vaast's that later found its way to Senlis. The dedication of Saint-Vaast itself is duly recorded on 21 February in the Saint-Geneviève book, as in *Ratoldus*.[81]

An Artesian origin for *St Petersburg* is clear on other grounds too. We have entries for St Aldegundis of Maubeuge (30 Jan.); St Vedastus

---

[81] See D. Muzerelle, *Manuscrits datés des Bibliothèques de France 1: Cambrai* (Paris, 2000), p. 14, and Leroquais, *Les sacramentaires*, I, 272–4. Borst, *Der karolingische Reichskalender*, I, 150, is clearly off track again when he assigns *St Petersburg* too to Cambrai ('Kalendarium Cameracense' [siglum c.5]).

(6 Feb.), though without the vigil and octave celebrated at the abbey; St Gaugericus, principal saint of Cambrai (11 Aug.), seat of the combined bishopric of Arras-Cambrai; St Hundegundis of Homblières (25 Aug.); St Eusebia of Hamage (18 Nov.); a good number of saints who were popular in the region, such as SS Richarius and Valericus, both with translations; and as one might expect, saints venerated in northern France at large. We also have a handful of feasts (some very striking) of wider general interest evidently deriving from martyrologies and necrologies:

JANUARY
3. St Genovefa of Paris.
8. St Lucian of Beauvais.
15. Deposition of St Remigius of Reims (the wrong day).

FEBRUARY
1. St Brigid of Ireland. St Ursus.

MARCH
17. St Patrick of Ireland.
21. St Benedict.

APRIL
1. St Valericus of Saint-Valéry.
26. Pope Gregory, perhaps his ordination. Deposition of St Richarius of Saint-Riquier.
27. 'Advent' of Pope Calixtus.

MAY
28. St Germanus of Paris.

JUNE
8. St Medard of Soissons.
14. Translation of St Anianus of Orléans.
17. St Avitus of Aurillac.

JULY
4. Translation of St Martin.
11. St Benedict.

16. 'Advent' of St Cassian.
20. St Wulmar of Samer.
25. St Firmin I of Amiens.

AUGUST
5. Deposition of St Cassian of Autun.
11. St Gaugericus of Cambrai.
20. St Philibert of Tournus.
31. St Paulinus of Trier.

SEPTEMBER
1. Translation of St Nazarius (to Lorsch).
22. St Maurice and companions.
17. St Lambert of Liège.
23. Pope Linus.
25. St Firminus I, Bishop of Amiens.

OCTOBER
1. St Remigius of Reims.
3. St Leger.
5. St Crista (apparently unattested elsewhere).
9. SS Denis, Rusticus and Eleutherius. Translation of St Richarius of Saint-Riquier.
25. SS Crispin and Crispinian of Soissons.
26. Translation of St Amand of Saint-Amand.

30. Pope Leo, possibly Leo V (d. 903) or Leo VI (d. 928), the only popes of the name whose obituaries are not otherwise known.
31. St Quentin of Saint-Quentin-en-Vermandois.

NOVEMBER
1. St Audomarus of Saint-Omer.
3. St Hubert of Liège.
17. Depostion of St Anianus of Orléans.

DECEMBER
1. St Eligius of Noyon.
5. St Crispinus, from Ado's martyrology.
12. St Valericus (translation at Saint-Valéry).
15. St Maximus of Orléans.
19. St Gregory of Auxerre.

The calendar of Saint-Vaast at Arras, as represented by *Ratoldus*, was clearly very different from the one adopted at the former cathedral.

GENERAL LITURGICAL CHARACTER OF THE SACRAMENTARY

In simple terms *Ratoldus* is a hybrid. A copy of the *Hadrianum*, that is to say, the sacramentary sent by Pope Hadrian to Charlemagne in the late 780s, lies at root; all else is built around that. As the collation tables at the end of this volume will indicate, the matter arranged around this 'core' descends from two or perhaps three well-known sources: a copy of the 'Supplement' to the *Hadrianum* probably compiled by Benedict of Aniane in the first decades of the ninth century; some sort of 'Eighth-Century Gelasian' sacramentary, perhaps one similar to Paris, Bibliothèque nationale de France, lat. 12048, the so-called 'Sacramentary of Gellone', a sacramentary-cum-pontifical prepared for Hildoard, bishop of Cambrai (d. 816 × 817), that found its way to Gellone soon thereafter; and a collection of *ordines*, principally for baptism and for obsequies.

As Hohler indicated, the sacramentary embodied in *Ratoldus* is, more specifically, particularly closely related to three others:[82]

---

[82] Hohler, 'Some service-books', 65, 221, notes 21 and 22.

Paris, Bibliothèque nationale de France lat. 11589: late-tenth-century, from the abbey of Saint-Méen in Brittany. Sanctoral separate.[83] Cues for the chant at mass are provided by the original scribe at the head of the formularies in the temporal and sanctoral. The sacramentary embodies propers for: Sidrac, Misac and Abednego (24 Apr.); St Guoetgualus (4 June); SS Eusebius and Méen (16 June); St Samson (28 July); St Malo (15 Nov.), with a vigil; and St Iudicael, King of Armorica, later a monk of the abbey (11 Dec.). As Doms Barré and Deshusses have noted, BNF lat. 11589 is one of a select group of books to name Alcuin in connexion with the votive masses encompassed: *Incipiunt missas dumno Alcuini per singulas ferias in ebdomada* (fol. 152v).[84] Also encompassed, on fols 157r–161r, are a series of votive masses in honour of groups of saints. Apostles and evangelists aside, those commemorated are: Innocent, Stephen, Denis, Rusticus and Eleutherius, Sebastian, Lawrence, Vincent, Tiburtius, Protus and Iacinthus, Cucuphas and Hermes, a list consonant principally with Saint-Denis, and partly with the claims of Saint-Médard's at Soissons.[85] By the twelfth century, the volume seems to have found its way to the abbey of Saint-Corneille de Compiègne, where a proper mass for the patron of the house, entitled *Delatio sancti Cornelii papae Compendio, idus martii*, was added on fol. 85v.

Orléans, Bibliothèque municipale 127 [105]: the so-called 'Sacramentary of Winchcombe', written either at Ramsey, or at Winchcombe in the late tenth century. A proper mass for St Kenelm (17 July) figures in the sanctoral, which is separate, as in BNF lat. 11589; and there is a second set of formulae for the saint, presum-

---

[83] For general descriptions of the book, see Delisle, 'Mémoire', 244–6; Leroquais, *Les sacramentaires*, I, 110–13; Duine, *Inventaire liturgique*, pp. 23–33. Fol. 80v is reproduced by Samaran and Marichal, *Catalogue des manuscrits en écriture latin*, III.ii, plate CCXLIVa.

[84] H. Barré and J. Deshusses, 'A la recherche du missel d'Alcuin', *EL* 82 (1968), 3–44, at 35–6. The materials provided for ordeals are ed. F. Zeumer, *Formulae Merovingici et Karolini Aevi*, MGH Legum Sectio 5: Formulae (Hanover, 1886), pp. 640–3.

[85] By the eleventh century Soissons was apparently claiming title to relics of SS Tiburtius, Marcellinus and Peter, Hermes, Protus and Iacinthus, and Marius, Martha, Audifax and Abacuc, all stolen away from Rome in 828 by Einhard, Charlemagne's biographer, who had them taken first to Aachen, then to the abbey of Mulheim, near Cologne. The stories are ed. G. Waitz, *Translatio et Miracula SS Marcellini et Petri auctore Einhardo*, and O. Holder-Egger, *Translatio SS Tiburtii, Marcellini et Petri ad S. Medardum*, MGH SS 15.i (Hanover, 1887), pp. 238–64 and 391–5. Where Saint-Denis is concerned, the link is likely to be Hilduin, whose priest was instrumental in the thefts. On the relics of SS Sebastian and Gregory acquired by Hilduin in Rome in 826, see below, note 96.

ably for use on 'low' Thursdays, among the votives (pages 274 and 280). Kenelm's name also appears in capitals in the *Nobis quoque* of the Canon of the Mass.[86] Other adjustments made in England include the provision of a distinctive votive for St Benedict, also to be found in Rouen, Bibliothèque municipale 274, the so-called 'Missal of Robert of Jumièges', a splendid early-eleventh-century copy of a sacramentary from Peterborough or (less probably) Ely, later owned by Robert, bishop of London (1044–51) and archbishop of Canterbury (1051–2).[87] Whether the prominence given to the name of St Germanus (of Paris) on page 203, and the presence of a secondary mass for the saint in October (pages 232–3), can be connected with Germanus, abbot of Winchcombe (*c.* 969–75) and, after an interlude at Fleury, abbot of the joint communities of Winchcombe and Ramsey at Ramsey (*c.* 978–92), remains to be seen. Germanus doubtless would never have taken the initiative in such matters, but the scribe might.[88] One would need to be sure though, that the texts in question were not simply copied mechanically from the model, something that cannot be established with confidence either way at present. Perhaps the most striking thing about *Winchcombe* in general terms is that a substantial section of its votives are laid out in a 'staggered' formation. Collects of the various masses encompassed come first, the corresponding secrets next, and finally the post-communions. A similar approach seems to have been followed by the man who arranged the masses of the dead in Laon, Bibliothèque municipale, 118, the much disordered (and incomplete) combined gradual, sacramentary and lectionary, of some choir master, possibly even abbot, of Saint-Denis. Indeed, there are signs that something similiar to the Laon book served as the model for *Winchcombe* as a

---

[86] Ed. A. Davril, *The Winchcombe Sacramentary*, HBS 109 (London, 1995). A partial synopsis of *Winchcombe*'s contents, still useful, is given by J. Wickham Legg, *Missale ad usum ecclesiae Westmonasteriensis*, 3 vols, HBS 1, 5 and 12 (1891–7) III, 1447–1628. For discussion of provenance and later history, see Delisle, 'Mémoire', 211–18; Gremont and Donnat, 'Fleury, le Mont Saint-Michel et l'Angleterre'.

[87] *The Winchcombe Sacramentary*, ed. Davril, pp. 218, 222, 225, nos 1514, 1543, 1573; *The Missal of Robert of Jumièges*, ed. H. A. Wilson, HBS 11 (London, 1896), p. 248.

[88] On Germanus, and for a good short account of the character of the sacramentary, see M. Lapidge, 'Abbot Germanus, Winchcombe, Ramsey and the Cambridge Psalter', in *Words, Texts and Manuscripts. Studies in Anglo-Saxon Culture presented to Helmut Gneuss on the Occasion of his Sixty-Fifth Birthday*, ed. M. Korhammer, K. Reichl and H. Sauer (Woodbridge, 1992), 99–129, esp. 103–5, 117–26. Note that the only names written in capitals in the texts encompassed in the sanctoral of Orléans BM 127 are those of SS Benedict, Kenelm, Germanus, Peter, and Denis. See *The Winchcombe Sacramentary*, ed. Davril, pp. 151, 170, 172, 194, 205, nos 939, 1101–5, 1120, 1123, 1315, 1406.

whole, for not only do both provide (unusually) a mass for the vigil of St Gregory, but they also give the same set of 'extra' prayers for the deposition of St Benedict (21 Mar.).[89] *Winchcombe* soon found its way overseas, travelling first to Mont-Saint-Michel 991 × 1009, then Fleury.

Paris, Bibliothèque nationale de France, lat. 2297: early-eleventh-century, probably from a house in the diocese of Dol. Closely written in two columns; sanctoral, beginning with St Felix, separate. Distinctive propers are provided for: Sidrac, Misac and Abednego; St Carilef of Le Mans (1 July); St Samson of Dol (28 July), with a vigil; St Victurus of Nantes (1 Sept.); and St Malo (15 Nov.), with a vigil. Also embodied is an ancient Gallican mass for SS Cyricus and Julitta (16 June). The remains of the first gathering of the book are preserved today as fols 45–47 and 49–50 of Paris, Bibliothèque nationale de France, lat. 894, a collection of fragments assembled by the seventeenth-century scholar Étienne Baluze. The leaves originally stood in the sacramentary as fols 1, 3–6 and 8. The proper order of the gathering as reconstructed by Delisle is: BNF lat. 894, fols 45, 46, 47, 49; BNF lat. 2297, fol. 7; then BNF lat. 894, fol. 50. The book contains important material in Old French.[90]

That all four descend from models originally compiled at Saint-Denis seems clear from their respective sanctoralia. Masses are provided for:

(i) The vigil, feast and octave of St Denis and companions (9 Oct.).[91]

(ii) St Genovefa of Paris (3 Jan.).

[89] For a description of the book, see below, p. lxvii. For the extra prayers provided for St Benedict's day, see R. Grégoire, 'Prières liturgiques médiévales en l'honneur de saint Benoit, sainte Scolastique et de saint Maur', Analecta Monastica 7, *Studia Anselmiana* 54 (Rome, 1965), 1–85, at 2, 5–7 and 19.
[90] See Delisle, 'Mémoire', 246–50; Leroquais, *Les sacramentaires*, I, 107–10; Duine, *Inventaire liturgique*, pp. 33–34; R. Haggenmüller, *Die Überlieferung der Beda und Egbert zugeschriebenen Bussbücher*, Europaischer Hochschulschriften 461 (Frankfurt am Main, 1991), pp. 89–90.
[91] Masses for the feast of the invention of St Denis (15 July) do not seem to have become popular until the tenth or perhaps even eleventh century, even though some sort of proper is specified in the calendar of Paris, Bibliothèque Saint-Geneviève 111, a sacramentary produced at Saint-Denis in the last quarter of the ninth century probably for Hadebertus, bishop of Senlis (*c.* 871–900). *CLLA*, no. 745. See Robertson, *Service Books*, pp. 7–8, 64, 69, 414–16, 470, with D. H. Turner, *The Missal of the New Minster, Winchester*, HBS 93 (London, 1962), pp. ix–x and 87, and M. Lapidge, 'The lost *passio metrica sancti Dionysii* by Hilduin of Saint-Denis', *Mittelateinisches Jahrbuch* 22 (1987), 56–80.

(iii) St Cucuphas of Barcelona (25 July), whose relics were brought to the abbey from an alien priory during Hilduin's abbacy (814–41). The community may have had title to them as far back as Abbot Fulrad's time (750–84).[92]

(iv) The vigil and feast of St Benedict (20 Mar.), and his translation (11 July), indicative of a Benedictine foundation. Ratoldus's scribe, unfortunately, seems to have created a nonsense of the relative distribution of the prayers.

(v) St Symphorian (22 Aug.). Patron of the oratory in which the relics of St Germanus of Paris were initially deposed. Indicative of Paris at large, though we must return to the details of the formulae provided in due course.

For Saint-Denis, the prayers adopted for the feasts of St Denis and companions (especially the octave) are decisive.[93] As for date, reference

---

[92] See Robertson, *Service Books*, pp. 30–31, with G. G. Meersseman, *Les capitules du diurnal de Saint-Denis*, Spicilegium Friburgense 30 (Fribourg, 1986), pp. 96–99, who prints the office for the day from Verona, Biblioteca Capitolare 88, a mid-ninth-century diurnal from the abbey. *CLLA*, no. 1627. Also see the entry in the martyrology of Ado, ed. Quentin, *Les martyrologes*, p. 507.

[93] It is well to note that masses for the vigil, feast and octave of St Denis, but with entirely different sets of prayers, are also to be found in the late-ninth-century supplement to Dusseldorf, Landes- und Universitätsbibliothek, D. 1, a sacramentary written for the confessors of the nuns of Essen in the 860s:

<32r> VIII ID. OCTB. VIGILIA SANCTORVM MARTYRVM DYONISII, RVSTICI ET ELEVTHERII
Beatorum martyrum dionisii, rustici, et eleutherii, natalicia ueneranda . . . glorificationis amore deuotior. Per dominum.
SVPER OBLATA. Munera populi tui domine propitius intende . . . fac gaudere suffragiis. Per.
AD COMPLENDVM. Omnipotens et misericors deus qui nos sacramentorum tuorum . . . et fidei consortio et digno seruitio. Per.

ITEM MISSA IN DIE
Presta quęsumus omnipotens deus <32v> ut sicut deuotissime christianus populus tuus . . . pio comprehendat affectu. Per.
ALIA. Annua martyrum tuorum domine dionisii rustici et eleutherii festa recolimus . . . capiamus a<u>gmentum. Per.
SVPER OBLATA. Oblata tibi sint domine munera populi tui . . . nobis intercessione sanctifica. Per.
PRAEFATIO. VD aeterne deus. Innumera laude diuinis dare uirtutibus et gloriosis preconiis . .<33r>. . et uirentibus paradisi floribus suos milites coronauit. Et ideo cum angelis.
AD COMPLENDVM. Sumptis domine sacramentis quesumus ut intercedentibus . . . proficiamus augmentum. Per.

to other books from Paris suggests that the models underlying *Ratoldus* and friends were probably compiled at some point, or rather points, in the first half of the tenth century, since the earliest sacramentaries to have come down to us from Saint-Denis and Notre Dame have considerably smaller sanctoralia:

Paris, Bibliothèque nationale de France, lat. 2290: mid- to late-ninth-century, probably written and decorated at Saint-Amand, certainly for use at Saint-Denis, as its calendar (fols 1–6) indicates. Probably commissioned by Gozlinus, abbot of Saint-Amand from 871 to 886, and of Saint-Denis from 878 to 884.[94] Large sections of the text, principally the temporal and sanctoral, run in line with the *Hadrianum*, but many archaic, presumably pre-Hadrianic, variants figure. Contains propers for the vigil and feast of St Denis but none for the other feasts mentioned above. Its votive masses are highly distinctive and not to be found in any of the other books edited by Deshusses. The collect of its *missa specialium sanctorum* begins: *Propitiare domine quaesumus nobis famulis tuis, per beatorum martyrum tuorum stephani dionysii rustici et eleutherii sebastiani laurentii ypoliti cucuphatis innocentii necnon sanctorum*

ITEM MISSA DE EODEM DIE

Deus qui hodierna die beatum dionisium uirtute constantię . . . et nulla eius aduersa formidare. Per.
SVPER OBLATA. Hostia domine quesumus quam in sanctorum tuorum . . . misericordię dona conciliet. Per.
AD COMPLENDVM. Quesumus omnipotens deus ut qui cęlestia alimenta . . . contra omnia aduersa muniamur. Per dominum.

XVII KL. NOV. OCTAVAS SANCTORVM MARTYRVM DIONISII RVSTICII ET ELEVTHERII

Praesta quesumus omnipotens deus ut qui sanctorum tuorum dionisii . . . eorum <33v> intercessionibus adiuuemur. Per.
SVPER OBLATA. Sacramentorum tuorum nobis domine pia non desit oratio . . . indulgentiam semper obtineat. Per dominum nostrum.
AD COMPLENDVM. Quesumus omnipotens deus ut qui celestia alimenta percepimus . . . contra omnia aduersa muniamur. Per.

Since this supplement appears to have been drawn up at Corvey, it seems reasonable to assume that the masses were assembled there, presumably during or shortly after the refuge of Hilduin of Saint-Denis, *c*. 830–31. The masses spread far and wide throughout Germany, also finding their way to England, though they were evidently never adopted in France. I have a full study of Dusseldorf D. 1 in hand.

94 For general descriptions, see Leroquais, *Les sacramentaires*, I, 19–21; Deshusses, *Le sacramentaire grégorien*, III, 34–5 (siglum 'R'); *idem*, 'Chronologie des grands sacramentaires de Saint-Amand', *RB* 87 (1977), 230–37. *CLLA*, no. 760. Extracts from the calendar are printed by Delisle, 'Mémoire', 324–5, and the contents listed in a synopsis by Robertson, *Service Books*, pp. 445–93, Appendix A (siglum N1).

confessorum martini hilarii ambrosii hieronimi augustini benedicti gregorii hilari merita gloriosa . . .; and the collect of its *missa pro defuncto*: *Beatorum martyrum tuorum dionysii rustici et eleutherii quaesumus domine*.[95] Saint-Denis had important relics of the saints mentioned in the first part of *Propitiare*. The position of the altars dedicated in their honour in the twelfth century is known from Abbot Suger's *De administratione* and *De consecratione*.[96] The series of saints named in the second part of the prayer (from Martin on) mirrors that of the book's *Communicantes*.

Paris, Bibliothèque nationale de France, lat. 2291: copied at Saint-Amand for the use of Gozlinus when bishop of Paris (884–6). Episcopal benedictions appear in place throughout.[97] In addition to the saints' masses embodied in the *Hadrianum* (which is not followed to the letter), BNF lat. 2291 provides for a number of 'Eighth-Century Gelasians', and, notably, SS Genovefa, Hilary, Scholastica, Benedict, Matthias, translation of Benedict, Mark, Symphorian, Maurice, Jerome, translation of German and the deposition of Remigius, and the vigil and feast of Denis and companions. The extended mass for St Jerome (prayers doubled) is also found in *Winchcombe*.[98] In the tenth century, several sets of additions were made at the front of the book. Particularly noteworthy are the mass for St Christopher; the two masses for St German, one with an episcopal benediction; and the necrology of Saint-Germain-des-Prés. Gozlinus had been abbot of Saint-Germain for a good spell

[95] Deshusses, *Le sacramentaire grégorien*, II, 51–2, 204, nos 1877, 2848.

[96] Ed. E. Panofsky, *Abbot Suger on the Abbey Church of St.-Denis and its Art Treasures*, 2nd ed. (Princeton, 1979), pp. 66–72, 98–99, 119. Also see E. B. Foley, *The First Ordinary of the Royal Abbey of St.-Denis in France*, Spicilegium Friburgense 32 (Fribourg, 1990), pp. 183–255. Hilduin, who obtained relics of SS Sebastian and Gregory the Great from Pope Eugenius II in 826 for Saint-Medard's at Soissons, presumably retained portions from Saint-Denis. For the translation, see the account of Odilo, a monk of Soissons, ed. O. Holder-Egger, *Ex translatione S. Sebastiani auctore Odilone*, MGH SS 15.i (Hanover, 1887), 377–91, esp. 381. A donation of Louis the Pious of 833, partially ed. *Gallia Christiana*, VII, 354, concerned principally with the endowing of the oratory of St Mary in the crypt of Saint-Denis, indicates that St Sebastian's day was one of only three (the others being the Purification of the Virgin, and SS Peter and Paul's) on which refection was to be granted to the monks from the revenues of land alloted. On the relics of St Hippolytus, which were probably brought to Saint-Denis by Hilduin from the church in Alsace at which they had initially been deposed by Fulrad, see R.-J. Hesbert, *Corpus Antiphonalium Officii*, 6 vols, Rerum ecclesiasticarum Documenta, Series maior, Fontes 7–12 (Rome, 1963–79) II, xii, note 2.

[97] For general descriptions, see Leroquais, *Les sacramentaires*, I, 56–8; Deshusses, *Le sacramentaire grégorien*, III, *idem*, 'Chronologie'. *CLLA*, no. 925.

[98] Deshusses, *Le sacramentaire grégorien*, II, 324–5, nos 3610–16; *The Winchcombe Sacramentary*, ed. Davril, pp. 191–2, nos 1292–99.

(867–884) before elevation to episcopal orders, and it may be that the book passed to the house soon after his death.[99] Conceivably the mass with the benediction is a copy of the one he was in the habit of using in Paris; but the matter needs further investigation. From Saint-Germain BNF lat. 2291 later passed to Saint-Denis. The name *Suggeri*, that of Suger, abbot of the house (1122–51), appears in the margin next to the *Communicantes*.

Laon, Bibliothèque municipale 118: an early-tenth-century lectionary and sacramentary, much disordered and incomplete. Sanctoral apparently separate, though only one gathering now remains (fols 214–19), beginning with the mass for St Agnes (21 Jan.) and ending with the mass for St Mark (25 Apr.). The late-ninth-century gradual, now fols 1–14, and 223, was probably prefixed at an early date. Fols 165–168 and 229–49 seem to be parts of another sacramentary, possibly of Saint-Germain. As Robertson has indicated, the original, Saint-Denis sections of Laon BM 118 contain the same set of ferial votives (fols 192v–207v) as BNF lat. 2290 (fols 121–39).[100] The temporal and sanctoral run in parallel with *Winchcombe*. Especially noteworthy is the provision of a mass for the vigil of St Gregory. Relics of the saint had been obtained, along with those of St Sebastian mentioned above, by Hilduin in Rome from Pope Eugenius II in 826 and deposed in the abbey of Saint-Médard at Soissons, of which Hilduin was abbot 822–30.[101] A fair copy of a list of Saint-Denis monks originally drawn up *c.* 867 figures on fol. 74v.[102] The book seems to have found its way into the hands of the Cistercians of Vauclair, near Laon, by the thirteenth century.

Even the most cursory of comparisons will indicate the measure of difference between *Ratoldus*'s sanctoral, for example, and that of BNF lat. 2290 (as set out by Leroquais).

Quite when the Sandionysian models underlying our four books, that

---

[99] All but the mass for St Christopher are ed. A. Wilmart, 'Un sacramentaire à l'usage de Saint-Germain-des-Près. Mentions nécrologiques relatives à ce monastère', *Revue Mabillon* 17 (1927), 279–94. On aspects of Gozlinus's career, see K. F. Werner, 'Gauzlin von Saint-Denis und die westfränkische Reichstellung von Amiens (März 880). Ein Beitrag zur Vorgeschichte von Odos Königtum', *Deutsches Archiv für Erforschung des Mittelalters* 35 (1979), 395–462.

[100] For general descriptions of the book, see Leroquais, *Les sacramentaires*, I, 64–8; *CLLA*, nos 927, 1267; Robertson, *Service Books*, pp. 359–66.

[101] See above, note 96.

[102] Ed. A. Wilmart, 'Les frères défunts de Saint-Denis au déclin du IXe siècle', *Revue Mabillon* 15 (1925), 241–57.

is to say *Ratoldus*, BNF lat. 11589, *Winchcombe* and BNF lat. 2297, found their way from Paris to their new 'homes' is more difficult to determine, however, for the texts transmitted are necessarily transmitted at second hand, perhaps even third hand in the case of *Ratoldus*. It is quite possible, for instance, that the originals were alive with different sets of additions. Yet for all that, certain preliminary observations do seem possible.

First, BNF lat. 2297's model appears to have been more advanced than others, since provision is made for St Christopher, patron of the church lying to the east of Notre Dame. The mass for his day is first attested as an addition in BNF lat. 2291, as has already been mentioned, and next, also as an addition probably of the later tenth century, in the Saint-Germain portions of Laon BM 118.[103] It is likely, therefore, that the Saint-Denis book at root did not arrive in Brittany until late in the century.

Second, *sanctoralia* as advanced as the ones embedded in *Ratoldus*, BNF lat. 11589 and *Winchcombe*, would be exceedingly precocious for the first or second decade of the tenth century. It seems best to suppose therefore, that the Saint-Denis model underlying *Ratoldus* came into the hands of the canons of Dol at Orléans in the 940s or 950s, and that it had been acquired initially by Count Hugh of Paris, the man who settled the community at the church of Saint-Symphorien.

Third, although we do not know how (or even when) the Winchcombe monks came by their model, transmission direct from Paris, rather than indirectly from some centre in Brittany, seems most likely, for there are not only no remnants of masses for Breton saints in the book's sanctoral, but perhaps more important, no significant invocations of Breton saints in the (augmented) Saint-Denis litany of the dead.[104]

---

[103] Note that the entry for the feast in the calendar of BNF lat. 2290 is an addition. See Leroquais, *Les sacramentaires*, I, 19.

[104] For the Saint-Denis order of the dead, as a whole, see below, pp. xcii–xciii. Although *Winchcombe*'s litany is evidently more advanced than the one given in BNF lat. 2290, ed. Delisle, 'Mémoire', 360–1 and Deshusses, *Le sacramentaire grégorien*, III, 285–8, no. 4500, the familial relationship between the two is clear nonetheless. Note for instance that the invocations of SS Denis and companions are followed immediately by that of St Sebastian. Even though a good deal of reordering has taken place, there are numerous other points of contact too. The emphasis given to the 'Acaunenses' in *Winchcombe*, first indicated by Lapidge, 'Abbot Germanus', 105, is probably to be connected with the presence of relics of the Theban Legion at Saint-Denis. See Suger, ed. Panofsky, with Foley, *The First Ordinary*, pp. 210–14. These probably date back to the seventh century, when

Fourth, as we shall see, BNF lat. 11589 probably embodies the oldest form of Saint-Denis text. Before we proceed any further however, it will be best to look at *Ratoldus* in more detail.

THE CANON OF THE MASS (nos 212–231)

Ratoldus's Canon, as has already been mentioned, is not homogeneous. All that remains of the original is the second half of the text, that is to say from the *Hanc igitur* to the *Agnus dei* (nos 222–231); the first half is new.[105] One cannot tell, therefore, whether the *Communicantes*, the one prayer that regularly contains indications of local use, had the names of saints connectable with Saint-Denis or, after adjustment, Orléans. The rest of the Canon is fairly 'bland' from a liturgical point of view. Later additions bring the *Nobis quoque* into line with Corbie use.

Collation shows that the original portions of *Ratoldus* contain only one variant of any note: the words *cum omnibus sanctis* in the prayer *Libera nos* (no. 230):

Libera nos quaesumus domine ab omnibus malis praeteritis, praesentibus et futuris, et intercedente beata et gloriosa semper uirgine dei genetrice maria, et beatis apostolis tuis, petro et paulo atque andrea, cum omnibus sanctis. Da propicius . . .

Reference to Deshusses's edition of the *Hadrianum* shows that only two early books have this incise in their main text:

Oxford, Bodleian Library, Auct. D. I. 20: a mid- to late-ninth-century sacramentary from the abbey of Saint-Gall that soon found its way to St Alban's at Mainz, where a calendar and a prefatory supplement bringing the text into line with local use were added.[106]

---

laus perennis was introduced on the model of Saint-Maurice-en-Valais. See Robertson, *Service Books*, pp. 13–18, for a summary of the evidence.

[105] For the Corbie additions, see below, pp. xliii–xlv.

[106] Its text is ed. Deshusses, *Le sacramentaire grégorien*, under the siglum 'F'. *CLLA*, no. 737. The calendar is ed. A. Merton, *Die Buchmalerei in St Gallen vom neunten bis zum elften Jahrhundert* (Leipzig, 1912), pp. 98–102.

and Modena, Biblioteca Capitolare, O. II. 7: a mid-ninth-century sacramentary, now incomplete, probably written for use at Modena.[107]

In later centuries, however, *cum omnibus sanctis* seems to have become the 'standard' reading, either because the words were thought to have been introduced at, and issued from Rome, or, more probably, because communities generally felt it expedient and sensible to make some mention of 'all' saints, instead of SS Peter, Paul and Andrew alone. At any rate, the form of text given in *Ratoldus*'s *Libera* must have been the form generally used at Saint-Denis in the tenth century, as the incise also appears in *Winchcombe* and BNF lat. 11589.[108] But generations of modifications seem to have carried the Canons of these books away from whatever textual norm prevailed. *Winchcombe*'s is perhaps the most 'eccentric', as it contains a private *Memento* for the priest, and a prayer to be said at communion, *Haec sacrosancta communio*; BNF lat. 11589 and *Ratoldus* are less so, but at key points one often has a 'variant' in its main text when the other has it as an interlineation.[109]

THE TEMPORAL

Comparison of the four sacramentaries, that is to say *Ratoldus*, *Winchcombe*, BNF lat. 11589 and BNF lat. 2297, reveals:

(i) that aside from a few disjunctions, which we shall come to in a moment, the general level of agreement between the books is quite exceptional. Indeed, from the Vigil of Epiphany to Easter the four run almost entirely in parallel, prayer by prayer. However, there are certain indications, here and there, to show that where the temporal alone is concerned, *Ratoldus* sides more with *Winchcombe*. Both, for instance, place the Gelasian prayers for the Pentecostal Ember masses after the first Sunday after the octave (*Dominica I post octauas*). In BNF lat.

---

[107] Its text is ed. Deshusses, *Le sacramentaire grégorien*, under the siglum 'G'. *CLLA*, no. 777.

[108] BNF lat. 2297's Canon does not survive.

[109] For example in the Memento of the dead, BNF lat. 11589 has in its main text *Ipsis domine et omnibus in christo quiescentibus*, whereas in *Ratoldus*, *domine*, a reading that is rare in the earliest copies of the *Hadrianum*, appears as a later addition.

11589 they follow the second Sunday. But since no trace of the formulae remain in BNF lat. 2297 it is difficult to be sure whether any 'Saint-Denis standard' existed.

(ii) that the Saint-Denis books from which *Ratoldus*, *Winchcombe*, BNF lat. 2297 and BNF lat. 11589 descend had elements in common with the pre-Hadrianic Gregorian book underlying Trent, Castel del Buon Consiglio, 1590, the famous early-ninth-century sacramentary of Trent. For the Thursday in the first full week of Lent, *Ratoldus* (nos 556–560), *Winchcombe* and BNF lat. 11589 give:[110]

	Trent	*11589*	*Winchcombe*	*Ratoldus*
Collect.	O. s. d. q. nobis	O. s. d. q. nobis	O. s. d. q. nobis	O. s. d. q. nobis
Alia.	C. qs. o. d. ut huius	C. qs. o. d. ut huius	Precamur	
Secret	Suscipientes dne.	Sacrificia	Sacrificia	Sacrificia
Preface		Quia conpetenter	Quia conpetenter	Quia conpetenter
Ad compl.	Auerte qs. dne	Auerte qs. dne.	Tuorum	Tuorum
<Alia>.			Da qs. dne. pop.	Da qs. dne. pop.

and in common with BNF lat. 2290, *Winchcombe* and BNF lat. 11589 also embody versions of the 'Trent' mass *Concede quesumus omnipotens deus ut ieiunia* for the third Sunday in Lent.[111] In *Ratoldus* and BNF lat. 2297 the forms seem to have been dispensed with.

(iii) that there is some disjunction in the manner in which prefaces were assigned to the Sundays after Pentecost. To summarise the situation: BNF lat. 11589 runs in line with *Winchcombe* from the first Sunday after the octave to the end of the series; BNF lat. 2297 runs in line with *Winchcombe* and BNF lat. 11589 from Sundays I–XX; and *Ratoldus* goes its own way. So for Sundays XXIV and XXV, which have, respectively, the collects *Largire quesumus* and *Familiam tuam*, three different prefaces figure for each mass:

SUNDAY XXIV

Book	*Preface*	*Supplement*
lat. 11589 and *Winch.*	Maiestatem tuam suppliciter deprecantes	XXII<II> post Pent.
lat. 2297.	Qui propterea iure punis errantes	XXII post Pent.
Ratoldus (no. 1897).	Et nos clementiam tuam exorare	XXIII post Pent.

---

[110] Unfortunately BNF lat. 2297 is defective at the point in question.

SUNDAY XXV

lat. 11589 and *Winch.*	Per quem sanctum et benedictum	XXV post Pent.
lat. 2297.	Et nos clementiam tuam exorare	XXIII post Pent.
Ratoldus (no. 1909).	Maiestatem tuam suppliciter deprecantes	XXII<II> post Pent.

Since all the forms adopted for the series of Sundays come from the Supplement to the *Hadrianum*, two things seem possible. First, that the proper prefaces did not appear in place in the Saint-Denis models but were extracted and inserted when the sacramentaries came to be recopied. Second, that the formulae had already been added at Saint-Denis by redactors who took very different approaches to the business of integrating the Supplement.

(iv) that the books, from time to time, go their own way. This is especially apparent in the masses provided for the Tuesday and Wednesday before Ascension Day, where there is absolutely no agreement at all, and during the Christmas period, where the older underlying order of formulae has been seriously disrupted. Perhaps the most idiosyncratic part of *Ratoldus*'s temporal is the section devoted to the Ember Saturday of Lent (beginning at no. 573). For there, distributed among the prayers of the fore-mass, we also find the *ordines* for the ordination of the various officers of the church that were extracted from the English pontifical, an arrangement that looks, at first glance, excessively awkward. Yet despite the apparent complexity of it all, once one has worked out what belongs where, the 'order of the day' is perfectly easy to follow in practice, as it is in the so-called 'Old' or 'Vatican Gelasian' sacramentary.[112] The prayers for mass, at any rate, are the same as those in the other books. Also noteworthy is the presence in *Ratoldus* of a mass for the feast of the vigil of St John the Evangelist (nos 277–279). The forms are only otherwise found in a fragmentary eleventh-century sacramentary from Benevento, and a tenth-century book from Utrecht published by Jacobus Pamelius in 1571.[113]

---

[111] Also see *The First Ordinary*, ed. Foley, p. 363.

[112] Ed. Mohlberg, *Liber Sacramentorum Romani aecclesiae*, pp. 23–9.

[113] K. Gamber, 'Fragmenta Liturgica', *Sacris Erudiri* 21 (1972–3), 241–66, at 242–3; J. Pamelius, *Liturgica Latinorum*, 2 vols (Cologne, 1571) II, 190. See Amalarius, *Liber Officialis*, Bk IV, cap. 40, ed. J. M. Hanssens, *Amalarii Episcopi Opera liturgica omnia*, 3 vols, Studi e Testi 138–40 (Vatican City, 1948–50) III, 530.

(v) that *Winchcombe* and Laon BM 118 probably preserve the oldest, or at least the 'purest' form of Saint-Denis arrangement.

THE BAPTISMAL ORDERS

Two sets of texts are provided in *Ratoldus*: an order for the preparation of the candidates for baptism (the 'scrutinies'); and an order for baptism itself on Holy Saturday. It will be best to take the two elements separately.

Order for the preparation of the catechumens (917–990)

That *Ratoldus*'s order for the preparation and instruction of the catechumens (in this case, the infants to be presented for baptism on Holy Saturday) was a physical insertion in the underlying Saint-Denis/ Orléans model seems to be borne out on four main counts. Nothing remotely related appears in *Winchcombe*, BNF lat. 11589 or 2297. Second, there is no entry for the section in the table of contents. Third, the text is not properly integrated in the temporal. Fourth, such orders are really only ever found at an early date in sacramentaries that were prepared for bishops or archbishops, the principal and perhaps best-known examples being:

> Vatican City, Biblioteca Vaticana Apostolica, Reg. lat. 316: the so-called 'Old' or 'Vatican Gelasian' sacramentary mentioned above, a book embodying two entirely unrelated sets of texts: an Italian sacramentary of the fifth or sixth century; and a Frankish pontifical of the seventh or early eighth century. The two were worked together in the mid eighth century to form the book as we have it today for some northern French bishop, possibly the bishop of Paris. The copying is thought to have been done at Chelles or Jouarre.[114] There is nothing whatsoever to suggest, contrary to what has sometimes been claimed, that any of the material preserved in Reg. lat. 316 was acquired from England, or from an Englishman. The *ordo*

---

[114] Ed. Mohlberg, *Liber Sacramentorum Romani aecclesiae*, pp. 32–3, 36, 39, 42–53, nos 193–9, 225–8, 254–7, 283–328.

scrutinorum descends, in large part, from a time when only three scrutinies were held. Seven later became the norm.[115]

Paris, Bibliothèque nationale de France, lat. 12048: the famous 'Sacramentary of Gellone' produced for Hildoard, bishop of Cambrai. Two orders are provided: the first, which appears in place in the temporal, is a hybrid, the result of a working together of something like the order given in the 'Vatican Gelasian' with an order similar to the one given later on among Gellone's votives. The second runs parallel with the text of *Ordo romanus* 11.[116]

Paris, Bibliothèque nationale de France, lat. 816: an 'Eighth-Century Gelasian' sacramentary written in the late eighth or early ninth century for some bishop of Angoulême, possibly Sideramnus (801–44), whose name figures as an addition on fol. 72r. As in *Gellone* I, the text is a sort of hybrid of old and new, but the updating appears to have been done rather more haphazardly. Sections of rubric that should, properly speaking, accompany the exorcisms at the beginning of the order are run together to form a sort of introduction to the candidates' examination.[117]

The sacramentary written at Reims for Godelgaudus, dean of the abbey of Saint-Remi, by the priest Lambert *c.* 800.[118] In view of its complement of episcopal benedictions, the book is likely to have been copied from a model from the cathedral nearby. The *ordo scrutinorum* is conjoint, as in *Ratoldus* and the 'Sacramentary of Angoulême', with the texts provided for use on Holy Saturday. Broadly agrees with *Angoulême*, but places the exposition of the *Pater noster* after the Creed, as in *Gellone* I.

Vatican City, Biblioteca Vaticana Apostolica, Vat. lat. 567: a fragmentary early-tenth-century sacramentary from Sens Cathedral.[119] The order embodied is a reduced and rearranged version of OR 11.

[115] For general discussion, see Henri Leclerq's article, 'Scrutin', *DACL* 15.i, 1037–52. For an arrangement of the scrutinies that may be even older than that of the 'Vatican Gelasian', see C. Lambot, *North Italian Services of the Eleventh Century*, HBS 67 (London, 1931), pp. 7–29, with G. Morin, 'Sur la date et la provenance de l'ordo scrutinorum du Cod. Ambros. T. 27 sup', *RB* 46 (1934), 216–23.
[116] Ed. Dumas and Deshusses, *Liber Sacramentorum Gellonensis*, I, 47–51, 56, 60, 64–73, nos 388–410, 449–53, 490–94, 525–64; and, I, 312–31, nos 2215–2303.
[117] Ed. Saint-Roch, *Liber Sacramentorum Engolismensis*, pp. 95–107, nos 682–729.
[118] The manuscript was destroyed in 1774. Its text is known from a transcript made by the antiquary Jean de Voison and printed by U. Chevalier, *Sacramentaire et martyrologe de l'abbaye de Saint-Remy*, Bibliothèque liturgique 7 (Paris, 1900). *CLLA*, no. 862. Also see Martimort, *La documentation liturgique*, p. 182, no. 256.
[119] Ed. A. Nocent, 'Un fragment de sacramentaire de Sens du Xe siècle', in *Miscellanea*

Monastic communities generally seem not to have copied the texts that came their way into practical service books, prefering to leave them in place in collections of *ordines*.[120]

As far as *Ratoldus*'s order is concerned, there is nothing quite like it anywhere. Rubric that appears to be invariable in other copies has been truncated or expanded throughout; and the exorcisms of salt and water which normally take place before the catechumens are exorcized have been dispensed with entirely (along with the rubric accompanying them). Perhaps the most significant departure from the rubrical norm, however, is that the deacon is explicitly instructed to dimiss the catechumens before the extracts from the gospels were read and to summon them back for the exposition afterwards. To take the example of the reading of St Matthew's Gospel. I give on the left the version of the text transmitted in *Ordo romanus* 11, which is also the one adopted in the Romano-German Pontifical; in the middle that of *Gellone*'s first order; and on the right *Ratoldus*'s:[121]

OR 11	*Gellone*	*Ratoldus* (nos 957–958)
Ipsa expleta, adnuntiat diaconus dicens: *State cum silentio, audientes intente.* Et tunc incipiens unus diaconus de super angulo primo altaris sinistro librum evangelii, praecedentibus ante eum duo candelabra cum turibulis ascendit ad legendum. Et legit: *Initium sancti evangelii secundum Matheum* usque *ipse enim salvum faciet populum suum a peccatis eorum.* Et postquam legerit, suscipit de eo subdiaconus ipsum evangelium super linteum et portat in sacrario.	*Dicat diaconus:* dominus uobiscum.	Dicat diaconus: Catecumini recedant, sicuti superius. Et postea dicit dominus uobiscum,
	Et legit inicium euangelii secundum matheum usque: ipse ẹnim saluum fatiit populum suum a peccatis eorum.	et incipiens legere initium sancti euangelii secundum matheum. Liber generationis usque ipse enim saluum faciet populum.
	Deinde adnunciat. State cum silentio; audientes intente.	Postquam legerit et adnuntiat diaconus dicens: Catecumini procedunt, state cum silentio, audientes intente.

liturgica in onore di sua eminenza il Cardinale Giacomo Lercaro, 2 vols (Rome, 1966–7) II, 649–794. *CLLA*, no. 866.

120 See Andrieu, *OR*, II, 365–79 (Ordo XI).

121 Andrieu, *OR*, II, 429–30, nos 46–7; *Liber Sacramentorum Gellonensis*, ed. Dumas and Deshusses, I, 66, nos 536–7. See also, *RGP*, I, 31–2 (*ordo* xcix, nos 133–8).

Et tractat presbiter his verbis: *Filii karissimi ne diutius ergo uos teneamus . . . est mathei persona.*	*Et tractat presbyter his uerbis.* Filii karissimi, ne dehutius ergo uos teniamus . . . est mathei persona.	Tractat presbyter his uerbis: Filii karissimi ne diutius ergo uos teneamus . . . est mathei persona.

Ratoldus is evidently a hybrid, and if indications are correct, a hybrid compiled from particularly uncommon materials, for the rubric *Et ascendet sacerdos ad altare dicet orationem ad missam*, which precedes the prayer *Da quesumus electis tuis* (no. 921) a short way into the order, is only otherwise to be found in Munich, Bayerische Staatsbibliothek, Clm 6425, a liturgical miscellany compiled in the early eleventh century for Egilbert, bishop of Freising (1006–39), and in Paris, Bibliothèque nationale de France, lat. 2399, an eleventh-century collection of *ordines* from Moissac. But neither of these books has anything else in common with *Ratoldus*, and in any case, the only real 'parallel' for *Ratoldus*'s general arrangement is presented by the *RGP,* which embodies a version of OR 11 in the shape of *Ordo romanus* 50. In both the forms for mass of the second scrutiny, properly speaking the *Missa Ebdomada IV,* or *Missa in Secundo Scrutinio* (nos 945–50), are positioned directly after the first.[122] But *Ratoldus* is too different, especially in points of detail, for any direct lineage to be traced. Quite where and at what sort of date this re-arranging took place is difficult to determine too: Orléans is certainly possible; but the order might equally well have been drawn up and incorporated at the instigation of Ratoldus.

The Baptismal Order (nos 991–1011, 1048–56)

If the order for the preparation of the catechumens was not already in place in the sacramentary underlying *Ratoldus* when it left Saint-Denis, the baptismal order and the Exultet almost certainly were.[123] Although some of the material encompassed seems to have been disarranged at some later point, presumably when the *ordo scrutinorum* and material from the English pontifical came to be copied in, the main lines of the

---

[122] See *OR*, II, 420, no. 9 (note) with *OR*, V, 134, note; and for descriptions of the books *OR*, I, 221–32 and 269–71. For the position of the mass for the scrutiny in the Romano-German Pontifical, see *RGP*, I, 29–30. Note too that its third mass is also embedded in the text of the order, as in *Ratoldus*.

[123] On the material for Holy Saturday extracted from the English pontifical (the short ordo for the blessing of the Paschal Candle and the forms for the blessing of the new fire and incense), see below, pp. clxiv–clxvi.

original are clear enough. In essence, the order is simply an expanded version of the order that first appears in BNF lat. 2290, the late-ninth-century sacramentary from Saint-Denis: and as one might expect, versions are also to be found in *Winchcombe* and BNF lat. 11589. BNF lat. 2297, however, was either fitted out with a different text to begin with, or had a new one added later. For the sake of convenience I give synopses of the orders here, noting where relevant the numbers assigned to the formulae in BNF lat. 2290 and *Winchcombe* by Doms Deshusses and Davril respectively:

BNF lat. 2290: lessons and prayers as prescribed in the *Hadrianum* (Deshusses, Ha 362–72); prayers *ad catecuminum faciendum* (TC 3901–15); forms for preparation of the candidate, namely *Nec te latet* and *Effeta* (TC 3916–7); a short exorcism followed by the renunciations, beginning *Abrenuntias* and ending with the signing of the chrism, *Et ego te linio* (TC 3936, 3918 and 3938); the Creed, indicated by incipit only; the blessing of the font, ending with the short formula for the inmixing and spargation of the chrism, *Fecundetur* (TC 3939–40 and 3942); the examination of the candidate (TC 3930); the baptism itself (TC 3920–21); and finally the vesting (TC 3943).

Winchcombe: Exultet and preface (Davril, nos 392a–b); lessons and prayers as prescribed in 'Gelasian' books (nos 393–407); prayers *ad catucuminum faciendum* (nos 408–22), followed by a reading from St Matthew's Gospel, *Tunc oblati sunt ei paruuli* (Matt. xix, 13); the long version of the Creed with the Lord's prayer (nos 423–4); forms for the preparation of the candidate, *Nec te latet* and *Effeta* (nos 426–7); the blessing of the font, ending with three short pieces: *Coniunctio olei*, *Coniunctio chrismatis*, *Fecundetur* (nos 428–429f); renunciations beginning *Abrenuntias*, then the signing of the chrismation *Ego te linio* (nos 430–31); the examination of the candidate (nos 432–3); the baptism itself (no. 434–5); and the vesting and consigning of the lamp (nos 436–7). A number of unique formulae, all noticed by Davril, appear throughout the order.

BNF lat. 11589, fols 45r–51r: Exultet and preface; five prayers and lessons as in the *Hadrianum*; rubric; two short pieces beginning *Signum*; prayers *ad catecuminum faciendum*; forms for the preparation of the candidate, namely *Nec te latet*, *Effeta*, and the series of renunciations beginning *Abrenuntias* followed by the chrismation *Ego te linio*; the long version of the Creed; forms for the blessing of font, the preface and short concluding pieces all as in *Ratoldus*; the examination of the candidate; the baptism; vesting. The order in BNF lat. 11589 continues with forms for the baptism of an infirm infant, and forms for the baptism of a convert.

BNF lat. 2297, fols 8r–11r: introductory rubric not found in the other books; the Exultet and preface; further lines of rubric; the lessons and prayers of the *Hadrianum*; prayers *ad catecuminum faciendum*, followed (as in *Winchcombe*) by a reading from St Matthew's Gospel, *Tunc oblati sunt*; the long version of the Creed with the Lord's prayer; forms for the preparation of the candidate, *Nec te latet*, *Effeta*, renunciations, with *Ego te linio* added later by the original scribe; forms for the blessing of font, but lacking the short pieces present in the other books; exorcism of water; the examination of the candidate; baptism; rubric but no forms for vesting and the consigning of the lamp. Mass of Holy Saturday follows.

No one order appears to be a direct descendent of the other. In any case, some books obviously had the prayers and lessons of the *Hadrianum* to begin with, others those of 'Eighth-Century Gelasians'. *Ratoldus* lies somewhere in between *Winchcombe* and BNF lat. 11589. The material common to *Ratoldus*, *Winchcombe* and BNF lat. 11589 is:

(i) the Exultet and Preface (*Ratoldus*, nos 1018–1019).

(ii) prayers and lessons (nos 1020–1046). BNF lat. 11589 has the Hadrianic series; *Winchcombe* the Gelasian.

(iii) the two short pieces beginning *Signum* (nos 991–92). As BNF lat. 11589. The pieces appear for the first time in BNF lat. 2291, the sacramentary written for Bishop Gozlinus.

(iv) prayers *ad catecuminum faciendum* (not the same selection in each, however), ending with *Ego te linio* (nos 993–1011).

(v) the text of the Creed (no. 968).

(vi) the blessing of the font with interpolated directions: *Hic diuiditur aqua in modum crucis*, *Hic signa*, *Hic tangis aquam*, *Hic muta uocem quasi lectionem legendum*, *Hic suffla ter in aqua*, *Hic ponunt caereos*, *Tunc spargat aquam in populo*, *Deinde misceat crisma cum aqua (in modum crucis) et dicit his verbis*, followed by *Fecundetur*, *Coniunctio olei* and *Coniunctio chrismatis* (nos 1048–50).

(vii) examination, baptism and vesting (nos 1051–56).

Aside from the variation in the number of lessons assigned, the principal divergences are really only of order and layout. We shall return to matters of layout in due course.[124]

THE SANCTORAL

In terms of physical arrangement alone, *Ratoldus* probably transmits most accurately the form of the original Saint-Denis model (or models) since its two propria – temporal and sanctoral – are still intermixed, as in the *Hadrianum* and the 'Eighth-Century Gelasian' books. BNF lat. 11589, BNF lat. 2297, and *Winchcombe*, all have theirs separate. To recombine the two if they had already been separated out at some earlier point in the line of transmission, would have been a wholly retrograde, not to say tedious step to take.

Although comparison of the *sanctoralia* is a relatively straightforward process in itself, analysis of the results is trickier, for we not only lack a fixed point of departure, but have at least four decades of reshaping to contend with: in the case of *Ratoldus*, from *c.* 940 when the underlying model issued forth from Saint-Denis to its eventual recopying *c.* 980; in the case of BNF lat. 2297 possibly much more. BNF lat. 2290 and lat. 2291, alas, are really too early to serve as 'controls'. Nonetheless, a 'basic' sanctoral does seem to be recoverable if we limit our view solely to feasts that are either common to all four books or shared by a combination of three. Feasts attested by three are marked with an asterisk and the names of the witnesses indicated in brackets:

DECEMBER
31. Silvester.

JANUARY
3. Genovefa* (2297 begins with St Felix).
13. Hilary* (as above).
14. Felix.

16. Marcellus.
16. Prisca.
19. Mary and Martha* (11589, 2297, *Ratoldus*).
20. Fabian.
20. Sebastian.
21. Agnes.
22. Vincent.

---

[124] See below, pp. clxv–clxix.

25. Conversion of Paul.
25. Proiectus* (11589, 2297, *Winch*).
28. Agnes.

FEBRUARY
2. Purification.
5. Agatha.
14. Valentine.
22. Cathedra Petri.

MARCH
12. Gregory (precedes the feast of St Peter's Chains in 11589).
20. Vigil of Benedict.
21. Benedict.
25. Annunciation.

APRIL
13. Eufemia.
14. Tiburtius, Valerianus and Maximus.
23. George.
28. Vitalis.

MAY
1. Philip and James.
3. Alex., Ev. and Theod.
3. Invention of the Cross.
6. John before the Latin Gate.
10. Gordian and Epimachus.
12. Pancras.
12. Nereus and Achilleus.
13. Mary ad Martyres.
25. Urban.

JUNE
1. Nichomedis.
2. Marcellinus and Peter.
9. Primus and Felician.
12. Basilides, Cyrinus, Nabor and Nazarius.
15. Vitus.
18. Mark and Marcellinus.

19. Gervase and Prothase.
23. Vigil of John the Baptist.
24. Prima missa.
24. Missa.
26. John and Paul.
28. Leo.
28. Vigil of Peter.
29. Peter.
30. Paul.

JULY
2. Processus and Martinian* (11589, 2297, *Ratoldus*).
4. Translation of Martin.
6. Octave of Apostles.
10. Seven Brothers.
11. Benedict.
25. James.
25. Cucuphas* (11589, 2297, *Ratoldus*).
29. Felix.
29. Simplicius, Faustinus and Beatrix.
30. Abdon and Sennes.
31. Germanus* (2297, *Ratoldus*, *Winch*).

AUGUST
1. Peter's Chains.
1. Maccabees.
3. Stephen.
6. Sixtus.
6. Felicissimus and Agapitus.
8. Cyriacus.
9. Vigil of Laurence.
10. Prima missa.
10. Missa.
11. Tiburtius.
13. Ypollitus.
14. Eusebius.
14. Vigil of Assumption.
15. Assumption.
17. Octave of Laurence.

18. Agapitus.
19. Magnus* (2297, *Ratoldus, Winch*).
22. Timothy.
22. Symphorian* (2297, *Ratoldus, Winch*).
25. Bartholomew.
27. Rufus.
28. Hermes.
28. Augustine.
29. Sabina.
29. Decollation of John the Baptist.
30. Felix and Audactus.

SEPTEMBER
1. Priscus.
8. Nativity of Virgin.
9. Gorgonius.
11. Protus and Iacinthus.
14. Exaltation of Cross.
14. Cornelius and Cyprian.
15. Nichomedis.
16. Eufemia.
16. Lucy and Geminian.
20. Vigil of Matthew.
21. Matthew.
22. Maurice.
27. Cosmas and Damian.
29. Michael.

OCTOBER
7. Mark* (11589, 2297, *Winch*).
8. Vigil of Denis.

9. Denis.
14. Calixtus* (11589, *Ratoldus, Winch*).
16. Octave of Denis.
18. Luke.
27. Vigil of Simon and Jude.
28. Simon and Jude.
31. Vigil of All Saints.

NOVEMBER
1. All Saints.
1. Cesarius.
8. Four Crowned Martyrs.
9. Theodore.
11. Mennas.
11. Martin.
21. Felicity.
21. Vigil of Cecilia.
22. Cecilia.
23. Clement.
24. Chrisogonus.
29. Saturninus.
29. Vigil of Andrew.
30. Andrew.

DECEMBER
7. Octave of Andrew* (2297, *Ratoldus, Winch*).
11. Damasus* (2297, *Ratoldus, Winch*).
13. Lucy.
21. Thomas.

With due reservations about the position or even presence of the mass for St Gregory, which is lacking in BNF lat. 2290 and misplaced in BNF lat. 11589 (possibly a result of a poor attempt to make good the deficiency), a sanctoral of this sort would be perfectly in order for a Saint-Denis book of the second third of the tenth century, as has already been mentioned.

Naturally, if sacramentaries from Saint-Denis regularly found their way to Brittany during the course of the tenth and eleventh centuries, this list will necessarily be highly reductive. For as we have already seen, BNF lat. 11589, which has few extras, is likely to descend from a model received at a relatively early date; and BNF lat. 2297, which embodies a great many, from one received perhaps as much as sixty or so years later, that is to say, anywhere in the period *c*. 960– 1000.

That BNF lat. 11589, BNF lat. 2297 and *Ratoldus* give masses for St Samson, and BNF lat. 2297, *Ratoldus* and *Winchcombe* a mass for St Jerome, simply indicates that these feasts were held to be important by the communities who owned the books in question, not that the feasts appeared in some sort of intermediate model stemming from Dol.

As one might expect, some feasts only appear in two books:

23 Jan.   SS Emerentiana and Macharius (11589 and 2297).
10 Feb.   St Scholastica (2297 and *Winch.*).
24 Feb.   St Matthias (2297 and *Winch.*).
24 Apr.   Sidrac, Misac and Abednego (11589 and 2297).
31 May   St Petronella (11589 and 2297).
18 June   Vigil of SS Gervase and Prothase (2297 and *Ratoldus*).
23 July   St Apollinaris (*Ratoldus* and *Winch.*).
7 Aug.   St Donatus (2297 and *Winch.*).
1 Oct.   SS Remigius, German and Vedastus (2297 and *Winch.*).
10 Nov.   Vigil of St Martin (11589 and 2297).
15 Nov.   St Malo (11589 and 2297).
29 Nov.   Chrisantus, Maurus and Darius (2297 and *Winch.*).

The masses for SS Emerentiana and Macharius, the Vigil of SS Gervase and Prothase, St Donatus, and SS Chrisantus, Maurus and Darius are standard 'Eighth-Century Gelasians'; those for St Scholastica, St Matthias, and SS Remigius, German and Vedastus, standard ninth- and tenth-century French texts. The only really distinctive feasts (and sets of formulae) are the 'Breton' ones: St Martin's vigil, with the prayers used at Tours; St Malo's day; and in *Ratoldus*, St Apollinaris's, which also has the prayers assigned at Tours, an indication perhaps that the mass was added to the book's sanctoral at much the same time as the masses for St Benedict, St Samson and SS Samson and Paternus came in.[125] *Winchcombe*'s principal mass for St Apollinaris contains elements of a set known and used at Wells some fifty years later. Its secondary mass,

---

[125] On the Breton propers for St Malo, see Duine, *Inventaire*, pp. 26–7; for St Apollinaris at Tours, Deshusses, *Le sacramentaire grégorien*, II, 313, nos 3545–7; and on the 'Breton' propers in *Ratoldus*, below, pp. lxxxviii–xc.

apparently an addition by the original English scribe, is the same as the one given in *Ratoldus* and at Tours.[126]

Finally, we have the feasts that are proper to individual books:

BNF lat. 11589

4 June	St Guoetgualus.
16 June	SS Eusebius and Meuuinus.
14 Nov.	Vigil of St Malo.
17 Dec.	St Iudicael.

The monks of Saint-Méen added only two types of feast to their Saint-Denis sanctoral: those of saints venerated fairly generally in Brittany (Sidrac, Misac and Abednego, and Malo), and those venerated locally.

Winchcombe

11 Mar.	Vigil of St Gregory.
25 Apr.	St Mark.
17 July	St Kenelm.
1 Oct.	St German alone.
4 Dec.	'Tumulatio' of St Benedict.

Of these, only the masses for St Kenelm and the 'tumulatio' of St Bene-dict, a feast commemorating the translation of the saint's relics to Fleury, are English insertions. The forms for St Mark's day, the vigil of St Gregory, and the secondary mass for St German, are likely to descend from the (specialised) Sandionysian model.[127]

BNF lat. 2297

27 Jan.	SS Policarp and Iulianus.
27 Jan.	St Iulianus alone.
10 Feb.	St Sotheris.
10 Feb.	SS Zoticus, Ireneus and Iacinthus.
14 Feb.	SS Vitalis, Felicula and Zeno.

---

[126] *The Winchcombe Sacramentary*, ed. Davril, pp. 169, 275, nos 1098–1100, 1910–12. The incipits of the prayers in Giso's book are indicated in Legg, *Missale ad usum ecclesiae Westmonasteriensis*, III, 1569–70.

[127] The mass for the vigil of St Gregory was once known at Reims too, as Reims BM 214, a late-tenth-century sacramentary from the abbey of Saint-Thierry; it turns its prayers into alternatives for the day (fol. 80r).

16 Feb.	St Iuliana.
19 Apr.	St Leo.
3 May	St Iuvenal.
16 June	SS Cyricus and Iulitta.
25 June	Vigil of SS John and Paul.
1 July	St Carilef.
7 July	St Marcial.
25 July	St Christopher.
27 July	Vigil of St Samson.
31 Aug.	St Victurus of Nantes.
8 Sept.	St Adrian.
28 Sept.	Vigil of St Michael.
1 Oct.	St Remigius alone.
13 Oct.	SS Adrian and Marcellus.
25 Oct.	SS Crispin and Crispinian.
31 Oct.	St Quentin.
13 Nov.	St Bricius.
18 Nov.	Octave of St Martin.

Ratoldus

St Vedastus, deposition and translation (nos 430–34, 1827–31): as has already mentioned, *Ratoldus* is deeply confused. The position is best illustrated with reference to Arras, Bibliothèque municipale 444, a thirteenth-century sacramentary from Saint-Vaast's published in synopsis by Louis Brou, which gives:[128]

IN VIGILIA SANCTI VEDASTI
Concede nos quesumus omnipotens deus uenturam beati Vedasti confessoris . . . et uenientem digna celebrare deuotione.
<SECRETA>. Accepta tibi sit domine nostrae deuotionis oblatio ut ad beati Vedasti confessoris . . . faciat nos uenire festiuitatem.
<POSTCOMMVNIO> Praesta nobis eterne largitor eius ubique protegi oratione . . . uotiuo preuenimus officio.

---

[128] Ed. Brou, *The Monastic Ordinal*, I, 81–2, 88. Also see the texts published from a privately owned thirteenth-century *missale parvum* by Z. H. Turton, *The Vedast Missal, or Missale parvum Vedastinum* (London, 1904), pp. 46–9.

IN DIE
Deus qui nos deuota beati Vedasti confessoris tui atque pontificis
. . . patrocinia sentiamus.
<SECRETA>. Hostias domine laudis tuis altaribus adhibemus
quas eius . . . peruenire laetitiam.
<POSTCOMMVNIO>. Beati Vedasti confessoris tui atque
pontificis domine precibus . . . eterna remedia capiamus.

INFRA OCTAVAS
Deus qui populo tuo eterne salutis beatum Vedastum . . . semper
habere mereamur in celis.
<SECRETA>. Omnipotens sempiterne deus maiestati tue oblata
. . . proficere ad salutem.
<POSTCOMMVNIO>. Sacramenta salutis nostre suscipientes
concede quesumus misericors deus . . . hec tue obtulimus
maiestati.

IN OCTAVAS SANCTI VEDASTI
Protegat nos domine beati Vedasti confessoris tui . . . perpetuam
defensionem sentiamus.
<SECRETA>. Indulgentiam nobis domine quesumus prebeant
hec munera . . . suffragiis offeruntur.
<POSTCOMMVNIO>. Adiuuet familiam tuam tibi domine
supplicando . . . extitit predicator.

TRANSLATIO CORPORIS SANCTI VEDASTI
Deus qui nos deuota. *Require tot. in deposit.*

In Brou's book, the forms assigned to the vigil and the deposition are
compositions by Alcuin, which appear first in Cambrai MM 162–3, the
late-ninth-century sacramentary from Saint-Vaast's, and later in
London, British Library, Loans 36/9 (formerly Phillips 3340), an early-
tenth-century sacramentary from Noyon, Rouen BM 274, the so-called
'Missal of Robert of Jumièges', and a number of others.[129] The prayers
for the octave are simply versions of the standard 'Gelasian' mass for
the octave of St Andrew; those for the mass *infra octauas* versions of
formulae originally composed for St Martin's day at Tours; and the mass
for the feast of the translation (1 Oct.) is the same as that for deposition.

[129] Deshusses, *Le sacramentaire grégorien*, I, 690–91, nos 59*–63*; Turner, 'A
10th–11th century Noyon sacramentary', 145, note 1; and *The Missal of Robert of
Jumièges*, ed. Wilson, p. 161.

In *Ratoldus* we encounter two sets of prayers, one for the deposition, the other notionally for the translation: and there are errors in each. On the deposition (nos 430–34) we have the propers normally assigned to the octave; and the 'translation', which has, one suspects by pure chance, the same prayers as Arras BM 444, is entitled NATALE SANCTI VEDASTI EPISCOPI.[130] No-one with any knowledge of the associations of the mass *Protegat nos* would have transferred it deliberately to a deposition. Only the blessing *Deus fundator fidei* (no. 433), which, ironically, is likely to have been extracted from the English benedictional and copied into its present position, is right.[131]

St Cuthbert (nos 459–463): extracted from the English pontifical and set in place in the sanctoral. We shall return to the forms provided in due course.[132]

St Benedict, feast in March; vigil of the feast, feast, and octave in July (nos 464–469, 1531–1538, 1544–1546): *Ratoldus* drastically rearranges the masses transmitted in the Saint-Denis model. For the deposition in March, the prayers must originally have been the ones given in BNF lat. 11589, BNF lat. 2297, and presumably before augmentation, *Winchcombe*:[133]

XIII KL. APR. VIGILIA SANCTI BENEDICTI ABBATIS
Concede nobis quesumus domine alacribus animis . . . uita complacuit. Per.
SECRETA. Oblata confessoris tui benedicti honore sint . . . effectum obtineat. Per.
POSTCOMMVNIO. Quos celestibus domine recreas alimentis . . . tuere periculis. Per.

[130] Note that formulae belonging to Alcuin's mass for the deposition were already being assigned to the translation as early as the tenth century. See Paris, Bibliothèque nationale de France, lat. 9433, the late-ninth- or early-tenth-century sacramentary from Echternach, ed. Hen, *The Sacramentary of Echternach*, pp. 303–5, nos 1456–62. The main text of the sacramentary is based on that of a book from Tours supplied by Alcuin. See N. A. Orchard, 'Some notes on the Sacramentary of Echternach', *Archiv für Liturgiewissenschaft* 43–44 (2002), 1–21.
[131] Note that blessings for the vigil of St Vedastus, as well as the day itself, are provided in the benedictional of Arras, Bibliothèque municipale 720 (fols 71r–v, 72r). See Leroquais, *Les pontificaux*, I, 37–8.
[132] See below, pp. cxxxvi–cxxxviii.
[133] See *The Winchcombe Sacramentary*, ed Davril, pp. 151–2, nos 939–54.

IN NATALE SANCTI BENEDICTI ABBATIS
Omnipotens sempiterne deus qui hodierna luce . . . consocientur et meritis. Per.
ALIA. Omnipotens sempiterne deus qui radiantibus . . . gaudiis admisceri. Per.
SECRETA. Oblatis domine ob honorem beati confessoris tui . . . indulgentiam peccatorum. Per.
PRAEFATIO. VD aeterne deus. Et te honorandi patris benedicti gloriosam caelebrantes . . . peruenire meretur. Per christum.
POSTCOMMVNIO. Perceptis tui corporis et sanguinis domine . . . fulciamur aeternis. Per.
ALIA. Fidelium tuorum domine quaesumus uota . . . interesse perpetuis. Per.

These are assigned in *Ratoldus* to 10 and 11 July, thereby displacing the standard Saint-Denis mass for the 11 July (preserved in BNF lat. 2297 and *Winchcombe*):

TRANSLATIO SANCTI BENEDICTI
Intercessio nos quaesumus domine beati benedicti . . . patrocino assequamur. Per.
SECRETA. Sacris altaribus domine hostias superpositas . . . prouenire deposcat. Per.
PRAEFATIO. VD aeterne deus. Et gloriam tuam profusis precibus . . .
POSTCOMMVNIO. Protegat nos domine cum tui perceptione . . . percipiamus suffragia. Per.

'Intercessio' in *Ratoldus* becomes the mass for the octave (18 July). What seems to have prompted the re-arrangement was the desire on the part of the community of Dol to introduce, for the feast in March, the prayers they had been in the habit of using in Brittany (nos 464–469). *Ratoldus's* formulae are essentially those adopted in the province of Tours.[134]

St Praxedis (nos 1547–1549): masses are relatively uncommon in the ninth and tenth centuries. *Ratoldus's* may have been introduced in an attempt to harmonise the sanctoral of the sacramentary with some standard gradual. Proper chant for the saint regularly appears in early

---

[134] Deshusses, *Le sacramentaire grégorien*, II, 299–300, nos 3458–3461.

graduals and antiphoners. The prayers for mass are versions of those assigned to the feast of St Prisca in the *Hadrianum*.[135]

SS Samson and Paternus (nos 1566–1568): only St Samson, patron of Dol, is named in the superscription. Both saints, however, are commemorated in the prayers, which are 'stock' formulae. Relics of St Paternus, secondary patron of Avranches, were apparently sent by Radbodus, prior of Dol, to King Æthelstan at some point in the late 920s, probably *c*. 926–7.[136] The relics kept at Avranches are likely to have been carried to Paris in the wake of the Viking invasions. The refugee community of Dol met refugees from Avranches and Bayeux on their way west to Paris.

St Samson alone (nos 1569–1572): the collects belong to the set normally assigned to the vigil of the feast, and the preface is proper to the day, as in BNF lat. 2297. The prayers are exceedingly lengthy:[137]

<32v> VI KL. AVG. VIGILIA SANCTI SAMSONIS
Omnipotens sempiterne et misericors deus qui in sanctis precipuae . . . exultare sacramentis. Per dominum.
SECRETA. Haec hostia domine quesumus deus noster quam tibi . . . gaudere sanctorum. Per.
PREFACIO. VD aeterne deus. Sursum cordibus et rectis hanc sanctam caelebrare diem . . <33r> . . restituuntur sanitati. Per christum.
POSTCOMMVNIO. Deus qui nos hanc diem in honore sancti samsonis . . . muniamur et precibus. Per dominum.

V KL. AVG. NATALE SANCTI SAMSONIS
Sacrosanctam adoneo annuam fratres karissimi . . . excolere debemus. Per dominum.
ALIA. Omnipotens sempiterne deus tribue nobis famulis tuis . . . possimus peruenire. Per.
SECRETA. Deus apostolorum, deus martyrum, deus confessorum . . . peruenire mereamur. Per.

---

135 Deshusses, *Le sacramentaire grégorien*, I, 118, nos 105–107. Carthusian communities took the same path. See Legg, *Missale ad usum ecclesiae Westmonasteriensis*, III, 1567.
136 See *Councils and Synods*, I, ed. Whitelock *et al.*, pp. 38–40, no. 9.
137 For a collation of the forms in view, see Duine, *Inventaire*, pp. 18–23, 28–34.

PREFACIO. VD aeterne deus. Cuius terribili trepidant corda caelestium . . <33v> . . non diuturno clamantes et dicentes.
POSTCOMMVNIO. Te quesumus domine conditor hac reformator . . . esse intercessorem. Per.
POSTCOMMVNIO. Saciasti nos domine de tuis sacratissimis muneribus . . . in tua beatitudine. Per dominum.

The forms introduced at Orléans doubtless originally ran in line with the ones preserved in BNF lat. 2297, but were recast (and shortened) when *Ratoldus* was copied out anew.

St Symphorian (nos 1678–1680): several ancient masses for the day exist, the earliest of which seems to be the one preserved in Vatican City, Biblioteca Apostolica Vaticana, Reg. lat. 317, the so-called 'Missale Gothicum', a mid-eighth-century sacramentary probably from Autun, the centre of the saint's cult.[138] BNF lat. 2291, *Ratoldus*, *Winchcombe* and BNF lat. 11589, on the other hand, embody versions of a completely different, and much 'newer', set of prayers, presumably issuing from Notre Dame. The forms transmitted in BNF lat. 2291, are, in synopsis:[139]

XI KALENDAS SEPTEMBRIS NATALE SANCTI SYMPHORIANI

Beati martyris tui symphoriani domine nos tuere praesidiis . . . aduersitatibus eruamur. Per.
SVPER OBLATA. Suscipe domine propicius orationem nostrum cum oblatione hostiarum super inpositis . . . et in opere efficaces. Per.
PREFATIO. VD aeterne deus. Et te in omnium martyrum triumphis laudare. Quoniam tuis donis atque muneribus . . . et eadem uincens coronam perpetuitatis promeruit. Per quem.
AD COMPLENDUM. Sacro munere satiati quaesumus omnipotens deus . . . iubeas adscisci colloquio.

These duly appear, in order, in *Winchcombe* and BNF lat. 11589.

---

[138] *Missale Gothicum*, ed. L. C. Mohlberg, Rerum ecclesiasticarum Documenta, Series maior, Fontes 5 (Vatican City, 1961), pp. 101–2, nos 414–18. *CLLA*, no. 210.
[139] Deshusses, *Le sacramentaire grégorien*, II, 317, nos 3566–9; *The Winchcombe Sacramentary*, ed. Davril, p. 181, nos 1197–1200. BNF lat. 2297, fol. 36v, has a set of prayers apparently unknown for St Symphorian elsewhere. They are *Perpetuis nos domine, Sacrificium nostrum tibi domine, Sumptis domine sacramentis quesumus.*

Ratoldus, however, makes changes. *Beati martyris tui*, the standard collect, makes way for a (Gallican) formula proper to a house dedicated to the saint, *Peculiari patroni festiuitatem annua recolentes*; the preface disappears; and a new Gallican postcommunion, *Interueniat pro nobis domine petimus sanctus tuus martyr symphorianus*, takes the place of *Sacro munere satiati*. The mass as it stands is clearly very odd indeed. However, if one supposes first, that these are the remnants of the forms introduced by the community of Dol at Orléans, and second, that the preface, doubtless a long, Gallican composition, if the collect is anything to go by, was tidied away as *Ratoldus* was being copied out, everything falls into place.

St Maurice, second mass (nos 1803–1805): the formulae, which are by no means common, may have been 'proper' at one time to the province of Reims, as the collect turns up (as an addition) in Reims BM 214, the late-tenth-century sacramentary from the abbey of Saint-Thierry, and insofar as other early books are concerned, nowhere else.[140]

THE COMMONS AND VOTIVES
(nos 2035–2193, 2215–2225, 2232–2238, 2286–2322)

With the commons and votives the relationship between the four books breaks down. Indeed, *Ratoldus* has no commons at all, an indication perhaps that the underlying sacramentary ceased to be a wholly practical book at some stage on its journey to Corbie. As far as the commons in the other three sacramentaries are concerned, *Winchcombe* probably transmits most accurately the forms provided in the Saint-Denis model, as the masses provided generally run in line with the set of seven (deriving ultimately from the Supplement, sections XLVIII–LIV) given in BNF lat. 2290, but with prefaces added.[141] The 'Saint-Denis core' is also detectable in BNF lat. 2297 and 11589, but it has clearly undergone much alteration, having been bulked out with material from other sources. In the case of BNF lat. 2297, which has the longer series of the

---

[140] Reims BM 214, fol. 106r (a late-tenth-century addition across the top of the page).
[141] Deshusses, *Le sacramentaire grégorien*, II, 253, 257, 262–3, 269, 276, 282, 287, nos 3149–51, 3176–8, 3212–14, 3254–6, 3309–11, 3350–52, 3387–89*.

two, the 'additions' are largely 'Eighth-Century Gelasian' in character and no doubt descend from the source that provided the 'new' Gelasian saints' masses for the sanctoral.

The sets of votive masses, that is to say, masses for special intentions, embodied in the four books look equally divergent. There are only scattered signs, here and there in *Winchcombe* and in BNF lat. 11589, of the numerous distinctive Saint-Denis propers transmitted in BNF lat. 2290.[142] If the sacramentaries did indeed have a common starting point, which is not an unreasonable assumption in view of the closeness of their other *propria*, it is much more likely to have been the Supplement, perhaps in company with a smaller set of 'Saint-Denis peculiars' than BNF lat. 2290 transmits.

As even the most cursory of inspections shows, *Ratoldus*'s set of votives is the simplest. Essentially the masses encompassed are, in order, those of sections LV, LXXXI, LXVII–LXX, LXXII–LXXIIII, LXXVI–LXXX, LXXXVI–XCVI, XCLII, LXXV, CXXX–CXLI, CXLV, XCVIIII, CI, CIIII–CXII and CIIII of the Supplement, with eleven additions, namely: seven masses originally composed by Alcuin, and four others.[143]

Elements of the Supplement, again all intact, form the backbone of *Winchcombe*'s votives too. As Davril has indicated (synoptic tables), the masses encompassed are: LXVIII, LXX, LXXI, LXXXVII, LXXVI, LXXVII, LXXVIIII, LXXX, XC, XCIIII, XCVI, XC, LXXXVIIII, XCI, LXXXXVIII, LXXII, LXXXIIII, C, CV, CVI, CVIIII. Other sets of prayers (*Winchcombe*, nos 1619–23, 1624–26, 1631–34, 1895–97) appear to have been copied from a sacramentary similar to the so-called 'First Sacramentary of Tours', a late-ninth-century book from the cathedral of St Maurice now divided between Tours, Bibliothèque municipale 184 and Paris, Bibliothèque nationale de France, lat. 9430, which may be a sign that *Winchcombe*'s underlying model came to England from Brittany, not directly from Paris. Any unwanted Breton saints' masses could easily have been dispensed with as the book, as we have it, was being copied out. But the matter requires further investigation.

BNF lat. 11589 and BNF lat. 2297, which both have an absolutely vast array of votives, go their own way. Of the two, the latter is perhaps

---

[142] *The Winchcombe Sacramentary*, ed. Davril, pp. 272–3, nos 1595, 1885–1888, 1889–1891; Deshusses, *Le sacramentaire grégorien*, II, 205, 225, nos 2852–4, 3003–5. BNF lat. 11589 only has (fol. 174v) the first of these two masses.
[143] See the collation table, pp. 501–508.

the most interesting, since we not only have as in *Winchcombe*, material from Tours, though in far greater profusion, and much rearranged, but we have elements (seven ferial votive masses) that are expressly said to be Milanese: *missae ambrosianae*.[144] Tours, perhaps, is hardly surprising as Dol was a suffragan. Milan, however, is quite remarkable.

THE *ORDO DEFUNCTORUM* (nos 2239–2285)

Reference to Deshusses shows that *Ratoldus*'s order runs in line with those embodied in two Carolingian sacramentaries: BNF lat. 2290 (edited under the siglum 'R'), which is, as we have seen, from Saint-Denis; and Stockholm, Kungliga Biblioteket, Holm A. 136, a sacramentary written at Saint-Amand in the third quarter of the ninth century for Ansegis, bishop of Sens (siglum 'T4').[145] Although none of the peculiar variants of BNF lat. 2290 are present – these are perhaps most pronounced in the introductory rubric – it seems reasonable to suppose, nonetheless, that the order as we have it in *Ratoldus* travelled with the underlying Saint-Denis model: and the feeling is further reinforced by the fact that copies also figure in two of *Ratoldus*'s relatives:

(i) BNF lat. 11589, fols 169r–173r. A good text, but with some adjustments. Sections of rubric have been condensed, and a further set of prayers provided for mass. In company with *Winchcombe*, the 'superscription' *Et deportatur usque ad sepulchrum*, is omitted.

(ii) *Winchcombe*. Agrees for the most part with *Ratoldus*, but omits *Et deportatur usque ad sepulchrum*, shortens the incipit of psalm 107 to

---

[144] BNF lat. 2297, fols 50v–54r.
[145] Versions of the order are also preserved in two books from Tours; in Cambrai BM 162–3, the late-ninth-century sacramentary of Saint-Vaast, Arras; and in Dusseldorf D. 1. See Deshusses, *Le sacramentaire grégorien*, III, 171–175. All diverge from *Saint-Denis* and *Sens*. The Tours books ('Tu1' and 'Tu2') have their own chant; Cambrai BM 162–3 ('S'), ends with an extra prayer; and Dusseldorf D. 1 ('W'), in company with 'S', 'Tu1' and 'Tu2', lacks the *orationes missales*. The Saint-Denis text seems to have been known to Amalarius. See C. A. Jones, *A Lost Work by Amalarius of Metz*, Henry Bradshaw Society, Subsidia II (London, 2001), pp. 136–140, 214–16.

Confitemini, and omits the superscription that follows (*Orationes ante sepulchrum*).[146]

BNF lat. 2297 (fols 86r–88v) sides with Tours, however, in giving at the end of the order, the prayer *Annue nobis domine ut anima.*[147]

ADDITIONS TO THE SACRAMENTARY AT CORBIE

The additions made at Corbie (all to the sacramentary, none to the 'pontifical'), were relatively few and are probably best dealt with more or less as they appear in the book:

Prayers for communion (nos i–x). Added on the verso of the first leaf (a singleton) at some point in the eleventh century. Most of the formulae are common enough. *Hec sacrosancta comistio corporis et sanguinis, Domine sancte pater omnipotens aeterne deus da mihi hoc corpus, Perceptio corporis et sanguini*, and *Domine iesu christe fili dei uiui qui ex uoluntate patris*, first appear with any regularity in sacramentaries and missals in the ninth and tenth centuries and probably do not go back much further than that.[148] *Sit nobis hoc sacramentum*, however, is much rarer and likely to be a Corbie proper as a superscription in a Corbie manuscript, reported by Mabillon and Martène, connects it with Paschasius Radbertus, abbot of Corbie (843–51): *ORATIO PASCHASII RATBERTI ante perceptionem Eucharistiae.*[149] Note that versions of the

---

146 Ed. Davril, *The Winchcombe Sacramentary*, pp. 260–70

147 Deshusses, *Le sacramentaire grégorien*, III, 175, note.

148 *Domine sancte pater omnipotens deus da mihi* and *Domine iesu christe* occur as late-ninth-century additions (fol. 214r) in Vatican City, Biblioteca Apostolica Vaticana, Ottob. lat. 313, a mid-ninth-century sacramentary from Paris. All formulae appear in place in the ordinary of BNF lat. 9432. See Leroquais, 'L'Ordo missae', 444, with *idem*, *Les sacramentaires*, I, 30, for the tenth-century additions to Le Mans, Médiathèque Louis Aragon, 77, a mid-ninth-century sacramentary probably written at Saint-Amand for use at Le Mans. On *Haec commixtio*, which is little more than a reformulation of the 'consecratory' prayer recommended in the long recension of *Ordo romanus* 1 (*Fiat commixtio*) and other sources, see B. Capelle, 'L'oraison "Haec commixtio et consecratio" de la messe romaine', in *Mélanges en l'honneur de Monseigneur Michel Andrieu*, ed. M. Nédoncelle and C. Vogel (Strasbourg, 1956), 65–78.

149 Mabillon, *Acta Sanctorum*, III.i, 136, notes that the prayer appeared in Corbie manuscript no. 462, evidently a copy of Paschasius's *De corpore et sanguine domini*, as Martène

commoner prayers already appear in place in the original portions of *Ratoldus*'s order for mass (nos 1114–19).

Canon of the Mass (nos 213–221). Supplied on a new gathering, fols 41–46, as a replacement for the original text, which now begins on fol. 47.[150] Something seems to have gone wrong, however, for the texts of the proper preface and *Sanctus* are not only given twice, but on fols 45r–v over an erasure (nos 215–16). It may be that the texts initially provided on the gathering did not dovetail properly with the original parts of the book. As Leroquais indicated, the new sections of the Canon run parallel with the ones added to BNF lat. 12051 at much the same date. Indeed, the two have a scribe in common. Both give the Corbie *Memento: Memento domine famulorum famularumque tuarum omnis congregationis beati petri apostoli tui* (no. 220).

Masses for the dedication of a church and the feast of the Invention of St Stephen (nos 193–201). Both are common enough. The former is an 'Eighth-Century Gelasian'; the latter appears regularly in northern French books of the eleventh and twelfth centuries, though its preface may well be proper.[151]

Mass for the feast of St Praecordius (nos 203–206). Relics of the saint were acquired by the community in 940. As has already been mentioned, an entry for the feast figures (as an addition) in *Ratoldus*'s calendar. The forms provided for mass are versions of prayers initially drawn up, probably by Alcuin, for use on the feast St Willibrord (7 Nov.) at Echternach. They were also adopted, in a series of separate initiatives, for St Birinus (4 Dec.) in England, and St Bertin (5 Sept.) at Saint-Bertin.[152]

---

printed the text at the end of his edition of Paschasius (1733). Since Martène's *texte de base* was Paris, Bibliothèque nationale de France, lat. 12299, an eleventh-century copy, made at Corbie, of a compilation originally drawn up at Saint-Vaast's, it presumably occurs in that. See *Paschasius Radbertus. De corpore et sanguine domini*, ed. B. Paulus, Corpus Christianorum continuatio Mediaevalis 16 (Turnhout, 1969), pp. xxxii–xxxiii. Paulus, however, makes no mention of the formula.

[150] Note that additions were made on fols 47 (a new *Memento)* and 48r (names for inclusion in the *Libera*) by one of the scribes who worked on the new gathering. See above, p. xliv.

[151] *Liber Sacramentorum Gellonensis*, ed. Dumas and Deshusses, I, 377–8, nos 2483–7; *Missale ad usum Westmonasteriensis*, ed. Legg, III, 1576.

[152] See N. A. Orchard, 'An Anglo-Saxon Mass for St Willibrord and its later liturgical uses', *ASE* 24 (1995), 1–10.

Nuptial mass and blessing of the candles (nos 207–211). Of the formulae provided, only *Deus inenarrabilis et inestimabilis* is at all unusual.[153]

Mass for the Fifth Sunday before Christmas (nos 9*–12*). A standard 'Eighth-Century Gelasian' with a preface taken from the 'Supplement'.[154]

Masses for St Mary Madgalen and St Nicholas (nos 3*–8*). Common enough. *Ratoldus* is one of the oldest witnesses to the mass for St Mary Magdalen, however.[155]

Votive masses (nos 15*–23*). Again, standard forms. The masses for relics and for invoking the grace of the Holy Spirit are compositions by Alcuin and common in sacramentaries of the ninth, tenth and eleventh centuries; the mass for someone lying sick descends from the 'Supplement'.[156]

Votive masses (nos 2323–37). Added as main texts, beginning where Scribe 1 left off (fol. 275, line 17). As has already been mentioned, the Corbie scribe may have been copying material from the underlying Saint-Denis model. The prayer *Suscipe sancta trinitas* (no. 2327) is first attested in BNF lat. 2290, the ninth-century sacramentary from the house; and the readings from the Apocalypse and St John's Gospel (nos 2325–6) first appear together in BNF lat. 2291, the sacramentary written for Gozlinus, bishop of Paris.[157]

Sermo Fulgentii (no. 2338). St Fulgentius, the fifth-century bishop of Ruspe, was evidently important at Corbie, as BNF lat. 12051 notes that a mass was to be held in his honour: PRID. KALENDAS JANVARII.

---

[153] A further example appears in BNF lat. 11589, fol. 84r.

[154] *Liber Sacramentorum Gellonensis*, ed. Dumas and Deshusses, I, 214–15, nos 1650, 1652, 1654, with Deshusses, *Le sacramentaire grégorien*, I, 559, no. 1695.

[155] See V. Saxer, *Le culte de Marie Madeleine en Occident*, Cahiers d'archéologie et d'histoire 3, ed. R. Louis (Paris, 1959), pp. 364, 367 and 369.

[156] Deshusses, *Le sacramentaire grégorien*, I, 455, nos 1392–4; II, 50–51, 126–7, nos 1870–72, 2330–33.

[157] *Suscipe sancta trinitas* is known later in books from Trent and Canterbury.

NATIVITAS SANCTI SILVESTRI PAPAE. *Eodem die sancti Fulgentii episcopi. Ratoldus*'s text is taken from Sermon 2.[158]

THE PONTIFICAL

The English pontifical to which Ratoldus had access supplied material for twelve main sections of text. These, to recapitulate, are:

(i) the order for the consecration of a church (nos 2–97).

(ii) the order for the election and consecration of a bishop (nos 98–128).

(iii) prayers for the consigning of an archbishop's pallium (nos 129–131).

(iv) forms for the coronation of a king and queen (nos 132–175).

(v) miscellaneous blessings and exorcisms of things (nos 176–192).

(vi) the mass for St Cuthbert (nos 459–463).

(vii) the penitential order for Ash Wednesday (nos 495–512).

(viii) orders for the consecration of church officers (nos 566–653).

(ix) blessings for Palm Sunday (nos 808–812).

(x) the suite of *ordines* for Holy Week (nos 836–881, 908–916, 1012–1017, 1047, 1056 and 1063), and the underlying structure of the Ordinary of the Mass, given as an order for Easter Sunday (nos 1068–1129).

(xi) an order for the visitation of the sick (nos 2194–2215).

(xii) blessings from the pontifical's benedictional copied into their proper place, service by service throughout the temporal and sanctoral, and occasionally among the votive masses. These will be dealt with in a separate section.

Not all of these texts were adopted without change, however. As we

---

[158] Ed. J. Fraipont, *Sancti Fulgentii episcopi Ruspensis Opera*, 2 vols, CCSL 91, 91A (Turnhout, 1968) II, 899–903.

shall see, a number were evidently adjusted to make them suitable for use on the continent, either as *Ratoldus* was being prepared, or at some earlier date, though probably not as far back as the 930s, as Hohler suggested. The pontifical is likely to have been relatively new on the continent when Ratoldus obtained it.

What also seems clear is that the book had much in common with the pontificals generally known as 'Claudius I' and 'Lanalet', on the one hand, and the so-called 'Egbert Pontifical', on the other. As is so often the case, all three transmit texts that are considerably older than their actual 'palaeographical' date. Indeed, *Claudius* and *Ratoldus* (less so the others) give us some idea of the type of pontifical adopted by Oda, archbishop of Canterbury (941–58), in the 950s, a time when the influence of liturgical books from Cambrai and Reims, not to mention Mainz (in the shape of the Romano-German Pontifical), must have been particularly strong.

It is well to say too that the English pontifical embodied in *Ratoldus* evidently had pictures. Not only was space left at the beginning of the order for the dedication of a church for full-page miniatures, possibly a depiction of the Alphabets to be marked out on the pavement during the course of the ceremony, as in *Robert*; but the short lines that follow the superscriptions of the services for the ordination of the major officers of the church may originally have been captions to 'illustrative' half-page panels in the body of the book, akin perhaps to the panels in Rome, Biblioteca Casanentense, 724 (I), the pontifical roll written for Landulfus, archbishop of Benevento (969–83) *c.* 969–70.[159] Indeed, if *Ratoldus*'s were initially devised for this sort of purpose, then there may be a case for supposing that Anglo-Saxon pontificals were, in the centuries following St Augustine's mission, arranged on the model of books, or even rolls, from central Italy. Certainly, as we shall see, the penitential tariff at Canterbury was written on a *rotulus*.[160]

[159] For reproductions in colour, see *Exultet: Rotuli liturgici del medioevo meridionale*, ed. G. Cavallo, G. Orofino and O. Pecere (Rome, 1994), pp. 79–85. Also see below, p. cxlvi. For hexameters accompanying miniatures in Ivrea, Biblioteca Capitolare 86 (31), a sacramentary written for Warmund, bishop of Ivrea (1001–1011), see the facsimile, ed. L. Bettazi, F. dell'Oro and L. Magnani, *Sacramentarium episcopi Warmundi* (Ivrea and Turin, 1990), with A. Ebner, *Quellen und Forschungen zur Geschichte und Kunstgeschichte des Missale Romanum im Mittelalter. Iter Italicum* (Freiburg-im-Breisgau, 1896), pp. 52–62.
[160] The subject of pontifical rolls and libelli is briefly addressed by N. K. Rasmussen, 'Unité et diversité des pontificaux latins', in *Liturgie de l'église particulière et liturgie de l'église universelle. Conférences Saint-Serge, XXIIe semaine d'études liturgiques, Paris, 30 juin–3 juillet, 1975*, ed. A. Pistoia, C. M. Triacca and A. M. Triacca, Biblioteca

Before we move on to examine *Ratoldus*'s pontifical in more detail though, it may be helpful to give brief details of the books regularly used for comparative purposes:

Leofric: Oxford, Bodleian Library, Bodley 579: the so-called 'Leofric Missal'. Despite its name, Bodley 579 is not a missal at all, but an early-tenth-century combined sacramentary, pontifical and ritual, with cues for the chant at mass supplied by the main French, or Lotharingian scribe. The original portions of the book are known as 'Leofric A'. To this central core a succession of additions were made at various dates. The material added by English scribes during the period *c.* 930–1020 in spaces originally left blank, or on gatherings newly inserted, is collectively known as 'Leofric B'; and the additions made at Exeter in the time of Bishop Leofric (1050–72) are 'Leofric C'.[161] It is principally 'Leofric A' and 'Leofric B' that concern us here. Generally speaking, 'A' has been attributed to the abbey of Saint-Vaast at Arras (dioc. Cambrai), chiefly on the grounds that an invocation of St Vedastus (6 Feb.), patron of the house, figures prominently in coloured capitals in the book's litany. But as Christopher Hohler indicated in 1975, the 'Saint-Vaast symptoms' are purely superficial.[162] 'Leofric A' was plainly written for use in England, possibly at Wells, but more likely Canterbury, as 'Leofric B' certainly originated there.[163]

Dunstan: Paris, Bibliothèque nationale de France, lat. 943: the 'Pontifical of St Dunstan'. As has long been realised, the book contains materials assembled by St Dunstan (d. 988), notably the copy of a papal privilege sent to him by Pope John XII (955–64) on fols 7–8.[164]

Ephemerides Liturgicae, Subsidia 7 (Rome, 1976), 393–410. Also see F. dell'Oro's edition of Asti, Biblioteca Capitolare, XIII, an eleventh-century ordination roll, 'Frammento di Rotolo Pontificale del seculo XI', in *Traditio et Progressio: studi liturgici in onore del Prof. Adrien Nocent OSB*, ed. G. Farnedi, Analecta Liturgica 12, Studia Anselmiana 95 (Rome, 1988), 177–204. But one must beware of using the notion of libelli too freely: libelli are simply small books. In many cases they simply contain excerpts from longer ones, conveniently set out on independent gatherings. They have no magical properties.

161 The book is ed. F. E. Warren, *The Leofric Missal* (Oxford, 1883), pp. 1–269, and more recently N. A. Orchard, *The Leofric Missal*, 2 vols, HBS 113–14 (London, 2002). *CLLA*, no. 950.

162 Hohler, 'Some service books', 78.

163 See Orchard, *The Leofric Missal*, I, 132–205.

164 The manuscript is described by R. Brotanek, *Texte und Untersuchungen zu altenglischen Literatur und Kirchengeschichte* (Halle, 1913), pp. 3–49, and 194–202; Leroquais, *Les pontificaux*, II, 6–10; Ker, *Catalogue of Manuscripts containing Anglo Saxon*, pp. 437–9, no. 364; and Rasmussen, *Les pontificaux*, pp. 258–315. P. Conner, *Anglo-Saxon Exeter. A Tenth-Century Cultural History* (Woodbridge, 1993), pp. 33–47 and

However, there are signs that the manuscript may not have been written for day-to-day use. For its order for the dedication of a church contains a piece of rubric (concerning aspergation) couched in the first person: *Ter dixi intrinsecus* [sc. *ecclesiam*] *propter imbuendam fidem trinitatis quam fatetur ecclesia, et semel extrinsecus propter unum, et non iteratum baptisma quod gerit exterius ecclesia.*[165] Dunstan would hardly have needed such a note himself. The pontifical has all the appearance of being a 'model' text; and in this respect it is worth recording that BNF lat. 943 is the earliest book to preserve a distinctively Anglo-Saxon version of the 'De officiis septem graduum' entitled *Item de VII gradibus aeclesiae quos adimplevit christus*, and a capitulary originally issued by Gerbaldus, bishop of Liège (787–809) in 801–2.[166] Both sets of texts figure in Paris, Bibliothèque nationale de France, lat. 10575, the late-tenth-century southern English pontifical known as the 'Egbert Pontifical', and in Rouen, Bibliothèque municipale, 368 the early-eleventh-century pontifical once owned by Lyfing, bishop of Crediton (1027–46), and now generally known as the 'Lanalet Pontifical'. *Lanalet* and *Egbert* have other elements in common too, as has long been known. In the 990s, BNF lat. 943 was at Sherborne, where an archiepiscopal letter to Bishop Wulfsige III (992–1001) was added on fols 2–3, and a list of Bishops of Sherborne entered on fol. 1. Both letter and list are in later hands.[167] At some point in the last third of the eleventh century the book found its way to Paris.[168]

86–94, has suggested that BNF lat. 943 was made at Exeter. R. Gameson, 'The origin of the Exeter Book of Old English poetry', *ASE* 25 (1995), 135–85, esp. 172–5, provides the necessary corrective and re-states the indisputable palaeographical case for Canterbury.

[165] Ed. Martène, *AER*, Bk I, cap. viii, art. xi, ordo 3, and W. H. Frere, *Pontifical Services*, 2 vols, Alcuin Club Collections 3–4 (Oxford, 1901) I, 25, note. I am grateful to Helen Gittos for pointing out the existence of this 'note' to me.

[166] See R. E. Reynolds, 'The De officiis VII graduum: its origins and early medieval development', *Medieval Studies* 34 (1972), 113–51; and Haggenmüller, *Die Überlieferung der Beda und Egbert zugeschriebenen Bussbücher*, pp. 89, 289, with *Ghärbald von Lüttich. Erstes Kapitular (Ghärbald I)*, ed. P. Brommer, MGH Capitula Episcoporum I (Hanover, 1984), pp. 3–21. The capitulary is appended in *Dunstan*, *Lanalet* and *Egbert* to an extract from the prologue (*Institutio illa*) of the pentitential of Egbert, archbishop of York.

[167] Rasmussen wrongly states that the letter is in a smaller version of the hand that wrote the body of the manuscript. The Conway Library of the Courtauld Institute of Art has a photograph of fol. 2. For a good summary of the literature surrounding BNF lat. 943, see J. Rosenthal, 'The Pontifical of St Dunstan', in *St Dunstan: His Life, Times and Cult*, ed. N. Ramsay, M. Sparks and T. Tatton-Brown (Woodbridge, 1992), 143–63.

[168] Ed. Martène, *AER*, Bk I, cap. viii, art. xi, ordo 3. See also Martimort, *La documentation liturgique*, p. 99, no. 236.

Egbert: BNF lat. 10575: the so-called 'Egbert Pontifical', a pontifical written in southern England in the last third of the tenth
century.[169] Provides an extensive series of forms for the consecrating
of women religious. The arrangement of the book is not always
straightforward, however: every so often material appears where one
least expects it. An order for the consecration of a cross, for instance,
is sandwiched between the orders for the consecration of a widow
and consecration of a nun; and the blessings and prayers for Maundy
Thursday, Good Friday and Holy Saturday at the end of the book are
given in no discernable order.[170] At some point in the course of the
eleventh century a further gathering was added, probably in England,
and not Evreux as has sometimes been contended, containing material that is distinctively English in character, as Canon Banting notes.
The order for Maundy Thursday provided in this section runs parallel
with the one embodied in *Ratoldus*.[171]

Robert: Rouen, Bibliothèque municipale 369, the 'Benedictional of
Archbishop Robert', so-called after a seventeenth-century inscription on fol. 1r: 'Benedictionarius Roberti Archiepiscopi', the
possible owners in view being Robert, archbishop of Rouen (990–
1037), or Robert of Jumièges, archbishop of Canterbury (1051–2; d.
1070). Despite its name, the book, as has long been recognised, is
actually a pontifical-cum-benedictional, probably drawn up at the
New Minster, Winchester, for Aethelgar, the abbot of the house who
later went on to become bishop of Selsey (988 – 990 × 992).[172] The
benedictional contains blessings for feasts of the most important
saints of New Minster (SS Grimbald and Iudoc), but not for those of
the Old Minster (St Swithun); and the order for the dedication of a
church embodies a litany in which St Benedict has a double invocation.[173] Aethelgar clearly felt perfectly entitled to impose elements of

---

[169] Ed. H. M. J. Banting, *Two Anglo-Saxon Pontificals*, HBS 104 (London, 1989), pp.
118–23. On the palaeography, see T. A. M. Bishop, *English Caroline Minuscule* (Oxford,
1971), p. 14, no. 16, plate XIV, with D. N. Dumville, *English Caroline Script and Monastic
History: Studies in Benedictinism A.D. 950–1030* (Woodbridge, 1993), p. 65.
[170] On the order for Maundy Thursday, ed. Banting, *Two Anglo-Saxon Pontificals*, pp.
128–31, see A. Chavasse, 'A Rome, le Jeudi Saint, au VIIe siècle, d'après un vieil ordo',
Revue d'histoire ecclésiastique 50 (1955), 21–35.
[171] Ed. Banting, *Two Anglo-Saxon Pontificals*, pp. 147–53.
[172] Ed. H. A. Wilson, *The Benedictional of Archbishop Robert*, HBS 24 (London, 1903).
A reproduction of fol. 101r (order for the dedication of a church) is given in *Le
répons-graduel Iustus ut Palma*, ed. A. Mocquereau, 2 vols, Paléographie musicale 2–3
(Solesmes, 1891–2) II, plate 178b.
[173] Ed. Wilson, *The Benedictional of Archbishop Robert*, pp. 39, 45 and 74. Note that St
Benedict's name is in capitals in the benediction provided for the feast of his translation.

his *alma mater* on the community at Selsey. The numerous *ordines* contained in his pontifical, however, must have been adapted from models initially supplied by, or obtained from, the Old Minster (the cathedral). Recent attempts to place the production of the book squarely in the eleventh century are unconvincing as they stand.[174] If by some chance Rouen BM 369 actually is as late as has been claimed, then the manuscript as we have it must simply be a more or less faithful copy of a text drawn up initially for Selsey, made either for 'display', or for some bishop collector.

Cambridge, Corpus Christi College 146: an early-eleventh-century English pontifical and benedictional.[175] With its benedictions for the feasts of SS Aelfheah I, Swithun, Aethelwold (two), the translation of St Aethelwold, St Birinus, and *quinta feria de sanctis in ecclesia Wentana ueteris coenobii quiescentibus*, Corpus 146 was clearly intended for use at Winchester, and not Canterbury as David Dumville and Laura Sole have recently proposed, though the earliest parts of the book may well have been copied from a Christ Church model by a scribe and musical notator who had been trained there.[176] Four possible owners are in view: Bishop Aelfheah II (984–1006); Cenwulf (1006); Aethelwold II (1006 × 1007 – 1012 × 1013); and Aelfsige II (1012 × 1013 – 1032). As Mildred Budny has noted, Corpus 146, like a number of other Winchester books, later found its way to Worcester, where substantial additions were made in Samson, bishop of Worcester's time (1096–1112).

Claudius: London, British Library, Cotton Claudius A. iii, fols 31–8, 106–36, 39–86, 137–50, generally known as 'Claudius I': a pontifical written in England in the first quarter of the eleventh century. Owned and annotated by Wulfstan I, bishop of Worcester (1002–16)

---

[174] D. N. Dumville, *Liturgy and the Ecclesiastical History of Late Anglo-Saxon England* (Woodbridge, 1992), p. 87, says the second quarter, R. Gameson, *The Role of Art in the late Anglo-Saxon Church* (Oxford, 1995), p. 30, note 110, says 'surely eleventh century'. Neither author seeks to provide dated comparative material in support of their respective hypotheses, nor makes any attempt to explain why a pontifical, a bishop's book, should have been drawn up according to the 'use' of New Minster.

[175] For a description of the manuscript, see M. R. James, *A Descriptive Catalogue of the Manuscripts in the Library of Corpus Christi College, Cambridge*, 2 vols (Cambridge, 1912) I, 332–5, with M. Budny, *Insular, Anglo-Saxon and Early Anglo-Norman Manuscript Art at Corpus Christi College, Cambridge*, 2 vols (Kalamazoo, 1997) I, 495–9.

[176] Dumville, *Liturgy*, p. 72, with L. M. Sole, 'Some Anglo-Saxon Cuthbert *liturgica*: the manuscript evidence', *RB* 108 (1998), 104–44, at 132. Dumville seems to find a Winchester provenance unthinkable on palaeographical grounds. But his arguments are, alas, somewhat circular.

and archbishop of York (1002–23).[177] Probably written for him at Worcester, since *Claudius* and Cambridge, Sidney Sussex College 100, a select pontifical associable on palaeographical grounds with Oswald, bishop of Worcester (961–71), evidently descend in parallel from a common ancestor.[178] The two books have the same distinctive series of formulae for the consecration of various church officers, but make no provision for the consecration of a bishop, an archiepiscopal duty. *Claudius* falls into four main sections, three of which end incomplete. Section 1 (fols 31–38v) contains copies in Latin and OE of the laws promulgated by King Ethelred at Eanham. Section 2 (fols 106–139v): a benedictional and order for Holy Thursday, left incomplete in the middle of a prayer. Section 3 (fols 39–86v): orders for the ordination of church officers, the dedication of a church, blessings, and a marriage order, perhaps ending complete as it stands. Section 4 (fols 137–150v): a second benedictional with integrated orders for Ash Wednesday and Holy Thursday. The text ends incomplete. In view of the presence of benedictions for SS Medard, Eligius and Nicasius, Section 4 is likely to embody a Reims benedictional similar to the one embodied in Reims BM 214, not a book from Soissons, as Turner suggested. The orders for Ash Wednesday and Holy Thursday evidently descend from the Reims model too, as we shall see.

Anderson: London, British Library, Add. 57337: an early-eleventh-century English pontifical-cum-benedictional once owned by Hugh Anderson, minister of the parish of Brainie, near Elgin.[179] Claimed by palaeographers and art-historians, probably correctly, for Christ Church, Canterbury.[180] Presumably made for an archbishop.

---

[177] Its text is ed. Turner, *The Claudius Pontificals*, pp. 1–88. See also Ker, *Catalogue of Manuscripts containing Anglo-Saxon*, pp. 177–8, no. 141; A. Prescott, 'The structure of English pre-Conquest benedictionals', *British Library Journal* 13 (1987), 118–58, at 139–41; M. Lapidge, *Anglo-Saxon Litanies of the Saints*, HBS 106 (London, 1991), p. 69; and P. Wormald, *The Making of English Law*, 2 vols (Oxford, 1999 and forthcoming) I, 191–5.

[178] The Sidney Sussex pontifical is ed. Banting, *Two Anglo-Saxon Pontificals*, pp. 156–70.

[179] Bought by the British Museum at Sotheby's, London, on 12 July 1971. Described and illustrated (in colour) in the catalogue of the sale. The contents of the manuscript as a whole are listed by Rasmussen, *Les pontificaux*, pp. 167–257. Also see Prescott, 'The structure', 135. Sarah Keefer and William Shipper have an edition in hand for the Henry Bradshaw Society.

[180] See Dumville, *English Caroline Script*, pp. 106–7. T. A. Heslop, 'The production of *de luxe* manuscripts and the patronage of King Cnut and Queen Emma', *ASE* 19 (1990), 151–91, at 169–70, has suggested that the presence of an invocation of St Bartholomew in *Anderson*'s short litany can be connected with the reputed arrival of relics of the saint at Christ Church in 1022 or 1023. However, invocations of St Bartholomew also occur in the short litanies of London, British Library, Add. 28188, and London, British Library, Cotton

Aelfheah (1005–12), Lyfing (1013–20) and perhaps even Aethelnoth (1020–38) are all possible.

Lanalet: Rouen, Bibliothèque municipale 368: the early-eleventh-century 'Lanalet Pontifical', so-called because an order of excommunication issued in the name of the monastery of 'Lanalet' (St German's in Cornwall) appears as an early addition on fol. 183r.[181] As Jane Toswell has demonstrated, the book was almost certainly written after *c.* 1020, as St Martial of Limoges is classed as an 'apostle' in the litany of the order for the visitation of the sick. The inscription in Old English on fol. 196r recording that the volume was once owned by a certain Bishop Lyfing is therefore likely to mean the Bishop Lyfing who ruled Crediton between 1027 and 1046, and not Lyfing, bishop of Wells (*c.* 999–1013), who has occasionally been suggested. Rouen BM 368 was probably originally made, however, for one of Lyfing of Crediton's predecessors: either Bishop Eadnoth of Crediton itself (*c.* 1011–1027), or Bishop Burhwold of Cornwall (*c.* 1011–27). The two sees were united in 1027. The book later found its way to Wells, where, among other things, blessings in honour of St Andrew, patron of the cathedral, were added.[182]

Other relevant sources will be described as necessary. To turn now to the constituent parts of *Ratoldus*'s pontifical.

The Order for the Dedication of a Church (nos 2–97)

Ratoldus's order, as it stands, does not appear complete in any other book. This, perhaps, will come as no surprise, for medieval *ordines* are generally highly variable in character and arrangement.[183] But

---

Vitellius A. vii, books that have no immediate connexion with Canterbury or any other house known to have possessed relics of the saint, significant or otherwise. But it is possible that both manuscripts (a benedictional and pontifical) descend indirectly from Canterbury models. See below, pp. cx–cxi. For their litanies, see Lapidge, *Anglo-Saxon Litanies of the Saints*, pp. 136–7 and 191–2.

[181] Ed. G. H. Doble, *Pontificale Lanaletense*, HBS 74 (London, 1937), pp. 130–8. A reproduction of fol. 47r (order for the dedication of a church) is given in *Le répons-graduel Iustus ut Palma*, ed. Mocquereau, II, plate 178a.

[182] See M. J. Toswell, 'St Martial and the dating of late Anglo-Saxon manuscripts', *Scriptorium* 51 (1997), 3–14. Dumville, *Liturgy*, p. 87, mistakenly takes Lyfing of Wells to be a possible owner. The added blessings in honour of St Andrew are ed. Doble, *Pontificale Lanaletense*, p. 143.

[183] *OR*, IV, 307–402 (*ordines* 41 and 42, with commentary); *RGP*, I, 124–73 (*ordo* xl, nos 1–150).

Ratoldus's sources are clear enough, nonetheless. Its principal constituents are:

(i) an order similar to the one preserved in BNF lat. 2290, the late-ninth-century sacramentary from Saint-Denis edited by Dom Deshusses. The first sections of rubric are particularly relevant (nos 2–5).[184]

(ii) an English order standing somewhere between the ones preserved in *Claudius* and *Lanalet*, though as we shall see, its opening sections were evidently suppressed. Fortunately, however, some of the material seems to have caught the redactor's attention. Two prayers proper to the entrance ceremonies appear out of place at the end of the order, that is to say, in the section relating to the consecration of an altar.

The order envisaged in *Ratoldus* is:

(1) On the eve of the dedication the relics to be deposed are taken by the bishop and his ministers to the old (*antequam*) church or chapel, where vigils are said through the night. In the morning the bishop goes to the new church to begin the dedication. At his command, twelve candles are lit, and all who are in the building are expelled, except for the archdeacon. The door is closed. The bishop with his ministers then repair to the old church to vest. The litany is recited for as long as is required. When it has been read through, a prayer and responses are said.

(2) The bishop and his ministers proceed to the door of the new church and the entrance dialogue begins, the bishop intoning *Tollite portas principes uestras*, the archdeacon replying from within, *Quis est iste rex gloriae*?

---

[184] Deshusses, *Le sacramentaire grégorien*, III, 200–2. Related rubric, it should be said, is also to be found in other books, notably: Paris, Bibliothèque nationale de France, lat. 1217, an early-tenth-century pontifical probably from Moissac or Cahors; and Besançon, Bibliothèque municipale 2168 (formerly Phillipps 9376), a copy of a pontifical from Besançon made at Tours in the mid eleventh century. But since the sacramentary embodied in *Ratoldus* descends from a book from Saint-Denis, there is no particular need to look further afield. On BNF lat. 1217, see Rasmussen, *Les pontificaux*, pp. 322–5, with Martimort, *La documentation liturgique*, p. 88, no. 88. The order is ed. Martène, *AER*, Bk I, art. xiii, ordo 7. On the Besançon pontifical, see Martimort, *La documentation liturgique*, pp. 69–70, with R. Jurot, *L'ordinaire liturgique du diocèse de Besançon (Besançon, Bibl. mun. MS. 101)*, Spicilegium Friburgense (Fribourg, 1999), p. 421, no. 5. The text of its order for the consecration of a church generally runs in line with that of the Romano-German Pontifical.

(3) Those outside the church perform three circuits of the exterior. After each circuit, the bishop knocks on the main door and sings *Tollite portas principes uestras* with its psalm and the *Gloria*. The response from the archdeacon is the same as before. When the bishop has knocked and the archdeacon answered for the third time, the bishop replies *Dominus uirtutum*, and the door is opened. On entering, he says the *Pax domini* three times, then *Crux pellit hostem* and *Crux christi triumphat*.

(4) The clergy begin the litany, and the bishop, in company with his ministers, prostrates himself at the altar while the *Agnus dei* is sung. When they have all arisen, the bishop does not say *Dominus uobiscum*, but 'Let us pray', and the deacon gives the direction, 'All kneel', followed a short time later, by 'Rise'. The bishop says the prayer *Magnificare*.

(5) When that has been done, the bishop proceeds to trace a cross (in the form of an X) on the pavement of the church with his staff, marking the letters of the alphabet out on the floor as he goes. The first arm is traced from the north-eastern corner of the church to the south-western, the second from the north-western corner to the south-eastern. Antiphons are sung on both legs of the 'journey'.

(6) The bishop then approaches the altar and says *Deus in adiutorium meum intende* three times with the *Gloria*, but not the *Alleluia*.

(7) The salt, water and ashes are exorcized and blessed. The bishop puts chrism in the water, and prepares the cement with which the relics are to be enclosed in the altar.

(8) The bishop asperges the four corners of the altar with water, then, circling it seven times, with hyssop. During these circuits the antiphon *Asperges* is sung.

(9) When the altar slab has been sprinkled, the bishop asperges the walls of the church facing the altar's right side. He returns to the altar. The other three walls of the church are asperged in turn.

(10) The bishop then asperges the pavement in the form of a cross while the antiphon *Fundamenta templi* is sung.

(11) Triple circuits of the church are undertaken, three times within, three times without, during which antiphons are sung. On these circuits the walls are again asperged.

(12) Having re-entered the church, the antiphon *O quam metuendus* is sung, followed by *Beati qui habitant*. The incense is prepared, and the prayer *Deus qui loca nomini* said. The church is censed.

(13) When the main consecratory prayers have been read through, the altar is veiled. The antiphon *Introibo ad altare dei* follows. The bishop then stands before the altar, washes it, and dries it. He sprinkles Holy Water over the slab.

(14) After the required prayers have been pronounced, the bishop censes the altar and marks a cross in its centre with Holy Oil. He anoints its four corners. Having censed the altar once more, he anoints it with chrism.

(15) The bishop then goes round church making crosses of chrism on its walls with his thumb. On a further circuit he censes the walls, saying the prayer *Omnipotens sempiterne deus effunde super hunc locum*.

(16) The altar is censed for a third time. The main consecratory prayers begin.

(17) When the prayers and confirmatory antiphon are over, the church goods are blessed: general vessels first, followed by the paten, chalice, corporal, sacerdotal vestments, and cross.

(18) Afterwards the cemetery is consecrated, and the gravestones are blessed. Last, in this part of the order, at any rate, is the blessing of the bells.

We then come to the order for the deposition of relics: *Incipit ordo quomodo in romana ecclesia sanctae reliquiae condantur*, the title of which derives from *Ordo romanus* 42.[185]

(19) The bishop returns to church in which the relics had been laid up overnight. As they are raised the litany is said, followed by a prayer.

(20) The relics are then borne on a bier in procession to the new church. Antiphons are sung as the procession proceeds, and at the door of the church, a halt is made for prayer. The bishop enters. Antiphons and further prayers ensue.

(21) When those are over, the bishop takes the relics from the priest who has charge of them, and places them on the altar, which has been veiled

---

[185] Ed. *OR*, IV, 397–402.

from the congregation. The bishop then inters the relics himself (*proprio manu*) in the altar's receptacle (*confessio*), making the sign of the cross both within it, and on the four corners of the altar, with chrism.

(22) Into the *confessio* he also puts in three particles of the host, and three of incense. The receptacle is then stopped up with the cement made earlier in the day. Antiphons are sung.

(23) After the altar has been washed, the bishop signs four crosses over the surface of the table with oil and chrism. Incised crosses are then made at the four corners of the table with a blade (*et designantur per quattuor angulos cum cultro*).[186] A prayer follows.

(24) The main altar is 'dressed' with holy water and censed. The bishop intones the antiphon *Ornauerunt faciem*.

(25) Thereafter the other altars in the church are 'dressed'. Mass follows.

(26) Throughout the week following the dedication, mass is publicly celebrated in the church. During this time there must be lamps, of wax or oil, before the altar; the day and night offices throughout the octave are to be with lights too.

The introductory rubric (nos 2–6). The rubric with which *Ratoldus*'s order begins looks to be composite in nature. The first few lines run parallel with the type of text transmitted in Oxford, Bodleian Library, Canon Lit. 359, a late-eleventh-century collectar-cum-pontifical from Arezzo Cathedral.[187] All rubric is given in capitals for the sake of convenience.

Canon Lit. 359	*Ratoldus*
INCIPIT ORDO CONSECRATIONIS ECCLESIARVM	INCIPIT ORDO AD ECCLESIAM DEDICANDAM.
PRIMITVS ENIM DECET VT EPISCOPVS CVM CLERICIS SVIS EAT AD ECCLESIAM VESPERTINO TEMPORE, ETSI EST IBI ALIA ECCLESIA RECONDANTVR IN EA RELIQVIAE, ET AGANTVR VIGILIAE.	PRIMITVS ENIM DECET VT EPISCOPVS CVM CETERIS MINISTRIS EAT AD ECCLESIAM ANTEQVAM ET IBI RECONDANT VESPERTINO IN TEMPORE RELIQVIAS, ET IVBEAT EXERCERE IBI VIGILIAS PER TOTAM NOCTEM.

[186] For examples, see J. Braun, *Der christliche Altar*, 2 vols (Munich, 1924) I, 288–98.
[187] On Canon. Lit. 359, see the brief description given by E. W. B. Nicholson, *Early Bodleian Music* (London, 1913), pp. lxxvi–lxxvii, plates XLI and XLII.

The next section, however, seems to have been extracted from the Saint-Denis book on which *Ratoldus*'s sacramentary was originally based: directions similar to those embodied in *Ratoldus* also appear in BNF lat. 2290. The presence of the responsory *Domine si conuersus fuerit populus tuus* (and the alternatives provided) in the two *ordines* is particularly striking:

BNF lat. 2290	*Ratoldus*
IN CRASTINA AUTEM VADIT PONTIFEX AD ECCLESIAM NOVAM QUAE SACRANDA EST CUM ALIQUIBUS MINISTRIS, ID EST DIACONO, ACOLITO VEL MANSIONARIO, SEU CUM HIS QUI ET NECESSARII FUERINT,	IN CRASTINA AVTEM EAT PONTIFEX AD ECCLESIAM QVAE SACRANDA EST,
ET ORDINET IN EA QUAE ORDINANDA SUNT. ET ILLUMINANTUR IPSIUS IUSSU DUODECIM CANDELAE PER CIRCUITUM ECCLESIAE, ET EMITTUNT FORAS OMNES ET CLAUDITUR OSTIUM.	ET ORDINET IN EA QVAE ORDINANDA SVNT ET INLVMINENTVR IVSSV SVO .XII. CANDELAE ET EXPELLVNTVR OMNES FORAS NISI SOLVS ARCHIDIACONVS CVM CLAVSO OSTIO IBI MANEAT.
TUNC PONTIFEX CUM SACRO ECCLESIASTICO COETU VADIT AD ECCLESIAM UBI PRIDI FUERUNT RELIQUIAE POSITAE,	TVNC PONTIFEX CVM SACRO ORDINE REDEAT AD ANTIQVAM ECCLĘSIAM ET INDVANT SE SACRIS VESTIBVS,
ET FACIAT LAETANIAM, PROUT HORA DICTAVERIT. QUA PERFECTA DICIT.	ET FATIAT LAETANIAM PROVT HORA DICTAVERIT. QVA EXPLETA DICAT HANC ORATIONEM.
OREMUS. Actiones nostras quesumus domine aspirando . . .et per te cepta finiatur. Per dominum nostrum ihesum christum.	OREMVS. Actiones nostras quesumus domine aspirando . . .et per te cepta finiatur. Per dominum nostrum iesum christum.
ET TUNC INCIPIENS RESPONSUM. Domine si conuersus fuerit.	ET TVNC INCIPIENS RESPONSORIVM. R. Domine si conuersus fuerit populus tuus.
ITEM ALIVD. Exaudisti domine orationem serui tui. INDE SI NECESSE FUERIT. Tu domine uniuersorum qui nullam habes indulgentiam. USQUE DUM VENIAT AD IANUAM CONSECRANDAE ECCLESIAE.	ITEM ALIVD. Exaudisti domine orationem serui tui. ITEM ALIVD. Tu domine uniuersorum qui nullam habes indulgentiam. ET TVNC OMNI COLLEGIONE PROCEDAT CANTANDO AD OSTIVM NOVAE ECCLESIAE.

AD QUAM CUM PERVENERIT FINITO RESPONSORIO, PERCUTIAT PONTIFEX SUPERLIMINARE DE CAMBOTTA SUA DICENS: Tollite portas principes.	FINITIS AVTEM RESPONSORIIS PERCVTIAT PONTIFEX OSTIVM ECCLESIAE DE BACVLO SVO DICENS: A. Tollite portas principes. Ps. Domini est terra.
	DEINTVS AVTEM MINISTER RESPONDENS DICAT: Quis est iste rex gloriae?

There are naturally some differences, especially towards the end of the section, but the relationship is otherwise clear enough. The last part of *Ratoldus*'s introductory rubric goes its own way, however:

BNF lat. 2290	Ratoldus
ET ITERUM PERCUTIENS, REPETAT SIMILITER. TERTIO AUTEM EANDEM ANTIPHONAM PRAECINENS, CANTENT OMNES PER CHOROS IPSUM PSALMUM. Domini est terra. CUM Gloria.	ET SIC PERGAT OMNIS LEGIO IN CIRCVITV ECCLAESIAE, TER CANTANDO HANC ANTIPHONAM, CVM PSALMO ET CVM GLORIA, TERTIO AVTEM PERCVSSO OSTIO AB EPISCOPO ET DICTO TOLLITE PORTAS, ET RESPONSO TER A MINISTRO QVIS EST ISTĘ REX GLORIAE, RESPONDEAT PONTIFEX: Dominus uirtutum ipse est rex gloriae.
ET HAC CANTILENA FINITA, INPINGAT OSTIUM ECCLESIAE PONTIFEX, ET FACIENS CRUCEM, DICAT EXCELSA UOCE. Pax huic domui. ET USQUE TERTIO REPETAT, ET POST EUM OMNES INTRANTES. DEINDE INCIPIAT CLERUS LAETANIAM.	ET APERTO OSTIO INTRANS DICAT TER. Pax huic domui. Crux pellit hostem. Crux christi triumphat.

In copies of the Romano-German Pontifical, *Dominus uirtutum* is alloted to the bishop alone to sing; English books, however, assign the piece to all those gathered at the church door. It does not figure at all in BNF lat. 2290. The 'antiphon' *Pax huic domui, Crux pellit hostem* and *Crux christi triumphat* occurs in all Anglo-Saxon pontificals but for *Dunstan*.[188]

The body of the order (nos 7–44). When we turn to subsequent sections of *Ratoldus*, material that is recognisably English becomes more plentiful. Particularly striking are:

---

[188] The relevant page in *Lanalet* is illustrated (primarily to show the notation) in Rankin, 'Neumatic notations', plate XV.

(i) the block of exorcisms ending with the blessing of ashes (nos 11–16). The sequence is only ever to be found in English books or in books copied from English models.

(ii) the extended text of the first exorcism of water (no. 12). I give the standard 'Roman' version on the left, *Ratoldus*'s on the right:[189]

'Roman'	Ratoldus
Exorcizo te creatura salis in nomine dei patris omnipotentis, et in nomine iesu christi filii eius, et spiritus sancti, et omnis incursio diaboli, omne fantasma omnisque inimici potestatem eradicare et effugare ab hac creatura aquę. Unde exorcizo te creatura aquę, per deum uiuum, per deum uerum, per deum sanctum, et per dominum nostrum iesum christum ut efficias aqua sancta, aqua benedicta, ubicumque effusa fueris, uel aspersa siue in domo, siue in agro, effugies omnem fantasiam, omnem inimici potestatem, spiritus sanctus habitet in domo hac. Per.	Exorcizo te creatura salis in nomine dei patris omnipotentis, et in nomine iesu christi filii eius et spiritus sancti, omnis uirtus aduersarii, omnis incursio diaboli, omne fantasma, omnes inimici potestas, eradicare et effugare ab hac creatura aquae. Vnde exorcizo te creatura aquae, per deum uiuum, per deum uerum, per deum sanctum, et per dominum nostrum iesum christum, ut efficiaris aqua sancta, aqua benedicta, ut ubicumque effusa fueris uel aspersa, siue in domo siue in agro, effuges omnem fantasiam et potestatem inimici. Quatinus consecratio huius sanctae aquae proficiat ad dedicationem huius ecclesiae ut per eam et per benedictionem diuinam auxiliante domine siue per os, et per manus atque officium nostrum, haec domus domini dei nostri diuinitus per gratiam spiritus sancti consecretur et perpetualiter ad inuocandum nomen domini consecrata permaneat, et spiritus sanctus habitet in domo hac. Per dominum.

The version embodied in *Ratoldus* figures in all the Anglo-Saxon books described above, except for *Leofric*: and to take two examples at random, it also figures in:

London, British Library, Harley 2892: the so-called 'Canterbury Benedictional', a benedictional and select pontifical written at Christ Church, Canterbury in the mid eleventh century.[190]

A pontifical seen by Dom Edmond Martène at the abbey of Lyre in Normandy, now lost. The book was plainly English, as its orders for the consecration of a cross and cemetery indicate. Lyre was a dependency of Bec, the house from which two successive archbishops of Canterbury came: Lanfranc (1070–87) and Anselm

---

[189] Deshusses, *Le sacramentaire grégorien*, III, 232, no. 4272.
[190] Ed. R. M. Woolley, *The Canterbury Benedictional*, HBS 51 (London, 1917), p. 130.

(1091–1109).[191] Contacts between Canterbury and Bec, and Bec and Lyre were close, especially in the twelfth century. Martène, it should be noted, managed to unearth some English books, also now lost, at Bec itself.[192]

In English books of the mid eleventh century (and later), however, versions of the section beginning *Quatinus* begin to multiply. The standard practice seems to have been to give the text of the exorcism in full once (and once only) in the order for the dedication of a church, its use in subsequent *ordines* being reduced to, and indicated by, a particularised form of *Quatinus*, the only part of the formula that really needed tailoring to particular occasions. So to give an example: in the main exorcism of water the form is *quatinus consecratio huius sanctę aquę proficiat ad dedicationem huius ecclesiae* (as in *Ratoldus*), but in the exorcism of water for the consecration of a cross we have *quatinus consecratio huius sanctę aquę proficiat ad consecratio huius crucis*. Since specialised incises of this sort emerge first in books associable with Archbishop Stigand (1052–70), namely BL Harley 2892 and London, British Library, Cotton Vitellius A. vii, a copy made at Exeter of the mid-eleventh-century pontifical of Stigand's brother, Aethelmar, bishop of North Elmham (1047–70), it seems reasonable to look for their origins in the early eleventh century.[193]

(iii) the incipit of the prayer *Deus creator et conseruator* (no. 17). Continental versions invariably begin *Creator et conseruator* or *Omnipotens sempiterne deus creator*.[194]

(iv) the antiphons for the aspersion of the walls of the church (nos 22–3). But these appear in *Ratoldus* without the accompanying prayers prescribed in *Dunstan* and *Lanalet*.[195]

[191] Ed. Martène, *AER*, Bk II, cap. xxiii, ordo 1. On the other material printed by Martène from the manuscript, see Martimort, *La documentation liturgique*, p. 143, no. 177.
[192] The *ordines* for the consecration of church officers, which are ed. Martène, *AER*, Bk I, cap. viii, *ordines* 11 and 12, run parallel to those given in *Robert*, ed. Wilson, *The Benedictional of Archbishop Robert*, pp. 115–30, and other English books.
[193] See Orchard, *The Leofric Missal*, I, 140–41
[194] Ed. Deshusses, *Le sacramentaire grégorien*, III, 178, no. 4089; *RGP*, I, 140 (*ordo* xl, no. 41).
[195] On the chant in English dedicatory orders, see T. Kozachek, 'The Repertory of Chant for Dedicating Churches in the Middle Ages: Music, Liturgy and Ritual', unpubl. doctoral dissertation, Harvard, 1995, pp. 117, 293–351, esp. 328–30, and Appendix II, pp. 365–9. The prayers in question are: *Hic benedictionem tuam, Solus et ineffabilis, Adiutor altissime deus*, and *Deus qui iacob famulo tuo preelecto*.

(v) the position of the antiphon *O quam metuendus* (no. 24). The Romano-German Pontifical and other related orders position this piece after the entrance litany.

(vi) the use of the office antiphon *Vidit iacob scalam* (no. 33).

(vii) the presence of the prayers *Omnipotens sempiterne deus effunde super locum* and *Deus qui de uiuis et electis lapidibus* (nos 35–6), both of which, technically speaking, belong to the mass for the day.

In order to illustrate the nature of the relationship of *Ratoldus* and *Claudius*, it may be helpful to lay the two texts out side by side. I give a full synopsis of *Ratoldus* on the left, *Claudius* on the right. Relevant portions of *Lanalet* are indicated on the right where direct parallels are lacking in *Claudius*. *Claudius*'s rubric is in capitals purely for convenience's sake.

Ratoldus	*Claudius*
DEINDE INCIPIAT CLERVS LAETANIAM ET PROSTERNAT SE EPISCOPVS CVM MINISTRIS ANTE ALTARE VSQVE DVM DICATVR AGNVS DEI.	DEINDE INCIPIT CLERUS LETANIA. ET CUM UENERINT ANTE ALTARE. PONTIFEX ET SACERDOTES PROSTERNANT SUPER STRAMENTA USQUE DUM DICANT *AGNUS DEI*.
	[*Claudius* (and *Lanalet*) give litany in full.]
VT AVTEM SVRREXERINT AB ORATIONE NON DICAT PONTIFEX DOMINVS VOBISCVM SED OREMVS TANTVM, ET DIACONVS DICAT. Flectamus genua. ET POST PAVLVLVM. Leuate.	UT AUTEM SURREXERINT AB ORATIONE NON DICIT PONTIFEX *DOMINUS UOBISCUM* SED TANTUM INCHOAT ET DICIT. *OREMUS.* ET DIACONUS UT SUPRA *FLECTAMUS GENUA.* ET ITERUM *LEUATE.*
[*Post paululum* as in *Dunstan*.]	
TVNC PONTIFEX DICAT HANC ORATIONEM. Magnificare domine deus noster in sanctis . . . hereditate lauderis. Per dominum.	SEQUITUR ORATIO. Magnificare domine deus noster in sanctis . . . hereditate lauderis. per.
	ANTIPHONA. Fundamenta templi.
DEINDE INCIPIAT PONTIFEX DE SINISTRO ANGVLO AB ORIENTE SCRIBENS PER PAVIMENTVM CVM CAMBVTA SVA HAEC ELEMENTA a. b. c. ET DICAT HANC ANTIPHONAM: Confirma hoc deus. PS. Exurgat deus. CVM GLORIA.	DEINDE INCIPIT PONTIFEX DE SINISTRO ANGULO AB ORIENTE, SCRIBENS PER PAUIMENTUM CUM CAMPUTTA SUA, ABECEDARIUM USQUE IN SINISTRO ANGULO OCCIDENTALIS BASILICĘ

DVM VADENS AD DEXTRVM ANGVLVM OCCIDENTALEM INCIPIENS ITERVM A DEXTRO ANGVLO ORIENTALI a. b. c. SCRIBENS VSQVE IN SINISTRVM OCCIDENTALEM ANGVLVM, CANENDO ANTIPHONAM ALIAM: Emitte spiritum tuum. PS. Benedic anima mea.

[*Lanalet* and numerous other *ordines* give the same instructions as *Ratoldus*, but in different words and with different antiphons.]

DEINDE VENIENS ANTE ALTARE ET DICAT TER: Deus in adiutorium. CVM GLORIA ABSQVE ALLELVIA.

DEINDE UENIENS ANTE ALTARE DICAT. Deus in adiutorium meum intende, cum Gloria absque alleluia.

DEINDE BENEDICENS SALEM ET AQVAM CVM CYNERE, ET DICAT HANC ORATIONEM: Deus qui ad salutem humani generis . . . ab omnibus sit inpugnationibus defensa. Per.

DEINDE BENEDICENS SALEM ET AQUAM CUM CINERE, DICAT HANC ORATIONEM. Deus qui ad salutem humani generis . . . ab omnibus sit inpugnationibus defensa. per dominum.

SEQVITVR EXORCISMVS AQVAE. Exorcizo te creatura aquae in nomine dei patris omnipotentis . . . et spiritus sanctus habitet in domo hac. Per dominum.

SEQUITVR EXORCISMUS AQUAE. Exorciszo te creatura aquae in nomine dei patris omnipotentis . . . et spiritus sanctus habitet in domo hac. per.

BENEDICTIO SALIS. Inmensam clementiam tuam omnipotens aeternae deus humiliter inploramus . . . inpugnatione spiritalis nequitiae. Per.

BENEDICTIO SALIS. Inmensam clementiam tuam omnipotens aeternę deus humiliter imploramus . . . inpugnatione spiritalis nequitiae. per dominum.

EXORCISMVS SALIS. Exorcizo te creatura salis per deum uiuum, per deum uerum . . . iudicare uiuos et mortuos et seculum per ignem.

EXORCISMUS SALIS. Exorcizo te creatura salis per deum uiuum per deum uerum . . . iudicare uiuos et mortuos et seculum per ignem.

BENEDICTIO CINERVM. Omnipotens sempiterne deus, parce metuentibus . . . et animae tutelam percipiant. Per dominum nostrum.

BENEDICTIO CINERUM. Omnipotens sempiterne deus parce metuentibus . . . et animae tutelam percipiant. per.

POST HOC MISCETVR SAL ET CYNIS FACIENS CRVCEM TER SVPER IPSAM AQVAM ET DICAT HANC ORATIONEM: Deus inuictae uirtutis auctor et inseparabilis imperii rex . . . poscentibus ubique adesse dignetur. Per.

POST HOC MISCEATUR SAL ET CINIS FACIENS CRUCEM TER SUPER IPSAM AQUAM ET DICAT. Deus inuictę uirtutis auctor et inseparabilis imperii rex . . . poscentibus ubique adesse dignetur. per dominum nostrum, etc.

DEINDE MISCETVR VINVM CVM AQVA ET DICAT HANC ORATIONEM: Deus creator et conseruator humani generis dator . . . ad consecrationem huius ecclesiae uel altaris proficiat. Per dominum.

DEINDE MISCEATUR VINUM CUM AQUA ET DICAT HANC ORATIONEM. Deus creator et conseruator humani generis dator . . . ad consecrationem huius ecclesiae uel altaris proficiat. per dominum nostrum, etc.

ET MITTAT IN EAM CRISMA ET
CONDAT EX IPSA AQVA CALCEM ET
FACIAT MALDAM VNDE RECLVDERE
DEBET IPSAS RELIQVIAS.

ET MITTAT IN EAM CRISMA, ET
CONDAT EX IPSA AQUA CALCEM, ET
FACIAT MALDAM, UNDE RECLUDERE
DEBET IPSAS RELIQUIAS.

DEINDE FACIAT CRVCEM DE DIGITO
SVO CVM IPSA AQVA IN DEXTRAM
PARTEM PER QVATTVOR CORNVA
ALTARIS CANTANDO ANTIPHONAM:
Asperges me domine ysopo et mundabor.

DEINDE FACIAT CRUCEM DE DIGITO
SUO CUM IPSA AQUA IN DEXTERAM
PARTEM PER QUATTUOR CORNUA
ALTARIS CANTANDO, ANTIPHONA.
Asperges me.

INDE VENIENS ANTE ALTARE CVM
YSOPO ASPERGET ILLVM ALTARE IN
CIRCVITV, SEPTEM VICIBVS
CANENDO AN. Asperges me domine
ysopo, CVM PSALMO. ET VADAT IN
CIRCVITV ALTARIS SPARGENDO.
DEINDE IN DEXTERA PARTE PER
PARIETES ECCLESIAE VSQVE DVM
VENIENS ANTE ALTARE SPARGET.

INDE VENIENS ANTE ALTARE CUM
YSOPO ASPERGET ILLUM ALTARE IN
CIRCUITU SEPTEM VICIBUS
CANENDO ANTIPHONAM. Asperges me
domine. CUM IPSO PSALMO, ET
VADAT IN CIRCUITU ALTARIS
SPARGENDO. DEINDE IN DEXTERA
PARTE PER PARIETES AECCLESIAE
USQUE DUM VENIAT ANTE ALTARE,
DEINDE ANTIPHONA. AN. Sanctificavit.

ITERVM TRIBVS VICIBVS DESVPER IN
CIRCVITV ALTARIS VEL ECCLESIAE
DEINTVS CVM ANTIPHONA.

ET SPARGENDO ITERUM TRIBUS
VICIBUS DESUPER IN CIRCUITU
ALTARIS, VEL ĘCCLESIE DEINTUS
CUM ANTIPHONA ET CUM PSALMO.
AN. In dedicatione huius templi.

VSQUE DUM VENIENS ITERUM ANTE
ALTARE ASPERGET DESUPER IN
CIRCUITU ECCLESIAE, ET MITTET EX
MINISTRIS ECCLESIE DUOS VEL
TRES QUI EXTRINSECUS ĘCCLESIĘ
PARIETES UNA VICE PSALLANT

ET TVNC SPARGET AQVAM PER
PAVIMENTVM IN MODVM CRVCIS ET
IN LONGITVDINE ET IN LATITVDINE
CANENDO ANTIPHONAM: Fundamenta
templi. PS. Fundamenta.

ITERUM IPSE PONTIFEX VADAT DE
IPSO ALTARI SPARGENDO PER
MEDIUM ECCLESIĘ IN LONGUM ET
IN LATUM FACIENDO CRUCEM
SUPER OMNE PAVIMENTUM CUM
ANTIPHONA. AN. Benedictus es. PL.
Benedicite.

DEINDE PER PARIETES INTRINSECVS
ECCLESIAE CANTANDO
ANTIPHONAM: Sanctificauit dominus
tabernaculum.
PS. Magnus dominus.
AN. In dedicatione huius templi.
PS. Laudate dominum de caelis.
A. Lapides praetiosi omnes muri.
PS. Lauda hierusalem.

[The antiphons given together at this point
in *Ratoldus* are distributed throughout the
orders embodied in *Claudius* and *Lanalet*.
Note that in the former *Sanctificavit* and *In
dedicatione* have already been used.]

A. Erit mihi dominus in deum et in lapis iste.
PS. Deus noster.
A. Haec est domus domini.
PS. Ecce quam bonum.

DEINDE PERGAT EXTRA ECCLESIAM CVM OMNI SCOLA SPARGENDO TER PER PARIETES IN CIRCVITV ET DESVPER CANENDO AN. Benedic domine domum istam.
PS. Deus misereatur nostri.
A. Ecce tabernaculum dei.
PS. Beati inmaculati.
AN. Benedic domine domum istam.

[Again, *Ratoldus*'s antiphons are distributed throughout *Claudius* and *Lanalet*. Note that *Ecce tabernaculum* is given below in *Claudius* (as in *Lanalet*) for the washing of the altar.]

FINITO HOC INGREDIATVR PONTIFEX IN ECCLESIAM CVM OMNI SCOLA ET INCIPIAT ANTIPHONAM. O quam metuendus est.
PS. Verba mea.
A. Qui habitat in adiutorio.
PS. Idipsum.
A. Beati qui habitant.
PS. Quam dilecta.

[*Ratoldus*'s text as *Lanalet*.]

ET TVNC PONAT INCENSVM IN ACERRA ET DICAT HANC ORATIONEM. OREMVS ET DIACONVS VT SVPRA. Deus qui loca nomini tuo dicata sanctificas . . . auxilium tuae misericordiae sentiatur. Per dominum.

ET VENIENS IN MEDIO ECCLESIĘ DICAT OREMUS. ET DIACONUS *FLECTAMUS GENUA*, POSTEA DICAT *LEUATE* ET DICAT EPISCOPUS HANC ORATIONEM. Deus qui loca nomini tuo dicata sanctificas . . . auxilium tuae misericordiae sentiatur. Per dominum.

ET TVNC EX INCENSO BONI ODORIS INFVMAT TOTAM ECCLESIAM, ET STANS IN MEDIO DICAT A. Domus mea domus orationis uocabitur. V. Narrabo nomen tuum. CVM GLORIA.

[*Ratoldus*'s chant normally used, as in *Ordo romanus* 41 and BNF lat. 2290, etc., for the asperging of the pavement.]

ITERVM DICAT OREMVS, ET DIACONVS VT SVPRA. Deus sanctificationum omnipotens dominator cuius pietas sine fine sentitur . . . in sanctae trinitatis fide catholica perseuerent. Per.

ITERUM DICAT *OREMUS* UT SUPRA SEQUITUR ORATIO. Deus sanctificationum omnipotens dominator cuius pietas sine fine sentitur . . . in sanctae trinitatis fide catholica perseuerent. Per.

PREFATIO IN MEDIO ECCLESIAE. VD aeterne deus. Adesto praecibus nostris, adesto sacramentis . . . perpetuo miserationis tuę munere gloriemur. Per christum.

PRĘFATIO IN MEDIO ĘCCLESIĘ. VD usque aeterne deus. Adesto praecibus nostris. Adesto sacramentis . . . perpetuo miserationis tuę munere gloriemur. per dominum.

IPSA EXPLETA INGREDIENDVM EST AD ALTARE POST EXTENSVM VELVM PSALLENDO ANTIPHONAM: Introibo ad altare dei ad deum qui laetificat iuuentutem meam. PS. Iudica me deus et discerne. DEINDE EAT ANTE ALTARE ET FVNDAT AQVAM SVPER ALTARIA ET ABSTERGAT LINTEO ET BENEDICAT TABVLAM ET AQVA SANCTA.

IPSA EXPLETA INGREDIENDUM EST AD ALTARE POST EXTENSUM VELUM PSALLENDO ANTIPHONAM. AN. Introibo ad altare dei ad deum qui laetificat iuuentutem meam. PL. Iudica me deus et discerne. TUNC VADAT ANTE ALTARE ET FUNDAT QUOD REMANSIT DE IPSA AQUA AD BASIM ALTARIS ET EXTERGATUR ALTARE DE LINTEO CUM ANTIPHONA. AN. Ecce tabernaculum. ET BENEDICAT TABULAM ALTARIS, QUAE TAMEN TABULA PRIUS LOTA ERIT EX AQUA SACRATA.

Singulare illud repropitiatorium quod se in ara crucis . . . legem scripsisti in tabulis. Per.

BENEDICTIO TABULAE. Singulare illud repropitiatorium quod se in ara crucis . . . legem scripsisti in tabulis. per dominum.

ITEM ALIA. Deus omnipotens uniuersarum rerum rationabilis artifex . . . fidei sit precipue dignum honore. Per.

ITEM ALIA. Deus omnipotens uniuersarum rerum rationabilis artifex . . . fidei sit precipue dignum honore. per.

POSTEA INCENSVM OFFERAT ET MITTAT OLEVM FACIENSQVE CRVCEM IN MEDIO ET IN QVATTVOR ANGVLIS ET DICAT. AN. Erexit iacob lapidem. PS. Quam dilecta.

POSTEA MITTAT OLEUM SUPER ALTARE IN MEDIO CRUCEM FACIENS ET SUPER QUATTUOR ANGULOS CUM ANTIPHONA. AN. Erexit iacob lapidem. PS. Quam dilecta.

ET UNGUAT MANU SUA IPSUM LAPIDEM SEMPER ET IN CIRCUITU IPSIUS ALTARIS, PER QUATTUOR CORNUA ALTARIS EXPLETO PSALMO MITTAT ITERUM OLEUM SICUT PRIUS CANENDO. ANT. Mane surgens iacob.

POST HAEC PONAT INCENSVM ET CRISMA, DICAT:
A. Ecce odor fili mei sicut odor.
PS. Ecce quam bonum.
A. Erit mihi dominus in deum.
PS. Deus noster.
A. Vidit iacob sumitas scalam.
PSS. Fundamenta.

IPSA EXPLETA ITA MITTAT CRISMA SIMILITER CANENDO. AN. Vidit iacob scalam. PL. Fundamenta eius.

DEINDE FACIENS CRVCES PER PARIETES IN CIRCVITV DE IPSO CRISMATE CVM POLLICE, DICAT AN. Sanctificauit dominus.
ALIA A. Lapides pretiosi.
PS. Lauda iherusalem.
ANT. Mane surgens iacob erigebat.

DEINDE IN CIRCUITU ECCLESIAE PER PARIETES A DEXTRO IN SINISTRO FACIENS CRUCEM CUM POLLICE. AN. O quam metuendus est locus iste. PL. Magnus dominus. ET ITERUM. AN. Lapides preciosi omnes. PL. Lauda ierusalem.

TVNC IN CIRCVITV INTRINSECVS MITTET INCENSVM BONI ODORIS ET DICAT, OREMVS. Omnipotens sempiterne deus effunde super hunc locum . . . et uotorum obtineatur effectus. Per.

[*Ratoldus* as *Lanalet* (and other English books); the prayer is unknown in this position in continental *ordines*.]

ITEM ALIA. Deus qui de uiuis et electis lapidibus . . . spiritalibus amplificetur augmentis. Per.

[*Ratoldus* as *Lanalet* (and other English books); the prayer is unknown in this position in continental *ordines*.]

TVNC EAT AD ALTARE, ET PONET INCENSVM ET DICAT ORATIONEM. Dei patris omnipotentis misericordiam dilectissimi fratres depraecemur . . . prumptus exauditor adsistat. Per.

INDE DICAT *OREMUS* ET DIACONUS UT SUPRA, ET DICAT EPISCOPUS. Dei patris omnipotentis misericordiam dilectissimi fratres deprecemur . . . promptus exauditor adsistat. per.

ALIA. Deus omnipotens in cuius honore altare hoc sub inuocatione nominis tui indigni consecramus . . . postulata concedas. Per.

ITERUM DICAT *OREMUS*, ET DIACONUS UT SUPRA, SEQUITUR ORATIO. Deus omnipotens in cuius honore altare hoc sub inuocatione nominis tui . . . postulata concedas. per dominum.

PRAEFATIO SVPER ALTARE. VD aeternae deus. Vt propensiori cura et adtentiori famulatu tibi seruitutis officia deferamus . . . in participatione earum uitam adquiramus sempiternam. Per christum.

PRAEFATIO SVPER ALTARE. VD aeterne deus. Vt propensiori cura et adtentiori famulatu tibi seruitutis officia deferamus . . . in participatione earum uitam adquiramus sempiternam. per dominum.

Maiestatem tuam domine imploramus humiliter . . . tuis uitam percipere aeternam mereamur. Per.

Maiestatem tuam domine imploramus humiliter . . . tuis uitam percipere aeternam mereamur. per.

III. A. Confirma hoc deus. CVM GLORIA.

DEINDE DICIT ANTIPHONO. AN. Confirma hoc. Cum gloria.

DEINDE BENEDICAT PONTIFEX LINTEAMINA ET OMNIA ORNAMENTA SEV VASA AD CVLTVM ECCLESIAE PERTINENTIA SVBDIACONIBVS ET ACOLITIS MANVVM TENENTIA CVM AQVA SANCTA ET INCENSO.

DEINDE TENENTIBUS SUBDIACONIBUS ET ACOLITIS LINTEAMINA, VEL OMNIA ORNAMENTA ECCLESIE, SEU VASA SACRA QUAECUMQUE AD CULTUM DEI ECCLESIĘ PERTINERE VIDENTUR, BENEDICAT EA PONTIFEX SICUT IN SACRAMENTARIO CONTINETUR.

OREMVS. Omnipotens et misericors deus, qui ab initio utilia . . . et sanguinis iesu christi filii tui domini nostri pareatur famulantibus. Qui tecum.

BENEDICTIO LINTEAMINUM, UEL OMNIA IN USUM BASILICAE. Omnipotens et misericors deus, qui ab initio utilia . . . et sanguinis ihesu christi filii tui domini nostri pareatur famulantibus. qui tecum.

THE SACRAMENTARY OF RATOLDUS

ALIA. Domine deus omnipotens sicut ab
initio hominibus utilia . . . tuta adque
defensa potens domine uasa. Per dominum.

[*Ratoldus* as *Lanalet.*]

BENEDICTIO AD OMNIA ORNAMENTA
ECCLAESIAE. Dignare domine deus
omnipotens rex regum, et dominus
dominantium . . . in suppremo meatu sine
fine constare credimus. Per dominum.

ITEM ALIA. Dignare domine deus
omnipotens rex regum et dominus
dominantium . . . in suppremo meatu sine
fine constare credimus.

Dignare domine deus omnipotens rex regum (no. 44), marks the end of
section III in *Ratoldus*.

Generally speaking five essential differences separate *Ratoldus* from
Claudius and *Lanalet*. First, the entrance ceremonies have been
dispensed with, and a new introductory section supplied. Second, where
Claudius and *Lanalet* normally keep to the text given in *Ordo romanus*
41, *Ratoldus* often gives either a paraphrase, or goes its own way
entirely. A case in point is the section dealing with ornaments:

OR 41, cap. 27	Claudius and Lanalet	Ratoldus
Deinde tenentes subdiaconi vel acolythi linteamina vel omnia ornamenta ecclesiae, seu vasa sacra quaecumque ad cultum Dei ad ecclesiam pertinere videntur benedicit pontifex sicut in sacramentorum continetur.	Deinde tenentibus subdiaconibus et acolitis linteamina, uel omnia ornamenta ecclesie, seu uasa sacra quaecumque ad cultum dei ecclesię pertinere uidentur, benedicat ea pontifex sicut in sacramentario continetur.	Deinde benedicat pontifex linteamina et omnia ornamenta seu uasa ad cultum ecclesiae pertinentia subdiaconibus et acolitis manuum tenentia cum aqua sancta et incenso.

Third, *Ratoldus*'s antiphons for the circuits of the church, inside and out,
are presented as a group, but without the prayers assigned in *Lanalet*
and other English books. Fourth, there is an enhanced interest in
incensation at various points throughout. Fifth, the order, taken as a
whole, is something of a hybrid, following *Claudius* for the most part,
but incorporating elements 'proper' to *Lanalet*.

That *Ratoldus* represents an advance on *Claudius* is clear enough
from the presence and position of the antiphon *O quam metuendus* and
its accompanying rubric; the prayers *Omnipotens sempiterne deus
effunde super hunc locum* and *Deus qui de uiuis et electis lapidibus* (nos
35 and 36); and the antiphons *Ecce tabernaculum* (no. 23) and *Erit mihi
dominus* (no. 33). That it cannot be a reworked version of *Lanalet*
emerges from even the briefest of glances at Doble's edition. The order
patently stands halfway between the two, a 'position' that can hardly
have been achieved by accident given the distinctiveness of the *ordines*
in view. Ratoldus's scribe must therefore have copied, more or less

accurately, what he had before him: and if he did make changes as he worked (besides the suppression of the entrance ceremonies), the changes made will have been very few and almost certainly limited to the wording of the rubric. The order effectively preserves, therefore, the work of an Englishman who had set about revising a text similar to the one in *Claudius*, but who had not yet hit upon the idea of drawing up something fully in line with *Lanalet*.

When we turn to sections IV–XI, that is to say, the formulae provided for the blessing of church goods (nos 45–70), *Claudius* again provides the best parallels, though there are some obvious differences, both of content and order. In section V, for instance, the blessing *Deus qui pro generis humani saluatione* (no. 51), to which we shall return in a moment, is evidently a 'newcomer'; in section IX, we have preliminary English versions of the forms given in the Romano-German Pontifical for the consecration of a cemetery (nos 59–61); and in section X, copies of the *RGP*'s blessings for a sepulchre (nos 62–64).[196] The other general point of departure from *Claudius* is the relative order in which the blessings are given. In company with *Dunstan* and *Lanalet*, *Ratoldus* presents an unbroken series. In *Claudius* the sets of formulae are interspersed with other material.

As for the blessings themselves, two evidently do not belong to the 'common stock' of formulae available throughout Europe during the middle ages. The first, which only appears in English books (*Dunstan* is probably the earliest), is the blessing of the corporal, *Deus qui pro generis humani salvatione*. As the following comparison will indicate, this was probably worked up, in part, from existing material, namely three 'Eighth-Century Gelasian' blessings: the 'Praefatio linteaminum' *Domine deus omnipotens sicut ab initio hominibus utilia*, the preface for the consecration of an altar *Domine sancte pater omnipotens qui post offendicula*, and the 'Benedictio altaris siue consecratio' *Domine omnipotens in cuius honore hoc sub inuocatione*. On the left, I give the

---

[196] For the forms for the consecration of a cemetery and the blessing of a sepulchre, which also stand side by side in the Romano-German Pontifical, see *RGP*, I, 192–4 (*ordines* liv–lv). Variants show that *Ratoldus*'s prayers for the consecration of a cemetery are a first English reworking of the German originals. In company with all other Anglo-Saxon pontificals *Ratoldus* gives *benedicere et sanctificare concedas, qui abrahae beato patriarche famulo tuo* instead of *benedicere et sanctificare digneris qui abrahae beati patriarchae famuli tui* in the prayer *Deus qui es totius* (no. 59); and its third prayer (no. 61) begins *Domine deus pastor*, again, as in other English books, instead of *Domine sancte pater*. But *Ratoldus* does not yet have the rubric and supplementary formulae of *Claudius* and friends.

relevant portions of these texts as they appear in BNF lat. 816, the famous late-eighth- or early-ninth-century sacramentary of Angoulême, on the right the cognate passages in *Ratoldus*:[197]

Angoulême	Ratoldus
	Deus qui pro generis humani saluatione uerbum caro factus es . . .
. . . sanctificare, benedicere, consecrareque digneris haec linteamina in usum altaris tui ad tegendum inuoluendumque corpus et sanguinem filii tui domini nostri iesu christi . . .	sanctificare, benedicere, consecrareque, digneris haec linteamina in usum altaris tui, ad consecrandum super ea siue ad tegendum inuoluendumque corpus et sanguinem filii tui domini nostri iesu christi,
	dignisque pareant famulantibus,
. . . ut quicquid sacro ritu super hoc immolabitur, sicut Melchisedech oblatum placeat tibi hoc holocaustum, et reportet per hoc praemium quisquis intulerit uotum . . .	ut quicquid sacro ritu super haec immolabitur, sicut melchisedech oblatum placeat tibi holocaustum, et reportet per hoc premium quicumque obtulerit uotum,
. . . tibi libamina accepta, sint grata, sint pinguia, et spiritus sancti tui semper rore perfusa . . .	. . . tibi libamina accepta, sint grata, sint pinguia, et spiritus sancti tui semper rore perfusa. Per dominum..

The second is the short prayer for the chrismation of a cross, *Omnipotens sempiterne deus qui per lignum perdito redemptionis* (no. 57). This appears in four out of five Anglo-Saxon pontificals that have come down to us, including the English abbatial benedictional-cum-pontifical embodied in Rouen, Bibliothèque municipale, 272, a mid-eleventh-century sacramentary from the abbey of Saint-Wandrille in Normandy.[198] It is unknown in continental books not copied from English models.

The enclosing of the relics (nos 71–97). As has already been mentioned, section XII, that is to say, the part of *Ratoldus*'s order containing the directions for the enclosing of the relics laid up the night before, is structured much as *Ordo romanus* 42. But on closer inspection the text again turns out to derive from a book standing somewhere between *Claudius* and *Lanalet*. Particularly English are:

---

[197] Ed. P. Saint-Roch, *Liber Sacramentorum Engolismensis*, CCSL 159C (Turnhout, 1987), pp. 303–4, 305, 308, nos 2026, 2029, 2041. The formulae are also conveniently edited with variants from other early books by Deshusses, *Le sacramentaire grégorien*, III, 179–80, 183, nos 4093, 4094 and 4105.

[198] For further comment, see Orchard, *The Leofric Missal*, I, 94.

(i) the secondary use of the antiphon *O quam metuendus* (no. 74) with its rubric.

(ii) the presence of the prayers *Deus qui uisibiliter omnia* (no. 76) and *Tabernaculum hoc ingredere* (no. 78). The latter is one of the formulae that the bishop would normally have pronounced on entering the church for the dedication. It only appears in English books.

(iii) the presence of the antiphon *Ornauerunt faciem*, which comes from the proper office for the day, and *Zacheae festinans* (no. 82), which was sung in England as the procession arrived at the front door for the service of dedication.[199] Again, this piece only occurs in English orders.

To illustrate the position, I print, as before, *Ratoldus*'s text on the left, *Claudius*'s on the right. Agreements with *Lanalet* have been indicated where appropriate.

Ratoldus	*Claudius*
INCIPIT ORDO QVOMODO IN ROMANA ECCLESIA SANCTAE RELIQVIAE CONDANTVR. PRIMVM EAT EPISCOPVS AD LOCVM IN QVO PRETERITA NOCTE RELIQVIAE CVM VIGILIIS FVERVNT ET ELEVET EAS CVM LAETANIA ET DAT ORATIONEM HANC: Aufer a nobis domine quaesumus iniquitates nostras, ut ad sancta sanctorum puris mereamur mentibus introire. Per.	INCIPIT ORDO QVOMODO IN SANCTA ROMANA ECCLESIA RELIQVIAE CONDANTVR. PRIMUM UADAT EPISCOPUS AD EUM LOCUM IN QUO RELIQUIAE PRAETERITA NOCTE CUM UIGILIIS FUERINT UT ELEUENT EAS ET FACIT LAETANIAM ET DICAT ORATIONEM HANC QUANDO LEUANTUR RELIQUIE̩. Aufer a nobis domine quaesumus iniquitate nostras, ut ad sanctarum puris mereamur mentibus introire. per.
DEINDE ELEVENT EAS CVM FERETRO CANTANDO ET PORTENT AD NOVAM CVM AN. Ambulate sancti dei ad locum destinatum. ALIA A. De hierusalem exeunt. A. Ecce populus. A. Cum iocunditate exibitis.	FINITA HAC ORATIONE, ELEUENT EAS CUM FERETRO, ET CUM MAGNO HONORE CANTANDO HAS ANTIPHONAS. Ambulate . . . in civitatem. Ambulate . . . ad locum. Ecce populus Cum iocunditate. [*Lanalet* has a more extensive set of antiphons].

[199] Note that *Ratoldus*'s order does not prescribe the saying of the litany on the three-fold processions round the exterior of the church prior to entering, a typically English characteristic. See H. Gittos, 'Sacred Space in Anglo-Saxon England: Liturgy, Architecture and Place', unpubl. D.Phil. thesis, Oxford, 2001, pp. 205–6.

PERGANT CVM CRVCIBVS, ET TVRRIBVLIS AD HOSTIVM NOVAE ECCLESIAE DICAT,

OREMVS. Deus qui in omni loco tuae dominationis . . . quae supplicat mereatur. Per.

DVM INTRAT EPISCOPVS DICAT AN. O quam metuendus est locus iste.

Domum tuam quaesumus domine clementer ingredere . . . huius fiat habitatio preclara. Per dominum nostrum iesum christum.

ITEM ALIA. Deus qui uisibiliter omnia contines . . . consolationis tuae beneficia consequantur. Per.

ITEM ALIA CVM A. Benedictus domine domum.

Tabernaculum hoc ingredire quaesumus omnipotens deus . . . ita benedicere et sanctificare eos et eum dignare. Per.

HAEC EXPLETA SVSCIPIAT EPISCOPVS RELIQVIAS A PRESBITERO ET PONAT EAS IN ALTARE NOVO EXTENSO VELO, INTER SE ET POPVLVM ET RECVNDET PROPRIO MANV IN CONFESSIONE ALTARIS ET FACIAT CRVCEM INTVS EX CRISMATE IN QVATTVOR ANGVLIS ITA DICENDO: In nomine patris et filii et spiritus sancti. Pax tibi. RP. Et cum spiritu tuo.

ET PONAT TRES PORTIONES CORPORIS DOMINI INTVS, ET TRES DE INCENSO. RECLVDANTVR TVNC RELIQVIAE CANENTES
AN. Exultabunt sancti in gloria.
PS. Laudate dominum de caelis.

A. Sub altare domini sedes. PS. Beati inmaculati.

CUM CRUCIBUS ET TURRIBULIS ET CANDELABRIS, MULTISQUE LUMINIBUS, CUMQUE PERUENERINT AD OSTIUM ECCLESIAE, DICAT EPISCOPUS ORATIONEM HANC AD OSTIUM. Deus in omni loco tuae dominationis . . . quae supplicat mereatur. per.

[*Ratoldus* as *Lanalet*.]

POSTQUAM INTRO PEDEM INTULERINT, DICAT ORATIONEM HANC: OREMUS. Domum tuam quaesumus domine clementer ingredere . . . huius fiat habitatio preclara. per.

[*Ratoldus* as *Lanalet*.]

[*Ratoldus* as *Lanalet*.]

[In *Lanalet*, *Tabernaculum* is used for the entrance ceremonies.]

IPSA EXPLETA, SUSCIPIT IPSAS RELIQUIAS A PUERO, ET PORTET EAS CUM LETANIA SUPER ALTARE NOUUM, EXTENSO UELO INTER EOS ET POPULUM, RECONDET PONTIFEX PROPRIA MANU IPSAS RELIQUIAS IN CONFESSIONE ALTARIS PER ANGUALAS QUATTUOR IN CRUCE ITA DICENDO. In nomine patris. R. Et cum spiritu tuo.

DEINDE PONAT TRES PORTIONES CORPORIS DOMINI INTUS IN CONFESSIONE ALTARIS, ET TRES DE INCENSO, ET RECLUDANTUR RELIQUIẸ IN CONFESSIONE CANENTES ANTIPHONAM. ANT. Exultabant.

ITEM ANTIPHONA, DUM PONUNTUR PIGNORA SACRA IN CONFESSIONE ALTARIS. ANT. Sub altare. PL. Beati inmaculati.

ET TVNC PONATVR TABVLA SVPER AQVAM FACIET CRVCES .IIII. EX OLEO ET SANCTAM CRISMAM ET DESIGNANTVR PER QVATTVOR ANGVLOS CVM CVLTRO ET DICAT PONTIFEX ORATIONEM HANC: Deus qui ex omni coaptione sanctorum . . . semper meritis adiuuemur. Per.

SUBPONATUR ETIAM TABULA SACRA, SUPER QUAM INFUNDATUR OLEUM SACRATUM ET POSTEA PER QUATTUOR ANGULOS ALTARIS EX IPSIS CRUX FIGURETUR, FINITO HOC, DICAT HANC ORATIONEM. Deus qui ex omni coaptione sanctorum . . . semper meritis adiuuemur. per.

POST HAEC VESTIATVR ALTARE CVM AQVA BENEDICTA ET INCENSO DICAT EPISCOPVS AN. Ornauerunt faciem templi. A. Zacheae festinans.

POST HAEC UESTIATUR ALTARE,

[*Ornauerunt* appears in place in *Lanalet*; *Zacheae* is generally the standard introductory antiphon for the main dedicatory order in English books.]

DVM ORNANTVR ALTARIA CANANTVR HAEC ET DICAT PONTIFEX ORATIONEM: Descendat quaesumus domine deus . . . corda dignanter emundet. Per.

ET DICATUR ORATIO. Descendat quaesumus domine deus . . . corda dignanter emundet. per.

ET TUNC ASPERGATUR AQUA CUM HYSOPO PER TOTAM ECCLESIAM, INDE REUERTATUR PONTIFEX IN SACRARIUM, CUM ORDINIBUS SUIS, ET INDUANT SE UESTIMENTIS ALIIS SOLLEMPNIBUS INTERIM ORNETUR ECCLESIA, ET ACCENDANTUR LUMINARIA MULTA,

XIII. DEINDE INCIPIAT CANTOR A. Terribilis est locus iste. DEINDE GLORIA IN EXCELSIS.

ET CANTOR INCIPIAT AD INTROITUM ANT. Terribilis.

Both *ordines* then give the formulae necessary for mass. In *Ratoldus* these form section XIII (nos 84–94). The order closes with two prayers for the consecration of a baptistery (nos 95–6) in section XIV; and a short piece of rubric (no. 97) relating to lights. This last combines the closing lines of *Ordo romanus* 42 with a section of rubric apparently running in line with the rubric normally occuring in English books, though it is possible, thanks to the looseness of its phrasing, to make it mean precisely the opposite:[200]

---

[200] Ed. Wilson, *The Benedictional of Archbishop Robert*, p. 100.

OR 42

ET POSTEA PER TOTAM EBDOMADAM
MISSA PUBLICA IN IPSA ECCLESIA
CELEBRETUR USQUE OCTO DIES
COMPLETOS

Ratoldus

ET POSTEA PER TOTAM
EBDOMADAM MISSA PVBLICA IN
IPSA ECCLESIA CELEBRETVR ET IN
IPSIS .VIII. DIEBVS,

Robert

SINE INTERMISSIONE INIBI
LUMINARIA ARDEANT, ET SI
SOLLEMNIS DOMUS EST
PRECIPIENTE EPISCOPO PER
TOTIDEM NOCTURNA DIURNAQUE
LAUS IBI CELEBRETUR.

IBI LVMINARIA ANTE ALTARE AVT
DE CERA AVT DE OLEO DEBENT
ESSE, ABSQVE LVMINARIBVS, ET
OFFICIIS NOCTVRNIS DIVRNISQVE
IN PREDICTIS .VIII. DIEBVS VLLO
MODO REPPERIATVR VSQVE DVM
.VIII. DIES COMPLEANTVR

Further work will doubtless distinguish more precise textual parallels for this passage, however.

Election and consecration of a Bishop (nos 98–131)

Ratoldus's order for the election and consecration of a bishop, first printed in full by Jean Morinus in 1655, is hybrid in nature, being part English, part 'continental' (as are a number of the additions made to the 'Leofric Missal' at Canterbury in the mid tenth century), and in places eccentrically arranged.[201] It consists of an open form of petition from the clergy and people of a church to their metropolitan, asking that such and such a man should be elected bishop (no. 98); formulae for the preparation of the candidate and his insignia of office (nos 99–108); formulae for the ordination itself (nos 109–128); and three prayers for recitation over the pallium, should the candidate be an archbishop (nos 129–131). Distinctively English are:

(i) the promissory formula *In nomine* (no. 101), which is an 'escapee' from the Christ Church archive, as we shall see.

(ii) the verse *Tu baculus nostrae* (no. 105) for the conferring of the baculus.

(iii) the second consecratory blessing, *Pater sancte* (no. 116), an ancient formula, perhaps introduced by St Augustine, and only known on the continent in books descending from English models.[202]

---

[201] Morinus, *Commentarius de sacris ecclesiae ordinationibus*, part II, 249–52. The texts added to Bodley 579 are ed. Orchard, *The Leofric Missal*, II, 399–403, nos 2331–47.

[202] For further commentary on this prayer, see N. A. Orchard, '*Pater sancte*: an ordina-

(iv) the text of the blessing *Spiritus sanctus septiformis*, which is partially embedded in *Ratoldus* in the prayer *Domine iesu christe tu praeeligisti* (no. 119). I print the forms given in *Robert* on the left and the hybrid formula of *Ratoldus* on the right:[203]

Robert	*Ratoldus*
Domine ihesu christe tu preelegisti apostolos tuos ut doctrina sua nobis preessent, ita etiam vice apostolorum hunc episcopum doctrinam docere et benedicere, et erudire digneris, ut inmaculatam vitam et illesam conservet, per omnia secula seculorum.	Domine iesu christe tu praeeligisti apostolos tuos, ut doctrina nobis praeessent, ita etiam uice apostolorum episcopos doctrinam docere, et benedicere, et erudire digneris, ut inmaculatam uitam et inlaesam conseruent,
Spiritus sanctus septiformis veniat super te,	quatenus spiritus sanctus septiformis ueniat super eos, et super nos omnes, et uirtus altissimi sine peccato una custodiat nos, et
et omnis benedictio quae in scripturis sanctis scripta est super te veniat. Confirmet te deus pater, et filius, et spiritus sanctus, ut habeas vitam aeternam, et vivas in secula seculorum. Amen.	omnis benedictio quae in scripturis sanctis scripta est super nos pariter ueniat, et confirmet nos deus pater, et filius et spiritus sanctus, ut habeamus uitam aeternam in saecula saeculorum.

In the majority of English pontificals that have come down to us, *Spiritus sanctus septiformis* normally follows *Pater sancte*, whilst *Domine iesu christe tu praeeligisti* follows *Omnipotens pater sancte deus aeterne*, the prayer said in England over the enthroned and consecrated candidate towards the end of the ceremonies of ordination. In *Ratoldus*, the two prayers have become a prayer of consecration.

(v) the chant, in particular the series of alternatives, which only has parallels in the material added to *Leofric* at Canterbury in Archbishop Wulfhelm or Oda's time, that is to say the 930s and 940s.[204]

Although the precise form of the English *ordo* is almost impossible to regenerate in detail, it can only really have resembled *Dunstan* and *Lanalet*, on the one hand; *Robert*, *Anderson*, and Corpus 146, on the other. These pontificals are in close agreement on the matter of episcopal ordinations. Indeed, the only differences of any great note between the two sets of books are that *Dunstan* and *Lanalet* make provi-

---

tion prayer used by the Anglo-Saxon church', *RB* 111 (2001), 446–63; *idem*, *The Leofric Missal*, II, 404, no. 2351.
[203] Ed. Wilson, *The Benedictional of Archbishop Robert*, pp. 127–8, 130.
[204] Ed. Orchard, *The Leofric Missal*, II, 403–4, nos 2342–5.

sion for the anointing of the candidate's head before the reading of *Pater sancte*, and 'omit' the prayer *Accipe baculum sacri regiminis*.

As far as the actual arrangement of the whole is concerned, we have, first, in section XV, the model petition, which goes under the superscription: *Electio quomodo a clero et a populo eligitur episcopus in propria sede cum consensu regis archipraesulisque omnique populo*:

> Domino francorumque meritis coequando pa<t>ri patrum domno .N. praesuli summo cunctus clerus omnisque populus sanctae .ill. ecclesiae multimodam in domino obtamus salutem. Igitur quoties aliqua pleps uestrae dictioni subdita a proprio fuerit uiduata pastore non aliunde nisi a uobis est implorandum auxilium. Quem ad hoc diuina praeordinauit maiestas, ut non solum uestros specialiter pascatis filios sed etiam rectores non habentibus, et spiritali pabulo indigentibus pastores tribuetis. Quapropter ad uestrae sanctitatis paternitatem fiducialiter nostras fundimus preces, poscentes uidelicet ut hunc .ill. summe honestatis, humilem uestrum famulum nobis pontificem ordinare indigemini. Cuius conuersationem et mores in quantum cognouimus laudamus, et ad tam dignum opus idoneum testificamus. Et quamdiu ad benedictionem (*sc*. ab benedictione) episcopali inmunes sumus eius doctrina et exemplo roborati, ad uiam salutis, domino miserante, quasi perdita onus (*sc*. ouis) et inuenta, redituros nos credimus. Quod decretum nostris manibus roboratum .ill. ecclesiae uestrae uobis dirigere statuimus. Anno incarnationis domini, et episcopatus uestri, et regi .ill. annorum illorum. Indictione tale, datarum tale.

> We, the clergy and people of church N., offer respectful greetings in the sight of the Lord to archbishop N., father of fathers, equal in honour to the Lord of the Franks. Whenever a congregation in your diocese has been deprived of a pastor, it is from none but you that help must be sought. To which end, the Lord has arranged that you will provide for your children, appointing pastors for those lacking spiritual sustenance, and rectors for those who have none. Therefore we faithfully pray that we might ordain bishop this man (his name), your humble servant, whose character and bearing, in our experience, is wholly praiseworthy; and whose fitness for such office is well attested. And although we lack episcopal blessing, his guidance and example strengthen us, and we believe that we may return, with God's mercy, to the way of salvation, much as a lost sheep that now has been found. We of church N., have resolved to direct to you this decree, authorised by our own hands, in the year of the Lord, year of your archiepiscopacy,

and year of King N's reign, such-and-such. Indiction such, day such.

The text is clearly an 'addition', prefixed in the copying, to the order transmitted in the English book. Since no other copy or version of the petition survives, all that can reasonably be deduced is that the document is northern French in origin – certain expressions also appear in petitions drawn up in the archdioceses of Sens and Reims – and that it was introduced either on behalf of, or perhaps even at the express request of, the bishop or archbishop for whom *Ratoldus* was made. The chances of it being an adjusted version of an English original seem slight.[205]

After the petition, we come to the formal admission of the candidate, which consists of a prayer to be said by the archbishop over the bishop elect (no. 99); a short admonition (no. 100); and a promissory formula or profession for the candidate himself (no. 101). The first two pieces descend from some copy of the Romano-German Pontifical, or an analogous source, and are relatively unexceptional; the same is not true of the third, however. For as Michael Richter has shown, the *promissio* is essentially an open version of the form used for the consecration of Herewine, bishop of Lichfield, 814 × 816. The copy that we have in *Ratoldus* evidently descends, therefore, from the English pontifical, all localisable references having been struck out in the copying.[206]

Section XVII consists solely of *Memor sponsionis* (no. 102), a prayer that regularly accompanies the conferring of the bishop's staff (*baculus*) in copies of the *RGP,* and now and again in non-standard books, the conferring of the ring (*anulus*), for which it is in some respects better fitted. *Ratoldus*, however, casts it as an *admonitio post promissionem*, which is also its stated function in 'Leofric B'.[207] Perhaps this was the formula's original function. Sections XVI and XVII seem to hang together logically enough.

When we turn to the sections that follow though, *Ratoldus* diverges markedly from standard medieval practice in placing the conferring and

[205] The Sens and Reims petitions are conveniently ed. PL 87 (cols 909–10, 911–12) along with many others (of widely varying dates) from France, Italy and Germany. See also *RGP*, I, 194 (*ordo* lvi, nos 1–5).
[206] Richter, *Canterbury Professions*, pp. xlviii–li. As Richter notes, the words *ecclesia Christi* were doubtless originally a reference to Christ Church, Canterbury, which the scribe misunderstood.
[207] Ed. *RGP*, I, 222 (*ordo* lxii, no. 43)

blessing of the episcopal ring and staff (sections XVII–XVIIII), or at least the formulae accompanying these actions, before the formulae prescribed for the consecration itself. Normally one would expect consecration to come first, anointing second, followed closely by the tradition of the insignia. That at least is how all surviving English orders are arranged and almost all those in books still in French collections. But there is one exception: the Albi pontifical, which positions the blessing of the ring and staff, along with the consigning of the Gospel book, before the main consecratory preface, *Deus honorum omnium*.[208] Clearly the Albi book did not serve as any sort of model, for the formulae provided are unique; but it shows nonetheless, that two houses might separately hit upon the same non-standard arrangement.

The rest of the order, that is to say, the last part of section XVIIII and sections XXI–XXIII in their entirety, hold fewer surprises. The forms for mass, all given more or less their proper place in the *ordo*, are essentially those of the *RGP*, while the principal prayers for the consecration, anointing and installation of the bishop descend from the English pontifical. We have in order: cues for the introit chant for mass (no. 108); the collects in full, and cues for the readings and graduals for the day (nos 109–114); the main consecratory blessing *Deus honorum omnium* (no. 115); the secondary blessing, *Pater sancte* (no. 116); forms for the anointing of the candidate's head and hands (nos 117–118); a blessing to be said over the consecrators (no. 119); cues for the gospel reading and offertory (nos 120–21); the remaining prayers and chant for mass (nos 122–27); a confirmatory prayer over the enthroned and consecrated bishop (no. 128); and finally, the prayers said as the pallium was consigned to an archbishop (nos 129–31). Collation shows that these last side with the many English texts that have come down to us, and the not the versions embodied in the Romano-German Pontifical.[209]

---

[208] Leroquais, *Les pontificaux*, I, 8–15. Rasmussen, *Les pontificaux*, pp. 49–50, seems to allude to the analogy.

[209] For example, in company with other Anglo-Saxon pontificals, *Ratoldus* gives *sanctis premia* at the end of the third prayer (no. 131), not *sanctus per omnia*, which is the standard reading of all copies of the Romano-German Pontifical. Along with *Anderson* and *Dunstan*, *Ratoldus* also provides the rubric *Hic detur pallium. Consecratio post pallium*, but it does not yet have the text of the note from Bede: either that, or the note was suppressed.

Coronation Order (nos 132–175)

Ratoldus, as has long been recognised, preserves the oldest surviving 'continental' text of the so-called 'Second English Coronation Order' (less commonly now, the 'Edgar Order'). The arrangement given in *Ratoldus*, variant readings and corrections aside, is repeated in no less than sixteen later French books. Six English pontificals of the late tenth and eleventh century transmit the text as it was known in England: *Dunstan*; *Robert*; Corpus 146; *Anderson*; *Claudius II*, a fragmentary early- to mid-eleventh-century pontifical from Christ Church, Canterbury; and London, British Library, Cotton Vitellius A. vii, the copy, made at Exeter, of Aethelmar of North Elmham's pontifical.[210] To outline the most obvious differences between the two families, I give a synopsis of *Ratoldus* on the left, *Robert* on the right:

Ratoldus	Robert
Petition of Bishops. *A uobis perdonari.*	Antiphon. *Firmetur manus tua.*
The King's response. *Promitto uobis.*	Prostration of King. *Te deum.*
Instructions for the enquiry of the bishops into the will of the people. *Te Deum.*	Promise. *Haec tria praecepta populo.*
Prostration of the King. *Te Deum.*	
Blessing. *Te inuocamus domine sanctae pater.*	Blessing. *Te inuocamus domine sancte pater.*
Alia. *Deus qui populis tuis uirtute.*	Alia. *Deus qui populis tuis uirtute.*
Alia. *In diebus eius oriatur.*	Item. *In diebus eius oriatur.*
Consecration. *Omnipotens sempiterne deus creator.*	Consecration. *Omnipotens sempiterne deus creator.*
Antiphon. *Vnxerunt salomonem.*	Antiphon. *Unxerunt salomonem.*
<Prayer continues>. *Vnde unxisti sacerdotes.*	Prayer. *Christe perunge . . . unde unxisti.*
Alia. *Deus electorum fortitudo.*	Alia. *Deus electorum fortitudo.*
Alia oratio. *Deus dei filius iesus christus.*	Alia oratio. *Deus dei filius iesus christus.*
Giving of ring. *Accipe anulum signaculum.*	Giving of ring. *Accipe anulum signaculum.*
Prayer. *Deus cuius est omnis potestas.*	Prayer. *Deus cuius est omnis potestas.*
	Antiphon. *Confortare et esto.*
Giving of sword. *Accipe hunc gladium.*	Giving of sword. *Accipe hunc gladium.*
Prayer. *Deus qui prouidentia tua.*	Prayer. *Deus qui prouidentia tua.*
Crowning. *Coronet te deus corona.*	Crowning. *Coronet te deus corona.*
Prayer. *Deus perpetuitatis dux uirtutum.*	Prayer. *Deus perpetuitatis dux uirtutum.*

[210] Ménard, *Liber sacramentorum*, pp. 278–85, prints *Ratoldus*'s text.

Giving of sceptre. *Accipe sceptrum regiae.*
Prayer. *Omnium domine fons bonorum.*

Giving of *uirga. Accipe uirgam uirtutis.*

Blessing. *Extendat omnipotens deus.*
Alia. *Benedic domine hunc praesulem.*

Designation. *Sta et retine ammodo.*
Enthronement. *Haec tria praecepta populo.*
Acclamation. *Viuat rex feliciter.*

Mass.

Giving of sceptre. *Accipe sceptrum regiae.*
Prayer. *Omnium domine fons bonorum.*

Giving of *uirga. Accipe uirgam uirtutis.*

Blessing. *Extendat omnipotens deus.*
Alia. *Benedic domine hunc praesulem.*
Antiphon. *Uiuat rex uiuat rex.*

Designation. *Sta et retine ammodo.*
Prayer. *Omnipotens deus det tibi.*
Alia. *Benedic fortitudinem principis.*

Despite the disjunctions at the beginning and end and the occasional adjustments throughout, the body of material employed and the sequence in which it appears is clearly the same. To take *Robert* and friends first.

As Bouman and Nelson have indicated, *Robert* (as representative) has elements in common with four other coronation orders, namely: the 'First English Coronation Order' as given in the Leofric Missal; the *ordines* assembled by Hincmar for the coronation of Charles the Bald in 869 and Louis the Stammerer in 877; an order similar to the so-called 'Erdmann Order', the earliest copy of which survives in a pontifical from Sens of *c.* 1000, now St Petersburg Public Library, Q. v. I. 35; and an order akin to the so-called 'Order of Eleven Forms', the earliest copy of which also survives in a book from Sens, or at least from a house in the archdiocese, now Leiden, Rijksuniversiteit, Vossianus lat. Q. 13, again, of *c.* 1000.[211] *Robert* shares:

(i) with the 'First English Order', the blessings *Te inuocamus*, *In diebus oriatur*, *Deus electorum*, *Deus perpetuitatis*; *Omnipotens deus det tibi* and *Benedic domine fortitudinem*; and the acclamation *Uiuat rex*, although the form of this last has been modified.

---

[211] C. A. Bouman, *Sacring and Crowning*, Bidragen van het Instituut voor middeleeuwe Geschiedenis der Rijks-Universiteit te Utrecht 30 (Groningen, Djakarta, 1957); J. L. Nelson, 'The second English *ordo*', in her *Politics and Ritual in Early Medieval Europe* (London, 1986), 361–74. The order in the Leofric Missal is ed. Orchard, *The Leofric Missal*, II, 427–32, nos 2458–66; the others, R. A. Jackson, *Ordines coronationis Franciae. Texts and ordines for the Coronation of Frankish and French Kings and Queens in the Middle Ages*, 2 vols (Philadelphia, 1995–2000) I, pp. 106–9, 117–19. 147–53 and 159–67, nos VII, VIII, XIII, and XIV.

(ii) with 'Erdmann', the prayers for the giving of the ring (*Accipe anulum signaculum* and *Deus cuius est omnis potestas*), the sword (*Accipe hunc gladium*), the crown (*Coronet te*), and the giving of the sceptre (*Accipe sceptrum regiae* and *Omnium domine fons*).

(iii) with the 'Order of Eleven Forms', the formulae for the giving of the virga (*Accipe uirgam uirtutis*), and the designation, *Sta et retine*, though as Bouman saw the text is pre-supposed in the rubric of the 'First English Order'.[212]

(iv) with Hincmar's *ordines*, the long form of the blessing *Extendat omnipotens deus dexteram*, a form that seems to have fallen out of fashion in France by the late ninth century. Erdmann reduces the formula to half its original length. Were it not for copies of the 'Second English Order', *Extendat* would have completely disappeared on the continent. *Ratoldus* and friends, however, drop the final clause (which is original), *Clerum ac populum*.[213]

Although there is no space here to enter into a detailed analysis of the relationships of these *ordines*, which are exceedingly complex, it does seem perfectly reasonable to suppose that parts of *Erdmann*, the 'Order of the Eleven Forms', and *Hincmar*, actually derive from English books, rather than the other way round. Hincmar evidently knew of and extracted material from the 'First English Order'; and perhaps more important, the 'Second English Order' looks to have held a far greater position of authority in France than 'Erdmann' and the 'Order of Eleven Forms' ever did. Where the constituent elements of the 'Second English Order' are concerned, one simply cannot assume a one-way traffic of material from the archdiocese of Sens, say, to Canterbury.

Turning now to *Ratoldus*, it has generally been supposed that the coronation order embodied in the book is a more or less faithful copy of an English original more primitive in arrangement than *Robert*, but with elements in place, notably the introductory section, that were later dispensed with in England. That *Ratoldus* does indeed transmit an earlier version of the 'Second English Order', is clear enough, as Bouman noted, from the way in which the prayer *Omnipotens sempiterne deus creator et gubernator* (no. 138) is presented.

---

212 Bouman, *Sacring and Crowning*, p. 88.
213 *Ibid.*, pp. 95–6.

Ratoldus	*Robert*
. . . et oleo gratiae spiritus sancti perunge.	. . . et oleo gratiae spiritus sancti perunge.
Hic ungatur oleo. Antiphona. Vnxerunt salomonem.	*Hic ungatur oleo, et haec cantetur antiphona.* Unxerunt salomonem.
Vnde unxisti sacerdotes, reges et prophetas . . .	Christe, perunge hunc regem in regimen, unde unxisti sacerdotes, reges et prophetas . . .

The resumption of the formula after the antiphon *Vnxerunt* (no. 139) in *Ratoldus* is awkward. In *Robert,* the difficulty of picking up with the subordinate clause *Vnde unxisti*, has been surmounted by the addition of an introductory phrase. Anyone knowing of the solution given in *Robert* would hardly have returned to state of affairs inherent in *Ratoldus*.

However, we are on not quite such firm ground when we come to the forms of petition and promise (nos 132–134) with which *Ratoldus*'s order begins. For these in theory could have been copied into the order on the continent, displacing the text of the three-fold promise, *Haec tria promissa,* as in *Robert*, in the process. One only need look a few pages back in *Ratoldus* to find a parallel instance of re-arrangement (in the order for the ordination of a bishop).

That the order was adjusted on the continent emerges in any case from the variant readings encompassed in the first half of the prayer *Omnipotens sempiterne deus creator,* that is to say, in the half that lies before the singing of the antiphon *Vnxerunt*. The position is best illustrated comparatively:

. . . respice propitius ad praeces nostrae humilitatis, et super hunc famulum tuum, quem supplici deuotione in regnum

Ratoldus	*Later French copies*	*Robert*
N. albionis totius uidelicet francorum		anglorum siue saxonum

pariter eligimus, benedictionum tuarum dona multiplica, eumque dextera tuae potentiae semper ubique circumda . . . et per tramitem iustitiae inoffenso gressu semper incedat, et totius

albionis	regni	regni N.

ecclesiam deinceps cum plebibus sibi annexis ita enutriat, ac doceat, muniat et instruat, contraque omnes uisibiles et inuisibiles hostes idem potenter regaliterque tuae uirtutis regimen amminstret, ut regale solium uidelicet

francorum	Saxonum, Merciorum, Nordan Himbrorumque	saxonum uel anglorum

sceptra (*Robert* has *sceptro*) non deserat, sed ad pristinę fidei pacisque concordiam eorum animos te opitulante reformet,

ut utrorumque horum

populorum debita subiectione fultus, condigno amore glorificatus, per longum uitae spatium paternae apicem gloriae tua miseratione unatim stabilire et gubernare mereatur.

Ratoldus's scribe, evidently finding *Albionis* as an interlinear or marginal alternative to *Saxonum, Merciorum, Nordan Himbrorumque*, the reading of the main text of the English pontifical he had before him ('Saxons, Mercians and Northumbrians' figures in numerous continental copies), introduced the alternative along with the new mention of the Frankish realm.

However, as Hohler and Nelson have pointed out, *Saxonum, Merciorum, Norhan Himbrorumque*, was probably not 'original' either. For the mention of 'both peoples' (*utrorumque horum populorum* and elsewhere *pariter eligimus* and *unatim*), suggests that at first only two were named. Logically, at any rate, this would seem to be the case. Quite what stood in place originally, of course, is difficult to say: 'Angles and Saxons', possibly; but if one allows that the prayer was drawn up on the continent, and borrowed by Englishmen, then the initial reading could easily have been something along the lines of 'Franks and Aquitinians', which was changed (at Canterbury) into 'Saxons, Mercians and Northumbrians', and only thereafter into 'Angles and Saxons', to make sense of the references that followed.[214] In any event, the mismatch of number (three peoples named, two referred to) does not seem to have bothered the French bishops and archbishops who, in succeeding centuries, had copies of the 'Second English Order' made.

References embedded in English versions of *Omnipotens sempiterne deus creator et gubernator* have also been used, it should be said, to 'date' the order. Essentially the point turns on the perceived meaning of the phrase *per longum uitae spatium paternae apicem gloriae tua*

---

[214] But even the Sens pontifical is not consistent, for its text first gives *Francorum et Equitanorum pariter eligimus*, then *ut Francorum regnum non deserat*, and *ut utrorumque horum populorum*. A thirteenth-century Portuguese text names no peoples at all but still manages to refer to 'two'.

miseratione unatim stabilire et gubernare mereatur. Three possibilities have been advanced:

(i) Percy Schramm's view: that the words imply that the order was drawn up for someone who had ruled for some time, and whose father had ruled before him.[215]

(ii) Christopher Hohler and Derek Turner's view, as expressed by Turner using, in his inimitable fashion, the royal 'we': 'Personally we feel that the phrase in question, if it has a special connotation, refers more to the success of the king who was the father than to anything about the son. The only English monarchs in the tenth century who had sons who became kings were Edward the Elder, Edmund and Edgar'. He then went on to make a case for Aethelstan, as Hohler had, suggesting that the man responsible for establishing the 'Second English Order' on the continent was Louis IV d'Outremer, returning to France from Æthelstan's court in 936, to be crowned king at Laon later that year. In effect, Hohler and Turner tacitly endorse what Morinus had said in 1655.[216]

(iii) Janet Nelson's view: that the order was produced in Alfred's last years, on the grounds first, that the 'unity' urged in *Ratoldus*'s version of the prayer *Omnipotens sempiterne deus creator* best fits Alfred's claim to rule over the Mercians and West Saxons, and second, that the forms for the consecration of a queen in the 'Second English Order' were originally included by the need or desire to consecrate Aedfflaed, Edward's wife.[217]

Clearly, as Turner said, none of these explanations will have any force at all if the words lack special connotation. Unfortunately it seems exceedingly hard to ascribe one. For the phrase hardly differs from its analogues in the 'Erdmann Order': *et ad paternum decenter solium*, and in the formula *Sta et retine*: *hucusque paterna successione tenuisti hereditario iure.*

As for the dissemination of the 'Second English Order' on the continent, the surviving manuscripts fall into two distinct families. Twelve

[215] P. E. Schramm, 'Die Krönung bei den Westfranken und Angelsachsen von 878 bis zum 1000', *Zeitschrift für Rechtsgeschichte* 55, Abt 23 (1934), 117–242.

[216] Turner, *The Claudius Pontificals*, pp. xxxi–xxxiii. For the views expressed by Morinus and Hohler, see above, pp. xvi–xvii and xxiv–xxvii.

[217] Nelson, 'The second English *ordo*', 365–7.

follow the arrangement of *Ratoldus*, four follow the arrangement of *Robert*: and unless one is prepared to suppose that the four preserve the text from which *Ratoldus* and the other twelve descend, it seems likely that at least two very different sorts of English order found their way across the channel. Since the earliest surviving continental analogue of *Robert* is a twelfth-century book from Reims, now Reims, Bibliothèque municipale 342, a post-Conquest date for the 'second wave' seems likeliest. But further work will have to be undertaken to determine precisely what class of English text was transmitted, for the four French derivatives of *Robert* give 'Saxons, Mercians, and Northumbrians', not 'Angles and Saxons'.

On the matter of the history of the order on the continent, Richard Jackson came to two principal conclusions: first, that the model from which *Ratoldus* descended (which he called x^1) was not that from which the other continental texts were copied (x^2), though he did not indicate expressly that four of the texts in view were arranged as *Robert*; and second, that the order was little known in France before 1100.[218] On the second point he is clearly right. On the first, however, there is room for doubt, for it seems quite possible that the 'variants' were either already in place in the English model or that deliberate emendations were made as the text was copied.

To take one example in the prayer *Deus dei filius iesus* (no. 142). *Ratoldus* and two other books, one from Arras, one from Cambrai, both of which we will come to in a moment, give the reading *temporalia regna*, which is supported by *Robert* and friends. All other continental texts have *temporali regno*, which appears as a variant at Arras. For all we know the English model had both readings, *temporalia regna* in the main text, *temporali regno* as an interlineation, or vice versa. Alternatively the pages may have been marked up later (or added to) with a view to showing how select passages were to be copied.

That Ratoldus (the man) obtained his English model from a house in the region of Arras may well be indicated by the fact that the two next best copies of the order were produced nearby, as has already been mentioned. The earliest appears in Cologne, Dombibliothek 141, the pontifical written in the mid eleventh century at Saint-Vaast's for use at

---

218 Jackson, *Ordines coronationis Franciae*, I, 168–75. Also see Ward, 'An early version of the Anglo-Saxon coronation ceremony'. Ward was the 'American' of Hohler's letter.

Cambrai.[219] As Jackson notes, the text of the order has been modified with material drawn from the Romano-German Pontifical. The second copy, which keeps more or less to the arrangement of the original, figures among the additions made at Cambrai in the mid eleventh century to Paris, Bibliothèque nationale de France, lat. 13313, a pontifical acquired from some cathedral in the archdiocese of Trier, if not Trier itself.[220]

Miscellaneous blessings (nos 176–192)

Ratoldus's miscellaneous blessings doubtless descend, along with the orders that precede it, from the English pontifical. The second benediction of an unguent (no. 186), is only otherwise found in *Egbert*; and the blessing for beer and wine (no. 190) only otherwise survives in *Egbert, Samson*, as a tenth-century addition in Durham Cathedral A. iv. 19, the so-called 'Durham Ritual', and in Rouen BM 272.[221] In view of the fact that blessings of unguents were particularly popular in England, it may well be that *Omnipotens sempiterne deus benedicere dignare hoc unguentum* (no. 185), a version of a fairly widespread formula for the blessing of bread, is English too.[222]

Mass for St Cuthbert (nos 459–463)

As Hohler and Prescott indicated, the mass for St Cuthbert, no. LXXXIII in the table of contents, was clearly copied into the sacramentary from the English pontifical. The prayers provided are an extraordinary mixture. The collect is a collect for 'martyrs' in the so-called Bangor Antiphoner, an Irish book of the late seventh century; the benediction is a proper for St Ambrose; and the postcommunion

---

[219] The order is edited separately by Jackson, *Ordines coronationis Franciae*, pp. 203–26 (Ordo XVI). For further references, see above, p. xlix.
[220] Its text is registered under the siglum 'B' in Jackson's edition of the 'Ratold Ordo'. For a description of the manuscript, see Leroquais, *Les pontificaux*, II, 175–9.
[221] *Two Anglo-Saxon Pontificals*, ed. Banting, pp. 139–40; Corpus 146, p. 298; *The Durham Collectar*, ed. A. Corrêa, HBS 107 (London, 1992), pp. 228–9, no. 638; and Rouen BM 272, fol. 259v.
[222] The earliest surviving version of the blessing is ed. Deshusses, *Le sacramentaire gregorien*, III, 255, n.4347.

occurs in the mass for the September translation of St Cuthbert given in London, British Library, Cotton Vitellius A. xviii, the sacramentary of Giso, bishop of Wells (1060–88). The secret has yet to be traced.

The preface, however, is a proper, and appears in something like its original form in the mass for 20 March added in the late tenth century, perhaps at Durham, to the 'Sidney Sussex Pontifical', a book associable with Oswald of Worcester:[223]

Sidney Sussex

\<VD aeterne deus\> In hac die migrationis ad christum sanctissimi sacerdotis cuðberhti, qui in primo continentissime et castissime, conuersationis monachorum in actuali uita exemplum sanctis factus, et postmodum multis annis theoricam in deserto secutus est uitam, solo aeternitatis dei amore pastus, et postea inuitus non sua uoluntate sed dei prouidentia ad ęcclesiarum consilio in episcopatus electus est gradum, qui semper uiriliter et fortiter contra carnem et sanguinem et aeris huius principes pugnauerat, cum galea spei salutis et lorica iustitię, et cum scuto fidei et gladio uerbi diuini uictoriam capiens, a dextris et sinistris protectus dei miles, hostium cuneos superabat et multa per eum dominus mirabilia fecit, et obitum suum diebus plurimis predicabat, regi et episcopo gubernationem plebis commendabat et ad desertum sanctum properabat, et spiritum suum cum cęlesti angelo et euangelico cetu deo patri omnipotenti emiserat te domine ergo deprecamur per intercessionem sancti cuðberhti episcopi ad portum felicitatis et ad cêlestia eius regna peruenire mereamur, cui adstant innumerabiles angelorum et archangelorum chori et dicunt, sanctus.

Ratoldus

VD aeterne deus. In hac die migrationis ad christum sanctissimi sacerdotis cutberhti, qui in primo continentissime et castissime conuersationis monachorum in actuali uita exemplum sanctis factus, et postmodum multis annis theoricam in deserto secutus est uitam, aeternitatis dei amore pastus.

Te ergo domine depraecamur, per intercessionem sancti cutberhti episcopi, ut ad portum felicitatis et ad caelestia regna peruenire mereamur. Cui adstant innumerabiles angelorum et archangelorum chori et dicunt. Sanctus. Sanctus. Sanctus.

The shortening is of the same order as the shortening applied to the equally wordy mass for St Samson.[224]

Hohler thought that *Ratoldus*'s mass stemmed from Glastonbury, arguing that Glastonbury was the one place in southern England where Irish material, namely the collect from the Antiphoner, must have been plentiful. As far as ultimate origins are concerned, this seems perfectly

[223] Ed. Banting, *Two Anglo-Saxon Pontificals*, pp. 169–170.
[224] See above, pp. lxxxviii–lxxxix.

possible. However, as I have indicated elsewhere, the versions of the mass embodied in *Sidney Sussex* and *Ratoldus* are likely to have had other starting points: for *Sidney Sussex*, Westbury-upon-Trym, the house at which Oswald of Worcester began his English career; for *Ratoldus*, Canterbury.[225] Indeed, the person who probably stands behind the dissemination of the mass as we have it in *Ratoldus* is Archbishop Oda, Oswald's uncle and sponsor. The collect, secret and postcommunion in *Sidney Sussex* are likely to be later replacements.

Penitential order for Ash Wednesday (nos 495–512)

The penitential order, as has already been mentioned, runs in line with the order embodied at the end of section 4 of *Claudius* (fols 137–150). Extensive searches have so far failed to turn up another version. That the order transmitted in *Claudius* and *Ratoldus* initially came to England from Reims seems clear on two counts. First, it appears as an integral part of the Reims benedictional embedded in *Claudius*. Second, English penitential orders for Holy Thursday show signs of having been compiled with material from Reims too. Particularly striking in this respect are the presence (in *Lanalet*, and numerous other English books) of the prayer *Dominus deus omnipotens rex regum et dominus dominantium*, and (in *Egbert* and *Lanalet* again) of the short form of episcopal absolution *Ego inmeritus et peccator episcopus*, formulae which apparently only otherwise appear together in the extracts printed by Morinus from an early pontifical once at the abbey of Saint-Remi, now lost: *Antiquissimus est codex in Abbatia sancti Remigii ad Durocorurum Rhemorum pertinens, literis Gothicis sive Langobardicis scriptus, ut videtur, in Gallia Belgica fit enim in eo mentio festorum S. Vedasti, Remigii, Germani, Martini. Continet potissimum varias Benedictiones Episcopales.* According to local Reims tradition, as related by Martène, Archbishop Turpin (*c.* 753–800) was reckoned to have been the volume's first owner, which is just possible.[226] *Dominus*

---

[225] See N. A. Orchard, 'A note on the English and German masses for St Cuthbert', *RB* 105 (1995), 79–98, with the judicious remarks of D. A. Bullough, 'A neglected early-ninth-century manuscript of the Lindisfarne Vita S. Cuthberti', *ASE* 27 (1998), 105–37.
[226] For the Reims book, see J. Morinus, *Commentarius historicus de disciplina in administratione sacramenti poenitentiae*, 2nd ed. (Antwerp, 1682), pp. 215, 542–3 (Bk IV,

rex regum dominus belonged to the main text; *Ego inmeritus*, an early addition.

Probably the most distinctive feature of the order as we have it in *Ratoldus* and *Claudius* is that the psalms are set out in place in between the prayers. In itself the arrangement is certainly not 'new'. Something similar was done at Tours, albeit in an entirely different sort of *ordo*, in the late ninth century, probably also at Noyon, half a century before that.[227] What does seem to be new though, is the application of such an arrangement to a set of 'standard' prayers; and reference to later books indicates that the order was very much at home in England. Versions survive in *Lanalet*, which makes few changes, and in BL Harley 2892 and BL Add. 28188, which jointly give a slightly later, and much augmented, Canterbury text.[228] It is well to note too, that a rather garbled reflex of the order survives in:[229]

Boulogne-sur-Mer, Bibliothèque municipale 84: a pontifical written by two main scribes for Lambert, bishop of Arras (1093–1115), and subsequently added to during the course of his episcopacy. As the book is not described by Leroquais, it may be useful to give a short digest of its contents: fols 2v–5v, an order for Ash Wednesday, exten-

cap. xviii, sect. 18, and Bk VIII, cap. xi, sect. 10), and Appendix, pp. 45–6; Martène, *AER*, Bk I, Syllabus (p. xxii), with Martimort, *La documentation liturgique*, p. 181, no. 255. *Dominus deus omnipotens rex regum* also figures in a later Reims pontifical, ed. Martène, *AER*, Bk I, cap. iv, art. vii, ordo 14. For some discussion of Turpin's book, see Rasmussen, *Les pontificaux*, pp. 418–19, and A. Mundó, 'Ordinis Romani LI indoles et tempus', *Liturgica* 2 (Montserrat, 1958), pp. 181–216, though neither takes account of Morinus's comments. Note that the Reims/Anglo-Saxon version of *Dominus deus omnipotens rex regum* differs considerably from the prayer of the same incipit given in *RGP*, II, 63–4 (*ordo* xcix, no. 244).

227 See the remarks of J. A. Jungmann, *Die lateinischen Bussriten in ihrer geschichtlichen Entwicklung*, Forschungen zur Geschichte des innerkirchlichen Liebens 3–4 (Innsbruck, 1932), pp. 55–8. The Tours *ordo* is ed. Deshusses, *Le sacramentaire grégorien*, III, 124–6, no. 429, and that of Noyon, Martène, *AER*, Bk I, cap. iv, art. vii, ordo 10. The former seems to have been particularly authoritative. Examples are found at Fulda, ed. G. Richter and A. Schönfelder, *Sacramentarium Fuldense saeculi X*, (Fulda, 1912), repr. HBS 101 (London, 1977), 43–6, nos 347–61; in the book ed. PL 101, cols 522–4; and in BNF lat. 2297, ed. Morinus, *Commentarius historicus*, Appendix, pp. 55–60.

228 *Pontificale Lanaletense*, ed. Doble, pp. 70–73; and *The Canterbury Benedictional*, ed. Woolley, pp. 13–17, with BL Add. 28188, fols 79v–84v. Note that similar arrangements, but with entirely different 'standard' prayers, are adopted in BNF lat. 13313 and Cologne, Dombibliothek 141. See S. Hamilton, *The Practice of Penance* (Bury St Edmunds, 2001), pp. 228–30.

229 I owe my knowledge of the existence of the book to the kindness of Richard Gameson. I should also like to record my thanks to Nathalie Picque of the IHRS in Paris, who supplied me with a microfiche in record time.

sively reworked; fols 5v–9r, decrees from Councils, and miscellaneous blessings; fols 9v–29v, an abriged version of the order for
Maundy Thursday transmitted in the *RGP*, interpolated with three
blessings (two of which are said, quite fantastically, to have been
composed by St Martial of Limoges), and notes on the rulings of
Councils; fols 30r–40r, orders for the consecration of church officers, generally falling in line with those in the *RGP*, but (i) with an
extended introduction as in Paris, Bibliothèque nationale de France,
lat. 953, a twelfth-century pontifical from a house in northern
France, later at Saint-Amand, and (ii) a substantial number of additions over erasures; fols 40v–47r, an order for the examination and
consecration of a bishop largely agreeing with the order embodied in
a group of four early manuscripts (B, G, K and L) of the *RGP* (*ordo*
lxiii); fols 47v–71r, an order for the dedication of a church and its
goods, the original litany, probably of Mainz, later brought into line
with the litanies elsewhere in the book (fols 11v–14r and
129r–131v); fols 71v–75v, an order for the sacring of a king, as in
manuscripts B, G, K and L of the *RGP* (*ordo* lxxii); fols 76r–77r, an
order for the Purification of the Virgin, much altered; fol. 77v, added
prayers for the making of a cleric; fols 78r–79r, blessings and prayers
for Ash Wednesday and Palm Sunday; fols 79v–82v, an order for the
consecration of a prior or abbot of a house of canons regular, in
which the professions, written in a sort of charter hand by the principal scribe, are made to the church of Arras; fols 82v–85v, an order
for the consecration of an abbot of a Benedictine house, the specimen
professions versions of those appointed in the preceding order,
followed at length by the 'English' blessing *Deus qui sub tue
maiestatis arbitrio*; fols 85v–87r, an order for the blessing of an
abbess, much rewritten; an order for the consecration of women religious, again, with later additions; fols 88v–89v, decrees from Councils relating to women religious (later additions); fol. 89v, an *oratio
ad mulierem uiduam*; fols 89v–90v, a further set of added decrees;
fols 90v–91r, a letter of 16 April 1102 from Pope Paschal II to
Lambert, bishop of Arras, confirming the standing of the restored
see; fol. 91v, a letter of Pope Nicholas I on papal obedience, with an
'annex' concerning the case of Guntar, archbishop of Cologne and
Theutgaud, bishop of Trier; fol. 92r, blessing of a widow, a mid-
twelfth-century addition; fols 92v–96v, an order for the consecration
of a cross; fols 97r–103r, two sermons of St Augustine for use on a
bishop's feast; fols 103r–115r, an order for Holy Saturday (little
rubric); fols 116r–120v, part of the Canon and Ordinary, and extracts
(from Papal correspondence) on various parts of mass; fols
120v–123r, mass for Easter Sunday; fols 123r–125v, an order for the

vigil of Pentecost; fols 125v–128v, a series of episcopal blessings mostly for Easter and Pentecost; fols 129r–131v, an order for the visitation of the sick with litany; fols 132r–136v, a second order for the visitation of the sick; fol. 137r, miscellaneous later material, including a prayer said to have been composed by Bede: *Deus omnipotens miserere supplici tuo*; fols 137v–138v, a list of popes from St Peter to Paschal II (the names of Urban II and Paschal II written by the original scribe in a larger hand); fol. 138v, a list of the archbishops of Reims from St Sixtus to Manasses (the names of Rainaldus and Manasses also written by the original scribe in a larger hand); fol. 139r, a list of the bishops of the see of Arras/Cambrai from St Vedastus to Gerardus II; fol. 139r, a list of the suffragans of Reims; fols 139r–152r, a collection of documentation, mostly in the form of letters, relating to the restoration of the see of Arras: *Incipiunt gesta quibus atrebatensium ciuitas sub Vrbano romanę et apostolicę sedis episcopo cameracensium excusso subiectionis iugo in antiquam reformatur dignitatem.*

Lambert could easily have obtained his order for Ash Wednesday from Reims, the metropolitan of Arras.

Ordinations of Church Officers (nos 566–653)

The forms provided in *Ratoldus* for the consecration and ordination of the remaining officers of the church (ostiary to priest) are laid out as an order of service, interspersed among the collects and lessons of the fore-mass of Ember Saturday in Lent.[230] Daunting though it may seem at first glance, the arrangement, which takes its cue from something akin to the *Ordo qualiter* of the Romano-German Pontifical, is in fact perfectly straightforward.[231] The prayers of the day are simply 'punctuated' by ordinations.

---

[230] On Ember days in general, see G. G. Willis, 'Ember Days', in his *Essays in Early Roman Liturgy*, Alcuin Club Collections 46 (London, 1964), 49–98.

[231] *RGP*, I, 13 (ordo xv). The text, which precedes the forms provided for the ordaining of the minor orders (psalmist to acolyte), runs: *Mensis primi, quarti, septimi et decimi, sabbatorum die, in xii lectionibus, ad sanctum Petrum, ubi missae celebrantur, postquam antiphonam ad introitum dixerint, per lectiones dat pontifex orationes.* The standard older form of *Mensis primi* appears in the succeeding order (ordo xvi) as an introduction to the ordination of priests, deacons and subdeacons. Also see Deshusses, *Le sacramentaire grégorien*, I, 602, no. 1800. No mention is made of *per lectiones*. Nor is any mention made in the many variant versions. The tradition of examining candidates for the major orders (deacon and priest) on Ember Wednesdays and Fridays, and ordaining them on Ember

To take an example. After the third collect of the fore-mass, *Protector noster aspice deus* (no. 585), we come to section CVI, which contains the forms provided for the ordination of exorcists (nos 586–8). The third lesson (from Maccabees) and its response follow (no. 589), and we then have the fourth collect *Adesto quaesumus domine supplicationibus nostris* (no. 590), which, in turn, sets off section CVII. The only other early books that openly allude to the relative positions of prayers, lessons and the formulae for ordinations, are:

Cologne, Dombibliothek 141, the mid-eleventh-century pontifical of Arras/Cambrai (fols 11v–22r). Prayers and readings are simply indicated by rubric: so, following the forms prescribed for the *ordo exorcistarum*, we have (fol. 14r): *Sequitur lectio tertia, cum gradale et oratione .iiii.*; and following the forms provided for the ordination of subdeacons (fol. 15r): *Tunc legatur lectio quarta cum gradale. Sequatur oratio quinta.* This is the arrangement prescribed in *Ratoldus*.

Besançon, Bibliothèque municipale 2168: a mid-eleventh-century copy, made at Tours and adjusted for local use, of a pontifical originally compiled at Besançon. Prayers and lessons are only mentioned explicitly in connexion with the ordination of ostiaries and lectors: *et tunc ordinantur uel benedicantur hostiarii. Postquam benedicti fuerint dicatur oratio de officio, quam sequatur lectio, postea responsum. Quo finito, recitentur nomina illorum qui lectores ordinandi sunt dicente cancellario, lectores qui ordinandi sunt accedant. Post benedictionem istorum, legatur .ii. lectio cum suo responso.* However, the ordinations of exorcists and subdeacons clearly took place in the same manner, as the ordinations of deacons and priests are expressly positioned at points following the 'hymn of the three children' (the collect *Deus qui tribus pueris mitigasti*

Saturdays goes back at least as far as the fifth century. See *Ordines romani* 34–40, ed. *OR*, III, 535–619, and IV, 3–286. Andrieu's commentaries are particularly useful. However, one must be aware that the texts printed vary in quality and status. *Ordines* 35A and 35B deal with the consecration of a bishop alone. The others are by and large mere outlines, sometimes based on eye-witness accounts, of the practice of particular popes and a very very few French and German bishops. Only *Ordo romanus* 35 says anything definite about the times at which the minor orders were ordained: *Subdiaconum uero uel ceteros gradus inferiores consuetudinem habet sedes apostolica die dominico uel ceteris festiuitatibus preclaris, in quibus pontifici conplacuerit uel quo tempore ipse missarum sollemnia agere uoluerit.* For some indication of just how sketchy the *ordines* generally are, see Canon Lit. 359, the late-eleventh-century pontifical from Arezzo, which gives, among other things, extensive instructions (fols 25r–28r) for 'explorations' of the lives of priests and deacons before ordination.

flammas), with which mass, proper, begins.[232] As in the books noted below (when relevant detail is actually given), the groups of prayers, lessons and responses belonging to the fore-mass are kept together.

Paris, Bibliothèque nationale de France, lat. 17334: a mid-twelfth-century pontifical from Soissons that later found its way to Saint-Corneille at Compiègne. As at Tours and Besançon, only the ordinations of ostiaries and lectors are explicitly mentioned: *Mensis primi, quarti, septimi et decimi sabbathorum die post decantatum missa introitum, data ab episcopo oratione, legatur prima lectio, et sequatur responsorium.* Forms for the ordination of the ostiary follow. The rubric then resumes: *Iterum dicatur collecta, legitur lectio, cantetur responsorium, inde uocantur lectores, et tradat eis episcopus codicem dicens.* No further rubric is provided for the minor orders.[233]

The pontifical drawn up by Durandus of Mende (d. 1289). Durand describes the arrangement for the minor and major orders, one by one. So, for the exorcists the rubric is: *Lectoribus ordinatis, presul accedit ad sedem suam et cantatur secundum responsorium, siue* Alleluia, *si sit infra octauam Pentecostes. Et dicuntur tertia collecta et tercia lectio,* and for the subdeacons: *Acolitis ordinatis, pontifex ad sedem accedit et cantatur quartum responsorium uel* Alleluia, *si sit infra octauam Pentecostes. Et dicuntur quinta collecta et quinta lectio.*[234]

and two fourteenth-century manuscripts of the so-called 'Pontifical of the Roman Curia', a compilation of the thirteenth century. The books in question are: Paris, Bibliothèque nationale de France, lat. 15619, owned by and probably made for Pierre du Colombier, bishop of Ostia (d. 1361); and Vatican City, Biblioteca Vaticana Apostolica, lat. 4748 (II), probably made for some late-fourteenth-century bishop of Modena. The text in question runs: *In qua parte seu quo loco misse conferri debeant minores ordines et subdiaconatus non dicitur hic, sed possunt competenter ordinari ostiarii inter primam et*

---

[232] The order is ed. Martène, *AER*, Bk I, cap. viii, art. xi, ordo 10. A full set of photographs of this important book is kept in the Conway Library of the Courtauld Institute of Art.

[233] The order is ed. Martène, *AER*, Bk I, cap. viii, art. xi, ordo 7. For a description of the book as a whole, see Leroquais, *Les pontificaux*, II, 208–11.

[234] Ed. M. Andrieu, *Le pontifical romain au moyen-âge*, 4 vols, Studi e Testi 86, 87, 88 and 99 (Vatican City, 1938–41) III, 338–73.

secundam lectionem siue propheticam, lectores inter secundam et tertiam, and so on.[235]

All these schemes will doubtless have been highly convenient for a bishop, archbishop, or pope who had large numbers of candidates to ordain.

When we turn to *Ratoldus*'s *ordines* in detail, however, it soon becomes clear that the texts embodied belong to a completely different (and older) tradition. In effect one has to differentiate between arrangement and content. *Ratoldus*'s principal relatives, as far as content is concerned, are:

BNF lat. 12050: the sacramentary written at Corbie in the mid ninth century probably for Odo, bishop of Beauvais (861–81).[236]

Albi, Bibliothèque Rochegude, 20: a mid-tenth-century pontifical possibly from the cathedral at Albi.[237]

Rome, Biblioteca Alessandrina, 173: a late-tenth or early-eleventh-century pontifical from Salzburg containing, among other things, an important Italian order for the examination and consecration of a bishop.[238]

and *Lanalet* and *Dunstan*.[239] As in *Ratoldus*, the rubric *Mensis primi*, in spite of the *RGP*, serves only to introduce the forms provided for the ordaining of deacons and priests (not subdeacons, or the grades of order as a whole); and the dialogue of the bishop and archdeacon, *Postulat haec mater sancta*, *Scis illum*, and *Quantum humana*, is followed by the 'Gelasian' proclamation *Auxiliante domino deo*, pronounced twice, and the short statement *Elegimus*, in which the titles of the candidates' churches were named.[240] The only book that might be said to parallel *Ratoldus* on grounds both of arrangement and content is BNF lat.

---

[235] Ed. Andrieu, *Le pontifical romain*, II, 329, note.

[236] Ed. Ménard, *Liber Sacramentorum*, pp. 232–40 (PL 78, cols 218–34).

[237] See Rasmussen, *Les pontificaux*, pp. 45–50.

[238] Ed. *RGP*, I, 20–36 (*ordo* xvi, nos 1–38). For a description of the book as a whole, see *OR*, I,

[239] Ed. Doble, *Pontifical Lanaletense*, pp. 49–58; Martène, *AER*, Bk I, cap. viii, art xi, ordo 3.

[240] For the 'Gelasian' forms, see Mohlberg, *Liber Sacramentorum Romani aecclesiae*, p. 24, nos 140–41. Note that entirely different versions of *Postulat* and *Quantum humana* are used when the dialogue precedes the forms appointed for the ordination of a psalmist or ostiary. See the late-ninth-century pontifical once at Beauvais now in Leyden, calendared by Rasmussen, *Les pontificaux*, pp. 159–63. A different set again is provided in some manuscripts of the Romano-German Pontifical, ed. *RGP*, I, 14 (*ordo* xv, nos 2–4).

17334, the mid-twelfth-century pontifical of Soissons. But the texts of its *ordines,* at key points, differ noticeably.

That *Ratoldus*'s *ordines* were extracted from the English pontifical to which Ratoldus had access, and not some continental source, is clear enough in any case:

(i) the instruction at the end of the rubric for the ordination of an ostiary, *Et ducat eos archidiaconus ad hostium,* and the short formula for commending charge of the church door, *Per hoc ostium traditur* (no. 576), a piece plainly echoing the one provided later on in *Ratoldus* for the deacon's stole, *Per hoc signum* (no. 620), are only otherwise found at an early date in Corpus 44 and BL Add. 28188.[241]

(ii) the blessing provided in the mass for the ordination of a deacon, *Benedicat uos deus misericordia plenus* (no. 627), never figures in truly continental books, as Andrew Prescott indicated in 1988.[242]

(iii) in company with *Dunstan* and *Lanalet, Ratoldus* dispenses with the standard direction *Respondet offerens,* or *Offerens,* prefixed to *Quantum humana,* and gives instead *Respondet archidiaconus.*

---

[241]   For the rubric and formula, see Corpus 44, p. 204, and BL Add. 28188, fol. 63r. Later descendents are: Oxford, Magdalen College, 226, the early-twelfth-century pontifical from Christ Church, ed. Wilson, *The Pontifical of Magdalen College,* p. 60 and note; and Douai, Bibliothèque municipale 67, a late-twelfth-century pontifical from Canterbury (the so-called 'Pontifical of Thomas à Becket') that later found its way to Marchiennes. For a short account of *Douai*'s contents, see Leroquais, *Les pontificaux,* I, 149–55. Five pontificals from northern France and one from Sweden seem to embody offshoots of the type of order given in these books. They are, roughly in order of date: Saint-Omer, Bibliothèque municipale 98, twelfth-century, origin unknown; Paris, Bibliothèque nationale de France, lat. 953, twelfth-century, origin unknown, later at the abbey of Saint-Amand; BNF lat. 17334, the mid-twelfth-century pontifical of Soissons, ed. Martène, *AER,* Bk I, cap. viii, art. xi, ordo 10; Amiens, Bibliothèque municipale 195, an early-thirteenth-century abbatial pontifical and collectar (with many later additions) from Corbie; Paris, Bibliothèque S. Geneviève 148, the pontifical of Pierre de Trégny, bishop of Senlis (1351–6); and Uppsala, Universitetsbibliothek, C. 441, of *c.* 1400, from Lund. For descriptions, see Leroquais, *Les pontificaux,* I, 15–18; II, 41–146, 250–54, 319–22; and Bengt Strömberg, *De pontifikala liturgin i Lund och Roskilde under medeltilden,* Studia Theologica Lundensia 9 (Lund, 1955), 246–60, at 247. The later French and Swedish texts are immediately distinguishable by the wording or their rubric: *Vocati hostiarii nominatim accedant per ordinem ad benedicendum. Hostiarius cum ordinatur . . . tradat episcopus claues ecclesie dicens. In nomine patris et filii et spiritus sancti. Sic agite quasi reddituri deo . . . Et tradat eis archidiaconus hostium ecclesie dicens. In nomine patris et filii et spiritus sancti. Per hoc hostium traditur uobis ministerium,* and so on. The introductory rubric in eleventh- and twelfth-century English books, however, is always: *Hac expleta electi ascendant ad sedem pontificis per nomina uocati ab archidiacono et benedicat eos ad quod uocati sunt. Per hoc ostium* is never introduced by *In nomine.*

[242]   See Prescott, 'The text of the Benedictional of Aethelwold', 141.

(iv) since 'bishops' are expressly mentioned in the rubric (no. 615), it seems reasonable to suppose that the order embodied in *Ratoldus* came from Canterbury, a conclusion reinforced not only by the material provided at the beginning of the book for the consecration of a bishop, but the hexameters set at the head of five of its forms: *Hic dentur claues queat ut captare fideles*; *Codex hic dabitur lectori rite legendus*; *Exorcismalis datur hic ex more libellus*; *Vrceus hic uacuus tripode denturque regendo*; *Hic calicem patenam cum sindone sistat et orcam.* These appear as marginal notes in *Claudius*.[243] Quite how far the verses go back is naturally difficult to say with any certainty, but it does seem possible that they were originally captions to pictures either in the English pontifical to which Ratoldus had access, or in the book from which that in turn descended.[244]

But the underlying English *ordines* seem, in one place at least, to have been retouched as they were copied.[245] For whereas *Dunstan* and *Lanalet* give the more usual neutral forms of the candidates' title, *de titulo ill. et ill.*, and stipulate only that a litany was to be said, *Ratoldus* provides the names of the tituli in view, St Mary's and St Peter's (no. 608), and gives the text of the litany, along with a set of invocations, in full (no. 611).[246] Potentially both titles and litany could be Roman, St Mary being Sta Maria Maggiore and St Peter's the Vatican basilica, and the 'blank forms' in *Dunstan* and *Lanalet* attempts at normalisation. But the close resemblance of *Lanalet*'s short litany for the dedication of a church to the one supplied in *Ratoldus* tends to rule that out: *Ratoldus*'s redactor, most probably, simply found a new use for the text that he found in the order for the dedication of a church embodied in the underlying English pontifical.[247]

---

[243] *The Claudius Pontificals*, ed. Turner, pp. 31, 32, 33, 34 (notes). The connexion was spotted by Banting, *Two Anglo-Saxon Pontificals*, p. xlii.

[244] For pictures in the tenth-century pontifical written in Beneventan script, see n. 159 above. Engravings of the pages were published by Séroux d'Agincourt, *Histoire de l'Art par les Monuments depuis sa décadence au IVe siècle jusqu'à son renouvellement au XVIe siècle*, 6 vols (Paris, 1823) V, plates XXXVII–XXXIX, and reprinted by W. B. Marriott, *Vestiarium Christianum* (London, 1868), plates XXXIV–XXXVI.

[245] In *Dunstan* and *Lanalet* the confirmatory prayer *Per hoc signum* has been suppressed.

[246] For an analogous instance of the insertion of specific references, see BNF lat. 17334, the mid-twelfth-century pontifical from Soissons, ed. Martène, *AER*, Bk I, cap. viii, art. xi, ordo 7, which gives St Mary and St Firmin.

[247] *Pontificale Lanaletense*, ed. Doble, p. 6. Note that *Ratoldus*'s compiler re-arranged other parts of the opening sections of the English order for the dedication of a church. See above, p. cxxi. The litany that appears in *Ratoldus*, as it turns out, is quite unsuited to its

Palm Sunday (nos 808–812)

In common with *Claudius* and a number of other books, *Ratoldus* provides three blessings for the day. The first, *Deus cuius filius pro salute generis humani*, is common enough, and need not detain us further. The second, *Omnipotens sempiterne deus qui dispersa congregas et congregata*, is much rarer, only otherwise occurring early on in Modena, Biblioteca Capitolare, O. II. 7, the mid- to late-ninth-century sacramentary probably of Modena itself. I give on the left the standard text of the formula from Cologne, Dombibliothek 88, an early- to mid-tenth-century sacramentary from Cologne (the blessing is a contemporary addition on fol. 178v, perhaps made when the book reached Trier); in the centre that of *Modena*; and on the right *Ratoldus*'s:[248]

Cologne	*Modena*	*Ratoldus*
Deus qui dispersa congregas et congregata conseruas qui populis obuiam iesu ramos portantibus benedixisti, benedic etiam hos ramos palmarum uel oliuarum, uel ceterarum arborum quos tui famuli ad nominis tui benedictionem suscipiunt, ut in quocumque loco introducti fuerint, tuam benedictionem consequantur, ut omni aduersa ualitudine effugata, dextera tua protegat quos redemit. Per eundem.	Omnipotens sempiterne deus qui dispersa congregas, et congregata conseruas qui populis obuiam christo iesu domino nostro ramis arborum oliuae palmaeque et ceterarum arborum, quos tui famuli ad honorem nominis tui et benedictionem laudemque suscipiunt et praesta ut in quocumque loco introducti fuerint tuae benedictionis consequantur effectum ut omnia aduersa ualitudine effugata, dextera tua protegat quos redemit. Per eundem.	Omnipotens sempiterne deus, qui dispersa congregas, et congregata conseruas, qui populis tuis obuiam iesum ramos portantibus benedixisti, benedic etiam hos ramos palme ceterarumue frondium, quos tui famuli ad honorem nominis tui et benedictionem suscipiunt, ut quocumque introducti fuerint, tuae benedictionis consequantur effectum, ut omnia aduersa ualitudine effugata, dextera tua protegat quos redemit. Per dominum.

position since there are no petitions for the candidates. One would expect at the very least: *Vt istos electos benedicere et consecrare digneris, te rogamus audi nos* (as in Canon Lit. 359, fol. 26r, for instance). The series provided, beginning *Per aduentum*, is more at home in longer litanies.

[248] A full set of digital pictures of Cologne, Dombibliothek, 88, is available at http://www.ceec.uni-koeln.de. For *Modena*, see Deshusses, *Le sacramentaire grégorien*, III, 242, no. 4334, who gives its variants as notes. The *Ratoldus-Modena* version of the text also figures in Bodleian Canon Lit. 345, the twelfth-century sacramentary from Pistoia (fols 59v–60r).

In view of the presence of the readings *Omnipotens sempiterne deus qui dispersa congregas, ad honorem nominis tui*, and *tuae benedictionis consequantur effectum*, it seems likely that the texts embodied in *Ratoldus* and *Modena* descend in parallel, and presumably at some remove, from some central or northern Italian original.[249]

That all three of *Ratoldus*'s formulae for the blessing of the palms were adopted, more immediately, from the English pontifical to which Ratoldus (the man) had access, seems to be indicated by the remarkable fact that *Deus qui temporibus noae famuli tui*, last in the series, is evidently only at home in England and Italy too, as Hermann Graf indicated in 1957.[250] The pre-Conquest books in which it occurs are, in approximate date order: *Egbert*; *Winchcombe*; Corpus 146; *Claudius*; Rouen BM 274, the so-called 'Missal of Robert of Jumièges'; BL Harley 2892; *Leofric* C; and BL Add. 28188.[251] Those from Italy: Florence, Biblioteca Riccardiana 299: a sacramentary probably written at some point close to the year 1113 for a house in Rome, possibly dedicated to SS Philip and James; and Vatican City, Biblioteca Apostolica Vaticana, S. Pietro F. 15: a mid-twelfth-century sacramentary from a house near Rome, possibly in Spoleto.[252] Further searches will doubtless uncover others.

Englishmen clearly had ready access to a store of Italian material, possibly a very old one, by and large unknown, or at least never used, in France and Germany. The rubric with which the order closes (no. 812) may originally have introduced directions, or perhaps even chant, for the procession.

---

[249] Note that BNF lat. 9433, *Winchcombe* and *Leofric* A have *deferunt* for *suscipiunt*, and *ualitudine depulsa* for *ualitudine effugata*.

[250] H. J. Graf, *Palmenweihe und Palmenprozession in der lateinischen Liturgie*, Veröffentlichungen des Missionspriesterseminars, St Augustin, Siegburg 5 (Kaldenkirchen, 1959), esp. 70–73, with Table V.

[251] *Two Anglo-Saxon Pontificals*, ed. Banting, p. 136; *The Winchcombe Sacramentary*, ed. Davril, p. 72, no. 335; Corpus 146, pp. 183–4; *The Claudius Pontificals*, ed. Turner, p. 63; *The Missal of Robert of Jumièges*, ed. Wilson, p. 84; *The Canterbury Benedictional*, ed. Woolley, p. 23; and BL Add. 28188, fol. 92r.

[252] For descriptions of these books, see Ebner, *Quellen und Forschungen*, pp. 45–50, 188–90.

Holy Thursday (nos 836–881)

Ratoldus's order is admirably clear. Essentially three interlocking ceremonies are provided for: an order for the absolution of the penitents expelled from church on Ash Wednesday; forms for mass; and an order for the consecration of the chrism. It will be best to deal with these in order.

The penitential order. The rubric supplied at the head of the order (nos 836–837, 842) sets out briefly the course of the ritual action:

(1) Entering the sacristry and vesting, though not putting on his *planeta* (chasuble), the bishop mixes the balsam with the oil thereby making ready the chrism. The bells are rung for mass.

(2) During the introit the bishop proceeds, without his pallium, from the sacristry with seven deacons in dalmatics, the subdeacons, and the acolytes with thuribules and censers. He salutes the altar, but does not take his place in the episcopal throne. Rather, he sits beside the altar, until it is time, later, to ascend.

(3) Mass proceeds. After the Kyrie, the bishop says the *Gloria in excelsis* and *Pax uobiscum*, as is the custom only on major feasts. The collect of mass and the Gospel over, the bishop takes his place in his throne, but does not say *Dominus uobiscum*. Instead, the penitential tariff is read from a roll (*rotula*) by the subdeacon.

(4) When that has been read through, the bishop first proceeds to an altar to pray, then to the ambo, which he ascends. From there, in line with Roman custom (*sicut ordo praecepit romanus*), he delivers a sermon to the congregation and the penitents.

(5) He returns thereafter to the altar, and in company with the congregation and those gathered outside the church, prostrates himself. The seven penitential psalms are sung.

(6) When these are finished, the bishop rises and offers prayers of absolution both for himself (a number of formulae are in the first person) and the congregation present. The texts of the prayers follow.

That the order for Holy Thursday as a whole descends from the English pontifical embedded in *Ratoldus* is clear on three principal counts.

First, as Christopher Jones has indicated, it only ever occurs in English books: *Claudius*, though the text is incomplete as it stands; *Egbert*, in a section probably copied from an English book in the late eleventh century; and Cambridge, Corpus Christi College 190, a collection of ecclesiastical legislation and other matter from Worcester.[253] Corpus 190 gives the rubric more or less in full, but reduces the number of prayers and gives only incipits.

Second, the short formula *Deus qui iustitiae tuae legis* (no. 848), which normally belongs in the version of the standard penitential prayer *Deus humani generis* given in the Romano-German Pontifical, is evidently a 'Canterbury proper', as it appears similarly 'out of context' in BL Harley 2892, the so-called 'Canterbury Benedictional'. To illustrate the position, I print the short, standard form of *Deus humani generis* given in the 'Supplement' on the left, that of the *RGP* in the middle, and the form in the 'Benedictional' right:[254]

Supplement	RGP	Canterbury Benedictional
Deus humani generis benignissime conditor, et misericordissime reformator,	Deus humani generis benignissime conditor et misericordissime formator, qui in reconciliatione lapsorum etiam me, qui misericordia tua primus indigeo, seruire effectibus gratiae tuae per sacerdotale ministerium uoluisti, ut cessante merito supplicis, mirabilior fieret indulgentia remittentis. *Deus, qui iustitiae tuae leges misericordiae semper multiplicatione moderaris, dum delinquentibus penitentiam adhibes, dum etiam malis prouidentiae*	Deus qui iustitię tuę leges misericordiae semper multiplicatione moderaris, dum delinquentibus poenitentiam tribuis, dum ab his ętiam prouidentię tuę dona non subtrahis, sed

---

[253] See Jones, 'The chrism mass in Anglo-Saxon England', in *Ritual and Belief*, ed. Bedingfield and Gittos. For the texts in question see: *The Claudius Pontificals*, ed. Turner, pp. 28–30; *Two Anglo-Saxon Pontificals*, ed. Banting, pp. 147–53; B. Fehr, *Die Hirtenbriefe Aelfrics in Altenglischer und Lateinischer Fassung*, Bibliothek der Angelsächsischen Prosa 11 (Hamburg, 1914), 249. As Banting and Jones note, the eleventh-century portions of *Egbert* contain material that is distinctively English, notably the prayer for the consigning of the *baculus*.

[254] Ed. Deshusses, *Le sacramentaire grégorien*, I, 453, no. 1385; *RGP*, II, 64–5 (*ordo* xcix, no. 245), with, for instance, *The Benedictional of Archbishop Robert*, ed. Wilson, p. 58, and *The Canterbury Benedictional*, ed. Woolley, p. 46.

	tuae dona non subtrahis, et	uindictam miserando
	uindictam miserendo	suspendis. Deus misericors,
	suspendis, Deus, qui	deus clemens, qui secundum
qui hominem inuidia diaboli	hominem inuidia diaboli ab	multitudinem . . .
ab eternitate . . .	aeternitate deiectum	

Canterbury clearly had access at an early date either to the version of
Deus qui humani transmitted by the *RGP,* or to the component parts
with which the prayer was interpolated. It is worth noting too that in the
'Benedictional', as in Ratoldus, *Deus qui iusticiae* is followed directly
by *Deus misericors, deus clemens*.

Third, the indicative form of absolution, *Absoluimus* (no. 851), has
an extra final clause only found in books from England and Fleury,
notably Corpus 146; Oxford, Bodleian Library, Laud misc. 482, a
mid-eleventh-century collection of penitential and confessional material
from Worcester, mainly in OE; London, British Library, Cotton
Vespasian D. xv, a late-twelfth-century select pontifical from Christ
Church, Canterbury that soon found its way to Exeter; and Orléans,
Bibliothèque municipale 123, the twelfth-century ritual from Fleury
printed by Dom Davril.[255] I give the standard form on the left, as in
Lanalet, and the lengthened version transmitted in *Ratoldus* and the
ritual on the right:[256]

Lanalet	*Ratoldus*
Absoluimus te uice beati petri apostolorum principis, cui dominus potestatem ligandi atque soluendi dedit, et quantum ad te pertinet accussatio et ad nos remissio, sit deus omnipotens tibi uita et salus, et omnibus peccatis tuis indultor. per eum qui uiuit et regnat per omnia saecula seculorum. Amen.	Absoluimus uos uice beati petri apostolorum principis, cui dominus ligandi atque soluendi potestatem dedit, et quantum ad uos pertinet accusatio, et ad nos remissio, sit uobis deus omnipotens uita et salus, et omnium peccatorum uestrorum indultor, et qui uobis compunctionem cordis dedit, det ueniam peccatorum, longeuamque uobis atque felicem uitam in hoc saeculo largiatur, et in futuro cum christo et omnibus sanctis eius, sine fine manentem. Per eundem dominum nostrum.

The conclusion must be that *Ratoldus* preserves a type of order, perhaps
altered here and there in the copying, current in England the first half of

[255] Corpus 146, pp. 190–191; B. Fehr, 'Altenglische Ritualtexte für Krankenbesuch,
heilige Ölung und Begräbnis', *Texte und Forschungen zur englischen Kulturgeschichte.
Festgabe für Felix Liebermann zum 20 Juli 1921*, ed. M. Förster and K. Wildhagen (Halle,
1921), pp. 20–67, at 62; *The Pontifical of Magdalen College*, ed. H. A. Wilson, HBS 39
(London, 1910) , pp. 237–8; and *The Monastic Ritual of Fleury (Orléans, Bibliothèque
Municipale, 123 [101])*, ed. A. Davril, HBS 105 (London, 1990), p. 120, no. 143.
[256] *Pontificale Lanaletense*, ed. Doble, p. 75.

the tenth century. That the order, as we have it, was redacted at Canterbury is assured. The 'episcopus' is instructed not to wear his pallium. Pallia were only worn by popes and archbishops, and the order is certainly not papal.[257]

In terms of overall arrangement, parallels are few and far between. Indeed, as Jungmann noted, the only other order explicitly to position the penitential order before the offertory is the one preserved in Paris, Bibliothèque de l'Arsenal 227, the so-called 'Pontifical of Poitiers', a pontifical probably written at Saint-Pierre, Rebais, for Rodulfus, archbishop of Bourges (d. 876).[258] But since *Poitiers* is otherwise unrelated, the practice may once have been common: in other words, 'timing' was simply a matter of local preference or convenience. At any rate, nothing whatsoever is said on the subject in the so-called *Ordines romani* published by Andrieu.

As far as the other English books are concerned, Corpus 190, as has already been mentioned, transmits the rubric in full, but not the prayers. *Egbert*, on the other hand, has 'extras', namely *Ego inmeritus et peccator episcopus* and *Omnipotens criminum absolutor et indultor peccaminum*, which are not to be found together elsewhere. That these are indeed late-eleventh-century interpolations, the one extracted from an order similar to *Lanalet*'s, the other either from some Italian book or a copy of the *RGP*, seems to be borne out by the mid-eleventh-century 'Canterbury Benedictional', which has neither.[259] *Ratoldus* evidently preserves an earlier state of affairs than *Egbert*.

---

[257] Archbishops evidently needed guidance on the matter. The order embodied in London, British Library, Additional 10048 (fols 37v–51v), a splendid late-twelfth-century sacramentary from Rouen, indicates that the pallium should be worn, as does the order provided in Besançon, Bibliothèque municipale 2168 (fols 21v–47r), the mid-eleventh-century Tours/Besançon pontifical. The latter is ed. Martène, *AER*, Bk IV, cap. xxii, under the heading *Antiqui ritus ecclesie Bisuntinae. Ex ms. Pontificali annorum circuiter 600.*

[258] Jungmann, *Die lateinischen Bussriten*, pp. 88–9.

[259] *Two Anglo-Saxon Pontificals*, ed. Banting, pp. 148–9. On *Ego inmeritus*, see above, n. 226. For *Omnipotens criminum absolutor et indultor*, a prayer proper to *ordines* for the visitation of the sick, see *RGP*, II, 167 (*ordo* cxliii, no. 45), and the order printed by Morinus, *Commentarius historicus*, Appendix, p. 28, from the so-called 'Codex Siculus', a book that found its way into the Barberini libary in the seventeenth century. It should also be said that *Egbert* provides antiphons for the mandatum at the end of Maundy Thursday, extracted from some fairly standard Roman or Romanized source. See Hesbert, *Corpus Antiphonalium Officii*, 6 vols, Rerum ecclesiarum Documenta, Series maior, Fontes 7–12 (Rome, 1963–79) I, 170, no. 1720.

Mass for the day and consecration of the chrism (nos 852–881). As in *Claudius*, *Egbert* and Corpus 190, the order moves straight on from the pentiential order to the consecration of the chrism. The 'shape' of the ritual action, which is given in detail, though sometimes ungrammatically, is:

(1) When the *Qui pridie* in the Canon of the Mass has been reached, three acolytes proceed from the sacristy, each accoutered with a long cloth (*sindon*) and bearing an ampulle with a tag (*breuiculum*) on it: one ampulle for the chrism, one for the oil for the catecumens, the third for the infirm.[260] The Canon meanwhile is read through to the words *sed ueniam quesumus largitor admitte.*

(2) The subdeacon then takes the cloth from the acolyte who has the oil for the catechumens, and turning towards the deacon offers the cloth to him. The deacon, taking it, puts it on and accepts the ampulle from the subdeacon. He bows to the bishop. The bishop kisses the ampulle, blows on it three times, and blesses it (saying the prayer *Emitte domine spiritum sanctum tuum*) so that those standing close by can hear.

(3) The oil is taken from the altar by the deacon and given to the subdeacon. Another deacon takes up the chalice, and mass proceeds up to the point where the *Pax domini* is said. The deacon says *Humiliate*, and the bishop pronounces the benediction *Benedicat uos qui per unigeniti*, followed by the *Pax domini*. He withdraws for a short time, remaining close to the altar.

(4) The deacon at the altar takes up a paten containing a portion of the host (*aliquam partem*) and hands it to the acolyte. The acolyte duly brings it before the bishop. The deacon brings the chalice. The bishop alone then communicates, and the host is reserved 'below' the altar (*sub altare*). The chalice containing the wine is placed on the right, the paten with the host in the middle, and an empty chalice on the left. The corpus is covered by the bishop and deacon with a clean corporal.

(5) The bishop then stands before the altar and prays. All the deacons stand, along with the subdeacons, in customary order. The subdeacon

---

[260] The closest parallel for *breuiculum* I have been able to find in a liturgical source appears in the section of rubric relating to the recluding of relics in an altar in Canon Lit. 359's order for the consecration of a church (fol. 6v): *Tunc breuiantur nomina sanctorum et mittantur cum reliquis in buxidem et ponantur .iiii. portiones corporis domini in simul et in tres de incenso et recludantur et sigillentur.*

takes the ampulle containing the balsam and oil (that is to say, the chrism) and puts on the cloth with which it had been wrapped. The deacon in turn takes the cloth from the subdeacon and puts it on. He then takes the ampulle to the altar, where he makes a threefold sign of the cross, and blows on it thrice. The chrism is blessed.

(6) The consecration. After the preface has been said, the chrism is removed from the altar by the officiating deacon and given to the subdeacon. The subdeacon gives it to an acolyte who goes to stand to the right of the altar. The ampulle is covered with the cloth. The subdeacon then takes from another acolyte the oil for baptisms, and having put on the cloth, gives the ampulle to a deacon, also with cloth.

(7) The deacon places the ampulle before the altar, and makes the three-fold sign of the cross, and blows on it thrice. It is then silently blessed by the bishop.

(8) The blessing over, the chrism is taken from the altar and given to the subdeacon, who gives it in turn to the acolyte. The bishop then takes up position at the right-hand corner of the altar, and the chrism is brought to him by the acolyte. Before the bishop kisses it, the signal is given to the cantor to begin the *Agnus Dei*. Having kissed the chrism, the bishop and acolyte retire to the right hand side of the choir.

(9) When the *Agnus Dei* has been sung for the first time, the priests one by one, and in order, approach to kiss the chrism, and proceed to the bishop for communion of the host. The bishop gives the kiss of peace to each, and once done, positions himself by the chalice which is on the left of the altar, to continue the communion. The cantor begins the chant.

(10) Thereafter, the chrism is adored and kissed by the others present, and they approach for communion, clergy first, then men, then women. While this is taking place, the bell for vespers is rung, and the cantor starts off a series of antiphons and psalms.

(11) The prayer *ad complendum* over, the bishop says *Dominus uobiscum*, and the deacon *Ite missa est*. They take refection. Thereafter, the washing of the feet, accompanied by a series of antiphons with psalms, and a hymn.

(12) The bishop then kisses the Gospel-book and those who stand by him. The Lord's prayer is said silently, then the preces, and the *oratio ad mandatum: Adesto quesumus domine officiis.*

(13) Last, they accept their portion of bread (*becellam panis*) and drink.[261] Compline begins.

In terms of general arrangement, the order that perhaps most resembles *Ratoldus*'s is the one set out in the modern Roman pontifical. Although extended comparison is not possible here, certain common characteristics are worth indicating: the attention given to the preparation of the ampulles in the sacristy, one for the oil for the infirm, and so on; the explanations of how the cloths are to be worn and the ampulles carried; the accounts of how the ampullae are to be passed from officer to officer; and above all, the level of detail provided throughout.

Needless to say there are points of contact with older *ordines* too, especially *Ordo romanus* 30B, a compilation redacted at Saint-Amand in the eighth century, which also provides incipits from the Canon of the Mass and mentions the signing of the cross on the chrism after it has been blown upon; and *Ordo romanus* 50, a text drawn up in the mid tenth century at Mainz and transmitted in the Romano-German pontifical, for the explicit mention of three ampulles, but none really come close otherwise: and there is certainly nothing that accounts for *Ratoldus*'s singularly precocious form in the earlier *Ordines romani* analysed by Andrieu.[262]

But it is difficult to determine the extent to which *Ratoldus* is 'original'. Some sort of Roman model seems possible, one perhaps that was only otherwise known, outside the Lateran, in England. But there are a number of elements that are evidently without parallel among the *ordines* and ninth- and tenth-century exegeses that have so far found their way into print, both in terms of the action envisaged and the wording used to describe it: namely, the use of *breuicula*; the details relating to the placing of the paten and the two chalices on the altar after the consecration of the sacrament; and the details relating to the communion of the church officers and congregation.

---

[261] The text as it stands is: *Deinde accipiant becellam panis et bibant ternis*, which means, taken literally: 'they then receive their portion of bread and drink in threes'. But *ternis* may have been a mis-reading of *ernis* ('they drink *from pitchers*').

[262] *Ordo romanus* 50, ed. *OR*, V, 186–244; *RGP*, II, 56–85 (*ordo* xcix, nos 212–302), with P. Salmon, 'Textes des ordines romani du Pontifical romano-germanique et de l'Ordinaire papal dans les sacramentaires des XIIe et XIIIe', in his *Analecta Liturgica*, Studi e testi 273 (Vatican City, 1974), 225–62. For recent Roman practice, see H. A. P. Schmidt, *Hebdomada Sancta*, 2 vols (Rome, 1956–7) I, 64–77.

Chant. The chant throughout is Roman, and perfectly standard. The only piece that does not appear in *Egbert* and Corpus 190 is the hymn *Tellus ac aethra* (no. 878), which may have been specially worked in on the continent, for the versions transmitted in Berlin, Deutsche Staatsbibliothek 693 (theol. qu. 15) and 694 (theol. qu. 11), a gradual and troper copied for Sigebert, bishop of Minden (1022–36), from models that had passed from Saint-Gall to Mainz, also omit the sixth verse.[263] However, since the 'missing' lines were later supplied in *Ratoldus*'s margins by the original scribe (Scribe 1), it seems likely that a second, complete, text was available for consultation. A number of faults in the appallingly corrupt main text also seem to have been corrected in the process.

Good Friday (nos 882–915)

The order, which is not to be found elsewhere, takes the following form:

(1) In accordance with normal 'Gelasian' practice, the bishop, at the ninth hour, proceeds with his ministers from the sacristy to the altar, and prays before it. Facing the congregation, he says: *Oremus*; and the deacon, *Flectamus genua*. The collect, Epistle, tract and its verses follow.

(2) After the *orationes sollennes* (nos 890–907), two deacons fetch the veiled cross and position themselves with it behind the altar, singing the first of the improperia (reproaches), *Popule meus*. Two priests standing before the cross reply *Agios o theos*, after which the Latin form, *Sanctus deus, sanctus fortis*, is sung by the choir.

(3) The cross is then carried forward a little way, accompanied by the singing of the second reproach *Ego quidem eduxi*, to which the priests and choir reply as before.

(4) A further carrying forward takes place, accompanied by the third reproach *Quid ultra debui facere*, and its replies.

(5) The cross is then brought before the altar, that is to say, to the congregation's side, and unveiled to the singing of the antiphon *Ecce lignum crucis* and its psalm (Ps. 50). This is undoubtedly the most dramatic part of the service.

(6) A threefold prostration before the cross follows, first by the bishop and the two deacons, then by clergy, and finally the congregation, women included. The prayers for the veneration are set out in a separate section, CLVIIII (nos 911–913).

(7) The choir then sings three antiphons: *Crucem tuam adoramus*, *Adoramus crucis*, and *Dum fabricator mundi*, followed by *Pange lingua gloriosi* (no. 910), the hymn often attributed (as in *Ratoldus*) to Venantius Fortunatus.

(8) The veneration over, two priests retire to the sacristry to fetch the host reserved on Holy Thursday. They place it on the paten. Subdeacons bear the chalice with unconsecrated wine. One priest accepts the paten, the other the chalice. Paten and chalice are set on the altar (no. 910).

(9) The bishop, sitting in his cathedra, blesses the congregation with the cross as the antiphon *Ecce lignum* is sung with its psalm (Ps. 118).

(10) After the cross has been returned to its place, the bishop proceeds to the altar and pronounces *Preceptis salutaribus monitis* and the rest (no. 915).

(11) Communion follows.

Ratoldus is by no means the earliest book to contain a fully worked out order for the Veneration of the Cross. Parallels are found in:[264]

Paris, Bibliothèque de l'Arsenal 227: the so-called 'Pontifical of Poitiers'.[265] Contains three independent parts: an extensive *ordo*, the

[263] See *Analecta Hymnica*, ed. G. M. Dreves, C. Blume and H. M. Bannister, 55 vols (Leipzig, 1886–1922) LI, 77–80. For descriptions of the two books, V. Rose, *Die Handschriften-Verzeichnisse der Königlichen Bibliothek zu Berlin*, 3 vols in 5 (Berlin, 1891–1919) II.ii, 682–90. The *ordines* for Holy Week embodied in Sigebert's sacramentary, now Berlin, Deutsche Staatsbibliothek 690 (theol. fol. 2), descend from the Romano-German Pontifical. See Rose, *Die Handschriften-Verzeichnisse*, II.ii, 676–79. For further comment on the Sigebert group, see *Le graduel romain. Étude critique par les moines de Solesmes*. II: *Les sources* (Solesmes, 1957), p. 34, and *Kunst und Kultur in Weserraum 800–1600. Ausstellung des Landes Nordrhein-Westfalen, Corvey, 28. 5–15. 9. 1966*, ed. H. Eichler and W. Eckhardt, 2 vols, 3rd ed. (Aschendorff Münster, 1966–7) II, 516–17 and 519–21, nos 204, 206 and 208. Note that *Tellus* appears alongside the standard 'Romano-Germanic' forms for Maundy Thursday in Besançon BM 2168, fols 45v–46r, ed. Martène, *AER*, Bk IV, cap. xxii. The text of the hymn was presumably added either at Tours or Besançon.
[264] S. Keefer, 'The Veneration of the Cross synaxis in Anglo-Saxon England', provides an excellent survey of the material.
[265] Ed. A. Martini, *Il cosidetto Pontificale di Poitiers*, Rerum Ecclesiasticarum

orationes sollennes first according to the *Hadrianum*, then according to Gelasian books; finally the actual order of service. The arrangement looks inconvenient, but may not have been so in practice, as the celebrant must have known off by heart how things were to proceed, and who was to say or sing what when.

The Romano-German Pontifical and its (many) relatives, among which is probably to be counted Vienna, Österreichisches Nationalbibliothek, lat. 1888, a mid- to late-tenth-century sacramentary from Mainz. But it may be that the Vienna book actually transmits an older text.[266]

Lerida, Archivo Capitular 14: a late-tenth- or early-eleventh-century pontifical from the cathedral of Roda, in northern Spain.[267]

Besançon, Bibliothèque municipale 2168: the pontifical copied at Besançon in the mid eleventh century from a model from Tours.[268]

and an eleventh-century pontifical probably from Angers cathedral, now lost.[269]

But all are formulated differently: and when there is common ground, it is usually due to the reliance of the respective redactors on the forms of rubric transmitted in copies of the so-called *Ordines romani*. The major points on which these 'Roman' texts could not be of much help, however, were: the singing of the reproaches, an ancient Frankish or north Italian practice only acknowledged by one very late and much interpolated *Ordo romanus* (OR 31); and the choice and arrangement of the prayers and antiphons said and sung while the cross was venerated.[270] These will have been extracted from whatever graduals, antiphoners, prayerbooks and collectars were to hand.

In *Ratoldus* the underlying text is plainly that of OR 28:

Documenta, Series Maior, Fontes 14 (Vatican City, 1979), pp. 190–209, nos 328–73. *CLLA*, no. 1555.
266 Ed. *RGP*, II, 86–93 (*ordo* xcix, nos 304–335).
267 Ed. J. R. Barriga Planas, *El Sacramentario, Ritual y Pontifical di Roda* (Barcelona, 1975), pp. 417–22 (*ordo* xli, nos 20–26). *CLLA*, no. 1573.
268 Ed. Martène, *AER*, Bk IV, cap. xxiii, ordo 8.
269 Ed. Martène, *AER*, Bk IV, cap. xxiii, ordo 10.
270 On the reproaches, see the entry by Ruth Steiner in *The New Grove Dictionary of Music and Musicians*, ed. S. Sadie, 20 vols (Washington, 1980) XV, 750–51.

Ordo romanus 28	*Ratoldus (nos 914–16)*
Presbiteri uero duo priores, mox ut salutauerint, intrant in sacrarium, uel ubi positum fuerit corpus domini, quod pridie remansit, ponentes eum in patena, et subdiaconus teneat ante ipsos calicem cum uino non consecrato et alter subdiaconus patenam cum corpore domini.	Post salutatam crucem, intrant duo presbiteri in sacrarium, uel ubi positum fuerit corpus domini, quod pridie remansit, ponentes eum in patenam, et subdiaconi teneant calicem ante ipsos cum uino non consecrato.
Quibus tenentibus, accipit unus presbiter patenam et alter calicem et deferunt super altare nudatum. Pontifex uero sedet dum persalutet populus crucem.	Vnus presbiter accipiat patenam, alter uero accipiat calicem ponat super altare. Pontifex uero sedeat in sede dum persalutat populus crucem.
Nam salutante pontifice uel populo crucem, canitur semper antiphona *Ecce lignum crucis, in quo salus mundi pependit. Venite adoremus.* Dicitur psalmus CXVIII.	Nam salutante pontifice, uel populo crucem, canitur semper AN. Ecce lignum crucis. PS. cxviii^{mum}.
Qua salutata et reposita in loco suo, descendit pontifex ante altare et dicit: *Oremus. Preceptis salutaribus. Pater noster.* Sequitur *Libera nos, quesumus, domine.*	Qua salutata et reposita in loco suo, descendat pontifex ante altare, et dicit. Oremus. Praeceptis salutaribus monitis. Pater noster qui es in caelis. Sed libera nos a malo. Libera nos quesumus domine.
Cum dixerint *Amen*, sumit de Sancta et ponit in calice nihil dicens. Et communicant omnes cum silentio et expleta sunt uniuersa. Et dicit pontifex: *In nomine patris et filii et spiritus sancti.* Resp.: *Et cum spiritu tuo.*	Cum dixerint Amen, sumat de sancto corpore et ponat in calice, nihil dicens. Et communicent omnes cum silentio et expleta sunt uniuersa,
Et post paulolum uesperam dicit unusquisque priuatim et sic uadunt ad mensam.	et post paululum uespera dicat unusquisque priuatim et sic uadunt ad mensam.

The decisive phrase is the last, *et post paululum uespera dicat unusquisque priuatim et sic uadunt ad mensam*, which does not appear in *Ordines romani* 23 to 27 and their numerous derivatives. In terms of the 'ritual' action encompassed in the order as a whole, *Ratoldus* has most in common with *Poitiers*, which also prescribes, in clear terms, 'bringing forwards' of the cross, but the 'relationship' otherwise can hardly be described as far-reaching.

Chant. Cues for three antiphons are provided: *Crucem tuam adoramus*, in various forms the standard piece for the occasion; *Adoramus crucis*, a piece unattested in 'standard' sources; and *Dum fabricator mundi*, an ancient text that appears first in the so-called 'Pontifical of Poitiers', and slightly later in Laon, Bibliothèque municipale 239, an early-tenth-century gradual probably originally from Laon, where it was used for Palm Sunday.[271] Of these, *Adoramus* (recte *Adoremus*) is clearly the most interesting, as versions have only otherwise come down to us in three sources that have found their way into print: the late-tenth- or early-eleventh-century pontifical from Roda in northern Spain; an early-eleventh-century noted gradual from Bologna, now Rome, Biblioteca Angelica 123; and a mid-eleventh-century gradual from Saint-Yrieix-la-Perche (just south of Limoges), now Paris, Bibliothèque nationale de France, lat. 903, which also gives the music.[272] The piece therefore seems to have been of extremely limited circulation. At Bologna and Saint-Yrieix its text is:

> Adoremus crucis signaculum, per quod salutis sumpsimus sacramentum in quo dominus noster quasi in statera seipsum pro pretio nostro pensauit, ut uita uendita fieret mors captiua, in quo ne mundus graui lapsi periret, sanctos pedes christus adfixit, et contra fortem fortior toti mundo triumphatorem ostendit. Hoc tamen plus est mirabile, quia qui toti mundo proficeret in una stans stipite cursum uictor impleuit. Ps. In nomine.

and that, presumably, will also have been its form in the graduals used by the men who compiled the orders embodied in *Roda* and *Ratoldus*. The cues suggest as much, at any rate.[273] Perhaps the most significant characteristic of the antiphon, however, aside from its disproportionate length in relation to *Crucem tuam* and other pieces transmitted in 'Roman' books, is that at all the houses in view, it invariably appears in company with *Dum fabricator*, and it may be that the two circulated together in some ancient (pre-Carolingian) and authoritative source. The

---

[271] *Il cosidetto Pontificale di Poitiers*, ed. Martini, p. 418 (*ordo* xli, no. 23); *Antiphonale missarum sancti Gregorii IXe–Xe siècle. Codex 239 de la Bibliothèque de Laon*, ed. P. Beyssac and A. Mocquereau, *Paléographie musicale* 10 (Tournai, 1909), pl. 87 (fol. 44r), with a cue, added later, for Good Friday, pl. 101 (fol. 51r).

[272] *El Sacramentario, Ritual y Pontifical di Roda*, ed. Barriga Planas, p. 418 (*ordo* xli, no. 23); *Venerabilis Viri J. M. Thomasi Opera omnia*, ed. A. F. Vezzosi, 7 vols (Rome, 1747–54) V, 83–88, at 85–6 . The antiphon remained current in Spain well into the sixteenth century. See the *Hores de la setmana sancta segons lo us del archbisbat de valencia* (Valencia, 1584), fol. cliii[v]. The text of *Adoremus* in all these instances is to be distinguished from the Greek-derived *Adoramus crucem tuam*. On this last, see T. F. Kelly, *The Beneventan Chant* (Cambridge, 1989), pp. 56, 81–2, 164, 207–14, 261.

[273] In later books the piece is re-assigned to the feast of the Exaltation of the cross and shortened to: *Adoremus crucis signaculum per quod salutis sacramentum*. See for instance, *Antiphonale Sarisburiense*, ed. W. H. Frere, Plainsong and Medieval Music Society, 4 vols (London, 1925) IV, plate 533.

appearance of *Dum fabricator* alone in some *ordines* – as in the Romano-German Pontifical, for instance – tends simply to indicate that one long piece was regarded as being quite enough for some choirs.

Prayers. That *Ratoldus* should have three prayers is perfectly in order. Three seems to have been the standard number throughout the middle ages. In the 'Pontifical of Poitiers' we have:[274]

> *Oratio siue confessio ad dominum iesum christum ante crucem.* Adoro te domine iesu christe deus eterne misericordie, deus pietatis et indulgentie . . . digneris me saluare et iustificare in te et per te saluator mundi, qui uiuis et regnas in saecula saeculorum. Amen.
>
> *Alia oratio ante crucem.* Domine iesu christe gloriosissime conditor . . . merear adistere mundus, qui uiuis, etc.
>
> *Item alia oratio ad sanctam et indiuiduam trinitatem.* Deus trine et une, scientiae lumen et gratiae pater . . . sine fine contemplari te, qui uiuis, etc.

in the Romano-German Pontifical and friends:[275]

> Domine iesu christe, deus uerus de deo uero, qui pro redemptione generis humani . . . perfidi sint incursione securi. Per te iesu christe, qui uiuis.
>
> *Oratio in secunda genuflexione.* Deus qui moysi famulo in uia squalentes heremi . . . et aeternae uitae participes esse mereamur. Qui cum patre.
>
> *Oratio in tertia genuflexione.* Domine iesu christe qui nos per crucis passionem hodierna die . . . ualeam peruenire, per te saluator mundi, qui cum patre et spiritu sancto uiuis et regnas.

and in the tenth-century pontifical now at Albi:[276]

> *Oracio ad crucem adorandam.* Adoro te domine iesu christe deus eterne misericordie, deus pietatis et indulgentie . . . saluare et iustificare in te et pro te salvator. (As in 'Poitiers')

[274] Ed. Martini, *Il cosidetto pontificale di Poitiers*, pp. 206–7, nos 367–9.
[275] Ed. *RGP*, II, 91–2, with *OR*, V, 254–5, and M. Gerbert, *Monumenta veteris liturgiae Alemmanicae*, 2 vols (Saint-Blaise, 1777–8) II, 84–6. Also see the early-eleventh-century order from Monte Cassino, ed. Dom T. Leutermann, 'Ordo Cassinensis Hebdomadae maioris (saec. XII)', *Miscellanea Cassinese* 20 (1941), 95–117, at 110–11.
[276] Calendared by Rasmussen, *Les pontificaux*, p. 83.

Domine iesu christe gloriosissime conditor mundi qui cum
splendor . . . merear adsistere mundus. Qui uiuis et regnas cum
deo patre.

Oracio Rabani de cruce. Deus omnipotens pater domini nostri
iesu christe qui hunigenitum . . . per unigenitum filium tuum
dominum nostrum mihi concedas. Qui tecum uiuit.

Ratoldus, however, has little in common with any of these. Rather, its
closest relations are *Egbert* and the eleventh-century manuscripts of the
Regularis Concordia, all of which embody relevant (Italian) versions of
Domine iesu christe adoro te in cruce and *Domine iesu christe
gloriosissime conditor* (nos 911–12).[277] *Egbert* and the *Concordia* naturally suggest that *Ratoldus*'s formulae were the forms generally
preferred in England.

Significant too is the close resemblance of *Ratoldus*'s third prayer,
Domine iesu christe qui pro nobis crucis (no. 913), which is also likely
to be Italian in ultimate origin, to a prayer transmitted in London,
British Library, Arundel 155, an early-eleventh-century psalter from
Christ Church, Canterbury, and Oxford, Bodleian Library, Tanner 169*,
a late-twelfth-century psalter-cum-prayerbook (and much, much more)
copied at Chester from a model compiled initially by Archbishop
Anselm. I give the Italian form on the left, that of *Ratoldus* in the
middle, and BL Arundel 155 on the right:[278]

---

[277] *Two Anglo-Saxon Pontificals*, ed. Banting, pp. 141–2; *The Regularis Concordia
Anglicae Nationis Monachorum Sanctimonialiumque. The Monastic Agreement of the
Monks and Nuns of the English Nation*, ed. T. Symons (London, 1953), pp. 44–5. The
manuscripts of the *Concordia* are London, British Library, Cotton Faustina B. iii, a
late-tenth- or early-eleventh-century miscellany from Christ Church, Canterbury; and
London, British Library, Cotton Tiberius A. iii, a mid-eleventh-century miscellany, also
from Christ Church. Numerous glosses in OE appear in Tiberius. On the *Concordia* in
general, see L. Kornexl, *Die Regularis concordia und ihre altenglische Interlinearversion
mit Einleitung und Kommentar*, Texte und Untersuchungen zur englischen Philologie 17
(Munich, 1993), and on the manuscripts, N. R. Ker, *Catalogue of Manuscripts Containing
Anglo-Saxon*, 2nd ed. (Oxford, 1991), pp. 196–7, 240–8. On the distinctive variants in the
prayers, see Gjerløw, *Adoratio Crucis*, pp. 17–18. *Domine iesu christe adoro te in cruce* (in
this form) and *Domine iesu christe gloriosissime conditor* are first attested together in
Rome, Biblioteca Nazionale 1349 (Sessorianus 71), a mid-ninth-century Italian
prayerbook that later found its way into the hands of Leopardus, abbot of Nonantola
(895–907). See A. Wilmart, 'Prières médiévales pour l'adoration de la Croix', *EL* 46
(1932), 22–65, at 29–30, with G. Gullotta and J. Ruysschaert, *Gli antichi cataloghi e i
codici della Abbazia di Nonantola*, 2 vols, Studi e Testi 182–182A (Vatican City, 1955), I,
121–3.

[278] Ed. PL 101, col. 506, with Wilmart, 'Prières', 30 and 37. The context of the formula
in Arundel 155 is best judged from F. Holthausen, 'Altenglische Interlinearversionen

Nonantola	Ratoldus	Arundel 155
Christe qui pro nobis crucis et mortis patibulum subiisti, ut mortis a nobis expelleres potestatem,	Domine iesu christe qui pro nobis crucis et mortis patibulum subisti, ut mortis a nobis expelleres potestates,	Domine iesu christe qui pro humano generi crucis patibulum sustinuisti
et sanguinis tui nos pretio liberares, miserere mei, qui sum humillimus seruus tuus, et ueniam mihi omnium meorum tribue peccatorum, meque coram adoranda cruce tua prostratum ab omnibus malis eripe, bonis tuis misericorditer tribue.	et sanguinis tui nos pretio liberares, miserere mihi humillimo famulo tuo, et ueniam mihi omnium meorum peccatorum, meque coram adorandam crucem tuam prostratum ab omnibus malis eripe, bonisque tuis misericorditer refice, qui cum patre et spiritu sancto uiuis et regnas ante omnia et nunc et semper et in eterna.	ac sanguinem tuum pro omnium nostrum fudisti, respice in me et miserere mei et dona mihi indulgentiam et remissionem omnium peccatorum, ac custodi me domine in posterum per uexillum sanctae crucis ab inlusionibus fantasmaticis satanae et perduc me ad uitam aeternam. Amen.

In the London and Oxford books *Domine iesu christe qui pro humani generi* follows the third prayer prescribed in the *Concordia*.

Although the evidence is perhaps less plentiful than one would like, the general picture seems clear enough. The English pontifical to which Ratoldus had access not only contained the substantial remains of an English order for Maundy Thursday and Holy Saturday (as we shall see), but an order for Good Friday containing prayers that stand in close relation to English books, a point not lost on Dom Symons: and the feeling of connexion is heightened by the fact that the *Concordia* too relies on sections of OR 28.

Whether Ratoldus's order for Good Friday was drawn up with the other orders for Holy Week necessarily depends on one's view of the detail. The bishop on Maundy Thursday, for instance, is called *episcopus*, whilst on Good Friday, he is *pontifex*. But this might not be quite so telling as it seems, for a number of 'Roman' *ordines* apparently use the terms interchangeably, describing the celebrant in different ways in succeeding sentences. What does seem significant, however, is the express mention of men and women, as in the order for Holy Thursday, something that is exceedingly rare. Such references only otherwise occur in generalised mass *ordines*.[279]

---

lateinischer Gebete und Beichten', *Anglia* 45 (1941), 230–54, 234–5. Note that *Christe qui pro nobis* was the only prayer assigned to the veneration at Valencia in the sixteenth century. See *Hores de la setmana sancta segons lo us del archbisbat de valencia*, fol. cliiii[r].
[279] See for example, *OR*, II, 92, 105, 162, 166, 218–19, 224, 247 and 332 (*Ordines romani* 1, 4, 5, 6 and 9).

Holy Saturday

As has already been indicated, the English pontifical contributed six elements for use on Holy Saturday: rubric relating to the blessing of the Paschal Candle (no. 1012); texts of blessings of the new fire (nos 1013–1014); texts of blessings of the incense (nos 1015–1017) a section of rubric relating to the procession and actions to be performed prior to the blessing of the font (no. 1047); rubric relating to the procession before mass (no. 1056); and the text of a blessing of the milk and honey (no. 1063). All were presumably set out originally in the form of an *ordo*, much as the order for Maundy Thursday. It will be best to deal with the relevant parts separately.

Order for the blessing of the Paschal Candle (no. 1012). In company with the *ordines* for Maundy Thursday and Good Friday, *Ratoldus's* short order for the blessing of the new fire and the lighting of the Paschal Candle is cast in terms of what the 'bishop' had to do:

(1) At the sixth hour the bishop proceeds to the sacristy with deacons and ministers and vests. Arrangements are to be as for the morning of Easter Sunday.

(2) The bishop orders new fire to be kindled either from glass or flint.

(3) He makes a cross of incense on the Paschal Candle and writes the year of the Lord and the letters Alpha and Omega on it.[280] The candle, garlanded, is then carried in procession in front of the bishop, all candelabra and thuribles unlit. When the procession enters the choir, the candle is set up.

(4) The bishop, having said a prayer, proceeds to the altar, and sits. He does not ascend to his throne until it is time for the *Gloria in excelsis*.

---

[280] The marking of the candle with the letters Alpha and Omega is also alluded to in Léon, Biblioteca Catedral 8, the tenth-century gradual from Léon ed. L. Brou and J. Vives, *Antifonario visigótico mozárabe de la Catedral de Léon*, Monumenta Hispaniae sacra 5.i (Madrid, 1959), p. 280. On the practice of inscribing the year of the Lord and the indiction, see Bede, *De temporum ratione*, ch. 47, transl. F. E. Wallis, *Bede: The Reckoning of Time* (Liverpool, 1999), p. 128, with A. J. MacGregor, *Fire and Light in the Western Triduum. Their use at Tenebrae and at the Paschal Vigil*, Alcuin Club Collections 71 (Collegeville, Minn., 1992), pp. 368–77. H. J. Feasey, *Ancient English Holy Week Practice* (London, 1897), esp. 179–234, is a mine of useful information; on more recent Roman customs, see Schmidt, *Hebdomada Sancta*, I, 124.

(5) The deacon, asking for the bishop's blessing, goes to the candle to consecrate it.

(6) The procession divides in two, one half going to the left, the other to the right.

(7) Meanwhile, the bishop, seated at his throne, blesses the new fire and the incense in such a way that those near him can hear.

(8) When the deacon approaches, the candle is lighted as the words *<rutilans> ignis accendit* in the Exultet preface are reached.

That the order was initially drawn up at Canterbury seems clear on three principal counts. First, two phrases, both striking, are also to be found in *Ratoldus*'s order for Maundy Thursday, namely: *hora sessionis*, and *non ascendat ad sedem usque ad tempus/horam*. The parallelism is hardly likely to be accidental: these expressions never appear in continental *ordines*.[281] Second, as Andrew MacGregor points out, the only other early book expressly to prescribe incensation either of the new fire or the candle is *Egbert*, which gives the instruction: *Benedictio incensi in sabbato sancti antequam benediceris cereum et ipsum debes mitti in cereum in ipso loco ubi dicitur* suscipe incensi (Blessing of the incense on Holy Saturday. Before you bless the candle you must 'apply' the incense at the point in the Exultet preface when the words *suscipe <sancte pater> incensi* are said). However, it should be mentioned that in numerous sources a cross indicates that some ritual action was to take place as these words were said.[282] Third, the marking of a cross on the candle with grains of incense at the beginning of the ceremony, and the lighting of the Paschal candle at the point when the words *accendit ignis* had been reached in the Exultet preface are practices prescribed by Lanfranc of Canterbury in his *Decreta*. Lanfranc doubtless took as his starting point older Christ Church ceremonial.[283]

---

[281] Note that the word *sessio* appears in a similar context in Amalarius, *Liber officialis*, Bk III, caps 5 and 10, ed. Hanssens, *Amalarii Episcopi Opera liturgica omnia*, II, 271, 290–92. Whether the compiler of *Ratoldus*'s order had this in mind remains to be seen.

[282] *Two Anglo-Saxon Pontificals*, ed. Banting, p. 138, and for discussion, MacGregor, *Fire and Light*, pp. 361–2. For texts with a cross in place, see Kelly, *The Exultet*, pp. 297.

[283] *The Monastic Constitutions of Lanfranc*, ed. D. Knowles and C. N. L. Brooke (Oxford, 2001), pp. 66–9, with MacGregor, *Fire and Light*, pp. 339–45, 360–65, 392–3, 440–43. Unfortunately the Rouen ordinal used by MacGregor as a (Norman) parallel for Lanfranc's *Decreta* is not of the eleventh century, but the late twelfth and Augustinian. See PL 147, cols 157–92. The order is headed: *Ordinarium Canonicorum Regularium S. Laudi Rotomagensis (Ex ms. codice eiusdem ecclesiae)*. The church of St Lô was founded in

Prayers for the blessing of the new fire (nos 1013–1014). The only other place in which relevant early versions of *Domine sancte pater omnipotens deus exaudi nos lumen indeficiens* and *Domine sancte pater omnipotens aeterne deus quod in nomine tuo* have turned up together and alone is in the margins of the early-eleventh-century 'Anderson' pontifical, as additions made close in time to the writing of the main text. Their presence, or at least re-emergence, in a Christ Church book indicates pretty clearly that at one point these were the preferred archiepiscopal formulae.[284]

The three blessings of the incense (nos 1015–1017). The first is the standard English form of an ancient Italian text. I print the Milanese version on the left from Bergamo, Biblioteca di S. Alexandro di Colonna, s. n., a late-ninth-century sacramentary from Bergamo, the version given in *Ratoldus* in the middle, and that of the Romano-German Pontifical on the right:[285]

Bergamo	*Ratoldus*	*RGP*
Domine deus omnipotens, cui adstat exercitus angelorum cum tremore quorum seruitus in uentum et ignem conuertitur, dignare respicere + Et benedicere hanc creaturam incensi, ut omnes languorum insidiae odorem ipsius sentientes effugiant, et separentur a plasma tua, quam praetioso sanguine redemisti, ut numquam laedatur a morsu antiqui serpentis. per.	Domine deus omnipotens cui adsistunt exercitus angelorum cum tremore, quorum seruitus in uento et igne conuertitur, dignare respicere et benedicere hanc creaturam incensi, ut omnes languores insidias odorem ipsius sentientes effugiant, et separentur a plasma tua, quos pretioso sanguine tuo redemisiti, et numquam ledantur a morsu antiqui serpentis. Per.	Domine deus omnipotens cui astat exercitus angelorum, dignare respicere et benedicere hanc creaturam incensi, ut omnes languorum daemonumque insidiae odorem ipsius sentientes fugiant et separentur a plasmate tuo, quod filii ui pretioso sanguine redemisti, ut numquam ledantur a morsu serpentis antiqui. Per.

As can readily be seen, the formula transmitted in the *RGP* differs considerably. That *Ratoldus's* text descends from the English pontifical

---

1114. See Cottineau, *Repertoire*, II, 2545. MacGregor generally seems to have worked on the assumption that *Ratoldus* was a Corbie book. A further more general difficulty is his use of the term 'Gallican', which appears to mean, as he takes it, almost anything not demonstrably 'papal'.

[284] See MacGregor, *Fire and Light*, pp. 159, 458, 463, with Rasmussen, *Les pontificaux*, p. 213.

[285] *Sacramentarium Bergomense*, ed. A. Paredi, Monumenta Bergomensiana 6 (Bergamo, 1962), p. 352, no. 1524; *RGP*, I, 162 (*ordo* xl, no. 109). A lengthened version of the formula occurs in Oxford, Bodleian Library, Canon. Lit. 345, a twelfth-century sacramentary from Pistoia (fol. 73v).

is indicated by the presence of *assistunt,* the standard 'Anglo-Saxon' reading.

The second prayer, *Omnipotens deus abraham, deus isaac, deus iacob, inmitte in hanc creaturam incensi odoris tui uirtutem,* which presumably also comes from the English book as it appears in the tenth-century Durham Collectar (though its purpose in this seems to have been to help speed the capture of goats and deer), *Egbert,* and the 'Canterbury pontifical' of the 1050s, is simply an adjusted version of a prayer that emerges first in the order of mass in Paris, Bibliothèque nationale de France, lat. 9432, an early-tenth-century sacramentary from Amiens.[286] I give the Amiens text on the left, that of *Ratoldus* in the middle, and the version embodied in the Romano-German Pontifical on the right:[287]

Amiens	*Ratoldus*	*RGP*
Deus omnipotens, Deus Abraham, Deus Isaac, Deus Iacob, immitte in hanc creaturam incensi uim odoris tui uel uirtutem, ut sit seruulis tuis uel ancillis munimentum, tutelaque defensionis, ne intret hostis in uiscera eorum, aditumque et sedem habere possit. Per te Ihesu, Christe.	Omnipotens deus abraham, deus isaac, deus iacob, inmitte in hanc creaturam incensi odoris tui uirtutem, ut sit seruulis uel ancillis tuis, munimentum tutelaque defensionis, ut non intret hostis in uiscera eorum, aditumque et sedem in ibi habere possit. Per te christe.	Deus omnipotens, Deus Abraham, Deus Isaac, et Deus Iacob, immitte in hanc creaturam incensi uel thimiamatis uim odoris tui atque uirtutem, ut sit seruis uel ancillis tuis munimentum, tutelaque defensionis, ne intret hostis in uiscera eorum, nec habitum ibi uel sedem possit habere. Per.

The text embodied in the *RGP* is, once again, visibly different. *Ratoldus*'s opening line does not appear elsewhere.

The third prayer, *Veniat ergo omnipotens deus,* is common enough, being the standard form in numerous 'Gelasian' books for the benediction of the new fire on Holy Saturday, and in others for the blessing of the incense. As MacGregor has indicated, the types are normally distinguishable by their variants: *super hunc incensum* in the case of the former, *super hoc incensum,* for the latter.[288] Reference to Anglo-Saxon pontificals shows, however, that there are two sub-types, both English. The first is simply an interpolated version of *Veniat . . . super hoc*

286 *The Durham Collectar*, ed. Corrêa, p. 229, no. 641; *Two Anglo-Saxon Pontificals*, ed. Banting, p. 138; BL Cotton Vitellius A. vii, fol. 40v; Corpus 44, pp. 120–21.
287 Ed. V. Leroquais, 'L'Ordo Missae du sacramentaire d'Amiens. Paris, Bibliothèque nationale, ms. lat. 9432 (IXe s.)', *EL* 41 (1927), 435–46, at 441; *RGP*, I, 162 (*ordo* xl, no. 108).
288 MacGregor, *Fire and Light*, pp. 168–9.

incensum, and appears in all but *Egbert, Lanalet, Claudius, Robert and Anderson*. The second, a much-shortened text, only survives in *Lanalet* and *Ratoldus*.[289]

Rubric relating to the procession to the font (no. 1047). The ritual action is simple enough.

(1) After the solemn prayers and readings have been delivered, the seven-fold litany is sung as the infants are catechized at the church door by a priest.

(2) The bishop then goes in procession to the font as the five-fold litany is sung.

(3) At the font, a deacon holds the gospel-book open before the bishop, another holds the crucifix, and another ministers to him. Two priests stand behind. The other deacons and the subdeacons arrange themselves on the right and left. The acolytes do not light the candles in their candelabras until the instruction *Accendite* is given by the deacon.

(4) The font is consecrated.

Perhaps the most striking things about this short order are the details relating to the deacons, and the instruction that the candles were to remain unlighted. It is normally stipulated, when specifics are actually given, that they should be lit.[290]

Rubric following the baptismal order (no. 1056). Following a section of text extracted from the *ordo scrutinorum* (*Illud autem praeuidendum . . .*), the course of the ritual action continues:

(1) The bishop returns in procession to the sacristy. He washes his hands and robes for mass. Meanwhile, in the choir, the cantor and choir intone the three-fold litany.

(2) When this has been sung through, the bishop proceeds in procession

---

[289] For the two Anglo-Saxon texts, see *The Leofric Missal*, ed. Orchard, II, 237, no. 1298, which gives the long version; and *Pontificale Lanaletense*, ed. Doble, pp. 17–18, for the short.

[290] Lanfranc, *Monastic Constitutions*, ed. Brooke and Knowles, pp. 66–71, says that the candelabras were to be lighted, along with the candles on and around the altar, at the command *Accendite*, implying perhaps that no prior lighting of the candelabras had taken place.

to his seat, and gives the nod for the deacon to issue the command *Accendite* for the lighting up of the church.

(3) The bishop then begins the *Gloria*. All the bells of the monasteries in the city are rung.

(4) Having finished the *Gloria*, he says *Pax uobis* and mass begins.

Again, the text is not to be found elsewhere. The only real point of note is the instruction relating to the ringing of the bells *per tota monasteria*. We are evidently in an important city.

Blessing of the milk and honey (no. 1063). As Pierre-Marie Gy indicated in 1959, *Ratoldus*'s text largely sides with the ancient Italian version of the prayer transmitted in *Leofric*, but shares a number of variants with the Romano-German Pontifical, as the following comparison will show:[291]

Leofric	*Ratoldus*	*RGP*
Benedic domine et has creaturas fontis, lactis, et mellis, et pota famulos tuos de hoc fonte perenni, qui es spiritus ueritatis, et enutri eos de hoc melle et lacte. Tu enim domine promisisti patribus nostris, abrahe, isaac, dicens, introducam uos in terram repromissionis, terram fluentem lac et mel. Coniunge domine famulos tuos spiritui sancto sicut coniunctum est hoc lac et mel, in christo ihesu domino nostro. Per quem omnia domine.	Benedic domine hanc creaturam lactis et mellis, et pota famulos tuos de hoc fonte perenni, quod est spiritus ueritatis, et enutri eos de hoc melle et lacte, tu enim domine promisisti patribus nostris, abrahę isaac et iacob dicens. Introducam uos in terram repromissionis, terram fluentem lac et mel. Coniunge domine famulos tuos spiritui sancto sicut coniunctum est hoc lac et mel in christo iesu domino nostro. Per quem haec omnia domine semper bona creas.	Benedic, domine, has creaturas lactis et mellis et pota famulos tuos fonte perhenni quod est spiritus ueritatis, et enutri eos de hoc lacte et melle. Tu enim, domine, promisisti patribus nostris Habrahae, Isaac, et Iacob dicens: Introducam uos in terram repromissionis, terram fluentem lacte et melle. Coniunge domine famulos famulos tuos spiritu caritatis et pacis sicut coniunctum est hoc lac et mel in Christo Iesu domino nostro. Qui tecum uiuit et regnat.

In common with the *RGP*, *Ratoldus* omits to mention the *fons* in its opening clause. However, the *RGP* cannot be the source, as *Ratoldus* does not give the distinctive variant: *spiritu caritatis et pacis*. In view of the fact that the prayer is exceptionally rare in Europe outside the *RGP*, it seems safe to assume that the text descends from the English pontifical, and that it was altered at some point in the mid tenth century.

[291] P.-M. Gy, 'Die Segnung von Milch und Hönig in der Osternacht', in *Paschatis Solemnia*, ed. B. Fischer and J. Wagner (Freiburg-in-Breisgau, 1959), 206–12.

The ordo missae (nos 1068–1129)

Ratoldus's ordinary, which is set as a sort of 'specimen' within the mass for Easter Sunday, is, as Edmund Bishop noted, arranged as a pontifical service.[292] The celebrant is the bishop, and his vesting is accompanied by a set of prayers only otherwise found in northern Europe in the late-tenth-century Canterbury portions of the so-called 'Leofric Missal'. The ritual action is set out in some detail:

(1) Before mass, the bishop goes to an oratory for private prayer.

(2) At the third hour, the sacerdotal garments are brought to him. On entering the sacristy (*secretarium*) to the south of the choir he says a prayer and proceeds to put on his lace-up gaiters, sandals, superhumerale, alb, cincture, *baltheus* (subcinctorium), stole, and tunic with small bells round the hem (*tunica refecta gyris in tintinabulis*), which are handed to him by a minister. As he vests, verses are said. Water and comb are brought. He then puts on his gloves, ring, chasuble, rationale (a sort of decorated breast-plate, or a humeral similar to a pallium), and maniple (*sudarium*).

(3) Deference is paid to the bishop by his attendants, and the procession of seven, five, or three ministers put in order. The priests walk to his right, deacons to his left. The subdeacon, flanked by acolytes (and others) with candelabrae and thuribles, holds the Gospel book in front of the bishop. When the choir are ready, the bishop nods for the introit to begin.

(4) The procession arrives at the entrance to the presbytery. The bishop kisses the Gospel book, and they all enter.

(5) The introit over, the bishop stands in the middle of the choir and says the prayer *Suscipe confessionem meam*. Indicating to the cantor that the psalm and its repetition should be sung, he kisses those around him, first to the left, then to the right. Thereafter, at his signal, the *Gloria patri* begins.

---

[292] For an analogous instance of an order for mass in a pontifical, see Paris, Bibliothèque nationale de France, lat. 820, fols 5v–8v, texts added at Sées in the twelfth century to a book originally produced for some eleventh-century bishop of Salzburg, described by Leroquais, *Les pontificaux*, I, 292–304. The order is ed. Marténe, *AER*, Bk I, cap. iv, ordo 13 (also PL 78, cols 245–51).

(6) Flanked by his ministers, the bishop then proceeds to the high altar. He prays. During this time of prayer, priest and deacon, priest and deacon, in order, kiss the corners of the altar. The bishop then kisses the Gospel book which is held up open for him by his ministers. The book is placed in the middle of the altar by the subdeacon. The *Kyrie eleison* begins.

(7) With ministers preceding in procession, the bishop goes to his seat (*solium*). The *Gloria in excelsis* is sung, and the collect pronounced.

(8) The subdeacon ascends the ambo, and reads the Epistle *Expurgate* (I Corinth. vii–viii). Gradual and Alleluia follow.

(9) The deacon then enters the choir with a thurible, and a second minister with the incense. They genuflect before the bishop, and the deacon proceeds to prepare the censer.

(10) Having sought and received the bishop's blessing, the deacon kisses the Gospel book and ascends to read the Gospel of the day *Maria Magdalena* (Marc. xvi, 1–7). When he has finished, he hands the book to the subdeacon so that it may be kissed by the bishop and those round him. The offertory is sung.

(11) The oblations having been collected, the bishop returns in procession to his seat, takes off his gloves, washes his hands, and 'enters' the *propiciatorium* (the 'Holy of Holies'), at which point the oblations are offered to him, then the incense, which he blesses.

(12) After prayers have been pronounced, the ministers arrange themselves around the altar: the deacon before, the subdeacon behind, and the bishop standing at it. With heads bowed, they say *Per omnia saecula saeculorum*. The secret follows.

(13) Acolytes then bring water and a basin for the deacon to wash his hands. When he has finished, the bishop begins the proper preface. The Canon of the Mass follows.

(14) After the Paschal blessing, *Deus uniuersae carnis*, the acolyte bearing the paten stands behind the deacons, bowing until the point at which the bishop says the *Nobis quoque*. The deacon who read the Gospel makes sure that the bishop signs the chalice with a cross and elevates it. He then goes back to his place; and the subdeacons, who were facing the altar when the remembrances and names of the living and dead were being recited, file past the deacon, heads bowed.

(15) After the Lord's prayer has been said, a subdeacon takes the paten from the acolyte and passes it to the deacon, who then gives it to the bishop. They return to the positions at which they stood before the Gospel was read until the blessing and kiss of peace have been given.

(16) The bishop meanwhile says *Per omnia saecula saeculorum*, and the closing line of the Lord's prayer. At his nod, the deacon readies the congregation for the bishop's blessing. The blessing follows.

(17) Taking up a particle of the host, the bishop says the *Pax domini*, and nods for the cantor to begin the *Agnus dei*. He kisses the archdeacon and the others.

(18) Turning to the altar, the bishop says the prayer *Haec sacrosancta commixtio* as he drops the particle into the chalice (the commingling). At the fraction, which follows, he says *Emittere digneris*. An antiphon is sung thereafter.

(19) Communion then takes place. The bishop, having taken communion himself, says three prayers, and proceeds to communicate his ministers: *siccum sacrificium* (the Holy Blood received separately from the chalice) for the priests and deacons, who receive the kiss of peace; *mixtum sacrificium*, for the subdeacons, who do not receive the kiss. The priests and deacons then drink briefly from the chalice, which is held by the subdeacon. At the bishop's nod the cantor begins the communion chant.

(20) The bishop returns to his *solium* and washes his hands. He returns to the altar to say the postcommunion.

(21) Turning to face the congregation, the bishop then gives the final blessing, and the deacon signals the dismissal, *Ite missa est*. The bishop kisses the altar and says a prayer silently.

Although the *ordo* appears, at first glance, to be perfectly straightforward, closer inspection shows it to be anything but, as Jungmann indicated in 1949.[293] Particularly striking are the instructions provided for

---

[293] See J. A. Jungmann, *The Mass of the Roman Rite. Its Origins and Development* (Missarum Sollemnia), transl. F. A. Brunner, 2 vols (New York, 1950). The principal published collections of *ordines* are Martène, *AER*, Bk I, cap. iv, art xii; Ebner, *Quellen und Forschungen*, pp. 295–356; *OR*, II, 3–362 (*ordines* 1–10); Leroquais, *Les sacramentaires*, I; and P. Salmon, 'L'*ordo missae* dans dix manuscrits du Xe au XVe siècle', in his *Analecta liturgica*, 197–221. Also see B. Baroffio, 'L'Ordo Missae del

vesting, embodying the 'Roman' bidding, *Iube benedicere*, as in *Ordo romanus* 1; the reference to the bishop's tunic being adorned with bells, an arrangement only otherwise alluded to by St Jerome; the details relating to communion; and the number of unusual formulae adopted, the most important of which must by any measure be the antiphon *Emitte angelum tuum domine ut dignetur* (no. 1116), sung at the fraction.[294] This is exceedingly rare. Indeed, as Dom Cagin showed, fewer than thirty examples of this 'relic' of pre-Gregorian Roman or early 'Gallican' practice have come down to us, mostly, as it turns out, in books from northern Italy and southern France, though there are one or two exceptions.[295]

Three types of text survive: one beginning *Emitte angelum tuum*, as in *Ratoldus*, the other two, which need not concern us further, *Emitte spiritum tuum*, a later 'normalisation', effectively bringing the incipit into line with the incipits of the standard offertory for Pentecost and the formula for the consecration of the Holy Oil on Maundy Thursday.[296] In terms of actual palaeographical date, *Ratoldus* seems to be the oldest surviving member of the 'Type 1' family, followed closely by: Paris, Bibliothèque nationale de France, lat. 9448, a splendid gradual-cum-troper from the abbey of Prüm, a short way to the south-east of Liège, which appears from a colophon to have been written between 986 and 1001; Monza, Biblioteca Capitolare, C. 12/75, an early-eleventh-century gradual from Monza; and Rome, Biblioteca Angelica 123, an early-eleventh-century gradual-cum-troper from Bologna.[297] All three give:

Rituale-Messale Vallicellano E. 62', in *Traditio et Progressio: studi liturgici in onore del Prof. Adrien Nocent OSB*, ed. G. Farnedi, Analecta Liturgica 12, Studia Anselmiana 95 (Rome, 1988), 44–79; and A. Odenthal, 'Zwei Formulare des Apologientyps der Messe vor dem Jahre 1000', *Archiv für Liturgiewissenschaft* 37 (1995), 25–45.

[294] For the tunic decorated with bells (described in Exodus XXVIII) see St Jerome's letter to Fabiola, ed. I. Hildberg and M. Kamptner, *Sancti Eusebii Hieronymi Epistolae*, Corpus Scriptorum Ecclesiasticorum Latinorum 54–55.ii, 3 vols in 5 (Vienna, 1910–96) I, 586–615, at 600 (Epistola LXIV), with Marriott, *Vestiarum Christianum*, pp. 10–27. The letter was known to, and extensively cited by, Amalarius, *Liber officialis*, Bk II, caps 15–26, ed. Hanssens, *Amalarii Episcopi Opera liturgica omnia*, II, 236–54, but he does not mention the bells. Note that Hrabanus Maurus, *Commentaria in Exodum*, Bk IV, cap. vii, ed. PL 108, cols 201–202, provides extensive discussion of the relevant biblical passages.

[295] P. Cagin, *Te deum ou illatio*, 2 vols (Appuldurcombe and Tournai, 1906–12) I, 215–31. Cagin, who was the first to draw attention to the significance of the piece, took it to be Roman. Alexandre Planchart, on the other hand, envisages a 'Gallican' origin. See his entry 'Troper' in the *New Grove Dictionary of Music* 25, 777–94, at 781.

[296] Deshusses, *Le sacramentaire grégorien*, I, 172, no. 334.

[297] On BNF lat. 9448, see the important entry in *Rhein und Maas. Kunst und Kultur*

Emitte angelum tuum domine et dignare sanctificare corpus et
sanguinem tuum, nos frangimus domine, tu dignare benedicere, ut
immaculatis manibus illud tractemus. O quam beatus uenter ille
christum meruit portare. O quam preciosa gemma et margarita
quam lucis mundi illustrat gratiam. O quam beati pedes illi qui
christum meruerunt sustinere. Cui angeli et archangeli offerunt
munera sempiterna et excelso regi alleluia.

Allowing for the presence of the variant *ut dignetur*, this, therefore, is
pretty much how the text must have appeared in the book or books on
which *Ratoldus*'s order was ultimately based.

Quite where the source issued from is, of course, difficult to determine at present. But an English origin may well be suggested by the fact
that a version of *Emittere digneris domine sanctum angelum* (no. 1115),
so obviously the antiphon's companion piece, also figures in BNF lat.
9433, the late-ninth- or early-tenth-century sacramentary of Echternach,
a book in large part arranged by Alcuin; so if Cagin is right about the
relative antiquity of both formulae (sixth or seventh century, rather than
tenth), we are liable to be in the presence of material brought north to
Canterbury from Rome, or northern Italy, by St Augustine and his
followers.[298] Other noteworthy elements embodied in *Ratoldus*'s order
are:

(i) *Via sanctorum omnium iesu christe* and *Omnipotens et misericors
deus qui sacerdotum ministerio* (nos 1069 and 1071), which are respectively standard 'Eighth-Century Gelasian' prayers for entering a church

800–1400, Ausstellung des Schnütgen-Museums der Stadt Köln, vom 14 Mai bis zum 23
Juli, 1972, ed. A. Legner, A. von Euw and J. M. Plotzek, 2 vols (Cologne, 1972) I, 186, no.
C13, with Samaran and Marichal, *Catalogue des manuscrits en écriture latin*, III.i, 117.
The Bologna manuscript is ed. J. Froger, *Le codex 123 de la Bibliothèque Angelica de
Rome (XIe siècle). Graduel et Tropaire de Bologna*, Paléographie Musicale 18 (Berne,
1969). *Emitte angelum tuum* is given in full on fol. 32v, and indicated by incipit on fols 41r
and 195v. *CLLA*, no. 1342.
[298] Ed. Y. Hen, *The Sacramentary of Echternach*, HBS 110 (London, 1997), p. 88, no.
xxiv. See N. A. Orchard, 'Some notes on the Sacramentary of Echternach', *Archiv für
Liturgiewissenschaft* 43–44 (2002), 1–21. Note, however, that *Echternach* reverses the
relative positions of the commingling and fraction. For the (unrelated) text used at
Echternach in later centuries, see Darmstadt, Landes- und Hochschulbibliothek, 1946, fols
2r–7v, the early-eleventh-century sacramentary from the abbey, ed. (in facsimile) F.
Unterkircher, *Echternacher Sakramentar und Antiphoner*, Codices selecti phototypice
impressi 74 (Graz, 1982).

and entering a sacristy. Both occur in Anglo-Saxon *ordines* for the consecration of an altar.[299]

(ii) *Totius honestatis auctor* (no. 1073) for the putting on of the stockings (*caligae*). The prayer appears as a late-eleventh-century addition in Cologne, Dombibliothek 141, fol. 189r, the mid-eleventh-century pontifical of Cambrai; as a prayer *ad cambagos* in an eleventh-century book from Rheinau that Martin Gerbert had found at Zürich; and in Toulouse, Bibliothèque municipale 122, a fifteenth-century pontifical from some German cathedral.[300] It probably also appears in Los Angeles, John Paul Getty Museum, Ludwig VII.2, the pontifical compiled for Daniel Zehnder, auxiliary bishop of Constance (1473–98). To judge from a photograph, Zehnder's book has the same sequence of prayers as Gerbert's.[301] Further searches will almost certainly bring other examples to light. Provisionally though, the series (as given in *Gerbert* and *Zehnder*) looks to be ancient, Roman in origin, and thoroughly at home in Switzerland. As is the case with the *ordines* published by Andrieu, we are probably dealing with material compiled by or for particular popes. In many parts of Europe, authoritative compilations such as the *RGP*, and later, Durandus's pontifical, seem to have swept older traditions aside.

(iii) *Indue me domine calciamentis iustitiae* (no. 1074) for the putting on of the outer sandal. A version beginning *Benedic domine iesu christe hęc calciamenta iustitię*, which is probably its original form, figures as an eleventh-century addition in Cologne, Dombibliothek, 141, fol. 189r; in the book from Rheinau mentioned above; and in John Paul Getty Museum, Ludwig VII.2.[302]

---

[299] The formulae are conveniently ed. Deshusses, *Le sacramentaire grégorien*, III, 239, nos 488–9; *Pontificale Lanaletense*, ed. Doble, p. 24.

[300] Leroquais, *Les pontificaux*, II, 356–7; Gerbert, *Monumenta*, II, 52. Gerbert published the prayer and those that follow it under the superscription: AD BENEDICENDUM ORNAMENTA PONTIFICALIA. *Ex Msc. Rhenaug. saec. XI*. But the book is not readily identifiable in the detailed catalogue of the Rheinau manuscripts at Zürich produced by L. C. Mohlberg, *Katalog der Handschriften der Zentralbibliothek, Zürich*. I: *Mittelalterliche Handschriften*, 2nd ed. (Zürich, 1951). The *Cod. Rhenaug. saec. XI circ.* from which Gerbert published extracts, *Monumenta*, II, 36–8, 71–2 and 93–5, is now Zürich, Zentralbibliothek, Rheinau 114, ed. A. Hänggi, *Der Rheinauer Rituale (Zürich Rh. 114, Anfang 12 Jh.)*, Spicilegium Friburgense 5 (Fribourg, 1959).

[301] I only know the prayers in Ludwig VII.2 from the colour plate published by A. von Euw and J. M. Plotzek, *Die Handschriften der Sammlung Ludwig*, 4 vols (Cologne, 1979–85) I, 297–301.

[302] See Gerbert, *Monumenta*, II, 52 with von Euw and Plotzek, *Die Handschriften*, I, plate opp. p. 300

(iv) The hexameters for vesting (nos 1075–1085), as in the late-tenth-century sections of the 'Leofric Missal'. *Ratoldus*, however, has three further sets: *Sanctifica tunicam* for the tunic; *Digna manus nostras* for the gauntlets; and *Pignore me fidei* for the episcopal ring. Vestiges of the series, which is probably Italian in ultimate origin, survive in Oxford, Bodleian Library, Canon. Lit. 345, a twelfth-century sacramentary from the cathedral at Pistoia.[303]

(v) The prayer for the ministering of the water, *Omnipotens et misericors deus precor clementiam* (no. 1081). Not traced elsewhere.

(vi) *solium*: the normal Latin word for 'throne' (as in numerous coronation *ordines*). Rarely used in a 'concrete' sense, however, in liturgical sources.[304] Generally speaking, the preferred terms are *sedes* and *cathedra*. But *solium* was certainly known and used of the archbishop's throne at Canterbury in the mid eleventh century, as the word appears twice in the order for the installation of a new primate provided in Cambridge, Corpus Christi College, 44, a pontifical prepared at St Augustine's abbey for Lanfranc, shortly before his arrival in England in 1070.[305]

(vii) *propitiatorium*: the Biblical word for the lid of the Ark of the Convenant (Exodus xxv, xxxvii, and many other mentions). The 'context' in *Ratoldus*, however, is that of Leviticus xvi, 1–2: *Locutusque est Dominus ad Moysen . . . et praecepit ei, dicens: Loquere ad Aaron fratrem tuum ne omni tempore ingrediatur sanctuarium, quod est intra uelum coram propitiatorio quo tegitur arca*. In this instance, *propitiatorium* is the 'mercy-seat', or place where incense was offered. But *Ratoldus* probably presents the word more in a figurative sense: after the bishop has washed his hands, the character of mass changes,

---

[303] The verses in *Leofric* and *Ratoldus* are registered by D. Schaller and E. Könsgen, *Initia Carminum latinorum saeculo undecimo Antiquiorum* (Göttingen, 1977), p. 770, no. 17365. The Pistoia book has (fol. 5v): *AD AMICTVM. Virtus summa*; *AD ALBAM. Vestibus angelicis*; *AD CINGVLVM. Scrutator cordis* and *Colla iugo subdenda*; and *AD PLANETAM. Summe assiste deus.*

[304] The word is generally only used for 'thrones' in the heavenly realm, as in the antiphon *Benedic domine domum istam* (no. 23); and in the prayer for the installation of a bishop, *Omnipotens pater sancte deus aeterne tu hominem*. See *RGP*, I, 199–200 (*ordo* lxii, no. 5).

[305] The order figures on pp. 260–78, with references to the *solium* of pp. 275* and 277. I have an edition of the text in hand. For plans of the church, see *Canterbury Cathedral Nave. Archaeology, History and Architecture*, The Archaeology of Canterbury, new series, ed. K. Blockley, M. Sparks and T. Tatton-Brown (Canterbury, 1997), pp. 100–110, esp. 102 and 105.

becoming a *sacrificium propitiatorium*, or propitiatory ceremony, for which oblations are brought.[306]

(viii) The short prayer of 'tradition' to be said over the incense, *Mitto incensum in odorem suauitatis* (no. 1095), which may simply be a reworked version of some standard formula, such as: *In nomine patris et filii et spiritus sancti benedicatur incensum istud et acceptabile fiat in odore suauitatis.*

(ix) The second prayer said during the incensation itself, *Placetur domine hoc timiamate* (no. 1099), which is only otherwise to be found in this form in an order printed by Martène, under the heading *Stabulensis monasterii ms., qui videtur olim fuisse ecclesiae Virdunensis,* from Brussels, Bibliothèque royale 2031–2032, an eleventh-century liturgical miscellany made up of material from different sources: the *ordo missae* (fols 1–18v); a calendar-obituary from the church of St Lawrence in Liège (fols 19–22); and a sacramentary-cum-lectionary with a separate gradual and sequenciary (fols 33–138) drawn up for the church of St James at Liège. The collection later found its way to Stavelot. But as Martimort indicated, the *ordo* is neither of Verdun or Stavelot, as Martène thought, nor demonstrably that of either house in Liège.[307] Indeed, in view of the fact that the bishop is mentioned in the introductory rubric, *Cum episcopus aut presbyter ad missam se praeparat,* and at points throughout, a cathedral – St Lambert's at Liège is certainly a possibility – must be in view.[308]

---

[306] For discussion of Leviticus XVI in precisely these terms, see Hrabanus Maurus, *Expositiones in Leuiticus*, Bk V, cap. iii, ed. PL 108, cols 414–15. Note that figurative language of a similar nature appears in the order for Maundy Thursday transmitted in Vatican City, Biblioteca Apostolica Vaticana, lat. 12989, a late-twelfth- or early-thirteenth-century sacramentary written from the Lateran, ed. Salmon, 'Textes des *ordines romani*', 246–9, at 249: *Deinde pontifex intrat ad sacrificandum, solus intra arcam, ut significat quod in Veteri Testamento scriptum est, quia solus pontifex <intrabat> semel in anno in sancta sanctorum.*

[307] Ed. Martène, *AER*, Bk I, cap. iv, art. xii, ordo 15. See Martimort, *La documentation liturgique*, pp. 207, 314–15, nos 303 and 559. *Stavelot* often agrees closely with the order preserved in Wolfenbüttel, Herzog August-Bibliothek, Helmst 1151, the so-called 'Missal of Flaccus Illyricus', a sacramentary written for Sigebert of Minden. The text is ed. PL 138, cols 1305–36. *CLLA*, no. 990. The twin orders embodied in London, British Library, Additional 18031, fols 4v–7v, and Additional 10832, fols 1r–2r, a two-volume missal from Stavelot, have nothing relevant in common with *Ratoldus*.

[308] The orders preserved in two books from St Lambert's, Bamberg, Staatsliche Bibliothek, Lit. 3, fols 11v–12v, a late-eleventh-century sacramentary, and Cologne, Dombibliothek 157, fols 9v–24v, a late-twelfth-century sacramentary, unfortunately have nothing relevant in common either with *Ratoldus* or *Stavelot*, so if the latter really came

Ratoldus and *Stavelot*, however, have precious little in common otherwise besides *Placetur.*

As for the 'origins' of the prayer, only two parallels have so far come to light. On the left I print the text given in the Seville Missal of 1485, in the middle that preserved in London, British Library, Cotton Titus D. xxvii, the first volume of a prayerbook written for Aelfwine, dean of Winchester in the 1020s, and on the right that of *Ratoldus* and *Stavelot:*[309]

Seville	*Aelfwine*	*Ratoldus/'Stavelot'*
Placare domine per hoc incensum mihi et populo tuo, parcens peccatis nostris, et quiescat ira et furor tuus, presta propicius, ut bonus odor simus tibi in uitam eternam.	Placare quaesumus domine hoc thimiamate, et miserere nostri parcens peccatis nostris, et praesta ut boni odoris simus tibi in uitam aeternam.	Placetur domine hoc timiamate uel incenso furor tuus contra me et contra locum istum et contra populum istum, et praesta propitius ut fumus boni odoris, tibi simus ad capiendam uitam aeternam. Per.

All three clearly spring from a common source, presumably more along the lines of the version adopted at Seville than at Winchester or in *Ratoldus*.

Viewed as a whole, *Ratoldus*'s order is something of a patchwork, a 'one-off', prepared specially for the book's intended owner. Three sources are readily identifiable: the collect, secret, preface and postcommunion for mass were doubtless extracted from the underlying (Saint-Denis) sacramentary; a tenth-century 'Lotharingian' order provided a selection of prayers to accompany certain actions at the altar; and the English pontifical provided, at the very least, prayers and verses for vesting, possibly even the outline of the order as a whole in the form of rubric deriving (in part) from an Italian source akin to *Ordo romanus* 1. As for the elements that are clearly non-Roman and non-Carolingian, an English source is just as likely as the 'Gallican' one envisaged by

from St Lambert's, it must have been non-standard not only in relation to normal practice at Liège but to practice in Lotharingia as a whole, and very much obsolete by the early eleventh century. A full set of digital pictures of the Cologne book is available at http://www.ceec.uni-koeln.de.
[309] *Aelfwine's Prayerbook (London, British Library, Cotton Titus D. xxvi + xxvii)*, ed. B. Günzel, HBS 108 (London, 1993), p. 117, no. 34. 3.

Jungmann.[310] Arras, *pace* Bishop, appears to have played no discernable part in the shaping of *Ratoldus*'s text.[311]

Order for the Visitation of the Sick (nos 2194–2214)

Ratoldus's order is extremely compact. There are no preliminary bless-ings or aspersions of the building in which the patient lies, nor any introductory chant. We have instead a short dialogue, a group of antiphons for use at points throughout the order, a series of unctions, and finally the closing prayers and mass. In general terms, the arrange-ment runs parallel to that of the 'Sacramentary of Winchcombe', which also gives the chant required as a free-standing group. But the relation-ship ends there. The order to which Ratoldus had access was clearly very different. Indeed, to judge by the antiphons provided, it must have been a forerunner of the types of order found in the 'Missal of Robert of Jumièges'; *Lanalet*; Bodleian, Laud misc. 482; and Cambridge, Corpus Christi College 422, the so-called 'Red Book of Darley', a combined votive missal, ritual and select breviary written at Winchester *c.* 1060 for use at Sherborne; and Boulogne Bibliothèque municipale 84, the pontifical of Lambert, bishop of Arras. These at any rate are apparently the only surviving books in which the series *Succurre domine infirmo*, *Cor contritum*, *Opem ferat*, *Dominus locutus est*, *Saluum fac seruum*, *Cadent a latere*, *Propitietur domine*, occurs.[312] *Ratoldus*, however, has

---

[310] Jungmann, *The Mass of the Roman Rite*, II, 78 n.11, for instance, states that the handwashing after the saying of the secret in *Ratoldus* is of 'ancient Gallic usage': in other words, it is neither demonstrably 'Roman' nor demonstrably 'Carolingian'. For Jungmann, pre-Conquest England hardly exists.

[311] In a letter to Armitage Robinson (11 Dec. 1916), Edmund Bishop noted: 'In the last chapter of his *Commentarius Praevius* to the Roman Ordos Mabillon mentions a Cambray and Arras Ordo recently published from Fr. Pithou's MSS. collections earlier than saec. XII in the new edition of "Codex Canonum Ecclesiae Romanae" . . . my memory of *many* years ago . . . seems to bring back to me that the vol. mentioned by Mabillon was published in 1684, a folio . . . Now it would be worth while to see if this Ordo shews any traces of the stylistic peculiarities of the Ratoldus *Ordo missae*. – The scrap given by Mabillon shews certain peculiarities of style.' The book Bishop had in mind was *Petri Pithoei comes theologus siue spicilegium ex sacra messe* (Paris, 1684), pp. 367–9. For details of the manuscripts Pithou used, see Martimort, *La documentation liturgique*, pp. 54–5. Unfortu-nately their text has no bearing whatsoever on *Ratoldus*, and the 'order' is in any case an office directory. For the order of mass used at Saint-Vaast in the early eleventh century, see Arras, Bibliothèque municipale 721, described by Leroquais, *Les sacramentaires*, I, 163–4.

[312] *The Missal of Robert of Jumièges*, ed. Wilson, pp. 286–95; *Pontificale Lanaletense*,

'strays': *Quia apud deum misericordia*, third in order, comes from Fleury (and is therefore in *Winchcombe*), and *Domine libera animam*, the last, is only otherwise to be found in Cambrai, Mediathèque municipale 223, a pontifical drawn up for some thirteenth-century bishop of the cathedral.

Cambrai also seems to have provided the introductory dialogue. I give on the left the oldest known form of the exchange from a ritual probably drawn up at Saint-Amand, or a house close by, in the late ninth or early tenth century; the version preserved in the Cambrai book in the middle; and *Ratoldus*'s (no. 2194) on the right:[313]

Saint-Amand	Cambrai	Ratoldus
Tunc sacerdos accedat ad infirmum, dicat. Vocasti? INFIRMVS DICAT. Desideraui tecum loqui, ut mihi poenitentiam et remissionem peccatorum tradas. SACERDOS DICAT. Det tibi dominus iesu christe ueniam, tamen si deus in te respexerit custodies illam? INFIRMVS RESP. Custodio. DEINDE SACERDOS AVDIAT CONFESSIONEM EIVS SICVT MELIVS INQVIRERE POTERIT AVT SCRIPTIS AVT VERBIS.	*Tunc dicit sacerdos ad infirmum.* Quid me huc uocasti frater? *Infirmus respondet.* Vt mihi tradas unctionem. *Et adiungit sacerdos.* Donet tibi dominus noster iesus ueram felicemque unctionem, tamen si respexerit et sanauerit dominus, custodies illam? *Respondet.* Custodiam.	Hic dicatur sacerdos ad infirmum. Quid me aduocasti, frater? Ille ait, ut mihi unctionem tradas. Dicit sacerdos ad eum. Donet tibi dominus noster iesus christus ueram facilemque unctionem, tam si te respexerit et sanauerit te deus, custodies illam? Respondet. Custodiam.

ed. Doble, pp. 131–39; B. Fehr, 'Altenglische Ritualtexte fur Krankenbesuch, heilige Ölung und Begräbnis', *Texte und Forschungen*, ed. Förster and Wildhagen, pp. 20–67; and Boulogne BM 84, fols 132r–136v. The sequence of antiphons in *Robert, Lanalet* and *Boulogne* is *Sana domine, Succurre domine, Sanet te iesus, Opem ferat, Dominus locutus est, Cor contritum, Saluum fac, Cadent a latere, Propicietur. Lanalet* and Laud misc. 482 add *Ne reminiscaris.*

[313] The Cambrai text is ed. Martène, *AER*, Bk II, cap. vii, art iv, ordo 19. The Saint-Amand text is reproduced in part by E. Palazzo, 'Les deux rituels d'un libellus de Saint-Amand (Paris, Bibliothèque nationale, lat. 13764)', in *Rituels. Mélanges offerts à Pierre-Marie Gy, o.p.*, ed. P. de Clerck and E. Palazzo (Paris, 1990), 423–36, fig. 3. A later version of the Saint-Amand *ordo* survives in Paris, Bibliothèque nationale de France, lat. 818, an eleventh-century sacramentary from Troyes. The text is ed. Martène, *AER*, Bk I, cap. vii, art. iv, ordo 3. Also see Martimort, *La documentation liturgique*, pp. 214–5, no. 316.

<table>
<tr><td>Tunc faciet crucem ex
cinere super pectus infirmi
et imponat cilicium super
caput eius.</td><td>Tunc sacerdos facit crucem ex
cinere cum aqua supra pectus
eius et imponit silentium
desuper.</td></tr>
</table>

Ratoldus and *Cambrai* side together in giving the non-standard *Donet tibi dominus*. Two possibilities confront us: first, that the text of the 'dialogue' was acquired from Arras (which lies twenty or so miles to the north-west of Cambrai) during the course of the making of *Ratoldus*; second, that the lines were already in place in the order transmitted in the English pontifical. Since we no longer have the model or models from which *Ratoldus* was assembled it is naturally difficult to be sure, but what tends to tip the balance in favour of the second is not only that vestiges of the 'Cambrai' dialogue survive, translated into OE, in two eleventh-century English books:[314]

Cambrai	*Corpus 422*
	Aefter þisum collectan bige se preost his cneowa aetforan ðam seocan mid gelimplicere
Tunc dicit sacerdos ad infirmum. Quid me huc uocasti frater? *Infirmus* *respondet.* Vt mihi tradas unctionem.	eadmodnisse and him þus cweðe: To hwi gecig dest þu, broðor, us hider to þe? Ðonne andswarige se seoca and þus cweðe: To þam þaet ge me smyrian sceoldon.

Cambrai	*Robert*
Tunc sacerdos faciet crucem ex cinere cum aqua super pectus eius et imponit cilicium desuper dicens . . .	Ðonne wyrce se sacerd cristes rodetacn mid þan halig waetere mid axun und mid þam axum ofer his breost and onlecge haeran oððe wyllen . . .

but that certain elements in English pontificals and benedictionals clearly descend from books drawn up initially for use by the bishops of Cambrai. The lines of descent are perhaps clearest in the benedictionals, which we shall come to in due course. It therefore seems best to suppose that an English order for the visitation of the sick, containing material originally assembled at Cambrai at some point in the tenth century, underlies the order embodied in *Ratoldus*.[315] Quite where the elements from the Romano-Germano Pontifical came in is impossible to say, but

314 See Fehr, 'Altenglische Ritualtexte', 49.
315 The dialogue certainly does not figure in the order added (at Cambrai) in the late ninth century to Cambrai, Mediathèque municipale, 164, the sacramentary written for Bishop Hildoard, *c.* 812. For a brief account of the character of the additions to the book, see N. A. Orchard, 'The ninth- and tenth-century additions to Cambrai, Mediathèque municipale, 164', *RB*, forthcoming.

they are there nonetheless in the shape of the formulae for unction and commendation.

Forms for the laying-on of hands (nos 2226–2231)

The first five prayers are simply copies of the formulae transmitted in Benedict of Aniane's 'Supplement' to the *Hadrianum*, and as such, presumably descend from the underlying Saint-Denis sacramentary. The sixth, however, is almost certainly English, for versions are only otherwise known in the original portions of the 'Leofric Missal' and in London, British Library, Royal 12. D. xvii, a mid-tenth-century collection of charms and recipes, probably from Winchester.[316]

THE BENEDICTIONAL

As both Hohler and Prescott have indicated, the English pontifical to which Ratoldus had access evidently embodied an extensive benedictional, its blessings now distributed throughout the sacramentary by Ratoldus's scribe, who made a fair job of copying them in.[317]

In terms of content and arrangement, the benedictional seems to have been something of a miscellany. In a peculiarly English fashion, it drew together material from two principal continental sources: a benedictional from Reims akin to the one preserved in Reims, Bibliothèque municipal 214, a late-tenth-century sacramentary-cum-pontifical from the cathedral that later found its way to the abbey of Saint-Thierry; and a benedictional from Cambrai similar to the one progressively compiled in the ninth and tenth centuries in Cambrai, Mediathèque municipale, 164, a copy of the *Hadrianum* (and the best that has come down to us) written for Bishop Hildoard at some point close to 812. A partial copy

---

[316] See *The Leofric Missal*, ed. Orchard, I, 109–112, and II, 437–8, no. 2479, with K. L. Jolly, *Popular Religion in Late Saxon England. Elf Charms in Context* (Chapel Hill, 1996), pp. 162–4. Distinctively, parts of the body are named in the prayer.

[317] See Prescott, 'The text of the Benedictional of Æthelwold', 135–42, with Hohler, 'Some service-books', 65.

of an unadulterated Reims benedictional survives in *Claudius* (fols 137r–150v), as has already been mentioned.[318]

That books from Cambrai were known in England is clear enough from the presence, in almost all the Anglo-Saxon benedictionals that have survived of a blessing for the feast of St Vedastus, the principal saint of the diocese: and this is not the only indication, as we shall see. Before we go any further, however, it may be useful first to show how *Ratoldus* lines up against its relatives. The books used for comparative purposes are:

Aeth.: London, British Library, Additional 49598, the splendid benediction copied by the scribe Godemann for Aethelwold, bishop of Winchester (963–84) in the early 970s.[319] An alternative blessing is provided for almost every feast encompassed. The benedictional was clearly part reference text, part practical book.

Camb.: Cambrai Médiathèque municipale 164, the sacramentary written for Hildoard, bishop of Cambrai. The main benedictional is a mid-ninth-century addition prefixed to the front of the volume on a set of gatherings newly supplied. Supplementary texts were appended on fols 241v–245v in the early tenth century. For the first set of blessings, I have used the system of numbering given by Deshusses. The second set is registered in Roman numerals, i–x.[320]

C 1: the first and longer of the two benedictionals embodied in *Claudius* (fols 106r-133r). The text looks to be 'complete'.[321]

C 2: the second benedictional embodied in *Claudius* (fols 137r–150v). The text begins with a blessing for the joint feast of SS Sebastian and Fabian (16 Jan.), and ends incomplete in the order for Maundy Thursday.[322]

Lan.: the benedictional embodied in *Lanalet*. Only the blessings have been assigned numbers. The *ordines* for Ash Wednesday, Maundy Thursday and Candlemas have not been taken into account.[323] Later additions have been signalled where appropriate.

---

[318] See above, pp. ci–cii.
[319] Ed. G. Warner and H. A. Wilson, *The Benedictional of St Æthelwold*, pp. 1–47. Also see the facsimile ed. A. Prescott, *The Benedictional of St Æthelwold* (London, 2002).
[320] Ed. Deshusses, *Le sacramentaire grégorien*, II, 356–64, nos 3811–47, with Orchard, 'The ninth- and tenth-century additions to Cambrai MM 164', forthcoming.
[321] Ed. Turner, *The Claudius Pontificals*, pp. 1–28.
[322] Ed. Turner, *The Claudius Pontificals*, pp. 74–88.
[323] Ed. Doble, *Pontificale Lanaletense*, pp. 65–108.

R: the benedictional of Reims Bibliothèque municipale 214, the late-tenth-century sacramentary-cum-pontifical from the church of Saint Thierry at Reims.[324]

In the last column I give the number assigned to the blessings (where they have been printed from other sources) in Dom Moeller's *Corpus Benedictionum Pontificalium*.[325]

For *Lan.*, *C 1*, *C 2*, and *Reims*, it has seemed best to cite page numbers first, then formulae numbers (for example, 112,2 is p. 112, second formula on that page) rather than number the blessings sequentially. It has also seemed best to separate out the blessings of the temporal from those of the sanctoral. I have included the forms for priests and deacons solely for convenience's sake: properly speaking they belong to the pontifical, or at least to the *ordines* embodied in it, much as the blessings for the dedication of a church (no. 92), the ordination of a bishop or archbishop (no. 124), and for the king (nos 168 and 173) belong with their respective *ordines*.

The principal abbreviations and contractions employed are: aet. = aeterne; ben. = benedicat; bm = beatum; d. = deus: dne = domine; dns = dominus; m. = misericors; o. = omnipotens; p. = pater; q. = qui; qs = quaesumus; s. = sancte. Brackets indicate that a formula is present but assigned to a different feast. Italics indicate an addition.

CHRISTMAS – PENTECOST

Ratold.	Feast	Incipit	Aeth.	Lan.	C 1	Reims	C 2	Camb.	CBP
235	Vig. Nat.	O. d. q. incarnatione	12	65,4	2,4	605,3		1738	1643
241	Nocte	Populum tuum qs. dne	13	65,5	3,1	606,2			1857
249	Mane	D. q. non solum genus	14	66,1		606,3			1021
257	Nat. Dom.	Ben. uos o. d. uestramque	15	66,2	3,2	607,1		1739	321
259	Alia.	D. q. genus humanum	16						931
271	Stephen	D. q. bm stephanum prot.	17	66,3		607,2		1740	854
283	Ioh. Ev.	O. d. dignetur uobis per	19	66,4		607,4		1741	1566
292	Innocents	O. d. pro cuius unigeniti	20	66,5		607,6		1742	1600
297	Alia.	C. qs. dne plebi tuae inn.	21			607,7			579
301	Dom. p. N.	O. d. adaperiat cor uestrum	(138)	(87,8)				(3842)	1523

[324] Ed. PL 78, cols 605–38. Text checked against a microfilm of the manuscript.
[325] *Corpus Benedictionum Pontificalium*, ed. E. Moeller, CCSL 162, 162A–C, 4 vols (Turnhout, 1980–1).

306	Vig. Oct.	O. s. d. q. per incarnatum		(97,1)	3,3	(608,1)			1797
307	Alia.	*Requ. in nat. i cf.* (not given)							
312	Oct. Dom.	O. d. cuius unigenitus	22	66,6	3,4	607,6		1743	1545
322	Dom I p. N.	D. q. unigenitum suum	23	67,1	4,1	607,8		3824	1168
331	Epiphany	D. lumen uerum q. unigen.	24	67,2	4,2	608,3		1744	732
344	Dom I p. Th.	D. q. filii sui temporalem	26	67,3	4,3	608,2		3825	926
351	Oct. Epiph.	D. q. presentem diem	25		4,4	608,5			1086
372	Dom II p. Th.	D. q. sua mirabili potestate	27	67,4	5,1	608,4		3826	1143
398	Dom III p. Th.	O. d. uos ab omnium	28	67,5	5,2	608,6		3827	1711
420	Dom IV p. Th.	Temptationum omnium	29	67,6	5,3	608,8		3828	2019
438	Dom V p. Th.	D. q. bonorum semen	30	67,7	5,4	608,9		3829	855
452	Dom VI p. Th.	D. q. mare suis pedibus	31	67,8	6,1	609,1		3830	1005
483	Septuag.	O. d. ita studium uestri	46	67,9	9,2	609,2		3813	1584
488	Sexag.	Det uobis dominus nosse	48	68,1	9,3	609,4		3814	632
493	Quinqu.	O. d. sua uos benedictione	50	68,2	9,4	609,6		3815	1694
517	Cap. ieiunii	Ben. uos dns ihs xps q. se	52		10,1	609,8			247
534	Quadrag.	Ben. uos o. d. q. quadrag.	53	73,2	10,2			1746	192
541	Fer. ii.	Benedic dne populum	54		9,5	609,7	(86,2)		101
553	Fer. iv.	Respice pastor bone super	55	(73,1)		610,1	(86,1)		1924
627	Deacon.	Ben. uos d. misericordia pl.	(120)	107,2	38,2				218
647	Priest.	D. fons indulgentiae	56	(88,6)		(614,9)	(86,3)		702
652	Alia.	O. s. d. respicere dignare		107,3	41,2				1803
657	Dom vacat.	O. d. ieiunii ceterarumque	57	73,3	11,1	610,2		1747	1576
662	Fer. ii.	D. q. es custos animarum	58			601,3	(86,4)		909
673	Fer. iv.	Ben. uos d. misericordia pl.	(120)	(107,2)	(38,2)				218
684	Fer. vi.	Ben. uobis d. nostri alloq.							169
695	Dom II.	O. d. ieiuniorum uestrorum		73,4		610,4		1748	1577
700	Fer. ii	O. det uobis copiam suae				610,5	(87,1)		1554
711	Fer. iv.	Respice dne de caelo et	(47)			(609,3)	(82,3)		1913
723	Fer. vi.	O. dns q. a muliere samarit.							
733	Dom III.	D. q. uos ad praesentium		73,5		610,6		1749	1193
740	Fer. ii.	Ben. uos o d. et omnem	59		11,2	610,7	(87,2)		286
752	Fer. iv.	D. q. genus humanum							
763	Fer. vi.	Ben. uos o. d. q. per humil.							
774	Dom IV.	Accendat in uobis dns uim		73,6		611,1		1750	8
789	Fer. iv.	Adesto o. d. huic populo	62	(88,7)		610,8	(87,3)		13
800	Fer. vi.	Ben. uos o. d. et mentes				611,2	(88,1)		288
816	Dom Palm.	Ben. uobis o. cui et iein.	60	75,2	11,3			1751	180
821	Fer. ii.	O. d. q. unigeniti sui pass.	61	75,3	11,4			1752	1671
833	Fer. iv.	D. q. pro mundi salute	63						1097

Ratold.	Feast	Incipit	Aeth.	Lan.	C 1	Reims	C 2	Camb.	CBP
864	Cena Dom.	Ben. uos d. q. per unigen.	64	82,4	12,1			1753	233
1064	Sabbato	D. q. de ecclesie tue intem.	66	*82,6*	12,2			1754	879
864	Pascha	Ben. uos o. d. hodierna	68	83,1	12,3	611,3			292
1133	Fer. ii.	D. q. pro uobis suscepit	70	83,2	12,4	611,4		3816	510
1143	Fer. iii.	D. q. uos lauit aqua sui lat.	71	83,3	13,1	611,5		3817	1207
1152	Fer. iv.	Dns d. noster uos perducat	72	83,4	13,2	611,6		3818	1268
1161	Fer. v.	D. q. inter orbis primordia	75		14,1				995
1170	Fer. vi.	C. m. d. huic plebi salutif.	(79)	(84,4)					576
1178	Sabbato	D. q. peracto senario				611,9			1076
1185	Dom.	D. cuius unigenitus hod.	76	84,1	14,2	611,10		1756	679
1209	Dom I p. Oct.	Omnipotentis dei et dom.	73	83,5	13,2	611,7			1815
1214	Dom II p. Oct.	Ben. uobis d. de caelis	74	83,6	13,4	611,8			216
1229	Dom III p. O.	D. q. calcatis inferni leg.	69	83,7				3820	859
1234	Dom IV p. O.	Ben. uos o. d. q. uos grat.	77	84,2	14,3	611,12		1757	314
1245	Litany	Benedic qs. dne uniuersam				612,3			112
1251	Die ii.	O. d. deuotionem nostram	85	84,5	15,2	611,13		1759	156
1257	Die iii.	Respice dne super hanc	86		15,3	611,14			1919
1264	Ascension.	Ben. uobis o. d. cuius unig.	88	84,6		612,4		1760	281
1276	Dom I. p. Asc.	Benedictionum suarum	87	84,7	15,4	612,5		3831	380
1277	Alia.	D. q. tartara fregisti	89			612,6			1152

PENTECOST – ADVENT

Ratold.	Feast	Incipit	Aeth.	Lan.	C 1	Reims	C 2	Camb.	CBP
1332	Sabbato.	Ben. uobis o. d. ob cuius	90	85,1	16,2			3821	186
1336	Pentecost.	D. q. hod. die discipulorum	91	85,2	16,3	612,7			948
1343	Fer. ii.	O. d. q. quinquagesimum	92			612,8			1659
1348	Fer. iii.	Ben. uobis o. d. q. cuncta	93	85,3	16,4	612,9			187
1353	Fer. iv	O. trinitas unus et uerus	94	85,4	17,1	613,1		3822	1804
1371	Sabbato	Dne iesu christe q. discip.	95			613,2			1258
1376	Oct. Pent.	Ben. uos trinitatis diuinae		101,7		(615,3)			350
1388	Dom II p. Oct.	Benedic dne istam omnem	(139)			613,3			98
1406	Fer. vi.	Benedic dne omnem istam							(98)
1418	Sabbato.	*Requ. in ext. die* (feria vi.)							
1424	Dom III p. O.	Propicietur dns cunctis	98	85,6	18,2	613,4		3832	1880
1440	Dom vacat.	Ben. uobis nostri oris alloq.		85,7	18,3	613,5		3833	169
1453	Dom V p. P.	Emundet dns conscientias	101	85,8	18,4	613,6		3834	1337
1481	Dom VI.	Agnoscat in nobis dns	99			613,7			22
1509	Dom VII.	Amoueat a uobis dns	105	86,1	19,2	613,8		3835	31

Ratold.	Feast	Incipit	Aeth.	Lan.	C 1	Reims	C 2	Camb.	CBP
1525	Dom VIII.	Ben. uos o. d. et per hab.				613,9			289
1542	Dom IX.	Sanctificet uos domini gr.	109	86,3	19,4	613,10		3836	1962
1564	Dom X.	Populi tui qs dne postul.				613,11			71
1590	Dom XI.	D. q. est uita mortalium	113	86,5	20,1	614,1		3837	921
1614	Dom XII.	Tribuat uobis dns caritatis				614,2			2024
1639	Dom XIII.	Gratie sue dono uos	117	86,7	20,3	614,3		3838	1388
1666	Dom XIV.	Ben. uobis celorum rector				614,4			239
1689	Dom XV.	Benedictio uos domini	121	86,9	20,5	614,5		3839	360
1727	Dom XVI.	Benedic dne hanc plebem				614,6			77
1749	Dom XVII.	O. dns peccatorum nostr.	125	87,1	21,2	614,7			1745
1763	Dom XVIII.	Ben. uos p. dni nri iesu chr.	(104)			615,1			1745
1782	Sabbato	Benedictionum suarum	155	(98,1)	(15,4)	(612,5)		(3831)	380
1787	Dom vacat.	Ben. uos o. d. et mentes	**	**		(611,2)			288
1809	Dom XX.	Adesto dne propicius plebi							
1835	Dom XXI.	Plebs tua dne qs nostram		(103,3)					1852
1853	Dom XXII.	Aspiciat uos rector aetern.	(114)			615,7	(83,1)		42
1868	Dom XXIII.	Dirigat uos dns in omni							
1898	Dom XXIV.	Ben. uos dns celorum							(156)
1910	Dom XXV.	Benedic dne populum		(88,5)		(614,8)		3847	101
1925	Dom XXVI.	Benedic uos p. dni nri iesu	(104)			(615,1)			340
1953	Dom XXVII.	D. inuisibilis inaestimabilis				(615,2)			725
1976	Adv I.	O. d. cuius unigeniti	2	88,1	1,1	616,6		3844	1544
1984	Adv II.	Cuius aduentus incarnationis	4	88,2	1,2	616,8		3845	663
2001	Adv III.	O. d. uos placito uultu	6	88,3	1,3	617,1		3846	1722
2007	Fer. iv.	D. q. es custos animarum	10		2,2	(610,3)			909
2012	Fer. vi.	Dns iesus christus q. sacr.	7			616,7			1307
2022	Sabbato	D. q. per angelum tuum	9			617,4			1072
2027	Dom vacat.	D. q. uos et prioris advent.	8	88,4	2,1	617,3		3847	1200

SANCTORAL

Ratold.	Feast	Incipit	Aeth.	Lan.	C 1	Reims	C 2	Camb.	CBP
379	Seb. & Fab.	D. q. triumphantibus pro	33	88,8	6,2	(621,1)	74,1		1160
386	Agnes.	Ben. uobis dns q. beate ag.	34	89,1	6,3		74,2		175
393	Vincent.	Ben. uobis dns celorum	35	89,2	6,4		74,3		156
403	Conv. Paul.	D. q. gratia sua bm paulum	36	89,3	7,2	617,5		3811	940
414	Purification.	O. d. q. unigenitum suum	39	91,5	7,3	617,6		1745	1674
425	Agatha.	Sanctifica dne ecclesiam	40	91,6	7,4	617,7			1956
433	Vedast.	D. fundator fidei et indult.	41	92,1	8,1	(618,3)	(76,3)		910
442	Valentine.	D. q. beatissimum ualent.	(43)		(8,2)	(620,6)			807

Ratold.	Feast	Incipit	Aeth.	Lan.	C 1	Reims	C 2	Camb.	CBP
447	Cath. Petri.	D. q. bm petrum apostolum	42	92,2	8,3	617,8			851
457	Gregory.	D. q. beatissimum greg.	(43)	92,3	8,2	(620,6)			807
462	Cuthbert	Dne d. omnium gratiarum	(45)	(93,2)		(621,2)	(75,3)		1254
467	Benedict	Dne d. omnium gratiarum	(45)	(93,2)		(621,2)	(75,3)		1254
474	Annunc.	D. q. cum te non capiunt	44	*92,5*	9,1	(619,3)			874
1219	Tib. & Val.	Ben. uobis dns beatorum	83	94,1					153
1224	George	Beati martyris sui georgii	(170)	94,2					57
1282	Ph. & Jas.	D. q. ecclesiam suam							905
1290	Inv. of Cross	O. d. det uobis sue bened.	84						310
1305	Pancras NA.	Respice dne hanc familiam		(95,2)			(76,2)		1916
1393	Medard	Dne iesu christe pastor							(1256)
1428	BCNN	Enutri qs dne plebem tuum					(76,1)		
1448	Gerv. & Prot.	Dne s. p. o. aet. d. respice		95,3			76,4		1266
1458	Vig. Ioh. B.	Deus q. bm iohannem	142	96,1		618,4	77,1		835
1466	Ioh. Bapt.	Ben. uobis. o. d. beati ioh.	141	96,2	17,3			1763	179
1494	Pet. & Paul	Ben. uobis o. d. q. nos beati	143	96,3	17,4	618,5			193
1504	Paul	D. q. in membris ecclesiae	144			618,6	77,2		981
1513	Pr. & Mart.	Respice dne hanc familiam		(95,2)					1916
1629	Lawrence	Corrobora gregem tuum				618,7	77,3		597
1657	Assumpt.	D. q. beatae marie partum	148	96,5	23,3	618,8			1053
1684	Barthol.	D. q. ecclesiam tuam	149	96,6		618,9	78,1		905
1708	Decoll. Ioh.	D. q. uos beati iohannis	150	96,7	24,2	619,1			1194
1722	Nat. BVM	O. d. sua uos dignetur		97,1	24,1				1697
1735	Prot. & Iac.	Respice dne hanc familiam		97,3			78,4		1916
1744	Exalt. Cross	D. q. redemisti genus	153	97,4		619,4	79,1		792
1795	Matthew	Benedic dne populum	154	97,5				ii	101
1818	Michael	Adesto plebi tuae m. d.				619,7	80,1	iii	14
1848	Denis	Exaudi dne preces suppl.				(619,5)	(79,2)	iv	1347
1888	All Saints	Respice dne qs de alto thr.				620,2	81,1	i	1923
1918	Martin	O. d. q. bm martinum				620,4		v	1609
1934	Cecilia	Sanctae trinitatis super	162	100,1	(23,2)			vi	1948
1940	Clement	O. d. uestrorum cordium	163	100,2			80,3	vii	1706
1948	Chrisogonus	O. d. deuotionem		100,3			81,2	viii	1561
1962	Vig. Andrew	O. d. sua uos locupletet	164	*143,5*	25,2			ix	1695
1967	Andrew	D. q. bm andream apost.	165	*143,6*	25,3			x	817
1991	Lucy	Ben. uos o. d. et ad omnem	(11)						286
1996	Thomas	Aperi dne ianuas caeli	(3)			(616,7)			37

VOTIVES

Ratold.	Feast	Incipit	Aeth.	Lan.	C 1	Reims	C 2	Camb.	CBP
2039	Trinity.	O. trinitas unus et uerus		101,6	(17,1)	(613,1)			1804
2045	Suffrag. SS	O. d. q. per incarnatum			(3,3)	(607,9)	(78,3)		1654
2050	Suffrag. Ang.	D. q. ad salutem nostram	(98,2)			(619,6)	(79,4)		779
2056	Wisdom.	O. d. sua uos clementia		(102,1)	(19,1)				1696
2068	Charity.	(D. q. redemisti genus)	(153)	(97,4)		(619,4)	(79,1)		(792)
2223	Infirm.	O. d. hunc infirmum uisita		110,2					1575

Several points emerge from the table. First, as far as the temporal is concerned, *Ratoldus* runs parallel:

(i) with *Aeth* from Christmas to Lent, though only *Lanalet* and *Claudius* give the blessings for the days either side of the octave of Christmas in the same order as *Ratoldus*.

(ii) with *Reims* and to a lesser extent *Lanalet* from the first Sunday in Lent to Easter. Note, however, that *Reims* has no forms for the week before Easter, and that *Aeth*, alone of the others, provides the blessing *Deus qui pro mundi salute* (no. 833) for the Wednesday. It is perhaps well to say too that *Ratoldus* provides for an unparalleled number of weekdays throughout the season. For the most part the blessings allotted to these only figure in English sources, a case in point being *Benedicat uos deus misericordia plenus*, for deacons and the Wednesday in the second week of Lent (nos 627 and 673).

(iii) with *Aeth*, *Lanalet* and *Claudius* from Easter to Pentecost. *Reims* has a very different set of forms for Sundays.

(iv) with *Reims* and *Reims* alone from the first to seventeenth Sunday after Pentecost. The order of blessings adopted for the series is not to be found elsewhere. After the seventeenth Sunday, *Ratoldus* goes its own way. Of all the books surveyed by Moeller, *Plebs tua domine quesumus* (no. 1835) only otherwise figures in *Lanalet* and *Egbert*, which are both from houses in the west country.

(v) with *Aeth* again during Advent itself.

Seven formulae, however, are not to be found in any other book: *Omnipotens deus qui a muliere samaritana*, for Friday in the second week of Lent (no. 723); *Deus qui genus humanum* and *Benedicat uos omnipotens deus qui per humilitatem*, for Wednesday and Friday in the third week of Lent (nos 752 and 763); *Benedic domine istam omnem*, for the Friday of the second week after Pentecost (no. 1388); *Adesto domine propicius plebi, Dirigat uos dominus in omni*, and *Benedicat uos dominus celorum*, for the twentieth, twenty-third and twenty-fourth Sundays after Pentecost (nos 1809, 1868 and 1898). *Ratoldus's* temporal is clearly a complex hybrid.

When we come to the sanctoral, the picture once again appears to be somewhat fragmented. If we put to one side the blessings that were generally popular throughout the early middle ages, five clearly defined sub-groups emerge:

(i) blessings that only survive in books written in England, namely *Enutri quesumus domine plebem*, for SS Basilides, Cyrinus, Nabor and Nazarius (no. 1428), which is assigned to the feast of SS Alexander and Eventius in the second benedictional of *Claudius*; *Respice domine hanc familiam*, for the feasts of SS Pancras, Nereus and Achilleus (no. 1305), SS Processus and Martinian (no. 1513), SS Protus and Iacinthus (no. 1735), but perhaps originally from the 'commons'; *Omnipotens deus sua uos dignetur*, for the Nativity of the Virgin (no. 1722); and *Omnipotens deus qui per incarnatum*, for the suffrage of saints (no. 2045).

(ii) 'Gallican' or 'Gregorian' blessings that are assigned, as in English benedictionals, to feasts other than the ones for which they were originally composed: *Deus qui triumphantibus*, for SS Sebastian and Fabian (no. 379); *Benedicat vobis dominus qui beati*, for St Agnes (no. 386); *Deus qui beatissimum*, for St Valentine (no. 442); *Benedicat uobis dominus beatorum*, for SS Tiburtius and Valerian (no. 1219); *Beati martyris sui*, for St George (no. 1224); and *Domine sancte pater omnipotens aeterne deus respice*, for SS Gervase and Protase (no. 1448).

(iii) blessings known in the late tenth century at Cambrai and in England: *Sanctae trinitatis super*, for St Cecilia (no. 1934); *Omnipotens deus uestrorum cordium*, for St Clement (no. 1940); *Omnipotens deus deuotionem uestram*, for St Chrisogonus (no. 1948); *Omnipotens deus sua uos locupletet* and *Deus qui beatum andream*, for the vigil and feast of St Andrew (nos 1962 and 1967).

(iv) formulae not found in other books: *Omnipotens deus det uobis sue benedictionis*, for the feast of the Invention of the Cross (no. 1290); and

Domine iesu christe pastor, for St Medard (no. 1393), which is based on a blessing for the twenty-first Sunday after Pentecost at Reims.

(v) blessings removed from the temporal and assigned to saints' days: *Benedicat uos omnipotens deus et ad omnem* (no. 1991), a standard form for the Sunday before Palm Sunday, for St Lucy; and *Aperi domine ianuas caeli* (no. 1996), the alternative Reims blessing for the fourth Sunday before Christmas, for St Thomas.

Although a certain amount of readjustment has evidently taken place, the main strands are clear enough. In terms of content and arrangement, the sanctoral is, in order, part Cambrai, part English, part Reims, and part 'Ratoldian' rearrangement. Presumably the English pontifical to which Ratoldus had access contained, like *Claudius,* two distinct and perhaps quite separate sets of texts: a benedictional from Cambrai that had already been adapted for use in England, and another, more or less unadjusted, from Reims. That *Ratoldus* should have turned out to be so odd is perhaps not altogether surprising. The two sets of blessings will largely have been incompatible, as they are in *Claudius.*

In effect, *Ratoldus* and *Claudius* provide us with a tantalising glimpse of the sort of texts that were used in England before the massive compilations of the second half of the tenth century – Æthelwold's benedictional, for example – gained an air of authority. If any one man was responsible for gathering the relevant material together, Archbishop Oda, as I have indicated elsewhere, would fit the bill perfectly.[326] The Cambrai benedictional that came to be adopted in England was clearly more advanced than the one embodied in Cambrai, Médiathèque municipale 164.

CONCLUSION

'Complete' sacramentary-cum-pontificals are rare. Only four other early examples have come down to us: Vat. Reg. lat. 316, the so-called 'Vatican Gelasian' sacramentary, a book probably prepared for some Bishop of Paris in the mid eighth century; BNF lat. 12048, the 'Sacramentary of Gellone', drawn up for Hildoard, bishop of Cambrai,

---

[326] Orchard, 'The ninth- and tenth-century additions to Cambrai MM 164', forthcoming.

at some point close to the year 800; Bodley 579, the sacramentary-cum-pontifical written by a scribe from Saint-Vaast probably for the use of Plegmund, archbishop of Canterbury (890–923); and Verona, Biblioteca Capitolare 87, an exceedingly long text produced for Wolfgang, bishop of Regensburg (972–94) in 993 or 994.[327] Like *Ratoldus*, all are highly complex.

Unfortunately in *Ratoldus*'s case the identity of the intended recipient is unknown. He was clearly to have been a bishop or archbishop, and his seat presumably not too far from Corbie: Amiens, Beauvais, even Cambrai, are all possible. Quite why the book should have been fitted out with a Saint-Vaast calendar and other Saint-Vaast matter, muddled though it may be, is hard to say. Perhaps Ratoldus had simply learnt that the requisite materials had been assembled at Arras.[328] At any rate, as Jean Morinus and Edmund Bishop indicated, there is no reason whatsoever to doubt that Ratoldus was the prime mover. The inscription states, *pace* Samaran and Marichal, that the whole book, and not just the piecemeal Corbie additions, was made to his order: *Abbatis domni stat mentio sancta Ratoldi. Istum qui fecit scribere quippe librum.*

Morinus may also have been on to something when he suggested that the book had been commissioned by Ratoldus before he became abbot (972). For at some point close to 957, Engrannus, a monk of Corbie, became bishop of Cambrai (d. *c.* 960), an event that could easily have occasioned the making of a book such as BNF lat. 12052.[329] Palaeographically, that would certainly be possible. That the manuscript ended up at Corbie simply means that the scribes who wrote it sent it back there, major decoration and some minor initials lacking, when their work had come to a halt.

As for the underlying texts that Ratoldus caused to be worked together, one would be hard pressed to find a more unlikely combination. The sacramentary began life at Saint-Denis, passing later to Orléans, perhaps then to Saint-Vaast's, presumably gathering additions on new leaves and in its margins on the way; and the pontifical evidently

---

[327] Ed. K. Gamber and S. Rehle, *Das Sakramentar-Pontifikale des Bischofs Wolfgang von Regensburg* (Verona, Bibl. Cap., Cod. LXXXVII), Textus patristici et liturgici 15 (Regensburg, 1985). *CLLA*, no. 940.

[328] Note that Saint-Vaast's also produced liturgical books for monastic and secular houses. See above, pp. xlviii and xxxi, on Cologne, Dombibliothek, 141 and BNF lat. 9436.

[329] See the *Gesta episcoporum Cameracensium*, ed. Bethmann, 414–15, 433–4, with *Gallia Christiana*, III, col. 17.

came from Canterbury. Of the two, the pontifical is perhaps the most interesting, for it not only shows that numerous texts that survive only in eleventh-century books, notably *Claudius*, *Lanalet*, *Dunstan*, and in one instance Corpus 44, were originally compiled at least as early as the mid tenth century, but that the archbishops of Canterbury and the bishops of Worcester had access to, and were in the habit of using, some of the most developed *ordines* of their day. Necessarily the link between Canterbury and Worcester will have been Oswald, Archbishop Oda's nephew; and it may even have been Oswald who took the underlying pontifical abroad in the first place. But the only parts of this English book that seem to have been at all influential are its coronation order; the *ordines* for the ordination of church officers, particularly their arrangement (imitated in Cologne, Dombibliothek 141); and a prayer here and there.

BIBLIOGRAPHY

Abercrombie, N., *The Life and Work of Edmund Bishop* (London, 1959).

Andrieu, M. (ed.), *Les ordines romani du haut moyen âge*, 5 vols, Spicilegium Sacrum Lovaniense 11, 23, 24, 28 and 29 (Louvain, 1931–61).

———, (ed.), *Le pontifical romain au moyen-âge*, 4 vols, Studi e Testi 86, 87, 88 and 99 (Vatican City, 1938–41)

Ashworth, H., Obituary of Louis Brou, *EL* 75 (1961), 356–61.

Banting, H. M. J. (ed.), *Two Anglo-Saxon Pontificals*, HBS 104 (London, 1989).

Baroffio, B., 'L'Ordo Missae del Rituale-Messale Vallicellano E. 62', in *Traditio et Progressio: studi liturgici in onore del Prof. Adrien Nocent OSB*, ed. G. Farnedi, Analecta Liturgica 12, Studia Anselmiana 95 (Rome, 1988), 44–79.

Barré, H., and J. Deshusses, 'A la recherche du missel d'Alcuin', *EL* 82 (1968), 3–44.

Barriga Planas, J. R. (ed.), *El Sacramentario, Ritual y Pontifical di Roda* (Barcelona, 1975).

Bernard, P., 'Benoît d'Aniane est-il l'auteur de l'avertissement "Hucusque" et du Supplément au sacramentaire "Hadrianum"?', *Studi medievali*, 3rd series, 39.i (1998), 1–120.

Bethman, L. C. (ed.), *Gesta Episcopum Cameracensium,* MGH SS 7 (Hanover, 1846).

Bettazi, L., F. dell'Oro and L. Magnani (eds), *Sacramentarium episcopi Warmundi* (Ivrea and Turin, 1990).

Beyssac, P., and A. Mocquereau (eds), *Antiphonale missarum sancti Gregorii IXe–Xe siècle. Codex 239 de la Bibliothèque de Laon*, Paléographie musicale 10 (Tournai, 1909).

Bishop, T. A. M., *English Caroline Minuscule* (Oxford, 1971).

Blockley, K., M. Sparks and T. Tatton-Brown, *Canterbury Cathedral Nave. Archaeology, History and Architecture*, The Archaeology of Canterbury, new series (Canterbury, 1997).

Bouman, C. A., *Sacring and Crowning*, Bidragen van het Instituut voor middeleeuwe Geschiedenis der Rijks-Universiteit te Utrecht 30 (Groningen, Djakarta, 1957).

Braun, J., *Die liturgische Gewändung* (Freiburg-im-Breisgau, 1907).

———, *Der christliche Altar*, 2 vols (Munich, 1924).

Brommer, P. (ed.), *Ghärbald von Lüttich. Erstes Kapitular (Ghärbald I)*, MGH Capitula Episcoporum I (Hanover, 1984), pp. 3–21.

Brotanek, R., *Texte und Untersuchungen zu altenglischen Literatur und Kirchengeschichte* (Halle, 1913).

Brou, L. (ed.), *The Monastic Ordinal of St Vedast's Abbey, Arras*, 2 vols, HBS 86–7 (1955–6).

———, and J. Vives (eds), *Antifonario visigótico mozárabe de la Catedral de Léon*, Monumenta Hispaniae sacra 5.i (Madrid, 1959).

———, 'L'ancien office de Saint Vaast, evêque d'Arras', *Etudes grégoriennes* 4 (1961), 7–42.

Budny, M., *Insular, Anglo-Saxon and Early Anglo-Norman Manuscript Art at Corpus Christi College, Cambridge*, 2 vols (Kalamazoo, 1997).

Bullough, D. A., 'A neglected early-ninth-century manuscript of the Lindisfarne Vita S. Cuthberti', *ASE* 27 (1998), 105–37.

Burkitt, F. C., 'Obituary of J. A. Robinson', *JTS* 34 (1933), 225–31.

Cabrol, F., and H. Leclercq (eds), *Dictionnaire d'archéologie chrétienne et de liturgie*, 30 vols in 15 (Paris, 1907–53).

Cagin, P., *Te deum ou illatio*, 2 vols (Appuldurcombe and Tournai, 1906–12).

Capelle, B., 'L'oraison "Haec commixtio et consecratio" de la messe romaine', in *Mélanges en l'honneur de Monseigneur Michel Andrieu*, ed. M. Nédoncelle and C. Vogel (Strasbourg, 1956), 65–78.

Cavallo, G., G. Orofino and O. Pecere (eds), *Exultet: Rotuli liturgici del medioevale meridionale* (Rome, 1994).

Chavasse, A., 'A Rome, le Jeudi Saint, au VIIe siècle, d'après un vieil ordo', *Revue d'histoire ecclésiastique* 50 (1955), 21–35.

Chevalier, U., *Sacramentaire et martyrologe de l'abbaye de Saint-Remy*, Bibliothèque liturgique 7 (Paris, 1900).

Conner, P., *Anglo-Saxon Exeter. A Tenth-Century Cultural History* (Woodbridge, 1993).

Corrêa, A. (ed.), *The Durham Collectar*, HBS 107 (London, 1992).

d'Achéry, L., and J. Mabillon, *Acta Sanctorum ordinis sancti Benedicti in saeculorum classes distributa*, 7 vols in 9 (Paris, 1668–85).

———, *Spicilegium sive Collectio veterum aliquot scriptorum qui in Galliae bibliothecis detulerant*, 2nd ed., 3 vols (Paris, 1723).

d'Agincourt, S., *Histoire de l'Art par les Monuments depuis sa décadence au IVe siècle jusqu'à son renouvellement au XVIe siècle*, 6 vols (Paris, 1823).

Davril, A. (ed.), *The Winchcombe Sacramentary*, HBS 109 (London, 1995).

Decreaux, J. (ed.), *Le sacramentaire de Marmoutier* (Autun 19 bis), 2 vols, Studi di Antichitá Cristiana 38 (Vatican City, 1985).

Delisle, L. V., *Inventaire des manuscrits latins conservés B la Bibliothèque Nationale sous les numéros 8823–18613*, 5 parts (Paris, 1863–71).

———, *Le Cabinet des Manuscrits de la Bibliothèque Nationale*, 3 vols in 4 (Paris, 1868- 81).

———, 'Mémoire sur d'anciens sacramentaires', *Mémoires de l'Academie des inscriptions et belles-lettres* 32.i (Paris, 1886).

dell'Oro, F., and H. Rogger (eds), *Sacramentarium Tridentinum*, Monumenta liturgica ecclesiae Tridentinae saeculo XIII antiquiora 2A (Trent, 1985).

———, 'Frammento di Rotolo Pontificale del seculo XI', in *Traditio et Progressio: studi liturgici in onore del Prof. Adrien Nocent OSB*, ed. G. Farnedi, Analecta Liturgica 12, Studia Anselmiana 95 (Rome, 1988), 177–204.

Deshusses, J. (ed.), *Le sacramentaire grégorien*, 3 vols, Spicilegium Friburgense 16, 24 and 28, 2nd ed. (Fribourg, 1979–85).

———, 'Le "Supplement" au sacramentaire grégorien: Alcuin ou saint Benoît d'Aniane?', *Archiv für Liturgiewissenschaft* 9 (1965), 48–71.

———, 'Chronologie des grands sacramentaires de Saint-Amand', *RB* 87 (1977), 230–37.

———, 'Sur quelques anciens livres liturgiques de Saint-Thierry: les étapes d'une transformation de la liturgie', *Saint-Thierry, une abbaye du VIe au XXe siècle*, ed. M. Bur (Saint-Thierry, 1979), 133–45.

Doble, G. H. (ed.), *Pontificale Lanaletense*, HBS 74 (London, 1937).

Dreves, G. M., C. Blume and H. M. Bannister (eds), *Analecta Hymnica*, 55 vols (Leipzig, 1886- 1922).

Duine, F., *Inventaire liturgique de l'hagiographie bretonne*, La Bretagne et les pays celtiques 16 (Paris, 1922).

Dumas A., and J. Deshusses (eds), *Liber Sacramentorum Gellonensis*, 2 vols, CCSL 159 and 159A (Turnhout, 1981).

Dummler, E., 'Aus Handschriften', *Neues Archiv* 5 (1880), 621–36.

Dumville, D. N., *Liturgy and the Ecclesiastical History of Late Anglo-Saxon England* (Woodbridge, 1992).

———, *English Caroline Script and Monastic History: Studies in Benedictinism A.D. 950- 1030* (Woodbridge, 1993).

Ebner, A., *Quellen und Forschungen zur Geschichte und Kunstgeschichte des Missale Romanum im Mittelalter. Iter Italicum* (Freiburg-im-Breisgau, 1896).

Eichler, H., and W. Eckhardt (eds), *Kunst und Kultur in Weserraum 800–1600. Ausstellung des Landes Nordrhein-Westfalen, Corvey, 28.5–15.9.1966*, 2 vols, 3rd ed. (Aschendorff Münster, 1966–7).

Escudier, D., 'Le scriptorium de Saint-Vaast d'Arras des origines au XIIe siècle. Contribution à l'étude des notations neumatiques du nord de la France', *Bibliothèque de l'Ecole des Chartes* 129, Position des thèses (1971), 27–48.

———, 'La notation musicale de Saint-Vaast d'Arras. Étude d'une particularité graphique', *Musicologie médiévale. Notations et Séquences*, ed. M. Huglo (Paris, 1987), 107–120.

Evans, J., *Time and Chance: The Story of Arthur Evans and his Forebears* (London, 1943).

Feasey, H. J., *Ancient English Holy Week Practice* (London, 1897).

Fehr, B., *Die Hirtenbriefe Aelfrics in Altenglischer und Lateinischer Fassung*, Bibliothek der Angelsächsischen Prosa 11 (Hamburg, 1914).

———, 'Altenglische Ritualtexte fur Krankenbesuch, heilige Ölung und Begräbnis', *Texte und Forschungen zur englischen Kulturgeschichte. Festgabe für Felix Liebermann zum 20 Juli 1921*, ed. M. Förster and K. Wildhagen (Halle, 1921), pp. 20–67.

Fenlon, I. (ed.), *Cambridge Music Manuscripts 900–1700* (Cambridge, 1982).

Foley, E. B. (ed.), *The First Ordinary of the Royal Abbey of St.-Denis in France*, Spicilegium Friburgense 32 (Fribourg, 1990).

Fraipont, J. (ed.), *Sancti Fulgentii episcopi Ruspensis Opera*, 2 vols, CCSL 91, 91A (Turnhout, 1968).

Frere, W. H., *Pontifical Services*, 2 vols, Alcuin Club Collections 3–4 (Oxford, 1901).

———, 'The Carolingian Gregorianum: its sections and their numbering', *JTS* 18 (1916), 47–55.

———, (ed.), *Antiphonale Sarisburiense*, Plainsong and Medieval Music Society, 4 vols (London, 1925).

Froger, J. (ed.), *Le codex 123 de la Bibliothèque Angelica de Rome (XIe siècle). Graduel et Tropaire de Bologna*, Paléographie musicale 18 (Berne, 1969).

Gamber, K., 'Fragmenta Liturgica', *Sacris Erudiri* 21 (1972–3), 241–66.

———, *Codices Latini Liturgici Antiquiores*, Spicilegia Friburgensis Subsidia, 2nd ed. (Fribourg, 1969), and Supplement (1988).

———, and S. Rehle (eds), *Das Sakramentar-Pontifikale des Bischofs Wolfgang von Regensburg* (Verona, Bibl. Cap., Cod. LXXXVII), Textus patristici et liturgici 15 (Regensburg, 1985).

Gameson, R., 'The origin of the Exeter Book of Old English poetry', *Anglo-Saxon England* 25 (1995).

———, *The Role of Art in the Late Anglo-Saxon Church* (Oxford, 1995).

Ganz, D., *Corbie in the Carolingian Renaissance*, Beihefte der Francia 20 (Sigmaringen, 1990).

Gasparri, F., 'Le scriptorium de Corbie', *Scrittura e civiltà* 15 (1991), 289–305.

Gerbert, M., *Monumenta Veteris Liturgicae Alemmanicae*, 2 vols (Saint-Blaise, 1777–8).

Gillert, K., 'Lateinische Handschriften in St Petersburg', *Neues Archiv der Gesellschaft für ältere deutsche Geschichtskunde*, Fünfter Band, Drittes Heft 5 (1880), 243–65.

Gittos, H., 'Sacred Space in Anglo-Saxon England: Liturgy, Architecture and Place', unpubl. D.Phil. thesis, Oxford, 2001.

———, and B. A. Bedingfield (eds), *Ritual and Belief*, HBS Subsidia 4 (London, forthcoming).

Gjerløw, L., *Adoratio Crucis* (Oslo, 1961).

Graf, H. J., *Palmenweihe und Palmenprozession in der lateinischen Liturgie*,

Veröffentlichungen des Missionspriesterseminars, St Augustin, Siegburg 5 (Kaldenkirchen, 1959).

Grégoire, R., 'Prières liturgiques médiévales en l'honneur de saint Benoit, sainte Scolastique et de saint Maur', Analecta Monastica 7, *Studia Anselmiana* 54 (Rome, 1965), 1–85.

Gremont, D., and L. Donnat, 'Fleury, le Mont Saint-Michel et l'Angleterre à la fin du Xe et au début du XIe siècle à propos du manuscrit d'Orléans no. 127 (105)', *Millénaire monastique de Mont Saint-Michel*, ed. J. Laporte *et al.*, 4 vols (Paris, 1966–7) I, 751–93.

Grenier, P., *Histoire de la ville et du comte de Corbie (des origines à 1400)*, 2 vols (Paris, 1910).

Guillotel, H., 'L'exode du clerge breton devant les invasions scandinaves', *Mémoires de la Société d'Histoire et d'Archéologie de Bretagne* 59 (1982), 269–315.

Gullotta, G., and J. Ruysschaert, *Gli antichi cataloghi e i codici della Abbazia di Nonantola*, 2 vols, Studi e Testi 182–182A (Vatican City, 1955).

Günzel, B. (ed.), *Aelfwine's Prayerbook (London, British Library, Cotton Titus D. xxvi + xxvii)*, HBS 108 (London, 1993).

Gy, P-M., 'Die Segnung von Milch und Hönig in der Osternacht', in *Paschatis Solemnia*, ed. B. Fischer and J. Wagner (Freiburg-in-Breisgau, 1959), 206–12.

Haggenmüller, R., *Die Überlieferung der Beda und Egbert zugeschreibenen Bussbücher*, Europäischer Hochschulschriften 461 (Frankfurt am Main, 1991).

Hamilton, S., *The Practice of Penance* (Bury St Edmunds, 2001), pp. 228–30.

Hanssens, J. M., *Amalarii Episcopi Opera liturgica omnia*, 3 vols, Studi e Testi 138–40 (Vatican City, 1948–50).

Hartzheim, J., *Catalogus historicus-criticus codicum MSS Bibliothecae Ecclesiae Metropolitanae Coloniensis* (Cologne, 1752).

Hen, Y. (ed.), *The Sacramentary of Echternach*, HBS 110 (London, 1997).

Hesbert, R.-J. (ed.), *Corpus Antiphonalium Officii*, 6 vols, Rerum ecclesiasticarum Documenta, Series maior, Fontes 7–12 (Rome, 1963–79).

Heslop, T. A., 'The production of *de luxe* manuscripts and the patronage of King Cnut and Queen Emma', *Anglo-Saxon England* 19 (1990), 151–91.

———, review of Dumville, *Early Caroline Script* in *JTS* 45.i (1994), 378–81.

Hildberg, I., and M. Kamptner (eds), *Sancti Eusebii Hieronymi Epistolae*, Corpus Scriptorum Ecclesiasticorum Latinorum 54–55.ii, 3 vols in 5 (Vienna, 1910–96).

Hohler, C., 'Some service-books of the Anglo-Saxon Church', in *Tenth Century Studies*, ed. D. Parsons (Leicester, 1975), pp. 60–83, and 217–27.

Holder-Egger, O. (ed.), *Translatio SS Tiburtii, Marcellini et Petri ad S. Medardum*, MGH SS 15.i (Hanover, 1887), pp. 391–5.

————, (ed.), *Ex translatione S. Sebastiani auctore Odilone*, MGH SS 15.i (Hanover, 1887), pp. 377–91.

————, (ed.), *Monumenta Vedastina Minora*, MGH SS 15.i (Hanover, 1887), pp. 399–402.

Holthausen, F., 'Altenglische Interlinearversionen lateinischer Gebete und Beichten', *Anglia* 45 (1941), 230–54.

Huglo, M. (ed.), *Musicologie médiévale. Notations et Séquences* (Paris, 1987).

Jackson, R. A., *Ordines coronationis Franciae. Texts and ordines for the Coronation of Frankish and French Kings and Queens in the Middle Ages*, 2 vols (Philadelphia, 1995- 2000).

James, M. R., *A Descriptive Catalogue of the Manuscripts in the Library of Corpus Christi College, Cambridge*, 2 vols (Cambridge, 1912).

Jolly, K. L., *Popular Religion in Late Saxon England. Elf Charms in Context* (Chapel Hill, 1996).

Jones, C. A., *A Lost Work by Amalarius of Metz*, Henry Bradshaw Society, Subsidia II (London, 2001).

————, 'The chrism mass in later Anglo-Saxon England', in *Ritual and Belief*, ed. Gittos and Bedingfield, HBS Subsidia (London, forthcoming).

Jungmann, J. A., *Die lateinischen Bussriten in ihrer geschichtlichen Entwicklung*, Forschungen zur Geschichte des innerkirchlichen Liebens 3–4 (Innsbruck, 1932).

————, *The Mass of the Roman Rite. Its Origins and Development* (Missarum Sollemnia), transl. F. A. Brunner, 2 vols (New York, 1950).

Jurot, R., *L'ordinaire liturgique du diocèse de Besançon (Besançon, Bibl. mun. MS. 101)*, Spicilegium Friburgense 38 (Fribourg, 1999).

Keefer, S., 'The Veneration of the Cross synaxis in Anglo-Saxon England', in *Ritual and Belief*, ed. Gittos and Bedingfield, HBS Subsidia (London, forthcoming).

Kelly, T. F., *The Beneventan Chant* (Cambridge, 1989).

Ker, N. R., *Catalogue of Manuscripts containing Anglo-Saxon* (Oxford, 1957).

Knowles, D., and C. N. L. Brooke (eds), *The Monastic Constitutions of Lanfranc* (Oxford, 2001).

Kornexl, L., *Die Regularis concordia und ihre altenglische Interlinearversion mit Einleitung und Kommentar*, Texte und Untersuchungen zur englischen Philologie 17 (Munich, 1993).

Kozachek, T., 'The Repertory of Chant for Dedicating Churches in the Middle Ages: Music, Liturgy and Ritual', unpubl. doctoral dissertation, Harvard, 1995.

Krusch, B. (ed.), *Vita S. Vedasti*, MGH rer. Meroving. 3 (Hanover, 1896), 399–412.

Lambot, C. (ed.), *North Italian Services of the Eleventh Century*, HBS 67 (London, 1931).

Lapidge, M., 'The lost *passio metrica sancti Dionysii* by Hilduin of Saint-Denis', *Mittelateinisches Jahrbuch* 22 (1987), 56–80.

————, (ed.), *Anglo-Saxon Litanies of the Saints*, HBS 106 (London, 1991).

————, 'Abbot Germanus, Winchcombe, Ramsey and the Cambridge Psalter', in *Words, Texts and Manuscripts. Studies in Anglo-Saxon Culture presented to Helmut Gneuss on the Occasion of his Sixty-Fifth Birthday*, ed. M. Korhammer, K. Reichl and H. Sauer (Woodbridge, 1992), 99–129.

Laporte, J., 'Quelques particularités du recueil des "Benedictiones Pontificales" de Durand de Mende', in *Mélanges en l'honneur de Monseigneur Andrieu*, ed. M. Nédoncelle and C. Vogel (Strasbourg, 1956), pp. 279–86.

————, *Le graduel romain. Étude critique par les moines de Solesmes. II: Les sources* (Solesmes, 1957).

Leclercq, H., 'Scrutin', *DACL* 15.i, 1037–52.

Legner, A., A. von Euw and J. M. Plotzek (eds), *Rhein und Maas. Kunst und Kultur 800–1400*, Ausstellung des Schnütgen-Museums der Stadt Köln, vom 14 Mai bis zum 23 Juli, 1972, 2 vols (Cologne, 1972).

Leroquais, V., *Les sacramentaires et les missels manuscrits*, 4 vols (Paris, 1924).

————, 'L'Ordo Missae du sacramentaire d'Amiens. Paris, Bibliothèque nationale, ms. lat. 9432 (IXe s.)', *EL* 41 (1927), 435–46.

————, *Les breviaires manuscrits*, 6 vols (Paris, 1934).

————, *Les pontificaux manuscrits*, 4 vols (Paris, 1937).

Leutermann, T., 'Ordo Cassinensis Hebdomadae maioris (saec. XII)', *Miscellanea Cassinese* 20 (1941), 95–117.

Levillain, L., *Examen critique des chartes mérovingiennes et carolingiennes d'abbaye de Corbie* (Paris, 1902).

Mabillon, J., *De re diplomatica libri VI*, 2 vols (Paris, 1681–1704).

MacGregor, A. J., *Fire and Light in the Western Triduum. Their use at Tenebrae and at the Paschal Vigil*, Alcuin Club Collections 71 (Collegeville, Minn., 1992).

Marriott, W. B., *Vestiarium Christianum* (London, 1868).

Martène, E., *De antiquis ecclesiae ritibus*, 1st ed. (Rouen, 1700–2).

Tractatus de antiqua ecclesie disciplina in diuinis celebrandis officiis (Lyons, 1706).

————, and U. Durand, *Thesaurus novus anecdotum*, 5 vols (Paris, 1717).

————, *De antiquis ecclesiae ritibus*, 2nd ed. (Antwerp, 1736–48).

Martimort, A. G., *La documentation liturgique de dom Edmond Martène*, Studi e Testi 279 (Vatican City, 1978).

Martini, A. (ed.), *Il cosidetto Pontificale di Poitiers*, Rerum Ecclesiasticarum Documenta, Series Maior, Fontes 14 (Vatican City, 1979).

Meersseman, G. G. (ed.), *Les capitules du diurnal de Saint-Denis*, Spicilegium Friburgense 30 (Fribourg, 1986).

Ménard, H. (ed.), *Diui Gregorii papae huius nominis primi, cognomento magni liber sacramentorum* (Paris, 1642), reprinted in PL 78, cols 25–240.

————, *Notae et obseruationes in librum sacramentorum Sancti Gregorii Magni Papae I* (Paris, 1641), reprinted in PL 78, cols 263–602.

Mocquereau, A. (ed.), *Le répons-graduel Iustus ut Palma*, 2 vols, Paléographie musicale 2–3 (Solesmes, 1891–2).

————, (ed.), *Le codex 903 de la Bibliothèque nationale de Paris (XIe siècle). Graduel de Saint- Yrieix.* Paléographie musicale 13 (Tournai, 1925).

Moeller, E. (ed.), *Corpus Benedictionum Pontificalium*, 4 vols, CCSL 162, 162A–C (Turnhout, 1980–81).

Mohlberg, L. C. (ed.), *Liber Sacramentorum Romani aecclesiae ordinis anni circuli*, Rerum ecclesiasticarum Documenta, Series maior, Fontes 4 (Rome, 1960).

————, (ed.) *Missale Gothicum*, Rerum ecclesiasticarum Documenta, Series maior, Fontes 5 (Vatican City, 1961).

Morin, G., 'Sur la date et la provenance de l'ordo scrutinorum du Cod. Ambros. T. 27 sup', *RB* 46 (1934), 216–23.

Morinus, J., *Commentarius de sacris ecclesiae ordinationibus* (Paris, 1655). A second edition appeared at Antwerp in 1695.

————, *Commentarius historicus de disciplina in administratione sacramenti poenitentiae*, 2nd ed. (Antwerp, 1682).

Mundó, A., 'Ordinis Romani LI indoles et tempus', *Liturgica* 2 (Montserrat, 1958), pp. 181–216.

Muzerelle, D., *Manuscrits datés des Bibliothèques de France. I: Cambrai* (Paris, 2000).

Nelson, J. L., 'The second English *ordo*', in her *Politics and Ritual in Early Medieval Europe* (London, 1986), 361–74.

Netzer, V., *L'introduction de la messe romaine sous les carolingiens* (Paris, 1910).

Nicholson, E. W. B., *Early Bodleian Music* (London, 1913).

Nocent, A., 'Un fragment de sacramentaire de Sens du Xe siècle', *in Miscellanea liturgica in onore di sua eminenza il Cardinale Giacomo Lercaro*, 2 vols (Rome, 1966–7) II, 649–794.

Odenthal, A., 'Zwei Formulare des Apologientyps der Messe vor dem Jahre 1000', *Archiv für Liturgiewissenschaft* 37 (1995), 25–45.

Omont, H., *Concordance des numéros anciens et des numéros actuels des manuscrits latins de la Bibliothèque Nationale* (Paris, 1903).

Orchard, N. A., 'An Anglo-Saxon Mass for St Willibrord and its later liturgical uses', *ASE* 24 (1995), 1–10.

————, '*Pater sancte*: an ordination prayer used by the Anglo-Saxon church', *RB* 111 (2001), 446–63.

————, 'Some notes on the Sacramentary of Echternach', *Archiv für Liturgiewissenschaft* 43- 44 (2002), 1–21.

———— (ed.), *The Leofric Missal*, 2 vols, HBS 113–114 (London, 2002).

————, 'The ninth- and tenth-century additions to Cambrai, Médiathèque municipale, 164', *RB*, forthcoming.

Palazzo, E., 'Les deux rituels d'un libellus de Saint-Amand (Paris, Bibliothèque nationale, lat. 13764)', in *Rituels. Mélanges offerts à Pierre-Marie Gy, o.p.*, ed. P. de Clerck and E. Palazzo (Paris, 1990), 423–36.

Pamelius, J., *Liturgica Latinorum*, 2 vols (Cologne, 1571).

Panofsky, E., *Abbot Suger on the Abbey Church of St.-Denis and its Art Treasures*, 2nd ed. (Princeton, 1979).

Paredi, A., *Sacramentarium Bergomense*, Monumenta Bergomensiana 6 (Bergamo, 1962).

Parsons, D. (ed.), *Tenth Century Studies* (Leicester, 1975).

Peigné-Delacourt, A. (ed.), *Monasticon Gallicanum. Collection de 168 planches de vues topographiques représentant les monastères de l'ordre de Saint-Benoît, Congrégation de Saint-Maur* (Paris, 1871).

Pitou, P., *Petri Pithoei comes theologus siue spicilegium ex sacra messe* (Paris, 1684).

Planchart, A., 'Troper', *New Grove Dictionary of Music* 25, 777–94.

Plotzek, J. (ed.), *Glaube und Wissen im Mittelalter. Katalogbuch zur Ausstellung, Erzbischöfliches Diozesanmuseum, Köln, 7. August bis 15. November, 1998*, (Munich, 1998).

Prescott, A., 'The structure of English pre-Conquest benedictionals', *British Library Journal* 13 (1987), 118–58.

————, 'The text of the Benedictional of St Æthelwold', in *Bishop Aethelwold: His Career and Influence*, ed. B. Yorke (Woodbridge, 1988), 119–47.

————, *The Benedictional of St Æthelwold* (London, 2002).

Quentin, H., *Les martyrologes historiques du moyen âge* (Paris, 1908).

Rankin, S., 'Neumatic notations in Anglo-Saxon England', in *Musicologie médiévale. Notations et Séquences*, ed. Huglo, 129–44.

Rasmussen, N. K., 'Unité et diversité des pontificaux latins', in *Liturgie de l'église particulière et liturgie de l'église universelle. Conférences Saint-Serge, XXIIe semaine d'études liturgiques, Paris, 30 juin–3 juillet, 1975*, ed. A. Pistoia, C. M. Triacca and A. M. Triacca, Biblioteca Ephemerides Liturgicae, Subsidia 7 (Rome, 1976), 393–410.

————, and M. Haverals, *Les pontificaux manuscrits du haut moyen âge, genèse du livre de l'évêque*, Spicilegium Sacrum Lovaniense 49 (Paris, 1998).

Reynolds, R. E., 'The De officiis VII graduum: its origins and early medieval development', *Medieval Studies* 34 (1972), 113–51.

Richter G., and A. Schönfelder (eds), *Sacramentarium Fuldense saeculi X* (Fulda, 1912), repr. HBS 101 (London, 1977).

Richter, M. (ed.), *Canterbury Professions*, Canterbury and York Society 67 (London, 1973).

Rose, V., *Die Handschriften-Verzeichnisse der Königlichen Bibliothek zu Berlin*, 3 vols in 5 (Berlin, 1891–1919).

Rosenthal, J., 'The Pontifical of St Dunstan', in *St Dunstan: His Life, Times and Cult*, ed. N. Ramsay, M. Sparks and T. Tatton-Brown (Woodbridge, 1992), 143–63.

Sainte-Marthe, D. de (ed.), *Gallia Christiana*, 13 vols (Paris, 1715–1865).

Saint-Roch, P. (ed.), *Liber Sacramentorum Engolismensis*, CCSL 159C (Turnhout, 1987).

Salmon, P., 'L'*ordo missae* dans dix manuscrits du Xe au XVe siècle', in his *Analecta liturgica*, Studi e testi 273 (Vatican City, 1974), 197–221.

———, 'Textes des ordines romani du Pontifical romano-germanique et de l'Ordinaire papal dans les sacramentaires des XIIe and XIIIe', in his *Analecta Liturgica*, 225–62.

Samaran C., and R. Marichal, *Catalogue des manuscrits en écriture latin portant des indications de date, de lieu ou de copiste*, 7 vols in 14 (Paris, 1959–85).

Saxer, V., *Le culte de Marie Madeleine en Occident*, Cahiers d'archéologie et d'histoire 3, ed. R. Louis (Paris, 1959).

Schaller, D., and E. Könsgen, *Initia Carminum latinorum saeculo undecimo Antiquiorum* (Göttingen, 1977).

Schmidt, H. A. P., *Hebdomada Sancta*, 2 vols (Rome, 1956–7).

Schramm, P. E., 'Die Krönung bei den Westfranken und Angelsachsen von 878 bis zum 1000', *Zeitschrift für Rechtsgeschichte* 55, Abt. 23 (1934), 117–242.

Sole, L. M., 'Some Anglo-Saxon Cuthbert *liturgica*: the manuscript evidence', *RB* 108 (1998), 104–44.

Sollerius, J. B., J. Pinius, G. Cuperus and P. Boschius, *Acta Santorum Julii* VI (Antwerp, 1729).

Staerck, A., *Les manuscrits latins conservés a la bibliothèque impériale de Saint-Petersbourg*, 2 vols (St Petersburg, 1910).

Steiner, R., 'Reproaches', *The New Grove Dictionary of Music and Musicians*, ed. S. Sadie, 20 vols (Washington, 1980) XV, 750–51.

Surcin, l'Abbé, *La paroisse de Saint-Paterne dans le passé et dans le présent* (Orléans, 1894).

Symons, T. (ed.), *The Regularis Concordia Anglicae Nationis Monachorum Sanctimonialiumque. The Monastic Agreement of the Monks and Nuns of the English Nation* (London, 1953).

Terroine A., and L. Fossier, *Chartes et Documents de l'Abbaye de Saint-Magloire*, 3 vols (Turnhout, 1976–98).

Toswell, M. J., 'St Martial and the dating of late Anglo-Saxon manuscripts', *Scriptorium* 51 (1997), 3–14.

Turner, D. H. (ed.), *The Missal of the New Minster, Winchester*, HBS 93 (London, 1962).

———, 'A 10th–11th century Noyon sacramentary', *Studia Patristica 5, Texte und Untersuchungen zur Geschichte der altchristlichen Literatur* 80, ed. F. L. Cross (Berlin, 1962), 143–51.

——, (ed.), *The Claudius Pontificals*, HBS 97 (London, 1971).

Turton, Z. H., *The Vedast Missal, or Missale parvum Vedastinum* (London, 1904).

Ultee, U., *The Abbey of St Germain des Près in the Seventeenth Century* (New Haven, 1981).

Vezzosi, A. F. (ed.), *Venerabilis Viri J. M. Thomasi Opera omnia*, 7 vols (Rome, 1747–54).

Vogel, C., and R. Elze (eds), *Le pontificale Romano-Germanique du dixième siècle*, 3 vols, Studi e Testi 226, 227 and 269 (Vatican City, 1963–72).

von Euw, A., and J. M. Plotzek, *Die Handschriften der Sammlung Ludwig*, 4 vols (Cologne, 1979–85).

Waitz, G. (ed.), *Translatio et Miracula SS Marcellini et Petri auctore Einhardo*, MGH SS 15.i (Hanover, 1887), pp. 238–64.

Wallis, F. E. (ed. and transl.), *Bede: The Reckoning of Time* (Liverpool, 1999).

Ward, P. L., 'An early version of the Anglo-Saxon coronation ceremony', *English Historical Review* 57 (1942), 345–61.

Wareham, A., 'St Oswald's family and kin', in *St Oswald of Worcester. Life and Influence*, ed. N. Brooks and C. Cubitt (Leicester, 1996), 46–63.

Warner, G., and H. A. Wilson (eds), *The Benedictional of St Æthelwold*, Roxburghe Club Publications (Oxford, 1910).

Werner, K. F., 'Gauzlin von Saint-Denis und die westfränkische Reichstellung von Amiens (März 880). Ein Beitrag zur Vorgeschichte von Odos Königtum', *Deutsches Archiv für Erforschung des Mittelalters* 35 (1979), 395–462.

Whitelock, D., M. Brett and C. N. L. Brooke, *Councils and Synods with other documents relating to the English Church I, A.D. 871–1204*, 2 vols (Oxford, 1981).

Wickham Legg, J. (ed.), *Missale ad usum ecclesiae Westmonasteriensis*, 3 vols, HBS 1, 5 and 12 (1891–7).

Willis, G. G., 'Ember Days', in his *Essays in Early Roman Liturgy*, Alcuin Club Collections 46 (London, 1964), 49–98.

Wilmart, A., 'Corbie, manuscrits liturgiques de', *DACL* 3.ii, cols 2913–2958.

——, 'L'index liturgique de Saint-Thierry', *RB* 30 (1913), 437–50.

——, 'Les frères défunts de Saint-Denis au déclin du IXe siècle', *Revue Mabillon* 15 (1925), 241–57.

——, 'Un sacramentaire à l'usage de Saint-Germain-des-Près. Mentions nécrologiques relatives à ce monastère', *Revue Mabillon* 17 (1927), 279–94.

——, 'Prières médiévales pour l'adoration de la Croix', *EL* 46 (1932), 22–65.

Wilson, H. A. (ed.), *The Missal of Robert of Jumièges*, HBS 11 (London, 1896).

——, (ed.), *The Benedictional of Archbishop Robert*, HBS 24 (London, 1903).

Woolley, R. M. (ed.), *The Canterbury Benedictional*, HBS 51 (London, 1917).
Wormald, P., *The Making of English Law*, 2 vols (Oxford: Blackwell, 1999, and forthcoming).
Zeumer, F. (ed.), *Formulae Merovingici et Karolini Aevi*, MGH Legum Sectio 5: Formulae (Hanover, 1886).

EDITORIAL PROCEDURE

All abbreviations (except for the dates of feasts given in superscriptions) have been silently expanded; e caudata is registered as ę. Sections of text written in orange minuscule are printed in italics; sections written in capitals, whether of orange or brown, are registered throughout in normal capitals. Indications of how the colours alternate will be found in the notes. The eleven entries written in orange in the calendar, however, have been printed in bold without further comment.

Passages written in a smaller than usual minuscule (chant, some sections of *ordines*, and so on) have been printed in smaller type; Corbie additions of the late tenth and eleventh centuries are in monospaced type. Punctuation throughout is, as far as possible, that of the manuscript.

Formulae in the main body of the book have been numbered in a continuous sequence 1–2338; formulae added in the margins, 1*–23*; and the material jotted on fol. A (a singleton), i–x.

THE TEXT

i In spiritu humilitatis.

ii Suscipe sancta trinitas hanc oblationem quam tibi offero in memoriam incarnationis, natiuitatis, passionis, rexurrectionis, ascensionisque domini nostri iesu christi, et in ueneratione beatissimę semper uirginis marię et omnium sanctorum qui tibi placuerunt, ab initio mundi, et eorum quorum hic nomina et reliquię habentur, ut illis proficiat ad honorem, nobis autem ad salutem, ut illi pro nobis intercedere dignentur in cęlis, quorum memoriam agimus in terris. Per.

<MISSA>

iii Omnium sanctorum intercessionibus quesumus domine gratia tua nos protegat, et christianis omnibus uiuentibus atque defunctis misericordiam tuam ubique prętende, ut uiuentes ab omnibus inpugnationibus sint tua opitulacione defensi, et defuncti remissionem mereantur suorum omnium accipere delictorum. Per dominum.

iv SVPER OBLATA. Oblationibus nostris omnipotens deus ob tuorum omnium sanctorum honorem ueniam nobis tribue peccatorum, et christianis omnibus uiuentibus atque defunctis, haec presens libatio et pręsentis uitae subsidia, et premia conferat sempiterna. Per dominum.

v POST COMMVNIONEM. Haec sacrificia que sumpsimus domine, meritis et intercessionibus omnium sanctorum nobis ad salutem proficiant, et christianis omnibus uiuentibus atque defunctis, te fauente aeterna ac temporalia bona adquirant.

3

vi Sit nobis hoc sacramentum tuum[1] domine iesu, ad uitam, sit ad remissionem peccatorum, fiat nobis hęc eucharistia ad uitam, et uiscera misericordi et graciam salutis sanitatemque animarum nostrarum. Amen.

vii DVM FRANGITVR CORPVS DOMINI ET MITTITVR IN CALICE. Hec sacrosancta comistio corporis et sanguinis domine nostri iesu christi fiat mihi et omnibus sumentibus salus mentis et corporis et ad[2] . . . eterna preparatio salutaris. Per eundem.

viii ORATIO AD RECIPIENDVM CORPVS DOMINI. Domine sancte pater omnipotens aeterne deus da mihi hoc corpus et sanguinem domini nostri iesu christi, ita sumere ut merear per hoc remissionem omnium peccatorum accipere, et cum spiritu sancto replere. Per eundem.

ix ALIA. Perceptio corporis et sanguinis tui domine iesu christe quem ego peccator indignus sumere presumo, oro ut non mihi proficiat ad iudicium neque ad condempnationem, sed sit mihi pro tua pietate ad salutem anime meę ad remissionem omnium peccatorum meorum saluator mundi.

x POST PERCEPTIONEM. Domine iesu christe fili dei uiui qui ex uoluntate patris cooperante spiritu sancto per mortem tuam mundum libera me per hoc sacrum corpus et sanguinem filii tui domini nostri iesu christi, a cunctis iniquitatibus et uniuersis malis, et fac me tuis obedire praeceptis, et[3] . . . numquam in perpetuum . . . Per eundem.

---

[1] Supplied interlinearly.
[2] The following word illegible.
[3] The following word illegible.

[1] In lines of orangy-red and green.
[2] Second *n* of *condantur* added interlinearly.

XXXVI. Oratio quando spargitur aqua in domo.

XXXVII. Benedictio domus.

XXXVIII. Benedictio ferri.

XXXVIIII. Consecratio ferri.

/f. Bv / XL. Martyriiologium siue compotum.

XLI. Qualiter missa romana celebratur.

XLII. In uigilia natalis domini ad nonam.

XLIII. In nocte de uigilia domini.

XLIIII. Ad sanctam anastasiam primo mane.

XLV. Ad sanctum petrum in die.

XLVI. Orationes de natale domini.

XLVII. In natale sancti stephani.

XLVIII. In natale sancti iohannis euangelistae nocte.

XLVIIII. Item in die ad missam.

L. In natale innocentum.

LI. Dominica .i. post natale domini.

LII. In natale sancti siluestri papae.

LIII. Benedictio in uigilia octabas domini.

LIIII. Octabas domini ad sanctam mariam.

LV. In natale sanctae genoucfę.

LVI. Dominica .ii. post octabas domini.

LVII. In uigilia epiphaniae.

LVIII. In die ad sanctum petrum.

LVIIII. Dominica .i. post theophania.

LX. Octabas epiphaniae, et depositio sancti hilarii episcopi.

LXI. Natale sancti felicis in pincis.

LXII. Natale sancti marcelli papae.

LXIII. Natale sanctae priscae uirginis.

LXIIII. Natale sanctorum mariae et marthae.

LXV. Dominica .ii. post theophania.

LXVI. Natale sanctorum sebastiani et fabiani.

LXVII. Natale sanctae agnę martiris.

LXVIII. Natale sancti uincentii martiris.

LXVIIII. Dominica .iii. post theophania.

LXX. Conuersio sancti pauli, et natale sancti proiecti martyris.

LXXI. Natale sanctae agnae secundo.

LXXII. Ypapanti ad sanctam mariam, benedictio super candelas.

LXXIII. Collecta ad sanctum adrianum.

LXXIIII. Item ad missam in die.

LXXV. Dominica .iiii. post theophania.

LXXVI. Natale sanctae agathę.

LXXVII. Natale sancti vedasti confessoris.

LXXVIII. Dominica .v. post theophania.

LXXVIIII. Natale sancti ualentini martyris.

LXXX. Cathedra sancti petri.

LXXXI. Dominica .vi. post theophania.

LXXXII. Natale sancti gregorii papae.

LXXXIII. Natale cuthberhti episcopi.

LXXXIIII. Natale sancti benedicti abbatis.

LXXXV. Annuntiatio sanctae mariae.

LXXXVI. In septuagesima.

LXXXVII. In sexagesima.

/f. Cr   / LXXXVIII. In quinquagesima.

LXXXVIIII. In capite ieiunii ordo qualiter agantur circa penitentes. Feria iiii.

XC. Item ad missam ad sanctam anastasiam.

XCI. Feria .v. statio ad sanctum georgium.

XCII. Feria .vi. ad apostolos iohannem et paulum.

XCIII. In quadragesima.

XCIIII. Feria .ii. ad sanctum petrum ad uincula.

XCV. Feria .iii. ad sanctam anastasiam.

XCVI. Feria .iiii. mensis .i. ad sanctam mariam maiorem.

XCVII. Feria .v. ad sanctum laurentium foris murum.

XCVIII. Feria .vi. ad apostolos.

XCVIIII. Oratio ad capillaturam.

C. Oratio ad clericum faciendum.

CI. Oratio ad barbas tundendas.

CII. Sermo de .vii. gradibus ecclesię.

CIII. Sabbato in .xii. lectionibus ad sanctum petrum.

CIIII. Ordinatio clericorum seu ostiarum.

CV. Ordinatio lectorum.

CVI. Ordinatio exorcistarum.

CVII. Ordinatio acolitorum.

CVIII. Capitula sancti gregorii.

CVIIII. Ordinatio subdiaconi.

CX. Ordo qualiter ordinandum romae.

CXI. Ordinatio diaconi.

CXII. Benedictio stolae siue planetae sacerdotis seu leuitae.

CXIII. Benedictio post stolas super omnes.

CXIIII. Ad consummandum diaconi officium.

CXV. Missa in die consecrationis diaconi.

CXVI. Item ad missam dicendam episcopus.

CXVII. Ordinatio presbiterorum.

CXVIII. Benedictio post casulas super omnes.

CXVIIII. Benedictio manuum sacerdotis.

CXX. Consummatio presbiterorum.

CXXI. Missa in die consecrationis prebiterorum.

CXXII. Dominica uacat.

CXXIII. Feria .ii. ad sanctum clementem.

CXXIIII. Feria .iii. ad sanctam balbinam.

CXXV. Feria .iiii. ad sanctam ceciliam.

CXXVI. Feria .v. ad sanctam mariam trans tyberim.

CXXVII. Feria .vi. ad sanctum uitalem.

CXXVIII. Sabbato ad sanctos marcellinum et petrum.

CXXVIIII. Dominica ad sanctum laurentium foris murum.

CXXX. Feria .ii. ad sanctum marcum.

CXXXI. Feria .iii. ad sanctam potentianam.

CXXXII. Feria .iiii. Ad sanctum Syxtum.

CXXXIII. Feria .v. ad sanctos cosmam et damianum.

CXXXIIII. Feria .vi. ad sanctum laurentium in lucina.

CXXXV. Sabbato ad sanctam susannam.

CXXXVI. Dominica ad hierusalem.

/f. Cv   / CXXXVII. Feria .ii. ad sanctos quattuor coronatos.

CXXXVIII. Feria .iii. ad sanctum laurentium in damasco.

CXXXVIIII. Feria .iiii. ad sanctum paulum.

CXL. Feria v. ad sanctum siluestrum.

CXLI. Feria vi. ad sanctum eusebium.

CXLII. Sabbato ad sanctum laurentium foris murum.

CXLIII. Dominica de passione ad sanctum petrum.

CXLIIII. Feria ii. ad sanctum chrisogonem.

CXLV. Feria iii. ad sanctum cyriacum.

CXLVI. Feria iiii. ad sanctum marcellum.

CXLVII. Feria v. ad sanctum apollinarem.

CXLVIII. Feria vi. ad sanctum stephanum.

CXLVIIII. Sabbato ad sanctum petrum quando elemosinas datur.

CL. Benedictio in ramis palmarum super palmas.

CLI. Missa in die.

CLII. Feria ii. statio ad sanctum nereum et achilleum.

CLIII. Feria iii. statio ad sanctam priscam.

CLIIII. Feria iiii. statio ad sanctam mariam.

8

f. Dr

---

[1] For *lucina*.

CXCIII. Die .ii. ad missam.

CXCIIII. Die tertio ad missam.

CXCV. In ascensione domini.

CXCVI. Orationes de ascensione domini.

CXCVII. In natale Sancti uitalis martiris.

CXCVIII. Item prefatio de ascensione domini.

CXCVIIII. Dominica .i. post ascensione domini.

CC. Natale apostolorum philippi et iacobi.

CCI. Natale sanctorum alexandri, euenti et teodoli.

CCII. Eodemque die inuentio Sanctae crucis.

CCIII. Natale sancti iohannis euangelistae.

CCIIII. Natale sanctorum gordiani, cyrilli <et> epimachi.

CCV. Sanctorum pancratii nerei, et achillei.

CCVI. Natale sanctę marię ad martyres.

CCVII. Natale sancti urbani papae.

CCVIII. Orationes in sabbato pentecosten ad lectiones.

CCVIIII. Orationes ad missam in sabbato pentecosten.

CCX. Die dominico ad sanctum petrum.

CCXI. Feria ii. statio ad sanctrum petrum ad uincula.

CCXII. Feria iii. statio ad sanctam anastasiam.

CCXIII. Feria iiii. statio ad sanctam mariam ad presepem.

CCXIIII. Feria v. ad apostolos.

CCXV. Feria vi.

CCXVI. Sabbato ad sanctum petrum in xii lectiones.

CCXVII. Oratio ad missam.

CCXVIII. Dominica octaua pentecosten.

CCXVIIII. Dedicatio basilicae Sancti nicomedis martyris.

CCXX. Natale sanctorum marcellini et petri.

CCXXI. Dominica ii. post pentecosten.

CCXXII. Natale sancti medardi.

CCXXIII. Natale Sanctorum primi et feliciani.

CCXXIIII. Mensis quarti, feria .iiii. ad sanctam mariam.

CCXXV. Feria vi ad apostolos.

CCXXVI. Sabbato ad sanctum petrum in xii lectionibus.

CCXXVII. Oratio ad missam.

CCXXVIII. Dominica uacat.

CCXXVIIII. Natale sanctorum basilidis, cyrini naboris et nazarii.

CCXXX. Natale Sancti uiti.

CCXXXI. Natale sanctorum marci et marcelliani.

CCXXXII. Dominica .iii. post octauas pentecosten.

f. Dv

CCXXXIII. Vigilia sanctorum Geruasii et protasii.
CCXXXIIII. Natale sanctorum Geruasii et protasii.
CCXXXV. Ebdomada .v. post pentecosten.
/ CCXXXVI. Vigilia sancti iohannis baptistę.
CCXXXVII. In prima missa.
CCXXXVIII. Item in die ad missam.
CCXXXVIIII. Orationes ad eiusdem.
CCXL. Natale Sanctorum iohannis et pauli.
CCXLI. Dominica vi. post pentecosten.
CCXLII. Natale Sancti leonis papae.
CCXLIII. Eodem die uigilia sancti petri apostoli.
CCXLIIII. Natale apostolorum petri et pauli.
CCXLV. Natale Sancti pauli apostoli.
CCXLVI. Dominica .vii. post pentecosten.
CCXLVII. Natale sanctorum processi et martiniani.
CCXLVIII. Translatio Sancti martini episcopi.
CCXLVIIII. Octauas apostolorum.
CCL. Dominica octaua post pentecosten.
CCLI. Natale septem fratrum.
CCLII. Eodem die uigilia sancti benedicti.
CCLIII. Natale sancti benedicti abbatis.
CCLIIII. Dominica .viiii. post pentecosten.
CCLV. Octauas Sancti benedicti abbatis.
CCLVI. Natale sanctae praxedis.
CCLVII. Natale sancti apollonaris.
CCLVIII. Natale sancti iacobi apostoli.
CCLVIIII. Eodem die sancti cucuphati.
CCLX. Dominica .x. post pentecosten.
CCLXI. Natale sancti samsonis.
CCLXII. Natale sanctorum felicis, Simplicii, faustini et beatricis.
CCLXIII. Item propria missa Sancti felicis.
CCLXIIII. Natale sanctorum abdon et sennes.
CCLXV. Natale Sancti germani.
CCLXVI. Dominica .xi. post pentecosten.
CCLXVII. Kl. aug. ad sanctum petrum ad uincula.
CCLXVIII. Eodem die natale machabeorum.
CCLXVIIII. Natale sancti stephani episcopi et martiris.
CCLXX. Natale Sancti sixti episcopi et martiris.
CCLXXI. Benedic uuae siue fabae.
CCLXXII. Eodem die natale sanctorum felicissimi et agapiti.

11

CCLXXIII. Dominica .xii. post pentecosten.

CCLXXIIII. Natale sancti cyriaci martyris.

CCLXXV. Vigilia Sancti laurentii martyris.

CCLXXVI. Natale sancti laurentii in prima missa.

CCLXXVII. Item in die ad missam.

CCLXXVIII. Natale sancti tyburtii martyris.

CCLXXVIIII. Dominica .xiii. post pentecosten.

CCLXXX. Natale Sancti ypoliti martiris.

CCLXXXI. Natale sancti eusebii confessoris.

CCLXXXII. Eodem die uigilia assumptionis sanctae mariae.

CCLXXXIII. Item in die assumptionis sanctae mariae.

CCLXXXIIII. Octabas Sancti laurentii.

/f. Er   / CCLXXXV. Dominica xiiii. post pentecosten.

CCLXXXVI. Natale sancti agapiti martyris.

CCLXXXVII. Natale Sanctae magnae.

CCLXXXVIII. Natale sancti timothei.

CCLXXXVIIII. Eodem die sancti simphoriani.

CCXC. Natale sancti bartholomei apostoli.

CCXCI. Dominica xv post pentecosten.

CCXCII. Natale Sancti Rufi.

CCXCIII. Natale sancti hermetis martyris.

CCXCIIII. Eodem die natale sancti augusti<ni> episcopi.

CCXCV. Natale sanctae sabinę uirginis.

CCXCVI. Eodem die decollationis sancti iohannis baptistae

CCXCVII. Natale sanctorum felicis audacti.

CCXCVIII. Natale sancti prisci.

CCXCVIIII. Natiuitas Sanctae mariae.

CCC. Dominica xvi. post pentecosten.

CCCI. Natale sancti gorgonii martiris.

CCCII. Natale Sanctorum proti et iacinti.

CCCIII. Natale sanctorum cornelii et cypriani.

CCCIIII. Eodem die exaltatio sanctae crucis.

CCCV. Dominica xvii. post pentecosten.

CCCVI. Natale sancti nicomedis martyris.

CCCVII. Natale sanctae eufemiae uirginis.

CCCVIII. Eodem die natale sanctorum luciae et geminiani.

CCCVIIII. Dominica .xviii. post pentecosten.

CCCX. Mensis septimi, feria iiii. ad sanctam mariam.

CCCXI. Feria vi. ad apostolos.

CCCXII. Sabbato ad sanctum petrum in xii lectiones.

12

CCCXIII. Dominica uacat.

CCCXIIII. Vigilia sancti mathei euangelistae.

CCCXV. Natale eiusdem.

CCCXVI. Natale sanctorum mauricii cum sociis suis.

CCCXVII. Item missa sanctorum mauricii.

CCCXVIII. Dominica xx. post pentecosten.

CCCXVIIII. Natale sanctorum cosmę et damiani.

CCCXX. Dedicatio basilicae Sancti michahelis.

CCCXXI. Orationes ad eiusdem.

CCCXXII. Natale sancti ieronimi.

CCCXXIII. Dominica xxi. post pentecosten.

CCCXXIIII. Natale sancti marci papae.

CCCXXV. Vigilia sanctorum dionisii rustici et eleutherii.

CCCXXVI. Natale sanctorum dionisii rustici et eleutherii.

CCCXXVII. Dominica xxii. post pentecosten.

CCCXXVIII. Natale Sancti calisti papae.

CCCXXVIIII. Octabas sanctorum dionisii rusticii et eleutherii.

CCCXXX. Natale Sancti lucę euangelistae.

CCCXXXI. Dominica xxiii. post pentecosten.

CCCXXXII. Vigilia apostolorum Symonis et iudę.

CCCXXXIII. Natale ipsorum.

CCCXXXIIII. Vigilia omnium sanctorum.

f. Ev   / CCCXXXV. Natale omnium sanctorum.

CCCXXXVI. Eodem die natale sancti caesarii martiris.

CCCXXXVII. Dominica xxiiii. post pentecosten.

CCCXXXVIII. Natale sanctorum quattuor coronatorum.

CCCXXXVIIII. Natale sancti teodori.

CCCXL. Dominica xxv. post pentecosten.

CCCXLI. Natale sanctae menne martiris.

CCCXLII. Eodem die Sancti martini episcopi.

CCCXLIII. Dominica xxvi. post pentecosten.

CCCXLIIII. Vigilia Sanctae caeciliae uirginis.

CCCXLV. Natale sanctae caeciliae.

CCCXLVI. Natale sancti clementis martiris.

CCCXLVII. Eodem die natale Sanctae felicitatis.

CCCXLVIII. Natale sancti grisogoni martyris.

CCCXLVIIII. Dominica xxviii. post pentecosten.

CCCL. Natale sancti Saturnini martyris.

CCCLI. Eodem die uigilia sancti andreae apostoli.

CCCLII. Natale sancti andreae.

13

CCCLIII. Dominica i. de aduentu domini.

CCCLIIII. Octauas Sancti andreae.

CCCLV. Dominica .ii. de aduentu domini.

CCCLVI. Natale sancti damasi papae.

CCCLVII. Natale sanctae luciae uirginis.

CCCLVIII. Natale sancti thomae apostoli.

CCCLVIIII. Dominica .iii. ad sanctum petrum.

CCCLX. Feria .iiii. ad sanctam mariam maiorem.

CCCLXI. Feria vi ad apostolos.

CCCLXII. Sabbato ad sanctum petrum in xii lectiones.

CCCLXIII. Dominica uacat.

CCCLXIIII. Orationes de aduentu domini.

CCCLXV. Missa de trinitate.

CCCLXVI. Missa ad suffragia sanctorum.

CCCLXVII. Missa ad suffragia angelorum.

CCCLXVIII. Missa de sapientia.

CCCLXVIIII. Missa de caritate, feria v.

CCCLXX. Missa de sancta cruce, feria vi.

CCCLXXI. Missa ad laudem Sanctę marię, feria uii.

CCCLXXII. Missa pro peccatis, feria ii.

CCCLXXIII. Missa pro temptatione carnis.

CCCLXXIIII. Missa pro petitione lacrimarum.

CCCLXXV. Missa specialis pro sacerdote.

CCCLXXVI. Item missa pro sacerdote.

CCCLXXVII. Missa uotiua.

CCCLXXVIII. Alia missa.

CCCLXXVIIII. Missa pro salute uiuorum.

CCCLXXX. Item pro familiaribus.

CCCLXXXI. Missa pro abbate uel congregatione.

CCCLXXXII. Orationes pro fratribus in uia dirigendis.

CCCLXXXIII. Orationes pro redeuntibus de itinere.

CCCLXXXIIII. Oratio in aduentu fratrum superueniendum.

/f. Fr   / CCCLXXXV. Missa pro iter agentibus.

CCCLXXXVI. Missa pro nauigantibus.

CCCLXXXVII. Missa pro pace.

CCCLXXXVIII. Missa pro quaecumque tribulatione.

CCCLXXXVIIII. Missa pro peste animalium.

CCCXC. Missa in[1] contentione.

---

[1] *pro* before correction.

14

CCCXCI. Missa contra iudices male agentes.

CCCXCII. Missa contra obloquentes.

CCCXCIII. Oratio ad pluuiam postulandam.

CCCXCIIII. Missa ad pluuiam postulandam.

CCCXCV. Oratio ad poscendam serenitatem.

CCCXCVI. Missa ad poscendam serenitatem.

CCCXCVII. Missa ad repellendam[1] tempestatem.

CCCXCVIII. Orationes matutinales.

CCCXCVIIII. Orationes uespertinales seu matutinales.

CCCC. Oratio in monasterio monachorum.

CCCCI. Oratio in refectorio.

CCCCII. Oratio in dormitorio.

CCCCIII. Oratio in cellario.

CCCCIIII. Oratio in scriptorio.

CCCCV. Oratio in hospitale.

CCCCVI. Oratio in domo infirmorum.

CCCCVII. Oratio in area.

CCCCVIII. Oratio in granario.

CCCCVIIII. Oratio in pistrino.

CCCCX. Oratio in coquina.

CCCCXI. Oratio in lardario.

CCCCXII. Oratio in caminata.

CCCCXIII. Oratio ad portam ciuitatis.

CCCCXIIII. Missa pro infirmis.

CCCCXV. Oratio ad sponsas benedicendas.

CCCCXVI. Benedictio uestium uirginum uel uiduę.

CCCCXVII. Incipit ordo unctionis.

CCCCXVIII. Missa pro infirmo in domo.

CCCCXVIIII. Inpositio manuum super energuminum.

CCCCXX. Orationes ad uisitandum infirmum.

CCCCXXI. Orationes in agenda mortuorum.

CCCCXXII. Missa in die antequam sepeliatur.

CCCCXXIII. Oratio iuxta feretrum.

CCCCXXIIII. Oratio ante sepultum.

CCCCXXV. Oratio post sepultum corpus.

CCCCXXVI. Missa unius defuncti.

CCCCXXVII. Missa in anniuersario unius defuncti.

CCCCXXVIII. Missa pro defuncto nuper baptizato.

---

[1] *repellandam* before correction.

CCCCXXVIIII. Missa pro defuncto desiderante penitentiam.

CCCCXXX. Missa plurimorum defunctorum.

CCCCXXXI. Item missa defunctorum.

CCCCXXXII. Item alia.

CCCCXXXIII. Missa in cymiteriis.

CCCCXXXIIII. Missa pro salute uiuorum uel in agenda mortuorum.

/f. Fv

/ I

INCIPIT ORDO AD ECCLESIAM DEDICANDAM

2 PRIMITVS ENIM DECET VT EPISCOPVS CVM CETERIS MINISTRIS EAT AD ECCLESIAM ANTEQVAM ET IBI RECONDANT VESPERTINO IN TEMPORE RELIQVIAS, ET IVBEAT EXERCERE IBI VIGILIAS PER TOTAM NOCTEM. IN CRASTINA AVTEM EAT PONTIFEX AD ECCLESIAM QVAE SACRANDA EST ET ORDINET IN EA QVAE ORDINANDA SVNT ET INLVMINENTVR IVSSV SVO .XII. CANDELAE ET EXPELLVNTVR OMNES FORAS NISI SOLVS ARCHIDIACONVS CVM CLAVSO OSTIO IBI MANEAT. TVNC PONTIFEX CVM SACRO ORDINE REDEAT AD ANTIQVAM ECCLĘSIAM ET INDVANT SE SACRIS VESTIBVS ET FATIAT LAETANIAM PROVT HORA DICTAVERIT. QVA EXPLETA DICAT HANC ORATIONEM.

3 OREMVS. Actiones nostras quesumus domine aspirando praeueni, et adiuuando prosequere, ut cuncta nostra operatio et a te semper incipiat, et per te cepta finiatur. Per dominum nostrum iesum christum.

4 ET TVNC INCIPIENS RESPONSORIVM. R. Domine si conuersus fuerit populus tuus. ITEM ALIVD. Exaudisti domine orationem serui tui. ITEM ALIVD. Tu domine uniuersorum qui nullam habes indulgentiam. ET TVNC OMNI COLLEGIONE PROCEDAT CANTANDO AD OSTIVM NOVAE ECCLESIAE.

5 FINITIS AVTEM RESPONSORIIS PERCVTIAT PONTIFEX OSTIVM ECCLESIAE DE BACVLO SVO DICENS: A. Tollite portas principes uestras et eleuamini portae aeternales. PS. Domini est terra. DEINTVS AVTEM MINISTER RESPONDENS DICAT: / Quis est iste rex gloriae?

/f. Gr

16

6 ET SIC PERGAT OMNIS LEGIO IN CIRCVITV ECCLAESIAE, TER CANTANDO HANC ANTIPHONAM, CVM PSALMO ET CVM GLORIA, TERTIO AVTEM PERCVSSO OSTIO AB EPISCOPO ET DICTO TOLLITE PORTAS, ET RESPONSO TER A MINISTRO QVIS EST ISTĘ REX GLORIAE, RESPONDEAT PONTIFEX: Dominus uirtutum ipse est rex gloriae. ET APERTO OSTIO INTRANS DICAT TER. Pax huic domui. Crux pellit hostem. Crux christi triumphat.

7 DEINDE INCIPIAT CLERVS LAETANIAM ET PROSTERNAT SE EPISCOPVS CVM MINISTRIS ANTE ALTARE VSQVE DVM DICATVR AGNVS DEI, VT AVTEM SVRREXERINT AB ORATIONE NON DICAT PONTIFEX DOMINVS VOBISCVM SED OREMVS TANTVM, ET DIACONVS DICAT: Flectamus genua. ET POST PAVLVLVM. Leuate.

8 TVNC PONTIFEX DICAT HANC ORATIONEM: Magnificare domine deus noster in sanctis tuis et hoc in templo aedificationis appare, ut qui omnia in filiis adoptionis operaris, ipse semper in tua hereditate lauderis. Per dominum.

9 DEINDE INCIPIAT PONTIFEX DE SINISTRO ANGVLO AB ORIENTE SCRIBENS PER PAVIMENTVM CVM CAMBVTA SVA HAEC ELEMENTA a. b. c. ET DICAT HANC ANTIPHONAM: Confirma hoc deus quod operatus es in nobis a templo sancto tuo quos est in hierusalem, alleluia alleluia. PS. Exurgat deus. CVM GLORIA. DVM VADENS AD DEXTRVM ANGVLVM OCCIDENTALEM INCIPIENS ITERVM A DEXTRO ANGVLO ORIENTALI a. b. c. SCRIBENS VSQVE IN SINISTRVM OCCIDENTALEM ANGVLVM, CANENDO / [1]ANTIPHONAM ALIAM: Emitte spiritum tuum et creabuntur et renouabis faciem terrae alleluia, alleluia. PS. Benedic anima mea domine deus meus.

10 DEINDE VENIENS ANTE ALTARE, ET DICAT TER: Deus in adiutorium meum intende domine ad adiuuandum me festina. CVM GLORIA ABSQVE ALLELVIA.

---

[1] Fols Gv and 1r blank.

11 DEINDE BENEDICENS SALEM ET AQVAM CVM CYNERE, ET DICAT HANC ORATIONEM: Deus qui ad salutem humani generis maxima quaeque sacramenta in aquarum substantia condidisti, adesto inuocationibus nostris, et elimento huic multimodis purificationibus praeparato, uirtutem tuae benedictionis infunde, ut creatura misterii tui tibi seruiens, ad abiciendos daemones, morbosque pellendas, diuinae gratiae sumat effectum, ut quicquid in domibus uel in locis fidelium haec unda resperserit, careat omni inmunditia, liberetur a noxa, non illic resideat spiritus pestilens, non aura corrumpens, discedant omnes insidiae latentis inimici, et si quid est quod aut incolomitati habitantium inuidet, aut quieti, aspersione huius aquae effugiat, ut salubritas per inuocationem tui nominis expetita, ab omnibus sit inpugnationibus defensa. Per.

12 SEQVITVR EXORCISMVS AQVAE. Exorcizo te creatura aquae in nomine dei patris omnipotentis, et in nomine iesu christi filii eius et spiritus sancti, omnis uirtus aduersarii, omnis incursio diaboli, omne fantasma, omnes inimici potestas, eradicare et effugare ab hac creatura aquae. Vnde exorcizo te creatura aquae, per deum uiuum, per deum uerum, per deum sanctum, et per dominum nostrum iesum christum, ut efficiaris aqua sancta, aqua bene/dicta, ut ubicumque effusa fueris uel aspersa, siue in domo siue in agro, effuges omnem fantasiam et potestatem inimici. Quatinus consecratio huius sanctae aquae proficiat ad dedicationem huius ecclesiae ut per eam et per benedictionem diuinam auxiliante domino siue per os, et per manus atque officium nostrum, haec domus domini dei nostri diuinitus per gratiam spiritus sancti consecretur et perpetualiter ad inuocandum nomen domini consecrata permaneat, et spiritus sanctus habitet in domo hac. Per dominum.

/f. 2r

13 BENEDICTIO SALIS. Inmensam clementiam tuam omnipotens aeternae deus humiliter inploramus, ut hanc creaturam salis, quam in usu generis humani tribuisti, benedicere et sanctificare tua pietate digneris. Vt sit omnibus sumentibus salus mentis et corporis, et quicquid eo tactum uel respersum fuerit, careat omni inmunditia omnique inpugnatione spiritalis nequitiae. Per.

14 EXORCISMVS SALIS. Exorcizo te creatura salis per deum uiuum, per deum uerum, per deum sanctum, per deum qui te per heliseum prophetam in aquam mitti iussit, ut sanaretur sterelitas aquae, ut efficaris sal exorcizatum in salutem credentium, ut sis omnibus sumentibus sanitas animae et corporis, et effugiat atque discedat ab eo loco quo aspersus fueris, omnis fantasia et nequitia, uel uersutia diabolicae fraudis, omnisque spiritus inmundus adiuratus, per eum qui uenturus est, iudicare uiuos et mortuos et seculum per ignem.

15 BENEDICTIO CINERVM. Omnipotens sempiterne deus, parce metuentibus, propitiare supplicibus et mittere digneris sanctum angelum tuum de caelis qui benedicat et sanctificet cyneres istos

f. 2v
ut sint remedium salubre omnibus nomen / tuum humiliter implorantibus, ac semetipsos pro conscientia delictorum suorum accusantibus, atque conspectui diuinę clementiae tuae facinora sua deplorantibus uel serenissimam pietatem tuam suppliciter obnixeque flagitantibus, praesta quaesumus per inuocationem nominis tui, ut quicumque eos super se asperserint pro redemptione peccatorum, corporis sanitatem et animae tutelam percipiant. Per dominum nostrum.

16 POST HOC MISCETVR SAL ET CYNIS FACIENS CRVCEM TER SVPER IPSAM AQVAM ET DICAT HANC ORATIONEM: Deus inuictae uirtutis auctor et inseparabilis imperii rex ac semper magnificus triumphator qui aduersae dominationis uires reprimis, qui inimici rugientis seuitiam superas, qui hostiles nequitias potens expugnas, te domine trementes et supplices depraecamur ac petimus, ut hanc creaturam salis et aquae dignanter accipias, benignus inlustres, pietatis tuae more sanctifices, ut ubicumque fuerit aspersa per inuocationem sancti tui nominis omnis infestatio inmundi spiritus abiciatur, terrorque uenenosi serpentis procul pellatur, et praesentia sancti spiritus nobis misericordiam tuam poscentibus ubique adesse dignetur. Per.

17 DEINDE MISCETVR VINVM CVM AQVA ET DICAT HANC ORATIONEM: Deus creator et conseruator humani generis dator gratiae spiritalis largitor aeternae salutis, tu domine mitte spiritum sanctum tuum super uinum hoc aquae mixtum, ut arma

19

uirtute caelestis defensionis, ad consecrationem huius ecclesiae uel altaris proficiat. Per dominum.

18 ET MITTAT IN EAM CRISMA ET CONDAT EX IPSA AQVA CALCEM ET FACIAT MALDAM VNDE RECLVDERE DEBET IPSAS RELIQVIAS.

19 DEINDE FACIAT CRVCEM DE DIGITO SVO CVM IPSA AQVA IN DEXTRAM PARTEM / PER QVATTVOR CORNVA ALTARIS CANTANDO ANTIPHONAM: Asperges me domine ysopo et mundabor.

/f. 3r

20 INDE VENIENS ANTE ALTARE CVM YSOPO ASPERGET ILLVM ALTARE IN CIRCVITV, SEPTEM VICIBVS CANENDO AN. Asperges me domine ysopo, CVM PSALMO. ET VADAT IN CIRCVITV ALTARIS SPARGENDO. DEINDE IN DEXTERA PARTE PER PARIETES ECCLESIAE VSQVE DVM VENIENS ANTE ALTARE SPARGET. ITERVM TRIBVS VICIBVS DESVPER IN CIRCVITV ALTARIS VEL ECCLESIAE DEINTVS CVM ANTIPIIONA.

21 ET TVNC SPARGET AQVAM PER PAVIMENTVM IN MODVM CRVCIS ET IN LONGITVDINE ET IN LATITVDINE CANENDO ANTIPHONAM: Fundamenta templi huius sapientia sua fundauit deus in quo dominum caeli conlaudant angeli surgant[1] uenti et fluant flumina non possunt ea mouere umquam fundata enim erat supra petram. PS. Fundamenta.

22 DEINDE PER PARIETES INTRINSECVS ECCLESIAE CANTANDO ANTIPHONAM: Sanctificauit dominus tabernaculum suum et haec est domus domini in qua inuocetur nomen eius de quo scriptum est erit nomen meum ibi dicit dominus. PS. Magnus dominus. AN. In dedicatione huius templi laudate deum omnis militia caelorum et omnis terra laudent nomen domini quia exaltatum est nomen eius solius. PS. Laudate dominum de caelis. A. Lapides praetiosi omnes muri tui et turres hierusalem gemmis aedificabuntur. PS. Lauda hierusalem. A. Erit mihi dominus in deum et lapis iste uocabitur domus dei. PS. Deus noster. [2]A.

---

[1] *surruant* before correction.
[2] *A.* and *H* of *Haec* supplied later in crimson ink.

Haec est domus domini firmiter aedificata benefundata est supra firmam petram. PS. Ecce quam bonum.

23 DEINDE PERGAT EXTRA ECCLESIAM CVM OMNI SCOLA SPARGENDO TER PER PARIETES IN CIRCVITV ET DESVPER CANENDO AN. Benedic domine domum istam / quam aedificaui nomini tuo uenientium in locum istum exaudi praeces in excelso solio gloriae tuae. PS. Deus misereatur nostri. A. Ecce tabernaculum dei cum hominibus et spiritus sanctus habitet[1] in uobis templum enim dei sanctum est quod estis uos pro cuius amore caelebrant honore gaudia templi tempore festi. PS. Beati inmaculati. AN. Benedic domine domum istam est omnes habitantes in ea quia tu domine dixisti pax huic domui benedic domine timentes te pusillis cum maioribus benedicti uos a domino qui fecit caelum et terram.

24 FINITO HOC INGREDIATVR PONTIFEX IN ECCLESIAM CVM OMNI SCOLA ET INCIPIAT ANTIPHONAM: O quam metuendus est locus iste uere non est hic aliud nisi domus dei et porta caeli. PS. Verba mea. A. Qui habitat in adiutorio altissimi in protectione dei caeli commorabitur. PS. Idipsum. A. Beati qui habitant in domo tua domine in saeculum saeculi laudabunt te. PS. Quam dilecta.

25 ET TVNC PONAT INCENSVM IN ACERRA ET DICAT HANC ORATIONEM. OREMVS ET DIACONVS VT SVPRA. Deus qui loca nomini tuo dicata sanctificas, effunde super hanc orationis domum gratiam tuam, ut ab omnibus hic inuocantibus nomen tuum auxilium tuae misericordiae sentiatur. Per dominum.

26 ET TVNC EX INCENSO BONI ODORIS INFVMAT TOTAM ECCLESIAM, ET STANS IN MEDIO DICAT A. Domus mea domus orationis uocabitur. V. Narrabo nomen tuum. CVM GLORIA.

27 ITERVM DICAT OREMVS, ET DIACONVS VT SVPRA. Deus sanctificationum omnipotens dominator cuius pietas sine fine sentitur. Deus qui caelestia simul et terrestria moderaris seruans misericordiam tuam populo tuo ambulanti ante conspectum gloriae tuae, exaudi preces seruorum / tuorum et

f. 3v

f. 4r

---

[1] *habitat* before correction.

praesta, ut sint oculi tui aperti super domum istam die ac nocte, hancque basilicam in honore sancti .il. sacris misteriis institutam clementissimus dedica, miseratus illustra, propitio splendore, clarifica et benedicito, omnemque hominem uenientem adorare te in hoc loco placatus admitte, propitius dignare respicere, et propter nomen tuum magnum, et manum fortem, et brachium excelsum, in habitaculo hoc supplicantes libens protege, dignanter exaudi, et aeterna defensione conserua, ut semper felices, semperque in tua religione laetantes, constanter in sanctae trinitatis fide catholica perseuerent. Per.

PREFATIO IN MEDIO ECCLAESIAE
Sursum corda. R. Habemus ad dominum.
Gratias agamus domino deo nostro. R. Dignum et iustum est.

28 VD aeternae deus. Adesto praecibus nostris, adesto sacramentis. Adesto etiam piis famulorum tuorum laboribus nobisque misericordiam tuam poscentibus. Descendat quoque in hanc ecclesiam tuam, quam sub inuocatione sancti nominis tui in honore sancti .il. indigni consecramus spiritus sanctus tuus septiformis gratiae hubertate perfusus, ut quotienscumque in hac domo tua sanctum tuum nomen fuerit inuocatum, eorum qui te inuocauerint, a te pio domino preces exaudiantur. O beata sancta trinitas, quae omnia purificas, omnia mundas, omnia exornas. O beata maiestas dei, quae cuncta imples, cuncta contines, cunctaque disponis. O beata et sancta manus domini, quae omnia sanctificas, omnia benedicis, omnia sacrificas. O

/f. 4v

sanctae / sanctorum deus, tuam clementiam humillima deuotione deposcimus, ut hanc ecclesiam per nostrae humilitatis famulatum, in honore sancti martyris tui .ill. purificare, benedicere, consecrareque digneris perpetua sanctificationis tuae hubertate. Hic quoque sacerdotes sacrificium tibi laudis offerant, hic fideles populi uota persoluant. Hic peccatorum onera soluantur, fideliumque lapsa reparentur. In hac ergo quaesumus domine domo tua spiritus sancti gratia egroti sanentur, infirmi restituantur, claudi curentur, leprosi mundentur, caeci illuminentur, demonia eiciantur. Cunctorum ergo debilium egrotationes te domine annuente pellantur, omnium et iam uincula peccatorum, absoluantur, ut omnes qui hoc templum beneficia iusta deprecaturi ingrediuntur, cuncta se impetrasse laetentur. Vt concessa misericordia quam praecamur, perpetuo miserationis tuę munere gloriemur. Per christum.

29 IPSA EXPLETA INGREDIENDVM EST AD ALTARE POST EXTENSVM VELVM PSALLENDO ANTIPHONAM: Introibo ad altare dei ad deum qui laetificat iuuentutem meam. PS. Iudica me deus et discerne. DEINDE EAT ANTE ALTARE ET FVNDAT AQVAM SVPER ALTARIA ET ABSTERGAT LINTEO ET BENEDICAT TABVLAM ET AQVA SANCTA.

II

30 Singulare illud repropitiatorium quod se in ara crucis nobis redimentis obtulit immolandum cuius praefiguratione patriarcha iacob lapidem erexit in titulum, quo fieret sacrificium et porta caeli desuper aperietur oraculum, suppliciter tibi[1] domine praeces fundimus ut metalli huius expoli/tam materiam supernis sacrificiis imbuendo, ipse tuae dotari sanctificationis ubertate percipias qui quondam lapideis legem scripsisti in tabulis. Per.

f. 5r

31 ITEM ALIA. Deus omnipotens uniuersarum rerum rationabilis artifex, qui inter ceteras creaturas formam lapidei metalli ad obsequium tui sacrificii condidisti, ut legis libatorium tuo praeparetur altari, annue dignanter huius institutor misterii, ut quicquid hic oblatum sacratumue fuerit nomini tuo assurgat, religioni proficiat, spei innitatur, fidei sit praecipue dignum honore. Per.

32 POSTEA INCENSVM OFFERAT ET MITTAT OLEVM FACIENSQVE CRVCEM IN MEDIO ET IN QVATTVOR ANGVLIS ET DICAT AN. Erexit iacob lapidem in titulum fundens oleum desuper. <PS.> <Q>uam dilecta.

33 POST HAEC PONAT INCENSVM ET CRISMA, DICAT A. Ecce odor filii mei sicut odor agri cui benedixit dominus. PS. Ecce quam bonum. A. Erit mihi dominus in deum et lapis iste uocabitur domus dei. PS. Deus noster. A. Vidit iacob scalam summitas eius caelos tangebat et descendentes angelos et dixit uere locus iste sanctus est. PSS. Fundamenta.

---

[1] *te* before correction.

34 DEINDE FACIENS CRVCES[1] PER PARIETES IN CIRCVITV DE IPSO CRISMATE CVM POLLICE, DICAT AN. Sanctificauit dominus. ALIA A. Lapides praetiosi. PS. Lauda iherusalem. ANT. Mane surgens iacob erigebat lapidem in titulum fundens oleum desuper uotum uouit domino uere locus iste sanctus est et ego nesciebam.

35 TVNC IN CIRCVITV INTRINSECVS MITTET INCENSVM BONI ODORIS ET DICAT OREMVS. Omnipotens sempiterne deus effunde super hunc locum gratiam tuam et omnibus in te sperantibus auxilium tui muneris osten/de, ut hic et sacramentorum uirtus et uotorum obtineatur effectus. Per.

/f. 5v

36 ITEM ALIA. Deus qui de uiuis et electis lapidibus aeternum maiestatis tuae condis habitaculum auxiliare populo supplicanti, ut quod ecclesiae tuae corporalibus proficit spatiis spiritalibus amplificetur augmentis. Per.

37 TVNC EAT AD ALTARE, ET PONET INCENSVM ET DICAT ORATIONEM. Dei patris omnipotentis misericordiam dilectissimi fratres depraecemur, ut hoc altare sacrificiis spiritalibus consecrandum uocis exoratus[2] officio, praesenti benedictione sanctificet, ut in eo semper oblationes famulorum suorum studio suae deuotionis impositas, benedicere et sanctificare dignetur, et spiritali placatus incenso, precanti familiae suae, prumptus exauditor adsistat. Per.

38 ALIA. Deus omnipotens in cuius honore altare hoc sub inuocatione nominis tui indigni consecramus, clemens et propitius praeces nostrae humilitatis exaudi, et presta ut in hac mensa sint tibi libamina accepta, sint grata, sint pinguia, et spiritus tui sancti semper rore perfusa, ut omni tempore in hoc loco supplicantis tibi familiae tuae anxietates releues, egritudines cures, preces exaudias, uota suscipias, desiderata confirmes, postulata concedas. Per.

PRAEFATIO SVPER ALTARE
Sursum corda. R. Habemus ad dominum.
Gratias agamus domino deo nostro. R. Dignum et iustum est.

---

[1] *CRVCEM* before correction.
[2] *exoramus* before correction.

24

39 VD aeternae deus. Vt propensiori cura et adtentiori famulatu tibi
/f. 6r seruitutis officia deferamus / hoc praesertim in tempore quo
religiosarum mentium habiturum reuerentia altare dedicamus.
Dignare igitur dominator domine hoc quaesumus altare caelesti
sanctificatione perfundere, et benedicere, ut sancti spiritus
illustratione praefulgeat. Sit illi usquoque apud te gratiae, cuius
fuit illud quod abraham pater fidei nostrae filium immolaturus
extruxit. Quod isaac in conspectu tuae maiestatis instituit, quod
iacob dominum magna uidens uisione erexit. Vt hic orantes
exaudias, hic oblata sanctifices, hicque superposita benedicas,
hinc quippe benedicta distribuas. Sit ergo ecclesiae tuae, titulus
sempiternus. Sit mensa caelestis, spiritalique conuiuio parata.
Tu enim domine proprio ore tuo hostias super eam impositas
benedicito, et benedicas suscipito, atque nobis omnibus tribue,
in participatione earum uitam adquiramus sempiternam. Per
christum.

40 Maiestatem tuam domine imploramus humiliter, ut altare hoc ad
suscipienda populi tui munera iniuncta potenter benedicere et
sanctificare digneris, et quod nunc a nobis indigni sub tui
nominis inuocatione, in honore et nomine sancti .ill. sacrosancti
crismatis unctione, est delibutum placeat tibi. Hoc altare maneat
perpetuum, ut quicquid deinceps super eo oblatum sacratumue
fuerit, dignum tibi fiat holocaustum, atque omnium hic
offerentium sacrificia, a te pio deo benigne suscipiantur, et per
ea peccatorum nostrorum et eorum uincula absoluantur, maculae
deleantur, ueniae impetrentur gratiae adquirantur. Quatinus una
/f. 6v cum sanctis et electis / tuis uitam percipere aeternam mereamur.
Per.

III
41 A. Confirma hoc deus. CVM GLORIA. DEINDE BENEDICAT
PONTIFEX LINTEAMINA ET OMNIA ORNAMENTA SEV
VASA AD CVLTVM ECCLESIAE PERTINENTIA
SVBDIACONIBVS ET ACOLITIS MANVVM TENENTIA
CVM AQVA SANCTA ET INCENSO.

42 OREMVS. Omnipotens et misericors deus, qui ab initio utilia et
necessaria hominibus praeparasti, templaque manu hominum
facta nomini tuo sancto dicari, tuaeque habitationis loca uocari

uoluisti, quique per famulum tuum moysen, uestimenta pontificalia et sacerdotalia seu leuitica, et alia quaeque diuersi generis ornamenta, ad cultum et decorem tabernaculi, et altaris tui fieri decreuisti, exaudi propitius praeces nostras, et omnia haec diuersarum specierum, ornamenta in husum huius basilice uel altaris ad honorem et gloriam tuam praeparata + purificare, + sanctificare, + benedicere, et consecrare, per nostrae humilitatis seruitutem digneris, ut et diuinis cultibus sacrisque misteriis apta existant, hisque confectioni corporis et sanguinis iesu christi filii tui domini nostri pareatur famulantibus. Qui tecum.

43 ALIA. Domine deus omnipotens sicut ab initio hominibus utilia et necessaria creasti et quemadmodum uestimenta pontificalia sacerdotibus et leuitis, ornamentaque et linteamina fieri famulo tuo moysi, per xl. dies docuisti, siue etiam ea quae sancta maria texuit et fecit in usum mynisterii tabernaculi foederis sanctificare, benedicere, consecrareque digneris haec linteamina /f. 7r in usum altaris tui / ad tegendum inuoluendumque corpus et sanguinem filii tui domini nostri iesu christi, qui tecum uiuit, fiant omnia ista protectione tua, tuta adque defensa potens domine uasa. Per dominum.

44 BENEDICTIO AD OMNIA ORNAMENTA ECCLAESIAE. Dignare domine deus omnipotens rex regum, et dominus dominantium, sacerdos omnium, pontifex uniuersorum, per quem una cum patre sanctoque spiritu facta sunt uniuersa, benedicere, consecrare, et sanctificare digneris uasa haec cum hoc altari, et linteaminibus ceterisque uasis, et quemadmodum officia tabernaculi testimonii, olim archam, oracula, cherubim, alas, uela, columnas, candelabra, altare argenteum, bases, tabulas deauratas, holocausti hostias, aereum altare cum aeneis uasis, tentoriis funibus, oleo unctionis, et ceteris aliis in figuram nostri per manus sanctorum sanctificasti sacerdotum, ita nunc manens in aeternum summus sacerdos sacerdotum, secundum ordinem melchisedech, ut diximus patenam hanc, et calicem hunc, et omnia instrumenta huius ecclesiae et altaris quae inter nostras manus habentur corde puro praecamur, ut benedicas, purificas, consecres, et consumes, quibus inter nos et aeternam unitatem, in suppremo meatu sine fine constare credimus. Per dominum.

26

IIII

45 CONSECRATIO PATENE FAC CRVCEM DE OLEO. Consecramus et sanctificamus hanc patenam ad conficiendum in ea corpus domini nostri iesu christi patientis crucem pro omnium nostra salute. Qui cum patre.

f. 7v

46 ITEM BENEDICTIO / PATENE ET FAC CRVCEM DE CRISMATE. Consecrare et sanctificare digneris domine patenam hanc, per istam et nostram benedictionem in christo iesu domino nostro. Amen.

V

47 AD CALICEM BENEDICENDVM. Oremus dilectissimi fratres, ut dominus deus noster calicem suum in ministerio consecrandum, caelestis gratiae inspiratione sanctificet, et ad humanam benedictionem plenitudine diuini fauoris accommodet. Per.

48 ITEM ALIA. Dignare domine deus noster calicem istum in usum misterii tui pia deuotione formatum, ea sanctificatione perfundere, quam melchisedech famuli tui sacratum calicem perfudisti et quod arte metallo effici non potest, altaribus tuis dignum fiat tua benedictione praetiosum atque sanctificatum. Per dominum nostrum iesum christum.

49 ALIA. Omnipotens deus trinitas inseparabilis manibus nostris, opem tuae benedictionis infunde, ut nostram benedictionem haec uasa sanctificentur, et corporis christi noua sepulchra spiritus sancti gratia perficiantur. Per dominum.

VI

50 ORATIO AD CORPORALEM BENEDICENDVM. Clementissime domine cuius inenarrabilis uirtus, cuius mynisteria archani mira caelebrantur, tribue quaesumus, ut hoc linteamen tuae propitiationis benedictione sanctificetur, ad consecrandum super illud corpus dei, et domini nostri iesu christi filii tui. Qui tecum.

51 ALIA. Deus qui pro generis humani saluatione uerbum caro factus es, et habitare totus in nobis non dedigna/tus es, quique

f. 8r

27

traditori tuo perfido osculum pium dedisti, dum pro omnium
uita pius uoluisti agnus mactari, atque in sindone ioseph lino
texta totum te inuolui permisisti. Respice propitius ad uota
nostra qui tua fideliter carismata amplecti cupimus, quaesumus
domine + sanctificare, + benedicere, + consecrareque digneris,
haec linteamina in usum altaris tui, ad consecrandum super ea
siue ad tegendum inuoluendumque corpus et sanguinem filii tui
domini nostri iesu christi dignisque pareant famulantibus ut
quicquid sacro ritu super haec immolabitur, sicut melchisedech
oblatum placeat[1] tibi holocaustum, et reportet per hoc premium
quicumque obtulerit uotum, te quoque humiliter rogamus ac
petimus, ut haec linteamina tuę sanctificationis spiritu et gratiae
tuae ubertate purifices et sanctifices, qui te pro nobis omnibus
sacrificium offerri uoluisti, et praesta ut per haec sint tibi
libamina accepta, sint grata, sint pinguia, et spiritus sancti tui
semper rore perfusa. Per dominum.

52 ITEM ALIA. Deus qui digne tibi seruientium imitari desideras
famulatum, respice propitius ad humilitatis nostri seruitutem, et
hoc corporale nomini tuo dicatum, seu haec linteamina seruitutis
nostrae usibus praeparata, caelestis uirtutis benedictione, +
sanctifica, + purifica, + et consecra, quatinus super eo, uel super
his spiritus sanctus tuus descendat, qui et populi tui oblationes
benedicat, et corda siue corpora, sumentium benignus perficiat.
Per dominum.

VII

53 BENEDICTIO VESTIMENTORVM SACERDOTALIVM SEV
LEVITICORVM. / Omnipotens sempiternę deus, qui per
moysen famulum tuum, pontificalia seu sacerdotalia, atque
leuitica uestimenta, ad explendum in conspectu tuo ministerium
eorum et ad decorem seu laudem nominis tui fieri decreuisti.
Adesto propitius inuocationibus nostris, et haec indumenta
sacerdotalia famuli uel sacerdotis tui ill. ut super gratia tua
irrigante tua ingenti benedictione per nostrae humilitatis
seruitium, + purificare, + benedicere, + consecrareque digneris,
ut diuinis cultibus, et sacris mysteriis apta et benedicta existant,
his quoque sacris uestibus sacerdotes siue leuitae tui induti,

/f. 8v

---
[1] *l* supplied later.

muniti et defensi ab omnibus inpulsionibus, seu temptationibus malignorum spirituum tuti esse mereantur, tuisque misteriis apte et condigne seruire et inherere atque in his placide et deuote perseuerare tribue. Saluator mundi. Qui uiuis.

54 ALIA ORATIO. Domine sancte pater omnipotens rex magnificus triumphator, qui sanctos patres nostros qui tibi in sacerdotali ordine placuerunt, diuersi generis ornamenta et uestimenta sacerdotalia fieri, et ornari sacerdotes tibi seruientes iussisti, exaudi propitius orationem nostram et hanc planetam famuli tui .ill. seu poderem, albam ac stolam cingulum orariumque dextera tua sancta, + benedicere, + sanctificare, + consecrareque et purificare digneris, quatinus haec uestimenta ministris et leuitis, ac sacerdotibus tuis ad diuinum cultum

f. 9r

ornandum et explen/dum proficiant, sanctisque altaribus tuis mundi et ornati his sacris uestibus ministraturi, inreprehensibilis in actu, et dictu, interius exteriusque appareant, tibique soli deo puro corde et mundo corpore, omnibus diebus uitae eorum inreprehensibiliter sanctorum patrum exempla sequentes seruire ualeant, hisque sacris ministeriis secundum tuam uoluntatem quando tibi placuerit expletis, caelestis regni gloriam cum omnibus nobis sibique commissis percipere mereantur. Per.

VIII

55 CONSECRATIO CRVCIS. Benedic domine hanc crucem tuam per quam eripuisti mundum a potestate demoniorum et superasti passione suggessorem peccati qui gaudebat in praeuaricatione primi hominis per uetitum lignum sanctifica domine istud signaculum passionis tuae ut sit inimicis tuis obstaculum et credentibus in te perpetuum perfice uexillum.

56 ITEM ALIA. Rogamus te domine sanctae pater omnipotens aeterne deus, ut digneris benedicere hoc lignum crucis tuae, ut remedium sit singulare generi humano, sit soliditas fidei, profectus bonorum operum, redemptio animarum, protectio ac tutela, contra saeua iacula inimicorum. Per dominum.

57 HIC PONATVR CRI<S>MA. Omnipotens sempiterne deus qui per lignum perdito mundo redemptionis tuae lignum crucis praedestinasti, quaesumus ut benedicere digneris hoc lignum

/f. 9v

similitudine crucis tuae signatum, et praepara in ea[1] tuis fidelibus / uirtutem, inimicis autem obstaculum, ad augendum nomini tuo credentium chorum uirtutẹ caelesti. Per.

58 ITEM CONSECRATIO CRVCIS. Omnipotens aeternae deus pater domini nostri iesu christi, tu conditor caeli, conditor angelorum et siderum, tu fundasti terram super stabilitatem suam, tu creasti mare, tu solus omnipotens deus sine principio et sine fine, benedic hanc crucem fabricatam, ad instar et ad imaginem crucis in qua passus est filius tuus unigenitus iesus christus pro salute mundi, quae erat diffusa rore proprio decorati sanguinis iesu christi filii tui + benedicimus, + et consecramus istam crucem in honore nominis tui et memoriam iesu christi filii tui ut sit + et benedicta + et consecrata haec crux inter misteria aecclesiastica in honore trinitatis, patris, et filii, et spiritus sancti. Qui uiuis.

VIIII

59 CONSECRATIO CYMITERII CANENTVR SEPTEM PSALMI, IN CIRCVITV INLVMINENTVR .IIII. CANDELAE. Deus qui es totius orbis conditor, et humani generis redemptor, cunctarumque creaturarum, uisibilium et inuisibilium, perfectus dispositor, te supplici uoce, ac puro corde exposcimus, ut hoc cymiterium siue poliandrum in quo famulorum famularumque tuarum corpora requiescere debent, post curricula huius uitae labentia, sanctificare, purgare, atque benedicere digneris, quique peccatorum remissionem per tuam magnam misericordiam in te fidentibus praestitisti, corporibus uero eorum / in hoc cymiterio quiescentibus, et tubam primi archangeli hic expectantibus, consolationem perpetuam largiter impertire. Per.

/f. 10r

60 ALIA. Domine sanctae pater omnipotens, trina maiestas et una deitas, pater et filius necne spiritus sanctus iustitiae auctor, ueniae largitor, bonorum dator, sanctitatis origo, karismatum distributor, omniumque ad te uenientium pius receptor, praesta propitius, ut hoc cymiterium in honore nominis tui compositum, benedicere et sanctificare concedas, qui abrahae beato

---

[1] *in ea* repeated but marked for omission.

patriarchae famulo tuo terram a filiis ebron comparatam causa sepulturae benedixisti, et qui populo israhelitico promissionis tellurem in aeuo durantem concessisti, famulorum famularumque tuarum corporibus in hoc cymiterium intrantibus quietis sedem et omni incursione malorum spirituum tutelam benignus largitor tribuas, ut post animarum corporumque resurrectionem, coadunantam te donante atque concedente beatitudinem sempiternam percipere mereantur. Per dominum.

61 ITEM ALIA. Domine deus pastor aeternae gloriae, lux et honor sapientię, custos et uigor prudentiae, salus aegrotantium, ualitudo potentium, mestorum solamen, uita iustorum, gloria humilium, te flagitamus, ut hoc sanctorum tuorum cymiterium ab omni spurcitiae iniquamento spirituum inmundorum custodire, mundare, benedicere digneris, atque corporibus humanis huic loco aduenientibus sinceritatem perpetuam *f. 10v* tribuere / non desinas, et quicumque baptismi sacramentum perceperint, et in fide catholica usque ad uitae terminum perseuerantes fuerint, atque decurso huius aeui termino corpora sua in hoc cimiterio requie commendauerint, angelicis tubis concrepantibus materia corporis, et animae unita praemia caelestium gaudiorum sempiterna percipiant. Per.

X

62 BENEDICTIO SEPVLCRI ET LOCVLI. Rogamus te domine sanctae pater omnipotens aeternae deus, ut digneris benedicere et sanctificare hoc sepulchrum et loculum in eo collocatum, ut sit remedium salutare in eo quiescenti, et redemptio animae eius, atque tutela et munimen contra seua iacula inimici. Per.

63 ALIA. Sanctificetur istud habitaculum domine deus per nostram supplicationem, et fugatur ab eo inmundus spiritus, per uirtutem domini nostri iesu christi placida requies corporum, quod postmodum collocabitur, te protegente ac conseruante maiestate tua iesu christe. Qui cum patre.

64 ALIA ORATIO. Adesto domine supplicationibus nostris, et nihil de nostra conscientia praesumentibus ineffabili miseratione tua nobis succurre, ut quod non habet nostrorum fiducia meritorum tuorum, conferat largitas inuicta donorum. Per dominum nostrum.

65 AD SIGNVM ECCLESIAE BENEDICENDVM. IN PRIMIS INTINGVAE .III. IN AQVA ET LAVES IN EA QVAE BENEDICENDA EST HIS VERBIS: / Benedic domine hanc aquam benedictione caelesti, et assistat super eam uirtus spiritus sancti ut cum hoc uasculum ad inuitandos filios ecclesiae praeparatum in ea fuerit tinctum, ubicumque sonuerit eius tinnibulum longe recedat uirtus inimicorum, umbra fantasmatum, incursio turbinum, percussio fulminum, laesio tonitruorum, calamitas temptestatum, omnis spiritus procellarum et cum clangorem illius audierint filii christianorum, crescat in eis deuotionis augmentum, ut festinantes ad piae matris gremium, cantent tibi canticum nouum in ecclesia sanctorum, deferentes in sono tubae praeconium modulationis per psalterium exultationis, per organum suauitatis, per timphanum iocunditatis, quatenus inuitare ualeant in templo sancto tuo suis obsequiis et precibus exercitum angelorum. Saluator mundi, qui uiuit et regnat.

66 POST HAEC CANTABIS PSALMOS SEX, IDEST LAVDA ANIMA MEA DOMINVM VSQVE IN FINE PSALTERII. INTERIM LAVES EVM DE AQVA CVM OLEO ET SALE, ET DIC: Deus qui per moysen legiferum tubas argenteas fieri precepisti, quas dum leuitae tempore sacrificii clangerent sonitu dulcedinis populus monitus ad te orandum fieret praeparatus, quarum clangore ortatus ad bellum tela[1] prosterneret aduersantium, praesta ut hoc uasculum tuae ecclesiae pr$e$paratum, sanctificetur ab spiritu sancto, ut per illius tactum / fideles inuitentur ad praemium, et cum melodia illius auribus insonuerit populorum crescat in eis deuotio fidei[2], procul pellantur omnes insidiae inimici, fragor grandinum, procella turbinum, impetus tempestatum, temperentur infesta tonitrua uentorum, flabra fiant salubriter ac moderate suspensa, prosternantur aeriae potestates dexter$e$ tuae uirtute, ut hoc audientes tintinnabulum tremescant et fugiant ante sanctae crucis uexillum, praesta saluator cui flectitur omne regnum caelestium, terrestrium et infernorum, et omnis lingua confitetur, quod dominus noster iesus christus absorta morte,

/f. 11r

/f. 11v

---

[1]   Over a longer word erased.
[2]   *fidelis* before correction.

per patibulum crucis, regnat in gloria dei patris cum spiritu sancto. Per omnia.

67 TVNC EXTERGIS EVM LINTEO ET DICAS. V. Vox domini super aquas deus maiestatis intonuit dominus super aquas multas. VSQVE IN FINEM PSALMI. POST HAEC TANGIS EVM DE CRISMATE .VII. VICIBVS FORIS INTVS QVATERNIS.

68 ORATIO. Omnipotens sempiternae deus, qui ante archam foederis per clangorum tubarum muros lapideos, quibus aduersantium cingebatur exercitus cadere fecisti, tu hoc tintinnabulum caelesti benedictione perfunde, ut ante sonitum eius longius effugentur ignita iacula inimici, percussio fulminum, impetus lapidum, laesio tempestatum, ut ad interrogationem propheticam. Quid est mare quod fugisti? suis motibus iordanica retro / acta fluenta respondeant. A faciae domini mota est terra, a faciae dei iacob. Qui conuertit petram in stagna aquarum, et rupim in fontes aquarum. Non nobis ergo domine non nobis, sed nomini tuo da gloriam. Super misericordia tua et ueritate tua, ut cum praesens uasculum sicut reliqua altaria uasa, sacro crismate tingitur, oleo sancto ungitur, quicumque ad sonitum eius conuenerint, ab omnibus inimici temptationibus liberi, semper fidei catholicae documenta sectentur. Saluator mundi cui flectitur omne genu caelestium, et terrestrium. Per.

69 TVNC PONES INCENSVM IN ACERNA ET MYRRAM ET FACIAT EVM ET FACIAT FVMVS INTVS ET EXTRA ET CANTES. V. Viderunt te aquę deus uiderunt te aquae. VSQVE IN FINEM PSALMI.

70 Omnipotens deus dominator christe, cui[1] secundum assumptionem carnis dormienti in naui, dum aborta tempestas mare conturbasset, te protinus excitato et imperante dissoluitur, tu necessitatibus populi tui benignus succurre, tu hoc tintinnabulum sancti spiritus rore perfunde, ut ante sonitum illius semper fugiat inimicus, inuitetur ad fidem populus christianus, hostilis terreatur exercitus, confortetur in domino

/f. 12r

---

[1] *qui* before correction.

33

/f. 12v

per eum populus euocatus, atque sicut per dauiticam citharam
delectatus desuper descendat spiritus sanctus, atque sicut[1] super
samuhel crinigerum agnum mactante[2] in holocaustum tuo rex
aeternae / imperio fragor aurarum, turbam reppulit aduersantem,
ita dum huius uasculi transit per nubila ecclesiae conuentum
manus seruet angelica credentium mentes et corpora saluet
protectio sempiterna. Per.

XII

71 INCIPIT ORDO QVOMODO IN ROMANA ECCLESIA
SANCTAE RELIQVIAE CONDANTVR
PRIMVM EAT EPISCOPVS AD LOCVM IN QVO
PRETERITA NOCTE RELIQVIAE CVM VIGILIIS
FVERVNT ET ELEVET EAS CVM LAETANIA ET DAT
ORATIONEM HANC: Aufer a nobis domine quaesumus
iniquitates nostras, ut ad sancta sanctorum puris mereamur
mentibus introire. Per.

72 DEINDE ELEVENT EAS CVM FERETRO CANTANDO ET
PORTENT AD NOVAM CVM AN. Ambulate sancti dei ad locum
destinatum. ALIA A. De hierusalem exeunt. A. Ecce populus. A. Cum
iocunditate exibitis.

73 PERGANT CVM CRVCIBVS, ET TVRRIBVLIS AD
HOSTIVM NOVAE ECCLESIAE DICAT OREMVS. Deus qui
in omni loco tuae dominationis dedicator adsistis, exaudi nos
quaesumus ut inuiolabilis huius ecclesiae permaneat
consecratio, ut beneficia tui muneris quae supplicat mereatur.
Per.

74 DVM INTRAT EPISCOPVS DICAT AN. O quam metuendus est
locus iste.

75 Domum tuam quaesumus domine clementer ingredere, et in
tuorum tibi cordibus fidelium perpetuam constituae mansionem,
ut cuius aedificatione substitit, huius fiat habitatio praeclara. Per
dominum nostrum iesum christum.

---

[1] *in* before correction.
[2] *mactantem* before correction.

76 ITEM ALIA. / Deus qui uisibiliter omnia contines, et tamen pro salute generis humani, signaculum tuae potentiae uisibiliter ostendis, templum hoc potentiae tuae habitatione inlustra, ut omnes qui huc depraecaturi conueniunt, ex quacumque ad te tribulatione clamauerint, consolationis tuae beneficia consequantur. Per.

77 ITEM ALIA CVM A. Benedictus domine domum.

78 Tabernaculum hoc ingredire quaesumus omnipotens deus sempiternae, et famulos tuos congregatos ad honorem et laudem beatę marię sacrae uirginis benedici, sicut benedicere dignatus es domus patriarcharum abraham, isaac et iacob, pusillis cum magnis, ita benedicere et sanctificare eos et eum dignare. Per.

79 HAEC EXPLETA SVSCIPIAT EPISCOPVS RELIQVIAS A PRESBITERO ET PONAT EAS IN ALTARE NOVO EXTENSO VELO, INTER SE ET POPVLVM ET RECVNDET PROPRIO MANV IN CONFESSIONE ALTARIS ET FACIAT CRVCEM INTVS EX CRISMATE IN QVATTVOR ANGVLIS ITA DICENDO: In nomine patris et filii et spiritus sancti. Pax tibi. RP. Et cum spiritu tuo.

80 ET PONAT TRES PORTIONES CORPORIS DOMINI INTVS, ET TRES DE INCENSO. RECLVDANTVR TVNC RELIQVIAE CANENTES AN. Exultabunt sancti in gloria. PS. Laudate dominum de caelis. A. Sub altare domini sedes accepistis intercedite pro nobis per quam meruistis. PS. Beati inmaculati.

81 ET TVNC PONATVR TABVLA SVPER AQVAM FACIET CRVCES .IIII. EX OLEO ET SANCTAM CRISMAM ET DESIGNANTVR PER QVATTVOR ANGVLOS CVM
CVLTRO ET DICAT PONTIFEX ORATIONEM HANC: / Deus qui ex omni coaptione sanctorum aeternum tibi condis habitaculum, da aedificationis tuae incrementa caelestia, ut quorum reliquias pio amore complectimur, eorum semper meritis adiuuemur. Per.

82 POST HAEC VESTIATVR ALTARE CVM AQVA BENEDICTA ET INCENSO DICAT EPISCOPVS AN.

Ornauerunt faciem templi coronis aureis et dedicauerunt altare domino qui facta est laetifia magna in populo. A. Zacheae festinans descende quia hodię in domo tua oportet me manere at ille festinans descendit et suscepit illum gaudens alleluia hodie huic domui salus a domino facta est alleluia.

83 DVM ORNANTVR ALTARIA CANANTVR HAEC ET DICAT PONTIFEX ORATIONEM: Descendat quaesumus domine deus noster spiritus sanctus tuus super hoc altare qui et populi tui dona sanctificet, et sumentium corda dignanter emundet. Per.

84 DEINDE INCIPIAT CANTOR A. Terribilis est locus iste. DEINDE GLORIA IN EXCELSIS.

85 COLLECTA AD MISSAM. Deus qui sacrandorum tibi auctor es munerum, effunde super hanc orationis domum benedictionem tuam, ut ab omnibus inuocantibus nomen tuum, defensionis auxilium sentiantur. Per dominum.

86 LECTIO LIBRI APOCALIPSIS IOHANNIS APOSTOLI. In diebus illis. Vidi ciuitatem sanctam hierusalem.

87 R. Locus iste a deo factus est. V. Deus cui adstat angelorum chorus. Alleluia. Adorabo ad templum.

88 SECVNDVM LVCAM. In illo tempore dixit iesus discipulis. Non est arbor bona.

89 OF. Domine deus in simplicitate. V. Maiestas. V. Fecit salomon.

90 SVPER OBLATA. Omnipotens sempiternae deus, altare nomini tuo dicatum caelestis uirtutis benedictione / sanctifica, et omnibus in te sperantibus auxilii tui munus ostende, et hic sacramentorum uirtus, et uotorum obtineatur affectus. Per dominum nostrum iesum christum.

/f. 14r

91 PRAEFATIO. VD aeternae deus, per christum. Per quem te suppliciter depraecamur, ut altare hoc sanctis usibus praeparatum, caelesti dedicatione sanctifices. Vt sicut melchisedech sacerdotis precipui oblationem dignatione mirabili suscepisti, ita imposita nouo huic altari munera semper acceptare digneris. Vt populus qui in hanc ecclesiae domum sanctam conuenit, per haec libamina caelesti sanctificatione saluatus, animarum quoque suarum salutem perpetuam consequatur. Et ideo.

92 BENEDICTIO. Benedicat et custodiat uos omnipotens deus, domumque hanc sui muneris praesentia illustrare, atque suę pietatis oculos super eam die ac nocte dignetur aperire. AMEN. Concedatque propitius, ut omnes qui ad dedicationem huius basilicae deuotae conuenistis, intercedente beato .ill. et caeteris sanctis tuis quorum reliquiae hic pio uenerantur amore, uobiscum hinc ueniam peccatorum uestrorum reportare ualeatis. AMEN.
Quatinus eorum interuentu ipsi templum sancti spiritus in quo sancta deus trinitas iugiter habitare dignetur efficiamini, post huius uitae labentis excursum, ad gaudia aeterna feliciter peruenire mere/amini. AMEN.
Quod ipse praestare dignetur. AMEN.

/f. 14v

93 CO. Domus mea domus orationis uocabitur.

94 AD COMPLENDVM. Quaesumus omnipotens deus ut hoc in loco quem nomini tuo indigni dedicauimus, cunctis petentibus aures tuae pietatis ac<c>ommodes. Per dominum nostrum.

XIIII

95 INDE PROCEDENS AD FONTES ET CONSECRET. Omnipotens sempiternae deus hoc baptisterium caelesti uisitatione dedicatum, spiritus sancti tui inlustratione sanctifica, ut quoscumque fons iste lauaturus est, trina ablutione purgati indulgentiam omnium delictorum tuo munere consequantur. Per.

96 ITEM ALIA. Multiplica domine benedictionem tuam, et spiritus tui munere fidem nostram corrobora, ut qui in hac fluenta descenderint, in libro uitae adscribi mereantur. Per.

97 ET POSTEA PER TOTAM EBDOMADAM MISSA PVBLICA IN IPSA ECCLESIA CELEBRETVR ET IN IPSIS .VIII. DIEBVS IBI LVMINARIA ANTE ALTARE AVT DE CERA AVT DE OLEO DEBENT ESSE, ABSQVE LVMINARIBVS,

ET OFFICIIS NOCTVRNIS DIVRNISQVE IN PREDICTIS
.VIII. DIEBVS VLLO MODO REPPERIATVR VSQVE DVM
.VIII. DIES COMPLEANTVR.

XV

98 ELECTIO QVOMODO A CLERO ET A POPVLO ELIGITVR
EPISCOPVS IN PROPRIA SEDE CVM¹ CONSENSV REGIS
ARCHIPRAESVLISQVE OMNIQVE POPVLO

/f. 15r

Domino francorumque meritis coequando pa<t>ri patrum
domno .N. praesuli summo cunctus clerus / omnisque populus
sanctae .ill. ecclesiae multimodam in domino obtamus salutem.
Igitur quoties aliqua pleps uestrae dictioni subdita a proprio
fuerit uiduata pastore non aliunde nisi a uobis est implorandum
auxilium. Quem ad hoc diuina praeordinauit maiestas, ut non
solum uestros specialiter pascatis filios sed etiam rectores non
habentibus, et spiritali pabulo indigentibus pastores tribuetis.
Quapropter ad uestrae sanctitatis paternitatem fiducialiter
nostras fundimus preces, poscentes uidelicet ut hunc .ill. summe
honestatis, humilem uestrum famulum nobis pontificem
ordinare indigemini. Cuius conuersationcm et mores in quantum
cognouimus laudamus, et ad tam dignum opus idoneum
testificamus. Et quamdiu ad benedictionem episcopali inmunes
sumus eius doctrina et exemplo roborati, ad uiam salutis,
domino miserante, quasi perdita onus et inuenta, redituros nos
credimus. Quod decretum nostris manibus roboratum .ill.
ecclesiae uestrae uobis dirigere statuimus. Anno incarnationis
domini, et episcopatus uestri, et regi .ill. annorum illorum.
Indictione tale, datarum tale.

XVI

99 ORATIO AB ARCHIEPISCOPO DICENDA POST
ELECTIONEM SVPER ELECTVM ET SVPER SE. Oremus
fratres ut deus et dominus noster iesus christus, nos et electum
nostrum gratia spiritus sancti inlustrare dignetur. Per.

/f. 15v

100 SEQVITVR AMMONITIO EPISCOPI. / Haec solita mente et
studio uigilanti conserua et tibi commissis nota facere cura, ut

¹ *COM* before correction.

38

unanimes uno ore conlaudetis deum de suis erga uos beneficiis
cui exibendus est honor et gloria. Per omnia.

101 PROMISSIO. In nomine altithroni conditoris regis aeterni, ego
.N. humilis christi famulus licet indignus ad episcopalem ill.
ecclesiae sedem electus ad regendam eam deoque seruatam,
suppliciter confiteor cum omnipotentis dei auxilio et quantam
uoluerit mihi gratiam superna sapientia reuelare, et uitam
commodare in hoc seculo quo dego sanctae saluatoris mundi .ill.
et uenerando patriarchi .ill. eiusque successoribus, quem
superna praeuidet gratia, et nobis praedestinat in patre deuota et
fideli mente semper deseruire et oboedire desidero, stabilemque
me esse permanentem, sine aliqua dissimulatione et
deceptatione omnibus diebus quamdiu spiritus est in naribus
meis, et uita comis fuerit numquam ad dexteram neque ad
sinistram ab illa sede .ill. ecclesiae quae caput est, sed sine
aliquo scrupulo diabolicę fraudis et humili deuotioni et sincera
mente illo praefato patri .ill. et successoribus eius, quem diuina
gratia ad illam sanctam sedem praedestinauit episcopum,
deseruire et oboedire omnibus uiribus meis deo omnipotenti
confiteor, et illam sanctam apostolicam fidem quam patres
nostri digne seruauerunt, cum omni humilitate et oboedientia
diuina, simus et hu/mana sicut praedecessores mei ipsa sede
sancta ecclesiae christi subiuncti sunt, semper seruare me uelle
humiliter per omnia fateor, et quod illi hic et ibi iuste plebi dei
praedicauerunt, et custodiendo impleuerunt hoc praedicare et
obseruare non cesso, fauente et uolente pio domino et saluatori
nostro iesu christo.

f. 16r

XVII

102 ITEM AMMONITIO POST PROMISSIONEM. Memor sis
sponsionis et desponsationis ecclesiasticae et dilectionis domini
dei tui in die qua assequutus es hunc honorem[1], caue ne
obliuiscaris illius.

---

[1] *no* supplied interlinearly.

XVIII

103 BENEDICTIO AD[1] ANVLVM EPISCOPI. Creator et conseruator humani[2] generis, dator gratię spiritalis, largitor aeternae salutis, tu domine permitte tuam benedictionem super hunc anulum, ut armata uirtute caelestis defensionis proficiat illis ad aeternam salutem. Per.

104 HIC DETVR ANVLVS IN DIGITO. Accipe[3] ergo anulum discretionis et honoris fidei signum, ut quae signanda sunt signes, et quae aperienda sunt prodas, quae liganda sunt liges, quae soluenda sunt solues, atque credentibus per fidem baptismatis, lapsis autem sed poenitentibus per ministerium reconciliationis ianuas regni caelestis aperias, cunctis uero de thesauro dominico noua et uetera proferas, ad aeternam salutem omnibus consolatus gratia domini nostri iesu christi. Qui cum patre et spiritu sancto uiuit et regnas.

XVIIII

105   BENEDICTIO BACVLI

/f. 16v   / Tu baculus nostrae, et rector per saecula uitae,
Istum sanctifica pietatis iure bacillum,
Quo mala sternantur, quo semper recta regantur.

106 HIC DETVR PASTORALIS BACVLVS. Accipe baculum sacri regiminis signum, ut inbecilles consolides, titubantes confirmes, prauos corrigas, rectos dirigas in uiam salutis aeternae, habeasque potestatem erigendi dignos, et corrigendi indignos, cooperante domino nostro iesu christo. Qui cum patre et spiritu sancto uiuit et regnat[4], per omnia.

107 ITEM ALIA DATIO. Accipe baculum pastoralis officii, et sis in corrigendis uitiis saeuiens, in ira iudicium sine ira tenens, cum iratus fueris, misericordia reminiscens. Per.

---

[1] Supplied interlinearly.
[2] *ni* supplied interlinearly.
[3] *e* supplied interlinearly.
[4] I have supplied the doxology normally attached to this prayer. *Ratoldus* gives: *q. p. i. s. s. c. h. i. per omnia*, which is not capable of expansion according to normal rules.

108 MODO SVRGENDI SVNT ET INCIPIATVR INTROITVM:
Elegit te dominus sibi in sacerdotem. PS. Exaudiat te deus. AD R. Mittat
tibi. ALIA. Sicut fui cum moysi. PS. Exaudiat te deus. ALIA. Benedixit te
hodie deus. PS. Deus deorum.

XX

109 ORATIO AD MISSAM IN DIE. Oremus dilectissimi nobis ut
huic uiro ad utilitatem ecclesiae prouehendo benignitas
omnipotentis dei gratiae suae tribuat largitatem. Per.

110 EPISTOLA. Karissimi. Fidelis sermo. Si quis episcopatum
desiderat.

111 R. Memor sit omnis sacrificii tui. V. Mittat tibi domine. V. Immola deo. TR.
Desiderium. ALL. Disposuit. ALL. Diffusa est gratia.

112 HIC ORDINANDVS EST EPISCOPVS ANTEQVAM
LEGATVR EVANGELIVM POST ALLELVIA. ET TVNC
DEBENT DVO EPISCOPI DEDVCERE ILLVM PER MANVS
EXTRA SECRETARIVM IN PRE/SENTIA ARCHIEPISCOPI
ANTE ALTARE, ET PROSTERNENS SE ET CAETERI
FACIANT LAETANIAM. FINITA, TENTENTES LIBRVM
EVANGELII SVPER SCAPVLAS ET ARCHIEPISCOPVS,
BENEDICAT EVM.

f. 17r

XXI

113 Adesto domine supplicationibus nostris omnipotens deus, et
quod humilitatis nostrae gerendum est, ministerio tuae uirtutis
impleatur effectu. Per.

114 ALIA. Propitiare supplicationibus nostris et inclinato super hunc
famulum tuum cornu gratiae sacerdotalis, benedictionis tuae in
eo effunde uirtutem. Per dominum nostrium iesum christum
filium tuum.

XXII

115 CONSECRATIO AB ARCHIEPISCOPO SOLO DICENDA.
Deus honorum omnium, deus omnium dignitatumque gloriae
tuae sacris famulantur ordinibus, deus qui moysen famulum
tuum secreti familiaris affectu, inter caetera caelestis documenta

culturae. De habitu quoque indumenti, sacerdotalis instituens, electum aaron, mistico amictu uestiri inter sacra iussisti, ut intelligentiae sensum de exemplis priorum caperet secutura posteritas, ne erudito doctrinae tuae ulli deesset aetati, cum apud ueteres reuerentia ipsa significationum spicies optineret, et apud nos certiora essent, experimenta rerum, quam enigmata

/f. 17v figurarum. Illius namque sacerdotii anterioris abitus nostrae / mentis ornatus est, et pontificalem gloriam non iam nobis honor commendat uestium, sed splendor animarum, quia et illa quae tunc carnalibus blandiebantur optutibus ea potius quae in ipsis erant intelligenda poscebant, et idcirco huic famulo tuo quem ad summi sacerdotii ministerium elegisti, hanc quesumus domine gratiam largiaris, ut quicquid illa uelamina in fulgore auri, in nitore gemmarum, in multimodi operis uarietate signabant, hoc eius moribus actibusque clarescat. Comple domine in sacerdote tuo mysterii tui summam, et ornamentis totius glorificationis instructum eum caelestis unigenti flore sanctifica. HIC PONATVR OLEVM SVPER CAPVT EIVS. Hoc domine copiose in eius caput influat, hoc in oris subiecta decurrat, hoc in totius corporis extrema descendat, ut tui spiritus uirtus et interiora eius repleat, et exteriora eius circumtegat. Abundet in eo constantia fidei, puritas dilectionis, sinceritas pacis. Sint spetiosi munere tuo pedes eius ad euangelizandam pacem, ad euangelizandum bona tua. Da ei domine mysterium reconciliationis[1] in uerbis et factis, et uirtutibus et signis et prodigiis. Sit sermo eius prędicatio, non in persuabilibus humanę sapientiae uerbis, sed in ostensione spiritus et uirtutis. Da ei domine claues regni caelorum, utatur nec glorietur potestate quam tribuis, in edificationem et non in

/f. 18r destructionem. / Quodcumque ligauerit super terram, sit ligatum et in caelis, et quodcumque soluerit super terram, sit solutum et in caelis. Quorum detenuerit peccata, detenta sint, et quorum dimiserit tu dimittas. Qui benedixerit ei sit benedictus, et qui maledixerit ei maledictionibus repleatur. Sit fidelis ei seruus et prudens, quem constituas dominum super familiam tuam, ut det illis cybum in tempore necessario, ut exibeat omnem hominem perfectum. Sit sollicitudine inpiger, sit spiritu feruens. Oderit

---

[1] *ci* supplied interlinearly.

superbiam, diligat ueritatem, nec eam umquam deserat, aut[1] lassitudine aut timore superatus. Non ponat lucem tenebras, nec tenebras lucem. Non dicat malum bonum, nec bonum malum. Sit sapientibus et insipientibus debitor, ut fructum de profectu omnium consequatur. Tribuas ei domine cathedram episcopalem ad regendam ecclesiam tuam, et plebem uniuersam. Sis ei auctoritas, sis ei firmitas, sis ei potestas. Multiplices super eum benedictionem, et gratiam tuam, ut ad exorandam misericordiam tuam tuo munere semper idoneus, tua gratia possit esse deuotus. Per.

116 ITEM ALIA SVPER EPISCOPO. Pater sanctae omnipotens deus, qui per dominum nostrum iesum christum ab initio cuncta creasti, et postmodum in fine temporum secundum pollicitationem quam habraham patriarcha noster acceperat, / ecclesiam quoque sanctorum congregatione fundasti, ordinatis rebus per quas legibus a te datis disciplinę religio regeneretur, praesta ut hic famulus tuus sit ministeriis cunctisque fideliter gestis officiis dignus, ut antiquitus instituta sacramentorum possit misteria caelebrare, per te in summum ad quod assumitur socerdotium consecretur. Sit super eundem benedictio tua, licet manu nostra sit. Praecipe domine huic pascere oues tuas ac tribue ut commissi gregis custodia sollicitus pastor inuigilet. Spiritus huic sanctus tuus caelestium carismatum diuisor adsistat, ut sicut ille electus gentium doctor instituit, sit iustitia non indigens, benignitate pollens, hospitalitate diffusus, seruet in exortationibus alacritatem, in persecutionibus fidem, in caritate patientiam, in ueritate constantiam, in heresibus ac uitiis omnibus odium sciat, in emulationibus nesciat. In iudiciis gratiosum esse sinas, et gratum esse concedas. Postremo omnia a te largiter discat, quae salubriter tuos doceat. Sacerdotium ipsum opus esse existimet, non dignitatem. Proficiant ei honoris augmenta, etiam ad incrementa meritorum, ut per haec sicut aput nos nunc adscisscitur in sacerdotium, ita aput te postea adsciscatur in regnum. Per dominum.

117 TVNC DEBET EI MANVS VNGERE. / Vnguantur manus iste et sanctificentur, et in te deo deorum ordinentur, ungo has

f. 18v

f. 19r

---

[1] *t* supplied later.

43

manus oleo sanctificato, et crismate unctionis purificato, sicut unxit moyses uerba oris sui manus sancti aaron germani sui, et sicut unxit spiritus sanctus per suos flatus manus omnium sacerdotum, et sicut iesus saluator omnium nostrorum, sanctas manus suorum apostolorum, ita unguentur manus et sanctificentur et consecrentur, ut in omnibus sint perfectae in nomine tuo pater filiique atque aeternae spiritus sanctae qui es unus ac summus deus omnium uiuorum et mortuorum manens in saecula saeculorum.

118 TVNC DEBET EI CAPVT VNGERE. Vngatur et consecretur caput tuum caelesti benedictione in ordine pontificali, in nomine patris, et filii, et spiritus sancti. Pax tibi. R. Et cum spiritu tuo.

119 Domine iesu christe tu praeelegisti apostolos tuos, ut doctrina nobis praeessent, ita etiam uice apostolorum episcopos doctrinam docere, et benedicere, et erudire digneris, ut inmaculatam uitam et inlesam conseruent, quatenus spiritus sanctus septiformis ueniat super eos, et super nos omnes, et uirtus altissimi sine peccato una custodiat nos, et omnis benedictio quae in scripturis sanctis scripta est super nos pariter ueniat, et confirmet nos deus pater, et filius et spiritus sanctus, ut habeamus uitam aeternam in saecula saeculorum.

120 ET TVNC LEGATVR EVANGELIVM, SECVNDVM LVCAM.
/f. 19v   / In illo tempore. Facta est contentio.

121 ET TVNC OFFERAT, PANEM ET VINVM, IPSE ET OMNES. OF. Inueni dauid seruum meum. <V.> Memor sit dominus. OF. Gloria et honore.

122 SVPER OBLATA. Haec hostia domine quaesumus emundet nostra delicta, et sacrificium caelebrandum subditorum tibi corpora, mentesque sanctificet. Per.

123 IN FRACTIONE. Hanc igitur oblationem seruitutis nostrae, sed et cuncte familiae tuae quam tibi offerimus et iam pro famulo tuo .ill. quem ad episcopatum ordinem promouere dignatus es, quaesumus domine ut placatus accipias, et propitius in eo tua

44

dona custodias, ut quod diuino consecutus est munere diuinis effectibus exsequatur. D<i>esque nostros in tua.

124 BENEDICTIO EPISCOPALIS IN DIE. Deus qui populis indulgendo consoleris, et amore dominaris, da spiritum sapientiae quibus tradidisti regimen disciplinae. AMEN.
Et de profectu sanctarum ouium fiant gaudia aeterna pastorum, et de electione eorum, gaudeant simul in aeternum. AMEN.
Et quidem dierum nostrorum numeros temporumque mensuras, maiestatis tuae potestate dispensas, ad humilitatis nostrae respice seruitutem, et pacis tuae abundantiae tempora nostra praetende et conserua. AMEN.
Collatis quoque in nos per gratiam tuam propitiare muneribus, et quem fecisti gradu episcopali sublimen, fac operum profectione tibi esse placabilem. AMEN.
Atque in eum affectum dirige cor plebis et praesulis, / ut nec pastori oboedientia gregis, nec gregi umquam desit cura pastoris. AMEN.
Quod ipse praestare dignetur.

f. 20r

125 ET TVNC COMMVNICANT OMNES EPISCOPI AD MANVS ARCHIEPISCOPI.

126 CO. Laetificabimur in salutari tuo et in nomine domini dei nostri magnificabimur. CO. Beatus seruus.

127 AD COMPLENDVM. Plenum quaesumus domine in nobis remedium tuae miserationis operare, et tales nos esse perfice, ut propitius nos ubique fouere digneris. Per dominum.

128 TVNC MITTENDVS EST IN CATHEDRA ET HAEC DICENDA ORATIO. Omnipotens pater sanctae deus aeternae, tu omnem ordinem dignatus es in caelestibus sedibus ordinare, ut ait psalmista. Domine in aeternum permanet uerbum tuum in caelo, angelos et archangelos suo tibi ordine mancipari, in ueteris testamenti priuilegio moysen et aaron et samuel inter eos in sacerdotibus suis, qui inuocant nomen eius, patriarchas, prophetas perungui ordinasti, in nouo per filium tuum iesum christum, apostolos sanctos suis ordinibus elegisti, primum petrum apostolum in cathedra honoris, et mathiam eiusdem

45

consortis in apostolatum, atque cathedra honoris enumerasti, et in numero sanctorum omnium apostolorum euocasti, ut spiritus sanctus ait per prophetam, in cathedra seniorum laudent dominum diuino nutu aeque de aliis haec illis contingerunt, et tu domine pro tua inmensa misericordia in nostris temporibus, / da similem gratiam fratri nostro .ill. ad instar sanctorum apostolorum tuorum sedentium in cathedra honoris et dignitatis, ut in conspectu maiestatis tuae, dignus honore appareat. Per eundem.

/f. 20v

XXIII

129 ORATIONES QVAE DICENDAE SVNT A DOMNO PAPA
SVPER ARCHIEPISCOPVM ANTE PALLEVM

Deus omnipotens pater qui non propriis suffragantibus meritis, sed sola ineffabili gratiae tuae largitate, istum famulum tuum .ill. populo tuo preesse iussisti, tribue ei per gratiam spiritus sancti tui, digne tibi persoluere ministerium sacerdotalis officii, et ecclesiasticis conuenienter seruire ministeriis, plebemque commissam, ad gloriam tui nominis te in omnibus protegente, gubernare concede. Per dominum.

130 ITEM ALIA. Deus innocentiae restituor et amator, dirige hunc famulum tuum .il. spiritus tui feruore, ut in fide inueniatur stabilis, et operibus tuis efficax, illuminare eum lumine sapientiae, munda eum et sanctifica, da ei consilium rectum, doctrinam sanctam, ut qui eum inter summos sacerdotes uoluisti numerare, concede ut quod humano ore eum uoluisti uocari, hoc in conspectu tuo per gratiam tuae pietatis possit fieri, ut cum electis tuis aeternae uitae beatitudinem percipere mereatur. Per dominum nostrum iesum christum filium tuum.

XXIIII

131 HIC DETVR PALLIVM. CONSECRATIO POST PALLEVM.

f. 21r

/ Domine sanctae pater omnipotens aeternae deus, rex regum et dominus dominantium, clementiam tuam humiliter exoramus, necnon et unigeniti filii tui domini nostri iesu christi, qui omnes aeterno pontificatu super eminens, solus sine macula sacerdotale ministerium impleuit, simulque sancti spiritus cuius septiformis gratia caelesti uirtute cuncta sanctificas, ut hunc famulum tuum .ill. diuinae prouidentiae gratia largiente, a

46

minoribus usque ad maiora per gradus ascendentem, supernae pietatis tuo gremio gratanter suscipias, et quia nobis indignis quos sedis apostolicae summęque ministros seruitutis non exigentibus meritis, sed dono clementiae tuae constituisti salutaribus indumentis, ad sacri altaris officium foras uestitus in praesenti apparet, ab omnibus criminum contagiis castigatus perpetua, spiritus tui sanctificatione intus impleri mereatur, uiuique fontis fluentibus irrigatum, uirtutum fructibus crescere, et coram omnibus claresc<er>e concedas, ut eius uita aliis possit exempla prebere. Sit ei honor pallei ornamentum animae, et unde aduenit fastigium uisibile, inde florescat amor inuisibilis, tua diuina potentia eum corroboret, tui filii uirtus uiscera eius fecundet, tui spiritus gratia interiora eius impleat, per te firmitatem / fidei catholicae non solum sibimet seruandi, sed etiam alios docendi causa conseruet, per te cathedre episcopalis ecclesiae uniuersalis scutum, non solum a spiritibus sed etiam a corporalibus huius saeculi, aduersitatibus habere mereatur, per te apostolicę dignitatis in caelis et in terris, soluendi et ligandi non solum corpora, sed et animas diuinas ditatus, gratia dominium suscipiat, ut ita dignis successibus deuote degens, ad destinata sanctis premia perueniens, aeternam accipiat beatitudinem. Per.

f. 21v

XXV
INCIPIT PERCVNCTATIO SIVE ELECTIO EPISCOPORVM AC CLERICORVM NECNON POPVLORVM AD REGEM CONSECRANDVM SIVE BENEDICENDVM

132 AMMONITIO EPISCOPORVM VEL CLERICORVM SEV POPVLORVM AD REGEM, DICENDA ITA, LEGATVR AB VNO EPISCOPO CORAM OMNIBVS. A uobis perdonari petimus, ut unicuique de nobis, et ecclesiis nobis commissis, canonicum priuilegium ac debitam legem, atque iustitiam conseruetis, et defensionem exibeatis, sicut rex in suo regno unicuique episcopo et ecclesiae sibi commissae per rectum exibere debet.

133 RESPONSIO REGIS. PROMITTO VOBIS ET PERDONO QVIA VNICVIQVE DE VOBIS ET ECCLESIIS VOBIS COMMISSIS, CANONICVM PRIVILEGIVM ET DEBITAM LEGEM ATQVE IVSTITIAM SERVABO, ET

/f. 22r

DEFENSIONEM QVANTVM POTVERO ADIVVANTE DOMINO EXIBEBO, / SICVT REX IN SVO REGNO, VNICVIQVAE EPISCOPO ET ECCLAESIAE SIBI COMMISSAE PER RECTVM EXIBERE DEBET.

134 DEINDE ALLOQVANTVR DVO EPISCOPI POPVLVM IN ECCLESIA, INQVIRENTES EORVM VOLVNTATEM. ET SI CONCORDES FVERINT, AGANT DEO GRATIAS OMNIPOTENTI DECANTANTES, TE DEVM LAVDAMVS. ET DVO EPISCOPI ACCIPIANT EVM PER MANVS, ET DEDVCANT ANTE ALTARE ET PROSTERNET SE VSQVE IN FINEM TE DEVM LAVDAMVS.

135 INVOCATIO SVPER REGEM. Te inuocamus domine sanctae pater omnipotens aeternae deus, ut hunc famulum tuum .N. quam tuae diuinę dispensationis prouidentia in primordio plasmatum, usque hunc praesentem diem, iuuenili flore laetantem crescere concessisti, eum tuae pietatis dono ditatum, plenumque gratia ueritatis de die in diem coram deo et hominibus ad meliora semper proficere facias, ut summi regiminis solium gratiae supernae largitate gaudens suscipiat, et misericordiae tuae muro ab hostium aduersitate undique munitus, plebem sibi commissam cum pace propitiationis et uirtute uictoriae, feliciter regere mereatur. Per dominum.

136 ITEM ORATIO. Deus qui populis tuis uirtute consulis et amore dominaris, da huic famulo tuo spiritum sapientiae cum regimine disciplinae, ut tibi toto corde deuotus in regni regimine maneat semper idoneus, / tuoque munere ipsius temporibus securitas ecclesiae dirigatur, et in tranquillitate deuotio christiana permaneat, ut in bonis operibus perseuerans, ad aeternum regnum te duce, ualeat peruenire. Per.

/f. 22v

137 ALIA. In diebus eius oriatur omnibus aequitas et iustitia, amicis adiutorium, inimicis obstaculum, humilibus solatium, elatis correctio, diuitibus doctrina, pauperibus pietas, peregrinis pacificatio, propriis in patria pax et securitas, unicuique secundum suam mensuram moderate gubernans, seipsum sedulus discat, ut tua irrigatus compunctione toto populo tibi placita prębere possit exempla, et per uiam ueritatis cum grege

gradiens sibi subdito, opes frugales habundanter adquirat, simul ad salutem non solum corporum, sed etiam cordium a te concessam cuncta accipiat. Sicque in te cogitatum animi consiliumque omne componens plebis gubernacula, cum pace simul et sapientia, semper inuenire uideatur. Teque auxiliante praesentis uitae prolixitatem percipiat, et per tempora bona usque ad summam senectutem perueniat, huiusque fragilitatis finem perfectum, ab omnibus uitiorum uinculis tuae pietatis largitate liberatus, et infinitae prosperitatis premia perpetua angelorumque aeterna / comercia consequatur. Per.

. 23r

XXVI

138 CONSECRATIO REGIS. Omnipotens sempiterne deus, creator ac gubernator caeli et terrae, conditor et dispositor angelorum et hominum, rex regum et dominus dominorum, qui abraham fidelem famulum tuum, de hostibus triumphare fecisti, moysi et iosuae populo tuo praelatis multiplicem uictoriam tribuisti, humilem quoque dauid puerum tuum regni fastigio sublimasti, eumque de ore leonis et de manu bestiae atque goliae, sed et de gladio maligno saul et omnium inimicorum eius liberasti, et salomonem sapientię pacisque ineffabili munere ditasti, respice propicius ad praeces nostrae humilitatis, et super hunc famulum tuum, quem supplici deuotione in regnum .N. albionis totius uidelicet francorum pariter eligimus, benedictionum tuarum dona multiplica, eumque dextera tuae potentiae semper ubique circumda, quatinus praedicti abrahę fidelitate firmatus, moysi mansuetudine fretus, iosuę fortitudine munitus, dauid humilitate exaltatus, salomonis sapientia decoratus, tibi in omnibus complaceat, et per tramitem iusticiae inoffenso gressu semper incedat, et totius albionis ecclesiam deinceps cum plebibus sibi annexis ita enutriat, ac doceat, muniat, et instruat, contraque omnes uisibiles et inuisibiles / hostes idem potenter regaliterque tuae uirtutis regimen amministret, ut regale solium uidelicet francorum sceptra non deserat, sed ad pristinę fidei pacisque concordiam eorum animos te opitulante reformet, ut utrorumque horum populorum debita subiectione fultus, condigno amore glorificatus, per longum uitae spatium paternae apicem gloriae tua miseratione unatim stabilire et gubernare mereatur, tuae quoque protectionis galea munitus, et scuto insuperabili iugiter protectus, armisque caelestibus circumdatus,

. 23v

obtabilis uictoriae triumphum de hostibus feliciter capiat, terroremque suae potentiae infidelibus inferat, et pacem tibi militantibus laetanter reportet. Virtutibus necnon quibus praefatos fideles tuos decorasti, multiplici honoris benedictione condecora, et in regimine regni sublimiter colloca, et oleo gratiae spiritus sancti perunge.

139 HIC VNGATVR OLEO. A. Vnxerunt salamonem sadoc sacerdos et nathan propheta regem in gion et accedentes laeti dixerunt uiuat rex in aeternum.

140 Vnde unxisti sacerdotes reges, et prophetas, ac martyres, qui per fidem uicerunt regna et operati sunt iustitiam, adque adempti sunt promissiones. Cuius sacratissima unctio super caput eius defluat, atque ad interiora descendat, et cordis illius intima /f. 24r penetret, et promissionibus / quas adempti sunt uictoriosissimi reges, gratia tua dignus efficiatur, quatinus et in praesenti saeculo feliciter regnet, et ad eorum consortium in caelesti regno perueniat, per dominum nostrum iesum christum filium tuum, qui unctus est oleo laetitiae prae consortibus suis, et uirtute crucis potestates aereas debellauit, tartara destruxit, regnumque diaboli superauit, et ad caelos uictor ascendit, in cuius manu uictoria, omnis gloria et potestas consistunt, et tecum uiuit et regnat in unitate eiusdem spiritus. Per.

141 ALIA. Deus electorum fortitudo et humilium celsitudo, qui in primordio[1] per effusionem diluuii crimina mundi castigare uoluisti, et per columbam ramum oliuę portantem pacem terris redditam demonst<r>asti, iterumque aaron famulum tuum per unctionem olei sacerdotem sanxisti, et postea per huius ingenti infusionem ad regendum populum israheliticum, sacerdotes reges ac prophetas perfecisti, uultumque ecclesiae in oleo exilarandum per propheticam famuli tui uocem dauid esse praedixisti, ita quaesumus omnipotens pater ut per huius creaturae pinguedinem, hunc seruum tuum sanctificare tua benedictione digneris, eumque in similitudine columbae pacem simplicitatis populo sibi commisso praestare, et exempla aaron /f. 24v in dei seruitio dili/genter imitari regnique fastigia in consiliis scientiae et aequitate iudicii semper adsequi, uultumque

---

[1] *primordia* before correction.

hilaritatis per hanc olei unctionem te adiuuante totius plebis paratum habere facias. Per.

142 ALIA. Deus dei filius iesus christus dominus noster qui a patre oleo exultationis unctus est prae participibus suis, ipse per praesentem sacri unguimus infusionem spiritus paracliti super caput tuum infundat benedictionem, eandemque usque ad interiora cordis tui penetrare faciat, quatinus hoc uisibili et tractabili dono, inuisibilia percipere et temporalia regna, iustis moderaminibus executo, aeternaliter cum eo regnare merearis. Per.

143 HIC DETVR ANVLVM. Accipe anulum signaculum uidelicet sanctae fidei, soliditatem regni, augmentum potentiae, per quae scias triumphali potentia hostes repellere, hereses destruere, subditos coadunare, et catholicae fidei perseuerabilitati conecti. Per.

144 ORATIO POST ANVLVM DATVM. Deus cuius est omnis potestas et dignitas, da famulo tuo pro spiritu suae dignitatis effectum, in qua te remunerante permaneat, semperque timeat, tibique iugiter placere contendat. Per dominum nostrum iesum christum filium tuum.

145 HIC CINGATVR EI GLADIVS AB ARCHIEPISCOPO.
f. 25r / Accipe hunc gladium cum dei benedictione tibi collatum, in quo per uirtutem spiritus sancti resistere, et eiecere omnes inimicos tuos ualeas, et cunctos sanctę dei ecclesiae aduersarios regnumque tibi commissum tutari, atque protegere castra dei, per auxilium inuictissimi triumphatoris domini nostri iesu christi, qui cum patre in unitate spiritus sancti uiuit et regnat, in saecula saeculorum.

146 ORATIO POST GLADIVM. Deus qui prouidentia tua caelestia simul et terrena moderaris, propitiare christianissimo regi nostro, ut omnis hostium suorum fortitudo uirtute gladii spiritualis frangatur, ac te pro illo pugnante penitus conteratur. Per.

147 HIC CORONETVR. Coronet te deus corona glorię atque iusticiae honore et opere fortitudinis, ut per officium nostrae benedictionis cum fide recta, et multiplici bonorum operum fructu, ad coronam peruenias regni perpetui, ipso largiente cuius regnum permanet in saecula saeculorum.

148 ORATIO POST CORONAM. Deus perpetuitatis, dux uirtutum cunctorum hostium uictor, benedic hunc famulum tuum, tibi caput suum inclinantem, et prolixa sanitate, et prospera felicitate eum conserua, et ubicumque, pro quibus auxilium tuum inuocauerit, cito adsis / et protegas ac defendas. Tribue ei quaesumus domine diuitias gratiae tuae, comple in bonis desiderium eius, corona eum in miseratione et misericordia, tibique domino pia deuotione iugiter famuletur. Per dominum nostrum.

/f. 25v

149 HIC DETVR SCEPTRVM. Accipe sceptrum regiae potestatis insigne, uirgam scilicet rectam regni, uirgam uirtutis, qua te ipsum bene regas sanctam ecclesiam, populumque uidelicet christianum tibi a deo commissum, regia uirtute ab improbis defendas. Prauos corrigas, rectos pacifices, et ut uiam rectam tenere possint, tuo iuuamine dirigas, quatinus de temporali regno ad aeternum regnum peruenias, ipso adiuuante cuius regnum et imperium, sine fine permanet in saecula saeculorum.

150 ORATIO POST SCEPTRVM. Omnium domine fons bonorum cunctorumque deus institutor profectuum, tribue quesumus famulo tuo .ill. adeptam bene regere dignitatem, et a te sibi prestitutum honorem dignare corroborare. Honorifica eum prae cunctis regibus terrae uberi eum benedictione locupleta, et in solio regni firma stabilitate consolida. Visita eum in sobole, pręsta ei prolixitatem uitae, in diebus eius semper oriatur iusticia, ut cum iocunditate et laetitia, aeterno glorietur in regno. Per dominum nostrum iesum christum.

/f. 26r

151 / TVNC DATVR EI VIRGA. Accipe uirgam uirtutis atque aequitatis, qua intelligas mulcere pios et terrere reprobos, errantes uiam doce, lapsisque manum porrige, disperdesque superbos, et releues humiles, et aperiat tibi hostium iesus christus dominus noster qui de seipso ait. Ego sum hostium per me si quis introierit saluabitur. Et ipse qui est clauis dauid et sceptrum domus israhel, qui aperit et nemo claudit, claudit et nemo aperit. Sit tibi adiutor qui educit uinctum de domo carceris sedentem in tenebris et umbra mortis, ut in omnibus sequi merearis eum, de quo propheta dauid cecinit. Sedes tua deus in saeculum saeculi uirga aequitatis uirga regni tui, et imitando ipsum qui dicit, diligas iusticiam et odio habeas iniquitatem, propterea unxit te deus deus tuus oleo laetitiae, ad exemplum illius quem ante saecula unxerat prae participibus suis. Iesum christum dominum nostrum.

152 TVNC DICATVR BENEDICTIO. Extendat omnis deus dexteram suae benedictionis, et effundat super te donum suae protectionis, et circumdet te muro felicitatis ac custodia suae propitiationis, sanctae mariae ac beati petri apostolorum principis, sanctique gregorii angelorum apostolici, atque omnium sanctorum intercedentibus meritis. AMEN.

f. 26v Indulgeat tibi dominus omnia mala quae / gessisti, et tribuat tibi gratiam et misericordiam quam humiliter ab eo deposcis, et liberet te ab aduersitatibus cunctis, et ab omnibus uisibilium et inuisibilium inimicorum insidiis. AMEN.

Angelos suos bonos semper et ubique qui te precedant comitentur et subsequantur ad custodiam tui ponat, et a peccato seu gladio et ab omnium periculorum discrimine, sua potentia liberet. AMEN.

Inimicos tuos ad pacis caritatisque benignitatem conuertat, et bonis omnibus te gratiosum et amabilem faciat, pertinaces quoque in tui insectatione et odio confusione salutari induat, super te autem sanctificatio sempiterna floreat. AMEN.

Victoriosum te atque triumphatorem de inuisibilibus atque uisibilibus hostibus semper efficiat, et sancti nominis sui timorem pariter et amorem, continuo cordi tuo infundat, et in fide recta ac bonis operibus perseuerabilem reddat, et pace in diebus tuis concessa, cum palma uictoriae te ad perpetuum regnum perducat. AMEN.

Et qui te uoluit super populum suum constituere regem, et in praesenti saeculo felicem aeternae felicitatis tribuat esse consortem. AMEN.

Quod ipse praestare dignetur.

/f. 27r **153** ITEM ALIA BENEDICTIO. / Benedic domine hunc praesulem principem, qui regna omnium regum a saeculo moderaris. AMEN.

Et tali eum benedictione glorifica, ut dauitica teneat sublimitate sceptrum salutis, et sanctificet propitiationis munere reperiatur locupletus. AMEN.

Da ei a tuo spiramine regere populum, sicut salomonem fecisti regnum optinere pacificum. AMEN.

Quod ipse praestare.

154 REGIS STATVS DESIGNATIO. Sta et retine ammodo quem hucusque paterna suggestione tenuisti hereditario iure tibi delegatum, per auctoritatem dei omnipotentis et per presentem traditionem nostram, omnium scilicet episcoporum ceterorumque dei seruorum, et quanto clerum sacris altaribus propinquiorem prospicis, tanto ei potiorem in locis congruis honorem impendere memineris, quatinus mediator dei et hominum te mediatorem cleri et plebis, in hoc regni solio confirmet, et in regnum aeternum secum regnare faciat. Iesus christus dominus noster, rex regum et dominus dominantium, qui cum deo patre et spiritu sancto.

155 Rectitudo regis est nouiter ordinati, et in solium sublimati. Haec tria praecepta populo christiano sibi subdito praecipere, in primis ut ecclesia dei et omnis populus christianus ueram pacem seruens in omni tempore. Aliud est ut rapacitates et omnes /f. 27v iniqui/tates omnibus gradibus interdicat. Tertium est, ut in omnibus iudiciis aequitatem et misericordiam praecipiat, ut illi et nobis indulgeat sua misericordia[1] clemens et misericors deus. Qui cum patre.

156 ET TVNC DEOSCVLETVR OMNIBVS CLERVM POPVLVMQVE ET DICAT VNVSQVISQVE VIVAT REX FELICITER IN SEMPITERNVM, TRIBVS VICIBVS VIVAT REX, VT SVPRA. VIVAT REX, VT SVPRA. ET POST EVANGELIVM OFFERAT REX AD MANVS ARCHIEPISCOPI OBLATIONEM ET VINVM. ET SIC PERAGATVR MISSA SVO ORDINE. DEINDE

---

[1]   *suam misericordiam* before correction.

COMMVNICETVR AB ARCHIEPISCOPO CORPORE ET
SANGVINE CHRISTI. ET SIC REFERANT DEO GRATIAS.
POST PERGANT AD MENSAM.

XXVII
ITEM AD REGINAM BENEDICENDAM

157 DEBET ENIM ADDVCI IN ECCLESIAM ET PROSTERNI
ANTE ALTARE. ELEVATA AB ORATIONE AB EPISCOPIS,
ET INCLINATO CAPITE DICAT ARCHIEPISCOPVS HANC
ORATIONEM: Adesto domine supplicationibus nostris, et quod
humilitatis nostrae gerendum est, ministerio tuae uirtutis
impleatur effectu. Per.

158 TVNC DEBET CAPVT EIVS VNGVI OLEO. In nomine patris,
et filii, et spiritus sancti, prosit tibi haec unctio olei in honorem
et confirmationem aeternam.

159 SEQVITVR ORATIO POST VNCTIONEM. Omnipotens
sempiternae deus, affluentem spiritum tuae benedictionis super
famulam tuam, nobis orantibus propitiatus infunde, ut quae per
manus nostrae impositionem hodie regina instituitur,
sanctificatione tua / digna et electa permaneat, ut nunquam
postmodum de tua gratia separetur indigna. Per.

f. 28r

160 TVNC DEBET EI ANVLVS MITTI DIGITO. Accipe anulum
fidei signaculum sanctae trinitatis quo possis omnes haereticas
prauitatis deuitare, et barbaras gentes uirtute tibi praestitere, ad
agnitionem ueritatis aduocare.

161 SEQVITVR ORATIO. Deus cuius est omnis potestas et
dignitas, da famulae tuę ill. signo tuae fidei prosperum, suae
dignitatis effectum, in qua tibi semper firma maneat, tibique
iugiter placere contendat.

162 TVNC DEBET INPONI CORONA IN CAPITE. Accipe
coronam gloriae honorem iocunditatis, ut splendida fulgeas, et
aeterna exultatione coroneris. Per dominum.

163 ITEM ORATIO. Omnium domine fons bonorum et cunctorum
dator, profectuum tribuę famulae tuae .ill. adeptam bene regere

dignitatem, et a te sibi praestitam in ea bonis operibus corrobora gloriam. Per dominum.

XXVIII
MISSA PRO REGIBVS

164 Deus regnorum omnium et christiani maxime protector imperii, da seruis tuis regibus nostris .ill. triumphum uirtutis tuae scienter excolere, ut qui tua constitutione sunt principes, tuo semper munere sine potentes. Per dominum nostrum iesum christum.

165 SVPER OBLATA. Suscipe domine preces et hostias ecclesiae tuae pro salute famuli tui .ill. supplicantis, et in protectione / fidelium populorum antiqua brachii tui operare miracula, ut superatus pacis inimicis, secura tibi seruiat christiana libertas. Per.

/f. 28v

166 PRAEFATIO. VD aeternae deus. Qui es fons inmarcessibilis lucis, et origo perpetuae bonitatis regum consecrator. Honorum hominum adtributor, dignitatumque largitor. Cuius incffabilem clementiam uotis omnibus exoramus, ut famulum tuum .ill. quem regalis dignitatis fastigio uoluisti sublimari, sapientiae ceterorumque uirtutum, ornamentis facias decorari. Et quia tui es muneris quod regnat, tuae sit pietatis quod feliciter agat. Quatinus in fundamento spei, fidei, caritatisque fundatus peccatorum labae abstersus, de uisibilibus et inuisibilibus hostibus triumphator effectus, subiecti populo augmento prosteritate et securitate exilaratus, cum eis mutua dileccione conexus. Et transitori regni gubernacula inculpabiliter teneat, et ad aeterni infinita gaudia, te miserante perueniat. Per christum dominum nostrum.

167 IN FRACTIONE. Hanc igitur oblationem famuli tui .ill. quam tibi ministerio officii sacerdotalis offerimus, pro eo quod in ipso potestatem imperii conferre dignatus es, propitius et benignus adsume, et exoratus nostra obsecratione concede, ut maies/tatis tuae protectione confidens, et aeuo augeatur et regno. Per dominum nostrum.

/f. 29r

168 BENEDICTIO. Omnipotens pater et genitus sanctus quoque flatus. Ordine mirifico disponens omnia regna. Conseruet tibi rex regnum per tempora longa. AMEN.
Quique super populum regnare suum uoluit te. Anitiam tibi uirtutem concedat habere. AMEN.
Sicque pie et iustae uiuens, post debita carnis. Quos hodie colimus sanctis iungi merearis. AMEN.
Quod ipse praestare.

169 AD COMPLENDVM. Deus qui ad praedicandum aeterni regis euangelium romanum imperium praeparasti, praetende famulis tuis principibus nostris arma caelestia, ut pax ecclesiarum nulla turbetur tempestate bellorum. Per dominum nostrum iesum.

XXVIIII
MISSA COTIDIANA PRO REGIBVS

170 Quesumus omnipotens deus, ut famulus tuus rex noster, qui tua miseratione suscepit regni gubernacula, uirtutum etiam omnium percipiat incrementa, quibus decenter ornatus, et uitiorum monstra deuitare, et ad te qui uia ueritas et uita es, gratiosus ualeat peruenire. Per dominum.

/f. 29v **171** SVPER OBLATA. Munera domine quaesumus oblata sanctifica, ut et nobis unigeniti tui corpus et sanguis fiant .ill. regi ad obtinendam animae corporisque salutem, et / per agendum iniunctum officium, te largiente usquequaque proficiant. Per.

172 PRAEFATIO. VD aeternę deus. Et pietatem tuam supplici deuotione exposcere, ut haec oblatio quam tibi pro famulo tuo .ill. offerimus, sit in oculis tuis semper accepta. Et sicut sanctos tuos fides recta prouexit ad coronam, ita eum deuotio perducat ad ueniam. Qualiter hae oblatione placatus, a cunctis eum emundes sordibus delictorum, et dites fructu operum bonorum. Per christum.

173 BENEDICTIO. Christus rex regum ex aeuo qui regnat in aeuum. Istum confortet regem sua iura tuentem. <AMEN>.
Quique illum conpsit tritauorum staemate regni. Praesidium tribuat reuerenter hoc retinendi. AMEN.

57

Inuictus quo hic cuncta agatisque suisque fideles. Vt pariter capiant palmas in fine perennes. AMEN.
Quod ipse.

174 AD COMPLENDVM. Haec domine oratio salutaris, famulum tuum ab omnibus tueatur aduersis, quatinus et ecclesiasticae pacis obtineat tranquillitatem, et post istius temporis decursum, ad aeternam perueniat hereditatem. Per dominum.

XXX

175 BENEDICTIO VEXILLI. Inclina domine iesu saluator omnium, et redemptor, aures tuae pietatis ad praeces nostrae humilitatis, et per interuentum beati / michahelis archangeli tui, omniumque caelestium uirtutum, praesta nobis auxilium dexterae tuae, ut sicut benedixisti abraham aduersus quinque reges triumphantem, atque dauid regem in tui nominis laude triumphales congressus exercentem, ita benedicere et sanctificare digneris uexillum hoc quod ob defensionem sanctae ecclesiae contra hostilem rabiem defertur, quatinus in nomine tuo fideles et defensores populi dei illud sequentes, per uirtutem sanctae crucis triumphum et uictoriam se ex hostibus adquisisse laetentur. Qui cum patre et spiritu sancto.

/f. 30r

XXXI

176 EXORCISMVS SALIS. Exorcizo te creatura salis, per deum uiuum, per deum uerum, per deum sanctum, per deum qui te per heliseum prophetam in aqua mitti iussit, ut sanaretur sterilitas aquae, ut efficaris sal exorcizatum in salutem credentium, et sis omnibus te sumentibus sanitas animae et corporis, et effugiat atque discedat ab eo loco quo aspersus fueris, omnis fantasia et nequitia uel uersutia diabolicae fraudis, omnisque spiritus mundus adiuratus, per eum qui uenturus est iudicare uiuos et mortuos et seculum per ignem.

XXXII

177 BENEDICTIO SALIS. Inmensam clementiam tuam omnipotens aeterne deus humiliter imploramus, ut hanc / creaturam salis, quam in usum generis humani tribuisti, + benedicere, + et sanctificare pro tua pietate digneris, ut sit omnibus sumentibus salus mentis et corporis, et quicquid eo tactum uel respersum

/f. 30v

fuerit, careat omni inmunditia, omnique inpugnatio spiritalis nequitiae. Per.

XXXIII

178 EXORCISMVS AQVAE. Exorcizo te creatura aquae in nomine dei patris omnipotentis, et in nomine iesu christi filii eius domini nostri, ut fias aqua exorcizata ad effugandam omnem potestatem inimici, et ipsum inimicum eradicare et explantare cum angelis suis apostaticis, per uirtutem domini nostri iesu christi, qui uenturus est iudicare uiuos et mortuos, et saeculum per ignem. Amen.

XXXIIII

179 BENEDICTIO AQVAE. Deus qui ad salutem humani generis maxima quęque sacramenta in aquarum substantia condidisti, adesto inuocationibus nostris, et elemento huic multimodis purificationibus praeparato, uirtutem tuae benedictionis effunde, ut creatura mysterii tui tibi seruiens, ad abiciendos daemones, morbosque pellendos, diuinae gratiae sumat effectum, ut quicquid in domibus uel in locis fidelium haec unda / resperserit, careat inmunditia, liberetur a noxa, non illic resideat spiritus pestilens, non aura corrumpens, discedant omnes insidiae latentis inimici. Et siquid est quod aut incolomitati habitantium inuidet, aut quieti aspersione huius aquae effugiat, ut salubritas per inuocationem tui nominis expetita, ab omnibus sit inpugnationibus defensa. Per dominum nostrum iesum christum.

/f. 31r

XXXV

180 HIC MITTATVR SAL IN AQVA. BENEDICTIO SALIS ET AQVAE PARITER. Deus inuictę uirtutis auctor, et inseparabilis imperii rex, ac semper magnificus triumphator, qui aduersae dominationis uires reprimis, qui inimici rugientis saeuitiam superas, qui hostiles nequitias potens expugnas, te domine trementes, et supplices depraecamur ac petimus, ut hanc creaturam salis et aquae dignanter accipias, benignus inlustres, pietatis tuae more sanctifices, ut ubicumque fuerit aspersa per inuocationem sancti tui nominis, omnis infestatio inmundi spiritus abiciatur, terrorque uenenosi serpentis procul pellatur, et praesentia sancti spiritus nobis misericordiam tuam poscentibus, ubique adesse dignetur. Per dominum nostrum iesum christum filium tuum, qui tecum uiuit et regnat deus, per omnia saecula.

XXXVI

/f. 31v   **181** ORATIO QVANDO AQVA SPARGITVR IN DOMO. / Exaudi nos domine sanctae pater omnipotens aeternae deus, ut mittere digneris[1] angelum tuum sanctum de caelis, qui custodiat, foueat, protegat, uisitet et defendat omnes habitantes in hoc habitaculo. Per dominum.

XXXVII

182 BENEDICTIO DOMVS. Adesto domine supplicationibus nostris, et hanc domum serenis oculis tuae pietatis inlustra. Descendat super habitantes in ea gratiae tuae larga benedictio, ut in his manufactis habitaculis, cum salubritate manentes, ipsi semper tuum sint habitaculum. Per dominum.

XXXVIII

183 BENEDICTIO FERRI. Benedic domine per inuocationem sanctissimi nominis tui ad manifestandum uerum iudicium tuum, hoc genus metalli ut omne demonum falsitate procul remota ueritas ueri iudicii tui, fidelibus tuis manifesta fiat. Per.

XXXVIIII

184 ITEM CONSECRATIO FERRI. Deus iudex iustus qui auctor pacis es, et iudicas aequitatem, te suppliciter rogamus, ut hoc ferrum ordinatum ad iustitiam, et[2] examinationem cuiuslibet dubietatis faciendam, benedicere et sanctificare digneris, ita ut si innocens de praedicta nominata causa, unde purgatio querenda est in hoc ignitum, et tua benedictione sanctificatum ferrum, manus uel pedes inmiserit illesus[3] appareat tua benignissima miseratione, si autem culpabilis atque reus te[4]

/f. 32r   comtempserit, qui iustus deus es / et omnia iuste et recte iudicas, ut per herbas uel qualiacumque[5] temptamenta siue molimina peccata sua contueri, contra ueritatis tuae examen uoluerit,

---

[1] Supplied interlinearly.
[2] Supplied interlinearly.
[3] The ending rewritten.
[4] Supplied interlinearly.
[5] *qualicumque* before correction.

iustissima misericors domine deus, ut[1] hoc uirtus tua in eo cum ueritate declaret[2], quatinus iustitiae tuae non dominetur iniquitas, sed subdatur falsitas ueritati, et ut ceteri uidentes, ab incredulitate sua liberentur. Per unigenitum dominum.

185 BENEDICTIO VNGVENTI AD MANDVCANDVM. Omnipotens sempiternae deus benedicere dignare hoc unguentum spiritali benedictione, ut sit omnibus com fide et reuerentia et gratiarum actione sumentibus salus mentis et corporis, et quę[3] contra omnes morbos et uniuersas cunctorum inimicorum insidias tutamentum, per dominum nostrum iesum christum filium tuum panem uitae qui de caelo descendit et dat uitam et salutem mundo, ipse benedicere hoc unguentum in nomine suo dignetur. Per dominum.

186 ITEM ALIA. Deus qui fecisti et creasti cunctis uiuentibus tuę largitatis alimoniam humanumque genus spiritalibus aescis ab oculis tuorum pręceptorum terrenisque substantiis tuorum donorum indesinenter te omnipotentem iesum obnixe petimus, ut haec tua dona tu ipse qui ea creasti / et nobis donasti hanc creaturam unguenti ex oleo et butiro et sagina, et ex uariarum herbarum genera confectum, perpetuam hac praeclaram benignitatem tuam sanctificare ac benedicere digneris, ut uescentibus gustantibusque ex eo largam tuae benedictionis sanitatem in uisceribus eorum clementer colloca, et praesentis uitae sospitatem et futurae beatitudinem misericorditer indulge. Per.

/f. 32v

187 ALIA. Deus uniuersae carnis, qui noe et filiis eius de mundis et inmundis animalibus praecepta dedisti, quique sibi sicut holera herbarum ad opus unctionis humana corpora perungi instituisti, postulamus itaque iesu benigne pietatem tuam, ut quisquis per aliqua incomoditate, seu infirmitate se de isto unguento peruncserit, siue pro dolore capitis, siue pro aliqua infirmitate gutturae degustare, aut inpedimentum abuerit, aut in pectore, siue in brachiis, siue in humeris uel in collo, necnon in cerebro

1 Supplied over an erasure.
2 Supplied over an erasure.
3 *atque* before correction.

siue in auriculis, aut in oculis, uel in manibus, siue in uentre, siue in genibus, aut in cruribus, pedibusue aut in nullo compagine membrorum, uel contra morsu serpentis, aut a morsu lupis, uel canis, percussus fuerit, aut ab illusionibus fraude / antiqui hostis delusus fuerit, per uirtutem tui nominis euacuetur adque euanescat omnique caelesti benedictione sanitatemque animae ac corporis per te christe consequantur. Qui uiuis.

/f. 33r

188 BENEDICTIO SEMINIS. Omnipotens sempiterne deus, creator generis humani, suppliciter tuam clementiam exoramus, ut hoc semen quod in tuo nomine serimus in agros nostros, caelesti benedictione benedicere, sanctificareque et multiplicare digneris, ut centesimum quadragesimumque fructum tua miseratione multiplicet, atque ad maturitatem perducas, ut per uniuersum orbem terrarum conlaudetur dextera tua. Per.

189 ALIA. Deus qui nos pastores in populo uocari uoluisti, praesta quaesumus ut hoc quod humano ore dicimus, in tuis oculis esse ualeamus. Per dominum.

190 BENEDICTIO AD CERVISAM VEL VINI. Benedic domine hunc potum et hoc uasculum, sicut benedixisti .vi. hydrias lapideas capientes metretas binas uel ternas, et uinum factum de aqua in chana galileae, sic benedicere digneris uinum istum uel ceruisam istam, ut sint sani inmaculati omnes homines qui ex eo bibituri sunt, per inuocationem nominis / tui domine. Qui uiuis et regnas.

/f. 33v

191 ORATIO SVPER VAS IN LOCO ANTIQVO REPERTVM[1]. Omnipotens sempiterne deus. Insere te officiis nostris, et haec uascula arte fabricata gentilium, sublimitatis tuae potentia. Ita emundare digneris, ut omni inmunditia depulsa, sint tuis fidelibus tempore pacis atque tranquillitatis utenda. Per.

192 BENEDICTIO PVTEI. Depraecamur domine clementiam pietatis tuae, ut aquam putei huius caelesti benedictione sanctifices, et ad communem uitam concedas salubrem. Et ita ex eo fugare digneris omnem diabolicae temptationis incursum. Vt

---

[1] *REPERTA* before correction.

quicumque ex eo abhinc hauserit bibere, uel in quibuslibet necessariis usibus, hausta aqua usus fuerit, totius uirtutis ac sanitatis dulcedine perfruatur. Vt tibi semper sanctificatori et saluatori omnium, domino gratias agere mereatur. Per dominum.

[1]MISSA IN ANNIVERSARIO DEDICATIONIS BASILICĘ

193 Deus qui nobis per singulos annos huius sancti templi tui consecrationis reparas diem, et sacris semper mysteriis, repraesentas incolumes, exaudi preces populi tui, et prĘsta ut quisquis hoc templum beneficia petiturus ingreditur, cuncta se impetrasse lĘtetur. Per.

194 SUPER OBLATA. Annue quaesumus domine precibus nostris, ut quicumque intra templi huius / cuius anniuersarium dedicationis diem caelebramus ambitum continemur, plena tibi atque perfecta corporis et animĘ deuotione placeamus, ut dum hĘc praesentia uota reddimus, ad Ęterna prĘmia, te adiuuante uenire mereamur. Per.

f. 34r

195 PREĘFACIO. [2]VD aeterne deus. Pro annua dedicatione tabernaculi huius, laudes tibi gratiasque referre. Cuius uirtus magna, pietas copiosa. Respice quaesumus de cĘlo, et uide, et uisita domum istam. Vt si quis mea nomini tuo supplicauerit libenter exaudias, et satis facientibus clementer ignoscas. Hic tibi sacerdotes tui sacrificium laudis offerant, hic fidelis populus uota persoluat. Hic peccatorum onera deponantur, hic fides sancta stabilitetur. Hic ipse inter bonum malumque discernas, cum causa interpellatus iudicaueris, quam non ignoras. Hic pietas absoluta redeat, hinc iniquitas emendata

---

[1] Nos 193–201 supplied by a Corbie scribe.
[2] Preface partly neumed.

discedat. Inueniat apud te domine locum uenię, quicumque satis faciens huc confugerit, et conscio dolore uictus, altaria tua riuis suarum elauerit lacrimarum. Hic si quando populus tuus, tristis męstusque conuenerit, adquiesce rogari, et rogatus indulge. Per christum.

196 AD COMPLETVM. Deus qui ecclesiam tuam sponsam uocare dignatus es, ut quę habebat gratiam per fidei deuotionem, haberet etiam ex nomine pietatem, da ut omnis hęc plebs nomini tuo seruiens, huius uocabuli consortio digna esse mereatur, et hoc in templo cuius anniuersarius dedicationis dies celebratur tibi collecta, te timeat, te diligat, te sequatur, ut dum iugiter per uestigia tua graditur, ad cęlestia promissa te ducente peruenire / mereatur. Qui uiuis.

/f. 34v

197 SUPER POPVLVM. Deus qui de uiuis et electis lapidibus ęternum maiestati tuę condis habitaculum, auxiliare populo supplicanti, ut quod ecclesię tuę corporalibus proficiat spatiis, spiritalibus amplificetur augmentis. Per.

MISSA IN INVENTIONE SANCTI STEPHANI

198 Deus qui es sanctorum tuorum splendor mirabilis, quique hodierna die beatorum martyrum tuorum, stephani, nichodemi, gamalielis atque abibon, corpora[1] inuentione gloriosa reuelasti, da nobis in ęterna lętitia, decorum societate gaudere. Per.

199 SECRETA. Munera tibi domine nostrę deuotionis offerimus quę et pro tuorum tibi grata sint

---

[1] Supplied interlinearly.

64

honore iustorum, et nobis salutaria te miserante reddantur. Per.

200 PREFATIO. [1]VD et salutare. Te quidem sine intermissione laudare omnipotens deus, qui primo martyri beato stephano, et praesentialiter perpetuum tribuis emolumentum, et eternaliter inmarcescibile contulisti brauium. Quatinus et laus illius ab humano ore numquam deficiat, et eius perpes corona, indeficienti fecunditate semper uirescat. Et ideo.

201 POSTCOMMVNIO. Sumpsimus domine sanctorum tuorum, stephani, nichodemi, gamalielis, atque abibon inuentionem celebrantes, sacramenta celestia, presta quaesumus ut quod temporaliter gerimus, eternis gaudiis consequamur. Per.

---

[1] Preface partly neumed.

/f. 35r **202**   /\<MARTYROLOGIVM SIVE COMPOTVM\>
                    \<IANVARIVS\>

I.   Iani prima dies et septima fine tenetur.   VII.

KL

1	A			IANR	OCTAVAE DOMINI. Romae passio sanctae martinae.
2	B	IIII	N		In antiochia natale sancti macharii abbatis.
3	C	III	N		Parisius, depositio sanctae genouefae uirginis. Et passio sancti petri qui et balsami.
4	D	II	N		Natalis sancti titi apostoli discipuli sancti pauli, et natalis sancti augentii.
5	E	NON		IANR	In siria natalis sancti symeonis qui in columpna stetit, et uigilia EPIPHANIAE.
6	F	VIII	ID		EPYPHANIA DOMINI. Lingonis ciuitate depositio sancti gregorii episcopi, et passio sanctae macrae.
7	G	VII	ID		Apud antiochiam natale sancti luciani presbiteri, qui in quattuor partes diuisus est.
8	H	VI	ID		Bellouagus passio sanctorum luciani, maxiani, et iuliani.
9	I	V	ID		Natalis sancti iuliani martyris, et basilissae uirginis, et sancti antonii presbyterii.
10	K	IIII	ID		Natalis sancti pauli primi anachoritae, qui a xvi. anno usque ad .cxiii. solus in heremo permansit.
11	L	III	ID		Eductio domini de egipto. In africa cartagine ciuitate natalis sancti saluii martyris.
12	M	II	ID		Natale sanctorum satiri et sancti archadii martirum.
13	N	IDVS		IANR	Octauae epiphaniae. Pictauis depositio sancti hilarii episcopi. Remis sancti Remigii archiepiscopi.
14	O	XVIIII	KL		¹Passio sancti felicis. In pincis.
15	P	XVIII	KL		²Depositio sancti mauri abbatis, et sancti macharii, et sancti isidori episcopi. Abbacuc et micheae prophetarum.
16	Q	XVII	KL		Natalis sancti marcelli papae. Arelato depositio sancti honorati episcopi. Perrona monasterio depositio sancti fursei confessoris.
17	R	XVI	KL		Lingonis ciuitate passio trium germanorum, speusippi, alasippi et melasippi, et depositio sancti sulpicii episcopi. Et depositio sancti antonii monachi.
18	S	XV	KL		Natalis sanctae priscae martyris. Romae dedicatio cathedrae sancti petri apostoli.
19	T	XIIII	KL		Hierosolimis marthae et mariae.

---

¹ Entry supplied over an erasure.
² Entries supplied over an erasure.

20	V	XIII	KL	Passio sanctorum fabiani papae, et sancti sebastiani, et sanctorum marii, marthae, audifax, et abbacuc.
21	A.	XII	KL	Romae passio sanctae agnę uirginis.
22	B.	XI	KL	Valentia ciuitate passio sancti uincentii diaconi, et natalis sancti anastasii monachi, et passio sancti potiti.
23	C.	X	KL	Natalis sanctae emerentianae uirginis, et sancti macharii, et passio parmenae diaconi.
24	D.	VIIII	KL	Antiocha ciuitate passio babilae episcopi, et trium paruulorum.
25	E.	VIII	KL	Conuersio sancti pauli apostoli, et natalis sancti preiecti martyris.
26	F.	VII	KL	In asia passio sancti policarpi, zmyrneorum episcopi.
27	G.	VI	KL	Natalis sancti iohannis chrisostomi. In africa sancti auiti.
28	H.	V	KL	Romae sanctae agnetis de natiuitate.
29	I.	IIII	KL	Treueris depositio sancti ualerii episcopi.
30	K.	III	KL	Molbodio monasterio, depositio sanctae aldegundis uirginis.
31	L.	II	KL	

/f. 35v

/ <FEBRVARIVS>

IIII. Ast februi quartae, praecedit tertia finem III.

KL

1	M.		FEBR	Passio sancti ignatii episcopi. Et depositio sanctae brigidae uirginis. Depositio sancti precordii confessoris. R. N.
2	N.	IIII	N	Ypapanti domini. R. XII.
3	O.	III	N	Natalis sanctę uualdredrudę uirginis.
4	P.	II	N	
5	Q.	NON	FEBR	Passio sanctae agathae uirginis. Et uigilia sancti VEDASTI EPISCOPI. R. XII.
6	R.	VIII	ID	**DEPOSITIO SANCTI VEDASTI**. Et sancti amandi episcoporum. R. N.
7	S.	VII	ID	VERIS INITIVM habet dies xci.
8	T.	VI	ID	
9	V.	V	ID	
10	.A	IIII	ID	Depositio sanctae scolasticae uirginis. Et passio sanctae sotheris uirginis. Et sanctorum zotici, yrenei et iacinthi martyrum. Et translatio sancte gertrudis. M.
11	.B	III		Lugduno desiderii episcopi.
12	.C	II	KL	Sancti basilii monachi, et depositio simplicii episcopi.

13	.D	IDVS	FEBR	Lugduno, depositio sancti stephani episcopi. In nicomidia, passio iuliani martyris.
14	.E	XVI	KL MARC	Passio sancti ualentini episcopi. Item ualentini, uitalis, felicule et zenonis. M.
15	.F	XV	KL	Taruenna, depositio sancti siluini episcopi. Diabolus retrorsum a domino captus recessit.
16	.G	XIIII	KL	Passio sanctae iuliana uirginis. R. III.
17	.H	XIII	KL	
18	.I	XII	KL	
19	.K	XI	KL	
20	.L	X	KL	
21	.M	VIIII	KL	Dedicatio ecclesiae sancti **VEDASTI**. Et natalis sancti uictorini.
22	.N	VIII	KL	Cathedra sancti petri, quam sedit apud antiochiam. R. N.
23	.O	VII	KL	In asia, sancti policarpi, cum aliis xii. martyribus.
24	.P	VI	KL	In iudea natalis sancti matthiae apostoli. Et inuentio capitis praecursoris. Hic fit bissextus. R. III.
25	.Q	V	KL	
26	.R	IIII	KL	
27	.S	III	KL	
28	.T	II	KL	

/f. 36r

/ <MARTIVS>

I. Martis prima necat cuius si cuspide quartae. IIII.

KL

1	A		MARC	Andegauis ciuitate, depositio sancti albini episcopi. Et alibi sancti donati. R. III.
2	B	VI	N	Natalis sancti lupi episcopi, et sanctorum eraclii, et pauli.
3	C	V	N	
4	D	IIII	N	Romae depositio sancti lucii papae, et passio sancti adriani cum aliis .xxii, et alibi .dccc. martyrum.
5	E	III	N	Passio sancti focae episcopi.
6	F	II	N	Passio sanctorum uictoris, et uictorini.
7	G	NONAS	MARC	Tiburtina ciuitate, passio sanctarum, perpetuae, et felicitatis uirginum. M.
8	H	VIII	ID	Prima incensio lunę paschalis.
9	I	VII	ID	Passio .xl. militum in sebasta ciuitate quorum gesta habentur.
10	K	VI	ID	Translatio corporis sancti uiti martyris ad nouam corbeiam.

11	L	V	ID		Depositio sancti uinditiani atrebatensis episcopi.
12	M	IIII	ID		Depositio sancti gregorii papae. In asia natalis sancti carpi episcopi. R. XII.
13	N	III	ID		In attica miluus apparet.
14	O	II	ID		Natale sancti leonis papae. Post istum locum non potest esse quadragesima.
15	P	IDVS		MARC	Abbatis domni stat mentio sancta ratoldi. Istum qui fecit scribere quippe librum.
16	Q	XVII	KL	APLIS	
17	R	XVI	KL		In hybernia natalis sancti patricii episcopi. Et depositio sanctae geretrudis uirginis. Adam et eua seducti sunt. Et translatio corporis sanctę balthildis reginę. R. III.
18	S	XV	KL		
19	T	XIIII	KL		
20	V	XIII	KL		Depositio sancti cutberhti episcopi.
21	A.	XII	KL		Depositio sancti **BENEDICTI ABBATIS. AEQVINOCTIVM**. R. XII.
22	B.	XI	KL		Primum pascha, et sedes epactarum.
23	C.	X	KL		
24	D.	VIIII	KL		Concurrentium locus.
25	E.	VIII	KL		Adnunciatio sanctae mariae. Et passio DOMINI NOSTRI IESV CHRISTI, et iacobi fratris eius. Adam plasmatus est et cunctis animantibus nomina inposuit. R. N.
26	F.	VII	KL		Albiniaco monasterio depositio sancti chilliani confessoris.
27	G.	VI	KL		Resurrectio DOMINI NOSTRI IESV CHRISTI.
28	H.	V	KL		
29	I.	IIII	KL		Romae ordinatio sancti gregorii papae.
30	K.	III	KL		
31	L.	II	KL		

/ <APRILIS>

X. Aprilis decimo est, undeno et fine minatur. XI.

KL

1	M.		APLIS	In aegipto, passio sanctorum uictoris et stephani. Liganau monasterio depositio sanci uualarici confessoris. R. III.
2	N.	IIII	N	Natalis sanctae theodosiae uirginis.
3	O.	III	N	Natalis sancti euagrii martyris.
4	P.	II	N	Mediolanis depositio ambrosii episcopi. R. III.
5	Q.	NON	APLIS	
6	R.	VIII	ID	
7	S.	VII		
8	T.	VI	ID	
9	V.	V	ID	Depositio sanctae mariae egiptiacae. Et in sirmio passio sanctarum .vii. uirginum.
10	.A	IIII	ID	
11	.B	III	ID	Romae depositio sancti leonis papae. Et in uia aurelia, depositio sancti iulii papae. M.
12	.C	II		
13	.D	IDVS	APRELIS	In calcedonia, sanctae eufemiae uirginis. M.
14	.E	XVIII	KL MAI	Romae uia appia, passio sanctorum tiburtii ualeriani et maximi. M.
15	.F	XVII	KL	
16	.G	XVI	KL	
17	.H	XV	KL	
18	.I	XIIII	KL	
19	.K	XIII	KL	
20	.L	XII	KL	
21	.M	XI	KL	
22	.N	X	KL	
23	.O	VIIII	KL	Passio sancti georgii martyris, et depositio sancti reguli confessoris. R. III.
24	.P	VIII	KL	Annanias, azarias, misahel, hac die de camino ignis ardentis sunt liberati.
25	.Q	VII	KL	Laetania maior, et passio sancti marci euangelistae. Vltimum pascha. M.
26	.R	VI	KL	Centulo monasterio depositio sancti **RICHARII CONFESSORIS**. R. III.
27	.T	V	KL	Romae natale sancti anastasii papae. Obiit Odo.
28	.V	IIII	KL	Egressio noe de archa. Rauenna, natalis sancti uitalis martyris. Et sancti christophori martyris. M.

29	A	III	KL	In alexandria, natalis sancti germani presbiteri.
30	B	II	KL	Romae, natale sancti quirini episcopi.

f. 37r

/ <MAIVS>

III. Tertius est maio lopus, est et septimus anguis. .VII.

KL

1 C   N   MAI   Initium praedicationis domini nostri iesu christi. Passio sancti iudae qui et quiriacus dictus est. Apostolorum philippi et iacobis. Agauno passio sancti sigismundi regis. Autisiodero, depositio sancti amatoris episcopi. R. XII.

2 D   VI   N

3 E   V   N   Hierosolimis. Inuentio sanctae crucis. Et natalis alexandri, euentii, et theodoli. R. III.

4 F   IIII   N   Autisiodero, depositio sancti corchodomi diaconi.

5 G   III   N   **ASCENSIO DOMINI AD CAELOS.** Autisiodero, passio iuuiniani lectoris.

6 H   II   N   Natale sancti iohannis apostoli ante portam latinam, quando a domiciano cęsare in feruentis olei dolium missus est. M.

7 I   NONAS   MAI

8 K   VIII   ID   Reuelatio basilicae sancti michahelis archangeli.

9 L   VII   ID   Natalis sancti cirini martyris, et alibi, .cccx^{torum}. martirum. ESTATIS INITIVM habet dies xci.

10 M   VI   ID   Beati iob patriarchae, et passio sanctorum gordiani et epimachi. M.

11 N   V   ID   Vienna depositio episcoporum mammerti et mammertini. In sirmia sancti montani.

12 O   IIII   ID   Passio sanctorum nerei, et achillei, atque panchratii. Et natalis sancti patris nostri epiphanii episcopi cipri. R. III.

13 P   III   ID   Romae dedicatio ecclesiae sanctae mariae ad martires, et depositio sancti seruatii episcopi. R. III.

14 Q   II   ID   Sancti patris nostri pachumii. In africa sancti maximini. QVADRAGISIMA ANTE FESTVM SANCTI iohannis.

15 R   IDVS   MAI   Spiritus sanctus super apostolos linguis apparuit. Hesperia, natale .vii^{tem}. pontificum. Primus pentecostes.

16 S   XVII   KL IVN   Ambianis ciuitate depositio sancti honorati episcopi.

17 T   XVI   KL   Niuiduno, natale sanctorum eraclii et pauli.

18 V   XV   KL   In egipto dioscori lectoris qui multa passus est.

71

19	A.	XIIII	KL	Romae, natale sanctae potentianae. Atrebas, depositio sancti hadulfi episcopi. M.
20	B.	XIII	KL	
21	C.	XII	KL	
22	D.	XI	KL	In corsica insula, passio sanctae iulianae uirginis.
23	E.	X	KL	Passio sancti desiderii episcopi.
24	F.	VIIII	KL	
25	G.	VIII	KL	Romae, passio sancti urbani papae. **AESTAS ORITVR**. M.
26	H.	VII	KL	In territorio autisioderensi, loco quociaco, passio sancti prisci martiris cum sociis suis.
27	I.	VI	KL	
28	K.	V	KL	Rauenna depositio sancti iohannis papae. Parisius depositio sancti germani episcopi. R. III.
29	L.	IIII	KL	Treueris depositio sancti maximini episcopi.
30	M.	III	KL	
31	N.	II	KL	Romae depositio sanctae petronillae uirginis. filię sancti petri. M.

/f. 37v

/ \<IVNIVS\>

X. Junius ın decimo quindenum a fine salutat. XV.

KL

1	O.			IVNII	Romae, dedicatio sancti nichomedis martiris. M.
2	P.	IIII	N		Romae natalis sanctorum marcellini et petri, et passio herasmi, et sancti bonifaciis martyris. R. III.
3	Q.	III	N		
4	R.	II	N		Translatio sancti **VEDASTI** in cripta, et passio sancti quirini episcopi.
5	S.	NONAS		IVNII	Passio sancti bonefacii archiepiscopi cum aliis seruis dei. Corbeia translatio sancti precordii confessoris. R. N.
6	T.	VIII	ID		
7	V.	VII	ID		
8	.A	VI	ID		Nouiomo depositio sancti medardi episcopi. Rotomago sancti gildardi episcopi. R. III.
9	.B	V	ID		Passio sanctorum primi et feliciani. M.
10	.C	IIII	ID		
11	.D	III	ID		Natale sancti barnabae apostoli.
12	.E	II	ID		Romae miliario .v. natale sanctorum basilidis, cirini, naboris, et nazarii martyrum. M.
13	.F	IDVS		IVNII	Vltimum pentecostes.
14	.G	XVIII	KL	IVLII	Passio sanctorum rufini et ualeri.

15	.H	XVII	KL	Natale sanctorum uiti, et modesti, et sanctae margaritae. R. N.
16	.I	XVI	KL	Cirici martiris, et iulittae matris eius, et cum eis .cccciiiiᵒʳ. martires.
17	.K	XV	KL	Aurelianis depositio auiti presbiteri.
18	.L	XIIII	KL	Passio sanctorum marci et marcelliani. M.
19	.M	XIII	KL	Mediolano passio sanctorum geruasii et protasii. R. III.
20	.N	XII	KL	In cesarea palestinae, depositio sancti eusebii historiographi. SOLSTITIVM.
21	.O	XI	KL	
22	.P	X	KL	Nola ciuitate natale sancti paulini episcopi et confessoris. R. III.
23	.Q	VIIII	KL	Vigilia sancti iohannis baptistae. M.
24	.R	VIII	KL	Natiuitas sancti iohannis baptistae. Et inuentio corporis sancti quintini martyris. R. XII.
25	.S	VII	KL	
26	.T	VI	KL	Natale sanctorum iohannis et pauli. Valentianas sancti saluii martiris. R. III.
27	A	V	KL	
28	B	IIII	KL	Vigilia apostolorum, et depositio sancti leonis papae. M.
29	C	III	KL	Natale apostolorum petri et pauli. R. N.
30	D	II	KL	Commemoratio sancti pauli apostoli. Lemodicas ciuitate depositio sancti martialis episcopi. R. N.

f. 38r

/ <IVLIVS>

XIII. Tredecimus iulii, decimo innuit ante kalendas. X.

KL

1	E		IVLII	In monte oreb depositio aaron sacerdotis, et octauae sancti iohannis, romae, sancti gagi papae. Natale sancti carilephi presbiteri. R. III.
2	F	VI	N	Romae natale sanctorum processi et marti<ni>ani. M.
3	G	V	N	Translatio corporis sancti thomae apostoli ab india, in edissa ciuitate. R. III.
4	H	IIII	N	Translatio sancti martini, et ordinatio, et dedicatio basilicae ipsius, et depositio sanctae bertae. R. III.
5	I	III	N	
6	K	II	N	Esaiae prophetae, et octauae apostolorum, et depositio sancti goari confessoris. R. III.

73

7	L	NONAS		
8	M	VIII	ID	
9	N	VII	ID	Senonis ciuitate depositio sancti eraclii episcopi.
10	O	VI	ID	Natale .vii. fratrum filiorum sanctae felicitatis, id est felicis, philippi, uitalis, martialis, alexandri, sil<u>ani, et ianuarii. M.
11	P	V	ID	Translatio sancti benedicti abbatis. R. XII.
12	Q	IIII	ID	
13	R	III	ID	
14	S	II	ID	
15	T	IDVS	IVLII	Corbẹia monasterio exceptio reliquiarum sancti dion<ys>ii. R. III.
16	V	XVII	KL AVG	
17	A.	XVI	KL	Sanctae simphorosae cum .vii. filiis, crescente, iuliano, nemesio, primitiuo, iustino, stacteo, eugenio, passi iubente adriano principe.
18	B.	XV	KL	
19	C.	XIIII	KL	
20	D.	XIII	KL	Corbeiae monasterio dedicatio sancti stephani martyris. R. N.
21	E.	XII	KL	Romae sanctae praxedis uirginis. Danihelis prophetae. M.
22	F.	XI	KL	Natale mariae magdalenae. Fontenella monasterio depositio sancti uuandregisili confessoris.
23	G.	X	KL	Rauenna passio sancti apollinaris episcopi et martiris. R. III.
24	H.	VIIII	KL	In tiro ciuitate natale sanctẹ christinẹ uirginis.
25	I.	VIII	KL	Natale sancti iacobi fratris iohannis euangelistae. Et passio sanctorum christophori et cucuphatis. R. XII.
26	K.	VII	KL	
27	L.	VI	KL	
28	M.	V	KL	Passio sancti pantaleonis, mediolano sancti nazarii, celsi pueri, et martiris, et sancti samsonis. Corbeia dedicatio sancti petri apostoli. R. N.
29	N.	IIII	KL	Romae passio sancti felicis papae. Et natale simplicii, faustini, beatricis. Trecas depositio sancti lupi episcopi. M.
30	O.	III	KL	Romẹ natale sanctorum abdon et sennen. Autisiodero depositio beati ursi episcopi. R. III.
31	P.	II	KL	Rauenna depositio sancti germani autisioderensis episcopi. R. III.

/ \<AVGVSTVS\>

I. Augusti nepa prima, fugat de fine secunda. II.

KL

1	Q.		AVG	Sancti petri ad uincula, et passio machabeorum vii. fratrum cum matre sua.
2	R.	IIII	N	Romae passio sancti stephani papae sub ualeriano imperatore.
3	S.	III	N	Inuentio sancti stephani protomartiris, et sanctorum gamalielis, abibi, et nichomedi.
4	T.	II	N	Natalis sancti iustini presbiteri, qui multos martires sepeliuit.
5	V.	NONAS	AVG	Augustiduno, sancti cassiani episcopi. Catalauis mimii episcopi. In brittania osualdi regis.
6	.A	VIII	ID	Romae passio sanctorum syxti papae, felicissimi et agapiti diaconorum, sub decio imperatore.
7	.B	VII	ID	In aritio sancti donati episcopi. Transfiguratio domini. Autumni initium habet dies xci.
8	.C	VI	ID	Romae passio sancti ciriaci diaconi, philadelfia sancti leonidis.
9	.D	V	ID	In italia passio sanctorum secundiani ueriani martialis. Romae sancti romani martiris.
10	.E	IIII	ID	Romae passio sancti laurentii archidiaconi.
11	.F	III	ID	Romae passio sancti tiburtii subdiaconi. Camaraco depositio sancti gaugerici episcopi.
12	.G	II	ID	
13	.H	IDVS	AVG	Romae natalis sancti yppoliti martiris. Pictauis depositio sanctae radegundis reginae.
14	.I	XVIIII	KL	SEPTEMBRIS Romae natalis sancti eusebii presbiteri.
15	.K	XVIII	KL	ASSVMPTIO SANCTAE MARIAE.
16	.L	XVII	KL	Mettis ciuitate, depositio sancti arnulfi episcopi.
17	.M	XVI	KL	Octauae sancti laurentii. In caesarea sancti mametis martiris.
18	.N	XV	KL	Praenestina ciuitate sancti agapiti martiris.
19	.O	XIIII	KL	Sancti magni cum sociis suis duorum milia d. et xcvii. Hierusolimis apparatio sanctę crucis.
20	.P	XIII	KL	Samuhelis prophetae, et depositio sancti filiberi. Cainone castro depositio sancti maximi.
21	.Q	XII	KL	Consecratio sanctę gertrudis uirginis.
22	.R	XI	KL	Romae natalis sancti timothei. Edua ciuitate passio sancti symphoriani.
23	.S	X	KL	Remis passio sanctorum timothei et apollonaris.

24	.T	VIIII	KL	In India natale sancti bartholomei apostoli. Rodomo depositio sancti audoeni episcopi.
25	A	VIII	KL	Natalis sancti genesii martiris.
26	B	VII	KL	Natalis sancti eleutherii episcopi.
27	C	VI	KL	In capua, natalis sancti rufi martiris.
28	D	V	KL	Romae natalis sancti hermetis martiris, et depositio sancti augustini episcopi.
29	E	IIII	KL	Pausatio helisei prophetae, et passio sancti iohannis baptistae, romae sanctae sabinae martiris.
30	F	III	KL	Passio sanctorum felicis et audacti.
31	G	II	KL	Treueris depositio sancti paulini episcopi.

/f. 39r

/ \<SEPTEMBRIS\>

III. Tertia septembris, uulpis ferit a pede dena. X.

KL

1	H		SEPTEMB	Iosue patriarchę, et passio sancti prisci. Senonis, sancti lupi episcopi. Ambianis, firmini episcopi.
2	I	IIII	N	
3	K	III	N	
4	L	II	N	Moysi prophetae, romae depositio sancti bonefacii episcopi. Cauillonis sancti marcelli martiris.
5	M	NONAS	SEPTB	Sithiu monasterio depositio sancti bertini abbatis.
6	N	VIII	ID	Zachariae prophetae. Romae passio sancti eleutherii episcopi.
7	O	VII	ID	Aurelianis depositio beati euurtii episcopi. Augustidono loco alisina passio sanctae reginę.
8	P	VI	ID	Natiuitas sanctae mariae. In nicomidia sancti adriani cum sociis suis .xxiii. martiribus.
9	Q	V	ID	Depositio sancti audomari episcopi, et passio sancti gurgonii.
10	R	IIII	ID	
11	S	III	ID	Romae passio sanctorum proti et iacinthi.
12	T	II	ID	
13	V	IDVS	SEPTB	
14	A.	XVIII	KL OCTOB	Exaltatio sanctae crucis, romae sancti cornelii papae. Kartaginę sancti cypriani episcopi et martiris.
15	B.	XVII	KL	Passio sancti nicomedis. Et in tullo leucorum, sancti apri confessoris.
16	C.	XVI	KL	In calcedonia, passio sanctae eufemiae. Romae sanctorum luciae et geminiani.

17	D.	XV	KL	Passio sancti lantberti episcopi.
18	E.	XIIII	KL	
19	F.	XIII	KL	
20	G.	XII	KL	Vigilia sancti matthei apostoli. Eleuatio corporis sancti amandi.
21	H.	XI	KL	Natalis sancti matthei apostoli et euangelistae, mediolano sancti uictoris.
22	I.	X	KL	Passio sancti mauricii cum sociis suis .vi. milia .dlxxxv. martiribus.
23	K.	VIIII	KL	Natalis sanctae teclae uirginis.
24	L.	VIII	KL	Conceptio sancti iohannis baptistae.
25	M.	VII	KL	Ambianis ciuitate passio sancti firmini episcopi. Lugduno sancti lupi episcopi.
26	N.	VI	KL	Cypriani episcopi, et iustinae uirginis, qui passi sunt sub claudio principe.
27	O.	V	KL	Natalis sanctorum cosmae, et damiani martirum.
28	P.	IIII	KL	
29	Q.	III	KL	Dedicatio basilicae sancti michahelis archangeli. Autisiodero depositio sancti fraterni episcopi.
30	R.	II	KL	In bethleem iuda, depositio sancti hieronimi presbiteri.

/ <OCTOBRIS>

III. Tertius octobris, decimus in ordine nectit. X.

KL

1	S.		OCT	Nobiliaco monasterio translatio sancti uedasti. Remis sancti remigii, germani, bauonis, piati.
2	T.	VI	N	Atrebatis depositio sancti scupilionis presbiteri. Et passio sancti leodegarii episcopi.
3	V.	V	N	
4	.A	IIII	N	Autisiodero natale sancti marsi presbiteri.
5	.B	III	N	
6	.C	II	N	
7	.D	NON	OCTOB	Natalis sancti marci papae, romae sancti lini papae et martiris, bituricas depositio sancti augustini episcopi.
8	.E	VIII	ID	**OCTAVAE SANCTI VEDASTI**. Antiochia dionisii episcopi et martiris.
9	.F	VII	ID	Parisius passio sanctorum dionisii, rustici et eleutherii diaconi. Abraham patriarchę.
10	.G	VI	ID	
11	.H	V	ID	
12	.I	IIII	ID	

13	.K	III	ID	
14	.L	II	ID	Natalis sancti calisti papae et martiris.
15	.M	IDUS	OCT	
16	.N	XVII	KL NOV	Sanctorum luciani, maxiani et iuliani martirum
17	.O	XVI	KL	Natalis sancti[1]
18	.P	XV	KL	Natalis sancti lucae euangelistae. In pago beluacensi, sancti iusti martiris. Ebroicas sancti aquilini episcopi.
19	.Q	XIIII	KL	Depositio sancti amati confessoris.
20	.R	XIII	KL	
21	.S	XII	KL	Sancti patris nostri hilarionis. Colonia passio sanctarum uirginum.
22	.T	XI	KL	
23	A	X	KL	Restitutio corporis sancti amandi episcopi.
24	B	VIIII	KL	
25	C	VIII	KL	Suessionis ciuitate passio sanctorum crispini et crispiniani.
26	D	VII	KL	Translatio sancti amandi episcopi, et ordinatio, et dedicatio basilicae ipsius.
27	E	VI	KL	Vigilia apostolorum symonis et iudae, et natalis sancti florentii.
28	F	V	KL	Natale apostolorum simonis et iudae.
29	G	IIII	KL	
30	H	III	KL	Tolosa ciuitate translatio sancti saturnini episcopi et martiris.
31	I	II	KL	Augusta uermandorum, passio sancti quintini.

/f. 40r

/ <NOVEMBRIS>

V. Quinta nouembris acus, uix tertia mansit in urna.   III.

KL

1	K		NOVB	Sollempnitas omnium sanctorum.
2	L	IIII	N	Natalis iuliani presbiteri et martiris, et passio sancti uictorini.
3	M	III	N	Depositio sancti hucberti episcopi, et passio sanctae agricolae.
4	N	II	N	Redonis sancti amantii episcopi.
5	O	NON	NOVEMB	Zachariae prophetae patris sancti iohannis baptistae, et natale sancti eusebii monachi.

---

[1] Remainder of line erased.

78

6	P	VIII	ID	Redonis depositio sancti melanii episcopi, et sancti uuinnoci confessoris.
7	Q	VII	ID	Depositio sancti uuilbrordi episcopi. Hiemis initium habet dies xcii.
8	R	VI	ID	Natalis sanctorum claudii, nicostrati, simphoriani, castorii atque simplicii. Eodem die .iiii^{or}. coronatorum, seueri, seueriani, uictorini et carpofori.
9	S	V	ID	Natale sancti teodori, et sancti ragnulfi martiris.
10	T	IIII	ID	Aurelianis depositio sancti monitoris episcopi.
11	V	III	ID	Turonis depositio sancti martini episcopi. Romae sancti mennae martiris. Lugduno, sancti uerani episcopi. Rauenna, sanctorum ualentini, feliciani, octaui, et felicis.
12	A.	II	ID	Agrippina sancti chuniberti confessoris.
13	B.	IDVS	NOVEB	Turonis depositio sancti briccii episcopi.
14	C.	XVIII	KL DEC	QVADRAGINTA ANTE NATIVITATEM DOMINI.
15	D.	XVII	KL	
16	E.	XVI	KL	
17	F.	XV	KL	Aurelianis sancti aniani episcopi, et sancti gregorii miraculorum factoris.
18	G.	XIIII	KL	
19	H.	XIII	KL	
20	I.	XII	KL	
21	K.	XI	KL	
22	L.	X	KL	Romae natalis sanctae ceciliae uirginis.
23	M.	VIIII	KL	Natalis sancti clementis papae, et sancti trudonis, et sanctae felicitatis.
24	N.	VIII	KL	Romae natalis sancti chrisogoni martiris.
25	O.	VII	KL	
26	P.	VI	KL	
27	Q.	V	KL	
28	R.	IIII	KL	
29	S.	III	KL	Romae passio sancti saturnini, crisanti, et dariae uirginis.
30	T.	II	KL	Passio sancti andreae apostoli.

/f. 40v

/ \<DECEMBRIS\>

VII. Dat duodena cohors, septem inde decemque decembris. X.

KL

1	V.		DECEMB	Nouiomo depositio sancti eligii episcopi.
2	.A	IIII	N	
3	.B	III	N	
4	.C	II	N	
5	.D	NON	DECEMB	
6	.E	VIII	ID	
7	.F	VII	ID	
8	.G	VI	ID	
9	.H	V	ID	
10	.I	IIII	ID	Barcinonis passio sanctae eulaliae uirginis.
11	.K	III	ID	Romae depositio sancti damasi papae. Et natalis sanctorum fusciani, uictorici et gentiani martirum.
12	.L	II	ID	Depositio sancti uualerici confessoris. Et natalis ermogenis, et donati, et .xxii. martirum.
13	.M	IDVS	DECB	Passio sanctae luciae uirginis sub pascasio. Camaraco depositio sancti autberti, et alibi, sancti iudoci confessoris.
14	.N	XVIIII	KL IANR	Remis passio sancti nicasii episcopi, et eutropiae sororis eius.
15	.O	XVIII	KL	Aurelianis depositio Maximi episcopi.
16	.P	XVII	KL	
17	.Q	XVI	KL	
18	.R	XV	KL	
19	.S	XIIII	KL	
20	.T	XIII	KL	Passio sanctae margaritae uirginis.
21	A	XII	KL	Natalis sancti thomae apostoli. SOLSTITIVM.
22	B	XI	KL	
23	C	X	KL	
24	D	VIIII	KL	**VIGILIA NATIVITATIS DOMINI NOSTRI IESV CHRISTI.**
25	E	VIII	KL	**NATIVITAS DOMINI NOSTRI IESV CHRISTI**, et passio sanctae anastasiae uirginis.
26	F	VII	KL	Passio sancti stephani protomartiris.
27	G	VI	KL	Sancti iohannis apostoli et euangelistae.
28	H	V	KL	Sanctorum innocentum.
29	I	IIII	KL	Sancti felicis.
30	K	III	KL	Sancti perpetui episcopi.
31	L	II	KL	Sancti siluestri papae. Et sanctae columbae uirginis.

Expliciunt .iiii^{or}. tempora anni, menses .xii., ebdomadae .lii. et una dies, dies .ccc^{li}. .lxv. et .vi. horae. Horae .viiii. .d.cclx., momenta .cccl.d.clx.

f. 41r

/ MISSA SANCTI PRĘCORDII CONFESSORIS

203 [1]Deus qui in diuersis nationum populis pręclaros uerę uitę fidei constituisti patronos, concede quaesumus ut omnes qui ad sanctissimi patronis nostri pręcordii festa conuenerunt, pręsentis prosperitatis gaudium, et futurę beatitudinis gloriam consequantur. Per.

204 SECRETA. Sit tibi quaesumus domine deus nostrę deuotionis oblatio acceptabilis, ut beato precordio confessore tuo intercedente, utrumque et tuę placeat maiestati et nostrę proficiat saluti. Per.

205 PREFATIO. [2]VD eterne deus. Qui beatum precordium confessorem tuum nobis patronum donare dignatus es. Qui quod uerbis credidit exemplo monstrauit. Cuius uita moribus effulsit egregia, cuius meritum miraculis illuxit. Cuius patrocinio gaudentes, tuam super nos predicamus gratiam habundanter effusam. Per christum.

206 POST COMMVNIONEM. Misteriis diuinis refecti domine deus, quaesumus ut beati pręcordii confessoris tui, ubique intercessione protegamur, pro cuius annua ueneratione hęc tuę obtulimus maiestati. Per.

f. 41v

/ [3]MISSA AD SPONSAS BENEDICENDAS

207 Exaudi nos omnipotens et misericors deus, ut quod nostro ministratur officio, tua benedictione potius impleatur. Per.

---

[1] Nos 203–211 supplied by Corbie scribes.
[2] Partly neumed.
[3] New hand.

ITEM AD SPONSAS BENEDICENDAS SINE MISSA
208 V. Manda deus uirtuti tuę, usque argento.

209 ORATIO. Deus abraham, deus isaac, deus iacob sit uobiscum, ipse coniungat uos, impleatque benedictionem[1] suam in uobis. Per.

210 BENEDICTIO. [2]Deus qui potestate uirtutis tuę de nichilo cuncta fecisti, qui dispositis uniuersitatis exordiis homini ad imaginem dei facto. Ideo inseparabile mulieris adiutorium condidisti, ut femineo corpori de uirili dares carne principium, docens quod ex uno placuisset institui, numquam liceret disiungi. Deus qui tam excellenti misterio coniugalem copulam consecrasti ut christi et ęcclesię sacramentum praesignares in fędere nuptiarum, deus per quem mulier iungitur uiro et societas / principaliter ordinata ea benedictio donatur, quę sola nec per originalis peccati pęnam, nec per diluuii est ablata sententia. Respice propicius super hanc famulam tuam quę maritali est iungenda consortio, tua se expetit protectione muniri. Sit in ea iugum dilectionis et pacis. Fidelis et casta nubat in christo, imitatrixque sanctarum permaneat feminarum. Sit amabilis ut rachel, sapiens ut rebecca, longeua et fidelis ut sarra, nichil in ea ex actibus suis ille autor praeuaricationis usurpet. Nexa fidei mandatisque permaneat. Vni thoro iuncta, contactus inlicitos fugiat, muniat infirmitatem suam robore disciplinę. Sit uerecundia grauis, pudore uenerabilis, doctrinis cęlestibus erudita. Sit fęcunda in sobole, sit probata et innocens, et ad beatorum requiem atque ad cęlestia regna

/f. 42r

---

[1] Second *e* supplied interlinearly.
[2] After empty line.

perueniat, et uideat filios filiorum suorum usque in terciam et quartam progeniam, et adoptatam perueniat senectutem. Per.

f. 42v

/ BENEDICTIO CANDELARVM IN PVRIFICATIONE SANCTĘ MARIAE

211 Deus inenarrabilis et inestimabilis potentię cuius unigenitus cum nostra humanitate hodierna die a matre in templo est presentatus, benedicere, et sanctificare digneris has candelas, in honore nominis tui consecrandas, et concede ut per intercessionem beatissimę dei genitricis[1] marię, quicumque hęc luminaria pro amore filii tui manibus gestauerint, temporali et

f. 43r

ęterna potiantur sospitate / et ubicumque istarum flamma fuerit accensa immundorum spirituum repellatur fallatia, et sic mereantur temporali perfrui lętitia, quatinus obuiam sponso per gentes, lampadarum lumine splendentes, ad nuptias uenturas in die iudicii ualeant peruenire cum sponso gaudentes. Per dominum.

f. 44r

212 / [2]IN NOMINE DOMINI. INCIPIT LIBER SACRAMENTORVM DE CIRCVLO ANNI A SANCTO GREGORIO PAPA ROMANA EDITVS. Q<V>ALITER MISSA ROMANA CELEBRATVR. HOC EST INPRIMIS INTROITVS QVALIS FVERIT STATVTIS TEMPORIBVS SIVE DIEBVS FESTIS SEV COTIDIANIS. DEINDE KYRIE ELEISON. ITEM DICITVR GLORIA IN EXCELSIS DEO. SI EPISCOPVS FVERIT TANTVMMODO DIE DOMINICO SIVE DIEBVS FESTIS A PRESBITERIS AVTEM MINIME DICITVR NISI SOLO IN PASCHA. QVANDO VERO LAETANIA AGITVR NEQVE GLORIA IN EXCELSIS DEO NEQVE ALLELVIA CANITVR. POSTMODVM DICITVR ORATIO. DEINDE SEQVITVR APOSTOLVS. ITEM

---

[1] *genetricis* before correction.
[2] Fol. 43v blank. Nos 212–221 are Corbie additions.

GRADALIS SIVE ALLELVIA. POSTMODVM LEGITVR
EVANGELIVM. DEINDE OFFERTORIVM, ET DI<CI>TVR
ORATIO SVPER OBLATA. QVA COMPLETA DICIT
SACERDOS EXCELSA VOCE.

/f. 44v **213** / [1]PER OMNIA SAECVLA SAECVLORVM. AMEN.
DOMINVS VOBISCVM.
ET CVM SPIRITV TVO.
SVRSVM CORDA.
HABEMVS AD DOMINVM.
GRATIAS AGAMVS DOMINO DEO NOSTRO.
DIGNVM ET IVSTVM EST.

214 [2]VERE DIGNVM ET IVSTVM EST, AEQVVM ET
SALVTARE, NOS[3] TIBI SEMPER ET VBIQVE GRATIAS
AGERE, DOMINE SANCTE PATER OMNIPOTENS AETERNE
DEVS PER CHRISTVM DOMINVM NOSTRVM. PER QVEM
MAIESTATEM TVAM LAVDANT ANGELI. ADORANT
DOMINATIONES. TREMVNT POTESTATES. CAELI
CAELORVMQVE VIRTVTES AC BEATA SERAPHIM SOCIA
EXVLTATIONE CONCELEBRANT. CVM QVIBVS ET
NOSTRAS VOCES VT ADMITTI IVBEAS DEPRECAMVR
SVPPLICI CONFESSIONE DICENTES: SANCTVS,
SANCTVS, SANCTVS, DOMINVS.

215 ET IDEO CVM ANGELIS ET ARCHANGELIS, CVM
TRONIS ET DOMINATIONIBVS. CVMQVE OMNI MILICIA
/f. 45v CAELESTIS / EXERCITVS, HYMNVM GLORIĘ TVAE,
CANIMVS SINE FINE DICENTES: SANCTVS, SANCTVS,
SANCTVS, DOMINVS, SABAOTH PLENI SVNT CĘLI ET
TERRA GLORIA TVA OSANNA IN EXCELSIS,
BENEDICTVS QVI VENIT IN NOMINE DOMINI OSANNA
IN EXCELSIS.

---

[1] Neumed.
[2] Neumed.
[3] Over an erasure.

216 Per omnia saecula saeculorvm. Amen.
Dominus uobiscum. Et cum spiritu tuo.
Sursum corda. Habemus ad dominum.
Gratias agamus domino deo nostro.
Dignum et iustum est.

f. 46r   **217** / VERE dignum et iustum est, aequum et
salutare, nos tibi semper et ubique gratias
agere, domine sancte pater omnipotens aeterne
deus, per christum dominum nostrum. Per quem
maiestatem tuam laudant angeli. Adorant
dominationes. Tremunt potestates. Caeli
cęlorumque uirtutes ac beata seraphim sotia
exultatione concelebrant. Cum quibus et
nostras uoces ut admitti iubeas deprecamur
supplici confessione dicentes. Sanctus,
Sanctus, Sanctus, dominus.

218 Et ideo cum angelis et archangelis, cum
thronis et dominationibus. Cumque omni
malicia cęlestis exercitus, hymnum glorię
tuae canimus sine fine dicentes: Sanctus,
sanctus, sanctus, dominus deus sabaoth pleni
sunt cęli et terra gloria tua osanna in
excelsis, benedictus qui uenit in nomine dei
osanna in excelsis.

219 TE igitur clementissime pater per iesum
f. 46v   christum filium tuum dominum nostrum /
supplices rogamus, et petimus uti accepta
habeas et benedicas, haec dona, + hęc munera,
+ hęc sancta, + sacrificia inlibata. In
primis quę tibi offerimus pro ęcclesia tua
sancta catholica, quam pacificare, custodire,
adunare, et regere digneris toto orbe
terrarum una cum famulo tuo papa nostro ill.
sedis apostolicę, necnon et antestite nostro
ill. et omnibus orthodoxis atque catholicę et
apostolicę fidei cultoribus.

220 Memento domine famulorum famularumque tuarum omnis congregationis beati petri apostoli tui omniumque propinquorum meorum, et quorum elemosinas suscepimus, seu qui mihi confessi sunt, necnon et quorum nomina super sanctum altare tuum scripta habentur, et omnium circumadstantium, quorum tibi fides cognita est et nota deuotio pro quibus tibi offerimus, uel qui tibi offerunt hoc sacrificium laudis pro se suisque omnibus pro redemptione animarum suarum, pro spe salutis et incolomitatis suę tibique reddunt uota sua aeterno deo uiuo et uero.

221 Communicantes et memoriam uenerantes inprimis gloriosę semper uirginis marię genetricis dei et domini nostri iesu christi. Sed et beatorum apostolorum ac martyrum tuorum, Petri, Pauli, Andreae, Iacobi, Iohannis, Thomę, Iacobi, Philippi, bartholomei, mathei, simonis, et taddei, lini, cleti, clementis, syxti, cornelii, cipriani, laurentii, chrisogoni, Iohannis et pauli, cosmę, et damiani[1] hilarii, martini, benedicti, gregorii, amandi[2], et omnium sanctorum tuorum. Sed et domine natalicium, cęlebrantes sanctorum tuorum martyrum ac confessorum perfectorum iustorum quorum hodie sollempnitas in conspectu glorię tuae celebratur. Quorum meritis precibusque concedas, ut in omnibus protectionis tuae muniamur auxilio. Per eundem christum[3] dominum nostrum.

---

[1] *Nicasii* added in left margin.
[2] *Remigii* added in right margin.
[3] Supplied interlinearly.

f. 47r **222** / [1]Hanc igitur oblationem seruitutis nostrae, sed et cunctae familiae tuae quaesumus domine ut placatus accipias, diesque nostros in tua pace disponas, atque ab aeterna damnatione nos eripi, et in electorum tuorum iubeas grege numerari. Per christum dominum nostrum.

223 Quam oblationem tu deus in omnibus quaesumus, + benedictam, + adscriptam, + ratam, + rationabilem, acceptabilemque facere digneris, ut nobis + corpus, + et sanguis fiat dilectissimi filii tui domini dei nostri iesu christi. Qui pridie quam pateretur, accepit panem in sanctas ac uenerabiles manus suas, et[2] eleuatis oculis in caelum, ad te deum patrem suum omnipotentem, tibi gratias agens, + benedixit, fregit dedit discipulis suis dicens. Accipite et manducate ex hoc omnes, hoc est enim corpus meum. Simili modo posteaquam caenatum est, accipiens et hunc praeclarum calicem in sanctas ac uenerabiles manus suas. Item tibi gratias agens, + benedixit, dedit discipulis suis dicens. Accipite et bibite ex eo omnes. Hic est enim calix sanguinis mei, noui et[3] aeterni testamenti mysterium fidei qui pro uobis et pro multis effundetur in remissionem peccatorum. Haec quotienscumque[4] feceritis in mei memoriam facietis.

224 Vnde et memores domine nos tui serui, sed et plebs tua sancta eiusdem[5] christi filii tui domini dei nostri, tam uenerandę natiuitatis quam et beatę passionis, / necnon ab inferis resurrectionis, sed et in caelos gloriosae ascensionis offerimus praeclarae maiestatis tuae, de tuis donis ac datis, + hostiam puram, + hostiam sanctam, + hostiam inmaculatam. + Panem sanctum uitae aeternae, + et calicem salutis perpetuae. Supraquę propitio[6] ac sereno uultu respicere digneris, et accepta habere, sicuti accepta habere dignatus es, munera pueri tui iusti abel, et sacrificium patriarchę nostri abrahę, et quod tibi obtulit summus sacerdos tuus melchisedech, sanctum sacrificium, inmaculatum hostiam. Supplices te rogamus omnipotens deus, iube haec

f. 47v

---

1 The original part of the book resumes.
2 Supplied interlinearly.
3 Supplied interlinearly.
4 *n* supplied interlinearly.
5 Supplied interlinearly.
6 *propitiatio* before correction.

perferri per manus sancti angeli tui in sublime altare tuum in conspectum diuinae maiestatis tuae, ut quotquot ex hac altaris participatione sacrosanctum filii tui, + corpus, + et sanguinem sumpserimus, omni benedictione caelesti et gratia repleamur. Per christum dominum nostrum.[1]

225 Memento etiam domine et eorum nominum[2] qui nos precesserunt cum signo fidei et dormiunt in somno pacis ill.[3] Ipsis domine[4] et omnibus in christo quiescentibus, locum refrigerii lucis et pacis, ut indulgeas depraecamur. Per christum dominum nostrum.

226 Nobis quoque peccatoribus famulis tuis, de multitudine miserationum tuarum sperantibus partem aliquam et societatem donare digneris / cum tuis sanctis apostolis et martyribus, cum Iohanne, Stephano, Mathia, Barnaba, Ignatio, Alexandro, Marcellino, Petro, Felicitate, Perpetua, Agatha, Lucia, Anastasia[5], et cum omnibus sanctis tuis. Intra quorum nos consortium, non aestimator meriti, sed ueniae quaesumus largitor admitte. Per christum.

/f. 48r

227 Per quem haec omnia domine semper bona creas, + sanctificas, + uiuificas benedicis et praestas nobis per ipsum, et cum ipso, et in ipso est tibi deo patri omnipotenti, in unitate spiritus sancti omnis honor et gloria.[6] Per omnia saecula saeculorum. Amen.

---

[1] Signe de renvoi for the *Memento* added in the left margin:

1* Memento mei queso domine et miserere, licet hec sancta indigne tibi sancte pater omnipotens aeterne deus meis manibus offerantur sacrificia, qui nec inuocare sanctum ac uenerabile nomen tuum dignus sum. Sed quoniam in honore, laude, et memoria gloriosissimi dilecti filii tui domini nostri iesu christi offeruntur, sicut incensum in conspectu diuine maiestatis tue cum odore suauitatis accendantur. Per eundem christum dominum nostrum.

[2] A small erasure follows.
[3] Supplied interlinearly.
[4] Supplied interlinearly.
[5] The names *Eutropia, Agna, Cecilia* added in right margin.
[6] Neumed.

228 OREMVS. Praeceptis salutaribus moniti, et diuina institutione formati audemus dicere.

229 Pater noster qui es in caelis. Sanctificetur nomen tuum. Adueniat regnum tuum. Fiat uoluntas tua, sicut in caelo et in terra. Panem nostrum cotidianum da nobis hodie. Et dimitte nobis debita nostra. Sicut et nos dimittimus debitoribus nostris, et ne nos inducas in temptationem. Sed libera nos a malo.

230 Libera nos quaesumus domine ab omnibus malis, praeteritis praesentibus et futuris, et intercedente beata et gloriosa semper uirgine dei genetrice maria, et beatis apostolis tuis, petro et paulo atque andrea, cum omnibus sanctis. Da propitius pacem in diebus nostris, ut ope misericordiae tuae adiuti, et a peccato / simus semper liberi, et ab omni perturbatione securi, per dominum nostrum iesum christum filium tuum. Qui tecum uiuit et regnat deus in unitate spiritus sancti, per omnia secula saeculorum.

/f. 48r

231 Pax domini sit semper uobiscum. R. Et cum spiritu tuo. Agnus dei qui tollis peccata mundi miserere nobis.

/f. 48v

/ XLII

VIII KL. IAN. VIGILIA NATALIS DOMINI HORA NONA[1].
STATIO AD SANCTAM MARIAM

232 *DEVS QVI NOS REDEMPTIONIS NOSTRAE ANNVA* expectatione laetificas, praesta ut unigenitum tuum quem redemptorem laeti suscepimus, uenientem quoque iudicem securi uideamus. Dominum nostrum iesum christum.

233 SVPER OBLATA. Da nobis quesumus omnipotens deus, ut sicut ad adoranda filii tui natalitia praeuenimus, sic eius munera capiamus sempiterna gaudentes. Qui tecum uiuit.

234 PRAEFATIO. VD per christum. Cuius hodie faciem in confessione praeuenimus, et uoce supplici exoramus, ut superuenturae noctis officiis, nos ita peruigiles reddat, ut sinceris mentibus, eius percipere mereamur natale uenturum. In

---

[1] A final letter erased.

quo inuisibilis ex substantia, uisibilis per carnem apparuit in nostram. Tecumque unus non tempore genitus, non natura inferior, ad nos uenit ex tempore natus. Per quem maiestatem tuam.

/f. 49r **235** BENEDICTIO SVPER POPVLVM. / Omnipotens deus qui incarnatione unigeniti sui mundi tenebras effugauit, et eius gloriosa natiuitate, hanc sacratissimam noctem inradiauit, effuget a uobis tenebras uitiorum, et inradiet corda uestra luce uirtutum. AMEN.
Quique eius sacratissimę natiuitatis gaudium magnum pastoribus ab angelo uoluit nuntiari, ipse super uos benedictionis suae gratissimum imbrem infundat, atque ipso pastore uos ad aeternorum gaudiorum, pascua aeterna perducat. AMEN.
Et qui per eius incarnationem terrena caelestibus sociauit, in aeternę pacis et bonę uoluntatis uos nectare repleat, et caelestis militiae, consortes efficiat. AMEN.
Quod ipse praestare dignetur, cuius regnum et imperium, sine fine permanet in saecula saeculorum.

236 AD COMPLENDVM. Da nobis domine quaesumus unigeniti tui filii recensita natiuitate respirare, cuius caelesti mysterio pascimur et potamur. Per eundem.

XLIII
DE NOCTE AD SANCTAM MARIAM

237 Deus qui hanc sacratissimam noctem ueri luminis fecisti inlustratione clarescere, da quaesumus ut cuius lucis mysteria in terra cognouimus, eius quoque gaudiis in caelo perfruamur. Qui tecum uiuit.

/f. 49v **238** SVPER OBLATA. / Accepta tibi sit domine quaesumus hodiernae festiuitatis oblatio, ut tua gratia largiente, per haec sacrosancta commercia in illius inueniamur forma, in quo tecum est nostra substantia. Qui tecum uiuit.

239 PRAEFATIO. [1]VD aequum et salutare. Quia per incarnati uerbi mysterium, noua mentis nostrae oculis lux tuae claritatis

---

[1] Partly neumed by a later scribe.

effulsit[1]. Vt dum uisibiliter deum cognoscimus, per hunc inuisibilium amore rapiamur. Et ideo cum angelis et archangelis cum thronis et dominationibus. Cumque omni militia caelestis exercitus, ymnum gloriae tuae canimus sine fine dicentes. Sanctus Sanctus.

240 Communicantes et noctem sacratissimam caelebrantes, qua beatae mariae intemerata uirginitas huic mundo edidit saluatorem. Sed et memoriam uenerantes eiusdem gloriosae semper uirginis mariae genitricis dei et domini nostri iesu christi. Sed et beatorum apostolorum.

241 BENEDICTIO. Populum tuum quaesumus domine pio fauore prosequere, pro quo dignatus es in hac sacratissima nocte tuam mundo praesentiam exhibere. AMEN.
A cunctis eum aduersitatibus paterna pietate custodi, pro quo in mundo hoc in tempore dignatus es ex uirgine nasci. AMEN.
Vt te redemptorem suum intellegat, / et tuam ueraciter gratiam comprehendat. AMEN.
Quod ipse praestare dignetur.

242 AD COMPLENDVM. Da nobis quaesumus domine deus noster, ut qui natiuitatem domini nostri iesu christi nos frequentare gaudemus, dignis conuersationibus ad eius mereamur pertinere consortium. Qui tecum uiuit.

XLIIII
MANE PRIMO AD SANCTAM ANASTASIAM

243 Da quaesumus omnipotens deus, ut qui noua incarnatione uerbi tui luce perfundimur, hoc in nostro resplendeat opere, quod per fidem fulget in mente. Per.

244 ALIA. Da quaesumus omnipotens deus, ut qui beatae anastasiae martyris tuae sollemnia colimus, eius apud te patrocinia sentiamus. Per.

245 SVPER OBLATA. Munera nostra quaesumus domine natiuitatis hodierna mysteriis apta proueniant, ut sicut homo genitus, idem

---

[1] First part of word over an erasure.

f. 50r

refulsit deus, sic nobis haec terrena substantia conferat quod diuinum est. Per eundem.

246 ALIA. Accipe quaesumus domine munera dignanter oblata, et beatae anastasiae suffragantibus meritis, ad nostrae salutis auxilium, prouenire concede. Per.

247 PRAEFATIO. [1]VD aequum et salutare. Quia nostri saluatoris hodie lux uera processit, quę clara nobis omnia et intellectu manifestauit et uisu. Et ideo cum angelis et archangelis.

/f. 50v **248** ITEM ALIA PRAEFATIO. / VD aequum et salutare. Nos tibi semper et ubique gratias agere, domine sanctae pater omnipotens aeternae deus. Qui ut de hoste generis humani maior uictoria duceretur, non solum per uiros uirtute martyrii, sed de eo etiam per feminas triumphasti. Et ideo.

249 BENEDICTIO. Deus qui non solum genus humanum condere, sed etiam te nascente uoluisti hominem de terris ad astra transire, praeces supplicum respice, ut qui te post longas tenebras hodie natum lumen agnoscunt, aeternę uisionis luce perfrui mereantur. AMEN.
Complectere hunc populum in ecclesia sinu, qui nobis processisti mariae de thalamo. AMEN.
Sit haec plebs tuis praeceptis oboedienter amabilis, sicut est partus uirginis, in origine singularis. Vt cum dies tui fulgoris effulserit, inuenias in illis quod recondas in horreo, pro quibus dignatus es in carne uenire de caelo. AMEN.
Quod ipse praestare dignetur.

250 AD COMPLENDVM. Huius nos domine sacramenti semper nouitas natalis instauret, cuius natiuitas singularis humanum reppulit uetustatem. Per eundem.

251 ALIA. Satiasti domine familiam tuam muneribus sacris, eius quaesumus semper interuentione nos refoue, cuius sollempnia caelebramus. Per dominum nostrum iesum.

---

[1] Partly neumed by a later scribe.

/ XLV
IN DIE NATALIS DOMINI

252 AD SANCTVM PETRVM. Omnipotens sempiterne deus, qui hunc diem per incarnationem uerbi tui, et partum beatae mariae uirginis consecrasti, da populis tuis in hac celebritate consortium, ut qui tua gratia sunt redempti, tua sint adoptione securi. Per eundem.

253 ALIA. Concede quaesumus omnipotens deus, ut nos unigeniti tui noua per carnem natiuitas liberet, quos sub peccati iugo uetusta seruitus tenet. Per eundem.

254 SVPER OBLATA. Oblata domine munera noua unigeniti tui natiuitate[1] sanctifica, nosque a peccatorum nostrorum maculis emunda. Per eundem.

255 PRAEFATIO. VD. Quia per incarnati uerbi mysterium, ut supra.

256 Communicantes et diem sacratissimum. Vt supra.

257 BENEDICTIO. Benedicat uos omnipotens dominus, uestramque ad supernam excitet intentionem, qui hunc sacratissimum diem, natiuitate filii sui fecit esse sollemnem. AMEN.
Et qui eum qui panis est angelorum, in preselpi ecclesiae cybum fecit esse fidelium animalium, ipse uos et in praesenti saeculo degustare faciat aeternorum gaudiorum dulcedinem, et in futuro perducat ad societatem aeternorum praemiorum. AMEN.
Quique eius infantiam uilibus uoluit indui pannis, ipse uos caelestium uestimentorum induat ornamentis.

/ <Q>uod ipse praestare dignetur.

258 AD COMPLENDVM. Praesta quaesumus omnipotens deus, ut natus hodie saluator mundi, sicut diuinae nobis generationis est auctor, ita et inmortalitatis sit ipse largitor. Qui tecum uiuit.

259 ITEM ALIA BENEDICTIO. Deus qui genus humanum uulneratum in protoplasto, nouo recuperasti antidoto, et cum te astra non capiant, habitasti mulieris in utero. AMEN.

---

[1] *natiuitatem* before correction.

Respice populum tuum de excelso habitaculo tuo, pro cuius redemptione dignatus es nasci in mundo, et nobis processisti mariae de thalamo. AMEN.

Et pietate sedula in te sit salus hominum, propter quod homo factus es creator angelorum, et de poenis ferialibus recuperator animarum. AMEN.

Quod ipse.

XLVI
ALIAE ORATIONES DE NATALE DOMINI

260 Concede quaesumus omnipotens deus, ut quos sub peccati iugo uetusta seruitus tenet, eos unigeniti tui noua per carnem natiuitas liberet. Qui tecum uiuit.

261 ALIA. Respice nos misericors deus, et mentibus clementer humanis nascente christo, summae ueritatis lumen ostende. Per eundem.

262 ALIA. Largire quaesumus domine famulis tuis fidei, spei, et caritatis augmentum, ut qui natiuitate filii tui domini nostri gloriantur, et aduersa mundi te gubernante non sentiant, et quae temporaliter / celebrare desiderant, sine fine percipiant. Per eundem.

/f. 52r

263 ALIA. Deus qui per beatae mariae uirginis partum, sine humana concupiscentia procreatum, in filii tui membra uenientis paternis fecisti praeiudiciis non teneri, praesta quaesumus, ut huius creaturae nouitate suscepta, uetustatis antiquae contagiis exuamur. Per eundem.

264 ALIA. Concede nobis omnipotens deus, ut salutare tuum noua caelorum luce mirabili, quod ad salutem mundi hodierna festiuitate processit, nostris semper innouandis cordibus oriatur. Per eundem.

265 ALIA. Deus qui humanae substantiae dignitatem, et mirabiliter condidisti, et mirabilius reformasti, da nobis quaesumus eius diuinitatis esse consortes, qui humanitatis nostrae fieri dignatus est particeps. Qui tecum.

266 ALIA. Omnipotens sempiternae deus, qui in filii tui domini nostri natiuitate tribuisti totius religionis initium, perfectionemque constare, da nobis quaesumus in eius portione censeri, in quo totius salutis humanae, summa consistit. Qui tecum.

267 ALIA. Da quaesumus domine populo tuo inuiolabilem fidei firmitatem, ut qui unigenitum tuum in tua tecum gloria sempiternum, in ueritate nostri corporis natum, de matre uirgine confitentur, et a praesentibus liberentur aduersis, et man/suris gaudiis inserantur. Per eundem dominum.

f. 53v

XLVII
VII KL. IAN. NATALE SANCTI STEPHANI MARTYRIS

268 Da nobis quaesumus domine imitari quod colimus, ut discamus et inimicos diligere, quia eius natalitia celebramus, qui nouit etiam pro persecutoribus exorare. <Per> dominum.

269 SVPER OBLATA. Suscipe domine munera pro tuorum commemoratione sanctorum, ut quod illos passio gloriosos, nos deuotio reddat innocuos. Per dominum.

270 PRAEFATIO. [1]VD aeterne deus. Beati stephani leuitae simul et martyris natalitia recolentes, qui fidei, qui sacrę militiae, qui dispensationis et castitatis egregiae, qui praedicationis mirabilisque constantiae, qui confessionis ac patientiae nobis exempla ueneranda proposuit. Et ideo natiuitatem filii tui merito prae caeteris passionis suae festiuitate prosequitur, cuius gloriae sempiternae primus martyr occurrit. Per christum.

271 BENEDICTIO. Deus qui beatum stephanum protomartyrem coronauit, et confessione fidei, et agone martyrii, mentes uestras circumdet, et in praesenti saeculo corona iustitiae, et in futuro[2] perducat uos ad coronam gloriae. AMEN.
Illius tribuat obtentu uobis, dei et proximi caritate semper exuberare, qui hanc studuit inter lapidantium impetus obtinere. AMEN.

---

[1] Partly neumed by a later scribe.
[2] *futoro* before correction.

/f. 53r / Quo eius exemplo roborati, et intercessione muniti, ab eo quem ille a dextris dei uidit stantem mereamini benedici. AMEN. Quod ipse praestare.

272 AD COMPLENDVM. Auxilientur nobis domine sumpta mysteria, et intercedente beato stephano martyre tuo, sempiterna protectione confirment. Per.

ALIAE ORATIONES

273 Omnipotens sempiterne deus, qui primitias martyrum in beati leuitae stephani sanguine dedicasti, tribue quaesumus ut pro nobis intercessor existat, qui pro suis etiam persecutoribus exorauit. Per.

274 ALIA. Deus qui nos unigeniti tui clementer incarnatione redemisti, da nobis patrocinia tuorum continuata sanctorum, quibus capere ualeamus salutaris mysterii portionem. Per dominum.

275 ALIA. Praesta quaesumus omnipotens deus, ut sicut diuina laudamus in sancti stephani passione magnalia, sic indulgentiam tuam piis eius praecibus subsequamur. Per dominum.

276 ALIA. Beatus martyr stephanus domine quaesumus pro fidelibus tuis suffragator accedat, qui dum bene sit tibi placitus, pro his etiam possit audire. Per dominum.

XLVIII
VI KL. IAN. NATALE SANCTI IOHANNIS EVANGELISTAE IN PRIMA MISSA

277 Deus qui per os beati apostoli tui iohannis, uerbi tui nobis archana reserasti, praesta quaesumus ut quod ille nostris auribus excellenter infudit, intelligentiae competentis eruditione capiamus. Per dominum.

/f. 53v 278 / SVPER OBLATA. Supplicationibus apostolicis beati iohannis euangelistae, quaesumus ecclesiae tuae domine commendetur oblatio, cuius magnificis praecibus eruditur. Per dominum.

279 AD COMPLENDVM. Beati iohannis euangelistae nos domine quaesumus merita prosequantur, et tuam nobis indulgentiam semper implorent. Per dominum nostrum.

XLVIIII
ITEM IN DIE AD MISSAM

280 Ecclesiam tuam domine benignus inlustra, ut beati iohannis euangelistae inluminata doctrinis, ad dona perueniat sempiterna. Per.

281 SVPER OBLATA. Suscipe munera domine quae in eius tibi sollemnitate deferimus, cuius nos confidimus patrocinio liberari. Per.

282 PRAEFATIO. [1]VD aeterne deus. Beati apostoli tui euangelistae iohannis, ueneranda natalicia recensentes, qui domini nostri iesu christi filii tui uocatione suscepta, terrenum respuit patrem, ut posset inuenire caelestem. Adeptus in regno caelorum sedem apostolici culminis, qui tantum retia carnalia contemserat genitoris. Quique ab unigenito tuo sic familiariter est dilectus, et immensae gratię muneribus adprobatus, ut eum idem dominus in cruce iam positus, uicarium suae matri uirgini filium subrogaret. Quatinus beatae genitricis / integritati, probati dilectique discipuli, uirginitas deseruiret. Nam et in cenae mysticae sacrosancto conuiuio, super ipsum uitae fontem, aeternum scilicet pectus recubuerat saluatoris. De quo perenniter manantia caelestis hauriens fluenta doctrinae, tam profundis ac mysticis reuelationibus est inbutus, ut omnem transgrediens creaturam, excelsa mente conspiceret, et euangelica uoce proferret, quod in principio erat uerbum, et uerbum erat apud deum, et deus erat uerbum. Et ideo.

/f. 54r

283 BENEDICTIO. Omnipotens deus, dignetur uobis per intercessionem beati iohannis apostoli et euangelistae benedicere, qui per eum archana uerbi sui uoluit ecclesiae reuelare. AMEN.
Concedat uobis ut quot ille spiritus sancti munere afflatus uestris

---

[1]   Partly neumed by a later scribe.

auribus infudit, eiusdem spiritus dona capere mente ualeatis. AMEN.

Quo eius documento de diuinitate nostri redemptoris edocti, et amando quod tradidit, et praedicando quod docuit, et exequendo quod iussit, ad dona peruenire mereamini, quae idem iesus christus dominus noster repromisit. AMEN.

Quod ipse praestare dignetur.

284 AD COMPLENDVM. Refecti cibo potuque caelesti deus noster, te supplices depraecamur, ut in cuius haec commemoratione percepimus, eius muniamur et praecibus. Per dominum.

/f. 54v   **285** / AD VESPERAS. Beati iohannis euangelistae quaesumus domine supplicatione placatus, et ueniam nobis tribuat, et remedia sempiterna concede. Per dominum.

286 ALIA. Beati euangelistae iohannis domine praecibus adiuuemur, ut quod possibilitas nostra non obtinet, eius nobis intercessione donetur. Per dominum.

287 ALIA. Sit domine quaesumus, beatus iohannes euangelista nostrae fragilitatis adiutor, ut pro nobis tibi supplicans, copiosus audiatur. Per dominum.

288 ALIA. Omnipotens sempiterne deus, qui huius diei uenerandam sanctamque laetitiam beati apostoli tui iohannis euangelistae festiuitate tribuisti, da ecclesiae tuae quaesumus, et amare quod credidit, et praedicare quod docuit. Per dominum.

L
V KL. IAN. NATALE INNOCENTIVM

289 Deus cuius hodierna die praeconium, innocentes martyres, non loquendo sed moriendo confessi sunt, omnia in nobis uitiorum mala mortifica, ut fidem tuam quam lingua nostra loquitur, etiam moribus uita fateatur. Per dominum.

290 SVPER OBLATA. Sanctorum tuorum nobis domine pia non desit oratio, quae et munera nostra conciliet, et tuam nobis indulgentiam semper obtineat. Per dominum.

291 PRAEFATIO. VD aeterne[1] deus. Et in praetiosis mortibus

paruulorum, quos propter nostri saluatoris infan/tiam, bestiali saeuitia herodes funestus occidit, inmensa clementiae tuae dona praedicare, in quibus fulget sola magis gratia quam uoluntas, et clara est prius confessio quam loquela. Ante passio, quam membra idonea passioni. Existunt testes christi, qui eius nondum fuerant agnitores. O infinita benignitas, o ineffabilis misericordia, quae pro suo nomine trucidatis, meritum gloriae perire non patitur, sed proprio cruore perfusis, et salus regenerationis adhibetur, et inputatur corona martyrii. Et ideo.

292 BENEDICTIO. Omnipotens deus, pro cuius unigeniti ueneranda infantia innocentum, cateruas herodis funesta peremit saeuitia, suae uobis benedictionis tribuat dona gratissima. AMEN.
Et qui eius concessit, ut unicum filium eius dominum nostrum, non loquendo sed moriendo confiterentur, concedat uobis ut fidem ueram quam lingua uestra fatetur, etiam mores probi et uita inculpabilis fateatur. AMEN.
Quique eos primitiuum fructum sanctae suae suscepit ecclesiae, cum fructu bonorum operum uos faciat peruenire, ad gaudia aeternae patriae. AMEN.
Quod ipse praestare dignetur.

293 AD COMPLENDVM. Votiua domine dona percepimus, quae sanctorum nobis praecibus et praesentis quaesumus uitae pariter, et aeternae tribuat conferre subsidium. Per dominum.

294 / ALIA. Deus qui licet sis magnus in magnis, mirabilia tamen gloriosius operaris in minimis, da nobis quaesumus in eorum caelebritate gaudere, qui filio tuo domino nostro testimonium prębuerunt etiam non loquentes. Per eundem dominum nostrum.

295 ALIA. Discat ecclesia tua deus, infantum quos hodie ueneramur exemplo sincera tenere pietate, quae illis prius uitam praestitit sempiternam, quam possint nosse praesentem. Per dominum.

296 ALIA. Adiuua nos domine quaesumus eorum depraecatione

---

[1]   *aeternae* before correction.

sanctorum, qui filium tuum humana necdum uoce profitentes, caelesti sunt pro eius natiuitate gratia coronati. Per dominum.

297 ITEM ALIA BENEDICTIO. Concede quaesumus domine plebi tuae innocentum gratiam, qui tibi consecrasti primitias martyrum, ab innocentia paruulorum. AMEN.
Seruetur hic populus purgatus baptismate, qui tibi placitam fecisti, innocentiam in cruore. AMEN.
Vt illuc eorum interuentu grex accedat post lauacrum, ubi felices paruuli perfusi rore sanguinis, gloriantur in perpetuum. AMEN.
Quod ipse praestare.

LI
DOMINICA I POST NATALE DOMINI

/f. 56r 298 Deus qui salutis aeternae beatae mariae uirginitate fecunda, humano generi praemia praestitisti, tribue quaesumus ut ipsam pro nobis intercedere / sentiamus, per quam meruimus auctorem uitae suscipere. <Per> dominum nostrum iesum christum.

299 SVPER OBLATA. Muneribus nostris quaesumus domine praecibusque susceptis, et caelestibus nos munda mysteriis, et clementer exaudi. Per dominum nostrum iesum christum.

300 PRAEFATIO. VD aeterne[1] deus. Et sursum cordibus erectis, diuinum adorare mysterium, ut quod magno dei munere geritur, magnis ecclesiae gaudiis caelebretur. Quoniam humana conditio ueteri terrenaque lege cessante, noua caelestique substantia mirabiliter restaurata profertur. Per christum.

301 BENEDICTIO. Omnipotens deus, adaperiat cor uestrum in lege sua, et humiliet animas uestras ad capienda dona caelestia. AMEN.
Quicquid uobis pro salute animarum uestrarum, os mortalitatis nostrae enarrat, acceptum uobis pietas diuina efficiat. AMEN.

---

[1] *aeternae* before correction.

Vt diuinis sermonibus animati, cum eis qui pro uobis inuigilant ad aeternam beatitudinem, mereamini peruenire illaesi. AMEN. Quod ipse praestare dignetur.

302 AD COMPLENDVM. Da nobis quaesumus domine deus noster, ut qui natiuitatem domini nostri iesu christi, nos frequentare gaudemus, dignis conuersationibus ad eius mereamur pertinere consortium. Per eundem.

LII
II KL. IAN. NATALE SANCTI SILVESTRI PAPAE

303 / Da quaesumus omnipotens deus, ut beati siluestri confessoris tui atque pontificis ueneranda sollemnitas, et deuotionem nobis augeat et salutem. Per dominum.

304 SVPER OBLATA. Sancti tui nos domine quaesumus ubique laetificent, ut dum eorum merita recolimus, patrocinia sentiamus. Per dominum nostrum iesum christum.

305 PRAEFATIO. VD aeterne[1] deus. Et in hac die quam transitu sacro beati confessoris tui .ill. consecrasti, quaesumus ergo clementiam tuam, ut des nobis illam sequi doctrinam, quam ille et uerbo docuit et opere compleuit. Quatinus nos adiuuari apud misericordiam tuam, et exemplis eius sentiamus et meritis. Per christum.

LIII
306 BENEDICTIO IN VIGILIA OCTABAS DOMINI. Omnipotens sempiterne deus. Qui per incarnatum uerbum unigenitum tuum dedisti lumen in saeculum, eius misericordiam suppliciter exoramus, ut qui ex gentibus sanctam eccelsiam fecundauit in grege, ab omni eam gentilitatis absoluat errore. AMEN.
Et qui in sequenti dię ut legis tolleret iugum, per legem est carnaliter circumcisus, huius populi spiritaliter dignetur circumcidere corda, atque omnia amputare radicitus uitia, ut sobrietatis studium, et non ębrietatis sectentur incommodum. AMEN.

---

[1] *aeternae* before correction.

Sint semper tua omnes protectione saluati, ut dum carnalem celebrare desiderant circumcisionem / tua sint firmati benedictione, ut callidi serpentis uenena possint euadere, et ad aeternam beatitudinem te praeuio feliciter ualeant peruenire. AMEN.

Quod ipse praestare.

307 ALIAM BENEDICTIONEM REQVIRE IN NATALE VNIVS CONFESSORIS.

308 AD COMPLENDVM. Praesta quaesumus omnipotens deus, ut de perceptis muneribus gratias exhibentes, beneficia potiora sumamus. Per dominum nostrum iesum christum.

LIIII
MENS. IAN. OCTABAS DOMINI AD SANCTAM MARIAM
309 Deus qui nobis nati saluatoris diem caelebrare concedis octauum, fac quaesumus nos eius perpetua diuinitate muniri, cuius sumus carnali commertio reparati. Qui tecum.

310 SVPER OBLATA. Praesta quaesumus domine, ut per haec munera quae domini nostri iesu christi archanae natiuitatis mysterio gerimus, purificatae mentis intelligentiam consequamur. Per dominum.

311 PRAEFATIO. VD per christum. Cuius hodie circumcisionis diem et natiuitatis octauum caelebrantes, tua domine mirabilia ueneramur. Quia quae peperit et mater et uirgo est, qui natus est, et infans et deus est. Merito caeli locuti sunt, angeli gratulati, pastores laetati, magi mutati, reges turbati, paruuli gloriosa passione coronati. Et ideo.

312 BENEDICTIO. Omnipotens deus. Cuius unigenitus hodierna die ne legem solueret, quam adimplere uenerat, corporalem
suscepit circumcisionem, spirituali[1] circumcisione / mentes uestras, ab omnibus uitiorum incentiuis expurget, et suam in uos infundat benedictionem. AMEN.

Et qui legem per moysen dedit, ut per mediatorem nostrum

---

[1] First *i* supplied interlinearly.

benedictionem daret, exuat uos mortificatione uitiorum, et faciat perseuerare in nouitate uirtutum. AMEN.

Quo sic in senarii numeri perfectione in hoc saeculo uiuatis, et in septenario numero inter beatorum spirituum agmina requiescatis, quatinus in octauo resurrectione renouati, iubilei remissione ditati, ad gaudia sine fine mansuri perueniatis. AMEN.

Quod ipse praestare dignetur.

313 AD COMPLENDVM. Haec nos communio domine quaesumus purget a crimine, et caelestis remedii faciat esse consortes. Per.

314 ALIA. Praesta quaesumus domine, ut quod saluatoris nostri iterata sollemnitate percepimus, perpetuae nobis redemptionis conferat medicinam. Per dominum.

LV
III NON. IAN. NATALE SANCTAE GENOVEFAE VIRGINIS

315 Beatae genouefae natalitia ueneranda, domine deus ecclesia tua deuota suscipiat, et fiat magnae deuotionis amore, et tantę fidei proficiat exemplum. Per dominum nostrum iesum christum.

316 SVPER OBLATA. Offerimus domine praeces et munera in honore sanctae genouefae gaudentes, praesta quaesumus ut et conuenienter haec agere, et remedium sempiternum ualeamus adquiri. Per dominum.

317 PRAEFATIO. / VD aeterne[1] deus. Beatae genouefae, natalicia recolentes. Vere enim huius honorandus est dies, quae sic terrena generatione processit, ut ad diuinitatis consortium perueniret. Per christum.

318 AD COMPLENDVM. Adiuuent nos quaesumus domine et haec mysteria sancta quae sumpsimus, et beatae genouefae intercessio ueneranda. Per.

---

[1] *aeternae* before correction.

LVI
DOMINICA I POST OCTABAS DOMINI

319 Omnipotens sempiterne deus, dirige actus nostros in beneplacito tuo, ut in nomine dilecti filii tui, mereamur bonis operibus abundare. Per eundem.

320 SVPER OBLATA. Concede quaesumus domine, ut oculis tuae maiestatis munus oblatum, et gratiam nobis deuotionis obtineat, et effectum beatae perennitatis adquirat. Per dominum nostrum.

321 PRAEFATIO. VD aeterne deus. Qui peccato primi parentis hominem a salutis finibus exulantem pietatis indulgentiam ad ueniam uitamque reuocasti, mittendo nobis unigenitum filium tuum, dominum et saluatorem nostrum. Per quem.

322 BENEDICTIO. Deus qui unigenitum suum misit ut mundum saluaret, eiusdem salutis uos participes efficiat, et in ea perseuerabiles reddat. AMEN.
Iram quae super infideles manet a uobis amoueat, et ab ea uos in perpetuum liberos efficiat. AMEN.
/f. 58v Spiritum filii sui uobis adtribuat, eiusque donis uos affa/tim exuberari concede. AMEN.
Quod ipse praestare dignetur.

323 AD COMPLENDVM. Per huius domine operationem mysterii, et uitia nostra purgentur et iusta desideria compleantur. Per.

LVII
IN VIGILIA EPIPHANIAE

324 Corda nostra quaesumus domine uenturae festiuitatis splendor inlustret, quo mundi huius tenebris carere ualeamus, et perueniamus ad patriam claritatis aeternae. Per.

325 SVPER OBLATA. Tribuae quaesumus domine, ut cum praesentibus immolamus sacrificiis et sumamus, quę uenturae sollemnitatis pia munera praelocuntur. <Per> iesum christum.

326 PRAEFATIO. VD aeterne[1] deus. Et te laudare mirabilem deum in omnibus operibus tuis, quibus sacratissima regni tui mysteria

---

[1]   *aeternae* before correction.

reuelasti. Hanc etenim festiuitatem dominicae apparitionis, index stella praecessit, quae natum in terra caeli dominum magis stupentibus nuntiaret. Vt manifestandus mundo deus et caelesti denuntiaretur indicio, et temporaliter procreatus, signorum temporalium ministerio panderetur. Et ideo.

327 AD COMPLENDVM. Inlumina quaesumus domine populum tuum, et splendore gratiae tuae cor eius semper accende, ut salutaris mundi stella famulante manifestata natiuitas, mentibus eorum et reueletur semper et crescat. Per dominum.

LVIII

VIII ID. IAN. EPIPHANIA AD SANCTVM PETRVM

'f. 59r   **328** / Deus qui hodierna die unigenitum gentibus stella duce reuelasti, concede propitius, ut qui iam te ex fide cognouimus, usque ad contemplandam speciem tuae celsitudinis perducamur. Per eundem.

329 SVPER OBLATA. Ecclesiae tuae quaesumus domine dona propitius intuere, quibus non iam, aurum, thus, et myrra profertur, sed quod eisdem muneribus declaratur, immolatur et sumitur. Per.

330 PRAEFATIO. VD aeterne[1] deus. Quia notam fecisti in populis misericordiam tuam, et salutare tuum cunctis gentibus declarasti. Hodiernum eligens diem, in qua ad adorandam ueri regis infantiam, excitatos de remotis partibus magos, clarior ceteris sideribus stella perduceret, et caeli ac terrae dominum corporaliter natum, radio suae lucis ostenderet. Et ideo.

331 BENEDICTIO. Deus lumen uerum, qui unigenitum suum hodierna die stella duce gentibus uoluit reuelare, sua uos dignetur benedictione ditare. AMEN.
Quo exemplo magorum, mystica domino iesu christo munera offerentes, spreto antiquo hoste spretisque contagiis uitiorum, ad aeternam patriam redire ualeatis, per uiam uirtutum. AMEN.

---

[1] *aeternae* before correction.

/f. 59v

Detque uobis ueram mentium innocentiam, qui super unigenitum suum spiritum sanctum demonstrari uoluit per columbam, eaque uirtute mentes uestrae exerceantur ad intelligenda diuine legis archana, qua in chana ga/lileae limpha est in uinum conuersa. AMEN.
Quod ipse praestare dignetur, cuius regnum.

332 Communicantes et diem sacratissimum caelebrantes, quo unigenitus tuus in tua tecum gloria coaeternus, in ueritate carnis nostrae uisibiliter corporalis apparuit. Sed et memoriam.

333 AD COMPLENDVM. Praesta quaesumus omnipotens deus, ut quae sollemni celebramus officio, purificatae mentis intelligentia consequamur. Per dominum.

ALIAE ORATIONES

334 Deus inluminator omnium gentium, da populis tuis perpetua pace gaudere, et illud lumen splendidum infunde cordibus nostris, quod trium magorum mentibus aspirasti. Per dominum.

335 ALIA. Deus cuius unigenitus in substantia nostrae carnis apparuit, praesta quaesumus ut per eum quem similem nobis foris agnouimus, intus reformari mereamur. Qui tecum.

336 ALIA. Omnipotens sempiternae deus fidelium splendor animarum, qui hanc sollemnitatem electionis gentium primitiis consecrasti, imple mundum gloria tua, et subditis tibi populis per luminis tui appare claritatem. Per dominum.

337 ALIA. Concede nobis omnipotens deus, ut salutare tuum noua caelorum luce mirabili, quod ad salutem mundi hodierna festiuitate processit, nostris semper innouandis cordibus oriatur. Per eundem.

/f. 60r

338 / ALIA. Da nobis quaesumus domine digne caelebrare mysterium, quod in nostri saluatoris infantiam miraculis coruscantibus declaratur, et corporalibus incrementis manifesta designatur humanitas. Per eundem.

106

339 ALIA. Praesta quaesumus omnipotens deus, ut saluatoris mundi stella duce manifestata natiuitas, mentibus nostris reueletur semper et crescat. Per dominum.

340 ALIA. Inlumina domine quaesumus populum tuum, et splendore gloriae tuae cor eius semper accende, ut saluatorem suum et incessanter agnoscat, et ueraciter adpraehendat. <Per> dominum nostrum iesum christum.

LVIIII
DOMINICA PRIMA POST THEOPHANIA

341 Vota quaesumus domine supplicantis populi caelesti pietate prosequere, ut et quae agenda sunt uideant, et ad implenda quae uiderint conualescant. Per.

342 SVPER OBLATA. Oblatum tibi domine sacrificium, uiuificet nos semper et muniat. Per.

343 PRAEFATIO. VD aeterne[1] deus. Quia cum unigenitus tuus in substantia nostrae mortalitatis apparuit, in noua nos inmortalitatis suae luce reparauit. Et ideo.

344 BENEDICTIO. Deus qui filii sui temporalem pueritiam fecit esse mirabilem, spiritu prudentiae corda uestra inlustrare ac docere dignetur. AMEN.

f. 60v

Quique eum parentibus temporaliter subdi uo/luit, ipse uos humilitatis et pietatis muneribus misericorditer informet. AMEN.

Et qui eum sapientia aetate et gratia proficere tribuit, spiritualium uobis profectuum incrementa propitius largiatur. AMEN.

Quod ipse praestare dignetur.

345 AD COMPLENDVM. Supplices te rogamus omnipotens deus, ut quos tuis reficis sacramentis, tibi etiam placitis moribus dignanter deseruire concedas. Per.

---

[1] *aeternae* before correction.

LX
IDVS IAN. OCTABAS EPIPHANIAE ET DEPOSITIO
SANCTI HILARII EPISCOPI

346 Deus cuius uestra genitus in substantia nostrae carnis apparuit. Require retro.

347 Deus cuius miseratione delinquentes mutuantur adueniam iusti transferuntur ad palmam, qui infusus corde beati hilarii antistitis quasi de tuo templo fidei responsa dedisti, concede propitius, ut qui tunc inclytum confessorem tuum fecisti caesarem non timere, eius intercessione ab spiritali hoste plebem protegas obsecrantem, ut cuius sollemnitate tripudiat, eius sit fida praece defensa. Per.

348 SVPER OBLATA. Vniuersitatis conditor et humani generis reformator, annuae quaesumus omnipotens deus praecibus nostris, ut qui miramur in doctore quod colimus, mereamur in munere quod placeamus, et sicut beato hilario confessori tuo atque pontifici dedisti, da ecclesiae tuae concordia memoriam gloriosam eo obtinente, ut sacrificium nostrum eius meritis tibi efficiatur acceptum. Per dominum nostrum.

/f. 61r **349** SVPER OBLATA. / Hostias tibi domine pro nati tui apparitione deferimus, suppliciter exorantes, ut sicut ipse nostrorum auctor est numerum, ita ipse sit misericors et susceptor. Iesus christus.

350 PRAEFATIO. VD Gratias agere. Vota soluere, munera consecrare, domine sanctae pater omnipotens aeterne[1] deus. Qui beatum hylarium confessorem tuum praeeligisti tibi sacratae confessionis tuae antistitem, ingenti lumine choruscantem, morum laenitate pollentem, fidei feruore flagrantem, eloquii fontem torrentem. Cui quae sit gloriatio ostendit concursus ad tumulum, purificatio incursorum, medela languentium, mirandarum signa uirtutum. Qui etsi hic natura fecit finem per transitum, illic uiuunt pontificis merita post sepulchrum, ubi praesentia saluatoris est iesu christi domine nostri. Per quem.

---

[1] *aeternae* before correction.

351 BENEDICTIO. Deus qui praesentem diem ita dignatus es eligere, ut et eum eligeres tot miraculis demonstrare, in quo te ad adorandum stella noua magos perduxit, et iordanis tuo baptismo sanctificari meruit, necnon et aquę pallor in chana galileae uinum produxit, esto quaesumus tuae familiae, ipse lux itineris qui stella indice clarificatus es rex salutis. AMEN.

Da plebi tuae redemptoris sui plenum cognoscere fulgorem, ut per eius incrementa ad perpetuam claritatem perueniat. AMEN.

f. 61v / Et qui dignatus es hodie ad iordanis fontem fons aquae uiuae descendere, et tuo baptismate sanctificare, tribuae populis tuis perpetuae pace gaudere, et splendore gratiae tuae semper accendere. AMEN.

Quod ipse praestare dignetur.

352 AD COMPLENDVM. Caelestis lumine quaesumus domine semper et ubique nos praeueni, ut mysterium cuius nos participes esse uoluisti, et puro cernamus intuitu, et digno percipiamus effectu. Per dominum nostrum.

353 AD COMPLENDVM. Deus fidelium remunerator animarum, praesta quaesumus, ut beati hylarii confessoris tui atque pontificis, cuius uenerandam caelebramus festiuitatem, eius praecibus indulgentiam consequamur. Per.

LXI

XVIIII KL. FEBR. NATALE SANCTI FELICIS IN PINCIS

354 Concede quaesumus omnipotens deus, ut ad meliorem uitam sanctorum tuorum exempla nos prouocent, quatinus quorum sollemnia agimus, etiam actus imitemur. Per.

355 SVPER OBLATA. Hostias tibi domine beati felicis confessoris tui dicatas meritis benignus adsume, et ad perpetuum nobis tribuę prouenire subsidium. Per dominum.

356 PRAEFATIO. VD aeterne[1] deus. Et confessionem sancti felicis memorabilem non tacere. Qui nec hereticis prauitatibus nec saeculi blandimentis, a sui status rectitudine potuit immutari.

---

[1] *aeternae* before correction.

/f. 62r Sed inter utraque discrimina ueritatis assertor, / firmitatem tuae fidei non dereliquid. Per christum.

357 AD COMPLENDVM. Quaesumus domine salutaribus repleti mysteriis, ut cuius sollemnitate caelebramus, eius orationibus adiuuemur. Per dominum.

LXII
XVII KL. FEBR. NATALE SANCTI MARCELLI PAPAE

358 Praeces populi tui quaesumus domine clementer exaudi, ut beati marcelli martyris tui atque pontificis meritis adiuuemur, cuius passione laetamur. Per.

359 SVPER OBLATA. Suscipe quaesumus domine munera dignanter oblata, et beati marcelli suffragantibus meritis, ad nostrae salutis auxilium, prouenire concede. Per dominum.

360 PRAEFATIO. VD aeterne[1] deus. Qui glorificaris in tuorum confessione sanctorum. Et non solum excellentioribus praemiis martyrum tuorum merita gloriosa prosequeris, sed etiam sacro mynisterio competentibus seruitiis exequentes, gaudium domini sui tribuis benignus intrare. Per christum.

361 AD COMPLENDVM. Satiasti domine familiam tuam muneribus sacris, eius quaesumus domine semper interuentione nos refoue, cuius sollemnia celebramus. Per dominum.

LXIII
XVI KL. FEBR. NATALE SANCTAE PRISCAE

362 Da quaesumus omnipotens deus, ut qui beatae priscae martyris tuae natalicia colimus, et annua sollemnitate laetemur, et tantae fidei proficiamus exemplo. Per dominum nostrum iesum christum.

/f. 62v **363** SVPER OBLATA. / Hostia domine quaesumus quam in sanctorum tuorum natalicias recensentes offerimus, et uincula nostrae prauitatis absoluat, et tuae nobis misericordiae dona conciliet. Per.

---

[1] *aeternae* before correction.

364 PRAEFATIO. VD per christum. Quem beata uirgo pariter et martyr .ill. et diligendo timuit, et timendo dilexit. Illique[1] coniuncta est moriendo, cui consecrauerat casta uiuendo. Et pro eo temporalem studuit sustinere poenam, ut ab eo perciperet gloriam sempiternam. Quae dum duplicem uoluit sumere palmam in sacri certaminis agone, et de corporis integritate, et de fidei puritate, laboriosius duxit longa antiqui hostis sustinere temptamenta, quam uitam praesentem cito amittere per tormenta. Quoniam cum in martyrio proponantur ea quae terreant, in carnis uero delectamentis ea quae mulceant, molestius sustinentur hostis occultus, quam superetur infestus. Cum ergo in utroque tui sit muneris quod uicit, quia nihil ualet humana fragilitas, nisi tua hanc adiuuet pietas, pro nobis quaesumus tuam pietatem exoret, quae a te accepit ut uinceret. Et quae unigeniti tui intrare meruit thalamum, intercessione sua inter mundi huius aduersa, nobis praestet auxilium. Per quem.

365 AD COMPLENDVM. Quaesumus domine salutaribus repleti mysteriis, ut cuius sollemnia caelebramus / eius orationibus adiuuemur. Per dominum nostrum.

f. 63r

LXIIII
XIIII KL. FEBR. NATALE SANCTORVM MARIAE ET MARTHAE

366 Exaudi domine populum tuum cum sanctorum tuorum tibi patrocinio supplicantem, ut temporalem uitae nos tribuas pace gaudere, et aeternae reperire subsidium. Per.

367 SVPER OBLATA. Praeces domine tuorum respice oblationesque fidelium, et ut tibi gratae sunt pro tuorum festiuitate sanctorum, et nobis conferant tuae propitiationis auxilium. Per.

368 AD COMPLENDVM. Sanctorum tuorum domine intercessione placatus, praesta quaesumus ut quae temporali caelebramus actione, perpetua saluatione capiamus. Per dominum nostrum.

---

[1] *quae* before correction.

LXV
DOMINICA II POST THEOPHANIAM

369 Omnipotens sempiterne deus, qui caelestia simul et terrena moderaris, supplicationes populi tui clementer exaudi, et pacem tuam nostris concede temporibus. Per.

370 SVPER OBLATA. Oblata domine munera sanctifica, nosque a peccatorum nostrorum maculis emunda. Per dominum.

371 PRAEFATIO. VD aeterne[1] deus. Semperque uirtutes et laudes tuas labiis exultationis effari. Qui nobis ad reuelandos istius uitae labores, diuersa donorum tuorum solatia, et munera salutarium gaudia contulisti, mittendo nobis iesum christum filium tuum dominum nostrum. Per quem.

/f. 63v **372** BENEDICTIO. / Deus qui sua mirabili potestate aquae uertit in uinum, uos a uetustate subtractos, in beatae uitae transferat nouitatem. AMEN.
Et qui nuptiis interesse uoluit, ut earum sua praesentia comprobaret bonum, ipse uobis castitatis et sobrietatis perpetuae conferat donum. AMEN.
Ipse etiam uobis sanctarum intelligentiam scripturarum spiritualem tribuat, qui aquas conuertendo in uinum hoc ipsum uoluit designare. AMEN.
Quod ipse praestare dignetur.

373 AD COMPLENDVM. Augeatur in nobis domine quaesumus tuae uirtutis operatio, ut diuinis uegetati sacramentis, ad eorum promissa capienda tuo munere prᶒparemur. Per dominum.

LXVI
XIII KL. FEBR. NATALE SANCTORVM SEBASTIANI ET FABIANI

374 Deus qui beatum sebastianum martyrem tuum uirtute constantiae in passione roborasti, ex eius nobis imitatione tribuae pro amore tuo prospera mundi despicere, et nulla eius aduersa formidare. Per.

---

[1] *aeternae* before correction.

375 ALIA. Infirmitatem nostram respice omnipotens deus, et quia pondus propriae actionis grauat, beati fabiani martyris tui atque pontificis intercessio gloriosa nos protegat. Per.

376 SVPER OBLATA. Accepta sit in conspectu tuo domine nostra deuotio, et eius nobis fiat supplicatione salutaris, pro cuius sollemnitate defertur. Per dominum.

f. 64r **377** ALIA. / Hostias tibi domine beati fabiani martyris tui dicatas meritis benignus adsume, et ad perpetuum nobis tribuae prouenire subsidium. Per.

378 PRAEFATIO. VD aeterne[1] deus. Quoniam martyris beati sebastiani pro confessione nominis tui uenerabilis sanguis effusus, simul et tua mirabilia manifestat quo perficis in infirmitate uirtutem, et nostris studiis dat profectum, et infirmis apud te praestat auxilium. Per christum.

379 BENEDICTIO. Deus qui triumphantibus pro te martyribus regiam caelestis aulae, potentiae dextera pandis, quique pro te dimicantes sic de coquis[2] incorporeis erumnis, ut uelut aurum rutilans excipias in supernis, exaudi uota praesentis populi tui, qui sanctis martyribus tuis fabiano et sebastiano in certamine uictoriam prestitisti. AMEN.
Sit plena huic ęcclesiae laetitia pro eorum triumphis obtineat ipsorum passio ueniam pro delicto, et effunde super eos dona spiritualium uirtutum, ut nihil in eos inimicus aut uiolenter subripiat, aut fraude decipiat. AMEN.
Et obtinentibus apud te beatis martyribus tuis fabiano et sebastiano quorum hodie festa caelebramus, per bonę conuersationis perseuerantiam ad tuam mereamur pertinere gratiam. AMEN.
Quod ipse praestare dignetur.

f. 64v **380** AD COMPLENDVM. / Sacro munere satiati supplices te domine depraecamur, ut quod debite seruitutis caelebramus officio, intercedente beato sebastiano martyre tuo saluationis tuae sentiamus augmentum. Per.

---

[1] *aeternae* before correction.
[2] *quoquis* before correction.

381 ALIA. Refecti participatione muneris sacri quaesumus domine deus noster, ut cuius exequimur cultum, sentiamus effectum. Per dominum nostrum iesum christum.

382 AD VESPERAS. Praesta quaesumus domine, ut intercedente beato sebastiano martyre tuo, et a cunctis aduersitatibus muniamur in corpore, et a prauis cogitationibus mundemur in mente. Per dominum nostrum.

LXVII
XII KL. FEBR. NATALE SANCTĘ AGNAE MARTYRIS
383 Omnipotens sempiterne deus, qui infirma mundi eligis ut fortia quaeque confundas, concede propitius ut qui beatę agnetis martyris tuae sollemnia colimus, eius apud te patrocinia sentiamus. Per.

384 SVPER OBLATA. Hostias domine quas tibi offerimus propitius suscipe, et intercedente beata agna martyre tua, uincula peccatorum nostrorum absolue. Per.

385 PRAEFATIO. VD aeterne[1] deus. Et diem beatae agnetis martyrio consecratam sollemniter recensere, quae terrenae generositatis oblectamenta despiciens, caelestem meruit dignitatem. Societatis humanae uota contemnens, aeterni regis est sociata consortio. Et praetiosam mortem sexus fragili/tate calcata pro christi confessione suscipiens, simul est facta conformis, et sempiternitatis eius et gloriae. Per quem maiestatem.

/f. 65r

386 BENEDICTIO. Benedicat uobis dominus, qui beatae agnae uirgini concessit, et decorem uirginitatis, et gloriam passionis. AMEN.
Et cuius opitulatione illa meruit, et sexus fragilitatem et persequentium rabiem deuincere uos possitis, et uestrorum corporum inlecebras, et antiqui hostis machinamenta superare. AMEN.
Quo sicut illa sexu fragili uirile nisa est certamen adire, et post certamen de hostibus triumphare, ita uos in hac mortalitate

---
[1] *aeternae* before correction.

114

uiuentes ualeatis, et antiquum hostem deuincere, et ad regna caelestia peruenire. <AMEN.>
Quod ipse praestare dignetur.

387 AD COMPLENDVM. Refecti cibo potuque caelesti deus noster te supplices exoramus, ut in cuius haec commemoratione percepimus, eius muniamur et praecibus. Per.

ALIAE ORATIONES
388 Praesta quaesumus domine mentibus nostris cum exultatione prouectum, ut beatae agnetis martyris tuae cuius diem passionis annua deuotione recolimus, etiam fidei constantiam subsequamur. Per.

389 ALIA. Crescat domine semper in nobis sanctae iocunditatis affectus, et beatae agnetis uirginis atque martyris tuae, ueneranda festiuitatis augeatur. Per.

XI KL. FEBR. NATALE SANCTI VINCENTII MARTYRIS
390 / Adesto quaesumus domine supplicationibus nostris, ut qui ex iniquitate nostra reos nos esse cognoscimus, beati uincentii martyris tui, intercessione liberemur. Per dominum.

391 SVPER OBLATA. Muneribus nostris quaesumus domine praecibusque susceptis, et caelestibus nos munda mysteriis, et clementer exaudi. Per dominum.

392 PRAEFATIO. VD per christum. Pro cuius nomine gloriosus leuita uincentius et miles inuictus, rabidi hostis insaniam interritus adiit, modestus sustinuit, securus irrisit. Sciens paratus esse, ut resisteret, nesciens elatus esse quod uinceret. In utroque domini ac magistri sui uestigia sequens. Qui et humilitatis custodiendae, et de hostibus triumphandi suis sequenda exempla monstrauit. Per quem.

393 BENEDICTIO. Benedicat uobis dominus caelorum rector et conditor, et det uobis tranquillitatem temporum, salubritatem corporum, salutemque animarum. AMEN.
Tribuatque uobis frugalitatis gaudium, interueniente beato

uincentio martyre suo, aeternitatis praemium, lumen clarissimum sempiternum. AMEN.
Et concedat uobis suae pietatis auxilium, ut cum cogitatione mens uideat, lingua uoce proferat, actio non offendat. AMEN.
Quod ipse praestare dignetur.

/f. 66r **394** AD COMPLENDVM. / Quaesumus omnipotens deus ut qui caelestia alimenta percepimus, intercedente beato uincentio martyre tuo, per haec contra omnia aduersa muniamur. Per.

LXVIIII
DOMINICA III POST THEOPHANIA

395 Omnipotens sempiterne deus, infirmitatem nostram propitius respice, atque ad protegendum nos dexteram tuae maiestatis extende. Per dominum.

396 SVPER OBLATA. Haec hostia domine quaesumus emundet nostra delicta, et sacrificium caelebrandum subditorum tibi corpora mentesque sanctificet. Per dominum.

397 PRAEFATIO. VD aeterne[1] deus. Et te omni tempore conlaudare et benedicere, quia in te uiuimus, mouemur et sumus. Et nullum tempus[2] nullumque momentum est, quod a beneficiis pietatis tuae uacuum transigamus. Variis etenim sollemnitatum causis, salutarium nobis operum tuorum et munerum, memoria praesentis uitę tempore exornat. Vnde et nos uel innouante laetitia praeteriti gaudii, uel permanentis boni tempus agnoscentes, indefessas maiestati tuae grates exsoluimus. Per christum.

398 BENEDICTIO. Omnipotens deus uos ab omnium peccatorum maculis emundet, qui leprosum supplicem tactu proprio dignatus est emundare. AMEN.
/f. 66v Quique centurionis seruum non aspernatus est / uisitare, ipse cordium uestrorum hospitium dignetur misericorditer introire. AMEN.

---

[1] *aeternae* before correction.
[2] Over an erasure.

Sicque uos fidei suae plenitudine informet, ut cum sanctis suis in caelorum regno accumbere concedat. AMEN.
Quod ipse praestare dignetur.

399 AD COMPLENDVM. Quos tantis domine largiris uti mysteriis, quaesumus ut effectibus eorum ueraciter aptare digneris. Per dominum nostrum iesum christum.

VIII KL. FEBR. IN CONVERSIONE SANCTI PAVLI

400 Deus qui uniuersum mundum beati pauli apostoli tui praedicatione docuisti, da nobis quaesumus ut qui eius hodie conuersionem colimus, per eius ad te exempla gradiamur. Per dominum.

401 SVPER OBLATA. Apostoli tui pauli quaesumus domine praecibus plebi tuae dona sanctifica, ut quae tibi grata sunt instituta, gratiora fiant patrocinio supplicantis. Per.

402 PRAEFATIO. VD aeterne[1] deus. Et maiestatem tuam suppliciter exorare, ut ecclesiam tuam beati pauli apostoli tui praedicatione edoctam, nulla sinas fallacia uiolari, et sicut nihil in uera religione manere dinoscitur quod non eius condierit disciplina, ita ad peragenda ea quae docuit, eius obtentu fidelibus tribuatur efficacia. Sentiatque credentium gentium multitudo eum pro se apud te intercessorem, quem habere cognouit / magistrum atque doctorem. Per christum.

403 BENEDICTIO. Deus qui gratia sua beatum paulum ex persecutore fecit apostolum, ipse uobis compunctionis pięque conuersationis dignetur impertire spiritum. AMEN.
Quique ei secretorum caelestium mysteria dignatus est reuelare, ipse uobis scripturarum suarum abdita dignetur aperire. AMEN.
Et qui ei perseuerantiam fidei constantiamque in persecutionibus inflexibilem dare dignatus est, eiusdem interuentionibus uestram infirmitatem donis spiritualibus roborare atque munire dignetur. AMEN.
Quod ipse praestare dignetur.

f. 67r

---

[1] *aeternae* before correction.

117

404 AD COMPLENDVM. Sanctifica quaesumus domine salutare mysterium, ut pro nobis eius non desit oratio, cuius nos donasti patrocinio gubernari. Per dominum.

405 SVPER POPVLVM. Praesta populo tuo domine quaesumus consolationis auxilium, et diuturnis calamitatibus laborantem, beati apostoli tui pauli intercessione, a cunctis tribulationibus erue. Per dominum.

LXXI
V KL. FEBR. NATALE SANCTAE AGNAE SECVNDO

406 Deus qui nos annua beatae agnetis martyris tuae sollemnitate laetificas, da quaesumus ut quam ueneramur officio, etiam piae conuersationis sequamur exemplo. Per.

/f. 67v   **407** SVPER OBLATA. / Super has quaesumus domine hostias benedictio copiosa descendat, quae et sanctificationum nobis clementer operetur, et de martyrum nos sollemnitatem laetificat. Per.

408 AD COMPLENDVM. Sumpsimus domine caelebritatis annuae uotiua sacramenta, praesta quaesumus ut et temporalis nobis uitae remedia praebeant et aeternae. Per.

III NON. FBR. YPAPANTI DOMINI AD SANCTAM MARIAM

409 BENEDICTIO SVPER CANDELAS. Domine iesu christe creator caeli et terrae, rex regum et dominus dominantium, exaudi nos indignos famulos tuos, clamantes et orantes ad te, praecamur te domine omnipotens aeternę deus, qui omnia ex nihilo creasti, et iussu tuo operę apum hanc ceram uel hunc liquorem aeuenire fecisti, et qui hodierna diae petitionem iusti symeonis implesti. Te humiliter deprecamur, ut has candelas ad usus hominum et animarum, siue in terra, siue in aquis, per inuocationem sanctissimi tui nominis, et per intercessionem sanctae mariae genetricis tuae, cuius hodie festa colimus, per precesque omnium sanctorum, + benedicere, + et sanctificare digneris, ut omnis haec pleps tua illas honorifice in manibus portantes, cantando, teque laudando, tu exaudies uoces illius de /f. 68r   caelo sancto tuo, / et de sede maiestatis tuae propitiusque sis

omnibus clamantibus ad te quos redemisti, pretio sanguinis tui.
Qui cum deo patre in unitate.

LXXIII

410 COLLECTA AD SANCTVM ADRIANVM. Erudi quaesumus
domine plebem tuam, et quae extrinsecus tribuis annua
deuotione uenerari, interius assequi gratiae tuae luce concede.
Per dominum nostrum iesum christum.

LXXIIII

411 ITEM AD SANCTAM MARIAM. Omnipotens sempiterne
deus, maiestatem tuam supplices exoramus, ut sicut unigenitus
filius tuus hodierna diae cum nostrae carnis substantia in templo
est praesentatus, ita nos facias purificatis tibi mentibus
praesentari. Per eundem.

412 SVPER OBLATA. Exaudi domine praeces nostras, et ut digna
sint munera quae oculis tuae maiestatis offerimus, subsidium
nobis tuae pietatis impende. Per.

413 PRAEFATIO. VD aeterne deus. Quia per incarnati uerbi
mysterium, noua mentis nostrae oculis, lux tuae claritatis
effulsit. Vt dum uisibiliter deum cognoscimus, per hunc
inuisibilium amore rapiemur. Et ideo.

414 BENEDICTIO. Omnipotens deus qui unigenitum suum
hodierna die in assumpta carne in templo uoluit praesentari,
benedictionis suę uos munere fultos bonis operibus faciat
exornari. <AMEN.>
/ Qui eum ut legem adimpleret, ministerium uoluit effici legis
mentes uestras instruat legis suae spiritalibus documentis.
AMEN.
Quo ei et pro turturibus castitatis seu caritatis munera offerre
ualeatis, et pro pullis columbarum spiritus sancti donis
exuberetis. AMEN.
Quod ipse praestare dignetur.

415 AD COMPLENDVM. Quaesumus domine deus noster ut
sacrosancta mysteria quae pro reparationis nostrae munimine
contulisti, intercedente beata semper uirgine maria, et pręsens
nobis remedium esse facias et futurum. Per.

416 ALIA ORATIO. Perfice in nobis quaesumus domine gratiam tuam qui iusti symeonis expectationem implesti, ut sicut ille mortem non uidit, priusquam christum dominum uidere mereretur, ita et nos uitam obtineamus aeternam. Per.

LXXV
DOMINICA IIII POST THEOPHANIA

417 Deus qui nos in tantis periculis constitutos pro humana scis fragilitate non posse subsistere, da nobis salutem mentis et corporis, ut ea quae pro peccatis nostris patimur, te adiuuante uincamus. Per.

418 SVPER OBLATA. Concede quaesumus omnipotens deus, ut huius sacrificii munus oblatum, fragilitatem nostram ab omni malo purget semper et muniat. Per.

/f. 69r
419 PRAEFATIO. VD aeterne[1] deus. Qui genus humanum praeuaricatione sua in ipsius originis / radice damnatum, per florem uirginalis uteri reddere dignatus es absolutum. Et hominem quem unigenitum creaueras, per filium tuum deum et hominem recreares. Et diabolus qui adam in fragili carne deuicerat, conseruata iustitia a deo carne uinceretur assumpta. Per quem.

420 BENEDICTIO. Temptationum omnium a uobis dominus pericula remoueat, et perturbationum procellas miseratus excludat. AMEN.
Temptatoris fraudes atque molimina dissoluat, et uos aduersus eum cautos atque inuincibiles faciat. AMEN.
Continuae pacis uobis munera tribuat, et uos in portu tranquillitatis ac securitatis propitiatus custodiat. AMEN.
Quod ipse praestare dignetur.

421 AD COMPLENDVM. Munera tua nos deus a delectationibus terrenis expediant, et caelestibus semper instruant alimentis. Per.

---

[1] *aeternae* before correction.

LXXVI
NON FEB. NATALE SANCTAE AGATHAE

422 Deus qui inter cetera potentiae tuae miracula etiam in sexu fragili uictoriam martyrii contulisti, concede propitius ut cuius natalitia colimus, per eius ad te exempla gradiamur. Per.

423 SVPER OBLATA. Suscipe munera domine quae in beatę agatae martyris tuae sollempnitate deferimus / cuius nos confidimus patrocinio liberari. Per.

/f. 69v

424 PRAEFATIO. VD per christum. Pro cuius nomine poenarum mortisque contemptum in utroque sexu fidelium, cunctis aetatibus contulisti. Vt inter fidelium martyrum palmas, agathen quoque beatissimam uirginem, uictrici patientia coronares. Quae nec minis territa, nec suppliciis superata, de diaboli saeuitia triumphauit, quia in tuae deitatis confessione permansit. Et ideo.

425 BENEDICTIO. Sanctifica domine ecclesiam tuam, qui beatam agathen uirginem et martyrem adquisisti fide, honorasti pudore, glorificasti certamine. AMEN.
Repleatur hic populus illo spiritu, qui martyri tuę affuit agathe cum eam ignis torreret, cum ungula raderet, cum aculeus infigeret, cum mamilla torqueret. AMEN.
Vt dum se sibi pro tuo amore abnegat, tuam collocetur in dexteram, cuius est electione uocata in gloriam. AMEN.
Quod ipse praestare dignetur.

426 AD COMPLENDVM. Auxilientur nobis domine sumpta mysteria, et intercedente beata agatha martyre tua, sempiterna protectione confirment. Per dominum.

ALIAE ORATIONES

/f. 70r

427 / Indulgentiam nobis domine beata agatha martyr imploret, quae tibi grata semper extitit, et merito castitatis, et tuae professione uirtutis. Per.

428 ALIA. Deus qui nos beatę agathae martyris tuae sollemnitate laetificas, da ut quam ueneramur officio, etiam piae conuersationis sequamur exemplo. Per.

429 ALIA. Beatae agathae martyris tuae domine precibus confidentes, quaesumus clementiam tuam, ut per ea quae sumpsimus, aeterna remedia capiamus. Per dominum.

LXXVII
VIII ID. FEBR. NATALE SANCTI VEDASTI CONFESSORIS

430 Protegat nos domine beati uedasti confessoris tui atque pontificis repetita sollemnitas, ut cuius patrocinia sine intermissione recolimus, perpetua defensione sentiamus. Per.

431 SVPER OBLATA. Indulgentiam nobis domine quaesumus praebeant haec munera largiorem, quae uenerabilis uedasti pontificis, suffragiis offeruntur. Per.

432 PRAEFATIO. VD aeterne deus. Et te in sanctorum tuorum uirtute laudare, quibus pro meritis suis beatitudinis praemia contulisti. Quoniam semper in manu tua sunt, et non tanget illos tormentum mortis, quos te custodiente beatitudinis synus intercludit, ubi perpetua semper exultatione laetantur, ubi etiam beatus summus confessor tuus .ill. / sociatus exultat. Petimus ergo ut memor sit miseriarum nostrarum, et de tua misericordia nobis impetret beatitudinis suae consortium. Per christum.

/f. 70v

433 BENEDICTIO. Deus fundator fidei, et indultor sacerdotii, congregatio plebis, sanctificatio confessoris, qui beatum uedastum ad hoc armasti uirtute, ut tibi militaret in fide, concede huic familiae tuae pro se hunc intercessorem, quem dedisti pontificem. AMEN.
Sit apud te nunc pro nobis assiduus intercessor, qui contra hereticos pro te extitit tunc assertor. AMEN.
Vt te tribuente populo crescat in numero, quo sacerdos sudauit in fide. AMEN.
Quod ipse praestare dignetur.

434 AD COMPLENDVM. Adiuuet familiam tuam tibi domine supplicando uenerandus pontifex uedastus, qui tui nominis extitit praedicator. Per dominum.

122

LXXVIII
DOMINICA V POST THEOPHANIA

435 Familiam tuam quaesumus domine, continua pietate custodi, ut quę in sola spe gratiae caelestis innititur, tua semper protectione muniatur. Per.

436 SVPER OBLATA. Hostias tibi domine placationis offerimus, ut et delicta nostra miseratus absoluas, et nutantia corda tu dirigas. Per.

437 PRAEFATIO. VD aeterne[1] deus. Et tibi hanc immolationis hostiam offerre, quae est salutifera / et ineffabile diuinę gratiae sacramentum. Quae offertur a plurimis, et unum christi corpus sancti spiritus infusione perficitur. Singuli accipiunt christum dominum, et in singulis portionibus totus est, nec per singulos minuitur, sed integrum se prebet in singulis. Propterea ipsi qui sumimus, communionem huius sancti panis et calicis, unum christi corpus efficimur, per ipsius itaque maiestatem te supplices exoramus, ut nos ab omnibus emundes contagiis uetustatis, et in nouitate uitae perseuerare concedas. Per quem.

f. 71r

438 BENEDICTIO. Deus qui bonorum semen in sua ecclesia serere consueuit, in uobis illud conseruare atque multiplicare numquam desistat. AMEN.
Zizaniorum superseminatorem a uobis procul repellat, et sui uerbi pabulo uos indesinenter reficiat. AMEN.
Quo cum dies iudicii aduenerit, a reprobis separati, ad dexteram iudicis sistamini, et in beatissimo ipsius regno collocemini. AMEN.
Quod ipse praestare dignetur.

439 AD COMPLENDVM. Quaesumus omnipotens deus, ut illius salutaris capiamus effectum, cuius per haec mysteria pignus accepimus. Per.

---

[1] *aeternae* before correction.

LXXVIIII
XVI KL. MART. NATALE SANCTI VALENTINI MARTYRIS

440 Praesta quaesumus omnipotens deus, ut qui beati ualentini martyris tui natalicia colimus, a cunctis malis imminentibus eius intercessione liberemur. Per.

/f. 71v **441** SVPER OBLATA. / Oblatis quaesumus domine placare muneribus, et intercedente beato ualentino martyre tuo, a cunctis nos defende periculis. Per.

442 BENEDICTIO. Deus qui beatissimum ualentinum martyrem tuum tanta familiaritate tibi iunxisti, ut etiam cum adhuc corpore habitaret in terris, iam tunc corde totus esset in caelis, respice preces praesentis familiae quae se gaudet tanti martyri sollemnia celebrare. AMEN.
Dignare eius intercessione tibi illas petitiones effundere, quas eligis libenter implere. AMEN.
Et qui festiuitatem hanc uenisse in terris sentiant, quam uidere uotis in caelis exobtant. AMEN.
Quod ipse praestare dignetur.

443 AD COMPLENDVM. Sit nobis domine reparatio mentis et corporis caeleste mysterium, ut cuius exequimur actionem sentiamus effectum. Per.

LXXX
VIII KL. MART. IN ANTIOCHIA CATHEDRA SANCTI PETRI

444 Deus qui beato apostolo petro conlatis clauibus regni caelestis, ligandi atque soluendi pontificium tradidisti, concede quaesumus ut intercessionis eius auxilio, a peccatorum nostrorum nexibus liberemur. Per.

445 SVPER OBLATA. Ecclesiae quaesumus domine praeces et hostias beati petri apostoli commendet oratio, ut quod pro illius gloria caelebramus nobis prosit ad ueniam.

/f. 72r **446** PRAEFATIO. / VD aeterne[1] deus. Et te laudare mirabilem deum in sanctis tuis, in quibus glorificatus es uehementer. Per quos

---

[1]   *aeternae* before correction.

124

unigeniti tui sacrum corpus exornas, et in quibus[1] ecclesiae tuae fundamenta constituis, quam in patriarchis fundasti, in prophętis praeparasti, in apostolis condidisti. Ex quibus beatum petrum apostolorum principem, ob confessionem unigeniti filii tui per os eiusdem uerbi tui confirmatum in fundamento domus tuae, mutato nomine caelestium claustrorum praesulem custodemque fecisti. Diuino ei iure concesso, ut quae statuisset in terris, seruarentur in caelis. In cuius ueneratione hodierna die maiestati tuae haec festa persoluimus, et gratiarum ac laudis hostiam immolamus. Per quem.

447 BENEDICTIO. Deus qui beatum petrum apostolum tuum ita reddidisti praecipium, ut sortiretur inter ipsos fidei principes principatum, et accepta te princeps in saeculo, caeli fieret ianitor, ut quos uult intromittat ciues in regno. AMEN.
Respice plebem tuam pietate solita, qui sacrosancto apostolo gressum firmasti per lubrica, et culpas abluisti per lamenta, obtineat apud te ueniam, pro corrigendis delictis, qui claudo fuit medela pro dirigendis uestigiis. AMEN.

f. 72v Vt ipso intercedente et te remunerante illuc / sibi greges commissos introducat per ueniam, quo pastor idemque ianitor tecum remuneratus exultet in gloriam. AMEN.
Quod ipse praestare dignetur.

448 AD COMPLENDVM. Laetificet nos domine munus oblatum, ut sicut in apostolo tuo petro te mirabilem deum praedicamus, sic per illum tuae sumamus indulgentiae largitatem. Per dominum.

LXXXI
DOMINICA VI POST THEOPHANIAM

449 Conserua populum tuum deus, et tuo nomini fac deuotum, ut diuinis subiectus officiis, et temporalia uiriliter et aeterna dona percipiat. Per.

450 SVPER OBLATA. Haec nos oblatio deus mundet quaesumus et renouet, et gubernet et protegat. Per.

---

[1] An erasure, perhaps of two words, follows.

451 PRAEFATIO. VD aeterne[1] deus. Ad cuius immensam pertinet gloriam, ut non solum mortalibus tua pietate succurreres, sed de ipsa etiam mortalitate nostra nobis remedium prouideres, et perditos quosque unde perierant, inde saluares. Per christum.

452 BENEDICTIO. Deus qui mare suis pedibus fecit esse calcabilem, uobis quicquid est noxium ipse substernat. AMEN. Contrarios inmundorum spirituum motus compescat, et uos in sua pace confirmet. AMEN.
Crucis suae nauim inter mundi fluctus gubernet, et in litus beatę perennitatis perducat. AMEN.
Quod ipse.

453 AD COMPLENDVM. Caelestibus domine pasti deliciis, quaesumus ut semper eadem per quę ueraciter uiuimus / appetamus. Per.

/f. 73r

LXXXII
IIII ID. MAR. NATALE SANCTI GREGORII PAPAE

454 Deus qui animae famuli tui gregorii aeternae beatitudinis praemia contulisti, concede propitius ut qui peccatorum nostrorum pondere premimur, per eius apud te precibus subleuemur. Per.

455 SVPER OBLATA. Annue nobis domine ut animę famuli tui gregorii prosit oblatio, quam immolando totius mundi tribuisti relaxari delicta. Per.

456 PRAEFATIO. VD aeterne[2] deus. Quia sic tribuis aecclesiam tuam sancti gregorii pontificis tui commemoratione gaudere, ut eam illius et festiuitate laetificas, et exemplo piae conuersationis exerceas. Et uerbo praedicationis erudias, grataque tibi supplicatione tuearis. Per christum.

457 BENEDICTIO. Deus qui beatissimum gregorium praesulem tuum tanta familiaritate iunxisti. REQVIRE RETRO IN NATALE SANCTI VALENTINI XVI KL. MAR.

---

[1] *aeternae* before correction.
[2] *aeternae* before correction.

458 AD COMPLENDVM. Deus qui beatum gregorium pontificem sanctorum tuorum meritis coaequasti, concede propitius ut qui commemorationis eius festa percolimus, uitae quoque imitemur exempla. Per.

LXXXIII
XIII KL. APL. NATALE SANCTI CVTBERHTI EPISCOPI

459 Sanctus et gloriosus cutberhtus martyr mirabilis atque potens anachorita, cuius in opere gaudet dominus, et in eius congregatione laetatur, intercessor obtimus et fortissimus protector / in deo, memento nostri semper in conspectu domini, praesta hic auxilium et in aeterna saecula. Per.

/f. 73v

460 SVPER OBLATA. Hoc sacro christi corpore et omnium sanctorum martyrum sociati simus deo patri praecamur sanctorum subsidia, ut dignenter exorare pro nobis in conspectu regni tui throno manenti sine fine et principio hic et in aeterna saecula. Per dominum.

461 PRAEFATIO. VD aeterne[1] deus. In hac die migrationis ad christum sanctissimi sacerdotis cutberhti, qui in primo continentissime et castissime conuersationis monachorum in actuali uita exemplum sanctis factus, et postmodum multis annis theoricam in deserto secutus est uitam, aeternitatis dei amore pastus. Te ergo domine depraecamur, per intercessionem sancti cutberhti episcopi, ut ad portum felicitatis et ad caelestia regna peruenire mereamur. Cui adstant innumerabiles angelorum et archangelorum chori et dicunt. Sanctus. Sanctus. Sanctus.

462 BENEDICTIO. Domine deus omnium gratiarum respicere dignare omnem hunc populum tuum, qui in honore tuo diuinis famulatur officiis, et quicquid sancto martyri tuo cutberhto hodierna die profuit ad beatitudinem, prosit huic ęcclesiae ad exemplum. AMEN.

Vt ipso intercedente sit in eis fides recta, imitabilis forma, casta sobrietas, hospitalis caritas, / spiritualis prudentia, alta sapientia, mens humilis, uita sublimis. AMEN.

/f. 74r

Vt cum ante tremendum iudicii diem in conspectu tuo

---

[1] *aeternae* before correction.

adstiterint, non damnandam, sed mitem ex ore tuo audiant, absolutionis sententiam. AMEN.
Quod ipse praestare dignetur.

463 AD COMPLENDVM. Satiatis domine munerum tuorum donis auxilium gratiae tuae rogatus impende, et auribus tuae pietatis nostras miserando preces benignus exaudi, ut meritis summi pastoris .ill. intercessione adiuuati in electorum tuorum numero aeterna in saecula recensemur. Per dominum.

LXXXIIII
XII KL. APRL. NATALE SANCTI BENEDICTI ABBATIS

464 Omnipotens aeterne deus, qui gloriosi benedicti abbatis exempla humilitatis triumphale nobis ostendisti iter, da quaesumus ut uiam tibi placidae oboedientiae, per quam uenerabilis pater benedictus inlesus antecedebat, nos praeclaris eius meritis adiuti, sine errore subsequamur. Per.

465 SVPER OBLATA. Paternis intercessionibus magnifici pastoris benedicti, quaesumus familiae tuę omnipotens deus commendetur oblatio, cuius uitalibus decoratur exemplis. Per.

466 PRAEFATIO. VD aeterne deus. Honorandi patris benedicti gloriosum caelebrantes diem, in quo hoc saeculum triste
/f. 74v   deserens, ad caelestis / patriae gaudia migrauit aeterna. Qui sancto spiritu repletus dono, monachorum gregi dignus pastor effulsit. Qui cuncta quae ammonuit dictis, sanctis impleuit operibus. Et uiam quam docebat carpere exemplis, monstrauit lucidis. Vt gloriosa monachorum plebs paterna intuens uestigia, ad perpetuę lucis aeternę uenire mereatur[1]. Per christum.

467 BENEDICTIO. Domine deus omnium gratiarum. REQVIRE RETRO IN NATALE SANCTI CVTBERHTI.

468 AD COMPLENDVM. Perceptis domine deus noster salutaribus sacramentis humiliter depraecamur, ut intercedente beato confessore tuo benedicto atque abbate, quae pro illius uenerando agimus obitu, nobis proficiat ad salutem. Per.

---

[1] *mereantur* before correction.

128

469 SVPER OBLATA[1]. Plebem nominis tui subditam domine propitius intuere, et intercedente beato benedicto abbate, consolationes tuas iugiter per caelestem gloriam dignanter operare. Per.

LXXXV[2]
VIII KL. APRL. ADNVNTIATIO SANCTAE MARIAE

470 Deus qui beatę uirginis utero uerbum tuum angelo adnuntiante carnem suscipere uoluisti, pręsta supplicibus tuis, ut qui uere eam dei genetricem credimus, eius apud te intercessionibus adiuuemur. Per eundem.

471 AD MISSAM. Deus qui hodierna die uerbum tuum beatae uirginis aluo coadunare uoluisti, fac nos ita peragere, ut tibi placere / ualeamus. Per dominum nostrum.

/f. 75r

472 SVPER OBLATA. In mentibus nostris domine uerae fidei sacramenta confirma, ut qui conceptum de uirgine deum uerum et hominem confitemur, per eius salutiferę resurrectionis potentiam, ad aeternam mereamur peruenire laet<it>iam. Per eundem.

473 PRAEFATIO. VD per christum dominum nostrum. Quem pro salute hominum nasciturum gabrihel archangelus nuntiauit, uirgo maria spiritus sancti cooperatione concepit. Vt quod angelica nuntiauit sublimitas, uirginea crederet puritas, ineffabilis perficeret deitas. Illius itaque obtamus te opitulante cernere faciem sine confusione, cuius incarnationis gaudemus sollemnitate. Quatinus purificati festiuitate cunctis purgati a uitiis, natalis eius interesse mereamur, sollemnibus festis. Per quem.

474 BENEDICTIO. Deus qui cum te non capiunt caeli dignatus es in templo uteri uirginalis includi, da ęcclesię tuę custodem angelum qui praedixit uirgini mariae ut conciperet dominum christum. AMEN.

---

[1] For *SVPER POPVLVM.*
[2] Added later in crimson.

Sanctificet gregem tuum illa benedictio, quae sine semine humano redemptorem uirginis formauit in utero. AMEN.

Et te protegente exultet ecclesia de congregato populo, sicut maria meruit gloriari de fruc/tu pretioso. AMEN.

/f. 75v

Quod ipse.

475 AD COMPLENDVM. Gratiam tuam domine mentibus nostris infunde, ut qui angelo nuntiante christi filii tui incarnationem cognouimus, per passionem eius et crucem ad resurrectionis gloriam perducamur. Per eundem.

476 SVPER POPVLVM. Protege domine famulos tuos subsidiis pacis, et beatę mariae patrociniis confidentes, a cunctis hostibus redde securos. Per dominum nostrum.

ALIAE ORATIONES

477 Beatae et gloriosę semper uirginis dei genetricis mariae nos quaesumus domine merita prosequantur, et tuam nobis indulgentiam semper implorent. Per.

478 ALIA. Beatae et gloriosae semper uirginis dei genetricis mariae, quaesumus omnipotens deus intercessio gloriosa nos protegat, et ad uitam perducat aeternam. Per.

479 ALIA. Porrige nobis deus dexteram tuam, et per intercessionem beatae et gloriosae semperque uirginis dei genetricis mariae, auxilium nobis supernae uirtutis impende. Per dominum.

LXXXVI
ORATIONES IN SEPTVAGESIMA AD SANCTVM LAVRENTIVM FORIS MVRVM

480 Preces populi tui quaesumus domine clementer exaudi, ut qui iuste pro peccatis nostris affligimur, pro tui nominis gloria misericorditer liberemur. Per.

481 SVPER OBLATA. Mentibus nostris quaesumus domine precibusque susceptis, et caelestibus nos munda mysteriis, et clementer exaudi. Per.

482 PRAEFATIO. / VD aeterne[1] deus. Quia per ea quae conspiciuntur instruimur, quibus modis ad inuisibilia tendere debeamus. Denique commonemur annuo[2] ducente successu[3], de praeteritis ad futura de uetustate in nouitatem uitae transire. Vt terrenis sustentationibus expediti, caelestis[4] doni capiamus desiderabilius ubertatem. Et per eum cibum qui beneficiis prorogatur alternis, perueniamus ad uictum sine fine mansurum. Iesum christum dominum nostrum.

483 BENEDICTIO. Omnipotens deus ita studium uestri cursus dirigere dignetur, ut brauium uos aeternae uitae compraehendere faciat. AMEN.
Et ita uos abstinentiae armis circumdet, ut nullis uitae huius oneribus a peruentione retardet. AMEN.
Quique uos uineam suam uocare uobisque sanctos operarios mittere dignatus est, ipse uos sua gratia dignetur excolere, ut denario uitę perennis remunerari non abnuat. AMEN.
Quod ipse praestare.

484 AD COMPLENDVM. Fideles tui deus per[5] tua dona firmentur, ut eadem et percipiendo requirant, et querendo sine fine percipiant. Per dominum.

LXXXVII
IN SEXAGESIMA AD SANCTVM PAVLVM

485 Deus qui conspicis quia ex nulla nostra actione confidimus,
concede propitius, ut contra / aduersa omnia doctoris gentium, protectione muniamur. Per dominum.

486 SVPER OBLATA. Oblatum tibi domine sacrificium, uiuificet nos semper et muniat. Per dominum.

487 PRAEFATIO. VD aeterne deus. Qui rationabilem creaturam ne temporalibus dedita bonis ad praemia sempiterna non tendat, ea dispensatione dignaris erudire, ut nec castigatione deficiat, nec

---

[1] *aeternae* before correction.
[2] Final letters over an erasure.
[3] *succensu* before correction.
[4] Final *s* supplied interlinearly.
[5] A small erasure follows.

prosperitatibus insolescat. Sed hoc potius fiat eius gloriosa deuotio, quo[1] nullis aduersitatibus obruta superetur. Per christum dominum nostrum.

488 BENEDICTIO. Det uobis dominus nosse mysteria regni dei, qui iam dare dignatus est auditum uerbi sui. AMEN.
Sicque manus uestras semini<s> sui copia repleat, ut in uobis illud sibi placitę, fructificare concedat. AMEN.
Et ita uos ab omni temptatione muniat, quatinus triceni, sexageni, atque centeni fructus, pro suę gratiae distributione, munificentia remunerari faciat. AMEN.
Quod ipse.

489 AD COMPLENDVM. Supplices te rogamus omnipotens deus, ut quos tuis reficis sacramentis, tibi etiam placitis moribus dignanter deseruire concedas. Per dominum.

LXXXVIII
IN QVINQVAGESIMA AD SANCTVM PETRVM

490 Preces nostras quaesumus domine clementer exaudi, atquc a peccatorum uinculis absolutos, ab omni nos aduer/sitate custodi. Per dominum.

/f. 77r

491 SVPER OBLATA. Haec hostia domine quaesumus emundet nostra delicta, et sacrificium celebrandum, subditorum tibi corpora mentesque sanctificet. Per.

492 PRAEFATIO. VD aeterne[2] deus. Et maiestatem tuam cernua deuotione exorare, ut modulum terrenae fragilitatis aspiciens, non in ira tua pro nostra prauitate nos arguas, sed inmensa clementia purifices, erudias consoleris. Qui cum sine te nihil possumus facere quod tibi sit placitum, tua nobis gratia sola praestabit, ut salubri conuersatione uiuamus. Per christum.

493 BENEDICTIO. Omnipotens deus sua uos benedictione confirmet, et imminenti quadragesimali abstinentiae abtos efficiat. AMEN.

---

[1] *quod* before correction.
[2] *aeternae* before correction.

Quique caeco supplicanti per diuinitatis substantiam lumen restituit, caecitatem cordis uestri clementissimus ac benignus inlustret. AMEN.

Quatinus uitiorum sordibus emundati, et caritatis ardore solidati, caelestem hereditatem percipere ualeatis inlaesi. AMEN.

Quod ipse praestare dignetur.

494 AD COMPLENDVM. Quaesumus omnipotens deus, ut qui caelestia alimenta percepimus, per haec contra omnia aduersa muniamur. Per dominum.

FERIA IIII CAPVT IEIVNII

f. 77v   **495** INCIPIT ORDO AD DANDAM PENITENTIAM. PSAL. / Domine ne in furore tuo .ii. PER TOTVM.

LXXXVIIII

496 Exaudi quaesumus domine supplicum praeces, et confitentium tibi parce peccatis, ut quos conscientiae[1] reatus accusat, indulgentia tuę miserationis absoluat. Per.

497 INDE DICITVR ALIVM PSALMVM[2]. Benedic anima mea dominum VSQVE Renouabitur ut aquilae iuuentus tua.

498 ORATIO. Adsit quaesumus domine huic famulo tuo, inspiratio gratię salutaris, quae cor eius fletuum ubertate resoluat, sicque macerando conficiat, ut iracundiae tuę motus idonea satisfactione compescat. Per.

499 PSL. Miserere mei deus VSQVE Redde mihi laetitiam.

500 ORATIO. Praeueniat hunc famulum tuum quaesumus domine tua misericordia, ut omnes iniquitates eius celeri indulgentia[3] deleantur. Per.

501 PSAL. Quid gloriaris in malitia VSQVE Videbunt iusti.

---

[1] *con* supplied interlinearly.
[2] *ALIVM PSALMVM* supplied later over an erasure.
[3] *indulgentiam* before correction.

502 OREMVS. Adesto domine supplicationibus nostris, nec sit ab hoc famulo tuo, clementiae tuae longinqua miseratio, sana uulnera, eiusque remitte peccata, ut nullis a te iniquitatibus separatus, tibi domino semper ualeat adherere. Per.

503 PS. Deus in nomine tuo. Totum.

504 OREMVS. Domine deus noster qui offensionem nostram non uinceris, sed satisfactione placaris, respice quaesumus domine ad hunc famulum[1] qui se tibi peccasse grauiter confitetur, tuum

/f. 78r

est enim ablutionem criminum dare, et ueniam praestare / peccantibus qui dixisti paenitentiam te malle peccatorum quam mortem concede ergo domine hoc ut tibi paenitentiae excubias celebret, et correctis actibus suis conferri sibi a te sempiterna gaudia gratuletur. Per.

505 DEINDE DICITVR. Pater noster. ET VERSVS. Miserere mei domine quoniam infirmus sum. Et anima mea turbata est ualde. Conuertere domine et eripe animam meam. Domine uide humilitatem mcam et laborem. Inlustra faciem tuam super seruum tuum. Saluum fac seruum tuum. Mitte ei domine auxilium de sancto. Domine exaudi orationem.

506 Da quaesumus domine huic famulo tuo, continuam purgationis suae obseruantiam paenitendo gerere, et ut hoc efficaciter implere ualeat, gratia eum tuae uisitationis preueniat et subsequatur. Per.

507 ALIA ORATIO. Deus cuius indulgentia nemo non indiget, memento famuli tui .ill. et qui lubrica terrenaque corporis fragilitate deceptus in multis deliquid, quaesumus ut des ueniam confitenti, parce supplici ut qui nostris meritis accusamur, ut miseratione saluemur. Per.

508 MODO SVRGENDI SVNT. BENEDICTIO CYNERIS. Deus qui non mortem sed paenitentiam desideras, peccatorum fragilitatem conditionis humanae benignissime respice, et hos cyneres quos causa pręferendae humilitatis atque promerendę

---

[1] Plural forms indicated interlinearly.

ueniae capitibus nostris imponi decernimus, benedicere pro tua
pietate digneris, ut qui nos in cynerem[1] et ob prauitatis nostrae
meritum in puluerem / reuersuros cognoscimus peccatorum
ueniam, et praemia paenitentibus repromissa, misericorditer
consequi mereamur. Per dominum.

509 ALIA. Omnipotens sempiternę deus, parce metuentibus,
propitiare supplicibus, et mittere digneris sanctum angelum
tuum de caelis, + qui benedicat, + et sanctificet cyneres istos, ut
sint remedium salubre omnibus nomen tuum humiliter
implorantibus ac semetipsos pro conscientia delictorum suorum
accusantibus, atque conspectui diuinae clementiae tuae facinora
sua deplorantibus uel serenissimam pietatem tuam suppliciter
obnixeque flagitantibus. Praesta quaesumus inuocationem
nominis tui, ut quicumque eas super se asperserint, pro
redemptione peccatorum corporis sanitatem anime tutelam
percipiant. Per dominum.

510 HIC MITTIT CYNERES SVPER CAPITA EORVM CVM
AQVA BENEDICTA ET EXPELLENTVR EXTRA
ECCLESIAM. INCIPITVR RESPONS. In sudore. ET
PROSTERNENT SE ANTE HOSTIVM. PS. Inclina domine.

511 ORATIO. Praecor domine clementiae et misericordiae tuae
maiestatem, ut famulo tuo ill. peccata et facinora sua confitenti
ueniam relaxare digneris, et praeteritorum criminum culpas
indulgeas, qui humeris tuis ouem perditam reduxisti, tu etiam
huic famulo tuo, placare domine tu huius precibus benignus

aspira, ut in confessione placabili per/maneat, fletus eius et
petitio perpetuam clementiam tuam celeriter exoret sanctisque
altaribus tuis, et sacris restitutus spei rursum aeternae
caelestique gloriae tuae mancipetur. Per.

512 ET POSTMODVM EANT IN CIRCVITV ECCLESIAE
CANTANDO AN.

---

[1] *uoluisti* erased.

XC

513 COLLECTA AD SANCTAM ANASTASIAM. Concede nobis domine praesidia militiae christianae sanctis inchoare ieiuniis, ut contra spiritales nequitias pugnaturi, continentiae muniamur auxiliis. Per.

514 ITEM AD SANCTAM SABINAM. Praesta domine fidelibus tuis ut ieiuniorum ueneranda sollemnia, et congrua pietate suscipiant, et secura deuotione percurrant. Per.

515 SVPER OBLATA. Fac nos quaesumus domine his muneribus offerendis conuenienter aptari, quibus ipsius uenerabilis sacramenti celebramus exordium. Per.

516 PRĘFATIO. VD aeterne[1] deus. Qui corporali ieiunio uitia comprimis, mentem eleuas, uirtutem largiris et praemium. Per christum.

517 BE<NE>DICTIO. Benedicat uos dominus iesus christus qui se a uobis uoluit benedici, et qui hoc quadragenario curriculo cuius hodie inchoatis exordium suo dedicauit ieiunio, uestrum suscipiat ieiunium, omnique uos repleat bono. AMEN.
Det uobis integram fidem, et abstinentiam tam salubrem, ut nec
/f. 79v   caro aescis deuicta luxuriet / nec mens afflicta degeneret. AMEN.
Sed ita sit uobis sanctificatum in diuino timore ieiunium, ut uitiis pariter atque corporibus abstinentię frena imponatis, et toti semper ab infestationibus inimici maneatis inlaesi, et pax iugiter quieta permaneat, in habitaculis uestris. AMEN.
Quod ipse praestare dignetur.

518 AD COMPLENDVM. Percepta nobis domine praebeant sacramenta subsidium, ut et tibi grata sint nostra ieiunia, et nobis proficiant ad medelam. Per.

519 SVPER POPVLVM. Inclinantes se domine maiestati tuae propitiatus intende, ut qui diuino munere sunt refecti, caelestibus semper nutriantur auxiliis. Per dominum.

---

[1] *aeternae* before correction.

XCI
FERIA V STATIO AD SANCTVM GEORGIVM

520 Deus qui culpa offenderis, paenitentia placaris, pręces populi tui supplicantis propitius respice, et flagella tuae iracundiae quae pro peccatis nostris meremur auerte. Per.

521 SVPER OBLATA. Sacrificiis praesentibus domine quaesumus intende placatus, ut et deuotioni[1] nostrae proficiant et saluti. Per.

522 AD COMPLENDVM. Caelestis doni benedictione percepta, supplices te deus omnipotens depraecamur, ut hoc idem nobis et sacramenti causa sit et salutis. Per.

f. 80r

523 SVPER POPVLVM. Parce domine parce populo tuo, ut dignis flagellationibus castigatus, in tua / miseratione respiret. Per.

XCII
FERIA VI AD APOSTOLOS IOHANNIS ET PAVLI

524 Inchoata ieiunia quaesumus domine benigno fauore prosequere, ut obseruantiam quam corporaliter exhibemus, mentibus etiam sinceris exercere ualeamus. Per dominum.

525 SVPER OBLATA. Sacrificium domine obseruantiae paschalis quod[2] offerimus, praesta quaesumus ut tibi et mentes nostras reddat acceptas, et continentiae promtioris nobis tribuat facultatem. Per dominum.

526 AD COMPLENDVM. Spiritum nobis domine tuae caritatis infunde, ut quos uno caelesti pane satiasti, tua facias pietate concordes. Per dominum.

527 SVPER POPVLVM. Tuere domine populum tuum, et ab omnibus peccatis clementer emunda, quia nulla ei nocebit aduersitas, si nulla dominetur iniquitas. Per.

---

[1] *ni* supplied interlinearly.
[2] *quod* supplied in margin.

137

SABBATO

528 Obseruationis huius annua caelebritate laetantes, quaesumus domine ut paschalibus actionibus inhęrentes, plenis eius effectibus gaudeamus. Per.

529 SVPER OBLATA. Suscipe domine sacrificium cuius te uoluisti dignanter immolatione placare, praesta quaesumus, ut huius operatione mundati, beneplacentium tibi nostrae mentis offeramus. Per.

530 AD COMPLENDVM. Caelestis uitae munere uegetati quaesumus domine, ut quod est nobis in praesenti uita mysterium, fiat aeternitatis auxilium. Per.

/f. 80v   / IN QVADRAGESIMA AD SANCTVM IOHANNEM IN LATERANIS

531 Deus qui ęcclesiam tuam annua quadragesimali obseruatione purificas, praesta familiae tuae, ut quod a te obtinere abstinendo nititur, hoc bonis operibus exequamur. Per.

532 SVPER OBLATA. Sacrificium quadragesimalis initii sollemniter immolamus, te domine depraecantes, ut cum epularum restrictione carnalium, a noxiis quoque uoluptatibus temperemur. Per.

533 PRAEFATIO. VD per christum. Qui continuatis quadraginta diebus et noctibus, hoc ieiunium non esuriens dedicauit. Postea enim esuriit, non tam cibum hominum, quam salutem. Nec escarum saecularium ępulas concupiuit, sed animarum desiderauit potius sanctitate. Cibus namque eius est, redemptio populorum. Cibus eius est, totius bonę uoluntatis affectus. Qui nos docuit operari non solum cybum qui terrenis dapibus apparatur, sed etiam eum qui diuinarum lectione percipitur. Per quem.

534 BENEDICTIO. Benedicat uos omnipotens deus, qui quadragenarium numerum in moysi et heliae necnon et mediatoris nostri ieiunio consecrauit, concedatque uobis ita transfigere praesentis uitae dispensationem, ut accepto a patrefamilias remunerationis denario, perueniatis ad peccatorum

138

f. 81v omnium remissionem / et ad gloriosam cum sanctis omnibus resurrectionem. AMEN.

Detque uobis spiritualium uirtutum inuictricia arma, quibus exemplo domini deuincere ualeatis antiqui hostis sagacissima temptamenta. AMEN.

Quo non in solo pane sed in omni uerbo quod de eius ore procedit, spiritualem alimoniam sumentes, per ieiuniorum obseruationem, et ceterorum bonorum operum exibitionem percipere mereamini, inmarcesibilem gloriae coronam. AMEN. Quod ipse.

535 AD COMPLENDVM. Tui nos domine sacramenti libatio sancta restauret, et a uetustate purgatos, in mysteriis salutaris faciat transire consortium. Per.

536 AD VESPERAS. Da nobis quaesumus omnipotens deus, et aeternae promissionis gaudia quaerere, et quęsita citius inuenire. Per dominum.

537 AD FONTEM. Adesto quaesumus domine supplicationibus nostris, et in tua misericordia confidentes, ab omni nos aduersitate custodi. Per dominum.

XCIIII

FERIA II AD SANCTVM PETRVM AD VINCVLA

538 Conuerte nos deus salutaris noster, et ut nobis ieiunium quadragesimale proficiat, mentes nostras caelestibus instrue disciplinis. Per.

539 SVPER OBLATA. Munera domine oblata sanctifica, nosque a peccatorum nostrorum maculis emunda. Per.

f. 81v 540 PRAEFATIO. / VD aeterne[1] deus. Qui das aescam omni carni, et nos non solum carnalibus, sed etiam spiritalibus aescis reficis. Vt non in solo pane uiuamus, sed in omni uerbo tuo, uitalem habeamus alimoniam. Nec tantum aepulando, sed etiam ieiunando pascamur. Nam ut et dapibus et poculis corpora, sic ieiuniis et uirtutibus animę saginantur, magnam in hoc munere

---

[1]   *aeternae* before correction.

salubritatem mentis ac corporis contulisti, quia ieiunium nobis uenerabile dedicasti. Vt ad paradysum de quo non abstinendo cecidimus, ieiunando sollemnius redeamus. Per christum.

541 BENEDICTIO. Benedic domine populum tuum et deuotum respice, humilitatem uide, gemitus suscipe, dolentes paterna pietate iube consolari. AMEN.

Prostratum alleua, dispersum congrega, adunatum conserua, esurientem ciba, sitientem pota, omnesque simul caelestibus donis irriga, dele in eis omnem peccati maculam, ut te gubernante ad gloriam perueniant sempiternam. AMEN.

Humiliata tibi omnium capita dexterae tuae benedictione sanctifica, ac benedicendo peccata relaxa, sanctique spiritus infunde carismata, ut sine ulla offensione maiestati tuae percepta adimpleant, et ad uitam aeternam te auxiliante perueniant. /
/f. 82r AMEN.

Quod ipse praestare.

542 AD COMPLENDVM. Salutaris tui domine munere satiati, supplices exoramus, ut cuius laetamur gustu, renoucmur effectu. Per dominum.

543 SVPER POPVLVM. Absolue domine quaesumus nostrorum uincula peccatorum, et quicquid pro eis meremur, propitiatus auerte. Per.

XCV
FERIA III AD SANCTAM ANASTASIAM

544 Respice domine familiam tuam, et praesta ut apud te mens nostra tuo desiderio fulgeat, quae se carnis maceratione castigat. Per.

545 SVPER OBLATA. Oblatis quaesumus domine placare muneribus, et a cunctis nos defende periculis. Per.

546 PRAEFATIO. VD per christum. In quo ieiunantium fides additur, spes prouehitur, caritas roboratur. Ipse est enim panis uiuus et uerus, qui substantia aeternitatis et aesca uirtutis est. Verbum enim tuum per quod facta sunt omnia, non solum humanarum mentium, sed ipse panis est angelorum. Hunc panem ministrare nobis non desinis, et ut eum indesinenter esuriamus hortaris. Cuius carne dum pascimur roboramur, et sanguine dum potamur abluimur. Per quem.

547 AD COMPLENDVM. Quaesumus omnipotens deus ut illius salutaris capiamus effectum, cuius per haec mysteria pignus accepimus. Per dominum.

f. 82v **548** SVPER POPVLVM. / Ascendant ad te domine praeces nostrae, et ab ecclesia tua cunctam repelle nequitiam. Per.

XCVI
FERIA IIII MENS. I

549 AD SANCTAM MARIAM MAIOREM. Praeces nostras quaesumus domine clementer exaudi, et contra cuncta nobis aduersantia, dexteram tuae maiestatis extende. Per dominum.

550 ALIA. Deuotionem populi tui domine quaesumus benignus intende, ut qui per abstinentiam macerantur in corpore, per fructum boni operis reficiantur in mente. Per.

551 SVPER OBLATA. Hostias tibi domine placationis offerimus, ut et delicta nostra miseratus absoluas, et nutantia corda tu dirigas. Per.

552 PRAEFATIO. VD aeterne deus. Qui in alimentum corporis humani frugum copiam prodire[1] iussisti, et in alimentum animarum, ieiunii nobis medicinam indidisti. Te itaque supplices inuocamus, ut tibi sit acceptabile ieiunium nostrum, et nos a cibis ieiunantes, a peccatis absoluas. Per christum.

553 BENEDICTIO. Respice pastor bone super hunc gregem, et tribuę ut qui terrenis abstinent cibis, spiritualibus pascantur alimoniis, et quem diuinis reficere tribuis sacramentis, ab omnibus propitius absolue peccatis. AMEN.
Da eis sic in diebus ieiuniorum suam componere uitam, ut non inueniantur uoluntates eorum a tua uoluntate dissimiles, sed sint
f. 83r semper / in omnibus tuis praeceptis obtemperantibus. AMEN.

---

[1] Two letters between *i* and *r* erased.

Et ita omnem hanc familiam tua benedictione sanctifica, ut eorum ieiunia oculis tuae pietatis sint semper accepta, et ad desideratum sanctae resurrectionis tuę diem, eos mundo corde et corpore pro tua pietate iubeas praesentari. AMEN.
Quod ipse.

554 AD COMPLENDVM. Tui domine perceptione sacramenti, et a nostris mundemur occultis, et ab hostium liberemur insidiis. Per dominum.

555 SVPER POPVLVM. Mentes nostras quaesumus domine lumine tuae claritatis inlustra, ut uidere possimus quae agenda sunt, et quę recta sunt agere ualeamus. Per dominum.

XCVII
FERIA V AD SANCTVM LAVRENTIVM FORIS MVRVM

556 Omnipotens sempiterne deus, qui nobis in obseruatione ieiunii et elemosinarum semine posuisti nostrorum remedia peccatorum, concede nos opere mentis et corporis, semper tibi esse deuotos. Per.

557 SVPER OBLATA. Sacrificia domine quaesumus propitius ista nos saluent, quae medicinalibus sunt instituta ieiuniis. Per dominum.

558 PRAEFATIO. VD aeterne deus. Quia competenter atque salubriter religiosa sunt nobis instituta[1] ieiunia, ut corporeae iocunditatis immoderatas coherceamus inlecebras. Et terrenae delectationis insolentia refrenata / purior atque tranquillior appetitus, ad caelestia contemplanda mysteria fidelium reddatur animarum. Per christum.

/f. 83v

559 AD COMPLENDVM. Tuorum nos domine largitate donorum, et temporalibus attolle praesidiis, et renoua sempiternis. Per.

560 SVPER POPVLVM. Da quaesumus domine populis christianis, et quae profitentur agnoscere, et caeleste munus diligere quod frequentant. Per.

---

[1]   *instututa* before correction.

142

FERIA VI AD APOSTOLOS

561 Esto domine propitius plebi tuae, et quam tibi facis esse deuotam, benigno refoue[1] miseratus auxilio. Per dominum nostrum.

562 SVPER OBLATA. Suscipe quaesumus domine munera nostris oblata seruitus, et tua propitius dona sanctifica. Per.

563 PRAEFATIO. VD aeterne[2] deus. Qui ieiunii obseruatione et elemosynarum gratissima largitione, nos docuisti nostrorum consequi remedia peccatorum. Vnde tuam imploramus clementiam, ut his obseruationibus et cęteris bonorum operum exhibitionibus muniti, ea operemur quibus ad aeterna gaudia consequenda, et spes nobis suppetat et facultas. Per christum.

564 POSTCOMMVNIO. Per huius domine operationem mysterii, et uitia[3] nostra purgentur, et iusta desideria impleantur. Per.

565 SVPER POPVLVM. Exaudi nos misericors deus, et mentibus nostris gratiae tuae lumen ostende. Per dominum.

/ XCVIIII

ORATIO AD CAPILLATVRAM

566 Omnipotens sempiterne deus, respice propitius super hunc famulum tuum .N. quem ad nouam tondendi gratiam uocare dignatus es, tribuens ei remissionem omnium peccatorum, adque ad caelestium donorum peruenire consortium. Per dominum nostrum.

f. 84r

---

[1] Over an erasure.
[2] *aeternae* before correction.
[3] Supplied interlinearly.

C
ORATIO AD CLERICVM FATIENDVM

567 Oremus dilectissimi fratres, dominum nostrum iesum christum, pro hoc famulo suo .N. qui ad deponendam comam capitis sui pro eius amore festinat, ut donet ei spiritum sanctum, qui habitum religionis in eo perpetuum conseruet, et a mundi impedimento uel saeculari desiderio cor eius defendat, ut sicut inmutatur in uultu, ita manus dexterae tuae ei uirtutis tribuat incrementa, ut ab omni cecitate humana oculos eius aperiat, et lumen ei aeternae gratiae concedat. Qui uiuit.

568 ALIA. Adesto domine supplicationibus nostris, et hunc famulum tuum benedicere dignare, cui in tuo sancto nomine habitum sacrę religionis imponimus, ut te largiente et deuotus in ęcclesia persistere, et uitam percipere mereatur aeternam. Per.

569 DVM TONDIS EVM DICIS ANTIPHONAM. A. Tu es domine qui restitues mihi hereditatem meam. V. Dominus pars hereditatis meae, cum gloria. A. Haec est generatio. Cum gloria. /f. 84v / A. Hic accipiet benedictionem a domino. PS. Domini est terra.

570 ORATIO POST TONSIONEM. Praesta omnipotens deus huic famulo tuo N. cuius hodie capitis comam pro diuino amore deposuimus, ut in tua dilectione perpetua maneat, et eum sine macula in sempiternum custodias. Per.

CI

571 ORATIO AD BARBAS TONDENDAS. Deus cuius spiritu creatura omnis incrementis adulta congaudet, exaudi praeces nostras super hunc famulum tuum ill. iuuenalis aetatis decore laetantem, et primis auspiciis ad tondendum, exaudi domine ut in omnibus protectionis tuae munitus auxilio, caelestem benedictionem accipiat, et praesentis uitae praesidiis gaudeat, et aeternae. Per.

CII
INCIPIT SERMO INNOCENTII PAPAE DE VII. GRADIBVS ECCLESIAE

/f. 85r   **572** Haec autem singulis gradibus obseruanda sunt tempora. Si ab infantia ecclesiasticis misteriis nostra didicerit exempla, et inter lectores usque in uicesimum annum continuata obseruatione perdurauerit, et indesimari aetati iam accesserit. Ita tamen, ut post baptismum statim se diuino cultui mancipare desiderat, et siue inter lectores, siue inter exorcistas quinque annis teneatur, et tunc catholicus, uel subdiaconus .iiii^{or}. annis fit, et sic ad benedictionem diaconatus si meretur accedat. In quo ordine quinque annis si inculpabiliter uixerit, herere debet, ut melius inueniat. Exinde suffragantibus meritis, per tot gradus datis propriae fidei documentis, si acutior uita illis ad bonos mores perduxe/rit, summum pontificatum sperare debebit, hac tamen lege seruata, neque bigamus, neque reuertens, siue poenitens, a maximis criminibus ad hos gradus possit admitti. Alioquin defensores ecclesiae, qui ex laicis fiunt unius uxores uiri, si in supradicta obseruatione teneatur, et si uita et moribus et scientia scripturarum meruerint, in ordine clericatus admittere debent.

CIII
SABBATO IN XII LECTIONES AD SANCTVM PETRVM

573 DICIT EPISCOPVS. Oremus. ET DIACONVS. Flectamus genua.

574 Populum tuum domine quaesumus propitius respice, atque ab eo flagella tuae iracundiae clementer auerte. Per.

CIIII
INCIPIT ORDINATIO CLERICORVM
Hic dentur claues queat ut captare fideles.

575 *Ostiarii cum ordinantur postquam ab archidiacono instructi fuerint qualiter in domo dei debeant conuersari. Tunc uocet archidiaconus omnes nominatim coram episcopo et ad suggestionem eius. Tradat eis episcopus claues ecclesiae de altari dicens*: Sic agite quasi reddituri deo rationem pro his rebus quae istis clauibus recluduntur.

576 ET DVCAT EOS ARCHIDIACONVS AD HOSTIVM ECCLESIAE ET DICAT. Per hoc ostium traditur uobis ministerium, ut sitis ianitores templi dei habeatisque potestatem recipiendi bonos et reiciendi indignos.

577 PRAEFATIO SVPER OSTIARIOS. Deum patrem omnipotentem suppliciter depraecemur, ut hos famulos suos .N. benedicere dignetur, quos in officium ostiariorum eligere / dignatus est, ut sit eis fidelissima cura in domo dei diebus ac noctibus ad distinctionem horarum certarum, ad inuocandum nomen domini, adiuuante domino nostro iesu christo qui cum eo uiuit.

/f. 85v

578 BENEDICTIO EIVSDEM. Domine sancte pater omnipotens aeterne deus, benedicere digneris hos famulos tuos .N. ostiarios ut inter ianitores ecclesiae pareant obsequia et inter electos tuos partem tuae mereantur habere mercedis. Per.

579 MODO LEGATVR LECTIO DEVTERONOMII DEINDE RESPONSORIVM. DICIT EPISCOPVS. Oremus. DIACONVS. Flectamus genua.

580 Deus qui nos in tantis periculis constitutos, pro humana scis fragilitate non posse subsistere, da nobis salutem mentis et corporis, ut ea quae pro peccatis nostris patimur, te adiuuante uincamus. Per.

CV

ORDINATIO LECTORVM

Codex hic dabitur lectori rite legendus.

581 *Lectores cum ordinantur faciat de illis uerbum episcopus ad plebem indicans eorum fidem ac uitam atque ingenium, post haec expectante plebe, tradat eis codicem esaię prophetę de quo lecturi sunt dicens:*

582 Accipite et estote uerbi dei relatores habitaturi, si fideliter impleueritis officium uestrum, partem cum his qui uerbum dei ministrauerunt, eligunt uos fratres uestri ut sitis lectores in domo dei uestri, et agnoscatis officium uestrum, et impleatis illud, potens est deus ut augeat uobis fidem.

/f. 86r **583** CONSECRATIO LECTORVM. / Domine sancte[1] pater omnipotens aeternae deus, benedicere digneris hos famulos tuos in officium lectorum, ut assiduitate lectionum distincti, atque

---

[1] *sanctae* before correction.

ordinati et agenda discant, et dicta opere compleant, et in utroque sanctae ecclesiae consulant. Per dominum.

584 MODO LEGATVR LECTIO DEVTERONOMI. DEINDE RESP. DICIT EPISCOPVS. Oremus. DIACONVS. Vt supra.

585 COLLECTA. Protector noster aspice deus, ut qui malorum nostrorum pondere praemimur, percepta misericordia libera tibi mente famulemur. Per.

CVI

ORDINATIO EXORCISTARVM

Exorcismalis datur hic ex more libellus.

586 *Exorciste cum ordinantur accipiant de manu episcopi libellum in quo scripti sunt exorcismi dicente episcopo:* Accipite et commendate memorię, et habetote potestatem imponendi manum super inerguminum, siue baptizatum, siue caticuminum.

587 CONSECRATIO EXORCISTARVM. Deum patrem omnipotentem supplices depraecemur, ut hos famulos suos .N. benedicere dignetur, in officium exorcistarum, ut sint spiritales imperatores ad abiciendos demones de corporibus obsessis cum omni nequitia eorum multiformi. Adiuuante domino.

588 BENEDICTIO. Domine sancte[1] pater omnipotens aeterne deus, benedicere digneris hos famulos tuos .N. in officium exor/cistarum, ut per impositionem manuum et oris officium eos eligere digneris, ut imperium habeant spirituum inmundorum cohercendorum, et probabiles sint, medici ecclesiae gratiae curationum, uirtute confirmati. Per dominum nostrum.

f. 86v

589 LECTIO MACHABEORVM ET RESP.

590 COLLECTA. Adesto quaesumus domine supplicationibus nostris, ut esse te largiente mereamur, et inter prospera humiles, et inter aduersa securi. Per.

---

[1] *sanctae* before correction.

CVII
ORDINATIO ACOLITORVM
Vrceus hic uacuus tripode denturque regendo.

591 *Acoliti cum ordinantur primum ab episcopo doceantur qualiter in officio sui agere debeant. Sed ab archidiacono accipiant ceroferarium cum cereo, ut sciant se ad accendenda ecclesiae luminaria mancipari. Ita dicente*:

592 Accipite hoc gestatorium luminis, ut per illud ualeatis aduersariorum tenebras effugare et uerissimum lumen quod inluminat omnem hominem uenientem in hunc mundum, fideliter inuenire.

593 *Detur eis urceum uacuum*: Accipite urceum ad effundendum uinum in eucharistia corporis christi.

594 BENEDICTIO ACOLITORVM. Omnipotens sempiterne deus, fons lucis et origo bonitatis, qui per iesum christum filium tuum qui est lumen uerum, mundum inluminasti eiusque passionis misterio redemisti, benedicere digneris hos famulos tuos .N. quos in acolitorum officium consccramus, / poscentes tuam clementiam, ut eorum mentes et corda lumine scientiae inlustres, et pietatis tuae rore inriges, ut ita perceptum misterium te auxiliante peragant, qualiter ad eternam remunerationem peruenire mereantur. Per eundem.

/f. 87r

595 CONSECRATIO ACOLITORVM. Domine sanctae pater omnipotens aeternae deus, qui per iesum christum filium tuum, in hunc mundum lumen claritatis misisti, et in cruce passionis tuae triumphum sanguinem et aquam ex latere pro genere humano dignatus es fundere, et per apostolos tuos in hoc saeculo lumen gratię spiritalis misisti. Ita benedicere digneris hos famulos tuos in officio acoliti, ut accendendum caritatis ecclesiae tuę et ad sugendum uinum et aquam ad conficiendum sanguinis tui in offerendo eucharistiam sanctis altaribus tuis fideliter subministrent. Accende domine eorum mentes et corda, ad amoris tui caeleste et gratiae, miserationis tuae uirtute confirma. Per.

CVIII
CAPITVLA SANCTI GREGORII

596 Sicut qui inuitatus rennuit, quaesitus refugit, sacris est altaribus remouendus, sic qui ultro ambit, uel inoportunis se ingerit, est proculdubio repellendus. Nam qui innititur ad altiora conscendere, quid agit nisi ut crescendo decrescat, cur non perpendit, quia benedictio illi in maledictum conuertitur? Quia ad hoc ut fiet hereticus promouetur.

597 LECTIO LIBRI SAPIENTIAE. REP. Vt supra.

f. 87v   **598** COLLECTA. / Praeces populi tui domine quaesumus clementer exaudi, ut qui iuste pro peccatis nostris affligimur, pro tui nominis gloria misericorditer liberemur. Per.

CVIIII
ORDINATIO SVBDIACONI
Hic calicem patenam cum sindone sistat et orcam.

599 [1]Subdiaconus uero cum ordinatur quia manus inpositionis non accipit patenam de manu episcopi accipiat uacuam et calicem uacuum, urceolum cum aqua ac manutergium. Exibeatur in conspectu episcopi patena et calix uacuus et dicat episcopus:

600 Videte cuius ministerium uobis tradetur, et ideo si usque nunc fuisti tardi ad ecclesiam modo debitis esse assidui, si usque nunc inhonesti[2], amodo casti, si usque nunc somnolenti, amodo uigiles, si usque nunc ebriosi, amodo sobrii. Oblationes quae ueniunt in altari, panes propositionis appellantur[3], de ipsis oblationibus tantummodo debet in altari poni quantum populum possit sufficere, ne aliquid putridum in sacrario remaneat. Pallae uero quae sunt in substratorio in alio uasi debent lauari in alio corporales, ubi pallae uel corporales lauate fuerint, nullum linteamen ibidem aliud debet lauari, et ipsa aqua in baptisterio debet uergi. Ideo uos admoneo ut tales uos exibeatis ut deo placere possitis.

601 ET TRADET EIS CALICEM ET PATENAM.

---

[1] Plural forms provided interlinearly throughout.
[2] *inhoneste* before correction.
[3] *appellentur* before correction.

ORDINATIO SVBDIACONORVM

/f. 88r **602** Oremus deum ac dominum nostrum ut super seruos suos .N. quos / ad subdiaconatus officium uocare dignatus est, infundat benedictionem et gratiam suam, ut in conspectu suo fideliter seruientes praedestinata sanctis praemia consequantur auxilianter. Per dominum.

603 BENEDICTIO SVBDIACONORVM. Domine sanctae pater omnipotens aeterne[1] deus, benedicere digneris famulos tuos hos quos ad subdiaconatus officium eligere dignatus es, ut eos sacrario tuo sancto, strenuosque sollicitos caelesti militiae instituas, et sanctis altaribus fideliter subministrent, et requiescat super eos spiritus domini, spiritus sapientiae et intellectus. AMEN. Spiritus consilii et fortitudinis. AMEN. Spiritus scientię et pietatis. AMEN. Reple eos spiritu timoris tui, ut eos in ministerio diuino confirmes, ut oboedientes factu atque dicto parentes tuam gratiam consequantur. Per dominum.

CX
ORDO QVALITER ORDINANDVM ROMAE

604 *Mensis primi, quarti, septimi, et decimi, sabbatorum die in duodecim lectionibus ad sanctum petrum, ubi missae caelebrantur. Postquam antiphonam et introitum dixerint. Data oratione.* DICAT ARCHIDIACONVS TALITER.

605 Postulat sancta mater ecclesia catholica ut hos praesentes subdiaconos ad onus diaconii, uel diaconos, ad onus presbiterii ordinetis.

606 INTERROGET EPISCOPVS. Scis illos dignos esse? RESPONDEAT ARCHIDIACONVS. Quantum humana /f. 88v fragilitas nosse sinit, et scio / et testificor ipsos dignos ad huius onus officii.

607 POSTEA ADNVNTIAT PONTIFEX POPVLVM DICENS: + Auxiliante deo et saluatore nostro iesu christo[2]. ITERVM DICIT: Auxiliante deo et saluatore nostro iesu christo. Elegimus

---

[1] *aeternae* before correction.
[2] The original scribe supplies the line in the lower margin.

in ordinem diaconii, siue praesbiterii, illum subdiaconum, uel diaconum.

608 TVNC NOMINAT ILLOS DE TITVLO SANCTAE MARIAE, VEL SANCTI PETRI, ET ALIORVM. Si quis autem habet aliquid contra hos uiros pro deo et propter deum cum fiducia exeat et dicat. Verumtamen memor sit communionis suae.

609 ET POST MODICVM INTERVALLVM, DICAT HANC ORATIONEM: Oremus fratres karissimi, ut deus omnipotens gratiam sancti spiritus sui, super nos electosque nostros dignetur fundere, ut in domo illius sancta digne maiestati illius designatis ordinibus ministrent. Ipso adiuuante qui uiuit et regnat deus.

610 ALIA. Ad praeces nostras quaesumus domine propitiatus intende, et leuitae tui sacris altaribus seruientes, et fidei ueritate fundati, et mente sint spiritali conspicui. Per.

611 INCIPIVNT CLERI LAETANIAS
Kyrie eleyson.
Christe eleyson.
Christe audi nos.
Sancta maria ora.
Sanctae michahel ora.
Sanctae gabrihel ora.
Sanctae raphahel ora.
Omnes sancti angeli orate.
Sanctę Iohannes ora.
Sanctae Petre ora.
Sanctae Paule ora.
Sanctae Andrea ora.
Omnes sancti apostoli orate.
Sanctę Stephane ora.
Sanctę Line ora.
Sanctę Clete ora.
Omnes sancti martyres orate.
Sanctę Siluester ora.
Sanctae Leo ora.
Sanctae Ambrosii ora.
Sanctae Agustine ora.

Omnes sancti confessores orate.
Sancta Felicitas ora.
Sancta Agnes ora.
Sancta Agatha ora.
/f. 89r / Omnes sanctae uirgines orate.
Omnes sancti orate.
Propitius esto libera nos domine.
Per aduentum tuum libera <nos> deus.
Per natiuitatem tuam libera <nos> deus.
Per circumcisionem tuam libera <nos> deus.
Per baptismum tuum libera <nos> deus.
Per ieiunium tuum libera nos <deus>.
Per crucem tuam libera nos deus.
Peccatores te rogamus <audi nos>.
Vt apostolicum nostrum.
Vt regem nostrum.
Vt episcopum nostrum.
Fili dei te rogamus iii.
Agnus dei qui tollis iii.
Christe audi nos iii.

612 FINITA LETANIA, SVRGAT EPISCOPVS AD ORATIONEM, LECTIONEM ET RESP. Quasi ut supra.

613 COLLECTA. Quaesumus omnipotens deus, uota humilium respice, atque ad defensionem nostram dexteram tuae maiestatis extende. Per dominum.

ORDINATIO DIACONORVM

614 *Diaconi uero cum ordinantur solus episcopus qui eos benedicat, manum super capita illorum ponat quia non ad sacerdotium sed ad ministerium consecrantur.*

615 ORATIO AD ORDINANDVM DIACONVM. OMNES EPISCOPI DICANT HAS: Oremus dilectissimi deum patrem omnipotentem super hos famulos tuos .N. quos in sacrum ordinem dignantur assumere, benedictionis suae gratiam clementer effundat, eisque donum consecrationis indulgeat, per quod eos ad prꝑmia aeterna perducat, auxiliante domino nostro iesu christo.

152

616 ALIA. Exaudi domine praeces nostras, et super hos famulos tuos, spiritum tuae benedictionis emitte, ut caelesti munere ditati, et tuae gratię possint maiestatis adquirere, et bene uiuendi aliis exemplum praebere. Per.

617 ITEM ALIA. Domine deus omnipotens praeces nostras clementer exaudi, ut quae nostro sunt gerenda seruitio, tuo / benignus prosequeris auxilio, et quos sacris ministeriis exequendis, pro nostra intelligentia credimus offerendos, tua potius electione iustifices. Per.

f. 89v

618 CONSECRATIO. Adesto quaesumus omnipotens deus honorum dator, ordinum distributor, officiorumque dispositor, qui in te manens innouans omnia et cuncta disponens, per uerbum tuum uirtutem sapientiamque tuam iesum christum filium tuum dominum nostrum, sempiterna prouidentia praeparas, et singulis quibusque temporibus aptanda dispensas. Cuius corpus ecclesiam tuam caelestium gratiarum uarietate distinctam, suorumque conexam discretionem membrorum, per legem mirabilem totius compaginis unitam, in augmentum templi tui crescere dilatarique largiris sacri muneris seruitutem, trinis gradibus ministrorum nomini tuo militare constituens. Electis ab initio leui filiis, qui mysticis operationibus domus tuae fidelibus excubiis permanentes, hereditatem benedictionis aeternae sorte perpetua possiderent. Super hos quoque famulos tuos quaesumus domine placatus intende, quos tuis sacrariis seruituros, in officium diaconatus suppliciter dedicamus. Et nos quidem tamquam homines diuini sensus et summe rationis ignari, horum uitam quantum possumus estimamus. / Te autem domine ea quae nobis ignota sunt non transeunt, te occulta non fallunt. Tu cognitor es secretorum, tu scrutator es cordium, tu eorum uitam caelesti poteris examinare iudicio, quo semper praeuales et amissa purgare, et ea quae sunt agenda concedere. Emitte in eos quaesumus domine spiritum sanctum, quo in opus ministerii fideliter exequendi, septiformis gratiae munere roborentur. Habundet in eis totius forma uirtutis, auctoritas modesta, innocentiae puritas, pudor constans, et spiritalis obseruatio disciplinae. In moribus eorum praecepta tua fulgeant, ut suae castitatis exemplo imitationem sancta plebs adquirat, et bonum conscientiae testimonium proferentes, in christo firmi et

f. 90r

stabiles perseuerent. Dignisque successibus de inferiori gradu, per gratiam capere potiora mereantur. Per dominum.

CXII

619 BENEDICTIO AD STOLAS SIVE AD PLANETAS SACERDOTALES SEV LEVITICAS. Deus inuictę uirtutis triumphator, et omnium rerum creator ac sanctificator, intende propitius praeces nostras, et has stolas siue[1] planetas leuitice ac sacerdotalis gloriae ministris tuis fruendas, tuos proprio ore, + benedicere, + ac sanctificare consecrareque digneris, omnesque eis utentes tuisque misteriis a nobis indignis consecratis, uel conse/crandis aptos, et tibi eis deuote et amabiliter seruientes, gratos efficere concedas, et nunc et per infinita saeculorum saecula.

/f. 90v

620 MODO PONENDE SVNT STOLAE IN VMERO. Per hoc signum tibi diaconatus officium humiliter imponimus, ut firmamentum mensae diuinae, tamquam sustentaculum columnarum esse possis. Et praeco regis caelestis, inreprehensibiliter existere merearis.

CXIII

621 BENEDICTIO POST STOLAS SVPER OMNES. In nomine sanctae trinitatis et unicę diuinitatis, accipie stolas quas uobis dominus per humilitatis nostrae famulatum, seu et per manus nostras accipiendas praeparauit, per quas sciatis sarcinam domini dei uestri ceruicibus uestris impositas, et ad humilitatem atque ad ministrationem uos esse conexos, et per quas uos cognoscant fratres uestri ministros dei esse ordinatos. Vt qui in diaconatus ministerio estis constituti, leuiticae benedictionis ordine clarescatis, et spiritali conuersatione praefulgentes, gratia sanctificationis eluceatis. Sed et in christo iesu firmi et stabiles perseueretis. Quatinus hoc quod per has stolas significatur in die districti iudicii, ante tribunal domini, sine macula representare ualeatis. Ipso adiuuante cui est honor et gloria in saecula.

622 ALIA. Domine sanctae spei, fidei, gratiae profectuum munerator, qui in caelestibus et terrenis / ministeriis angelorum

/f. 91r

---

[1] *ad* erased.

154

ubique dispositis, per omnia elementa uoluntatis tuae diffundis affectum. Hos quoque famulos tuos speciali affectu intueri digneris, ut tu<i>s obsequiis expediti sanctis altaribus ministri puri clarescant, et indulgentiae prioris gradu eorum quos apostoli tui in septenarium numerum beato stephano duce, atque spiritu sancto auctore elegerunt digni existant, et uirtutibus uniuersis quibus tibi seruire oportet instructi polleant. Per.

CXIIII

623 AD CONSVMANDVM DIACONATVS OFFICII. Commune uotum permaneat communis oratio prosequatur, ut hi totius ecclesiae praece, qui in diaconatus ministerio preparantur et leuiticae benedictionis spiritali conuersationis praefulgentes, per gratiam sanctificationis eluceant. Per.

CXV
HVCVSQVE V GRADVS.
MISSA IN DIE CONSECRATIONIS DIACONI

624 Ad praeces nostras quaesumus domine propitiatus intende, et leuitae tui sacris altaribus seruientes, et fidei ueritate fundati, et mente sint spiritali conspicui. Per dominum nostrum.

625 SVPER OBLATA. Suscipe quaesumus domine hostias leuitarum tuorum quibus mentium integritates, tuo nomine consecratas, et terrenis contagiis expiari, et caelestibus contulisti propinquare consortes. Per dominum nostrum.

/f. 91v **626** IN FRACTIONE. / Hanc igitur oblationem quam tibi offerimus pro famulis tuis, quod ad diaconatus ordinem promouere dignatus es, quaesumus domine placatus suscipias, ut quod eis diuino munere contulisti, in eis propitiatus dona custodi, diesque nostros.

627 BENEDICTIO. Benedicat uos deus misericordia plenus, pietate inmensus, maiestate gloriosus, uirtute praecipuus. AMEN.
<M>ultiplicetur pax in diebus uestris, saturitas in tempore, temperies in aere, fructus in germine, ut dum uos pius miserator locupletat, et in suam hereditatem propitius introducat. AMEN.
Benedicat in uobis dominus imagines quas plasmauit, et det misericordiam quam promisit, custodiatque animas uestras quas

155

redemit, seruando gratiam quam profudit, ut impleatis quae praecepit, et ille custodiat quod donauit. AMEN. Quod ipse.

628 POSTCOMMVNIO. Haec nos communio domine purget a crimine, et caelestibus remedii faciat esse consortes. per.

629 LEGATVR LECTIO DANIEL ET DIACONVS. Vt supra.

630 COLLECTA. Actiones nostras quaesumus domine et aspirando praeueni, et adiuuando prosequere, ut cuncta nostra operatio, et a te semper incipiat, et per te cepta finiatur. Per.

631 ITEM AD MISSAS DICAT EPISCOPVS. DOMINVS VOBISCVM. DIACONVS. Vt supra.

XCVI¹

632 COLLECTA. Deus qui tribus pueris mitigasti flammas ignium, concede propitius / ut nos famulos tuos non exurat flamma uitiorum. Per.

/f. 92r

CXVII
ORDINATIO PRESBITERORVM

633 Presbiteri cum ordinantur episcopo eos benedicente, et manus super capita eorum tenente, etiam omnes presbiteri qui praesentes sunt manus suas super scapulas eorum teneant, et archidiaconus nomina eorum et sanctorum titulorum locis incongruis prout decet denominat.

634 ORATIO SVPER PRESBITEROS DVM ORDINANTVR. Oremus dilectissimi deum patrem omnipotentem super hos famulos suos quos ad presbiterii munus elegit, caelestia dona multiplicet, et qui eius dignatione suscipiunt, ipsius digne exequantur auxilium. Per dominum nostrum.

635 ALIA. Exaudi nos domine deus noster et super hos famulos tuos benedictionem sancti spiritus et gratia sacerdotalis effunde uirtutem, ut quos tuae pietatis aspectibus offerimus

---

¹ For *CXVI.*

consecrandos, perpetua muneris tui largitate consequaris. Per dominum.

CONSECRATIO PRESBITERI
DOMINVS VOBISCVM. RESP. ET CVM SPIRITV TVO.
SVRSVM CORDA. RESP. HABEMVS AD DOMINVM.
GRATIAS AGAMVS DEO NOSTRO. RESP. DIGNVM ET
IVSTVM EST.

636 Vere quia dignum et iustum est, aequum et salutare, nos tibi semper et ubique gratias agere. Domine sanctae pater omnipotens aeternae deus. Honorum auctor et distributor omnium dignitatum, per quem proficiunt uniuersa, per quem cuncta firmantur. Amplificatis semper in melius naturae rationalis incrementis, / per ordinem congrua ratione dispositum. Vnde et sacerdotales gradus, atque officia leuitarum sacramentis mysticis instituta creuerunt. Vt cum pontifices summos regendis populis praeficisces, ad eorum societatis et operis adiumentum sequentis ordinis uiros, et secundę dignitatis eligeres. Sic in heremo per septuaginta uirorum prudentium mentes, moysi spiritum propagasti. Quibus ille adiutoribus usus in populo, innumeras multitudines facile gubernauit. Sic et in eleazaro et in ithamar filiis aaron paternę plenitudinis habundantiam transfudisti, ut ad hostias salutares et frequentioris[1] officii sacramenta, ministerium sufficeret sacerdotum. Hac prouidentia domine apostolis filii tui, doctores fidei comites addisti, quibus illi orbem totum, secundis praedicatoribus impleuerunt. Quapropter infirmitati quoque nostrae domine quaesumus haec adiumenta largire, qui quanto magis fragiliores sumus, tanto his pluribus indigemus. Da quaesumus omnipotens pater, in hos famulos tuos presbiterii dignitatem, innoua in uisceribus eorum spiritum sanctitatis acceptum. A te deus secundi meriti munus obtineant, censuramque morum, exemplo conuersationis suae insinuent. Sint probi cooperatores ordinis nostri, eluceat in eis totius forma iustitiae. Vt bonam rationem dispensa/tionis sibi creditę reddituri, aeternae beatitudinis praemia consequantur. Per christum dominum.

---

[1] *frequentiores* before correction.

637 MODO CONVERTAT STOLAM IN COLLO ET INDVANTVR CASVLA. Per haec indumenta stolam et casulam salutis indui merearis, et aeternae perpetuitatis plenitudinem cum sanctis sacerdotibus christo ministrante capescere ualeas.

CXVIII

638 BENEDICTIO POST CASVLAS SVPER OMNES. Benedictio dei patris, et filii, et spiritus sancti, descendat super uos, et his sacerdotalibus uestibus induti, protecti, et muniti esse ualeatis ab omnibus inpugnationibus malignorum spirituum et sitis benedicti in nomine domini nostri, et in uirtute spiritus sancti in ordine sacerdotali, et offeratis hostias placabiles pro peccatis atque offensionibus omnipotenti deo. Cui est honor et gloria.

639 CONSECRATIO MANVVM. Consecrentur manus istę, quaesumus domine de oleo sancto et de chrismate sancto, et sanctificentur per istam unctionem sanctamque benedictionem, ut quęcumque benedixerint benedicta sint, et quaecumque sanctificauerint sanctificata permaneant.

640 VNGVATVR CAPVT. Vnguatur caput tuum et consecretur caelesti benedictione in ordine sacerdotali in nomine patris, et filii, et spiritus sancti. AMEN. Pax tibi.

CXVIIII

641 ITEM BENEDICTIO MANVVM SACERDOTVM. Benedic domine has manus, et sanctifica, sacerdotum tuorum .il. ad /f. 93v consecrandas hostias, / quae pro delictis atque neglegentiis populi offeruntur, et ad cetera benedicenda quae ad usus populi necessaria sunt, et praesta quaesumus ut quaecumque benedixerint, benedicentur, et quaecumque sacrauerint sacrentur, saluator.

CXX

642 CONSVMMATIO PRESBITERORVM. Sit nobis communis oratio fratres, ut hi qui in adiutorium et utilitatem uestrae salutis eliguntur, presbiteratus benedictionem diuini muneris indulgentiam consequantur, et sancti spiritus sacerdotalia dona priuilegio uirtutum, ne impares loco depraehendantur obtineant. Per.

158

643 ITEM ALIA. Sanctificationum omnium auctor cuius uera consecratio, cuius plena benedictio est, tu domine super hos famulos tuos .ill. quos presbeteratus honore dedicamus, gratiam tuae benedictionis infunde, ut grauitate actuum probent se esse omnium seniores, his instituantur disciplinis quas tito et timotheo paulus instituit, ut in lege tua omnipotens deus die ac nocte meditantes quod legerint credant, quod crediderint doceant, et quod docuerint imitentur. Iustitiam, constantiam, misericordiam, fortitudinem, in se ostendant, exemplo probent, ammonitionem confirment, ut purum atque inmaculatum ministerii donum custodiant, et per obsequium plebis tuae corpore[1] et sanguine filii tui / inmaculata benedictione transformentur, et inuiolabilem caritatem, et in uirum perfectum, in mensuram aetatis plenitudinis christi, in die iustitiae aeterni iudicii, conscientia pura, fide plena spiritu sancto pleni appareant. Per dominum.

644 MODO LEGATVR EPISTOLA, TRACTVS ET EVANGELIVM, ET TVNC OFFERVNT OMNES SACRATAS OBLATIONES.

645 SVPER OBLATA. Praesentibus sacrificiis domine ieiunia nostra sanctifica, ut quod obseruantia nostra profitetur extrinsecus, interius operetur. Per.

646 PRAEFATIO. VD aeterne[2] deus. Inluminator et redemptor animarum nostrarum. Qui nos per primum adam abstinentiae lege uiolata paradyso eiectos, fortioris ieiunii remedio ad antiquae patriae beatitudinem per gratiam reuocasti. Nosque pia institutione docuisti, quibus obseruationibus a peccatis omnibus liberemur. Quem laudant angeli.

647 BENEDICTIO. Deus fons indulgentiae, suscipiat propitius litationem abstinentiae uestrae. AMEN.
Impleat corda uestra suarum delectationibus hostiarum, et det uobis posse suis parere praeceptis. AMEN.

---

[1] *uel corpus* supplied interlinearly.
[2] *aeternae* before correction.

159

Vt quod non potestis carnali ex infirmitate perficere, ipsius gratiae ubertate mereamini adimplere. AMEN.
Quod ipse praestare dignetur.

/f. 94v **648** AD COMPLENDVM. / Sanctificationibus tuis omnipotens deus, et uitia nostra curentur, et remedia nobis aeterna proueniant. Per.

CXXI
MISSA IN DIE ORDINATIONIS PRESBITERI

649 Exaudi domine supplicum praeces, et deuoto toto pectore famulantes, perpetua defensione custodi, ut nullis perturbationibus impediti, liberam seruitutem tuis semper exhibeamus officiis. Per.

650 SVPER OBLATA. Tuis domine quaesumus operare mysteriis, ut haec tibi munera dignis mentibus offeramus. Per.

651 PRAEFATIO. VD aeterne[1] deus. Effunde caelestem benedictionem super hos famulos tuos .ill. qui sc hodie humiliauerunt in ordine presbiteratus sub dextera tua, protege eos protectione diuina et fugiant ab eis uniuersa peccata, sciant sibi hodie bona desideria esse praeparata, et regni caelestis sancta conquirant lucra, pareant semper diuinis praeceptis, ut te adiuuante uincant incendia carnis. Da eis perfectos sensus, quibus omnia quae hodie audierunt et inuenerunt te protegente custodiant. Per christum.

652 BENEDICTIO. Omnipotens sempiterne deus, respicere dignare de altissimo regni tui solio, super hos presbiteros benedictionem tuam toto corde postulantes, ut quos pretioso sanguine filii tui redimere uoluisti, non permittas ullis aduersitatibus maculari. AMEN.

/f. 95r / Da eis domine tempora tranquilla, quieta et pacifica, et laetitiam spiritalem, habeant sine fine per tempora, daque eis sapientiam rectam, patientiam probatam, abstinentiae uirtutem, et uitam tribue perennem. AMEN.

---

[1] *aeternae* before correction.

Da eis cor quod te cognoscant, da sensus quibus te intellegant, da intellectus quibus terram despiciant, caelum aspiciant, peccata odiant, iustitiam diligant. AMEN. Quod ipse.

653 AD COMPLENDVM. Hos quos reficis domine diuinis sacramentis, tuis attolle benignus auxiliis, et tuae redemptionis effectum, et misteriis capere mereamur et moribus. Per dominum.

CXXII
DIE DOMINICA VACAT

654 Deus qui conspicis omni nos uirtute destitui, interius exteriusque custodi, ut et ab omnibus aduersitatibus muniamur in corpore, et a prauis cogitationibus mundemur in mente. Per dominum.

655 SVPER OBLATA. Sacrificiis praesentibus domine quaesumus intende placatus, ut et deuotioni nostrae proficiant et saluti. Per.

656 PRAEFATIO. VD aeterne[1] deus. Et maiestatem tuam suppliciter exorare, ut mentibus nostris medicinalis obseruantiae, munus infundas. Et qui neglegentibus etiam subsidium ferre non desinis, beneficia prebeas potiora deuotis. Per christum dominum nostrum.

/f. 95v **657** BENEDICTIO. / Omnipotens deus ieiunii caeterarumque uirtutem dedicator atque amator, sua uos benedictione sanctificet. <AMEN.>
Accendat in uobis pie deuotionis affectum, et praebeat supplicantibus suum benignus auditum. AMEN.
Quatinus mentes uestrae sinceris purgate ieiuniis, bonorum omnium exuberent[2] incrementis. AMEN.
Quod ipse prestare dignetur.

---

[1] *aeternae* before correction.
[2] Second *e* supplied interlinearly.

658 AD COMPLENDVM. Supplices te rogamus omnipotens deus, ut quos tuis reficis sacramentis, tibi etiam placitis moribus deseruire concedas. Per dominum.

CXXIII
FERIA II AD SANCTVM CLEMENTEM

659 Praesta quaesumus omnipotens deus, ut familia tua quae se affligendo carne ab alimentis abstinet, sectando iustitiam a culpa ieiunet. Per.

660 SVPER OBLATA. Haec hostia domine placationis et laudis, tua nos propitiatione dignos efficiat. Per.

661 PRĘFATIO. VD aeternae deus. Et pietatem tuam supplici deuotione deposcere, ut ieiunii nostri oblatione placatus, et peccatorum nobis concedas ueniam, et nos a noxiis liberes insidiis. Per christum.

662 BENEDICTIO. Deus qui es custos animarum et corporum, dignare hanc familiam tuam brachio tuae defensionis protegere, ut nullis inimicorum antiquorum hostium insidiis, corpora nostra patiaris illudi, sed semper cum domino / nostro iesu christo maneamus inlaesi. AMEN.

/f. 96r

Da huc ic[1] familiae tuae fidei calore, continentię rigorem, fraternitatis amorem, abstinentię uirtutem. AMEN.

Et sic quicquid dicto, facto uel cogitationibus peccauerunt, pietas ac benignitas, clementiae ac misericordiae tuae resoluere ac indulgere dignetur. AMEN.

Quod ipse praestare dignetur.

663 AD COMPLENDVM. Haec nos communio domine purget a crimine, et caelestibus remediis, faciat esse consortes. Per.

664 SVPER POPVLVM. Adesto supplicationibus nostris omnipotens deus, et quibus fiduciam sperandae pietatis indulges, consuetę misericordiae tribue benignus effectum. Per dominum

---

[1] For *huic*.

CXXIIII
FERIA III AD SANCTAM BALBINAM

665 Perfice quaesumus domine benignus, in nobis obseruantia sanctae subsidium, ut quae te auctore facienda cognouimus, te operante impleamus. Per.

666 SVPER OBLATA. Sanctificationem tuam nobis domine his mysteriis placatus operare, quae nos et a terrenis purget uitiis, et ad caelestia dona perducat. Per.

667 PRAEFATIO. VD aeterne[1] deus. Qui ob animarum medelam ieiunii deuotione castigari corpora praecepisti. Concede quaesumus ut corda nostra ita pietatis tuae ualeant exercere mandata, ut ad tua / mereamur te opitulante peruenire promissa. Per christum.

f. 96v

668 AD COMPLENDVM. Vt sacris domine reddamur digni muneribus, fac nos tuis quaesumus oboedire mandatis. Per.

669 SVPER POPVLVM. Propitiare domine supplicationibus nostris, et animarum nostrarum medere languoribus, ut remissione percepta, in tua semper benedictione laetemur. Per dominum nostrum iesum christum.

CXXV
FERIA IIII AD SANCTAM CECILIAM

670 Populum tuum domine propitius respice, et quos ab aescis carnalibus praecipis abstinere, a noxiis quoque uitiis cessare concede. Per.

671 SVPER OBLATA. Hostias domine quas tibi offerimus propitius respice, et per haec sancta commercia uincula peccatorum nostrorum absolue. Per.

672 PRAEFATIO. VD per christum dominum nostrum. Per quem humani generis reconciliatione, mirabili dispensatione operatus es. Praesta quaesumus, ut sancto purificati ieiunio, et tibi toto

---

[1] *aeterne* before correction.

corde simus subiecti, et inter mundanae prauitatis insidias, te miserante perseueremus inlaesi. Per quem.

673 BENEDICTIO. Benedicat uos deus misericordia plenus. Require retro in sabbato in missa diaconi.

674 AD COMPLENDVM. Sumptis domine sacramentis, ad redemptionis aeternae, quaesumus proficiamus[1] augmentum. Per.

675 SVPER POPVLVM. Deus innocentiae restitutor et amator, dirige ad te tuorum corda seruorum / ut spiritus tui feruore concepto, et in fide inueniantur stabiles, et in opere efficaces. Per.

/f. 97r

CXXVI
FERIA V AD SANCTAM MARIAM TRANS TYBERIM

676 Praesta nobis domine quaesumus auxilium gratiae tuae, ut ieiuniis et orationibus conuenienter intenti, liberemur ab hostibus mentis et corporis. Per.

677 SVPER OBLATA. Praesente sacrificio nomini tuo nos domine ieiunia dicata sanctificent, ut quod obseruantia nostra profitetur exterius, interius operetur effectum. Per.

678 PRĘFATIO. VD aeterne[2] deus. Et tuam concelebrationem ieiunii pietatem deuotis mentibus obsecrare, ut qui peccatis ingruentibus malorum pondere praemimur, et a peccatis omnibus liberemur, et libera tibi mente famulemur. Per christum.

679 AD COMPLENDVM. Gratia tua nos quaesumus domine non derelinquat, quae nobis opem semper adquirat. Per.

680 SVPER POPVLVM. Adesto domine famulis tuis, et perpetuam benignitatem largire poscentibus, ut his qui te auctore et

---

[1] Over an erasure.
[2] *aeternae* before correction.

gubernatore gloriantur, et congregata restaures, et restaurata conserues. Per.

CXXVII
FERIA VI AD SANCTVM VITALEM

681 Da quaesumus omnipotens deus, ut sacro nos purificante ieiunio, sinceris mentibus ad sancta uentura facias peruenire. Per.

682 SVPER OBLATA. Haec in nobis sacrificia deus, et actione permaneant, et operatione firmentur. Per.

683 PRĘFATIO. / VD aeterne[1] deus. Qui delinquentes perire non pateris, sed ut ad te conuertantur et uiuant hortaris. Poscimus itaque pietatem tuam ut a peccatis nostris tuae seueritatis suspendas uindictam, et nobis obtatam misericorditer tribuas ueniam. Nec iniquitatum nostrarum moleste prouocet ad ultionem, sed ieiunii obseruatio, et morum emendatio, te flectat ad peccatorum nostrorum remissionem. Per christum.

684 BENEDICTIO. Benedicat uobis deus nostri alloquio, et cor uestrum sinceri amoris copulet nexu perpetuo. <AMEN.>
Floreatis rerum praesentium copiis, iustitia adquisitis, gaudeatis perenniter, fructibus sincerissime caritatis. AMEN.
Tribuat uobis dominus dona perennia, ut per tempora feliciter dilatata, percipiatis gaudia sempiterna. AMEN.
Quod ipse praestare dignetur.

685 AD COMPLENDVM. Fac nos domine quaesumus accepto pignore salutis aeternę sic tendere congruenter, ut ad eam peruenire possimus. Per.

686 SVPER POPVLVM. Da quaesumus domine populo tuo salutem mentis et corporis, ut bonis operibus inherendo, tuae semper uirtutis mereatur[2] protectione defendi. Per.

---

[1] *aeternae* before correction.
[2] *mereamur* before correction.

CXXVIII
SABBATO AD SANCTOS MARCELLINVM ET PETRVM

/f. 98r **687** Da quaesumus domine nostris effectum ieiuniis salutarem, ut castigatio carnis assumpta, ad nostra/rum uegetationum transeat animarum. Per.

688 SVPER OBLATA. His sacrificiis domine concede placatus, ut qui propriis oramus absolui delictis, non grauemur aeternis. Per.

689 PRAEFATIO. VD aeterne[1] deus. Et tuam iugiter exorare clementiam tuam, ut mentes nostras quas conspicis terrenis affectibus pregrauari, medicinalibus tribuas exonerari, et per afflictionem corporum, proueniat nobis robur animarum. Per christum.

690 AD COMPLENDVM. Sacramenti tui domine diuina libatio, penetrabilia nostri cordis infundat, et sui participes potenter efficiat. Per.

691 SVPER POPVLVM. Familiam tuam quaesumus domine continua pietate custodi, ut quae in sola spe gratiae caelestis innititur, caelesti etiam protectione muniatur[2]. Per.

CCXXVIIII
DIE DOMINICA AD SANCTVM LAVRENTIVM FORIS MVRVM

692 Quaesumus omnipotens deus, uota humilium respice, adque ad defensionem nostram dexteram tuae maiestatis extende. Per dominum.

693 SVPER OBLATA. Haec hostia domine quaesumus emundet nostra delicta, et sacrificium celebrandum, subditorum tibi corpora, mentesque sanctificet. Per.

694 PRAEFATIO. VD aeterne deus. Et te suppliciter exorare, ut cum abstinentia corporali, mens quoque nostra[3] declinet illicita[4]. Et
/f. 98v qui terrenas delectationes et carnales epulas abnegamus, /

---

[1] *aeternae* before correction.
[2] *muniamur* before correction.
[3] Word following erased.
[4] *illicito* before correction.

humanę uoluntatis, praues intentiones[1] amputemus. Quatinus ad sancta sanctorum fideliter salubriterque capienda, competenti ieiunio ualeamus aptari, tanto nobis certi propensius iugiter adfutura, quanto fuerimus eorum institutionibus gratiores. Per christum.

695 BENEDICTIO. Omnipotens deus ieiuniorum uestrorum uictimas clementer accipiat, et sua uos benedictione dignos efficiat. AMEN.

Mentes uestras ita parsimoniae bona contra uitia muniat, praeceptorum suorum doctrinis erudiat, caritatis dona repleat, ut uos in omnibus sibi placere concedat. AMEN.

Quatinus praesentis quadragesime diebus deuotissime caelebratis, ad paschalia festa purificatis cordibus accedere ualeatis. AMEN.

Quod ipse.

696 AD COMPLENDVM. Cunctis nos domine reatibus et periculis propitiatus absolue, quos tanti mysterii tribuis esse participes. Per.

CXXX

FERIA II AD SANCTVM MARCVM

697 Cordibus nostris quaesumus domine benignus infunde, ut sicut ab aescis corporalibus abstinemus, ita sensus quoque nostros a noxiis retrahamur excessibus. Per.

698 SVPER OBLATA. Munus quod tibi domine nostrae seruitutis offerimus, tu salutare nobis perfice sacramentum. Per.

699 PRAEFATIO. VD aeterne[2] deus. Et clementiam tuam cum omni / supplicatione praecari, ut per hanc ieiuniorum obseruationem, crescat nostrae deuotionis affectus, et nostras actiones religiosus exornet affectus. Quatinus te auxiliante et ab humanis semper retrahamur excessibus et monitis inherere ualeamus te largiente caelestibus. Per christum dominum nostrum.

f. 99r

---

[1] *prauis intentionibus* before correction.
[2] *aeternae* before correction.

700 BENEDICTIO. Omnipotens deus det uobis copiam suae benedictionis, et conferat in uobis prẹmium aeternẹ salutis. AMEN.

Sicque quadragesimalis obseruantiae inchoata ieiunia sibi reddat placabilia, ut ab eo inmarcescibilia, ualeatis percipere dona repromissa. AMEN.

Concedatque hoc sanctae trinitatis atque indiuiduae unitatis clementia, cuius regnum et imperium sine fine permanet in saecula saeculorum. AMEN.

<Q>uod ipse praestare dignetur.

701 AD COMPLENDVM. Presta quaesumus omnipotens et misericors deus, ut quae ore contingimus, pura mente capiamus. Per.

702 SVPER POPVLVM. Subueniat nobis domine misericordia tua, ut ab imminentibus peccatorum nostrorum periculis, te mereamur protegente saluari. Per dominum.

CXXXI
FERIA III AD SANCTAM POTENTIANAM

703 Exaudi nos omnipotens et misericors deus, et continentiae salutaris propitius nobis dona concede. Per.

704 SVPER OBLATA. Per haec ueniat quaesumus domine sacramenta nostrae redemptionis effectus, qui nos et ab humanis / retrahat semper excessibus, et ad salutaria cuncta perducat. Per dominum.

/f. 99v

705 PRAEFATIO. VD aeterne[1] deus. Qui peccantium non uis animas perirẹ sed culpas, et peccantes non semper continuo iudicas, sed ad paenitentiam prouocatos expectas. Auerte quaesumus a nobis quam meremur iram, et quam obtamus super nos effunde clementiam, ut sacro purificati ieiunio, electorum tuorum adscissi mereamur collegio. Per christum.

706 AD COMPLENDVM. Sacris domine mysteriis expiati, et ueniam consequamur et gratiam. Per.

---

[1] *aeternae* before correction.

707 SVPER POPVLVM. Tua nos domine protectione defende, et ab omni semper iniquitate custodi. Per dominum.

CXXXII
FERIA IIII AD SANCTVM SYXTVM

708 Praesta nobis quaesumus domine, ut salutaribus ieiuniis eruditi, a noxiis quoque uitiis abstinentes, propitiationem tuam facilius impetremus. Per.

709 SVPER OBLATA. Suscipe quaesumus domine praeces populi tui cum oblationibus hostiarum, et tua mysteria caelebrantes, ab omnibus nos defende periculis. Per.

710 PRAEFATIO. VD aeterne[1] deus. Tuamque misęricordiam suppliciter exorare, ut ieiuniorum nostrorum sacrosancta mysteria, tuae sint pietati[2] semper accepta. Concedasque ut quorum corpora abstinentiae obseruatione macerantur, mentes quoque / uirtutibus et caelestibus institutis exornentur. Per christum.

f. 100r

711 BENEDICTIO. Respice domine de caelo, et uide et uisita uineam istam quam plantauit dextera tua, spirituales exhibeant fructus, et caelestes diligant actus, ut sine uitio in hoc saeculo transigant uitam, ut possint promereri perpetuam. <AMEN.>
Fragilem solida, contritum releua, inualidum robora, ualidumque confirma, pietate alleua, caritate aedifica, castitate munda, sapientia inlumina, misericordia serua. AMEN.
Proficiant huic praecepto fidei uigilantia, amoris tui perseuerantia, morum temperantia, misericordiae prouidentia, actuum disciplina, ut post concessam miserationis indulgentiam, non abicias eos promissionis tuae munificentia, sed perducas ad ueniam, quos tibi adoptasti per gratiam. AMEN.
Quod ipse pręstare dignetur.

712 AD COMPLENDVM. Sanctificet nos domine qua pasti sumus mensa caelestis, et a cunctis erroribus expiatos, supernis promissionibus reddat acceptos. Per.

---

[1] *aeternae* before correction.
[2] *pietatis* before correction.

713 SVPER POPVLVM. Concede quaesumus omnipotens deus, ut qui protectionis tuae gratiam quaerimus, liberi a malis omnibus, secura tibi mente seruiamus. Per dominum nostrum.

/f. 100v

/ CXXXIII
FERIA V AD SANCTOS COSMAM ET DAMIANVM

714 Deus qui peccantium animas non uis perire sed culpas, contine quam meremur iram, et quam praecamur super nos effunde clementiam, ut de merore gaudium tuae misericordiae consequi mereamur. Per.

715 ALIA. Magnificet te domine sanctorum tuorum cosmae et damiani beata sollemnitas[1], quia et illis gloriam sempiternam, et opem nobis ineffabilem prouidentiae contulisti. Per.

716 SVPER OBLATA. In tuorum domine praetiosa morte iustorum sacrificium illud offerimus, de quo martyrium sumpsit omne principium. Per dominum.

717 PRAEFATIO. VD aeterne deus. Et tuam inmensam clementiam supplici uoto deposcere, ut nos famulos tuos, et ieiunii maceratione castigatos, et cęteris bonorum operum exhibitionibus eruditos, in mandatis tuis facias perseuerare sinceros, et ad[2] paschalia festa peruenire inlesos. Sicque pręsentibus subsidiis consolemur, quatinus ad aeterna gaudia pertingere mereamur. Per christum.

718 AD COMPLENDVM. Sit nobis domine sacramenti tui certa saluatio, quae cum beatorum tuorum cosmae et damiani, meritis imploratur. Per.

719 SVPER POPVLVM. Subiectum tibi populum quaesumus domine propitiatio caelestis amplificet, et tuis semper faciat / seruire mandatis. Per.

/f. 101r

---

[1] Letters erased in the middle of the word.
[2] *et ad* supplied over an erasure.

CXXXIIII
FERIA VI AD SANCTVM LAVRENTIVM IN LVCINA[1]

720 Ieiunia nostra quaesumus domine benigno fauore prosequere, ut sicut ab alimentis in corpore, ita a uitiis ieiunemus in mente. Per.

721 SVPER OBLATA. Respice domine propitius ad munera quae sacramus, ut et tibi grata sint, et nobis salutaria semper existant. Per.

722 PRAEFATIO. VD per christum dominum nostrum. Qui ad insinuandum humilitatis suae mysterium, fatigatus resedit ad puteum. Qui a muliere samaritana aquae sibi petiit porrigi potum, qui in ea creauerat fidei donum. Et ita eius sitire dignatus est fidem, ut dum ab ea aquam peteret in ea ignem diuini amoris accenderet. Imploramus itaque tuam inmensam clementiam, ut contemnentes tenebrosam profunditatem uitiorum, et relinquentes noxiarum hydriam cupiditatum, et te qui fons uitae et origo bonitatis es semper sitiamus, et ieiuniorum nostrorum obseruatione tibi placeamus. Per quem.

723 BENEDICTIO. Omnipotens dominus qui a muliere samaritana aquae sibi petiit porrigi potum, ille tribuat in uobis spiritale donum. AMEN.
Et qui eius sitienti animo refocillauit uiuo fonte, auferat a uobis omnia delicta quae perpetrastis longo ex tempore. AMEN.

f. 101v / <S>itis semper in hoc saeculo fide repleti, et ab omni malo defensi, ut ab ipso in iudicio perenniter mereamini benedici. AMEN.
Quod ipse.

724 AD COMPLENDVM. Huius nos domine perceptio sacramenti mundet a crimine, et ad caelestia regna perducat. Per.

725 SVPER POPVLVM. Praesta quaesumus omnipotens deus, ut qui in tua protectione confidimus, cuncta nobis aduersantia, te adiuuante uincamus. Per dominum.

SABBATO AD SANCTAM SVSANNAM

726 Praesta quaesumus omnipotens deus, ut qui se affligendo carne ab alimentis abstinent, sectando iustitiam a culpa ieiunent. Per.

---

[1] *LVCANA* before correction.

THE SACRAMENTARY OF RATOLDUS

727 SVPER OBLATVM. Concede quaesumus omnipotens deus, ut huius sacrificii munus oblatum, fragilitatem nostram ab omni malo purget semper et muniat. Per.

728 PRĘFATIO. VD aeterne[1] deus. Qui ieiunii quadragesimalis obseruationem in moyse et elia dedicasti, et unigenito filio tuo legis et prophetarum, nostroque omnium domino exornasti. Tuam igitur inmensam bonitatem supplices exposcimus, ut quod ille iugi ieiuniorum compleuit continuatione, nos adimplere ualeamus, illius adiuti largissima miseratione. Et adimplentes ea quae praecepit, dona percipere mereamur quae promisit. Per quem.

/f. 102r **729** AD COMPLENDVM. / Quaesumus omnipotens deus, ut inter eius membra numeremur, cuius corpori communicauimus et sanguini. Per dominum nostrum.

730 SVPER POPVLVM. Praetende domine fidelibus tuis dexteram caelestis auxilii, ut et te toto corde perquirant, et quae digne postulant consequi mereantur. Per.

CXXXVI

DIE DOMINICA AD HIERVSALEM

731 Concede quaesumus omnipotens deus, ut qui ex merito nostrae actionis affligimur, tuae gratiae consolatione respiremus. Per dominum.

732 SVPER OBLATA. Sacrificiis praesentibus domine quaesumus intende placatus, ut et deuotioni nostrae proficiant et saluti. Per dominum nostrum.

733 PRAEFATIO. VD aeterne[2] deus. Et te creatorem omnium de praeteritis fructibus glorificare, et de uenturis suppliciter exorare. Vt cum de perceptis non inuenimur ingrati, de percipiendis non iudicemur indigni. Sed exibita toties sollempni deuotione ieiunia, cum subsidiis corporalibus profectum quoque capiamus animarum. Per christum.

---

[1] *aeternae* before correction.
[2] *aeternae* before correction.

734 BENEDICTIO. Deus qui uos ad praesentium dierum quadragesimalium medietatem dignatus est perducere, ipse sua uos miseratione dignetur benedicere. AMEN.

Abstinentiam uestram praeteritam et futuram, ita sibi placitam reddat, / ut sicut ab illicitis cybis, ita uos etiam a uitiis omnibus abstinere concedat. AMEN.

Quo de praeteritis et de futuris spiritualium carismatum frugibus ei grates persoluentes, ad sanctum pascha peruenire possitis indempnes. AMEN.

Quod ipse praestare dignetur.

735 AD COMPLENDVM. Da nobis misericors deus, ut sancta tua quibus incessanter explemur, sinceris tractemus obsequiis, et semper fideli mente sumamus. Per.

736 ALIA ORATIO AD MISSAM. Deus qui in deserti regione multitudinem populi tua uirtute satiasti, in huius quoque saeculi transeuntis excursu, uictum nobis spiritalem ne deficiamus impende. Per dominum.

CXXXVII

FERIA II AD SANCTOS QVATTVOR CORONATOS

737 Praesta quaesumus omnipotens deus, ut obseruationes sacras annua deuotione recolentes, et corpore tibi placeamus et mente. Per dominum.

738 SVPER OBLATA. Oblatum tibi domine sacrificium, uiuificet nos semper et muniat. Per.

739 PRAEFATIO. VD aeterne[1] deus. Et tuam suppliciter misericordiam implorare, ut exercitatio ueneranda, ieiunii salutaris nos a peccatorum nostrorum maculis purgatos reddat, et ad supernorum ciuium societatem perducat, ut et hic deuotorum actuum sumamus augmentum, et illic ad aeternae

bea/titudinis percipiamus emolumentum. Per christum.

---

[1] *aeternae* before correction.

740 BENEDICTIO. Benedicat uos omnipotens deus, et ad omnem rectam obseruantiae plenitudinem totius honestatis instituat. AMEN.
Sit in uobis castitatis studium, modestia morum, innocentis uitae sinceritas, fidei integritas, concordiae caritas, continentiae uirtus, benignitatis affectus, ad te oculos tendant, de te caelesti assumant, ut te uotis expectent, se claris actibus ornent. AMEN.
Vt consequenter cum sanctis pro premiorum multorum probitate referamus deo gratias, et praesentium bonorum, et futurorum munerum largitori. AMEN.
Quod ipse praestare dignetur.

741 AD COMPLENDVM. Sumptis domine salutaribus sacramentis, ad redemptionis aeternae, quaesumus proficiamus augmentum. Per.

742 SVPER POPVLVM. Deprecationem nostram quaesumus domine benignus exaudi, et quibus supplicandi praestas affectum, tribue defensionis auxilium. Per.

CXXXVIII
FERIA III AD SANCTVM LAVRENTIVM IN DAMASCO

743 Sacrae nobis quaesumus domine obseruationis ieiunia, et piae conuersationis augmentum, et tuae propitiationis continuum praestaet auxilium. Per.

744 SVPER OBLATA. Haec hostia domine quaesumus emundet
/f. 103v   nostra delicta, et sacrificium caelebrandum subditorum / tibi corpora mentesque sanctificet. Per.

745 PRAEFATIO. VD aeterne[1] deus. Per mediatorem dei et hominum iesum christum dominum nostrum. Qui mediante die festo ascendit in templum docere, qui de caelo descendit, mundum ab ignorantiae tenebras liberare. Cuius descensus, genus humanum doctrina salutari instruit, mors a perpetua morte redimit[2], ascensio ad caelestia regna perducit. Per quem te summe pater poscimus, ut eius institutione edocti, salutaris

---

[1] *aeternae* before correction.
[2] *redemit* before correction.

174

parsymoniae deuotione purificati, ad tua perueniamus promissa securi. Per quem.

746 AD COMPLENDVM. Huius nos domine perceptio sacramenti mundet a crimine, et ad caelestia regna perducat. Per.

747 SVPER POPVLVM. Miserere domine populo tuo, et continuis tribulationibus laborantem, propitius respirare concede. Per.

CXXXVIIII
FERIA IIII AD SANCTVM PAVLVM

748 Deus qui et iustis praemia meritorum et peccatoribus per ieiunium ueniam praebes, miserere supplicibus tuis, ut reatus nostri confessio, indulgentiam ualeat percipere delictorum. Per.

749 ALIA. Praesta quaesumus omnipotens deus, ut quos ieiunia uotiua castigant, ipsa quoque deuotio sancta laetificet, ut terrenis affectibus mitigatis, facilius / caelestia capiamus. Per dominum.

750 SVPER OBLATA. Supplices domine te rogamus, ut his sacrificiis peccata nostra mundentur, quia tunc ueram nobis tribuis, et mentis et corporis sanitatem. Per.

751 PRĘFATIO. VD per christum. Qui inluminatione[1] suae fidęi tenebras expulit mundi, et genus humanum quod primę matris uterus profuderat caecum, incarnationis suae mysterio reddidit inluminatum. Fecitque filios adoptionis, qui tenebantur uinculis iustae damnationis. Per ipsum te petimus ut tales in eius inueniamur iustissima examinatione, quales facti sumus in lauacri[2] salutaris felicissima regeneratione. Vt eius incarnationis medicamine imbuti, sacrosancti lauacri ablutione loti, parsimoniae deuotione ornati, ad aeterna gaudia perueniamus inlęsi. Per quem.

752 BENEDICTIO. Deus qui genus humanum quod primae uterus matris profuderat cęcum, suae incarnationis misterio reddidit

[1] *ne* supplied interlinearly.
[2] *lauacris* before correction.

inluminatum, ipse abstergat ab oculis uestri cordis omnem caliginem peccatorum. AMEN.

Et qui ex sputo fecit lutum, et ex ipso liniuit oculos a natiuitate ceci, ilico post lauationem reddidit uisum, ille uobis misericorditer tribuat lumen clarissimum sempiternum. AMEN.

/f. 104v / Dignosque uos in bonis operibus faciat, ubique uos a malo custodiat, et in paradyso post obitum lumen indefectiuum concedat. AMEN.

Quod ipse.

753 AD COMPLENDVM. Sacramenta quae sumpsimus domine deus noster, et spiritalibus nos repleant alimentis, et corporalibus tueantur auxiliis. Per.

754 SVPER POPVLVM. Pateant aures misericordiae tuae domine praecibus supplicantum, et ut petentibus desiderata concedas, fac eos quae tibi sunt placita postulare. Per.

CXL

FERIA V AD SANCTVM SILVESTRVM

755 Praesta quaesumus omnipotens deus, ut quos ieiunia uotiua castigant, ipsa quoque deuotio sancta laetificet, ut terrenis affectibus mitigatis, facilius caelestia capiamus. Per.

756 SVPER OBLATA. Purifica nos misericors deus, ut ecclesiae tuae praeces quae tibi gratae sunt pia munera deferentes, fiant expiatis mentibus gratiores. Per dominum.

757 PRAEFATIO. VD aeterne[1] deus. Cuius bonitas hominem condidit,[2] iustitia damnauit, misaericordia redemit. Te humiliter exoramus, ut sicut per inlicitos appetitus a beata regione decidimus, sic ad aeternam patriam per abstinentiam redeamus. Sicque moderetur tua miseratione nostra fragilitas, ut et transitoriis subsidiis nostra sustentetur mortalitas, et per

/f. 105r bonorum operum incrementa, / beata adquiratur inmortalitatis. Per quem.

---

[1] *aeternae* before correction.
[2] *in* erased.

758 AD COMPLENDVM. Caelestia dona capientibus quaesumus domine non ad iudicium peruenire patiaris, quod fidelibus tuis ad remedium prouidisti. Per dominum.

759 SVPER POPVLVM. Populi tui deus institutor et rector, peccata quibus inpugnatur expelle, ut semper tibi placitus, et tuo munimine sit securus. Per.

CXLI
FERIA VI AD SANCTVM EVSEBIVM

760 Deus qui ineffabilibus mundum renouas sacramentis, praesta quaesumus ut ecclesia tua aeternis proficiat institutis, et temporalibus non destituatur auxiliis. Per dominum.

761 SVPER OBLATA. Munera nos domine quaesumus oblata purificent, et te nobis iugiter faciant esse placatum. Per.

762 PRAEFATIO. VD per christum. Qui est dies aeternus, lux indeficiens, claritas sempiterna. Qui sic sequaces suos in luce praecepit ambulare, ut noctis aeternae ualeant caliginem euadere, et ad lucis patriam feliciter peruenire. Qui per humilitatem assumptae humanitatis lazarum fleuit, per diuinitatis potentiam uitae reddidit, genusque humanum quadrifica peccatorum mole obrutum, ad uitam reducit. Per quem petimus ieiunii obseruatione, a peccatorum nostrorum nexibus solui, aeternae uitae felicitati[1] reddi, et sanctorum coetibus / connumerari. Per quem.

f. 105v

763 BENEDICTIO. Benedicat uos omnipotens deus, qui per humilitatem assumptae humanitatis lazarum fleuit, per diuinitatis potentiam manus ac pedes dissoluit, uitaeque reddidit, ille uos a funibus peccatorum absoluat, ut caliginem noctis aeternae ualeatis euadere, et feliciter ad lucis patriam peruenire. AMEN.
Resuscitet uos de uitiorum sepulchris, qui eum quatriduanum iam foetentem lacrimabiliter ab inferis resuscitauit. AMEN.
Et qui ei in hoc mundo praestitit per aliquot spatium

---

[1] *felicitatis* before correction.

conditionem uiuendi, ipse in regno uobis aeterno tribuat cum illo mansionem sine fine uiuendi. AMEN.
Quod ipse.

764 POSTCOMMVNIO. Haec nos quaesumus domine participatio sacramenti, et propriis reatibus indesinenter expediat, et ab omnibus tueatur aduersis. Per.

765 SVPER POPVLVM. Da quaesumus omnipotens deus, ut qui infirmitatis nostrae conscii de tua pietate confidimus, sub tua semper pietate gaudeamus. Per dominum.

CXLII
SABBATO AD SANCTVM LAVRENTIVM FORIS MVROS

766 Fiat domine quaesumus per gratiam tuam fructuosus nostrae deuotionis affectus, quia tunc nobis proderunt suscepta ieiunia, si tuae sint placita pietati. Per.

/f. 106r **767** / Oblationibus quaesumus domine placare susceptis, et a te nostras etiam rebelles compelle propitius uoluntates. Per.

768 PRAEFATIO. VD aeterne[1] deus. Misericordiae dator, et totius bonitatis auctor. Qui ieiuniis, orationibus et elemosinis peccatorum remedia, et uirtutum omnium tribuis incrementa. Te humili deuotione praecamur, ut qui ad haec agenda saluberrimam dedisiti doctrinam, ad complendum indefessam tribuas efficaciam, ut oboedienter tua exequentes praecepta, feliciter tua capiamus promissa. Quem laudant.

769 AD COMPLENDVM. Tua nos domine quaesumus sancta purificent, et operationis suae perficiant esse placitos. Per.

770 SVPER POPVLVM. Deus qui sperantibus in te misereri potius eligis quam irasci, da nobis digne flere mala quae fecimus, ut tuae consolationis gratiam inuenire ualeamus. Per.

---

[1] *aeternae* before correction.

CXLIII
DIE DOMINICA DE PASSIONE AD SANCTVM PETRVM

771 Quaesumus omnipotens deus, familiam tuam propitius respice, ut te largiente regatur in corpore, et te seruante custodiatur in mente. Per.

772 SVPER OBLATA. Haec munera domine quaesumus et uincula nostrae prauitatis absoluant, et tuae nobis misericordiae dona concilient. Per.

f. 106v **773** PRAEFATIO. / VD aeternae deus. Maiestatem tuam propensius implorantes, ut quanto magis dies salutifere festiuitatis accedit, tanto deuotius ad eius digne caelebrandum proficiamus paschale mysterium. Per christum.

774 BENEDICTIO. Accendat in uobis dominus uim sui amoris, et per ieiuniorum obseruantiam infundat in uobis donum suae benedictionis. AMEN.
Sic ei parsimoniae uictimas offeratis, ut contriti ei cordis et humilitatis sacrificio placeatis. <AMEN.>
Quatinus oratio uestra, ieiuniis et elemosinae alis subuecta, ita ad aures uestri conditoris ascendat, ut uos aeternę beatitudinis heredes, et supernorum ciuium consortes efficiat. AMEN.
Quod ipse praestare dignetur.

775 AD COMPLENDVM. Adesto nobis domine deus noster, et quos tuis mysteriis recreasti, perpetuis defende praesidiis. Per.

CXLIIII
FERIA II AD SANCTVM CHRISOGONVM

776 Sanctifica quaesumus domine nostra ieiunia, et cunctarum nobis propitius indulgentiam largire culparum. Per.

777 SVPER OBLATA. Concede nobis domine deus noster, ut haec hostia salutaris, et nostrorum fiat purgatio delictorum, et tuae propitiatio maiestatis. Per.

778 PRAEFATIO. VD aeternae deus. Te suppliciter exorantes, ut sic
f. 107r nostra sanctificentur ieiunia / quo cunctorum nobis peccatorum proueniat indulgentia. Quatinus adpropinquante unigeniti filii

179

tui passione, bonorum operum tibi placere ualeamus exibitione. Per quem.

779 AD COMPLENDVM. Sacramenti tui quaesumus domine participatio salutaris, et purificationem nobis prebeat et medelam. Per dominum.

780 SVPER POPVLVM. Da quaesumus domine populo tuo salutem mentis et corporis, ut bonis operibus inherendo, tua semper mereamur protectione defendi. Per.

CXLV
FERIA III AD SANCTVM CYRIACVM

781 Nostra tibi domine quaesumus sint accepta ieiunia, quae nos et[1] expiando gratiae tuae dignos efficiant, et ad remedia perducant aeterna. Per.

782 SVPER OBLATA. Hostias tibi domine deferimus immolandas, quę temporalem consolationem significent, ut promissa certius non desperemus aeterna. Per.

783 PRAEFATIO. VD aeterne[2] deus. Et te deuotis mentibus supplicare, ut nos interius exteriusque restaures, et parsimonia salutaris, a peccatorum sordibus purges. Et quos illecebrosis[3] delectationibus non uis impediri, spiritalium uirtutum facias uigore muniri. Et sic in rebus transitoriis foueas, ut perpetuis inherere concedas. Per christum.

/f. 107v **784** AD COMPLENDVM. / Da quaesumus omnipotens deus, ut quae diuina sunt iugiter exequentes, donis mereamur caelestibus propinquare. Per dominum.

785 SVPER POPVLVM. Da nobis domine quaesumus perseuerantem in tua uoluntate famulatum, ut in diebus nostris et merito et numero populus tibi seruiens augeatur. Per.

---

[1] Supplied in margin.
[2] *aeternae* before correction.
[3] *inlecebrosis* before correction.

CXLVI
FERIA IIII AD SANCTVM MARCELLVM

786 Sanctificato hoc ieiunio deus, tuorum corda fidelium miserator inlustra, et quibus deuotionis prestas affectum, praebe supplicantibus pium benignus auditum. Per dominum.

787 SVPER OBLATA. Annuae misericors deus, ut hostias placationis et laudis, sincero tibi deferamus obsequio. Per.

788 PREFATIO. VD aeterne[1] deus. Et te supplici deuotione exorare, ut per ieiunia quae sacris institutis exequimur, a cunctis reatibus emundari mereamur. Tuamque percipere ualeamus propitiationem, qui praeparamur ad celebrandam unigeniti filii tui passionem. Per quem.

789 BENEDICTIO. Adesto omnipotens deus, huic populo tuo uerbis hodie mysticis informato, ut fiat illis inluminatio mentis, et praeparatio cordis. AMEN.
Proficiat in eis illa praetiosa benedictio tua plenius ad salutem, qui in hac die de sacris tuis cordis et corporis, susceperunt in aures. AMEN.

f. 108r

/ Sis illis protector et dominus in aeternum, sicut fuisti israhelitis praemonente moyse in subsidio, et aegyptiis in exterminio, ut non praemerentur oneroso seruitio. AMEN.
Et ne ulterius grauentur mole peccaminum, dignare circa eos diuinum impertiri praesidium, ut tibi famulari ualeant in aeternum. AMEN.
Quod ipse praestare dignetur.

790 AD COMPLENDVM. Caelestis doni benedictione percepta supplices te deus omnipotens depraecamur, ut hoc idem nobis et sacramenta causa sit et salutis. per.

791 SVPER POPVLVM. Adesto supplicationibus nostris omnipotens deus, et quibus fiduciam sperande pietatis indulges, consuete misericordiae tribue benignus effectum. Per.

---

[1] *aeternae* before correction.

CXLVII
FERIA V AD SANCTVM APOLLINAREM

792 Praesta quaesumus omnipotens deus, ut dignitas conditionis humanae, per immoderantiam sauciata, medicinalis parsimoniae studio reformetur. Per.

793 SVPER OBLATA. Domine deus noster qui in his potius creaturis quas ad fragilitatis nostrae subsidium condidisti, tuo quoque nomini munera iussisti dicanda constitui, tribuę quaesumus ut et uitae nobis praesentis auxilium, et aeternitatis efficiant sacramentum. Per.

794 PRĘFATIO. VD aeterne[1] deus. Qui sic nos tribuis sollemne tibi deferre ieiunium, ut indulgentiae tuae speremus nos percipere subsidium. / Sic nos instituis ad caelebranda paschalia festa, ut per haec adquiramus gaudia sempiterna. Per christum.

/f. 108v

795 AD COMPLENDVM. Quod ore sumpsimus domine mente capiamus, et de munere temporali, fiat nobis remedium sempiternum. Per.

796 SVPER POPVLVM. Esto quaesumus domine propitius plebi tuae, ut quae tibi non placent respuentes, tuorum potius repleantur[2] delectationibus mandatorum. Per.

CXLVIII
FERIA VI AD SANCTVM STEPHANVM

797 Cordibus nostris domine benignus infunde, ut peccata nostra castigatione uoluntaria cohibentes, temporaliter potius maceremur, quam suppliciis deputemur aeternis. Per.

798 SVPER OBLATA. Praesta nobis misericors deus, et[3] digne tuis seruire semper altaribus mereamur, et eorum perpetua participatione seruari. Per.

---

[1] *aeternae* before correction.
[2] *repleatur* before correction.
[3] *ut* before correction.

799 PRAEFATIO. VD aeterne deus. Cuius nos misericordia praeuenit ut bene agamus, subsequitur ne frustra agamus, accendit intentionem qua ad bona opera peragenda inardescamus tribuit efficatiam, qua haec ad perfectum perducere ualeamus. Tuam ergo clementiam indefessis uocibus obsecramus, ut nos ieiunii uictimis a peccatis mundatos, ad caelebrandum unigeniti filii tui domini nostri passionem facias esse deuotos. Per quem.

f. 109r   **800** / BENEDICTIO. Benedicat uos omnipotens deus, et mentes uestras ad boni actus intelligentiam, benignus institutor erudiat, et praestet uobis uelle quae praecipit, inspiret quae diligit, et tribuat quod oportet, atque omni uos bono spiritualium munerum cum praesentium rerum, subministratione locupletet. AMEN.

Vt uos in fide firmet, in temptatione adiuuet, in conuersatione castiget, in uirtute multiplicet, ex infirmitate releuet, in anxietate laetificet. AMEN.

In prosperitate praeparet, in iniquitate emendet, in tranquillitate sublimet, infundat gratiam, indulgeat offensam, ingerat disciplinam. AMEN.

Quod ipse praestare dignetur.

801 AD COMPLENDVM. Sumpti sacrificii domine perpetua nos tuitio non derelinquat[1], et noxia semper a nobis cuncta depellat. Per dominum.

802 SVPER POPVLVM. Concede quaesumus omnipotens deus, ut qui protectionis tuae gratiam quęrimus, liberati a malis omnibus, secura tibi mente seruiamus. Per.

CXLVIIII

SABBATO AD SANCTVM PETRVM QVANDO
ELEMOSINA DATVR

803 Proficiat quaesumus domine plebs tibi dicata piae deuotionis affectu, ut sacris actionibus erudita, quanto maiestati tuae fit gratior, tanto donis potioribus augeatur. Per.

---

[1]   *de* marked for omission.

804 SVPER OBLATA. Cunctis nos quaesumus domine reatibus et
periculis pro/pitiatus absolue, quos tanti mysterii tribuis esse
consortes. Per dominum.

/f. 109v

805 PRAEFATIO. VD aeternae deus. Cuius nos fides excitat, spes
erigit, caritas iungit. Cuius miseratio gratuita purificat, quos
conscientiae reatus accusat. Te igitur cum interno rugitu
depraecamur, ut carnalis alimoniae refrenatione castigati, ad
caelebrandum paschale mysterium, inueniamur idonei. Per
christum.

806 AD COMPLENDVM. Diuini satiati muneris largitate,
quaesumus domine deus noster, ut huius semper participatione
uiuamus. Per dominum.

807 SVPER POPVLVM. Tueatur quaesumus domine dextera tua
populum tuum depraecantem, et purificatum dignanter erudiat,
ut consolatione praesenti, ad futura bona proficiat. Per.

CL

808 BENEDICTIO IN RAMIS PALMARVM. Deus cuius filius pro
salute generis humani de cęlo descendit ad terras, et
adpropinquante hora passionis hierosolimam asino uenire, et a
turbis rex apellari ac laudari uoluit, + benedicere digneris hos
palmarum caeterarumue frondium ramos, ut omnes qui eos
laturi sunt, ita benedictionis tuae dono repleantur, quatinus in
hoc saeculo hostis antiqui temptamenta superare, et in futuro
cum palma uictoriae, / et fructu bonorum operum, tibi ualeant
apparere. Per.

/f. 110r

809 ITEM ALIA. Omnipotens sempiterne deus, qui dispersa
congregas, et congregata conseruas, qui populis tuis obuiam
iesum ramos portantibus benedixisti, benedic etiam hos ramos
palme ceterarumue frondium, quos tui famuli ad honorem
nominis tui et benedictionem suscipiunt, ut quocumque
introducti fuerint, tuae benedictionis consequantur effectum, ut
omni aduersa ualitudine effugata, dextera tua protegat quos
redemit. Per dominum.

810 ITEM ALIA. Deus qui temporibus noae famuli tui, per columbam ramum oliuę uirentibus foliis in ore deferentem post diluuii effusionem, pacem hominibus redditam nuntiare uoluisti, et qui unigenito tuo domino nostro hierosolimam properanti, pueros hebreorum cum ramis palmarum obuiam uenientes, laudesque concinnentes, osanna concrepare uoluisti, + benedicere, + et sanctificare digneris hos ramos palmarum, diuersarumque frondium uel florum, ut accipientes in manibus nostris cum palma uictoriae, et fructu bonorum operum, tibi placere ualeamus, atque ad resurrectionis gloriam, te largiente peruenire mereamur. Per.

811 MODO LEGENDVM EST EVANGELIVM A DIACONO, SECVNDVM MATHEVM. / In illo tempore. Cum adpropinquasset iesus hierosolimis, et uenisset bethphage ad montem, et reliqua.

f. 110v

812 DEINDE ACCIPIVNT PALMAS ET RAMOS ARBORVM CANENDE SVNT ANTIPHONAE IN CIRCVITV ECCLESIAE VEL IN CIRCVITV CIVITATIS.

CLI

MISSA IN DIE

813 Omnipotens sempiterne deus, qui humano generi ad imitandum humilitatis exemplum, saluatorem nostrum carnem sumere et crucem subire fecisti, concede nobis[1] propitius, et[2] patientię ipsius habere documenta, et resurrectionis eius[3] consortia mereamur. Per.

814 SVPER OBLATA. Concede quaesumus domine, ut oculis tuae maiestatis munus oblatum, et gratiam nobis deuotionis obtineat, et effectum beatae perennitatis adquirat. Per.

815 [4]PRAEFATIO. VD per christum. Per quem nobis indulgentia largitur, et pax per omne saeculum praedicatur. Traditur cunctis

---

[1] Supplied interlinearly.
[2] *ut* before correction.
[3] Supplied in margin.
[4] Partly neumed.

credentibus disciplina, ut sanctificatos non possit dies uenturus excipere. Cum angelis[1].

816 BENEDICTIO. Benedicat uobis omnipotens deus, cui et ieiuniorum maceratione, et praesentium dierum obseruatione placere studeatis. AMEN.
Concedatque uobis ut sicut ei cum ramis palmarum ceterarumue frondium praesentari studistis, ita cum palma uictoriae et fructu bonorum operum / ei post obitum apparere ualeatis. AMEN.
Quique unigeniti filii eius passionem puro corde creditis, mente deuota uenerari studeatis, ad resurrectionis eius festa, et uestrae remunerationis praemia ipsius fulti munimine ueniatis. AMEN.
Quod ipse praestare dignetur.

/f. 111r

817 POSTCOMMVNIONEM. Per huius domine operationem misterii, et uitia nostra purgentur, et iusta desideria compleantur. Per.

CLII
FERIA II STATIO AD SANCTVM NEREVM ET
ACHILLEVM

818 Da quaesumus omnipotens deus, ut qui in tot aduersis ex nostra infirmitate deficimus, intercedente unigeniti filii tui passione respiremus. Per.

819 SVPER OBLATA. Haec sacrificia nos omnipotens deus, potenti uirtute mundatos, ad suum faciant puriores uenire principium. Per dominum.

820 PRAEFATIO. VD per christum. Cuius nos humanitas colligit, humilitas aerigit, traditio obsoluit, poena redemit. Crux saluificat, sanguis emaculat, caro saginat. Per quem te summe pater cum ieiuniorum obsequiis obsecramus, ut ad eius caelebrandam passionem, purificatis mentibus accedamus. Per quem.

---

[1] *Cum angelis* added by a later scribe and neumed.

821 BENEDICTIO. Omnipotens deus qui unigeniti sui passione tribuit uobis humilitatis exemplum, concedat uobis per eandem humilitatem percipere suę bene/dictionis ineffabile donum. AMEN.
Ipsius resurrectionis percipiamus consortia, cuius patientiae ueneramini documenta. AMEN.
Quo ab eo sempiternae uitae munus percipiatis, per cuius temporalem mortem aeternam uos euadere creditis. AMEN.
Quod ipse.

f. 111v

822 AD COMPLENDVM. Praebeant nobis domine diuinum tua sanctam feruorem, quo eorum pariter et actu delectemur et fructu. Per dominum.

823 SVPER POPVLVM. Adiuua nos deus salutaris noster, et ad beneficia recolenda, quibus nos instaurare dignatus es, tribuę uenire gaudentes. Per.

CLIII
FERIA III STATIO AD SANCTAM PRISCAM

824 Omnipotens sempiternę deus, da nobis ita dominicę passionis sacramenta peragere, ut indulgentiam percipere mereamur. Per.

825 SVPER OBLATA. Sacrificia nos quaesumus domine propensius ita restaurent, quae medicinalibus sunt instituta ieiuniis. Per dominum.

826 PRA<E>FATIO. VD per christum. Cuius salutiferę passionis, et gloriosę resurrectionis dies adpropinquare noscuntur, in quibus et antiqui hostis superbia triumphatur, et nostrae redemptionis mysterium caelebratur. Vnde poscimus tuam inmensam clementiam, ut sicut in eo solo / consistit totius nostrae saluationis summa, ita per eum tibi sit ieiuniorum et actuum nostrorum semper uictima grata. Per.

/f. 112r

827 AD COMPLENDVM. Sanctificationibus tuis omnipotens deus, et uitia nostra curentur[1], et remedia nobis sempiterna proueniant. Per.

[1] A long erasure follows.

828 SVPER POPVLVM. Tua nos misericordia deus, et ab omni subreptione uetustatis expurget, et capaces sanctae nouitatis efficiat. Per.

FERIA IIII STATIO AD SANCTAM MARIAM

829 Praesta quaesumus omnipotens deus, ut qui nostris excessibus incessanter affligimur, per unigeniti tui passionem liberemur. Per dominum.

830 ALIA. Deus qui pro nobis filium tuum crucis patibulum subire uoluisti, ut inimici a nobis expelleres potestatem, concede nobis famulis tuis, ut resurrectionis gratiam consequamur. Per.

831 SVPER POPVLVM. Purifica nos misericors deus, ut ecclesiae tuae praeces quae tibi gratę sunt pia munera deferentes, fiant expiatis mentibus gratiores. Per.

832 PRAEFATIO. VD per christum. Qui innocens pro impiis uoluit pati, et pro sceleratis indebite condempnari, cuius mors delicta nostra detersit, et resurrectio iustificationem nobis exhibuit. Per quem tuam pietatem supplices exoramus, ut sic nos hodie a peccatis emacules, ut cras uenerabilis caenae dapibus saties. Hodie accipies confessio/nem nostrorum peccaminum, et cras tribuas spiritualium incrementa donorum. Hodie ieiuniorum nostrorum uota suscipias, et cras nos ad sacratissimae caenae conuiuium introducas. Per quem.

/f. 112v

833 BENEDICTIO. Deus qui pro mundi salute uerbum caro factus es, et habitasti totus in nobis, qui post caenae mysterium traditori perfido pium dedisti osculum, pro uita omnium pius uoluisti agnus occidi, respice uota supplicum, quia tua uirtute laetatur multitudo angelorum. AMEN.
Da illis toto corde te colere, seque cauere, te semper diligere, et se ubique munire. AMEN.
Adsis protector ecclesiae, qui pro nobis passus es iniurias sinagogae. AMEN.
Quod ipse.

834 AD COMPLENDVM. Largire sensibus nostris omnipotens deus, ut per temporalem filii tui mortem quam misteria ueneranda testantur, uitam nobis dedisse perpetuam confidamus. Per dominum.

835 SVPER POPVLVM. Respice domine quaesumus super hanc familiam tuam, pro qua dominus noster iesus christus non dubitauit manibus tradi nocentium, et crucis subire tormentum. Per dominum nostrum.

CLV
INCIPIT ORDO IN CAENAE DOMINI

836 [1]IN DIE IN CAENA DOMINI, VENIENS IN SACRARIVM EPISCOPVS, ET INDVENS SE SACRIS VESTIBVS

/f. 113r EXCEPTO PLANETA / MISCEAT BALSAMVM CVM OLEO VNDE CHRISMA CONFICI DEBET, ET PVLSATIS SIGNIS CANATVR AD MISSAM. AN. Nos autem gloriari oportet. PS. Deus misereatur.

837 ET PROCEDAT EPISCOPVS DE SACRARIO SINE PALLIO CVM DIACONIBVS .VII[TEM]. QVI OMNES SINT DALMATICIS INDVTI, ET TOTIDEM SVBDIACONI ET ACOLITI CVM TVRIBVLIS AC CEROFERARIIS ET SALVTATO ALTARI, NON ASCENDAT IPSA DIE AD SEDEM, SED IVXTA ALTARE VSQVE AD HORAM SESSIONIS STET. POSTQVAM CANATVR KYRRIE. QVA EXPLETA, DICAT EPISCOPVS. Gloria in excelsis deo. ET POSTEA PAX VOBISCVM, ETIAM NON SOLEAT DICIRE EPISCOPVS NISI TANTVMMODO DIEBVS FESTIS. DEINDE SEQVITVR ORATIO COLLECTA. Deus a quo et iudas. QVA FINITA, SEDEAT EPISCOPVS, ET LEGATVR EPISTOLA, ET CANTATVR RESPONSORIVM.

838 Deus a quo et iudas reatus sui poenam, et confessionis suae latro praemium sumpsit, concede nobis tuae propitiationis effectum, ut sicut in passione sua iesus christus dominus noster diuersa utrisque[2] intulit stipendia meritorum, ita nobis ablato uetustatis errore, resurrectionis suae gratiam largiatur. Qui tecum.

---

[1] Text of nos 836, 837 and 842 in alternating lines of orange and brown.
[2] *utriusque* before correction.

839 EPISTOLA. Conuenientibus uobis in unum.

840 R. Christus factus est pro nobis. V. Propter quod et deus exaltauit.

841 EVANG. Ante diem festum paschae. Sciens iesus quia uenit eius hora. VSQVE. ut quemadmodum ego feci uobis ita et uos faciatis.

/f. 113v

842 POSTEA SEDEAT EPISCOPVS IN SEDE IVXTA ALTARE, ET NON DICAT DOMINVS VOBISCVM, SED ARCHIDIACONVS / LEGAT CORAM EO ET POPVLO ROTVLAM, IN QVA CONTINENTVR QVAEDAM INDITA DE POENITENTVM RECONCILIATIONE. POST HOC ORET EPISCOPVS ANTE SANCTVM ALTARE. HOC EXPLETO, PERGAT AD AMBONEM, ET ASCENDAT IN EVM. FACIATQVE SERMONEM TAM POPVLIS QVAM POENITENTIBVS, SICVT ORDO PRAECIPIT ROMANVS. TVNC REDEAT ANTE ALTARE, ET PROSTERNENS SE TAM ILLE QVAM OMNIS POPVLVS ETIAM POENITENTES, TAM ILLI QVI INTVS SVNT QVAM EXTRA. ET CANTENT .VII. PSALMOS. FINITIS HIS PSALMIS, SVRGAT SOLVS ET DICIT HAS ORATIONES, TAM PRO SE QVAM PRO POPVLO.

843 Adesto domine supplicationibus nostris, et me qui etiam misericordia tua primus indigeo clementer exaudi, mihique quem non electione meriti, sed dono gratiae tuae constituisti operis huius ministrum, da fidutiam tui muneris gratiam exequendi, et ipse in nostro ministerio, quod tuae pietatis est operare. Per dominum.

844 ALIA. Praesta quaesumus domine his famulis tuis dignum poenitentiae fructum, ut ecclesiae tuae sanctae reconciliati, a cuius integritate deuiarant peccando, admissorum reddantur innoxii ueniam consequendo. Per dominum nostrum iesum christum filium tuum.

CLVI

/f. 114r **845** ABSOLVTIO. / Sicut principali[1] sententia constat, quia in multis offendimus omnes, ingemiscimus. Ita principali sententia

---

[1] *principalis* before correction.

consolamur, quia si confiteamur peccata nostra, fidelis et iustus est iesus christus, conditor et redemptor ac saluator noster, quem habemus aduocatum iustum apud patrem, et est propitiatio pro peccatis nostris, et interpellat pro nobis fideliter confitentibus, et dimittat nobis peccata nostra, et emundaet nos ab omni iniquitate. Quapropter fratres nostri confitentes peccata uestra per ecclesiasticam apostolicę auctoritatis potestatem, quam dominus noster iesus christus tradidit discipulis suis, et apostolis suis dicens. Accipite spiritum sanctum, quorum remiseritis peccata, remittuntur eis, et per eosdem apostolos suos, ipsorum successoribus quorum uices licet indigni tenemus, etsi non merito tamen nomine atque officii susceptione eandemque potestatem donauit, et in se credenti fideliter dixit. Fiat tibi secundum fidem tuam. Gratia et potentia sua et[1] uirtute sancti spiritus, qui est remissio omnium peccatorum, dimittat nobis omnia peccata nostra, liberet nos ab omni malo, conseruet nos in omni opere bono, et perducat nos ad uitam aeternam, et ad sanctorum consortium supernorum ciuium. Amen.

f. 114v   **846** / ALIA. [2]Deus humani generis, benignissime conditor et misericordissime reformator, qui hominem inuidia diaboli ab aeternitate deiectum, unici filii tui sanguine redemisti, uiuifica hunc famulum tuum quem nullatenus mori desideras, et qui non derelinquis deuium, assume correctum, moueant pietatem tuam quaesumus domine huic famulo tuo .ill. lacrimosa suspiria, tu eius medere uulneribus, tu iacentis manum porrige salutarem, ne ecclesia tua aliqua sui corporis portione uastetur, nec grex tuus detrimentum sustineat, ne de familiae tuae damno inimici exultet, ne renatum lauacro salutari mors secunda possideat. Tibi ergo domine supplices praeces, tibi fletum cordis effundimus, tu parce confitentibus, ut sic in hac mortalitate peccata sua te adiuuante defleant, quatinus in tremendi iudicii die, sententiam dampnationis aeternę euadat, et nesciat quod terret in tenebris, quod stridet in flammis, atque ab erroribus uia[3] ad iter reuersi[4] iustitiae, nequaquam ultra uulneribus saucietur, sed integrum sit

---

[1] Supplied interlinearly.
[2] Plural forms (later) provided interlinearly throughout.
[3] A final letter erased.
[4] A final letter erased.

eis adque perpetuum, et quod gratia tua contulit, et quod misericordia reformauit. Per.

847 ITEM ALIA. [1]Praecor domine clementiam tuam, ut huic famulo tuo peccata sui et facinora / confitenti donare ueniam, et praeteritorum criminum culpas relaxare digneris, qui humeris tuis ouem perditam reduxisti, qui publicani confessione placatus es. Tu etiam domine in huic famulo tuo praecibus benignus aspira, ut in flebili confessione persistens pietatem tuam caeleriter et indifficulter exorent, ac sacris altaribus mysteriis restituti[2], aeternae uitae praemia consequatur. Per.

/f. 115r

848 ITEM ALIA. Deus qui iustitia[3] tuae legis misericordiae semper multiplicationem moderaris, dum delinquentibus poenitentiam, dum ab his etiam prouidentiae tuae dona non subtrahis, et uindictam miserando suspendis. Per.

849 ALIA. Deus misericors, deus clemens, qui secundum multitudinem miserationum tuarum peccata poenitentium deles, et praeteritorum culpas, uenia[4] remissionis euacuas, respice propitius super hos famulos tuos et has famulas tuas, et remissionem sui omnium peccatorum suorum toto corde confessione poscentes depraecatus exaudi, renoua in eis piissime pater, quicquid terrena fragilitate corruptum, uel quicquid diabolica fraude uiolatum est, et in unitate corporis ecclesiae tuę perfecta remissione restituae, miserere domine gemituum, miserere lacrimarum, et non haben/tes[5] fiduciam nisi in tua misericordia, ad sacramentum reconciliationis admitte. Per.

/f. 115v

850 ALIA. Maiestatem tuam domine supplices depraecemur, ut his famulis tuis .ill. longo squalore poenitentiae maceratis, miserationis tuae ueniam largiri digneris, ut nuptiali ueste recepta, ad regalem mensam unde eiecti fuerant, mereantur introire. Per dominum.

---

1 Plural forms provided interlinearly throughout.
2 A final letter erased.
3 *iustitiae* before correction.
4 *ueniam* before correction.
5 Final letters over an erasure.

851 ITEM ALIA. Absoluimus uos uice beati petri apostolorum principis, cui dominus ligandi atque soluendi potestatem dedit, et quantum ad uos pertinet accusatio, et ad nos remissio, sit uobis deus omnipotens uita et salus, et omnium peccatorum uestrorum indultor, et qui uobis compunctionem cordis dedit, det ueniam peccatorum, longeuamque uobis atque felicem uitam in hoc saeculo largiatur, et in futuro cum christo et omnibus sanctis eius, sine fine manentem. Per eundem dominum nostrum.

852 [1]TVNC CONVERTAT SE EPISCOPVS AD ALTARE, ET SALVTAT POPVLVM ET DICIT. DOMINVS VOBISCVM. RESP. ET CVM SPIRITV TVO. OREMVS. ET TVNC CANATVR OFFERTORIVM, CVM VERSIS AC OFFERVNT PRESBITERI SACRA ILLA OBLATA. QVIBVS EXPLETIS, INCIPATVR MISSA SOLITO ORDINE.

853 OF. DEXTERA DOMINI FECIT VIRTVTEM.

854 SECRETA. Ipse tibi quaesumus domine sanctae pater omnipotens deus, sacrificium / nostrum reddat acceptum, qui discipulis suis in sui commemoratione hoc fieri, hodierna traditione monstrauit. Iesus christus dominus noster. Qui tecum.

/f. 116r

855 PRAEFATIO. VD aeterne[2] deus. Et clementiam tuam suppliciter exorare, ut spiritalis lauacri baptismo renouandis, creaturam crismatis in sacramentum perfectę salutis uiteque confirmes. Vt sanctificatione unctionis infusa, corruptione primae natiuitatis absorta, sanctum uniuscuiusque templum, acceptabilis uitae innocens odor redolescat. Vt secundum constitutionis tuae sacramentum regio, et sacerdotali propheticoque honore perfusi, uestimento incorrupti muneris induantur. Per christum.

856 ALIA. [3]VD per christum dominum nostrum. Quem in hac nocte inter sacras ępulas increpantem, mens sibi conscia traditoris ferre non potuit, sed apostolorum relicto consortio, sanguinis

---

[1] In alternating lines of orange and brown.
[2] *aeternae* before correction.
[3] Partly neumed.

/f. 116v

pretium a iudaeis accepit, ut uitam perderet quam distraxit. Caenauit igitur hodie proditor mortem suam, et cruentis manibus panem de manu saluatoris exiturus accepit. Vt saginatum cybo maior pęna constringeret, quem nec sacrati cybi collatio[1] ab scelere reuocaret. Patitur itaque dominus noster iesus christus filius tuus, cum hoste nouissimum participare conuiuium, a quo se nouerat continuo esse tradendum. / Vt exemplum innocentiae mundo relinqueret, et passionem suam pro saeculi redemptione suppleret. Pascit igitur mitis deus inmitem iudam, et sustinet pius crudelem conuiuam. Qui merito laquei sui[2] periturus erat, quia de magistri sanguine cogitarat. O dominum per omnia patientem, o agnum inter suas epulas mitem. Cybum eius iudas in ore ferebat, et quibus eum traderet persecutores aduocabat. Sed filius tuus dominus noster tamquam pia hostia, et immolari se tibi pro nobis patienter permisit, et peccatum quod mundus commiserat relaxauit. Per quem.

857 Communicantes et diem sacratissimum caelebrantes, quo dominus noster iesus christus pro nobis est traditus. Sed et memoriam uenerantes.

858 Hanc igitur oblationem seruitutis nostrae, sed et cunctae familiae tuae, quam tibi offerimus ob diem in qua dominus noster iesus christus tradidit discipulis suis corporis et sanguinis sui misteria caelebranda, quaesumus domine ut placatus accipias.

859 Qui pridie quam pro nostra omnium salute pateretur, hoc est hodie, accepit panem in sanctas ac uenerabiles.

860 [3]DEINDE TRES ACCOLITI PROCEDANT DE SACRARIO INDVTI SINDONIS CVM AMPVLLIS TRIBVS ET VNAQVAQVE HABEAT BREVICVLVM ID EST CRISMA SANCTA IN VNO / IN ALIO OLEO AD BAPTIZANDVM. IN TERTIO OLEO AD INFIRVMVM. ET CANATVR SECRETO

/f. 117r

---

[1] Letters erased in the middle of the word.
[2] *laqueo* suo before correction.
[3] Text of nos 860, 861, 863, 865, 866 in alternating lines of orange and brown.

SECVNDVM ORDINEM. Vsque sed ueniam quaesumus largitor admitte.

861 ET TVNC SVBDIACONVS ACCIPIENS SINDONEM AB ACCOLITO VBI EST OLEO AD INFIRMVM, ET CONVERTENS AD DIACONVM, ET OFFERAT DIACONO. DIACONVS AVTEM ACCIPIENS ITERVM SINDONEM ET INVOLVENS SE ACCIPIENSQVE AMPVLLAM DE MANV SVBDIACONI, ET HVMILLIME SVBMINISTRAT EPISCOPO. EPISCOPVS AVTEM DEOSCVLETVR AMPVLLAM, ET SVFFLET IN EA TER, ET BENEDICAT, VT IPSI CIRCVMSTANTES AVDIRE POSSINT.

862 Emitte domine spiritum sanctum tuum paraclytum de caelis in hanc pinguedinem oliuae quam de uiridi ligno producere dignatus es ad refectionem corporis, ut tua sancta benedictione sit omni ungenti tangenti tutamentum mentis et corporis, ad euacuandos omnes dolores, omnesque infirmitates, omnem egritudinem corporis, unxisti sacerdotes, reges, prophetas, et martyres, crisma tuum perfectum domine a te benedictum, permanens in uisceribus nostris, in nomine domini nostri iesu christi. Per quem haec omnia domine semper bona creas.

/f. 117v **863** TOLLITVR IAM DICTVM OLEVM A DIACONO AB ALTARI QVOD ACCIPIAT SVBDIACONVS AB / EODEM DIACONO. ET ALTER DIACONVS ACCIPIAT CALICEM, ET TVNC AD VLTIMVM PERAGATVR SECRETA MISSA IN ORDINE SVO, VSQVE PAX DOMINI DICATVR. DICIT DIACONVS. Humiliate uos ad benedictionem. QVIBVS HVMILIATIS TRADATVR SANCTA BENEDICTIO AB EPISCOPO CVNCTIS.

CLVII
864 BENEDICTIO IPSO DIE SVPER POPVLVM. Benedicat uos deus qui per unigeniti filii sui passionem, uetus pascha in nouum uoluit conuerti, concedatque uobis ut expurgato ueteris fermenti contagio noua in uobis perseueret conspersio. AMEN.
Et qui ad caelebrandam redemptoris nostri caenam mente deuota conuenistis, aeternarum dapium uobiscum aepulas reportetis. AMEN.

Ipsiusque opitulante clementia mundemini a sordibus peccatorum, qui ad insinuandum humilitatis exemplum lauare pedes uoluit discipulorum. AMEN.

Quod ipse prestare dignetur.

865 ET TVNC DICIT PAX DOMINI. DEINDE SECEDAT PARVMPER IVXTA ALTARE PONTIFEX, ET DIACONVS ACCIPIAT PARTEM ALIQVAM SVPRA ALTARE, DE DOMINI CORPORE CVM PATENA AC TRADAT EAM ACCOLITO, QVI DEFERAT ILLAM ANTE EPISCOPVM. ET DIACONVS CVM CALICE CVM PRETIOSO SANGVINE, QVIBVS APORTATIS COMMVNICAT IPSE[1] EPISCOPVS SOLVS TANTVMMODO DE EO SIMVL CVM SANGVINE
/f. 118r PRETIOSO. AC POSTEA / REPORTETVR SVB ALTARE, ID EST SACROSANCTVM CORPVS SANGVISQVE PRAETIOSISSIMVS, ET PONATVR CALIX IN QVO CONTINETVR SANGVIS DOMINI, IN DEXTERA PARTE ALTARIS, ET PATENA CVM CORPORE DOMINI IN MEDIO, ET DEFERATVR ALIVS CALIX VACVVS, QVI PONATVR EX SINISTRA ALTARIS PARTE, ET TVNC COOPERIATVR CORPVS IAM DICTVM AC SANGVINIS DOMINI DE SINDONE MVNDA AB EPISCOPO ET DIACONO.

866 STETQVE ITERVM EPISCOPVS ANTE ALTARE VT ANTEA ET ORET, ET DIACONI STENT ERECTI SIMVL CVM SVB DIACONIBVS RETRO TERGA ILLIVS, QVIBVS ASTANTIBVS ITA VELVTI STETERANT IN ORDINE, ACCIPIAT SVBDIACONVS AB ACCOLITO AMPVLLAM VBI MIXTVM FVERAT BALSAMVM CVM OLEO. QVAE HABET BREVICVLVM CHRISMATIS DE EADEM SINDONE SE INVOLVENS. ET ITERVM DIACONVS A SVBDIACONO SIMILITER REINVOLVENS, ET DEFERATVR AB EADEM DIACONO EADEM AMPVLLA ANTE ALTARE. QVA ALLATA, FACIAT SVPER EAM TER SIGNVM CRVCIS, SVFFLETQVE IN EA TER, ET TVNC BENEDICAT CRISMA SICVTI MOS EST.

---

[1]   *SE* before correction.

867 CONSECRATIO CRISMATIS. Oremus fratres karissimi, ut deus omnipotens hoc misterium corporis filii tui domini nostri iesu christi gerulum benedictione sanctificationis tutamine defensionis et donationis implere dignetur orantibus nobis. Per eundem.

f. 118v **868** ALIA. / Omnipotens sancta trinitas deus manibus nostris opem tuae benedictionis infunde, ut per nostram benedictionem hoc uasculum sanctificetur et corporis christi nouum sepulchrum spiritus sancti gratia perficiatur. Per.

INCIPIT BENEDICTIO CRISMA PRINCIPALIS.
Sursum corda. R. Habemus ad dominum.
Gratias agamus domino deo nostro. R. Dignum et iustum est.

869 VD aeterne[1] deus. Qui in principio inter caetera bonitatis et pietatis tuae munera[2] terram producere fructifera ligna iussisti[3], interque huius pinguissimi liquoris ministre oliuae nasceretur quarum fructus sacro crismati deseruiret. Nam et dauid prophetico spiritu gratiae tuae sacramenta praenoscens, uultus nostros in oleo exhilarandos esse cantauit. Et cum mundi crimina diluuii quondam expiaret effusio similitudinem futuri muneris columba demonstrans, per ramum oliuae pacem terris redditam nuntiauit. Quod in nouissimis diebus uel temporibus manifestis est, affectibus declaratum, cum baptismatis aquis omnium criminum commissa delentibus haec olei unctio uultus nostros iocundos efficit ac serenos, inde etiam moysi famulo tuo mandatum dedisti, ut aaron fratrem suum prius aqua lotum, per f. 119r infusionem huius ungenti constitueret sacerdotem. / Accessit ad hoc amplior honor cum filius tuus iesus christus dominus noster lauari a iohanne undis iordanicis exegisset. Vt spiritu sancto in columbe similitudinem desuper misso, unigenitum tuum in quo tibi obtime complacuisset testimonio subsequentis uocis ostenderes. Et hoc illud esse manifestissime comprobares, quod eum oleo laetitiae prae consortibus suis ungendum dauid propheta caecinisset. Te igitur deprecamur domine sanctae pater omnipotens aeternae deus, per eundem iesum christum

---

[1] *aeternae* before correction.
[2] *munere* before correction.
[3] A final letter erased.

dominum nostrum filium tuum, ut huius creaturae pinguedinem sanctificare tua benedictione digneris, et sancti spiritus ei admiscere uirtutem cooperante potentia christi tui, a cuius sancto nomine chrisma nomen accepit. Vnde unxisti sacerdotes reges prophetas, et martyres, ut sit his qui renati sunt ex aqua et spiritu sancto, chrisma salutis eosque aeternae uitae participes, et caelestis gloriae facias esse consortes. Per eundem.

870 [1]QVO BENEDICTO, REMOVEATVR AB ALTARI, A IAM SEPEFACTO DIACONO, AC TRADAT SVBDIACONO. SVBDIACONVS QVOQVE ACCOLITO TRADAT, ET PERGAT STARE IN DEXTERAM PARTEM ALTARIS, HABENS EANDEM AMPVLLAM COOPERTAM DE SINDONE EX QVO EST INVOLVTVS. DEINDE ACCIPIAT SVBDIACONVS AB ALIO ACCOLITO OLEVM AD BABTIZANDVM, DE EANDEM SINDONE SE INVOLVENS, /f. 119v ET QVOD ACCIPIT DIACONVS, SIMILITER / INVOLVTVS, ET DEFERAT ILLVD ANTE ALTARE, IPSOQVE APORTATO FACIAT SVPER ILLVD, TER, CRVCIS SIGNVM, SVFFLETQVE IN EO TER, AC TVNC BENEDICAT ILLVD TACITE EPISCOPVS.

871 ORATIO. Deus qui uirtute sancti spiritus tui inbecillarum mentium rudimenta confirmas, te oramus domine ut uenturis ad beatae regenerationis lauacrum tribuas, per unctionem istius creaturae purgationem mentis et corporis, ut si quae illis aduersantium spirituum inhesere reliquiae ad tactu sanctificati olei huius abscedant. Nullus spiritalibus nequitiis locus, nulla refugiis uirtutibus sit facultas, nulla insidiantibus malis latendi licentia relinquatur. Sed uenientibus ad fidem seruis tuis, et sancti spiritus tui, operatione mundandis, sit unctionis huius praeparatio, utilis ad salutem quam etiam caelestis regenerationis natiuitate in sacramento sunt baptismatis adepturi. Per dominum.

872 QVO BENEDICTO REPORTETVR A DIACONO AB ALTARI, ET TRADATVR SVBDIACONO, ET RVRSVS SVBDIACONVS ACCOLITO TRADAT, QVIBVS OMNIBVS

---

[1] Text of nos 870, 872 and 873 in alternating lines of orange and brown.

PATRATIS, STET EPISCOPVS IN DEXTERAM PARTEM
ALTARIS CORNV, ET DEFERATVR CHRISMA AB
ACCOLITO ILLI AD OSCVLANDVM. ANTEQVAM AVTEM
DEOSCVLETVR, INNVAT CANTORI INCIPIT AGNVS DEI.
DEOSCVLATOQVE AB EPISCOPO CHRISMATE,
SECEDAT ACCOLITVS / CVM CHRISMATE PROPE
CHORVM IN DEXTERAM PARTEM, ET CANTATO TER
AGNVS DEI, ACCEDANT PRIMVM PRESBITERI,
VNVSQVISQVE IN ORDINE SVO AD DEOSCVLANDVM
SANCTVM CHRISMA, ET TVNC PERGANT AD
EPISCOPVM COMMVNICARE DE SACRO DOMINI
CORPORE. QVO TRADENTE ILLIS EPISCOPO,
DEOSCVLARI DEBET VNVMQVEMQVE PRESBITERVM
ET PERGAT AD CALICEM SANGVINIS QVI IN SINISTRA
TENEATVR, VT AVTEM PRESBITERI INCIPERINT
COMMVNICARE, INCIPIT CANTOR COMMVNIONEM.
Hoc corpus quod pro uobis. PS. Iudica me. ET POST HANC
CANATVR. ALIA. Dominus iesus postquam caenauit. PS. Beati
inmaculati.

f. 120r

873 ET SIC DEMVM SEQVENS ORDO, CHRISMA AVTEM
ADORETVR A CVNCTIS ET DEOSCVLETVR AC
COMMVNICENT OMNES CLERICI, ET POST HOS VIRI,
AC FEMINE, ET INTERIM DONEC POPVLVS
COMMVNICET, PVLSANTVR SIGNIS VESPERTINE
CANANTVR.

874 ET CANTOR INCIPIT. A. Calicem. <P>S. Credidi. A. Cum his qui
oderunt. PS. Ad dominum cum tribularer. A. Ab hominibus iniquis. PS.
Eripe me. A. Custodi me a laqueo. PS. Domine clamaui. A.
Considerabam. PS. Voce mea. A. De manu filiorum. PS. Benedictus
dominus. V. Christus factus est pro nobis. IN EVANGELIVM.
Caenantibus autem. A. Accepto pane. A. Si male locutus sum.

875 AD COMPLENDVM. Refecti uitalibus alimentis quaesumus
domine deus noster, ut quod tempore nostrae mortalitatis
exequimur, inmortalitatis tuae munere consequamur. Per.

876 DICAT EPISCOPVS. Dominus uobiscum. R. Et cum spiritu tuo. ET
DIACONVS. Ite missa est. R. Deo gratias.

199

877 ET EAT VNVSQVISQVE AD MENSAM, DEINDE POST REFECTIONEM PRANDII, LAVANTVR PEDES, ET DVM HAEC AGANTVR, CANANTVR HAEC ANTIPHONAE, CVM RECIPROCIS PSALMIS. / Mandatum nouum. PS. Beati inmaculati. A. In diebus illis. PS. Magnus dominus. A. Postquam surrexit dominus. PS. Deus misereatur nostri. A. Ante diem festum. A. Vos uocatis me. A. Si ego dominus et magister. PS. Beati immaculati. A. Diligamus nos inuicem. A. Ecce quam bonus. A. In hoc cognoscent omnes. PS. Magnus dominus.

/f. 120v

YMNVM DE PASSIONE DOMINI

878 [1]Tellus ac ethra iubilant[2] in magni caena principis quę protoplausti pectora[3], uitae purgauit ferculo[4].

Hac nocte factor omnium potenti sat misterio[5] carnem suam cum sanguine in aescam transfert animae.

A celsis surgens dapibus praebens formam mortalibus humilitatis gratia petri petens uestigia.

Pallet[6] seruus[7] obsequio, cum angelorum dominum ferendo limpham[8] linteo cernit caeno[9] procumbere.

Permitte simon ablui acta figurant mistica dum summus ima[10] baiulat[11], quid cinisque seruit cineri[12].

Trux luppe iuda pessimę fers agno[13] miti basia dans membra loris[14] regia que sorde[15] tergunt saecula.

---

[1] Partly neumed.
[2] *iubilent* before correction.
[3] *pectore* before correction.
[4] *fercula* before correction.
[5] *potentis at mysteria* before correction.
[6] *Pollet* before correction.
[7] *seruuus* before correction.
[8] *limphum* before correction.
[9] *caena* before correction.
[10] A letter erased in the middle of the word.
[11] *baiulot* before correction.
[12] *cinisque dolus ruminat* before correction. The missing sixth verse supplied in the margin (and neumed) by the original scribe: Laeua tortoris accubat, uerbique fauos aggerat quos inter hostem denotat necis quod dolos ruminat.
[13] *uaesana* before correction.
[14] *laris* before correction.
[15] A final letter erased.

Nexi soluuntur hodie carnis ac[1] cordis carcere, unguem[2] sacratur[3] chrismatis spes inde crescit miseris.

Victori mortis inclitam[4] pangamus laudis gloriam, cum patre sancto spiritu qui nos redemit obitu.

879 HAEC EXPLETA OSCVLETVR EPISCOPVS EVANGELIVM ET OMNES QVI CIRCVM EO STANT. DEINDE DICANT DOMINICAM ORATIONEM TACITE. FINITA, DICAT EPISCOPVS ET NE NOS INDVCAS. Ecce quam bonum. Suscepimus deus. Tu mandasti. Tu lauasti pedes discipulorum. Opera manuum tuarum.

880 Adesto quaesumus domine officii nostrae seruitutis qui dignatus es lauare pedes tuis discipulis ne despicias opera manuum nostrarum, quae nobis retinenda mandasti, ut sicut hic exteriora abluuntur inquinamenta, sic ad te omnium nostrorum interiora lauentur / peccata. Per dominum.

f. 121r

881 Deinde accipiant becellam panis et bibant ternis. Post eant ad completorium.

CLVIII

FERIA VI QVOD EST PARASCEVE

882 HORA NONA PROCEDAT PONTIFEX DE SACRARIO CVM SVIS MINISTRIS ANTE ALTARE AD ORANDVM. ORATIONE FINITA, DICAT PONTIFEX AD POPVLVM. OREMVS. ET DIACONVS. Flectamus genua.

883 Deus a quo et iudas. Require retro.

884 EPLA. Haec dicit dominus deus. In tribulatione sua.

885 TRACT. Domine audiui. V. In medio duorum. V. In eo dum conturbata sunt. V. Deus a libano. V. Operuit caelos.

---

[1] *a* before correction.
[2] *ungem* before correction.
[3] Over an erasure.
[4] Over an erasure.

886 ORATIO. Deus qui peccati ueteris hereditaria mortem in qua posteritatis genus omne successerat, christi tui domini nostri passione soluisti dona ut conformes eidem facti[1], ut sicut imaginem terrene[2] naturę necessitate portauimus, ita imaginem caelestis gratiae sanctificatione portemus, unigeniti filii tui domini nostri iesu christi. Qui tecum.

887 LECTIO LIBRI EXODI. In diebus illis. Dixit dominus ad moysen et aaron in terra aegypti.

888 TRACT. Eripe me domine ab homine malo. V. Qui cogitauerunt. V. Acuerunt. V. Custodi me domine. V. Qui cogitauerunt. V. Et funes. V. Dixi domino. V. Domine domine uirtus. V. Ne tradas me. V. Caput circuitus. V. Verumtamen.

889 PASSIO DOMINI NOSTRI IESV CHRISTI, SECVNDVM IOHANNEM. In illo tempore. Egressus est iesus trans torrentem.

890 ORATIONES QVAE DICENDA SVNT. Oremus dilectissimi nobis imprimis[3] pro ęcclesia sancta dei, ut eam deus et dominus noster pacificare et custodire / dignetur toto orbe terrarum, subiciens ei principatus et potestates, detque nobis quietam et tranquillam uitam degentibus, glorificare deum patrem omnipotentem.

/f. 121v

OREMVS. ET ADNVNTIAT DIACONVS. Flectamus genua.

891 Omnipotens sempiterne deus qui gloriam tuam omnibus in christo gentibus reuelasti, custodi opera misericordiae tuae ut ecclesia toto orbe diffusa, stabili fide in confessione tui nominis perseueret. Per dominum nostrum.

892 Oremus et pro beatissimo papa nostro .ill. ut deus et dominus noster qui elegit eum in ordinem episcopatus, saluum atque incolumem custodiat ecclesiae suae sanctae ad regendum populum sanctum dei.

---

[1] *confirmes eadem facto* before correction.
[2] *terreni* before correction.
[3] Supplied in margin by original scribe.

893 OREMVS. Omnipotens sempiterne deus. Cuius iudicio uniuersa fundantur, respice propitius ad praeces nostras, et electum nobis antistitem tua pietate conserua, ut christiana plebs quae tali gubernatur auctore, sub tanto pontifice credulitatis suae meritis augeatur. Per dominum nostrum iesum christum.

894 Oremus et pro omnibus episcopis, presbiteris, diaconibus, subdiaconibus, accolitis, exorcistis, lectoribus, ostiariis, confessoribus, uirginibus, uiduis, et pro omni populo sancto dei.

895 OREMVS. Omnipotens sempiterne deus. Cuius spiritu totum corpus ecclesię sanctificatur et regitur, exaudi nos pro uniuersis ordinibus supplicantes, ut gratiae tuae munere / ab omnibus tibi gradibus fideliter seruiatur[1]. Per dominum nostrum iesum christum.

896 Oremus et pro christianissimo imperatore nostro, ut deus et dominus noster subditas illi faciat omnes barbaras nationes, ad nostram perpetuam pacem.

897 OREMVS. Omnipotens sempiterne deus. In cuius manu sunt omnium potestates, et omnia iura regnorum, respice ad romanorum siue francorum, benignus imperium, ut gentes quae in sua feritate confidunt, potentiae tuae dextera comprimantur. Per dominum nostrum.

898 Oremus et pro catecuminis nostris, ut deus et dominus noster adaperiat aures praecordiorum ipsorum ianuamque misericordiae, ut per lauacrum regenerationis accepta remissione omnium peccatorum, et ipsi digni inueniantur in christo iesu domino nostro.

899 OREMVS. Omnipotens sempiterne deus. Qui ecclesiam tuam noua semper prole fecundas, auge fidem et intellectum caticuminis nostris ut renati fonte baptismatis adoptionis tuae, filiis adgregentur. Per.

[1] *seruiantur* before correction.

203

900 Oremus dilectissimi nobis deum patrem omnipotentem[1], ut cunctis mundum purget erroribus, morbos auferat, famem depellat, aperiat carceres, uincula dissoluat, peregrinantibus reditum, infirmantibus sanitatem, nauigantibus portum salutis indulgeat.

/f. 122v **901** OREMVS. / Omnipotens sempiterne deus, moestorum consolatio, laborantium fortitudo, perueniant ad te praeces de quacumque tribulatione clamantium, ut omnes sibi in necessitatibus suis misericordiam tuam gaudeant adfuisse. Per dominum.

902 Oremus et pro hereticis et scismaticis, ut deus ac dominus noster eruat eos ab erroribus uniuersis, et ad sanctam matrem ecclesiam catholicam adque apostolicam reuocare dignetur.

903 OREMVS. Omnipotens sempiterne deus, qui saluas omnes, et neminem uis perire, respice ad animas diabolica fraude deceptas, ut omni heretica prauitate deposita, errantium corda resipiscant, et ad ueritatis tuae redeant unitatem. Per.

904 Oremus et pro perfidis iudaeis, ut deus et dominus noster auferat uelamen de cordibus eorum, ut et ipsi cognoscant iesum christum dominum nostrum.

905 [2]OREMVS. Omnipotens sempiterne deus, qui etiam iudaicam perfidiam a tua misericordia non repellis, exaudi praeces nostras quas tibi pro illius populi obcaecatione deferimus, ut agnita ueritatis tuae luce quae est christus, a suis tenebris eruantur. Per dominum.

906 Oremus et pro paganis, ut deus omnipotens auferat iniquitatem a cordibus eorum, et relictis idolis suis conuertantur ad deum uiuum et uerum, et unicum filium eius iesum christum dominum nostrum, cum quo uiuit et regnat cum spiritu sancto deus. Per[3].

---

[1] *omnipotenti* before correction.
[2] In the left margin, a note by a Corbie scribe: *Hic nostrum nullus debet modo flectere corpus. Ob populi noxam ac pariter rabiem.*
[3] *omnia saecula saeculorum* supplied in the lower margin by a Corbie scribe.

f. 123r **907** OREMVS. / Omnipotens sempiterne deus, qui non mortem
peccatorum sed uitam semper inquiris, suscipe propitius
orationem nostram, et libera eos ab idolorum cultura, et adgrega
ecclesiae tuae sanctae, ad laudem et gloriam nominis tui. Per
dominum nostrum.

908 ¹POST HAS ORATIONES PERGANT DVO DIACONI IN
SACRARIVM AVT RETRO ALTARE, CANTANT: Populle
meus. PRESBITERI VERO DVO STANT ANTE CRVCEM,
CVM SALVTATIONE RESPONDEANT: Agyos, o theos. ITEM
CHORVS: Sanctus deus sanctus fortis. DEPORTETVR CRVX
PAVLVLVM IN ANTEA, ET ITERVM CANTANT DIACONI:
Ego quidem eduxi te per desertum. PRESBITERI VERO: Agyos, o
theos. ET CHORVS ITERVM: Sanctus deus sanctus fortis. ITEM
DEPORTATVR PAVLVLVM: Quid ultra debui facere. Agyos. ITEM:
Sanctus deus.

909 ITERVM TERTIO DEPORTETVR CRVX ANTE ALTARE, ET
DISCOOPERIETVR LINTEO QVO ERAT PRECINCTA A
DVOBVS PRESBITERIS ET DICANT IPSI ELEVATA VOCE.
A. Ecce lignum crucis. PS. Deus misereatur.

910 TVNC VENIENS PONTIFEX CVM DVOBVS DIACONIBVS
PROSTERNENS SE TER ET ADORANTES CRVCEM MORE
SOLITO. POST HOS SEQVVNTVR SACERDOTES ET
LEVITẸ, DEINDE OMNIS CLERVS, EXINDE OMNIS
POPVLVS FEMINEOQVE SEXVS. INTERIM CANTAT HAS
ANTIPHONAS: Crucem tuam adoramus domine. PS. Beati inmaculati.
A. Adoramus crucis. A. Dum fabricator mundi. YMNVS FVRTVNATI.
Pange lingua gloriosi.

CLVIIII
911 HAEC ORATIONES QVAE SVNT AD CRVCEM
ADORANDAM. Domine iesu christe adoro te in cruce
ascendentem spineam coronam in capite portantem, depraecor
te ut ipsa crux liberet me de angelo percutienti. Adoro te in
f. 123v cruce / uulneratum felle et aceto potatum. Depraecor te ut tua
uulnera remedium sit anime meae. Adoro te in sepulchro posito,

¹ Text of nos 908, 909, 910 in alternating lines of orange and brown.

depraecor te ut tua mors sit uita mea. Adoro te descendentem ad inferos, et liberantem captiuos, depraecor te ut me non dimittas ibidem introire. Adoro te resurgentem a mortuis, ascendentem in caelum, sedentem ad dexteram patris, praecor te miserere mei. Adoro te saluatorem uenturum et iudicaturum, depraecor te ut in tuo sacro aduentu, non intres in iudicio cum me peccatore, sed ante dimittas quam iudices, christe saluator mundi qui uiuis et regnas. Per omnia saecula saeculorum. Amen.

912 ALIA. Domine iesu christe gloriosissime conditor mundi, qui cum sis splendor gloriae aequalis patri sanctoque spiritui carnem immaculatam assumere dignatus es, et gloriosissimas sanctas tuas palmas crucis patibulo permisisti configi, ut claustra inferi dissipares, et humanum genus de morte liberares. Miserere mihi misero oppresso facinore, ac nequitiarum labe sordidato, non me digneris derelinquere gloriosae domine, sed digneris mihi indulgere quod malum egi. Exaudi me domine prostratum ad adorandam tuam sanctam crucem, ut in his sacris sollemnibus tibi merear assistere mundus. Qui uiuis.

913 ALIA. Domine iesu christe qui pro nobis crucis et mortis
/f. 124r   patibulum subisti, ut mortis a nobis expelleres / potestates, et sanguinis tui nos pretio liberares, miserere mihi humillimo famulo tuo, et ueniam mihi omnium meorum peccatorum, meque coram adorandam crucem tuam prostratum ab omnibus malis eripe, bonisque tuis misericorditer refice, qui cum patre et spiritu sancto uiuis et regnas ante omnia et nunc et semper et in ęterna.

914 [1]POST SALVTATAM CRVCEM, INTRANT DVO PRESBITERI IN SACRARIVM, VEL VBI POSITVM FVERIT CORPVS DOMINI, QVOD PRIDIE REMANSIT, PONENTES EVM IN PATENAM, ET SVBDIACONI TENEANT CALICEM ANTE IPSOS CVM VINO NON CONSECRATO. VNVS PRESBITER ACCIPIAT PATENAM, ALTER VERO ACCIPIAT CALICEM PONAT SVPER ALTARE. PONTIFEX VERO SEDEAT IN SEDE DVM PERSALVTAT POPVLVS

---

[1]   Text of nos 914–16 in alternating lines of orange and brown.

CRVCEM. NAM SALVTANTE PONTIFICE, VEL POPVLO[1]
CRVCEM, CANITVR SEMPER. AN. Ecce lignum crucis. PS.
cxviii[mum].

915 QVA SALVTATA ET REPOSITA IN LOCO SVO,
DESCENDAT PONTIFEX ANTE ALTARE, ET DICIT.
OREMVS. Praeceptis salutaribus monitis. Pater noster qui es in caelis.
Sed libera nos a malo. Libera nos quaesumus domine. CVM DIXERINT
Amen, SVMAT DE SANCTO CORPORE ET PONAT IN
CALICE, NIHIL DICENS.

916 ET COMMVNICENT OMNES CVM SILENTIO ET
EXPLETA SVNT VNIVERSA, ET POST PAVLVLVM
VESPERA DICAT VNVSQVISQVE PRIVATIM, ET SIC
VADVNT AD MENSAM.

DENVNTIATIO PRO SCRVTINIO QVOD IN DOMINICA
MEDIO QVADRAGESIMAE POST EVANGELIVM A
DIACONO PRONVNTIANTVR HIS VERBIS:

f. 124v   **917** / Scrutinii diem dilectissimi fratres, quo electi nostri diuinitus
instruantur inminere cognoscite. Ideoque sollicita deuotione
succedentes illa feria .ii. et .iiii. siue .vi. circa horam diei sextam,
conuenire dignemini ut caelesti mysterium quo diabolus cum
sua pompa distruitur, et ianua regni caelestis aperitur, inculpabili
deo iubente ministerio peragere ualeamus. Per.

918 [2]VT AVTEM VENERINT AD ECCLESIAM SCRIBVNTVR
NOMINA INFANTVM AB ACCOLITO ET VOCANTVR
ANTE OSTIVM ECCLESIAE, PER NOMINA SICVT
SCRIPTI SVNT ET STATVVNTVR MASCVLI IN
DEXTERAM PARTEM, FEMINE IN SINISTRAM, ET DAT
ORATIONES PRESBITER SVPER EOS HIS VERBIS.

919 ORATIO SVPER ELECTOS AD CATICVMINOS
FATIENDOS. Omnipotens sempiterne deus pater domini nostri.

---

[1]   Final letter supplied over an erasure.
[2]   Most sections of 'rubric' throughout the order in alternating lines of orange and brown.

920 INDE VERO POSTQVAM FVERINT A PRESBITERO
CATECIZATI, MANEANT FORIS ANTE OSTIVM
ECCLESIAE EXPECTANTES HORAM QVANDO
REVOCENTVR. TVNC PRIMVM INCIPIENS CLERVS AN.
Dum sanctificatus fuero in uobis.

921 ET ASCENDET SACERDOS AD ALTARE DICET
ORATIONEM AD MISSAM. Da quaesumus domine electis
nostris digne atque sapienter, ad confessionem tuae laudis
accedere, ut dignitati pristinae quam originali transgressione[1]
perdiderant, perpetuam gratiam reformentur. Per.

922 ET VOCANTVR INFANTES AB ACCOLITO PER NOMINA
VEL ORDINEM SICVT SCRIPTI SVNT, ET ADMONENTVR
A DIACONO ITA: CATICVMINI PROCEDANT. ET
/f. 125r   ORDINANTVR MASCVLI IN DEXTRIS, / FEMINE VERO A
SINISTRIS ET ADMONENTVR A DIACONO ITA: ORATE
ELECTI, FLECTITE GENVA.

923 POSTQVAM ORAVERINT ITERVM DICIT: LEVATE.
COMPLETE ORATIONEM VESTRAM IN VNVM ET
DICITE. AMEN

924 ITEM DICIT DIACONVS: SIGNATE ILLOS. ACCEDITE AD
BENEDICTIONEM.

925 TVNC PRIMVM VENIENS ACOLITVS. FACIT CRVCEM IN
FRONTIBVS SINGVLORVM, INPONIT MANVM SVPER
EOS DANS ORATIONEM EXCELSA VOCE, HIS VERBIS:
DEVS ABRAHAM.

926 DEINDE SVPER FEMINAS. DEVS CAELI, DEVS TERRAE.

927 ITEM SVPER MASCVLOS. DEVS INMORTALE.

928 ITEM SVPER FEMINAS. DEVS ABRAHAM.

929 ITEM SVPER MASCVLOS. Exorcizo te inmunde spiritus.

---

[1]   First *s* supplied interlinearly.

930 ITEM SVPER FEMINAS. Exorcizo te inmunde spiritus.

931 ITEM SVPER MASCVLOS VEL FEMINAS, ORATIO. Aeternam ac iustissimam.

932 ET ITERVM ADMONENTVR A DIACONO ITA: Orate electi, flectite genua, leuate, complete orationem uestram in unum et dicite. Amen.

933 ITEM DICIT DIACONVS: State cum disciplina, silentio.

934 Inde reuertatur sacerdos ad sedem suam et legitur lectio quae in capitulare commemorat.

935 INDE SEQVITVR RESPONSORIVM. Et admonentur a diacono ita dicendo. CATECVMINI RECEDANT. SI QVIS CATECVMINVS EST RECEDAT. OMNES CATECVMINI EXEANT FORAS.

936 ET EGREDIENTVR OMNES EXPECTANTES PRO FORIBVS VSQVE DVM COMPLETAE FVERINT MISSARVM SOLLEMNIA. DEINDE LEGITVR EVANGELIVM DE IPSA DIE PERTINENTEM. ET OFFERVNTVR OBLATIONES A PARENTIBVS VEL QVI EOS SVSCEPTVRI SVNT.

937 ORATIO SVPER OBLATAM. Miseratio tua deus ad haec percipienda mysteria, famulos tuos quaesumus et proueniat competenter, et deuota conuersatione perducat. Per.

f. 125v **938** INFRA HACTIONEM VBI DICIT. / Memento domine famulorum famularumque tuarum qui electos tuos suscepturi sunt ad sanctam gratiam baptismi tui.

939 ET TANGIS ET RECITANTVR NOMINA VIRORVM AC MVLIERVM QVI IPSOS INFANTES SVSCEPTVRI SVNT ET INTRA SE OMNIVM CIRCVMADSTANTIVM QVORVM TIBI FIDES COGNITA EST.

940 ITEM INFRA HACTIONEM. Hanc igitur oblationem domine ut propitius suscipias deprecamur, quam tibi offerimus pro famulis et famulabus tuis quos ad aeternam uitam et beatum gratiae tuae donum elegere atque uocare dignatus es. Per christum dominum nostrum. Quam oblationem.

941 ET RECITANTVR NOMINA ELECTORVM. POSTQVAM RECENSETA FVERINT, DICIS. Hos domine fonte baptismatis innouandos, spiritus tui munere ad sacramentorum tuorum plenitudinem poscimus pręparari. Per christum dominum nostrum. Diesque nostros.

942 POST COMMVNIONEM. Adesto domine quaesumus redemptionis effectibus, ut quos sacramentis aeternitatis institutis, eosdem protegas dignanter aptandos. Per.

943 <ALIA.> Suppliciter domine sacra familia munus tuae miserationis expectat, concede quaesumus ut quod te iubente desiderat, te largiente percipiat. Per.

944 FINITA VERO MISSARVM SOLLEMNIA COMMVNICANT OMNES. DEINDE ADNVNTIAT PRESBITER QVALEM DIEM VOLVERIT IPSA EBDOMADA VT REVERTANTVR ITA DICENDO. ILLA FERIA VENIENTE, COLLEGITE /
/f. 126r   VOS TEMPORIVS AD ECCLESIAM ILLAM. ET ORDINETVR SCRVTINIVM SICVTI PRIVS.

ALIA MISSA PRO SCRVTINIO SECVNDO
945 Omnipotens sempiterne deus, ecclesiam tuam spiritali fecunditate multiplica, ut qui sunt generatione terreni, fiat regeneratione caelestes. Per.

946 DEINDE ACOLITVS ADMONEAT SICVTI SVPERIVS, ET DIACONVS VOCAT SICVTI SVPERIVS. CATICVMINI PROCEDANT. POSTEA LEGATVR LECTIO ET RESPONSORIVM CANATVR.

947 SECRETA. Remedii sempiterni munera domine laetantes offerimus, suppliciter exorantes, ut eadem nos et digne uenerari, et pro saluandis congruenter exhibere perficias. Per.

948 INFRA ACTIONEM, VBI SVPRA.

949 POST COMMVNIONEM. Tu sempiterne quaesumus domine tuam adtolle benignus familiam, tu dispone correctam, tu propitius tuere subiectam, tu guberna perpetua benignitate saluandam. Per.

950 ITEM ALIA. Tu famulis tuis quaesumus domine bonos mores placatus instituae, tu in eis quod tibi placitum sit dignanter infunde, ut et digni sint et tua ualeant beneficia promereri. Per.

951 SEQVENTI VERO EBDOMADA ITEM VNVM DIEM QVALE SACERDOS ADNVNTIAVERIT, FACIAT AVRIVM APERTIONVM HOC MODO. VENIVNT AD ECCLESIAM DE QVO EIS FVERIT ADNVNTIATVM ET CLAMAT DIACONVS DICENS. CATECVMINI PROCEDANT.

f. 126v

952 ET VOCANTVR INFANTES PER NOMINA SICVTI PRIVS VT SCRIPTI SVNT, ET STATVVNTVR SICVT DIXIMVS, MASCVLI AD DEXTERAM, FEMINĘ AD SINISTRAM ET CANVNT ANTIPHONAM AD INTRO/ITVM. IPSA EXPLETA, ADMONENTVR A DIACONO VT PRIVS VT ORENT. DEINDE DANS PRESBITER ORATIONEM.

ITEM MISSA PRO SCRVTINIO TERTIO, IN AVRIVM APERTIONVM

953 Concede domine electis nostris ut sanctis edocti mysteriis, et renouentur fonte baptismatis, et inter ecclesiae tuae membra numerentur. Per.

954 SEDIT POSTEA IN SEDE SVA, ET INPONVNT ACCOLITI MANVS SVPER IPSOS INFANTES VT PRIVS. DEINDE PRESBITERI HOC ORDINE EXPLETO, ITERVM ADMONENTVR A DIACONO VT ORENT, VT SVPRA. ET VT SVRREXERINT AB ORATIONE DICAT DIACONVS: SIGNATE ILLOS ET STATE CVM DISCIPLINA ET SILENTIO. ET LEGVNTVR DVAE LECTIONES QVAS IN CAPITVLARE COMMEMORAT. ET SEQVITVR RESPONSORIVM.

955 INDE VERO PROCEDVNT DIACONI DE SACRARIO CVM .IIII^{OR}. EVANGELIIS, PRECEDENTIBVS ILLIS DVOBVS CANDELABRIS CVM TVRIBVLIS CANTANTES. Sitientes uenite ad aquas.

956 ET PONVNT QVATTVOR EVANGELIA SVPER ALTARE, IN .IIII^{OR}. ANGVLOS, ET TRACTAT PRESBITER HIS VERBIS ANTEQVAM ALIQVIS EORVM LEGAT. Aperturi uobis filii karissimi euangelia, id est uerba diuina, prius ordinem insinuare debemus, quid est euangelium, et unde descendat, et cuius in eo uerba ponuntur, et quare quattuor sint qui haec gesta scripserunt, uel qui sunt ipsi quattuor, qui diuino spiritu adnuntiante per prophetam signati sunt, ne forte sine hac ordinis ratione uel causa stuporem uobis inminentibus relinquamus, et quia ad hoc uenistis, ut aures uobis aperiantur, ne incipiat sensus uester obtundi, euangelium dicitur / propriae bona adnuntiatio, quae utique adnuntiatio est iesu christi domini nostri. Descendit autem euangelium ab eo quod adnuntiet, et ostendat quod his qui per prophetas suos loquebatur, uenit in carnem sicut scriptum est, qui loquebatur ecce adsum. Explicantes autem breuiter quid sit euangelium, uel qui sunt hii quattuor qui per prophetam antea monstrati sunt. Nunc sua quaeque nomina singulis adsignemus iudiciis. Ait enim propheta ezechihel, et similitudo uultus eorum, ut facies hominis, et facies leonis a dextris illius, et facies uituli, et facies aquilae a sinistris illius, hii quattuor has figuras habentes, euangelistas esse, non dubium est. Sed nomina eorum qui euangelia scripserunt, haec sunt matheus, marcus, lucas, iohannes.

/f. 127r

957 DICIT DIACONVS: CATICVMINI RECEDANT. SICVTI SVPERIVS ET POSTEA DICIT DOMINVS VOBISCVM, ET INCIPIENS LEGERE INITIVM SANCTI EVANGELII SECVNDVM MATHEVM. Liber generationis, VSQVE IPSE ENIM SALVVM FACIET POPVLVM. POSTQVAM LEGERIT ET ADNVNTIAT DIACONVS DICENS: CATECVMINI PROCEDVNT, STATE CVM SILENTIO, AVDIENTES INTENTE.

958 TRACTAT PRESBITER HIS VERBIS: Filii karissimi ne diutius ergo uos teneamus exponimus uobis quam rationem et quam

212

f. 127v

figuram unusquisque in se contineat, et quare matheus in se figuram hominis habeat, quia initio suo nihil aliud agit nisi natiuitatem saluatoris, pleno ordine generationis enarrat, sic enim coepit, liber generationis iesu christi / filii dauid, filii abraham. Videtis quia non inmerito huic hominis adsignata persona est, quando ab hominibus natiuitatis initium comprehendit, nec inmerito ut diximus huic mysterio adsignata est mathei persona.

959 ET ADNVNTIAT DIACONVS VT SVPRA: SI QVIS CATECVMINVS EST RECEDAT. ET POSTEA DICIT DOMINVS VOBISCVM, INITIVM SANCTI EVANGELII SECVNDVM MARCVM VSQVE TV ES FILIVS MEVS DILECTVS. ITA ADNVNCIAT DIACONVS STATE CVM SILENTIO, VT SVPRA.

960 SEQVITVR PRESBITER HIS VERBIS: Marcus euangelista leonis gerens figuram a solicitudine incipit dicens. Vox clamantis in deserto parate uiam domini, siue quia regnat inuictus, huius leonis multifaria inuenimus exempla ut non uacet dictum illud. Iuda filius meus catulus leonis de germine mihi, ascendisti recubans dormiuit ut leo, et sicut catulus leonis qui exsuscitauit eum.

961 DICIT DIACONVS: CATECVMINI RECEDANT, VT SVPRA. POSTEA LEGAT INITIVM SANCTI EVANGELII SECVNDVM LVCAM, VSQVE PARARE DOMINO PLEBEM PERFECTAM. ITEM ADNVNTIAT DIACONVS: CATECVMINI PROCEDANT, VT SVPRA.

962 PROSEQVITVR PRESBITER HIS VERBIS: Lucas euangelista uituli spetiem gestat, ad cuius instar saluator noster est immolatus. Hic enim christi euangelium locutus, sic coepit de zacharia et helisabeth, de quibus iohannes baptista in summa natus est senectute, et ideo lucas uitulo comparatur, quia duo cornua, duo testamenta, et quattuor pedum ungulę, quattuor euangelia, quasi tenera firmitate nascentia, in se /plenissime continebat.

f. 128r

963 ET DICIT DIACONVS VT SVPRA: CATECVMINI RECEDANT, ET LEGIT INITIVM SANCTI EVANGELII SECVNDVM IOHANNEM, VSQVE PLENVM GRATIAE ET VERITATIS. ITERVM PRONVNTIAT DIACONVS VT SVPRA: CATECVMINI PROCEDANT.

964 ITEM PROSEQVITVR HIS VERBIS. Iohannes habet similitudinem aquilae, eo quod nimis alta petierit. Ait enim. In principio erat uerbum, et uerbum erat apud deum et deus erat uerbum, hoc erat in principio apud deum. Et dauid dixit de persona christi, renouabitur sicut aquilae iuuentus tua. Idem iesu christi domini nostri, quia resurgens a mortuis ascendit in caelos, unde iam uobis conceptis, praegnans gloriatur ecclesia, omne festiuitate uotorum, ad noua tendere christianae legis exordia, ut aduenienti die uenerabilis paschae lauacro baptismatis renascentis, sicut sancti omnes mereamini fidele munus infantiae a christo iesu domino nostro percipere, qui uiuit et regnat in saecula saeculorum. Amen.

965 INCIPIT PRAEFATIO SYMBOLI AD ELECTOS. ITEM ANTEQVAM DICAS SYMBOLVM HIS VERBIS PROSEQVERIS. Dilectissimi nobis accepturi sacramenta baptismatis, et in nouam creaturam sancti spiritus procreandi fidem, quam credentes iustificati estis, toto corde concipite, et animis uestris uera conuersatione mutatis ad deum qui mentium uestrarum est inluminator, accedite suscipientes euangelici symboli sacramentum a domino inspiratum, ab apostolis /f. 128v institutum, cuius pauca / quidem uerba sunt, sed magna mysteria. Sanctus enim spiritus qui magistris ecclesiae ista dictauit, tali eloquio talique breuitatem salutiferam concedit fidem, ut quod credendum uobis est semperque profitendum, nec intelligentiam possit latere, nec memoriam fatigare. Intentis itaque animis symbolum discite, et quod uobis sicut accepimus tradimus, non alicui[1] materiae quae corrumpi potest, sed paginis uestri cordis scribite, confessio itaque fidei quam suscepistis, hoc inchoatur exordio.

---

[1] *alicuius* before correction.

966 POST HAEC ACCIPIENS ACCOLITVS VNVM EX IPSIS INFANTIBVS MASCVLVM, TENENS EVM IN SINISTRO BRACHIO PONENS MANVM SVPER CAPVT, ET INTERROGAT PRESBITER GRECAE: ΠΥΑΠΟΑΜ ZOTICIN KYPION YMON, IESVM CHRISTVM. RESPONDIT ACCOLITVS. EAINICTIN. ITERVM DICIT PRĘSBITER, ADNVNTIAO AWN TIAYTIN, AYTW TWTW GNOCTIC. ET DICAT ACCOLITVS SYMBOLVM GRECAE DECANTANDO, TENENS MANVM SVPER CAPVT INFANTIS.

967 HOC FINITO, ITERVM ACCIPIENS ALTER ACCOLITVS EX IPSIS INFANTIBVS FEMINAM SICVT SVPRA, ET INTERROGAT PRESBITER LATINAE: QVA LINGVA CONFITENTVR DOMINVM NOSTRVM. RESPONDIT ACCOLITVS: LATINAE. ITERVM DICIT PRESBITER ADNVNTIA FIDEM IPSORVM QVALITER CREDANT.

968 PONENS MANVM ACCOLITVS SVPER CAPVT INFANTIS, ET DICIT SYMBOLVM DECANTANDO: Credo in unum deum patrem omnipotentem, factorem caeli et terrae, uisibilium omnium, et inuisibilium, et in unum dominum iesum christum filium dei unigenitum, et ex pa/tre natum ante omnia saecula, deum de deo, lumen de lumine, deum uerum de deo uero, genitum non factum consubstantialem patri[1] per quem omnia facta sunt, qui propter nos homines et propter nostram salutem descendit de caelis, et incarnatus est de spiritu sancto ex maria uirgine, et homo factus est, crucifixus etiam pro nobis sub pontio pilato, passus et sepultus est, et resurrexit tertia die secundum scripturas, et ascendit in caelum, sedet ad dexteram patris, et iterum uenturus est cum gloria, iudicare uiuos et mortuos, cuius regni non erit finis, et in spiritum sanctum dominum et uiuificantem, qui ex patre filioque procedit, qui cum patre et filio, simul adoratur et cum glorificatur, qui locutus est per prophetas, et unam sanctam catholicam, et apostolicam ecclesiam, confiteor unum baptisma in remissionem peccatorum, et expecto resurrectionem mortuorum, et uitam uenturi saeculi. Amen.

f. 129r

---

[1] *patris* before correction.

215

969 HOC EXPLETO, PROSEQVITVR PRESBITER HIS VERBIS: Haec summae, fidei nostri dilectissimi nobis, haec uerba sunt symboli, non sapientiae humana sermone facta, sed uera diuinitus ratione disposita, quibus compraehendendis atque seruandis, nemo non idoneus, nemo non aptus, et hic dei patris et filii, una et aequalis pronuntiatur potestas, hic unigenitus dei de maria uirgine et spiritu sancto secundum carnem natus ostenditur, hic eiusdem crucifixio, ac sepultura, ac die tertia resurrectio praedicatur, hic ascensio ipsius super caelos et /f. 129v confessio / in dextera paternae maiestatis agnoscitur, uenturusque ad iudicandos uiuos et mortuos declaratur, hic spiritus sanctus in eadem qua pater et filius deitate indiscretus accipitur. Hic postremo ecclesiae uocatio, peccatorum remissio, et carnis resurrectio perdocetur. Vos itaque dilectissimi ex uetere homine in nouum reformamini, et de carnalibus spiritales, de terrenis incipite esse caelestes secura et inconcussa fide, credite resurrectionem quae facta est in christo etiam in nobis omnibus esse complendam, et hoc secuturos in toto corpore quod praecessit in capite, quem et ipsum quod percepturi estis baptismi sacramentum in omnibus spetiei exponit formam. Ibi quaedam enim ibi mors, et quaedam resurrectio caelebratur, uetus homo deponitur, et nouus adsumitur. Peccator aquas ingreditur, et iustus egreditur. Ille abicitur qui traxit ad mortem, suscipitur .ill. qui reduxit ad uitam, per cuius gratiam uobis confertur ut filii dei sitis, non carnis uoluntate editi, sed sancti spiritus uirtute generati, et ideo hanc breuissimam plenitudinem. Ita debeatis uestris cordibus inherere, ut omni tempore praesidio huius confessionis utamini. Inuicta est enim semper talium armorum potestas, et contra omnes uobis insidias diaboli, tamque bonis christi militibus profutura. Diabolus qui hominem temptare non desistit, munitos uos hoc symbolo semper inueniat, et deuicto aduersario cui renuntiatis gratiam /f. 130r domini incorrup/tam, et inmaculatam usque in finem. Ipsum quem confitemini protegente seruetis, ut in quo peccatorum remissionem accipiatis, ut in eo gloriam resurrectionis habeatis. Ergo dilectissimi praefatum symbolum fidei catholicae in praesenti cognouistis, nunc euntes edocemini, nullo mutato sermone. Potens est enim dei misericordia quae et uos ad baptismi fidem currentes perducat, et nos qui uobis mysteria

tradimus, una uobiscum ad regna caelestia faciat peruenire. Per
eundem.

970 ITEM PRAEFATIO, ET AMMONENTVR A DIACONO.
ORATE DILECTI, VT SVPRA.

971 ET DICIT PRESBITER: Dominus et saluator noster iesus
christus inter cetera sacra praecepta discipulis suis petentibus
quemadmodum orare deberent, non solum formam orationis
concessit, uerum etiam qua mente et puritate praecaretur,
ostendit in praesenti sacra haec lectio demonstrauit, tu autem
cum orabis intra in cubiculum tuum, et clauso ostio ora patrem
tuum. Cubiculum quod nominat, non occultam domum ostendit,
sed cordis nostri secretum. Id est ut a mala cogitatione pectus
nostrum mystica fidei claue claudamus, ac labiis clausis
incorrupta mente deo loquamur, deus noster fidei non uocis
auditor est, ergo unde sermo est. Id est sapientia christus
dominus noster.

HANC ORATIONEM NOS DOCVIT, VT ITA OREMVS.
PATER NOSTER QVI ES IN CAELIS.

972 Haec liberatis uox est et plena fiducia, ergo his uobis moribus
est uiuendum, ut filii dei et fratres christi esse possitis. / Nam
patrem suum deum qua temeritate dicere praesumit, qui ab eius
uoluntate degenerat. Vnde uos dilectissimi dignos exhibete
adoptionem diuinam, quoniam scriptum est, quodquod autem
crediderunt in eum, dedit eis potestatem filios dei fieri.

SANCTIFICETVR NOMEN TVVM.

973 Id est non quod deus nostris sanctificetur orationibus qui semper
est sanctus, sed petimus ut nomen eius sanctificetur in nobis, ut
qui in baptismate eius sanctificamur, in id quod esse coepimus
perseueremus.

ADVENIAT REGNVM TVVM.

974 Deus namque noster quando non regnat maxime cuius regnum
est inmortale, sed cum dicimus ueniat regnum tuum, nostrum
regnum petimus aduenire a deo nobis promissum, christi
sanguine et passione quęsitum.

f. 130v

FIAT VOLVNTAS TVA SICVT IN CAELO ET IN TERRA.

975 Id est in eo fiat uoluntas tua, ut quod tu uis in caelo, hoc nos in terra positi inreprehensibiliter faciamus.

PANEM NOSTRVM COTIDIANVM DA NOBIS HODIE.

976 Hic spiritalem cybum intelligere debemus, christus enim panis est noster, qui dixit ego sum panis uiuus qui de caelo descendi, quae cotidianum dicens. Ita nos semper inmunes praecepit esse peccati, ut digni simus caelestibus alimentis.

ET DIMITTE NOBIS DEBITA NOSTRA, SICVT ET NOS DIMITTIMVS DEBITORIBVS NOSTRIS.

977 Hoc pactum est significans non nos aliter peccatorum ueniam posse promereri, nisi prius[1] nos in nobis delinquentibus aliis ueniam relaxemus, sicut in euangelio dominus noster dicit. Nisi dimiseritis pecca/ta hominibus, nec uobis pater uester dimittit peccata uestra.

/f. 131r

ET NE NOS INDVCAS IN TEMPTATIONEM.

978 Id est ne nos patiaris induci ab eo qui temptat prauitatis auctorem. Nam dicit scriptura. Deus enim intentator malorum est, diabolus uero est temptator ad quem euincendum. Dominus dicit. Vigilate et orate, ne intretis in temptationem.

SED LIBERA NOS A MALO.

979 Hoc ideo ait, quia dixit apostolus. Nescitis quid uobis oporteat orare, unde dominus omnipotens ita a nobis orandus est, ut quicquid humana fragilitas cauere aut uitare non praeualet, hoc ille ut possimus propitius nobis conferre dignetur. Iesus christus dominus noster, qui uiuit.

980 ET AMMONENTVR A DIACONO. ORATE ELECTI, FLECTITE GENVA, VT SVPRA.

981 ET DICIT PRESBITER: Audistis dilectissimi dominicae orationis sancta mysteria, nunc euntes ea uestris cordibus inuocate, ut ad exoranda ac percipiendam dei misericordiam, perfecti in christo esse possitis, potens est enim dominus deus

---

[1] *prous* before correction.

noster et uos qui ad fidem curritis, ad lauacrum aquae
regenerationis perducat, et nos qui uobis mysterium fidei
catholicae tradidimus, una uobiscum ad caelestia regna faciat
peruenire. Qui uiuit et regnat cum deo patre.

982 HOC EXPLETO, ITERVM ADMONETVR A DIACONO VT
SVPRA VT EXEANT. *Egressi uero parentes cum infantibus
eorum et iterum ingrediuntur in ecclesia tam parentes quam et
hii qui ipsos infantes suscepturi sunt cum oblationibus eorum /
et offeruntur pro ipsis. Ipsi uero infantes expectantes pro foribus
donec consumentur missarum solemnia. Expletas uero missas,
communicant omnes preter ipsos infantes, et iterum adnuntiat
presbiter qualem diem uoluerit ut reuertantur ad scrutinium.*

f. 131v

983 *Ita tamen pensandum est, ut a primo scrutinio qui incipit tertia
ebdomada in quadragesima, usque in sabbato sancto .vii.
scrutinia esse debent, secundum formam septem dona spiritus
sancti.*

984 *Sabbatorum die mane reddunt infantes symbolum, prius
catecizas eos.* INPOSITA SVPER CAPITA EORVM MANV,
HIS VERBIS. Nec te latet satanas.

985 SECRETA. Exaudi nos omnipotens deus, et famulos tuos, quos
fidei christianae primitiis imbuisti, huius sacrificii tribuas
operationem mundari. Per.

986 INFRA ACTIONEM, VT SVPRA.

987 POSTCOMMVNIO. Concurrat domine quasumus populus tuus,
et toto tibi corde subiectus obtineat, ut ab omni perturbatione
securus, et saluationis suae gaudia prumptus, exerceat et pro
regerandis benignus exoret. Per.

988 AD POPVLVM. Deus qui cum salute hominum semper es, nunc
tamen populum gratiam abundantiorae multiplicas, respice
propitius ad electionem tuam, ut paternae protectionis auxilio, et
regenerandos munias et renatos. Per.

989 FINITA MISSA ITEM ADMONENTVR AB ARCHIDIACONO
/f. 132r / HIS VERBIS. CATICVMINI RECEDANT, VT SVPRA.

990 ITERVM DICIT DIACONVS: Filii karissimi, reuertimini in locis uestris expectantes horam qua possit circa uos dei gratia baptismum operari.

FERIA VII. ORATIO AD CATICVMINVM FACIENDVM

991 *Signum saluatoris domini nostri iesu christi, in frontem tui pono.*

992 *Signum saluatoris domini nostri iesu christi in pectus tuum pono.*

CLX

993 ORATIO. Omnipotens sempiterne deus pater domini nostri iesu christi, respice dignare super hunc famulum tuum .ill. quem ad rudimenta fidei uocare dignatus es, omnem cecitatem cordis ab eo expelle, disrumpe omnes laqueos satanae quibus fuerat colligatus, aperi ei domine ianuam pietatis tuae, ut signo sapientiae tuae imbutus, omnium cupiditatum foetoribus careat, et ad suauem odorem praeceptorum tuorum laetus tibi in ecclesia tua deseruiat, et proficiat de die in diem, ut idoneus efficiatur accedere ad gratiam baptismi tui percepta medicina. Per dominum.

994 ALIA. Praeces nostras quaesumus domine clementer exaudi, et hunc electum tuum crucis dominice, cuius inpressione eum signamus uirtute custodi, ut magnitudinis gloriae rudimenta seruans, per custodia mandatorum tuorum, ad regenerationis gloriam peruenire mereatur. Per dominum.

/f. 132v **995** ITEM ALIA. / <Deus> qui humani generis ita es conditor, ut sis etiam reformator, propitiare populis adoptiuis, et nouo testamento sobolem nouae prolis adscribae, ut filii promissionis quod non potuerunt assequi per naturam, gaudeant se recepisse per gratiam. Per.

CLXI

996 BENEDICTIO SALIS DANDVM CATECVMINVM. Exorcizo te creatura salis in nomine dei patris omnipotentis, et in caritate

220

domini nostri iesu christi, et in uirtute spiritus sancti, exorcizo te per deum + uiuum, et per deum uerum, qui te ad tutelam humani generis procreauit, et populo uenienti ad credulitatem per seruos tuos consecrari praecepit, ut in nomine sanctae trinitatis efficiaris salutare sacramentum, ad effugandum inimicum. Proinde rogamus te domine deus noster, ut hanc creaturam salis, sanctificando sanctifices, benedicendo benedices, ut fiat omnibus accipientibus perfecta medicina permanens in uisceribus eorum, in nomine domini nostri iesu christi, qui uenturus est iudicare uiuos et mortuos et saeculum per ignem.

997 HANC ORATIONEM EXPLETA, ACCIPIAT SACERDOS DE EODEM SALE ET PONAT IN ORE INFANTIS DICENDO ILLI: Accipe sal sapientiae propitiatus in uitam aeternam.

998 <BENEDICTIO POST DATVM SALEM>. Deus patrum nostrorum, deus uniuerse conditor ueritatis, te supplices exoramus, ut hunc fa/mulum tuum .ill. respicere digneris propitius, ut hoc primum patibulum salis gustantem non diutius esurire permittas, quominus cybo expleatur caelesti, quatinus sit semper domine spiritu feruens, perduc eum ad noue regenerationis lauacrum, ut cum fidelibus tuis promissionum tuarum aeterna praemia consequi mereatur.

/f. 133r

999 ITERVM FAC CRVCEM IN FRONTIBVS EIVS, DIC HANC ORATIONEM: Deus abraham, deus isaac, deus iacob, deus qui moysi famulo tuo in monte synai apparuisti, et filios israhel de terra aegypti eduxisti, deputans eis angelum pietatis tuae, qui custodiret eos die ac nocte, te quaesumus domine ut mittere digneris sanctum angelum tuum, ut similiter custodiat et hunc famulum tuum, et perducat eum ad gratiam baptismi tui.

1000 Ergo maledicte diabole recognosce sententiam tuam, et da honorem deo uiuo et uero, da honorem iesu christo filio eius et spiritui sancto, et recede ab hoc famulo dei, quia istum sibi deus et dominus noster iesus christus ad suam sanctam gratiam et benedictionem fontemque baptismatis dono uocare dignatus est, et hoc signum sancte crucis quod nos fronti eius damus, tu maledicte diabole numquam audeas uiolare, per christum dominum nostrum, qui cum patre et spiritu sancto uiuit et regnat. Per omnia.

/f. 133v **1001** ITEM SVPER FEMINAS. / Deus caeli, deus terrae, deus angelorum, deus archangelorum, deus prophetarum, deus martyrum, deus confessorum, deus uirginum, deus omnium bene uiuentium, deus cui omnis lingua confitetur, et omne genu flectitur, caelestium terrestrium et infernorum, te inuoco domine super hanc famulam tuam .ill. ut perducere eam digneris ad gratiam baptismi tui. Ergo maledicte.

1002 SVPER MASCVLOS. Deus inmortale praesidium omnium postulantium, liberatio supplicum, pax rogantium, uita credentium, resurrectio mortuorum, te inuoco domine super hunc famulum tuum .ill. qui baptismi tui donum petens aeternam consequi gratiam spiritali regeneratione desiderat, accipe eum domine et quia dignus es dicere, petite et accipietis, quaerite et inuenietis, pulsate et aperietur uobis. Petenti itaque porrige et ianuam pande, pulsanti, ut aeternam caelestis lauacri benedictionem consecutus, promissa tui muneris regna percipiat.

1003 Audi maledicte satanas, adiuratus per nomen aeterni dei et saluatoris nostri filii eius, cum tua uictus inuidia tremens gemensque discede, nihil tibi sit commune cum seruo dei iam caelestia cogitanti renuntiatori tibi a saeculo tuo, et beatae inmortalitatis uictori, da igitur honorem aduenienti spiritui
/f. 134r sancto qui ex summa / caeli arce descendens, pro turbatis fraudibus tuis diuino fonte purgatum pectus, id est sanctificatum deo templum, et habitum perficiat ut ab omnibus poenitus noxiis praeteritorum criminum liberatus seruus dei gratias perenni deo referat semper, et benedicat nomen eius sanctum, in saecula saeculorum. Per dominum, qui uenturus.

1004 ITEM SVPER FEMINAS. Deus abraham deus isaac deus iacob, deus qui tribus israel de aegyptia seruitute liberatos, per moysen famulum tuum de custodia mandatorum tuorum in deserto monuisti, et susannam de falso crimine liberasti, te suplex deprecor domine, ut liberes et hanc famulam tuam, et perducere eam digneris ad gratiam baptismi tui. Ergo maledicte diabole.

222

1005 ITEM SVPER MASCVLOS. Exorcizo te immunde spiritus. In nomine patris et filii et spiritus sancti, ut exeas et recedas ab hoc famulo dei .N. Ipse enim tibi imperat maledicte damnate, qui pedibus super mare ambulauit, et petro mergenti dexteram porrexit. Ergo.

1006 ITEM SVPER FEMINAM. Exorcizo te inmunde spiritus per patrem et filium et spiritum sanctum, ut exeas et recedas ab hac famula dei. Ipse enim imperat maledicte damnate, qui caeco nato oculos aperuit, et quatriduanum lazarum de monumento suscitauit. Ergo ut supra.

f. 134v **1007** ITEM SVPER MASCVLVM ET FEMINAM. / Aeternam ac iustissimam pietatem tuam deprecor domine sancte pater omnipotens aeterne deus, luminis et ueritatis super hunc famulum tuum, ut digneris eum inluminare lumine intelligentiae tuae, munda eum et sanctifica, da ei scientiam ueram, ut dignus efficiatur accedere ad gratiam baptismi tui, teneat firmam spem, consilium rectum, doctrinam sanctam, ut aptus sit ad percipiendam gratiam baptismi tui. Per.

1008 ORATIO IN SABBATO SANCTO AD CATECIZANDVM INFANTES. Nec te latet satanas imminere tibi poenas, imminere tibi tormenta, imminere tibi diem iudicii, diem supplicii sempiterni, diem qui uenturus est uelut clibanus ardens, in quo tibi atque uniuersis angelis tuis aeternus ueniet interitus, proinde damnate da honorem deo uiuo et uero, da honorem iesu christo filio eius et spiritui sancto, in cuius nomine atque uirtute precipio tibi quicumque es spiritus inmunde ut exeas et recedas ab hoc famulo dei, quem hodie deus et dominus noster iesus christus ad suam sanctam gratiam et benedictionem, fontemque baptismatis uocare dignatus est, ut fiat eius templum per aquam regenerationis, in remissionem omnium peccatorum, in nomine domini nostri iesu christi, qui uenturus est.

f. 135r **1009** INDE VERO TANGAT EI NARES ET AVRES / DE SPVTO, ET DICIT AD AVREM. Effeta, quod est adaperire, in odorem suauitatis. Tu autem effugare diabole, adpropinquabat enim iudicium dei.

1010 POSTEA VERO TANGAT EI PECTVS ET INTER SCAPVLAS DE OLEO EXORCIZATO CRVCEM FACIENDO CVM POLICE. ET VOCATO NOMINE EIVS DICAT: Abrenuntias satanas? R. Abrenuntio. Et omnibus operibus eius? R. Abrenuntio. Et omnibus pompis eius? R. Abrenuntio.

1011 Et ego te lineo[1] oleo salutis in christo iesu domino nostro.

1012 *Hora sexta ingrediatur pontifex in sacrarium cum laeuitis et ministris, et induant se sacris uestibus, et ordinent se sicuti in crastina die paschae continetur, et iubeat adquiri nouum ignem, cum ampulla a sole inluminatum, siue a silice excussum. Deinde faciant crucem de incenso in caereo, et scribatur anni domini, atque A. et W., et tunc portetur caereus ante episcopum cum processione cum candelabris et turibulis, tamen sine lumine, et sic stipatus incedat episcopus in medio choro et ibi ponatur caereus. Episcopus autem finita oratione, pergat ad altare, et ibi hora sessionis sedeat. Non ascendat ad sedem usque ad tempus*

/f. 135v

dum dicat. Gloria in excelsis deo. Inde leuita postu/lans benedictionem ab episcopo, eat ad cereum et consecret, processio uero diuidet se pars in dextera, et pars in sinistra. Interim episcopus sedendo, benedicat ignem et incensum, ut audiant circumstantes. Cereus uero non inluminetur, usquedum peruenerit diaconus. Ignis accendit.

CLXIII

1013 BENEDICTIO IGNIS. Domine sancte[2] pater omnipotens deus, exaudi nos lumen indeficiens, tu es sanctae conditor omnium luminum, benedic domine hoc lumen, quod a te sanctificatum atque benedictum est, qui inluminasti omnem mundum, ut ab eo lumine accendamur, et inluminemur igni claritatis tuae, sicut ignem inluminasti moysi. Ita inluminabis cordibus et sensibus nostris, ut ad uitam aeternam peruenire mereamur. Per dominum nostrum.

---

[1] A second *te* supplied interlinearly.
[2] *sanctae* before correction.

1014 ALIA. Domine sancte pater omnipotens aeterne deus, quod in nomine tuo et filii tui ac domini nostri iesu christi et spiritus sancti, benediximus et sanctificauimus ignem hunc, adiuua nos. Qui uiuis et gloriaris.

CLXIIII

1015 BENEDICTIO INCENSI. Domine deus omnipotens cui adsistunt exercitus angelorum cum tremore, quorum seruitus in uento et igne conuertitur, dignare respicere et benedicere hanc creaturam incensi, ut omnes languores insidias odorem ipsius sentientes effugiant, et separentur a plasma tua, quos / pretioso sanguine tuo redemisiti, et numquam ledantur a morsu antiqui serpentis. Per.

f. 136r

1016 ALIA. Omnipotens deus abraham, deus isaac, deus iacob, inmitte in hanc creaturam incensi odoris tui uirtutem, ut sit seruulis uel ancillis tuis, munimentum tutelaque defensionis, ut non intret hostis in uiscera eorum, aditumque et sedem inibi habere non possit. Per te christe.

1017 ITEM ALIA. Veniat ergo omnipotens deus, super hoc incensum, larga tuae benedictionis infusio, ut quodcumque ex huius aliquid purificationis ministerio fuerit deportatum, expulsa diabolice fraudis nequitia, uirtus tuae maiestatis adsistat. Per.

CLXV

1018 CONSECRATIO CEREI. [1]Exultet iam angelica turba caelorum, exultent diuina mysteria, et pro tanti regis uictoria, tuba intonet salutaris. Gaudeat se tellus tantis inradiata fulgoribus, et aeterni regis splendore lustrata totius orbis se sentiat amisisse caliginem. Letetur et mater ecclesia tanti luminis adornata fulgoribus, et magnis populorum uocibus haec aula resultet. Quapropter adstantibus uobis fratres karissimi, ad tam miram sancti huius luminis claritatem, una mecum, quaeso, dei omnipotentis misericordiam inuocate, ut qui me non meis meritis intra leuitarum numerum dignatus est adgregare / luminis sui gratia infundente cerei huius laudem implere perficiat. Per dominum.

f. 136v

---

[1]   Neumed throughout.

Dominus uobiscum. R. Et cum spiritu tuo.
Sursum corda. R. Habemus ad dominum.
Gratias agamus domino deo nostro. R. Dignum et iustum est.

1019 PRAEFATIO EIVSDEM. [1]Vere quia dignum et iustum est. Vt inuisibilem deum omnipotentem patrem filiumque unigenitum dominum nostrum iesum christum, sanctum quoque spiritum, toto cordis ac mentis affectu et uocis mysterio personare. Qui pro nobis aeterno patri adae debitum soluit, et ueteris piaculi cautionem pio cruore detersit. Haec sunt enim festa paschalia, in quibus uerus ille agnus occiditur, eiusque sanguis postibus consecretur. In quo primum patres nostros, filios israhel eductos de aegypto rubrum mare sicco uestigio transire fecisti. Haec igitur nox est, quae peccatorum tenebras columne inluminatione purgauit. Haec nox est quae hodie per uniuersum mundum in christum credentes, a uitiis saeculi segregatos, et caligine peccatorum reddit gratiae sociatque sanctitati. Haec nox est in qua distructis uinculis mortis, christus ab inferis uictor ascendit. Nihil enim nasci nobis profuit, nisi redimi profuisset. O mira circa nos, tuae pietatis dignatio. O inaestimabilis dilectio caritatis, ut seruum redimeres, filium tradidisti. O certę /f. 137v necessarium adae peccatum nostrum / quod christi morte deletum est. O felix culpa, quae talem ac tantum meruit habere redemptorem. O beata nox, quae sola meruit scire tempus et horam, in qua christus ab inferis resurrexit. Haec nox est, de qua scriptum est, et nox ut dies inluminabitur, et nox inluminatio mea in deliciis meis. Huius igitur sanctificatio noctis, fugat scelera, culpas lauat, et reddit innocentiam lapsis, mestis laetitiam. Fugat odia, concordiam parat, et curuat imperia. In huius igitur noctis gratia, suscipe sancte pater incensi hu+ius sacrificium uespertinum. Quod tibi in hac cerei oblatione sollempni, per ministrorum manus de operibus apum, sacrosancta reddit ecclesia. Sed iam columne huius praeconia nouimus, quam in honore dei rutilans ignis accendit. Qui licet diuisus in partes mutuati luminis detrimenta non nouit. Alitur[2] liquentibus cęris[3] quas in substantiam pretiosae huius lampadis

---

[1] Neumed throughout.
[2] *Aliter* before correction.
[3] *cęreis* before correction.

mater eduxit. O uere beata nox, quae expoliauit aegyptios, ditauit aebreos. Nox in qua terrenis caelestia iunguntur[1]. Oramus te domine, ut caereus iste in honorem nominis tui conse+cratus, ad noctis huius caliginem destruendam indeficiens perseueret, in odorem suauitatis acceptus, supernis luminaribus misceatur. Flammas eius, lucifer matutinum inueniat. Ille in qua lucifer, qui nescit occasum. Ille qui regressus ab in/feris, humano generi serenus inluxit. [2]Precamur ergo te domine, ut nos famulos tuos omnem clerum et deuotissimum populum, una cum papa nostro .ill. quiete temporum concessa in his paschalibus gaudiis conseruare digneris. Per dominum.

/f. 137v

CLXVI
ORATIONES PER SINGVLAS LECTIONES IN SABBATO SANCTO

1020 In principio erat uerbum.

1021 Deus qui mirabiliter creasti hominem, et mirabilius redemisti, da nobis contra oblectamenta peccati mentis ratione persistere, ut mereamur ad gaudia aeterna peruenire. Per.

1022 Noae.

1023 ORATIO. Deus incommutabilis uirtus, lumen aeternum, respice propitius ad totius ecclesię tuae mirabile sacramentum, et opus salutis humanae perpetuę dispositionis effectu tranquillus operare, totusque mundus experiatur, et uideat deiecta erigi, inueterata nouari, et per ipsum redire omnia in[3] integrum, a quo sumpsere principium.

1024 Temptauit deus abraham.

1025 ORATIO. Deus fidelium pater summe, qui in toto orbe terrarum promissionis tuae filios diffusa adoptione multiplicas, et per paschale sacramentum abraham puerum tuum, uniuersarum

---

[1] *iungitur* before correction.
[2] An alternative text of the *Precamur* in the upper left corner of fol. 137v erased and illegible.
[3] Supplied interlinearly.

sicut iurasti gentium efficis patrem, da populis tuis digne ad gratiam tuae uocationis intrare. Per dominum.

1026 Factum est in uigilia matutina. TRACT. Cantemus domino.

/f. 138r **1027** ORATIO. / Deus cuius antiqua miracula etiam nostris seculis coruscare sentimus, dum quod uni populo a[1] persecutione aegyptia liberando, dexterę tuae potentia contulisti, id in salutem gentium per aquam regenerationis operaris, praesta ut et in abrahae filios et in israheliticam dignitatem, totius mundi transeat plenitudo. Per.

1028 Haec est hereditas.

1029 ORATIO. Deus qui ecclesiam tuam semper gentium uocatione multiplicas, concede propitius, ut quos aqua baptismatis abluis, continua protectione tuearis. Per.

1030 Audi israhel. TRACT. Vinea facta est.

1031 ORATIO. Deus incommutabilis uirtus, et lumen aeternum, respice propitius ad totius ecclesiae mirabile sacramentum, et da famulis tuis ut hoc quod deuote agimus, etiam rectitudine uitae teneamus. Per.

1032 Et facta est super me manus domini.

1033 ORATIO. Deus qui nos ad caelebrandum paschale sacramentum utriusque testamenti paginis imbuisti, da nobis intelligere misericordias tuas, ut ex perceptione praesentium numerum firma sit expectatio futurorum. Per.

1034 Adpraehendent.

---

[1] Supplied interlinearly by original scribe.

1035 [1]ORATIO. Deus qui diuitias misericordiae tuae in hac praecipuę nocte largiris, propitiare uniuerso ordini sacerdotalis officii, et omnes gradus famulatus nostri perfecta delictorum remissione sanctifica, ut / ministraturos regeneratricis gratiae tuae nulli esse obnoxios patiaris offensae. Per.

/f. 138v

1036 Dixit dominus ad moysen et aaron in terra aegypti. TRACT. Adscende caelum.

1037 ORATIO. Omnipotens sempiterne deus, qui in omnium operum tuorum dispensatione mirabilis es, intelligant redempti tui non fuisse excellentius, quod initio factus est mundus, quam quod in fine sęculorum pascha nostrum immolatus est christus. Qui tecum.

1038 Factum est uerbum domini ad ionam.

1039 ORATIO. Deus qui diuersitatem omnium gentium in confessione tui nominis adunasti, da nobis et uelle et posse quod praecipis, ut populo ad aeternitatem uocato, una sit fides mentium, et pietas actionum. Per.

1040 Scripsit moyses.

1041 ORATIO. Deus celsitudo humilium, et fortitudo rectorum, qui per sanctum moysen puerum tuum, ita erudire populos tuos sacri carminis tui decantatione uoluisti, ut illa legis iteratio fieret, etiam nostra directio, excita in omnem iustificatarum gentium plenitudinem potentiam tuam, et da lętitiam mitigando terrorem, ut omnium peccatis tua remissione deletis[2], quod denuntiatum est in ultionem, transeat in salutem. Per.

1042 Nabuchodonosor.

---

[1]   In the left margin, a note: *Ista dicatur antequam legatur, in principio.* In the right margin, the text of the preferred collect:

2* Deus qui in omnibus ęclesię tuę filiis sanctorum prophetarum uoce manifestasti, in omni loco dominationis tuę satorem te bonorum seminum, et electorum palmitum esse cultorem, tribue quaesumus populis tuis qui et uinearum apud te nomine censentur et segetum, ut spinarum et tribulorum squalore resecato, digni efficiantur fruge fecunda. Per.

[2]   Final letters rewritten.

1043 ORATIO. Omnipotens sempiterne deus, spes unica mundi, qui prophetarum tuorum praeconio, praesentium temporum declarasti mysteria, auge populi tui uota placatus, quia in nullo fidelium, nisi ex tua inspiratione, / proueniunt quarumlibet incrementa uirtutum. Per.

/f. 139r

1044 TRACTVS DE PS. XLI. Sicut ceruus desiderat.

1045 ORATIO. Omnipotens sempiterne deus respice propitius ad deuotionem populi renascentis, qui sicut ceruus aquarum tuarum expetit fontem, et concede propitius ut fidei ipsius sitis, baptismatis mysterio animam corpusque sanctificet. Per dominum.

1046 ALIA ORATIO IN EODEM PSALMO. Concede quaesumus omnipotens deus, ut qui festa paschalia agimus, caelestibus desideriis accensi fontem uitae sitiamus. Per.

1047 *Modo incipienda est prima laetania, septena. Interim unus presbiter catecizat infantes ad hostium ecclesiae. Deinde procedat episcopus ad fontes cum tota processione, peragant secunda laetania, quina, et exinde consecret fontes. Vnus uero diaconus teneat euangelium ante oculos eius, et alter crucifixum. Duo autem presbiteri stent retro illius, et tertius ministret ei, diaconi et subdiaconi a dextro et a sinistro stent. Acoliti uero, cum candelabris et candelis sine lumine perseuerent coram episcopo, usquedum dicatur a diacono. Accendite.*

BENEDICTIO FONTIS
Dominus uobiscum. R. Et cum spiritu tuo.

CLXVII

1048 ORATIO. Omnipotens sempiterne deus, adesto magne pietatis tuae mysteriis, adesto sacramentis et ad creandos nouos populos, quos tibi fons baptismatis parturit, / spiritum adoptionis emitte, ut quod nostrae humilitatis gerendum est, mynisterio, tuae uirtutis impleatur effectu. Per dominum.

/f. 139v

Dominus uobiscum. R. Et cum spiritu tuo.

Sursum corda. R. Habemus ad dominum.

Gratias agamus domino deo nostro. R. Dignum et iustum est.

1049 CONSECRATIO FONTIS. VD aeterne[1] deus. Qui inuisibili potentia sacramentorum tuorum mirabiliter operaris effectum. Et licet nos tantis mysteriis exequendis simus indigni, tu tamen gratiae tuae dona non deserens, etiam ad nostras praeces aures tuae pietatis inclina. Deus cuius spiritus super aquas inter ipsa mundi primordia ferebatur, ut iam tunc uirtutem sanctificationis aquarum natura conciperet. Deus qui nocentis mundi crimina per aquas abluens, regenerationis speciem in ipsa diluuii effusione signasti, ut unius elementi eiusdemque mysterio, et finis esset uiciis et origo uirtutum. Respice domine in faciem ecclesiae tuae, et multiplica in ea regenerationes tuas, qui gratiae tuae affluentis impetus, laetificas ciuitatem tuam, fontemque baptismatis aperis toto orbe terrarum gentibus innouandis, ut tuae maiestatis imperio, sumat unigeniti tui gratiam de spiritu sancto. HIC DIVIDITVR AQVA IN MODVM CRVCIS. + Qui hanc aquam regenerandis hominibus praeparatam, archana sui luminis / admixtione fecundet, ut sanctificatione concepta, ab immaculato diuini fontis utero, in nouam renata creaturam progenies caelestis emergat. Et quos aut sexus in corpore, aut aetas discernit in tempore, omnes in unam pariat gratia mater infantiam. Procul ergo hinc iubente te domine, omnis spiritus inmundus abscedat, procul tota nequitia diabolice fraudis assistat. Nihil hic loci habeat contrariae uirtutis admictio, non insidiando circumuolet, non latendo subripiat, non inficiendo corrumpat. Sit haec sancta et innocens creatura, libera ab omni inpugnatoris incursu, et totius nequitiae purgata discessu. Sit fons uiuus, aqua regenerans, unda purificans. Vt omnis hoc lauacro salutifero diluendi, operante in eis spiritu sancto, perfectae purgationis indulgentiam consequantur. HIC SIGNA. Vnde benedico te creatura aquę, per deum uiuum, per deum sanctum, qui te in principio uerbo separauit ab arida, cuius spiritus super te ferebatur, qui te de paradyso manare iussit, et in quattuor fluminibus totam terram rigare praecepit. HIC TANGIS AQVAM. Qui te in deserto amaram suauitate indita

f. 140r

---

[1]   *aeternae* before correction.

fecit esse potabilem, et sitienti populo de petra produxit. Benedico te et per iesum christum filium eius unicum dominum nostrum / qui te in chana galileae signo admirabili sua potentia conuertit in uinum, qui pedibus super te ambulauit, et a iohanne in iordane in te baptizatus est, qui te una cum sanguine de latere suo produxit, et discipulis suis iussit ut credentes baptizarentur in te dicens. Ite docete omnes gentes baptizantes eos in nomine patris et filii et spiritus sancti. HIC MVTA VOCEM QVASI LECTIONEM LEGENS. Haec nobis praecepta seruantibus, tu deus omnipotens clemens adesto, tu benignus aspira. HIC SVFFLA TER IN AQVA. tu has simplices aquas, tuo ore benedicito, ut praeter naturalem emundationem quam lauandis possunt adhibere corporibus, sint etiam purificandis mentibus efficaces. HIC PONVNT CAEREOS. Descendat in hanc plenitudinem fontis uirtus spiritus tui, totamque huius aquae substantiam regenerandi fecundet effectu, hic omnium peccatorum maculae deleantur, hic natura ad imaginem tuam condita, et ad honorem sui reformata principii, cunctis uetustatis squaloribus emundetur, ut omnis homo hoc sacramentum regenerationis ingressus, in uere innocentiae nouam infantiam renascatur. Per dominum nostrum iesum christum filium tuum, qui uenturus est. TVNC SPARGAT AQVAM IN POPVLO.

/f. 140v

/f. 141r **1050** DEINDE / MISCEAT CHRISMA CVM AQVA ET DICAT HIS VERBIS. Fecundetur et sanctificetur fons iste hoc salutifere chrismate. In nomine patris et filii et spiritus sancti. Coniunctio chrismatis huius sanctificationis et aqua baptismatis. In nomine patris et filii et spiritus sancti. Coniunctio olei unctionis et aquae baptismatis in nomine.

1051 *Et tunc a patronibus deportentur infantes coram episcopo, episcopus uero dicat singulis, quod nomen uocaris. Patronus uero dicat nomen eius, episcopus dicat.* Credis in deum patrem omnipotentem creatorem caeli et terrae? R. Credo. Credis in iesum christum filium eius unicum dominum nostrum natum et passum? R. Credo. Credis in spiritum sanctum, sanctam ecclesiam catholicam, remissionem peccatorum, carnis resurrectionem? R. Credo.

1052 INTERROGET EPISCOPVS. Vis baptizari? R. Volo.

232

1053 *Deinde baptizat sacerdos sub trina mersione, tantum sanctam trinitatem semel inuocans. Ita dicendo.* Et ego baptizo te in nomine patris, *et mergat semel,* et filii, *et mergat iterum,* et spiritus sancti, *mergatque tertio.*

1054 *Vt autem surrexerit a fonte, faciat sacerdos signum crucis de chrismate cum pollice in uertice eius, dicens hanc orationem*: Deus omnipotens pater domini nostri iesu christi, qui te regenerauit ex aqua et spiritu sancto, quique dedit tibi remissionem peccatorum omnium, ipse te linit chrismate salutis, in christo iesu domino nostro in uitam aeternam in saecula saeculorum.

1055 ET VESTIETVR INFANS VESTIMENTIS SVIS. Accipe uestem candidam quam perferas ante tribunal christi in uitam aeternam, et uiuas in saecula saeculorum. Amen.

f. 141v **1056** *Illud autem praeuidendum est baptizatis, ut nullus / cibum accipiant, nec ablactentur antequam communicent post missam. Episcopus autem cum processione redeat in sacrarium, lauetque manus. Induet se aliis uestis. Interim cantor cum omni scola in medio choro, faciat tertiam laetaniam. Hoc peracto, pergat episcopus ad sedem cum omni processione, et annuente illo, dicat diaconus.* Accendite. *Episcopus autem inchoat.* Gloria in excelsis deo, *et ilico pulsantur omnia signa per tota monasteria, finito autem* Gloria in excelsis deo, *dicat pontifex*: Pax uobis.

CLXVIII

1057 ORATIO. Deus qui hanc sacratissimam noctem gloria dominicę resurrectionis inlustras, conserua in noua familiae tuae progenie[1] adoptionis spiritum quem dedisti, ut corpore et mente renouati, puram tibi exhibeant seruitutem. Per dominum nostrum.

1058 EPISTOLA. ALLELVIA. Confitemini. TRACT. Laudate dominum. EVANGELIVM.

---

[1] Final *e* rewritten.

1059 SVPER OBLATA. Suscipe domine quaesumus praeces populi tui cum oblationibus hostiarum, ut paschalibus initiata mysteriis, ad aeternitatis nobis medelam te operante proficiant. Per dominum nostrum.

1060 PRAEFATIO. [1]VD aequum et salutare. Te quidem omni tempore, sed in hac potissimum nocte gloriosius conlaudare et praedicare[2], cum pascha nostrum immolatus est christus. Ipse enim uerus est agnus, qui abstulit peccata mundi. Qui mortem nostram mo/riendo destruxit, et uitam resurgendo reparauit. Et ideo cum angelis.

/f. 142r

1061 Communicantes et noctem sacratissimam celebrantes, resurrectionis domini nostri iesu christi secundum carnem. Sed et memoriam uenerantes. Inprimis.

1062 INFRA ACTIONEM. Hanc igitur oblationem seruitutis nostrae, sed et cunctae familiae tuae quam tibi offerimus, pro his quoque quos regenerare dignatus es ex aqua et spiritu sancto, tribuens eis remissionem omnium peccatorum, quaesumus domine ut placatus.

CLXVIIII

1063 BENEDICTIO LACTIS ET MELLIS. Benedic domine hanc creaturam lactis et mellis, et pota famulos tuos de hoc fonte perenni, quod est spiritus ueritatis, et enutri eos de hoc melle et lacte, tu enim domine promisisti patribus nostris, abrahę isaac et iacob dicens. Introducam uos in terram repromissionis, terram fluentem lac et mel. Coniunge domine famulos tuos spiritui sancto sicut coniunctum est hoc lac et mel in christo iesu domino nostro. Per quem haec omnia domine semper bona creas.

CLXX

1064 BENEDICTIO SVPER POPVLVM. Deus qui de ecclesiae tuae intemerato utero nouos populos producens, eam uirginitate manente, noua semper prole fęcundat, fidei spei et caritatis uos

---

[1] Partly neumed.
[2] *di* supplied interlinearly.

munere repleat, et suae in uobis benedictionis dona infundat. AMEN.

f. 142v / Et qui hanc sacratissimam noctem redemptoris nostri resurrectione uoluit inlustrare, mentes uestras peccatorum tenebris mundatas uirtutum copiis faciat coruscare. AMEN.

Quo eorum qui modo renati sunt innocentiam imitari certetis, et uascula mentium uestrarum exemplo praesentium luminum inlustretis, ut cum bonorum operum lampadibus ad huius sponsi thalamum, cui resurrectionem celebratis, cum prudentibus uirginibus intrare possitis. AMEN.

Quod ipse praestare.

1065 INTERIM DVM COMMVNICET POPVLVS, INCHOAT CANTOR. A. Alleluia. PS. Laudate dominum omnes gentes. AN. IN EVANGELIVM. Vespere autem. PS. Magnificat.

1066 POST HOC SVRGAT EPISCOPVS DE SEDE ET PERGAT AD ALTARE, DICAT COLLECTAM. Spiritum nobis domine tuae caritatis infunde, ut quos sacramentis paschalibus satiasti, tua facias pietate concordes. Per dominum.

1067 POST HAEC DICIT DIACONVS: ITE MISSA EST.

1068 *Dominica in die sancto paschae, primo antequam episcopus missam celebrat, ingredietur quoddam oratorium, et secundum cordis compunctionem, seipsum libamine orationis deo offerat.*

CLXXI

1069 DICAT HANC ORATIONEM: Via sanctorum ominum iesu christe, qui ad te uenientibus claritatis gaudium contulisti, introitum templi istius, spiritus sancti luce perfunde, qui locum f. 143r istum sanctorum martyrum nomine uel sanguine / consecrasti, praesta quaesumus omnipotens deus, ut omnes isti intercedentes obtineant ueniam pro delictis, ab omnibus liberentur angustiis. Impetrent quicquid petierint, pro necessitatibus suis placere semper praeualeant coram oculis tuis, quatinus per te et per sanctum petrum militem tuum muniti, mereamur aulam paradysi introire. Per.

235

1070 *Hora diei tertia, arma sibi deferantur sacerdotalia, quae induet extra chorum sinistrae partis, in loco secretarii, dum introierit in secretarium dicat hanc orationem.*

1071 ORATIO. Omnipotens et misericors deus, qui sacerdotem ministerio ad tibi seruiendum et supplicandum, ut ita dignaris quaesumus inmensam clementiam tuam, ut quicquid modo uisitamus uisites, quidquid benedicimus benedicas, sitque ad nostrae humilitatis introitum, sanctorum tuorum meritis, fuga demonum, angeli pacis ingressus. Per.

1072 *Primo quidem minister deferat caligas usque ad genu tendentes et dicat*: Tu domine obtamus, iubeas benedicier omnes.

1073 RESPONDET EPISCOPVS: Totius honestatis auctor, omnipotens deus ad reprimendas antiqui hostis uersutias, per nostrae seruitutis mysterium, iube sanctificari has caligas, ut et in gressu resplendeat euangelii ueritas, et mente fidei exerceatur integritas. Per omnia.

1074 DEINDE MINISTER DET SANDALIA, ET DICAT VT SVPRA. RESPONDET EPISCOPVS: Indue me domine calciamentis iustitiae, quem iohannes uidit uesti/tum podere ut possim tibi omni tempore cum timore seruire. Per omnia.

/f. 143v

1075 POST HAEC VERO ORNET SE CAETERIS INDVMENTIS, ET MINISTER ADMINISTRET SVPERHVMERALE, ET DICAT: IVBE DOMINE BENEDICERE. RESPONDET EPISCOPVS:
Virtus summa deus cunctorum rector opimus,
Tu benedic nostrum, quo nunc ornamur amictum,
Vt seruire tibi ualeamus corde pudico.
Per omnia.

1076 POSTEA MINISTRET EI ALBAM, ET DICAT VT SVPRA.
Vestibus angelicis induti rex pietatis,
Possimus libare pii libamen odoris,
Clemens et prauae purges contagia mentis,
Ac citius delenda malae contagia mentis.
Per omnia.

1077 POSTEA MINISTRET EI CINGVLVM, ET DICAT VT SVPRA.
Scrutator cordis et caste mentis amator,
Tu lumbos praecinge meos deus intime iudex,
Mortificans prauos in casto corpore gestus.
Per omnia.

1078 POSTEA DETVR EI BALTEVM PVDICITIAE ET DICAT MINISTER, VT SVPRA. RESPONDET EPISCOPVS: Rogo te altissime deus sabaoth pater sancte, ut me castigare digneris accingere, et meos lumbos balteo tui timoris ambire, ac renes cordis mei tuae caritatis igne urere, ut pro peccatis meis possim intercedere, et adstantis populi peccatorum ueniam promereri, ac pacificas singulorum hostias immolare. Per.

f. 144r **1079** TVNC MINISTER OFFE/RAT EI STOLAM IOCVNDITATIS, GERENS VITAM GEMINĘ CONTEMPLATIONIS, ET DICAT VT SVPRA. RESPONDET EPISCOPVS.
Colla iugo subdenda tuo deus alme sacrato,
Ad cuius dignum praetiosa morte sepulchrum,
Virtus angelica consederat ordine mundo.
Per omnia.

1080 SVPER HAEC ITAQVE MINISTRETVR EI TVNICA GYRIS IN TINTINABVLIS MYRICE REFECTA, ET DICAT MINISTER VT SVPRA. RESPONDET EPISCOPVS.
Sanctifica tunicam qua nunc superinduor istam,
Omnipotens aeternae deus, sine numine cuius,
Nil humana ualet deuoti condere uirtus,
Et qui me sacris uoluisti uestibus uti,
Da seruire tibi iudex pie mente fideli.
Per omnia.

1081 DEINDE MINISTRETVR EI AQVA AD MANVS, ET PECTEN AD CAPVT, ET DICAT MINISTER, VT SVPRA. <RESPONDET EPISCOPVS:> Omnipotens et misericors deus, precor clementiam tuam, ut me audaciter accedentem non sinas perire, sed dignare lauare, ornare, et laeniter suscipere. Per omnia.

1082 TVNC MINISTRETVR EI MANICĘ VT SVPRA.
<RESPONDET EPISCOPVS:>
Digna manus nostras christi custodia seruet,
Vt tractare quaeant nostrae monumenta salutis.
Per.

1083 POSTEA DETVR EI ANVLVS IN DEXTERA MANV,
DESVPER MANICA. DICAT MINISTER VT SVPRA.
<RESPONDET EPISCOPVS:>
Pignore me fidei signatum pacis et arra,
Custodi dextra rex benedictae tua.
Per omnia.

1084 POSTEA MINISTRETVR EI CASVLA, TANDEM VERO /
/f. 144v   RATIONALE COHERENS VINCTIM SVPERHVMERALI.
ET DICAT MINISTER VT SVPRA. RESPONDET
EPISCOPVS.
Spes aeternae deus cunctorum certa salusque,
Tu memor esto mei, toto te corde petenti,
Exequar ut dignus caelestis munia uitae.
Dumque meis manibus tractatur mystica uirtus,
Dispereat quicquid contraxerat ordo ueternus.
Per omnia.

1085 DETVRQVE MANVI LEVAE MANVPVLVS CASTITATIS
ET DICAT MINISTER. Iube domine benedicere. RESPONDET
EPISCOPVS:
Qui super astra sedes qui regni sceptra tueris,
Summus adesto deus mihimet tua iussa sequenti,
Ac leuem capiti complexibus adhibe dextram,
Auxiliumque mihi tribuas, per cuncta benignus,
Vt ualeam casta tibi sistere perpeti uita.
Per omnia.

1086 *Cum omni quoque diligentia episcopus ueneretur a suis, eo*
autem rationabiliter flamineato accedat ordinatim omnis
processio .vii. aut .v. aut .iii. etsi non presbiter et diaconus, pres-
byter quoque ad dexteram, et diaconus ad sinistram,
subdiaconus uero ante oculos eius teneat euangelium, qui etiam
stipatus sit duobus acolitis aut pluribus cum candelabris et

turibulis. Interim sane praeparet se schola, et cantor eorum medius, annuente episcopo inchoat A. Resurrexi. PS. Domine probasti me. *Properante episcopo ad templi uestibulum, et ad hostium secretarii osculetur euangelium, et postea cum omni diligentia incedant.*

f. 145r **1087** / *Finitoque introitu, ingrediatur medius pontifex cum collegio processionis, eo autem adstante et orante, dicat hanc orationem*: Suscipe confessionem meam unica spes salutis meae domine deus meus, quia gula, ebrietate, fornicatione, libidine, tristitia, accedia, somnolentia, negligentia, ira, cupiditate, inuidia, malitia, odio, detractione, periurio, falsitate, mendacio, uana gloria, leuitate, ac superbia perditus sum, et omnino cogitatione, locutione, actione, atque omnibus sensibus exstinctus, qui iustificas impios, et uiuificas mortuos, uiuifica me, et resuscita me, et miserere mei, deus meus. Per.

1088 *Annuente episcopo incipiatur psalmus a cantore, cum introitu reciprocante. Interim quoque osculetur omnes sibi circumdatos. Incipiens sinistre, alternatimque ueniens dextre. Hoc autem expleto episcopus signo digiti sui inchoet cantor*: Gloria patri.

1089 *Et properet episcopus ad altare stipantibus ministris, dicat hanc orationem*: Indignum me domine sacris tuis esse fateor, qui innumeris cotidiae peccatis fuscor, quid ego blandis te domine uerbis rogare praesumo, quem inprobis sepissime factis offendo. Tu enim domine mihi medicinam ingeris egro, ego sanitati meae contraria ago, legem tuam domine sacris paginis inditam lego, sanam uero disciplinam, infelix negligo ad tuum quidem altare
f. 145v quasi deuotus accedo, sed a pre/ceptis tuis contumaci corde recedo, da ergo mihi domine quaeso cor conpunctum, quod ueraciter odio habeat peccatum, meum est si donaueris delicta deflere, tuum est ea ut niuem cito delere, et licet palmam amisserim inimico fraudante ad ueniam salutem perueniam te miserante, tibi deo est honor regnum regi cunctorum cuncta regnanti, in saecula saeculorum. Amen.

1090 *Mora quidem orationis facta, sicut ordinati sunt alter alterutrum presbiteri et diaconi osculentur altaris cornua, et ultimus episcopus ministrantibus illis osculetur euangelium ab ipsis* *eleuatum et apertum, a subdiacono scilicet in altaris medio positum, et tunc canatur*: Kyrrie eleyson.

1091 *Et ipsis ducentibus, perueniat episcopus ad solium, et tunc incipiat*: Gloria in excelsis deo. Et in terra pax hominibus bone uoluntatis, laudamus te. Benedicimus te. Adoramus te. Glorificamus te, gratias agimus tibi propter magnam gloriam tuam. Domine deus rex caelestis, deus pater omnipotens. Domine fili unigenite iesu christe, domine deus. Agnus dei, filius patris. Qui tollis peccata mundi, miserere nobis. Qui tollis peccata mundi. Suscipe depraecationem nostram. Qui sedes ad dexteram patris. Miserere nobis. Quoniam tu solus sanctus. Tu solus dominus. Tu solus altissimus, iesu christe. Cum sancto spiritu in gloria dei patris. Amen.

1092 POST HAEC AVTEM CANATVR MISSA SECVNDVM SVI VISVM. ET ADNVNTIAT EPISCOPVS: Pax uobis. R. Et cum spiritu tuo.

CLXXII
1093 ORATIO. *DEVS QVI HODIERNA DIE PER VNIGENITVM[1] TVVM* aeternitatis nobis aditum deuicta morte / reserasti, uota nostra quae praeueniendo aspiras, etiam adiuuando prosequere. Per dominum nostrum.

/f. 146r

1094 *Exinde procedat subdiaconus in ambonem, et legat epistolam*: Expurgate. R. Haec dies. All. Pascha nostrum.

1095 *Incedat siquidem diaconus cum turibulum, aliusque minister cum turae genuflectentes ad genua sedentis episcopi, et mittat incensum, fumum suauis odoris et dicat*: Mitto incensum in odorem suauitatis, et in nomine sanctae et indiuiduae trinitatis.

1096 *Et diaconus postulans inclinato capite benedictionem et dicat*: Iube domine benedicere. RESPONDET EPISCOPVS. Dominus sit in corde tuo et in ore ad proferendam euangelii lectionem. *Accipiens ipse euangelium et deosculetur eum et altare, et ascendat in ambonem adnuntianti uerba aeternae felicitatis. Legatur euangelium*: Maria magdalenae.

---

[1] *NI* supplied interlinearly.

1097 *Finito euangelio, portetur euangelium a subdiacono ut osculetur episcopus et omnes post illum, et dicat episcopus*: Dominus uobiscum. R. Et cum spiritu tuo. *Oremus. Tunc incipiat*: OF. Terra tremuit.

1098 *Eo autem finito et oblatione recepta, cum omni processione reuertatur ad solium, et exuat manicas, lauetque manus, et sic ingrediatur propiciatorium et omnis processio offerat sibi oblationem, et ad ultimum incensum, et dicat has orationes dum incensatur*: Domine deus noster supplici deuotione deposcimus, ut si/cut suscepisti munera abel, noae, aaron, zachariae, et samuhel, et omnium sanctorum tuorum, sic et manu nostra peccatrice suscipere digneris incensum istud in odorem suauitatis, et remissionem omnium peccatorum nostrorum. Per dominum.

1099 ALIA. Placetur domine hoc timiamate uel incenso furor tuus contra me et contra locum istum et contra populum istum, et praesta propitius ut fumus boni odoris, tibi simus[1] ad capiendam uitam aeternam. Per.

1100 *Postea uero ordinent se more ecclesiastico, hoc est diaconi ante altare, subdiaconi retro, episcopus in medio, quia in ore duorum uel trium stat omne uerbum. Inclinantes capita quousque dicatur*: Per omnia saecula saeculorum. R. Amen.

1101 ET DICAT HANC ORATIONEM SVPER OBLATA. Suscipe domine quesumus preces populi tui, cum oblationibus hostiarum. *Require retro in sabbato sancto.*

1102 *Tunc uero post hanc erigunt se et accoliti ministrent aquam ad manus diaconum, et manutergium, et dicat pontifex alta uoce*: Per omnia saecula saeculorum. R. Amen. Sursum corda. R. Habemus ad dominum. Gratias agamus domino deo nostro. R. Dignum et iustum est.

1103 PRAEFATIO. VD aequum et salutare. Te quidem omni tempore, ut supra.

---

[1] *sumus* before correction.

1104 DVM DICATVR SANCTVS, INCLINANT SE OMNES, ET EPISCOPVS DICAT HANC ORATIONEM INTERIM: Deus qui non mortem sed poenitentiam desideras peccatorum me[341] miserum fragilemque peccatorem / a tua non repellaes pietate, neque aspicias ad peccata et ad scelera mea, et inmundas turpesque cogitationes meas, quibus flebiliter a tua disiungor uoluntate, sed ad misericordia tua, et ad fidem deuotionemque eorum, qui per me peccatorem tuam expetunt misericordiam, et quia me indignum medium inter te et populum tuum fieri uoluisti, fac me dignum talem ut possim tuam exorare misericordiam, pro me et pro eodem populo tuo, et adiunge uoces nostras uocibus sanctorum angelorum tuorum, ut sicut illi te laudant incessanter et infatigabiliter, in aeterna beatitudine, ita nos quoque eorum interuentu, mereamur laudare te inculpabiliter, in hac peregrinatione. Per dominum.

/f. 147r

1105 Te igitur clementissime pater.

1106 Communicantes et memoriam uenerantes, ut supra.

1107 Hanc igitur oblationem seruitutis nostrae, ut supra.

CLXXIII
1108 ANTEQVAM DICATVR PER QVEM HAEC OMNIA, BENEDICTIO CARNIS. Deus uniuersae carnis, qui noae et filii eius de mundis et inmundis animalibus praecepta dedisti, quique sibi sicut holera herbarum humano generi quadrupedia munda aedere permisisti, qui et agnum in aegypto moysi et populo tuo, in uigilia paschae comedere praecepisti. In figuram agni domini nostri iesu christi, cuius[2] sanguinem omnia primogenita, in aegypto percutere precepisti, / reseruans populum tuum agni sanguine prenotatum, dignare domine omnipotens benedicere et sanctificare has ouium carnes, ut quicumque ex populis tuis fidelibus comederint, omni benedictione caelesti, et gratia tua saturati, repleantur in bonis. Per quem haec omnia domine semper bona creas sanctificas uiuificas.

/f. 147v

---

[1] Supplied interlinearly.
[2] *In figuram agni domini nostri iesu christi, cuius* written over an erasure.

1109 *Accolitus uero cum patena stet retro diacono, inclinans se cum diaconibus usque dicat episcopus. Nobis quoque peccatoribus. Diaconus igitur qui euangelium legit, inde praecauens quod super calicem episcopus faciat signum crucis, et preueniat sibi subleuens calicem in conspectu domini, et reuertatur ad locum suum, cito siquidem subdiaconi a retro altari ubi memoria uel nomina uiuorum et mortuorum nominauerunt uel recitauerunt, procedunt post diaconum inclinantes capita.*

1110 *Dominica oratione finita, accipiat subdiaconus patenam de manu accoliti, et det diacono, et ille deferat episcopo, et post haec stabilientur in loco quo erant, antequam legeretur euangelium, quousque benedictio et pacis osculum fuerint finita.*

1111 *Deinde dum dicat episcopus*: Per omnia saecula saeculorum. R. Amen. *Post dominicam orationem, et dum finierit*: Libera nos a malo. *Annuente episcopo, dicat diaconus*: Humiliate uos ad benedictionem, *et populus*: R. Deo gratias.

/ CLXXIIII

1112 *Et episcopo dicat hanc benedictionem*: Benedicat uos omnipotens deus, hodierna interueniente paschali sollempnitate, et ab omni miseratus dignetur defendere prauitate. AMEN.
Et qui ad aeternam uitam in unigeniti sui resurrectione uos reparat, in ipsius aduentu inmortalitatis uos gaudiis uestiat. AMEN.
Et qui expletas ieiuniorum siue passionis dominicę diebus paschalis festi gaudia celebratis, ad ea festa quae non sunt annua sed continua, ipso opitulante exultantibus animis ueniatis. AMEN.
Quod ipse praestare dignetur.

1113 ET INDE ACCIPIENS PARTEM CORPORIS DOMINI ET DICAT. Pax domini sit semper uobiscum. R. Et cum spiritu tuo. ET ANNVENTE EPISCOPO DICAT CANTOR. Agnus dei qui tollit peccata mundi. INTERIM OSCVLETVR ARCHIDIACONVM ET CETEROS.

1114 INDE VERTENS SE AD ALTARE DICAT HANC ORATIONEM: Dominus uobiscum. R. Et cum. Haec sacrosancta commixtio corporis, et sanguinis domini nostri iesu christi, fiat omnibus sumentibus salus mentis et corporis, et ad uitam capiendam aeternam, praeparatio salutaris. Per dominum.

1115 DVM FRANGITVR CORPVS. Emittere digneris domine sanctum angelum tuum, ad sacrum et inmortale mysterium, scilicet corpus et sanguinem tuum, nos enim frangimus domine illud, tu dignare benedicere, et praesta ut inmaculatis sensibus et ma/nibus illud tractare ualeamus, et digne sumere. Per dominum nostrum.

/f. 148v

1116 A. Emitte angelum tuum domine ut dignetur.

1117 POST HAEC ITAQVE COMMVNICENT SE OMNES SINGILLATIM, EPISCOPVS QVOQVE EOQVE COMMVNICATO, DICAT ORATIONES HAS: Perceptio corporis et sanguinis tui domine iesu christe qua ego indignus praesumo sumere, non mihi ueniat ad iudicium et condemnationem, sed pro tua pietate prosit mihi, ad tutamentum mentis et corporis. Qui cum patre in unitate.

1118 ALIA. Domine iesu christe fili dei uiui, qui ex uoluntate patris cooperante spiritu sancto per mortem tuam mundum uiuificasti, libera me per hoc sacrum corpus et sanguinem tuum, a cunctis iniquitatibus et uniuersis malis meis, et fac me tuis oboedire praeceptis, et a te numquam in perpetuum separari. Qui cum patre.

1119 ALIA. Domine sancte pater omnipotens aeternę deus, da mihi hoc corpus et sanguinem domini nostri iesu christi ita sumere, ut merear per hoc remissionem omnium peccatorum meorum accipere, et tuo sancto spiritu repleri, quia tu es benedictus, et praeter te non est alius, cuius regnum gloriosum permanet in saecula saeculorum. Amen.

1120 *Et episcopus communicet presbiteros et diaconibus cum osculo pacis, sicco tamen sacrificio, et subdiaconibus sine osculo, mixto sacrificio, et diaconi et presbiteri sumatim gustent cum calice tenente subdiacono / de ipso sanguine. Interim cantor*

/f. 149r

incipiat annuente episcopo: COM. Pascha nostrum. PS. Domine probasti me. CVM GLORIA.

1121 *Hoc autem expleto, sedeat episcopus in solio et lotis manibus tertio reuertatur ad altare et dicit collectam.*

1122 AD COMPLENDVM. Spiritum nobis domine tuae caritatis infunde, ut quos sacramentis paschalibus satiasti, tua facias pietate concordes. Per dominum nostrum.

1123 *Postea dicat episcopus conuertens ad populum*: Dominus uobiscum. R. Et cum spiritu tuo. *Annuente episcopo, dicat diaconus*: Ite missa est. R. Deo gratias. *Episcopus autem deosculatur altare cum silentio, dicit hanc orationem.*

1124 OREMVS. Placeat tibi deus sancta trinitas obsequium seruitutis meę, et praesta ut sacrificium quod oculis tuae maiestatis indignus obtuli, tibi sit acceptabile, mihique et omnibus pro quibus illud obtuli, sit te miserante propitiabile. Per dominum.

1125 AD SANCTVM IOHANNEM AD VESPERVM. Concede quaesumus omnipotens deus, ut qui resurrectionis dominicae sollemnia colimus, innouatione tui spiritus a morte animae resurgamus. Per eundem dominum.

1126 AD FONTES. Praesta quaesumus omnipotens deus, ut qui resurrectionis dominicae sollemnia colimus, ereptionis nostrae suscipere laetitiam mereamur. Per.

1127 AD SANCTAM ANDREAM. Praesta quaesumus omnipotens deus, ut qui gratiam dominicae resurrectionis agnouimus, ipsi per amorem spiritus a morte animae resurgamus. Per.

/ CLXXV

1128 PRAEFATIO IN SABBATO SANCTO. VD aeterne deus. Te quidem omni tempore, sed in hac potissimum nocte gloriosius conlaudare et praedicare, per christum dominum nostrum. Qui inferorum claustra disrumpens, uictoriae suae clara uexilla suscepit, et triumphato diabolo uictor a mortuis resurrexit. O noctem quae finem tenebris ponit, et aeternae lucis uiam pandit.

O noctem quae uidere meruit et uinci diabolum, et resurgere christum. O noctem in qua tartara spoliantur, sancti ab inferis liberantur, caelestis patriae aditus aperitur. In qua in baptismate delictorum turba perimitur, filii lucis oriuntur, quos exemplo dominicae matris sine corruptione sancta mater ecclesiae concipit, sine dolore parit, et cum gaudio ad meliora prouehit. Et ideo cum angelis.

CLXXVI

1129 DOMINICA IN PASCHA. VD usque aeterne deus. Te quidem omni tempore, sed in hoc potissimum die gloriosius praedicare, cum pascha nostrum immolatus est christus. Per quem ad aeternam uitam filii lucis oriuntur, fidelibus regni caelestis atria reserantur, et beati lege commertii diuinis humana mutantur, quia nostrorum omnium mors, cruce christi perempta esse, et in /f. 150r resurrectione eius, omnium uita resurrexit. / Quem in susceptione mortalitatis, deum maiestatis agnoscimus, et in diuinitatis gloria deum et hominem confitemur, qui mortem nostram moriendo destruxit, et uitam resurgendo restituit. Et ideo.

CLXXVII
FERIA II IN ALBIS. STATIO AD SANCTVM PETRVM

1130 Deus qui sollemnitate paschali mundo remedia contulisti, populum tuum quaesumus caelesti dono prosequere, ut et perfectam libertatem consequi mereatur, et ad uitam proficiat sempiternam. Per.

1131 SVPER OBLATA. Suscipe domine quaesumus preces populi tui cum oblationibus, ut supra.

1132 PRAEFATIO. VD aeterne deus. Et te suppliciter exorare, ut fidelibus tuis dignanter impendas, quo et paschalia capiant sacramenta, et desideranter expectent uentura, ut in mysteriis quibus renati sunt permanentes, ad nouam uitam his operantibus perducantur. Per christum.

1133 BENEDICTIO. Deus qui pro uobis suscepit iniuriam crucis, laetitia uos innouet resurrectionis. AMEN.

246

Et qui pendenti secum in cruce latroni amisit delictum, uos soluat a cunctis nexibus peccatorum. AMEN.

Vt redemptionis uestrae mysterium et digne conseruetis in opere, et locupletius aeterna perfruamini remuneratione. AMEN.

Quod ipse.

1134 Communicantes, ut supra. Hanc igitur, ut supra

1135 AD COMPLENDVM. Spiritum nobis domine, ut supra.

f. 150v **1136** / AD VESPERVM. Concede quaesumus omnipotens deus, ut festa paschalia quae uenerando colimus, etiam uiuendo teneamus. Per.

1137 AD FONTES. Concede quaesumus omnipotens deus, ut qui peccatorum nostrorum pondere premimur, a cunctis malis imminentibus, per haec paschalia festa liberemur. Per.

1138 AD SANCTVM ANDREAM. Deus qui populum tuum de hostis callidi seruitute liberasti, praeces eius misericorditer respice, et aduersantes ei tua uirtute prosterne. Per dominum.

CLXXVIII

FERIA III. AD SANCTVM PAVLVM

1139 Deus qui ecclesiam tuam nouo semper foetu multiplicas, concede famulis tuis ut sacramentum uiuendo teneant, quod fide perceperunt. Per.

1140 SVPER OBLATA. Suscipe domine fidelium preces cum oblationibus hostiarum, ut per haec pie deuotionis officia, ad caelestem gloriam transeamus. Per.

1141 PREFATIO. VD usque per christum dominum nostrum. Qui oblatione sui corporis remotis sacrificiorum carnalium, obseruationibus seipsum tibi sacram hostiam agnumque inmaculatum summus sacerdos pro salute nostra immolauit. Per quem.

1142 Communicantes. Et hanc igitur, ut supra.

1143 BENEDICTIO. Deus qui uos lauit aqua sui lateris, et redemit effusione cruoris, ipse in uobis confirmet gratiam adeptae redemptionis. AMEN.

/f. 151r / Per quem renati estis ex aqua et spiritu sancto, ipse uos caelesti consociet regno. AMEN.

Quique dedit uobis initia sanctae fidei, ipse conferat et perfectionem boni operis, et plenitudinem caritatis. AMEN.

Quod ipse.

1144 AD COMPLENDVM. Concede quaesumus omnipotens deus, ut paschalis perceptio sacramenti, continua in nostris mentibus perseueret. Per dominum.

1145 AD VESPERAS. Concede quaesumus omnipotens deus, ut qui paschali festiuitatis sollemnia colimus, in tua semper sanctificatione uiuamus. Per.

1146 AD FONTES. Praesta quaesumus omnipotens deus, ut per haec paschalia festa quae colimus, deuoti in tua semper laude uiuamus. Per dominum.

1147 AD SANCTVM ANDREAM. Deus qui conspicis familiam tuam omni humana uirtute destitui, paschali interueniente festiuitate, tui eam brachii protectione custodi. Per.

CLXXVIIIII

FERIA IIII. AD SANCTVM LAVRENTIVM FORIS MVRVM

1148 Deus qui nos resurrectionis dominicae annua sollemnitate laetificas, concede propitius, ut per temporalia festa quae egimus, peruenire ad gaudia aeterna mereamur. Per.

1149 SVPER OBLATA. Sacrificia domine paschalibus gaudiis immolamus, quibus ecclesia mirabiliter et pascitur et nutritur. Per dominum.

/f. 151v **1150** PRAEFATIO. / VD aeterne deus. Et pietatem tuam indefessis praecibus implorare, ut qui paschalis festiuitatis sollemnia colimus, in tua semper sanctificatione uiuamus. Quo per temporalis festi obseruationem, peruenire mereamur ad

248

aeternorum gaudiorum continuationem. Per christum dominum nostrum.

1151 Communicantes. Et hanc igitur.

1152 BENEDICTIO. Dominus deus noster uos perducat ad arborem uitae, qui uos eruit de lacu miseriae. AMEN.
Ipse uobis aperiat ianuam paradysi, qui confregit portas inferni. AMEN.
Ipse uos eruat a flagello, et in regnum suum perducat confitentes, qui pati dignatus est pro impiis innocens. AMEN.
Quod ipse.

1153 AD COMPLENDVM. Ab omni nos quaesumus domine uetustate purgatos, sacramenti tui ueneranda perceptio, in nouam transferat creaturam. Per.

1154 AD VESPERAS. Praesta quaesumus omnipotens deus, ut huius paschalis festiuitas mirabile sacramentum, et temporalem nobis tranquillitatem tribuat, et uitam conferat sempiternam. Per.

1155 AD FONTES. Deus qui nos per paschalia festa laetificias, concede propitius ut ea quae deuote agimus, te adiuuante fideliter teneamus. Per dominum nostrum.

/f. 152r **1156** AD SANCTVM ANDREAM. / Tribue quaesumus omnipotens deus, ut illuc tendat christianae deuotionis effectus, quo tecum est nostra substantia. Per dominum nostrum.

CLXXX
FERIA V. AD APOSTOLOS

1157 Deus qui diuersitatem gentium in confessione tui nominis adunasti, da ut renatis fonte baptismatis, una sit fides mentium, et pietas actionum. Per dominum.

1158 SVPER OBLATA. Suscipe quaesumus domine munera populorum tuorum propitius, ut confessione tui nominis et baptismate renouati, sempiternam beatitudinem consequantur. Per dominum nostrum.

1159 PRAEFATIO. VD usque per christum dominum nostrum. Qui nos per paschale mysterium aedocuit uetustatem uitae relinquere, et in nouitate spiritus ambulare, a quo perpetuae mortis superatur aceruitas, et aeternę uitae fidelibus tribuitur integritas. Per quem.

1160 Communicantes. Et hanc igitur.

1161 BENEDICTIO. Deus qui inter orbis primordia subducto fluctu pelagi terras uario germine fecundasti, concede pastor optime gregem tuum tuam resurrectionem celebrantem perennibus pascuis introduci. AMEN.
Vt te custode sic oues gubernentur et agni, ut locus nullus pateat in praeda raptori. AMEN.
Sed erepti de fauce lupi, paradysi mereantur floribus epulari. AMEN.

/f. 152v / Quod ipse praestare dignetur.

1162 AD COMPLENDVM. Exaudi domine preces nostras, ut redemptionis nostrae sacrosancta commertia, et uitae nobis conferant praesentis auxilium, et gaudia sempiterna concilient. Per dominum nostrum.

1163 AD VESPERAS. Deus qui nobis ad celebrandum paschale sacramentum liberiores animos praestitisti, doce nos et metuere quod irasceris, et amare quod precipis. Per.

1164 AD FONTES. Da quaesumus omnipotens deus, ut ecclesia tua et suorum firmitate membrorum, et noua semper fecunditate laetetur. Per.

1165 AD SANCTVM ANDREAM. Multiplica quaesumus domine fidem populi tui, ut cuius per te sumpsit[1] initium, per te consequatur augmentum. Per dominum nostrum.

---

[1] *sumptit* before correction.

CLXXXI
FERIA VI. AD SANCTAM MARIAM AD MARTYRES

1166 Omnipotens sempiternę deus, qui paschale sacramentum in reconciliationis humanae fędere contulisti, da mentibus nostris ut quod professione celebramus, imitemur affectu. Per.

1167 SVPER OBLATA. Hostias quaesumus domine placatus assume, quas et pro renatorum expiatione peccati deferimus, et pro acceleratione caelestis auxilii. Per.

1168 PRAEFATIO. VD per christum dominum nostrum. Per quem supplices exposcimus, ut cuius muneris pignus acce/pimus, manifesta dona conprehendere ualeamus. Et quae nobis fideliter speranda paschale contulit sacramentum, per resurrectionis eius adtingere mereamur ineffabile mysterium. Per quem.

/f. 153r

1169 Communicantes. Et hanc igitur.

1170 BENEDICTIO. Concede misericors deus, huic plebi salutifera paschae sollemnia caelebranti, omne suum uelle in tua uoluntate plantare, et sperare quod tibi placuerit, et impetrare sibimet quod oportet. AMEN.
Te oculis intendat, corde teneat, uoce concinat, et uoto requirat. AMEN.
Euitet quod uetueris, eligat quod iusseris, amplectatur quod dicis, impleat quod placaris, ut in eo mysticę pietatis tuae sacramento perfecto, promte suum diligat dominum, qui sanguine tuo noua mercede intelligit se redemptum. AMEN.
Quod ipse.

1171 AD COMPLENDVM. Respice quaesumus domine populum tuum, et quem aeternis dignatus es renouare mysteriis, a temporalibus culpis tribue[1] dignanter absolue. Per.

1172 AD VESPERAS. Deus per quem nobis et redemptio uenit et praestatur adoptio, respice in opera misericordiae tuae, ut in christo renatis, et aeterna tribuatur hereditas, et uera libertas. Per eundem.

---

[1] Supplied interlinearly.

1173 AD FONTES. Adesto quaesumus domine familiae tuae, et
/f. 153v dignanter impende, ut quibus fidei gratiam / contulisti, et
coronam largiaris aeternam. Per dominum.

CLXXXII
SABBATO AD SANCTVM IOHANNEM

1174 Concede quaesumus omnipotens deus, ut qui festa paschalia
uenerando egimus, per haec contingere ad gaudia aeterna
mereamur. Per.

1175 SVPER OBLATA. Concede quaesumus domine semper nos per
haec mysteria paschalia gratulari, ut continua nostrae
reparationis operatio, perpetuae nobis fiat causa laetitiae. Per.

1176 Communicantes. Et hanc igitur, ut supra.

1177 PRAEFATIO. VD usque per christum dominum nostrum. Per
quem supplices exposcimus, ut cuius muneris pignus accepimus,
manifesta dona comprehendere ualeamus. Et quae nobis
fideliter speranda paschale contulit sacramentum, per
resurrectionis eius adtingere mereamur, ineffabile mysterium.
Per quem.

1178 BENEDICTIO. Deus qui peracto senario numero die sacro
sabbati ad omnibus operibus quieuisti, exaudi praeces
supplicum, ad dona tuae clementiae fideliter occurentium.
AMEN.
Praepara sensus eorum ad te suscipiendum, ut ipsi tibi propriae
mereantur effici templum. AMEN.
Et ita praesentes famulos in hac uita protegas, ut in aeternam
requiem, tecum dominator admittas. AMEN.
Quod ipse.

/f. 154r **1179** AD COMPLENDVM. / Redemptionis nostrae munere uegetati
quaesumus domine, ut hoc perpetuae salutis auxilium, fides
semper uera perficiat. Per dominum.

1180 AD VESPERVM. Deus totius conditor creaturae famulos tuos
fonte renouasti baptismatis, quosque gratiae tuae plenitudine
solidasti, in adoptionis sortę facias dignanter adscribi. Per.

1181 AD FONTES. Deus qui multiplicas ecclesiam tuam in sobole renascentium, fac eam gaudere propitius, de suorum profectibus filiorum. Per dominum nostrum.

CLXXXIII
DIE DOMINICO POST ALBAS

1182 Praesta quaesumus omnipotens deus, ut qui paschalia festa peregimus, haec te largiente moribus et uita teneamus. Per.

1183 SECRETA. Suscipe munera quaesumus domine exultantis ecclesiae, et cui causam tanti gaudii praestitisti, perpetuum fructum concede laetitiae. Per.

1184 PRAEFATIO. VD aeterne deus. Et te suppliciter obsecrare, ne nos ad illum sinas redire actum, cui iure dominatur inimicus. Sed in hac potius absolutione persistere, per quam diabolus extitit filio tuo uincente captiuus. Et ideo.

/f. 154v **1185** BENEDICTIO. Deus cuius unigenitus hodierna die discipulis suis ianuis clausis dignatus est apparere, suae uos benedictionis dono locupletare, et caeles/tis uobis regni ianuas dignetur aperire. AMEN.
Et qui ab eorum pectoribus ad tactu sui corporis uulnus amputauit dubietatis. Concedat ut per fidem qua eum resurrexisse creditis, omnium delictorum maculis careatis. AMEN.
Et qui eum cum thoma deum et dominum creditis, et cernuis uocibus inuocatis, ab eo et in saeculo a malis omnibus tueri, et in futuro sanctorum caetibus adsciri ualeatis. AMEN.
Quod ipse praestare dignetur.

1186 AD COMPLENDVM. Quaesumus domine deus noster, ut sacrosancta mysteria quae pro reparationis nostrae munimine contulisti, et praesens nobis remedium esse facias et futurum. Per dominum.

1187 AD VESPERVM AD SANCTOS COSMAM ET DAMIANVM. Largire quaesumus domine fidelibus tuis indulgentiam placatus et pacem, ut pariter ab omnibus mundentur offensis, et secura tibi mente deseruiant. Per.

CLXXXIIII
ALIAE ORATIONES PASCHALES

1188 Deus qui omnes in christo renatos genus regium et sacerdotale fecisti, da nobis et uelle et posse quę praecipis, ut populo ad aeternitatem uocato, una sit fides mentium, et pietas actionum. Per.

1189 ALIA. Deus qui pro salute mundi sacrificium paschale fecisti, propitiare supplicationibus nostris, ut interpellans[1] pro nobis pontifex summus, nos per id quod nostri est similis reconciliet, per id / quod tibi est aequalis absoluat, iesus christus filius tuus. Qui tecum.

/f. 155r

1190 ALIA. Praesta nobis omnipotens et misęricors deus, ut in resurrectione domini nostri iesu christi, percipiamus ueraciter portionem. Per eundem.

1191 ALIA. Concede quaesumus omnipotens deus, ut ueterem cum suis actionibus hominem deponentes, illius conuersatione uiuamus, ad cuius nos substantiam paschalibus remediis transtulisti. Per eundem.

1192 ITEM ALIA. Deus qui ad aeternam uitam in christi resurrectione nos reparas, imple pietatis tuae ineffabile sacramentum, ut cum in maiestate sua saluator noster aduenerit, quos fecisti baptismo regenerari, facias beata inmortalitate uestiri. Per eundem.

1193 ALIA. Gaudeat domine plebs fidelis, et cum propriae recolit saluationis exordia, eius promoueatur augmentis. Per dominum nostrum.

1194 ITEM ALIA. Familiam tuam quaesumus domine, dextera tua perpetuo circumdet auxilio, ut paschali interueniente sollemnitate, ab omni prauitate defensa, donis caelestibus prosequatur. Per dominum nostrum.

---

[1]   Second *n* supplied interlinearly.

1195 ITEM ALIA. Fac omnipotens deus, ut qui paschalibus remediis innouati, similitudinem terreni parentis euasimus, ad formam caelestis transferamur auctoris. Per dominum nostrum.

1196 AD COMPLENDVM DIEBVS FESTIS. Praesta quaesumus f. 155v domine deus noster, ut qui sollemni caelebramus /officio, purificatae mentis intelligentiam consequamur. Per.

1197 ALIA. Caelesti lumine quaesumus domine semper et ubique nos praeueni, ut mysterium cuius nos participes esse uoluisti, et puro cernamus intuitu, et digno percipiamus effectu. Per dominum nostrum.

CLXXXV
IDVS APRIL. NATALE SANCTAE EVFEMIAE
1198 Concede nobis omnipotens deus, sanctae martyris eufemiae, et exultare meritis, et beneficia referre suffragiis. Per dominum nostrum.

1199 SVPER OBLATA. Muneribus domine te magnificamus oblatis, quibus in sanctae nobis eufemiae et gaudia nobis aeterna concilias, et patrocinia sempiterna largiaris. Per.

1200 PRAEFATIO. VD aeterne deus. Et in[1] hac sollemnitate tibi laudis hostias immolare, qua beatae eufemiae martyris tuae passionem uenerando recolimus, et tui nobis gloriam debitis praeconiis magnificamus. Per christum.

1201 AD COMPLENDVM. Sanctae nos martyris eufemiae precatio tibi domine grata comitetur, et tuam nobis indulgentiam poscere non desistat. Per dominum nostrum iesum christum.

MISSA IN PASCHA ANNOTINVM
1202 Deus per cuius prouidentiam nec preteritorum momenta deficiunt, nec ulla superest expectatio futurorum, tribue f. 156r permanentem peractae quam recolimus sollemnitatis effectum, / ut quod recordatione percurrimus, semper in opere teneamus. Per dominum.

[1] Supplied interlinearly.

1203 SVPER OBLATA. Clementiam tuam domine suppliciter exoramus, ut pachalis muneris sacramentum, quod et fide recolimus, et spe desideramus, intenti perpetua dilectione capiamus. Per.

1204 PRAEFATIO. VD aeterne deus. Et redemptionis nostrae festa recolere, quibus humana substantia uinculis praeuaricationis exuta, spem resurrectionis per renouatam originis dignitatem adsumpsit. Et ideo.

1205 AD COMPLENDVM. Tua nos quaesumus domine quae sumpsimus sancta purificent, et operationis suae remedio nos tibi perficiant esse placitos. Per dominum nostrum iesum christum[1] filium tuum.

DOMINICA I POST OCTAVAS PASCHĘ

1206 Deus qui in filii tui humilitate iacentem mundum erexisti, fidelibus tuis perpetuam laetitiam concede. Vt quos perpetuae mortis eripuisti casibus, gaudiis facias sempiternis perfrui. Per eundem.

1207 SVPER OBLATA. Benedictionem domine nobis conferat salutarem, sacra semper oblatio, ut quod agit mysterio, uirtute perficiat. Per.

1208 PRAEFATIO. VD aeterne deus. Et inmensam bonitatis tuae
/f. 156v pietatem humiliter exorare, ut ignorantiam nostrae / mortalitatis adtendens, et tua inspiratione nos facias postulare quod rectum, et tua clementia tribuas impetrare quod poscimus. Per christum.

1209 BENEDICTIO. Omnipotentis dei et domini nostri benedictionibus repleamini, cuius estis sanguine praetioso redempti. AMEN.
Eius nos indeficiens repleat gratia, cuius ineffabilis plasmauit potentia. AMEN.
Et qui uobis in hoc mundo praestitit conditionem nascendi, ipse in regno aeterno tribuat mansionem sine fine uiuendi. AMEN.
Quod ipse.

---

[1] Supplied interlinearly.

1210 AD COMPLENDVM. Praesta nobis omnipotens deus, ut uiuificationis tuae gratiam consequentes, in tuo semper munere gloriemur. Per dominum nostrum iesum christum.

CLXXXVII
DOMINICA II POST OCTAVAS PASCHAE

1211 Deus qui errantibus ut in uiam possint redire, iustitiae ueritatis tuae lumen ostendis, da cunctis qui christiana professione censentur, et illa respuere quae huic inimica sunt nomini, et ea quae sunt apta sectari. Per dominum.

1212 SVPER OBLATA. His nobis domine mysteriis conferatur, quo terrena desideria mitigantes, discamus amare caelestia. Per.

1213 PRAEFATIO. VD per christum dominum nostrum. Qui de uirgine nasci dignatus, per passionem et mortem a perpetua nos morte liberauit, et resurrectione sua, aeternam nobis uitam contulit. Per quem.

/f. 158r **1214** / [1]BENEDICTIO. Benedicat uobis deus de caelis omnipotens, qui per crucem et sanguinem passionis suae uos dignatus est redimere in terris. AMEN.

Ipse uos renouet a uetustate peccati, qui pro uobis dignatus est crucifigi, uosque ad caelestia suscitet regna, qui pro uobis inferna penetrauit. AMEN.

Vitam[2] suam dominus uobis tribuat, qui mortem uestram suscepit et perdidit. AMEN.

Quod ipse.

1215 AD COMPLENDVM. Sacramenta quae sumpsimus domine, et spiritalibus nos instruant alimentis, et corporalibus tueantur auxiliis. Per dominum nostrum.

---

[1] The foliation jumps from 156 to 158.
[2] *V* supplied later in crimson.

CLXXXVIII
XVIII KL. MAI. NATALE SANCTORVM TYBVRTII, ET VALERIANI

1216 Praesta quaesumus omnipotens deus, ut qui sanctorum tuorum tyburtii, ualeriani et maximi sollemnia colimus, eorum etiam uirtutes imitemur. Per.

1217 SVPER OBLATA. Hostia haec quesumus domine quam in sanctorum tuorum nataliciis recensentes offerimus, et uincula nostrae prauitatis absoluat, et tuae nobis misęricordiae dona conciliet. Per dominum nostrum.

1218 PRAEFATIO. VD aeterne deus. Et te in sanctorum martyrum tuorum festiuitate laudare, qui semper es mirabilis in tuorum commemoratione sanctorum, et magnae fidaei largiris affectum, et tolerantiam tribuis passionum, et antiqui hostis facis superari machinamentum. Quo egregii martyres tui ad capiendam supernorum / beatitudinem praemiorum, nullis impediantur retinaculis blandimentorum. Et ideo.

/f. 158v

1219 BENEDICTIO. Benedicat uobis dominus beatorum martyrum suorum tyburtii et ualeriani suffragiis, et liberet ab aduersitatibus cunctis. AMEN.
Commendet uos eorum intercessio gloriosa, quorum in conspectu eius est mors praetiosa. AMEN.
Vt sicut illi per diuersa genera tormentorum, caelesti regni sunt sortiti hereditatem, ita uos eorum mereamini consortium per bonorum operum exibitionem. AMEN.
Quod ipse.

1220 AD COMPLENDVM. Sacro munere satiati supplices te domine depraecamur, ut quod debitę seruitutis celebramus officio, saluationis tuae sentiamus augmento. Per dominum.

CLXXXVIIII
VIIII KL. MAI. NATALE SANCTI GEORGII MARTYRIS

1221 Deus qui nos beati georgii martyris tui meritis et intercessione laetificas, concede propitius ut qui eius beneficia poscimus, dona tuae gratiae consequamur. Per.

1222 SVPER OBLATA. Munera domine oblata sanctifica, et intercedente beato georgio martyre tuo, nos per haec a peccatorum nostrorum maculis emunda. Per.

1223 PRAEFATIO. VD per christum dominum nostrum. Pro cuius nominis ueneranda confessione beatus martyr georgius diuersa supplicia sustinuit, et ea deuincens / coronam perpetuitatis promeruit. Per quem.

/f. 159r

1224 BENEDICTIO. Beati martyris sui georgii intercessione uos dominus benedicat, et ab omni malo defendat. AMEN.
Extendat in uos dexteram suae propitiationis, qui eum suscepit per supplicia passionis. AMEN.
Quo eius in caelo mereamini habere consortium, cuius deuotis mentibus in terra caelebratis triumphum. AMEN.
Quod ipse praestare dignetur.

1225 AD COMPLENDVM. Supplices te rogamus omnipotens deus, ut quos tuis reficis sacramentis, intercedente beato georgio martyre tuo, tibi etiam placitis moribus dignanter tribuas deseruire. Per dominum nostrum.

CXC
DOMINICA III POST OCTAVAS PASCHAE

1226 Deus qui fidelium mentes unius efficis uoluntatis, da populis tuis, id amare quod praecipis, id desiderare quod promittis, ut inter mundanas uarietates, ibi nostra fixa sint corda, ubi uera sunt gaudia. Per.

1227 SVPER OBLATA. Deus qui nos per huius sacrificii[1] ueneranda commercia unius summae diuinitatis participes esse fecisti, praesta quaesumus ut sicut tuam cognoscimus ueritatem, sic eam dignis moribus adsequamur. Per dominum.

1228 PRAEFATIO. VD aeterne deus. Et tui misęricordiam muneris postulare, ut tempora quibus post / resurrectionem suam dominus noster iesus christus cum discipulis suis corporaliter

/f. 159v

---

[1]   *sacrifisii* before correction.

habitauit. Sic ipso opitulante pia deuotione tractemus, quatinus in his omnium uitiorum sordibus careamus. Per quem.

1229 BENEDICTIO. Deus qui calcatis inferni legibus captiuitatem nostram resoluta catenarum compage dignatus est ad libertatis praemia reuocare, ipse uobis praestet ita hanc uitam transire, ut in illam perpetuam ipso duce possitis intrare. AMEN.
Et ita praebeat uobis feruorem catholicae fidei, ut sancti aduentus illius sitis expectatione securi. AMEN.
Vt quicumque hic meruerunt purgari unda baptismi, ibi praesentari ualeant pio iudici candidati. AMEN.
Quod ipse praestare dignetur.

1230 AD COMPLENDVM. Adesto domine deus noster, ut per haec quae fideliter sumpsimus, et purgemur a uitiis, et a periculis omnibus exuamur. Per dominum iesum christum filium tuum.

CXCI
DOMINICA IIII POST OCTAVAS PASCHAE

1231 Deus a quo bona cuncta procedunt, largire supplicibus, ut cogitemus te inspirante quae recta sunt, et te gubernante eadem faciamus. Per dominum.

1232 SVPER OBLATA. Suscipe domine fidelium preces cum oblationibus hostiarum, ut per haec pię deuotionis officia, ad caelestem gloriam transeamus. Per dominum nostrum.

/f. 160r **1233** PRAEFATIO. / VD aeterne deus. Et maiestatem tuam indefessis praecibus exorare, ut mentes nostras bonis operibus semper informes. Quia sic erimus praeclari muneris prompta sinceritate cultores, si ad meliora iugiter transeuntes, paschale mysterium studeamus habere perpetuum. Per christum dominum.

1234 BENEDICTIO. Benedicat uos omnipotens deus, qui uos gratuita miseratione creauit, et in resurrectione unigeniti sui spem nobis resurgendi concessit. AMEN.
Resuscitet uos de uitiorum sepulchris, qui eum resuscitauit a mortuis. AMEN.
Vt cum eo sine fine feliciter uiuatis, quem resurrexisse a mortuis ueraciter creditis. AMEN.
Quod ipse.

1235 AD COMPLENDVM. Tribue nobis domine caelestis mensae uirtutis societatem, et desiderare quae recta sunt, et desiderata percipere. Per.

CXCII
VII KL. MAI. LAETANIA MAIOR[1] AD SANCTVM LAVRENTIVM IN LVCANA

1236 Mentem familiae tuae quaesumus domine intercedente beato laurentio martyre tuo, et munere conpunctionis aperi, et largitate pietatis exaudi. Per.

1237 AD SANCTVM VALENTINVM. Deus qui culpas delinquentium districte feriendo percutis, fletus quoque lugentium non recuses, ut qui pondus tuae animaduersionis cognouimus, etiam pietatis gratiam sentiamus. Per.

1238 / AD CRVCEM. Parce domine quaesumus parce populo tuo, et nullis iam patiaris aduersitatibus fatigari, quos praetioso filii tui sanguine redemisti. Per.

f. 160v

1239 AD PONTEM MOLBI. Deus qui culpas nostras piis uerberibus percutis, ut nos a nostris iniquitatibus emundes, da nobis et de uerbere tuo proficere, et de tua citius consolatione gaudere. Per.

1240 IN ATRIO. Adesto domine supplicationibus nostris, et sperantes in tua misaericordia intercedente beato petro apostolo tuo caelesti protege benignus auxilio. Per dominum.

1241 ALIA IN ATRIO. Praesta quaesumus omnipotens deus, ut ad te toto corde clamantes, intercedente beato petro apostolo tuo tuae pietatis indulgentiam consequamur. Per.

1242 AD MISSAM. Praesta quaesumus omnipotens deus, ut qui in afflictione nostra de tua pietate confidimus, contra aduersa omnia tua semper protectione muniamur. Per.

---

[1]   *MAIORA* before correction.

1243 SVPER OBLATA. Haec munera domine quaesumus, et uincula nostrae prauitatis absoluant, et tuae nobis misęricordiae dona concilient. Per.

1244 PRAEFATIO. VD aeterne deus. Et te auctorem[1] et sanctificatorem ieiunii conlaudare, per quod nos liberas a nostrorum debitis peccatorum. Ergo suscipe ieiunantium praeces, atque ut nos a malis omnibus / propitiatus eripias, iniquitates nostras quibus merito adfligimur, placatus absolue. Per christum.

/f. 161r

1245 BENEDICTIO. Benedic quaesumus domine uniuersam familiam tuam, ad gaudia perpetuae resurrectionis feliciter euocatam. AMEN.
Rectissimum catholicę fidei tramitem teneat, et in una trinitatis confessione consistat. AMEN.
Nulla eos a rectitudine ecclesiastici dogmatis prauae assertionis impietas deuitet, ut nec supertextu nominis christiani ueritatis praesidio nudet, sed in eadem unitatis fide manentes, effici mereantur regni caelestis heredes. AMEN.
Quod ipse.

1246 AD COMPLENDVM. Vota nostra quaesumus domine pio fauore prosequere, ut dum dona tua in tribulatione percepimus, de consolatione nostra in tuo amore crescamus. Per.

1247 SVPER POPVLVM. Purifica quaesumus domine tuorum corda fidelium, ut a terrena cupiditate mundati, et praesentis uitae periculis exuantur, et perpetuis donis firmentur. Per dominum nostrum.

CXCIII
DIE SECVNDO AD MISSAM
1248 In ieiunio hoc afflicti corpore et corde contriti, frequentamus ad te praeces clementissime deus, ut cum abstinentia corporali, abstinentia nobis uitiorum donetur, ut restricto corpore ab aepulis, tu qui es refectio uera, in nostris cordibus oriaris. Per.

---

[1] *augtorem* before correction.

f. 161v **1249** / SVPER OBLATA. Oblatis quaesumus domine placare muneribus, et a cunctis nos defende periculis Per dominum.

1250 PRAEFATIO. VD aeterne deus. Et maiestatem tuam suppliciter exorare, ut non nos nostrae malitiae, sed indulgentiae tuae praeueniat semper affectus. Qui nos a noxiis uoluptatibus indesinenter expediat, et a mundanis cladibus dignanter eripiat. Per christum dominum nostrum.

1251 BENEDICTIO. Omnipotens deus deuotionem uestram dignanter intendat, et suae uobis benedictionis dona concedat. AMEN.
Indulgeat uobis mala omnia quae gessistis, et tribuat ueniam quam ab eo deposcitis. AMEN.
Sicque ieiunii uestri et praecum uota suscipiat, ut a uobis aduersa omnia quae peccatorum retributione mereamini auertat, et donum in uos spiritus paracliti infundat. AMEN.
Quod ipse.

1252 AD COMPLENDVM. Praetende nobis domine misaericordiam tuam, ut quae uotis expetimus conuersatione, tibi placita consequamur. Per dominum.

1253 SVPER POPVLVM. Praesta populo tuo domine quaesumus consolationis auxilium, et diuturnis calamitatibus laborantem, propitius respirare concede. Per.

CXCIIII
DIE TERTIO AD MISSAM

1254 Miserere iam quaesumus domine intercedente beata et gloriosa semperque uirgine dei genetrice maria populo tuo, et continuis

f. 162r tribulationibus laborantem / celeri propitiatione laetifica. Per.

1255 SVPER OBLATA. Oblatis quaesumus domine placare muneribus, et a cunctis nos defende periculis. Per.

1256 PRAEFATIO. VD aeterne deus. Vt quia tui est operis, sed quod tibi placitum est, aut cogitemus, aut agamus, tu nobis semper et intelligendi quae recta sunt, et exequendi tribuas facultatem. Per christum.

263

1257 BENEDICTIO. Respice domine super hanc familiam tuam subiectam tibi benedictionum tuarum dona poscentem, rege eam de superioribus tuis, et ubertatem frugum ei largire. AMEN.

Libera eam a diebus malis et a perturbatione bellorum, et da ei tempora tranquilla atque pacifica, ut te custode peruigili ac pastore aeterno[1] et in presenti tempore consistat secura, et ad aeterna gaudia perueniat libera. AMEN.

Et qui quondam misericors misertus es turbae tecum triduo permanenti, simili nunc dignatione hanc miserere plebi tibi ieiuniis et hymnis innixius supplicanti. AMEN.

Quod ipse.

1258 AD COMPLENDVM. Praesta quaesumus omnipotens deus, ut diuino munere satiati, et sacris mysteriis innouemur et moribus. Per dominum nostrum.

1259 SVPER POPVLVM. Memor esto quaesumus domine fragilitatis
/f. 162v humanae, ut qui iuste uerberas peccatores, parce propitiatus / afflictis. Per dominum nostrum iesum christum.

CXCV

IN ASCENSIONE DOMINI

1260 Concede quaesumus omnipotens deus, ut qui hodierna die unigenitum tuum redemptorem nostrum ad cęlos ascendisse credimus, ipsi quoque mente in caelestibus habitemus. Per eundem.

1261 SVPER OBLATA. Suscipe domine munera, quae pro filii tui gloriosa ascensione deferimus, et concede propitius, ut a praesentibus periculis liberemur, et ad uitam perueniamus aeternam. Per eundem.

1262 PRAEFATIO. VD per christum. Qui post resurrectionem suam omnibus discipulis suis manifestus apparuit, et ipsis cernentibus est eleuatus in caelum, ut nos diuinitatis suae tribueret esse participes. Et ideo.

---

[1] First letters rewritten.

1263 Communicantes et diem sacratissimum celebrantes, quo dominus noster unigenitus filius tuus unitam sibi fragilitatis nostrae substantiam in gloriae tuę dextera[1] collocauit. Sed et memoriam.

1264 BENEDICTIO. Benedicat uobis omnipotens deus, cuius unigenitus hodierna die caelorum alta penetrauit, et uobis ubi ille est ascendendi aditum patefecit. AMEN.
Concedat propitius ut sicut post resurrectionem suam discipulis uisus est manifestus, ita uobis in iudicium ueniens uideatur placatus. AMEN.

Et qui eum consedere patri in sua maiestate / creditis, uobiscum manere usque in finem saeculi, secundum suam promissionem sentiatis[2]. AMEN.
Quod ipse praestare dignetur.

1265 AD COMPLENDVM. Praesta nobis quaesumus omnipotens et misericors deus, ut quae uisibilibus mysteriis sumenda percepimus, inuisibili consequamur effectu. Per dominum.

CXCVI
ALIAE ORATIONES DE ASCENSIONE DOMINI

1266 Adesto domine supplicationibus nostris, ut sicut humani generis saluatorem consedere tecum in tua maiestate confidimus, ita usque ad consummationem saeculi manere nobiscum, quemadmodum est pollicitus sentiamus. Qui tecum.

1267 ALIA. Deus cuius filius in alta caelorum potenter ascendens, captiuitatem nostram sua duxit uirtute captiuam, tribue quaesumus ut dona quae suis participibus contulit largiatur et nobis. Iesus christus dominus noster.

1268 ALIA. Da quaesumus omnipotens deus illuc subsequi tuorum membra fidelium, quo caput nostrum principium praecessit. Per dominum nostrum.

---

[1] *dextere* before correction.
[2] Final letters rewritten.

CXCVII
IIII KL. MAI. NATALE SANCTI VITALIS MARTYRIS

1269 Praesta quaesumus omnipotens deus, ut intercedente beato uitale martyre tuo, et a cunctis aduersitatibus liberemur in corpore, et a prauis cogitationibus mundemur in mente. Per.

1270 SVPER OBLATA. Accepta tibi sit in conspectu tuo domine /f. 163v nostra deuotio, et eius nobis fiat suppli/catione salutaris, pro cuius sollemnitate defertur. Per.

1271 AD COMPLENDVM. Refecti participatione muneris sacri quaesumus domine deus noster, ut cuius exequimur cultum, sentiamus effectum. Per dominum nostrum.

CXCVIII

1272 ITEM PRAEFATIO DE ASCENSIONE DOMINI. VD aeterne deus. Et in hac praecipuae die, quo iesus christus filius tuus dominus noster, diuini consummato fine mysterii, dispositionis antiquę munus expleuit, ut scilicet et diabolum caelestis operis inimicum, per hominem quem subiugarat aelideret, et humanam reduceret ad superna dona substantiam. Et ideo.

CXCVIIII
DOMINICA I POST ASCENSIONE<M> DOMINI

1273 Omnipotens sempiterne deus, fac nos tibi semper et deuotam gerere uoluntatem, et maiestati tuae sincero corde seruire. Per dominum.

1274 SVPER OBLATA. Sacrificia nos domine immaculata purificent, et mentibus nostris supernae gratiae dent uigorem. Per.

1275 PRĘFATIO. VD per christum dominum nostrum. Qui generi humano nascendo subuenit, cum per mortem passionis mundum deuicit, per gloriam resurrectionis uitae aeternae aditum patefecit. Et per suam ascensionem ad caelos nobis spem ascendendi donauit. Per quem.

1276 BENEDICTIO. Benedictionum suarum super nos dominus /f. 164r imbrem infundat, et claritatis suae thesauros caeles/tes uobis aperiat. AMEN.

Faciat uos dominus uitae aeternae participes, et regni caelestis coheredes. AMEN.

Dignam in uobis habitationem spiritus sanctus inueniat, ut eius gloriosa maiestas placide in uestris cordibus requiescat. AMEN. Quod ipse.

1277 ITEM BENEDICTIO DE ASCENSIONE DOMINI. Deus qui tartara fregisti resurgens, aperuisti caelos ascendens, ut populi illuc per fidem ascenderent, ubi te apostoli intrare uiderunt, respice ascendens caelum propter quos dignatus es descendere in infernum. AMEN.

Sit eis quod te exaltasti protectio, quibus fuit unicum quod te humiliasti remedium. AMEN.

Vt in die iudicii non sint sinistri numero, qui te sedere ad patris dexteram confitentur in caelo. AMEN. Quod ipse.

1278 AD COMPLENDVM. Repleti domine muneribus sacris, da quaesumus ut in gratiarum semper actione maneamus. Per dominum.

CC
KL. MAI. NATALE APOSTOLORVM PHILIPPI ET IACOBI

1279 Deus qui nos annua apostolorum tuorum philippi et iacobi sollemnitate laetificas, praesta quaesumus ut quorum gaudemus meritis, instruamur exemplis. Per dominum.

1280 SVPER OBLATA. Munera domine quae pro apostolorum tuorum phylippi et iacobi sollemnitate deferimus, pro/pitius suscipe, et mala omnia quae meremur auerte. Per dominum nostrum.

1281 PRAEFATIO. VD aeterne deus. Qui ecclesiam tuam in apostolica soliditate firmasti, de quorum consortio sunt beatus phylippus et iacobus, quorum passionis hodie festum ueneramur poscentes, ut sicut eorum doctrinis instituimur, ita exemplis muniamur, et praecibus adiuuemur. Per christum.

1282 BENEDICTIO. Deus qui ecclesiam suam in apostolicis tribuit consistere fundamentis, benedicere uobis dignetur beatorum apostolorum phylippi et iacobi, intercedentibus meritis. AMEN.

f. 164v

Defendatque uos a cunctis aduersis apostolicis praesidiis, qui uos eorum uoluit ornari, et munerare exemplis et documentis. AMEN.

Quo per eorum intercessione perueniatis ad aeternae patriae hereditatem, per quorum doctrinam tenetis fidei integritatem. AMEN.

Quod ipse.

1283 AD COMPLENDVM. Quaesumus domine salutaribus repleti mysteriis, ut quorum sollemnia caelebramus, eorum orationibus adiuuemur. Per dominum.

CCI

V NON. MAI. NATALE SANCTORVM ALEXANDRI,
EVENTI, ET THEODOLI

1284 Praesta quaesumus omnipotens deus, ut qui in sanctorum alexandri, euenti, et theodoli, natalicia colimus, a cunctis malis imminentibus / eorum intercessionibus liberemur. Per dominum.

/f. 165r

1285 SVPER OBLATA. Super has quaesumus hostias domine benedictio copiosa descendat, quae et sanctificationem nobis clementer operetur, et de martyrum nos sollemnitate laetificet. Per.

1286 POST COMMVNIONEM. Refecti participatione muneris sacri quaesumus domine deus noster, ut quorum exequimur cultum, sentiamus effectum. Per dominum nostrum.

CCII

EODEM DIE INVENTIO SANCTAE CRVCIS

1287 Deus qui in praeclara salutiferae crucis inuentione passionis tuae miracula suscitasti, concede ut uitalis ligni praetio, aeternae uitae suffragia consequamur. Per.

1288 SVPER OBLATA. Sacrificium domine quod immolamus placatus intende, ut ab omni nos exuat bellorum nequitia, et per uexillum sanctae crucis filii tui ad conterendas potestates, et aduersariorum insidias, nos in tuae protectionis securitate constituat. Per dominum.

1289 PRAEFATIO. VD per christum dominum nostrum. Qui per passionem crucis mundum redemit, et antiqui arboris amarissimum gustum crucis medicamine indulcauit, mortemque quae per lignum uetitum uenerat, per ligni tropheum deuicit. Vt mirabili suae pietati dispensatione, / qui per ligni gustum a florigera sede discesseramus, per crucis lignum ad paradysi gaudia redeamus. Per.

f. 165v

1290 BENEDICTIO. Omnipotens deus det uobis suae benedictionis emolumentum, qui per unigeniti sui passionem et crucis patibulum, dignatus est redimere genus humanum. AMEN.
Concedatque uobis ut quae sit longitudo, latitudo, sublimitas et profundum, eiusdem crucis sagaci mente comprehendere, et perfecto opere imitari ualeatis. AMEN.
Quatinus uosmetipsos[1] abnegando crucemque gestando, ita in praesentis uitae stadio[2], redemptorem nostrum possitis sequi, ut ei inter choros angelorum mereamini post obitum asciri. AMEN. Quod ipse.

1291 AD COMPLENDVM. Repleti alimonia caelesti et spiritali poculo recreati quaesumus omnipotens deus, ut ab hoste maligno defendas, quos per lignum sanctae crucis filii tui arma iustitiae, pro salute mundi triumphare iussisti. Per.

1292 AD VESPERVM. Deus cui cunctae oboediunt creature, et omnia in uerbo tuo fecisti in sapientia, supplices quaesumus ineffabilem clementiam tuam, ut quos per lignum sanctae crucis filii tui pio cruore dignatus es redimere, tu qui es lignum uitae, paradysique reparator, omnibus intercedentibus dira / serpentis uenena extingue, et per gratiam spiritus sancti, poculum salutis semper infunde. Per dominum.

f. 166r

---

[1] *nosmetipsos* before correction.
[2] *studio* before correction.

CCIII
II NON. MAI. NATALE SANCTI IOHANNIS
EVANGELISTAE ANTE PORTAM LATINAM IN
FERVENTIS OLEI DOLEVM MISSVS

1293 Deus qui conspicis quia nos undique mala nostra perturbant, praesta quaesumus ut beati iohannis apostoli tui intercessio gloriosa nos protegat. Per dominum nostrum.

1294 SVPER OBLATA. Muneribus nostris quaesumus domine praecibusque susceptis, et caelestibus nos munda mysteriis, et clementer exaudi. Per dominum.

1295 AD COMPLENDVM. Refecti domine pane caelesti, ad uitam quaesumus nutriamur aeternam. Per dominum nostrum.

CCIIII
VI ID. MAI. NATALE SANCTORVM GORDIANI, CYRILLI
ADQVE EPIMACHI

1296 Da quaesumus omnipotens deus, ut qui beatorum martyrum gordiani atque epimachi sollemnia colimus, eorum apud te intercessionibus adiuuemur. Per.

1297 SVPER OBLATA. Hostias tibi domine beatorum martyrum gordiani atque epimachi, dicatas meritis benignus adsume, et ad perpetuum nobis tribue[1] prouenire subsidium. Per.

1298 POSTCOMMVNIONEM. Quaesumus omnipotens deus, ut qui caelestia alimenta percepimus, intercedentibus sanctis tuis gordiano atque epimacho, per haec contra omnia aduer/sa muniamur. Per.

/f. 166v

CCV
IIII ID. MAI. NATALE SANCTORVM PANCRATII, NEREI,
ET ACHILLEI

1299 Praesta quaesumus omnipotens deus, ut qui beati pancratii martyris tui natalicia colimus, a cunctis malis imminentibus, eius intercessionibus liberemur. Per.

---

[1] *tribuae* before correction.

1300 SVPER OBLATA. Munera quaesumus domine tibi dicata sanctifica, et intercedente beato pancratio, per eadem nos placatus intende. Per.

1301 POSTCOMMVNIO. Beati pancratii martyris tui domine intercessione placatus, praesta quaesumus, ut quae temporaliter celebramus actione, perpetua saluatione capiamus. Per dominum nostrum.

ITEM ALIA

1302 Semper nos domine martyrum tuorum nerei, achillei et pancratii foueat quaesumus beata sollemnitas, et tuo dignos reddat obsequio. Per.

1303 SVPER OBLATA. Sanctorum tuorum domine nerei, achillei et pancratii tibi grata confessio, et munera nostra commendent, et tuam nobis indulgentiam semper implorent. Per.

1304 PRAEFATIO. VD aeterne deus. Quoniam ad te constantiam fides, a te uirtutem sumit infirmitas. Et quicquid in persecutionibus seuum est, quicquid in morte terribile, nominis tui facis confessione superari. Vnde benedicimus te domine in operibus tuis, teque in sanctorum tuorum nerei, achillei, et pancratii / prouectione laudamus. Per christum.

f. 167r

1305 BENEDICTIO. Respice domine hanc familiam tuam serenis obtutibus, et largis eam infunde benedictionibus, ut in uiam recti itineris gressus dirigant, et fidei suae stabilem, firmitatem teneant. AMEN.
Hanc sanctis suffragantibus meritis, beatorum martyrum tuorum, nerei, achillei, et pancratii, quorum annuam festiuitatem deuotis mentibus exercent, perseuerantiam boni operis, usque in finem habere ualeant. AMEN.
Vt praemia destinata sanctis in aeterna beatitudine possideant sine fine, et cum eis sicuti est deum facie ad faciem uisu indefectiuo mereantur uidere. AMEN.
Quod ipse.

1306 AD COMPLENDVM. Quaesumus domine ut beatorum martyrum tuorum, nerei, achillei, et pancratii depraecationibus, sacramenta quae sumpsimus, ad tuae nobis fiant placationis augmentum. Per dominum.

CCVI
III ID. MAI. NATALE SANCTAE MARIAE AD MARTYRES

1307 Concede quaesumus omnipotens deus, ad eorum nos gaudia aeterna pertingere, de quorum nos uirtute tribuis annua sollemnitate gaudere. Per.

1308 SVPER OBLATA. Super has quaesumus domine hostias benedictio copiosa descendat, quae et sanctificationem nobis clementer operetur, et de martyrum nos sollemnitate laetificet. Per.

/f. 167v **1309** POSTCOMMVNIO. / Supplices te rogamus omnipotens deus, ut quos tuis reficis sacramentis, tibi etiam placitis moribus, dignanter deseruire concedas. Per dominum nostrum.

CCVII
VIII KL. IVN. NATALE SANCTI VRBANI PAPAE

1310 Da quaesumus omnipotens deus, ut qui beati urbani martyris tui atque pontificis sollemnia colimus, eius apud te intercessionibus adiuuemur. Per

1311 SVPER OBLATA. Haec hostia domine quaesumus emundet nostra delicta, et sacrificium caelebrandum, subditorum tibi corpora mentesque sanctificet. Per.

1312 POSTCOMMVNIO. Refecti participatione muneris sacri quaesumus domine deus noster, ut cuius exequimur cultum, sentiamus effectum. Per.

CCVIII
INCIPIVNT ORATIONES DE PENTECOSTEN DIE
SABBATO ANTE DECENSVM FONTIS

1313 LECTIO LIBRI GENESIS. Temptauit deus.

1314 Deus qui in abrahę filii tui opere, humano generi oboedientiae exempla praebuisti, concede nobis et nostrae uoluntatis

272

prauitatem frangere, et tuorum praeceptorum rectitudinem in omnibus adimplere. Per.

1315 LECTIO LIBRI DEVTERONOMII. Scripsit moyses canticum. CANTICVM. Adtende caelum.

1316 COLLECTA. Deus qui nobis per prophetarum ora praecepisti temporalia relinquere, atque ad aeterna festinare, da famulis tuis ut quae a te iussa cognouimus, implere caelesti inspiratione ualeamus. Per.

f. 168r **1317** / LECTIO ESAIAE PROPHETAE. Adpraehendent septem mulieres. CANTICVM. Vinea facta est.

1318 Deus qui nos ad caelebrandum praesentem festiuitatem utriusque testamenti paginis instruis, da nobis intelligere misericordiam tuam, ut ex perceptione praesentium munerum, firma sit expectatio futurorum. Per dominum nostrum.

1319 LECTIO HIEREMIAE PROPHETAE. Audi israhel.

1320 Deus incommutabilis uirtus et lumen aeternum, respice propitius ad totius ęcclesiae mirabile sacramentum, et da famulis tuis, ut hoc quod deuote agimus, etiam rectitudine uitae teneamus. Per.

1321 ORATIO DE PSALMO XLI. Sicut ceruus.

1322 Omnipotens sempiterne deus, qui hanc sollemnitatem aduentus sancti spiritus consecrasti, da nobis quaesumus ut caelestibus desideriis accensi, fontem uitae sitiamus. Per eiusdem.

ALIAE ORATIONES DICENDAE

1323 Omnipotens sempiterne deus, qui paschale sacramentum quinquagenta dierum uoluisti mysterio contineri, praesta ut gentium facta dispersio diuisione linguarum, ad unam confessionem tui nominis caelesti munere congregetur. Per.

1324 ALIA. Deus qui sacramento festiuitatis hodiernae, uniuersam ęcclesiam tuam in omni gente et natione sanctificas, in totam

f. 168v mundi latitu/dinem, spiritus tui dona diffunde. Per eiusdem.

273

1325 ALIA. Annue misericors deus, ut qui diuina praecepta uiolando paradysi felicitate decidimus, ad aeternae beatitudinis redeamus accensum, per tuorum custodiam mandatorum. Per.

1326 ALIA. Da nobis quaesumus domine per gratiam spiritus tui paracliti, nouam spiritalis obseruantiae disciplinam, ut mentes nostras sacro purificante ieiunio, cunctis reddantur eius muneribus aptiores. Per dominum.

CCVIIII
ORATIONES AD MISSAM IN SABBATO PENTECOSTEN POST ASCENSVM FONTIS

1327 Praesta quaesumus omnipotens deus, ut claritatis tuae super nos splendor effulgeat, et splendor tuae lucis corda eorum, qui per gratiam tuam renati sunt sancti spiritus inlustratione confirmet. Per.

1328 SVPER OBLATA. Munera domine quaesumus oblata sanctifica, et corda nostra sancti spiritus inlustratione emunda. Per.

1329 PRAEFATIO. VD per christum. Qui ascendens super omnes caelos, sedensque ad dexteram tuam, promissum spiritum sanctum hodierna die in filios adoptionis effudit. Quaproper profusis gaudiis, totus in orbe terrarum mundus exultat, sed et supernae uirtutes atque angelicę potestates, ymnum gloriae tuae concinunt, sine fine dicentes sanctus.

1330 Communicantes et diem sacratissimum pentecosten praeuenientes, quos spiritus sanctus apostolis innume/ris linguis aparuit. Sed et memoriam.

/f. 169r

1331 IN FRACTIONE. Hanc igitur oblationem seruitutis nostrae, sed et cunctae familiae tuae quam tibi offerimus, pro his quoque quos regenerare dignatus es ex aqua et spiritu sancto, tribuens eis remissionem omnium peccatorum. Quaesumus domine ut placatus.

1332 BENEDICTIO. Benedicat uobis omnipotens deus, ob cuius paracliti spiritus aduentum, mentes uestras ieiunii obseruantia

274

praeparatis, et praesentem diem sollemnibus laudibus honoratis. AMEN.

Instar modo renatorum infantium talem innocentiam habeatis, ut templum sancti spiritus ipso tribuente esse possitis. AMEN.

Atque idem spiritus sanctus ita uos hodie sua habitatione dignos efficiat, ut cras se uestris mentibus uobiscum perpetim habitaturus infundat, et peracto praesentis uitae curriculo, uos ad caelestia regna perducat. AMEN.

Quod[1] ipse praestare dignetur.

1333 AD COMPLENDVM. Sancti spiritus domine corda nostra mundet infusio, et sui roris intima aspersione fecundet. Per dominum.

CCX
DIE DOMINICO AD SANCTVM PETRVM

1334 Deus qui hodierna die corda fidelium, sancti spiritus inlustratione docuisti, da nobis in eodem spiritu recta sapere, et de eius semper consolatione gaudere. Per dominum.

f. 169v 1335 / SVPER OBLATA, PRAEFATIO, COMMVNICANTES, HANC IGITVR, VT SVPRA.

1336 BENEDICTIO IN DIAE. Deus qui hodierna die discipulorum mentes spiritus paracliti infusione dignatus est inlustrare, faciat uos sua benedictione repleri, et eiusdem spiritus donis exuberare. AMEN.

Ille ignis qui super discipulos apparuit, peccatorum uestrorum sordes expurget, et sui luminis infusione corda uestra perlustret. AMEN.

Quique dignatus est diuersitatem linguarum in unius fidei confessione adunare, in eadem uos faciat fide perseuerare, et per hanc ab spe ad speciem peruenire. AMEN.

Quod ipse.

1337 POST COMMVNIO. Sancti spiritus domine, ut supra.

---

[1] *Q* supplied later in crimson.

1338 AD VESPERAS. Deus qui discipulis tuis spiritum sanctum paraclitum in ignis feruore tui amoris mittere dignatus es, da populis tuis in unitate fidei esse feruentes, ut in tua semper dilectione permaneant, et in fide inueniantur stabiles, et in opere efficaces. Per dominum.

1339 ITEM ALIA. Praesta quaesumus domine ut a nostris mentibus carnales amoueat spiritus sanctus affectus, et spiritalia nobis dona potenter infundat. Per dominum nostrum iesum christum filium tuum.

CCXI
FERIA II STATIO AD SANCTVM PETRVM AD VINCVLA

/f. 170r **1340** / Deus qui apostolis tuis sanctum dedisti spiritum, concede plebi tuae petitionis effectum, ut quibus dedisti fidem, largiaris et pacem. Per.

1341 SVPER OBLATA. Propitius domine quaesumus haec dona per uirtutem sancti spiritus sanctifica, et hostiae spiritalis oblatione suscepta, nosmetipsos tibi perfice munus aeternum. Per.

1342 PRAEFATIO. VD per christum dominum nostrum. Qui promissum spiritum paraclitum super discipulos misit, qui principio nascentis ecclesiae cunctis gentibus inbuendis, et deitatis scientiam inderet, et linguarum diuersitatem, in unius fidei confessionem sociaret. Per quem tuam maiestatem supplices exoramus, ut cuius caelebramus aduentum, eius multimode gratia capiamus effectum. Per quem.

1343 BENEDICTIO. Omnipotens deus, qui quinquagesimum diem futurae remissionis munere figurasti, quo gratia sancti spiritus inebriati, apostoli mente una locuti sunt ore diuerso, respice hanc ecclesiam quam ex gentibus congregari linguarum uarietate signasti. AMEN.
Da consolationem inter praessuras saeculi, qui nobis aequalem tibi ipsi consolatorem spiritum misisti. AMEN.
/f. 170v   Et te propitiante sit ipse nunc plebis huius / custodia, qui dedit discipulis tunc doctrinam. AMEN.
Quod ipse praestare.

1344 POSTCOMMVNIO. Adesto domine quaesumus populo tuo, et quem mysteriis caelestibus imbuisti, ab hostium furore defende. Per.

CCXII
FERIA III STATIO AD SANCTAM ANASTASIAM

1345 Adsit nobis domine quaesumus uirtus spiritus sancti, quae et corda nostra clementer expurget, et ab omnibus tueatur aduersis. Per.

1346 SVPER OBLATA. Purificet nos domine quaesumus muneris praesentis oblatio, et dignos sacra participatione perficiat. Per dominum nostrum.

1347 PRAEFATIO. VD per christum dominum nostrum. Qui spiritus sancti infusione repleuit corda fidelium, qui sua admirabili operatione, et sui amoris ignem accenderet, et per diuersitatem linguarum gentes in unitate fidei solidaret. Cuius dono petimus, et inlecebrosas a nobis excludi uoluntates, et spiritales in nobis extrui, plantarique uirtutes. Per quem maiestatem.

1348 BENEDICTIO. Benedicat uobis omnipotens deus, qui cuncta ex nihilo creauit, et uobis in baptismate per spiritum sanctum remissionem omnium peccatorum tribuit. AMEN.
Quique eundem spiritum sanctum in igneis linguis discipulis suis dedit, ipsius illustratione corda uestra perlustret, atque in sui amorem iugiter / accendat. AMEN.
Quatinus eius dono a cunctis uitiis emundati, ipsiusque opitulatione ab omnibus aduersitatibus defensi, templum illius effici mereamini. AMEN.
Quod ipse.

f. 171r

1349 AD COMPLENDVM. Mentes nostras quaesumus domine spiritus sanctus diuinis reparet sacramentis, quia ipse est remissio omnium peccatorum. Per dominum nostrum.

CCXIII
FERIA IIII STATIO AD SANCTAM MARIAM AD PRAESEPEM

1350 Mentes nostras quaesumus domine paraclitus qui a te procedit inluminet, et inducat in omnem sicut tuus promisit filius ueritatem. Qui tecum.

1351 SVPER OBLATA. Praesta quaesumus omnipotens et misericors deus, ut spiritus sanctus adueniens templum nos gloriae suae dignanter habitando perficiat. Per dominum nostum.

1352 PRAEFATIO. VD per christum. Per quem discipulis spiritus sanctus in terra datur ob dilectionem proximi, et de caelo mittitur propter dilectionem tui. Cuius infusio petimus, ut in nobis peccatorum sordes exurat, tui amoris ignem nutriat, et nos ad amorem fraternitatis accendat. Per quem.

1353 BENEDICTIO. Omnipotens trinitas, unus et uerus deus pater et filius, et spiritus sanctus, det uobis se desiderare fideliter, /f. 171v agnoscere ueraciter, diligere / sinceriter. AMEN.
Aequalitatem atque incommutabilitatem suae essentiae, ita uestris mentibus infigat, ut ab ea numquam uos quibuscumque fantasiis aberrare permittat. AMEN.
Sicque uos in sua fide et caritate perseuerare concedat, ut per eam postmodum ad suam manifestationem uisionemque inter mirabilem introducat. AMEN.
Quod ipse.

1354 AD COMPLENDVM. Sumentes domine caelestia sacramenta quaesumus clementiam tuam, ut quod temporaliter gerimus, aeternis gaudiis consequamur. Per.

CCXIIII
FERIA V AD APOSTOLOS

1355 Da quaesumus ecclesiae tuae misericors deus, ut spiritu sancto congregata, hostili nullatenus incursione turbetur. Per dominum.

1356 SVPER OBLATA. Sacrificia domine tuis oblata conspectibus, ille ignis diuinus assumat, qui discipulorum christi tui per spiritum sanctum corda succendit. Per.

1357 PRAEFATIO. VD per christum. Per quem pietatem tuam suppliciter petimus, ut spiritus sanctus corda nostra clementer expurget, et sui luminis inradiatione perlustret, ut in eo qui gratiarum largitor est recta sapiamus, et de eius consolatione imperpetuum gaudeamus. Per quem.

1358 POSTCOMMVNIO. Sumpsimus domine sacri dona mysterii humiliter depraecantes, ut quae in tui commemoratione / nos facere praecepisti, in nostrae proficiant infirmitatis auxilium. Per dominum.

CCXV

FERIA VI

1359 Praesta quaesumus omnipotens et misericors deus, ut spiritus sanctus adueniens, templum nos gloriae suae dignanter habitando perficiat. Per.

1360 SVPER OBLATA. Sacrificia domine tuis oblata conspectibus, ut supra.

1361 PRAFATIO. VD aeterne deus. Et maiestatem tuam suppliciter exorare, ut spiritus paraclitus ad nos ueniat, et nos inhabitando templum suae maiestatis efficiat. Quod cum unigenito filio tuo clementi respectu, semper digneris uidere, et tuae inhabitationis fulgore in perpetuum perlustra. Per quem.

1362 POSTCOMMVNIO. Annue misericors deus, ut qui diuina praecepta[1] uiolando a paradisi felicitate decidimus, ad aeterne beatitudinis redeamus accessu, per tuorum custodiam mandatorum. Per dominum.

CCXVI

SABBATVM AD SANCTVM PETRVM IN XII LECTIONES

1363 Mentibus nostris domine quaesumus spiritum sanctum tuum benignus infunde, cuius et sapientia conditi sumus, et prouidentia gubernamur. Per.

---

[1] Letters erased in the middle of the word.

279

1364 ALIA. Illo nos igne quaesumus domine spiritus sanctus inflammet, quem dominus noster iesus christus misit in terram, et uoluit uehementer accendi. Qui tecum uiuit et regnat.

/f. 172v **1365** ITEM ALIA. / Deus qui ad animarum medelam ieiunii deuotione castigari corpora praecepisti, concede nobis propitius et mente et corpore, semper tibi esse deuotos. Per dominum nostrum.

1366 ALIA. Praesta quaesumus omnipotens deus, ut salutaribus ieiuniis eruditi, ab omnibus etiam uitiis abstinentes, propitiationem tuam facilius impetremus. Per dominum nostrum.

1367 ALIA. Praesta quaesumus omnipotens deus, sic nos ab aepulis carnalibus abstinere, ut a uitiis inruentibus pariter ieiunemus. Per dominum.

CCXVII

1368 ORATIO AD MISSAM. Deus qui tribus pueris mitigasti flammas ignium, concede propitius ut nos famulos tuos non exurat flamma uitiorum. Per.

1369 SVPER OBLATA. Vt accepta tibi sint domine nostra ieiunia, praesta nobis quaesumus huius munere sacramenti purificatum tibi pectus offerre. Per.

1370 PRAEFATIO. VD aeterne deus. Et tuam omnipotentiam deuotis praecibus implorare, ut nos spiritus tui lumen infundat, cuius nos sapientia creat, pietas recreat, et prouidentia gubernat. Qui cum a tua substantia nullo modo sit diuersus, sed tibi et unigenito tuo consubstantialis et coaeternus, diuersitate tamen donorum, /f. 173r replet tuorum / corda fidelium. Et ideo.

1371 BENEDICTIO. Domine iesu christe qui discipulis tuis sanctum dedisti spiritum, ecclesiae tuae catholicae dona largire, ut quicumque sunt ex aqua et spiritu sancto renati, semper sint eius protectione muniti. AMEN.
Redundet in eis caritas diffusa, per spiritum sanctum quae operiat ac superet omnem multitudinem peccatorum. AMEN.

Et requiescat in istis propitius, qui quondam requieuit in apostolis gloriosus. AMEN.
Quod ipse.

1372 AD COMPLENDVM. Prebeant nobis domine diuinum tua sancta feruorem, quo eorum pariter et actu delectemur et fructu. Per dominum nostrum.

CCXVIII
DOMINICA OCTAVAS PENTECOSTEN

1373 Timentium te domine saluator et custos, auerte ab ecclesia tua mundanae sapientiae oblectamenta fallacia[1], ut spiritus tui eruditione informandos[2], prophetica et apostolica potius instituta quam philosophiae uerba delectent, ne uanitas mendaciorum decipiat, quos eruditio ueritatis inluminat. Per eundem.

1374 SVPER OBLATA. Remotis obumbrationibus carnalium uictimarum, spiritalem tibi summe pater hostiam supplici seruitute deferimus, quae miro ineffabilique mysterio et immolatur semper /et ea dum semper offertur, pariterque et deuotorum munus et remunerantis esse praemium. Per.

/f. 173v

1375 PRAEFATIO. VD <aeterne deus.> Qui cum unigenito filio tuo et spiritu sancto, unus est deus, unus est dominus. Non in unius singularitate personae, sed in unius trinitate substantiae. Quod enim de tua gloria reuelante te credimus, hoc de filio tuo, hoc de spiritu sancto, sine differentiae discretione sentimus. Vt in confessione uerae sempiternaeque deitatis, et in personis proprietas, et in essentia unitas, et in maiestate adoretur aequalitas. Quam laudant.

1376 BENEDICTIO. Benedicat uos trinitatis diuinae maiestas, et una deitas pater et filius et spiritus sanctus, talesque inueniat dies examinationis, quales emisit fons regenerationis. AMEN.
Benedicat uos dominus, qui auctor est omnium et conditor

---

[1] *fallaciae* before correction.
[2] *in* supplied interlinearly.

sempiternus, corpus uestrum seruet immaculatum, et animas uestras misericorditer tueatur. AMEN.

Sicque uos ab omni crimine peccatorum reddat innoxios, ut in uobis maneat spiritus sanctus, et securi praestolemini aduentum eius. AMEN.

Quod ipse.

1377 AD COMPLENDVM. Laetificet nos quaesumus domine sacramenti ueneranda sollemnitas, pariterque mentes nostras et /f. 174r corpora, spiritali sanctificatione fecundet, et castis gau/diis semper exerceat. Per dominum nostrum.

CCXVIIII
KL. IVN. DEDICATIO BASILICAE SANCTI NICOMEDIS MARTYRIS

1378 Deus qui nos beati nicomedis martyris tui meritis et intercessione laetificas, concede propitius ut qui eius beneficia poscimus, dona tuae gratiae consequamur. Per.

1379 SVPER OBLATA. Munera domine oblata sanctifica, et intercedente beato nicomede martyre tuo, nos per haec a peccatorum nostrorum maculis emunda. Per dominum.

1380 AD COMPLENDVM. Supplices te rogamus omnipotens deus, ut quos tuis reficis sacramentis, intercedente beato nicomede martyre tuo, tibi etiam placitis moribus, dignanter tribuas deseruire. Per.

CCXX
IIII NON. IVN. NATALE SANCTORVM MARCELLINI ET PETRI

1381 Deus qui nos annua beatorum martyrum marcellini et petri sollemnitate laetificas, praesta quaesumus ut quorum gaudemus meritis, prouocemur exemplis. Per.

1382 SVPER OBLATA. Hostia haec quaesumus domine quam in sanctorum tuorum natalicia recensentes offerimus, et uincula nostrae prauitatis absoluat, et tuae nobis misęricordiae dona conciliet. Per dominum nostrum iesum christum filium tuum.

f. 174v **1383** PRAEFATIO. / VD aeterne deus. Apud quem semper est praeclara uita sanctorum, quorum nos mors praetiosa laetificat et tuẹtur. Quapropter martyrum tuorum, marcellini et petri, gloriosa recensentes natalicia, laudes tibi referimus, et magnificentiam tuam supplices exoramus, ut quorum sumus martyria uenerantes, beatitudinis mereamur esse consortes. Per christum.

1384 AD COMPLENDVM. Sacro munere satiati, supplices te domine depraecamur, ut quod debitẹ seruitutis celebramus officio, saluationis tuae sentiamus augmentum. Per dominum.

CCXXI
DOMINICA II POST PENTECOSTEN

1385 Deus in te sperantium fortitudo, adesto propitius inuocationibus nostris, et quia sine te nihil potest mortalis infirmitas, praesta auxilium gratiae tuae, ut in exequendis mandatis tuis, et uoluntate tibi et actione placeamus. Per dominum nostrum.

1386 SVPER OBLATA. Hostias nostras domine tibi dicatas placatus assume, et ad perpetuum nobis tribue prouenire subsidium. Per.

1387 PRAEFATIO. VD aeterne deus. Qui ẹcclesiae tuae filios sicut non cessas erudire, ita nos desinis adunare. Vt et scientiam te
f. 175r miserante recta / faciendi, et possibilitatem capiant exsequendi. Per christum dominum nostrum.

1388 BENEDICTIO. Benedic domine istam omnem familiam, qui gratiam benedictionis tuae desiderant inuenire, propriam manu de caelis emitte, et capita singulorum continge. AMEN.
Descendat super hos omnis gratia benedictionis tuae, sicut descendit ros super faciem terrae. AMEN.
Manus tuae sentiant tactum, spiritus sancti percipiant gaudium, ut benedicti permaneant in aeternum. AMEN.
Quod ipse.

1389 AD COMPLENDVM. Tantis domine repleti muneribus, praesta quaesumus ut et salutaria dona capiamus, et a tua numquam laude cessemus. Per dominum.

CCXXII
VI ID. IVN. NATALE SANCTI MEDARDI

1390 Deus qui sanctam nobis diei huius sollemnitatem in honore sancti medardi confessoris tui atque pontificis consecrasti, adesto familię tuae praecibus, et dona ut cuius festa celebramus, eius merito et auxilio subleuemur. Per.

1391 SVPER OBLATA. Respice domine quaesumus populum tuum[1], ad tua sacramenta currentem, et praesentem festiuitatem sancti confessoris tui atque pontificis medardi, ut quod in honore nominis tui detulerunt, cunctis proficiat adueniam. Per.

/f. 175v **1392** / <PRAEFATIO.> VD <aeterne deus.> Te domine sancte[2] pater omnipotens aeterne deus, qui beatum medardum confessorem tuum atque pontificem laetificas in regno tuo, in beatitudine semper sine fine. Vbi omnia possit uidere, in tua claritate cum omnibus sanctis, ubi est temperantia spiritalis, ubi refrigerium ineffabile[3], et laetitia inenerrabilis. Vbi praesentia saluatoris filii tui domini nostri iesu christi, in quem semper laetantes prospicere desiderant angeli. Cum quibus.

1393 BENEDICTIO. Domine iesu christe pastor bone gregem tuum custodi, et intercessione beati medardi confessoris tui quicquid postulauerint clementer concede. AMEN.
Da eis ante conspectum tuum cum iustitia uiuere, et cum misericordia eos iudicare dignare. AMEN.
Da eis credulitatem in fide, da uirtutem in labore, da prosperitatem in tempore, da laetitiam in pace. AMEN.
Quod ipse.

1394 AD COMPLENDVM. Gratias tibi agimus domine deus noster, qui nos caelesti medela reparare dignatus es, da quaesumus peccatis nostris ueniam, sicut beato medardo confessori tuo, dedisti sedem pontificatus. Per.

---

[1] Endings of *populum tuum* rewritten in black ink.
[2] *sanctae* before correction.
[3] *ineffabili* before correction.

CCXXIII
V ID. IVN. NATALE SANCTORVM PRIMI ET FELICIANI

1395 Fac nos domine quaesumus sanctorum primi et feliciani semper festa sectari, quorum suffragiis protectionis / tuae dona sentiamus. Per.

f. 176r

1396 SVPER OBLATA. Fiat domine quaesumus hostia sacranda placabilis praetiosi celebritate martyrii, quae et peccata nostra purificet, et tuorum tibi uota conciliet famulorum. Per dominum nostrum.

1397 AD COMPLENDVM. Quaesumus omnipotens deus, ut sanctorum tuorum caelestibus mysteriis caelebrata sollemnitas, indulgentiam nobis tuae propitiationis adquirat. Per.

CCXXIIII
MENSIS QVARTI FERIA .IIII. AD SANCTAM MARIAM

1398 Concede nobis domine praesidia militiae christianae sanctis inchoare ieiuniis, ut contra spiritales nequitias pugnaturi, continentia muniamur auxilii. Per dominum nostrum.

1399 ALIA. Omnipotens et misericors deus, apta nos tuae propitius uoluntati, quoniam sicut eius praetereuntes tramitem deuiamus, sic integro tenore dirigamur, ad illius semper ordinem recurrentes. Per dominum nostrum.

1400 SVPER OBLATA. Sollemnibus ieiuniis expiatos suo nos domine mysterio congruentes, hoc sacrum munus efficiat, quia tanto nobis salubrius aderit, quanto id deuotius sumpserimus. Per.

1401 <PRAEFATIO.> VD aeterne deus. Quia post illos laetitiae dies quos in honore domini a mortuis resurgentis, et in caelo ascendentis exegimus, / postque perceptum sancti spiritus donum, necessaria nobis ieiunia sanctae prouisa sunt, ut pura conuersatione uiuentibus, quae diuinitus sunt ecclesię conlata permaneant. Per christum.

f. 176v

1402 AD COMPLENDVM. Quos ieiunia uotiua castigant, tua domine sacramenta uiuificent, ut terrenis affectibus mitigatis, facilius caelestia capiamus. Per dominum.

1403 <SVPER POPVLVM.> Gratias tibi referat domine corde subiecto, tua semper ecclesia, et consequenter obtineat, ut obseruationes antiquas, iugiter recensendo proficiat in futurum. Per dominum.

CCXXV
FERIA VI AD APOSTOLOS

1404 Fiat tua gratia domine fructuos cor nostrae deuotionis affectus, quia tunc nobis proderunt suscepta ieiunia, si tuae sint placita pietati. Per dominum nostrum.

1405 SVPER OBLATA. Omnipotens sempiterne deus, qui non sacrificiorum ambitione placaris, sed studio piae deuotionis intendis, da familiae tuae spiritum rectum et habere cor mundum, ut fides eorum haec dona tibi conciliet, et humilitas oblata commendet. Per.

1406 BENEDICTIO. Benedic domine omnem istam familiam, quae gratiam benedictionis tuae inuenire desiderat. AMEN.

/f. 177r Propriam manum de caelis emitte, et capita / singulorum continge. AMEN.

Descendat super hanc plebem gratia benedictionis tuae, sicut descendit ros et pluuiae, ad irrigandam superficiem terrae. AMEN.

Quod ipse.

1407 AD COMPLENDVM. Annue quaesumus omnipotens deus, ut sacramentorum tuorum gesta recolentes, et temporali securitate releuemur, et erudiamur legalibus institutis. Per.

1408 SVPER POPVLVM. Fideli populo domine misaericordiam tuam placatus impende, et praesidia corporis copiosa tribue supplicanti. Per.

CCXXVI
SABBATO AD SANCTVM PETRVM IN XII LECTIONIBVS

1409 Praesta domine quaesmus famulis tuis ut tales nos concedas fieri tuae gratiae largitate, quatinus[1] bona tua et fiducialiter impetremus, et sine difficultate sumamus. Per.

---

[1] Supplied in margin.

1410 ALIA. Da nobis domine quaesumus regnum tuum iustitiamque semper inquirere, ut quibus indigere nos perspicis, clementer facias abundare. Per dominum nostrum.

1411 ALIA. Deus qui nos de praesentibus adiumentis esse uetuisti sollicitos, tribue quaesumus ut pie sectando quae tua sunt, uniuersa nobis salutaria condonentur. Per dominum nostrum.

1412 ALIA. Deus qui misericordia tua[1] praeuenis non petentes, da nobis affectum maiestatem tuam iugiter depraecandi[2], ut pietate perpetua suppli/cibus potiora concedas. Per.

f. 177v

1413 ALIA. Deus qui non despicis corde contritos, et afflictos miseriis populum tuum ieiunii ad te deuotione clamantem propitiatus exaudi, ut quos humiliauit aduersitas, attollat reparationis tuae prosperitas. Per dominum nostrum.

1414 ALIA. Deus qui tribus pueris. Require retro in sabbato pentecosten.

CCXXVII

ITEM ALIA AD MISSAM

1415 Deus cuius adorandę potentia maiestatis flammae seuientis incendium sanctis tribus pueris in splendorem demutatum est animarum, ecclesiae tuae similibus adesto remediis, ut de grauioribus mundi huius aduersitatibus propitiatione caelesti populus tuus liberetur[3]. Per.

1416 SVPER POPVLVM. Domine deus noster qui in his potius creaturis, quas ad fragilitatis nostrę praesidium condidisti, tuo quoque nomini munera iussisti dicanda constitui[4], tribuae quaesumus, ut et uitae nobis praesentis auxilium, et aeternitatis efficiant sacramentum. Per.

---

[1] *misericordiam tuam* before correction.
[2] *depraecantes* before correction.
[3] Supplied in margin.
[4] *constituit* before correction.

1417 PRĘFATIO. VD aeterne deus. Et tibi sanctificare ieiunium, quod nos ad aedificationem animarum, et castigationem corporum seruare docuisti, quia restrictis corporibus animae saginantur, in[1] quo exterior homo nostra affligitur, dilatatur / exterior. Memento domine ieiuniorum nostrorum et misęricordiarum tuarum, quas pectoribus pie semper ieiunantibus contulisti, ut non solum a cibis sed etiam a peccatis omnibus abstinentes, deuotionis tibi ieiunio. Per christum.

/f. 178r

1418 BENEDICTIO. Require in externa die.

1419 AD COMPLENDVM. Sumptum quaesumus domine uenerabile sacramentum, et praesentis uitae subsidio, nos foueat et aeternae. Per dominum nostrum.

1420 SVPER POPVLVM. Proficiat domine quaesumus plebs tibi[2] dicata piae deuotionis affectu, ut sacris actibus erudita, quanto maiestati tuae fit gratior, tanto donis potioribus augeatur. Per dominum nostrum.

CCXXVIII

DOMINICA III POST OCTAVAS PENTECOSTEN

1421 Sancti nominis tui domine timorem pariter et amorem fac nos habere perpetuum, quia numquam tua gubernatione destitues[3], quos in soliditatae tuae dilectionis instituis. Per.

1422 SVPER OBLATA. Oblatio nos tuo nomini dicanda purificet, et de die in diem ad caelestis uitae transferat actionem. Per.

1423 PRAEFATIO. VD aeterne deus. Cuius hoc mirificum opus ac salutare mysterium fuit, ut perditi dudum atque prostrati de diabolo et mortis aculeo, ad hanc gloriam / uocaremur. Qua nunc genus electum, sacerdotiumque regale, populus adquisitionis, et gens sancta uocaremur. Agentes igitur indefessas gratias, sanctamque munificentiam tuam praedicantes, maiestati tuae

/f. 178v

---

[1] *ex* before correction.
[2] Supplied interlinearly.
[3] Final letters rewritten.

haec sacra deferimus, quae nobis ipse salutis nostrae, auctor christus instituit. Per quem.

1424 BENEDICTIO. Propitietur dominus cunctis iniquitatibus uestris, et sanat omnes languores uestros. AMEN.
Redimetque de interitu uitam uestram, et satiet in bonis omnibus desiderium uestrum. AMEN.
Auferat a uobis cor lapideum, et det uobis cor carneum. AMEN.
Quod ipse.

1425 AD COMPLENDVM. Sumptis muneribus domine quaesumus, ut cum frequentatione mysterii, crescat nostrae salutis effectus. Per dominum.

CCXXVIIII
II IDVS IVN. NATALE SANCTORVM BASILIDIS, CYRINI, NABORIS ET NAZARII

1426 Sanctorum basilidis, cyrini, naboris, et nazari, quaesumus domine natalicia nobis uotiua resplendeant, et quod illis contulit excellentiam sempiternam, fructibus nostrae deuotionis adcrescat. Per dominum.

1427 SVPER OBLATA. Pro sanctorum basilidis, cyrini, naboris et nazari, sanguine uenerando hostias, tibi domine sollemniter immolamus, tua mirabilia / pertractantes, per quem talis est perfecta uictoria. Per dominum nostrum.

/f. 179r

1428 BENEDICTIO. Enutri quaesumus domine plebem tuam in fructibus sanctis et in operibus benedictis, et sanctorum martyrum tuorum basilidis, cyrini, naboris, et nazari, quorum natalicia colimus, eorum intercessionibus fac illis tali sobole germinare, quibus ad te mereantur introire, et sine fine paradysum possidere. AMEN.
Cruce pascantur, ligno sanentur, quod plantatum secus decursus aquarum, da eis fidei fructum, et fructu regni caelestis patiantur, et benedici in die iudicii mereantur. AMEN.
Hierusalem habitatores efficiantur caelestis et cum angelis in caelestibus gaudere mereantur regnis. AMEN.
Quod ipse praestare dignetur.

1429 AD COMPLENDVM. Semper domine sanctorum martyrum basilidis, cyrini, naboris, et nazari sollemnia caelebramus, et eorum patrocinia iugiter sentiamus. Per.

CCXXX
XVII KL. IVL. NATALE SANCTI VITI

1430 Da ecclesiae tuae domine quaesumus sancto uito intercedente superbe non sapere, sed tibi placita humilitate proficere, ut proterua despiciens, quaecumque matura sunt libera exerceat caritate. Per dominum.

/f. 179v **1431** SVPER OBLATA. / Sicut gloriam diuinae potentiae munera pro sanctis oblata testantur, sic nobis effectum domine tuae saluationis impendant. Per.

1432 PRAEFATIO. VD <aeterne deus.> Beati uiti martyrio gloriantes, cui admiranda gratia[1] in tenero adhuc corpore, et necdum uirili more maturo, uirtutem fidei, et patientiae fortitudinem tribuisti, ut saeuitiae persecutoribus non cederet constantia puerilis, et inter acerba supplicia, nec sensu potuit terreri, nec frangi etate, ut gloriosior fieret eius[2] corona martyrii. Et ideo.

1433 AD COMPLENDVM. Refecti domine benedictione sollemni, quaesumus ut per intercessionem sancti uiti medicina sacramenti, et corporibus nostris prosit et mentibus. Per.

CCXXXI
XIIII KL. IVL. NATALE SANCTORVM MARCI ET MARCELLIANI

1434 Praesta quaesumus omnipotens deus, ut qui sanctorum marci et marcelliani natalicia colimus, a cunctis malis imminentibus, eorum intercessionibus liberemur. Per.

1435 SVPER OBLATA. Munera domine tibi dicata sanctifica, et intercedentibus beato marco, et marcelliano, per eadem nos placatus intende. Per dominum nostrum.

---

[1] Supplied later over an erasure.
[2] Rewritten over an erasure.

1436 AD COMPLENDVM. Salutaris tui domine munere satiati supplices exoramus, ut quorum laetamur gustu, renouemur effectu. Per.

CCXXXII
DOMINICA VACAT

/f. 180r **1437** / Depraecationem nostram quaesumus domine benignus exaudi, et quibus supplicandi praestas affectum, tribue defensionis auxilium. Per dominum.

1438 SVPER OBLATA. Munera domine oblata sanctifica, ut tui nobis unigeniti corpus et sanguis fiant. Per eundem.

1439 PRAEFATIO. VD aeterne deus. Quoniam illa festa remeant, quibus nostrae mortalitati procuratur immortale commercium, ac temporali uitae subrogatur aeternitas, et de peccati pena, peccata mundantur. Mirisque modis conficitur de perditione saluatio, ut status conditionis humanae, qui per felicitatis insolentiam uenit ad tristitiam, humilis et modestus ad aeterna gaudia redeat per merorem. Per christum.

1440 BENEDICTIO. Benedicat uobis nostri oris alloquio, et cor uestrum sinceri amoris copulet nexu perpetuo. AMEN.
Floreatis rerum praesentium copiis iustitia adquisitis, gaudeatis perenniter fructibus sincerissime caritatis. AMEN.
Tribuat uobis dominus dona perennia, ut post tempora feliciter dilatata, percipiatis gaudia sempiterna. AMEN.
Quod ipse.

1441 AD COMPLENDVM. Haec nos communio domine purget a crimine, et caelestis remedii faciat esse consortes. Per.

CCXXXIII
/f. 180v ## XIIII KL. IVL. VIGILIA SANCTORVM MAR/TYRVM
GERVASII ET PROTASII

1442 Martyrum tuorum domine geruasii et protasii, natalicia praeeuntes, supplices te rogamus, ut quos caelesti gloria sublimasti, tuis adesse concede fidelibus. Per.

1443 SVPER OBLATA. Sacrificium domine quod pro sanctis martyribus geruasio, et protasio, praeuenit nostra deuotio, quorum merita nobis augeant te donante suffragium. Per dominum nostrum.

1444 AD COMPLENDVM. Sumpti sacrificii domine perpetua nos tuitio non relinquat, et noxia semper a nobis cuncta depellat. Per.

CCXXXIIII
XII KL. IVL. NATALE SANCTORVM GERVASII
ET PROTASII

1445 Deus qui nos annua sanctorum tuorum geruasii et protasii sollemnitate laetificas, concede propitius, ut quorum gaudemus meritis, accendamur exemplis. Per.

1446 SVPER OBLATA. Oblatis quaesumus domine placare muneribus, et intercedentibus sanctis tuis, a cunctis nos defende periculis. Per dominum.

1447 PRAEFATIO. VD per christum dominum nostrum. Pro cuius nominis confessione beati martyres geruasius et protasius passi, in caelesti regione aeternis perfruuntur gaudiis, et pro eorum sollemni recordatione, ecclesia religiosis / exultat officiis. Per quem.

/f. 181r

1448 BENEDICTIO. Domine sanctae pater aeternae omnipotens deus, respice propitius hunc populum tuum, qui benedictionum tuarum dona desiderat, et praesta ut in omnibus tuis praeceptis, pia ueneratione tibi deseruiat. AMEN.

Quatinus omni sanctitate firmatus retributionis diem sine metu confusionis expectet, et sanctam ac sacratissimam hodiernam festiuitatem beatorum scilicet geruasii et protasii martyrum caelebrans grata uota sollemnitate illorum accepta, in conspectu maiestatis tuae offerat. AMEN.

Ac beatorum consortio sanctorum aggregatus, aeternae uitae praemia consequi mereatur, et a te aeterna exultatione per perpetua benedictione ditetur. AMEN.

Quod ipse.

1449 AD COMPLENDVM. Haec nos communio domine purget a crimine, et intercedentibus sanctis tuis, caelestis remedii faciat esse consortes. Per dominum.

CCXXXV
EBDOMADA V POST PENTECOSTEN

1450 Protector in te sperantium deus, sine quo nihil est ualidum nihil sanctum, multiplica super nos misericordiam tuam, ut te rectore te duce, sic transeamus per bona temporalia, ut non amittamus aeterna. Per.

f. 181v **1451** SVPER OBLATA. / Respice domine munera supplicantis ecclesiae, et saluti credentium perpetua sanctificatione sumenda concede. Per.

1452 PRAEFATIO. VD aeterne[1] deus. Quoniam illa festa remeant, quibus nostrae mortalitati procuratur inmortale commertium, ac temporali uitae subrogatur aeternitas, et de peccati poena, peccata mundantur. Mirisque modis conficitur de perditione saluatio, ut status conditionis humanae, qui per felicitatis insolentiam uenit ad tristitiam, humilis et modestus, ad aeterna gaudia redeat per merorem. Per christum.

1453 BENEDICTIO. Emundet dominus conscientias uestras ab omni malitia, et repleat sanctificatione perpetua. AMEN.
Vota uestra clementer intendat, et peccata omnia propitiatus indulgeat. AMEN.
Quae piae optatis miseratus tribuat, et quae pauescitis pius propugnator, procul[2] repellat. AMEN.
Quod ipse praestare.

1454 AD COMPLENDVM. Sancta tua nos domine sumpta uiuificent, et misericordiae sempiternae praeparent expiatos. Per.

---

[1]   *aeternae* before correction.
[2]   Supplied interlinearly.

CCXXXVI
VIIII KL. IVL. VIGILIA SANCTI IOHANNIS BABTISTAE

1455 Praesta quaesumus omnipotens deus, ut familia tua per uiam salutis incedat, et beati iohannis praecursoris hortamenta sectando, ad eum quem praedixit / secura perueniat. Per dominum.

/f. 182r

1456 SVPER OBLATA. Munera domine oblata sanctifica, et intercedente iohanne baptista, nos per haec a peccatorum nostrorum maculis emunda. Per.

1457 PRAEFATIO. [1]VD aeternae deus. Exibentes sollemne ieiunium, quo beati iohannis baptistae natalicia praeuenimus. Cuius genitor dum eum dubitat nasciturum, sermonis amisit officium, et eo nascente et sermonis usum, et prophetiae suscepit donum. Cuiusque genetrix senio confecta, sterilitate multata, in eius conceptu, non solum sterilitatem amisit, fecunditatem adquisiuit, sed etiam spiritum sanctum quo matrem domini et saluatoris agnosceret accepit. Per quem.

1458 BENEDICTIO. Deus qui beatum iohannem baptistam magnum nuntiasti per angelum, maximum declarasti per uerbum, qui clausus in utero reddidit obsequium domino, matrem repleuit gaudio, patris linguam soluit a uinculo, cerne placato uultu, confrequentantem hodie populum ad tanti praeconiis occursum. AMEN.
Ascendit uox illius ad aures altissimi, qui maternis uisceribus ante mundi dominum nouit confiteri quam nasci. AMEN.
Vero intercedente purgetur haec plebs a cri/mine, cuius auctorem lauacri sacra dextera tinxit in fonte. AMEN.
Quod ipse.

/f. 182v

1459 AD COMPLENDVM. Beati iohannis baptistae nos domine praeclara comitetur oratio, et quem uenturum esse praedixit, poscat nobis fore placatum. Per.

---

[1] Partly neumed later.

294

CCXXXVII
VIII KL. <IVL.>. IN PRIMA MISSA SANCTI IOHANNIS

1460 Concede quaesumus omnipotens deus, ut qui beati iohannis baptistae sollemnia colimus, eius apud te intercessione muniamur. Per.

1461 SVPER OBLATA. Munera domine oblata sanctifica, et intercedente beato iohanne baptista, nos per haec a peccatorum nostrorum maculis emunda. Per.

1462 AD COMPLENDVM. Praesta quaesumus omnipotens deus, ut qui caelestia alimenta percepimus, intercedente beato iohanne baptista, per haec contra omnia aduersa muniamur. Per dominum.

CCXXXVIII
IN DIE AD MISSAM IN NATALE EIVSDEM

1463 Deus qui praesentem diem honorabilem nobis in beati iohannis natiuitate fecisti, da populis tuis spiritalium gratiam gaudiorum, et omnium fidelium mentes, dirige in uiam salutis aeternae. Per.

1464 SVPER OBLATA. Tua domine muneribus altaria cumulamus, illius natiuitatem honore debito caelebrantes, qui saluatorem mundi et cecinit affu/turum[1], et adesse monstrauit. Dominum nostrum.

/f. 183r

1465 PRAEFATIO. [2]VD aeterne[3] deus. Et in die festiuitatis hodiernę qua beatus iohannes exortus est, tuam magnificentiam collaudare[4]. Qui uocem matris domini nondum aeditus sensit, et adhuc clausus utero aduentum salutis humanae prophetica exultatione significauit. Qui et genetricis sterilitatem conceptus abstulit, et patris linguam natus absoluit. Solusque omnium prophetarum, redemptorem mundi, quem pronuntiauit ostendit. Et ut sacrę purificationis effectum, aquarum natura conciperet, sanctificandis iordanis fluentis, ipsum baptismo baptismatis lauit auctorem. Et ideo.

---

[1] *adfuturum* before correction.
[2] Partly neumed later.
[3] *aeternae* before correction.
[4] *conlaudare* before correction.

1466 BENEDICTIO. Benedicat uobis omnipotens deus, beati iohannis baptistae intercessione, cuius hodie natalicia caelebratis, concedatque ut cuius sollemnia colitis, patrocinia sentiatis. AMEN.

Illius obtentu ab omnibus aduersis tuaeamini, et bonis operibus perfruamini, qui aduentum redemptoris mundi necdum natus cognouit, matris sterilitatem nascendo abstulit, patris linguam natus absoluit. AMEN.

Quatinus ipsius agni quem ille digito ostendit, cuius immolatione estis redempti, ita uirtutum lanis uestiri, et /f. 183v innocentiam ualeatis imitari, / ut ei in aeternae patriae felicitate possitis adiungi. AMEN.

Quod ipse.

1467 AD COMPLENDVM. Sumat ęcclesia tua deus beati iohannis baptistae generatione laetitiam, per quem suae regenerationis cognouit auctorem. Dominum nostrum.

1468 AD VESPERAS. Deus qui nos beati iohannis baptistae concedis natalicio perfrui, eius nos tribue meritis adiuuari. Per dominum.

1469 AD FONTES. Omnipotens sempiterne deus, da cordibus nostris illam tuarum rectitudinem semitarum, quam beati iohannis baptistae, in deserto uox clamantis edocuit. Per dominum.

CCXXXVIIII
ALIAE ORATIONES

1470 Deus qui conspicis quia nos undique mala nostra contristant, per praecursorem gaudii, corda nostra laetifica. Per dominum.

1471 ALIA. Da quaesumus omnipotens deus intra sanctae ecclesiae uterum constitutos, eo nos spiritu ab iniquitate nostra iustificari, quo beatum iohannem intra uiscera materna docuisti. Per.

1472 ITEM ALIA. Deus qui nos annua beati iohannis baptistae, sollemnia frequentare concedis, praesta quaesumus ut et deuotis eadem mentibus cęlebraemus, et eius patrocinio promerente, plenae capiamus securitatis augmentum. Per.

f. 184r **1473** ALIA. / Omnipotens et misaericors deus, qui beatum iohannem baptistam tua prouidentia destinasti, ut perfectam plebem christo domino praepararet, da quaesumus ut familia tua huius intercessione praeconis, et a peccatis omnibus exuatur, et ad eum quem prophetauit peruenire mereatur. Iesum christum filium tuum.

CCXL
VI KL. IVL. NATALE SANCTORVM IOHANNIS ET PAVLI

1474 Quaesumus omnipotens deus, ut nos geminata laetitia, hodiernae festiuitatis excipiat, quae de beatorum iohannis et pauli glorificatione procedit, quos eadem fides et passio, uere fecit esse germanos. Per.

1475 SVPER OBLATA. Hostias tibi domine sanctorum martyrum tuorum iohannis et pauli, dicatas meritis benignus assume, et ad perpetuum nobis tribue[1] prouenire subsidium. Per.

1476 PRAEFATIO. [2]VD per christum dominum nostrum. Pro cuius amore gloriosi martyres iohannes et paulus, martyrium non sunt cunctati subire, quos in nascendi lege iunxit germanitas, in gremio matris ęcclesiae fidei unitas, in passionis acerbitate ferenda unius amoris sociaetas. Per quem nos petimus eorum praecibus adiuuari, quorum festa noscitur uenerari. Per quem.

1477 AD COMPLENDVM. Sumpsimus domine sanctorum tuorum sollemnia caelebrantes sacramenta caelestia, praesta quaesumus / ut quod temporaliter gerimus, aeternis gaudiis consequamur. Per.

f. 184v

DOMINICA VI POST PENTECOSTEN

1478 Da nobis domine quaesumus, ut et mundi cursus pacificus nobis tuo ordine dirigatur, et ęcclesia tua tranquilla deuotione lętetur. Per.

1479 SVPER OBLATA. Oblationibus quaesumus domine placare susceptis, et a te nostras etiam rebelles compelle propitius uoluntates. Per dominum.

---

[1] *tribuae* before correction.
[2] Partly neumed later.

1480 PRAEFATIO. [1]VD aeterne deus. Et omnipotentiam tuam iugiter implorare, ut nobis et praesentis uitę subsidium, et aeternae tribuas praemium sempiternum. Quo sic mutabilia bona capiamus, ut per haec ad incommutabilia dona peruenire ualeamus. Sic temporalis laetitiae tempora transeant, ut eis gaudia sempiterna succedant. Per christum dominum nostrum.

1481 BENEDICTIO. Agnoscat in uobis dominus proprium signum, et suum uobis misericorditer conferat donum. AMEN.
Bella comprimat, famen auferat, pacem tribuat, inimici insidias longe repellat. AMEN.
Merentium gemitus uideat, uocem uestri doloris exaudiat, et lacrimas ab omni facie tergat, alternamque uobis dilectionem indulgeat, et perfectam caritatem concedat. AMEN.
Quod ipse praestare.

/f. 185r **1482** AD COMPLENDVM. / Mysteria nos domine sancta purificent, et suo munere tueantur. Per dominum nostrum.

CCXLII
IIII KL. IVL. NATALE SANCTI LEONIS PAPAE
1483 Deus qui beatum leonem pontificem sanctorum tuorum meritis coaequasti, concede propitius ut qui commemorationis eius festa percolimus, uitae quoque imitemur exempla. Per dominum.

1484 SVPER OBLATA. Annue nobis domine ut animae famuli tui leonis haec prosit oblatio, quam immolando totius mundi tribuisti relaxari delicta. Per dominum nostrum.

1485 POSTCOMMVNIO. Deus qui animae famuli tui leonis aeternae beatitudinis praemia contulisti, concede propitius ut qui peccatorum nostrorum pondere praemimur, eius apud te precibus[2] subleuemur. Per dominum nostrum.

CCXLIII
EODEM DIE VIGILIA SANCTI PETRI APOSTOLI
1486 Praesta quaesumus omnipotens deus, ut nullis nos permittas perturbationibus concuti, quos in apostolicae confessionis petra solidasti. Per dominum.

---

[1] Partly neumed later.
[2] *praecibus* before correction.

1487 SVPER OBLATA. Munus populi tui domine quaesumus apostolica intercessione sanctifica, nosque a peccatorum nostrorum maculis emunda. Per.

1488 PRAEFATIO. [1]VD aequum et salutare. Te domine suppliciter exorare, ut gregem / tuum pastor aeterne[2] non deseras, sed per beatos apostolos tuos continua protectione custodias. Vt hisdem[3] rectoribus gubernetur, quos operis tui uicarios eidem contulisti praesse pastores. Et ideo.

f. 185v

1489 AD COMPLENDVM. Quos caelesti domine alimento satiasti, apostolicis intercessionibus ab omni aduersitate custodi. Per.

1490 AD VIGILIAM IN NOCTE. Deus qui ęcclesiam tuam apostoli tui petri fide et nomine consecrasti, quique beatum illi paulum ad praedicandum gentibus gloriam tuam sociare dignatus es, concede ut omnes qui ad apostolorum tuorum sollemnia conuenerunt, spiritali remuneratione ditentur. Per dominum.

CCXLIIIII
III KL. IVL. NATALE APOSTOLORVM PETRI ET PAVLI

1491 Deus qui hodiernam diem apostolorum tuorum petri et pauli martyrio consecrasti, da ęcclesiae eorum in omnibus sequi praeceptum, per quos religionis sumpsit exordium. Per.

1492 SVPER OBLATA. Hostias domine quas nomini tuo sacrandas offerimus, apostolica prosequatur oratio, per quam nos expiari tribuis et defendi. Per.

1493 PRAEFATIO. [4]VD aeterne[5] deus. Apud quem cum beatorum apostolorum continuata festiuitas, triumphique caelestis perpetua, et aeterna sit caelebritas, nobis tamen eorum festa, annuis recursibus / tribuis frequentare. Vt et illorum passioni sit[6] ueneratio, ex nostra deuotione, et nobis auxilium proueniat de

f. 186r

---

[1] Partly neumed later.
[2] *aeternae* before correction.
[3] *Vt his* over an erasure.
[4] Partly neumed later.
[5] *aeternae* before correction.
[6] *sint* before correction.

299

eorum sanctissima intercessione. Per christum dominum nostrum.

1494 BENEDICTIO. Benedicat uobis omnipotens deus, qui uos beati petri saluberrima confessione in ecclesiasticae fidei fundauit soliditate. AMEN.
Et quos beati pauli sanctissima instruxit praedicatione, sua tueatur gratissima defensione. AMEN.
Quatinus petrus claue, paulus sermone, utrique intercessione, ad illam uos certent patriam introducere, ad quam illi, alter cruce, alter gladio, hodierna die peruenire. AMEN.
Quod ipse.

1495 AD COMPLENDVM. Quos caelesti domine alimento satiasti, apostolicis intercessionibus ab omni aduersitate custodi. Per.

1496 AD VESPERAS. Deus qui apostolo tuo petro, conlatis clauibus regni caelestis ligandi atque soluendi pontificium tradidisti, concede ut intercessionis eius auxilio[1], a peccatorum nostrorum nexibus liberemur. Per dominum.

1497 ALIA. Omnipotens sempiterne deus, qui ecclesiam tuam in apostolica soliditate fundatam, ab infernorum eruis terrore

/f. 186v portarum praesta / ut in tua ueritate persistens, nulla recipiat consortio perfidorum. Per.

1498 ALIA. Familiam tuam domine propitius intuere, et apostolicis defende praesidiis, ut eorum praecibus gubernetur, quibus nititur te constituente principibus. Per dominum.

1499 ALIA. Exaudi nos deus salutaris noster, et apostolorum tuorum nos tuere praesidiis, quorum donasti fideles esse doctrinis. Per.

1500 ALIA. Protege domine populum tuum, et apostolorum patrocinio confidentem, perpetua defensione conserua. Per dominum nostrum.

1501 ALIA. Esto domine plebi tuae sanctificator et custos, ut apostolicis munita praesidiis, et conuersatione tibi placeat, et secura mente deseruiat. Per.

---

[1] First letters rewritten.

CCXLV
II KL. IVL. NATALE SANCTI PAVLI APOSTOLI

1502 Deus qui multitudinem gentium beati pauli apostoli praedicatione docuisti, da nobis quaesumus ut cuius natalicia colimus, eius apud te patrocinia sentiamus. Per.

1503 SVPER OBLATA. Ecclesię tuae quaesumus domine praeces et hostias apostolica commendet oratio, ut quod pro illorum gloria caelebramus, nobis prosit ad ueniam. Per.

1504 BENEDICTIO. Deus qui in membris ecclesiae uelud geminatum lumen quo caue/antur tenebrae, fecisti petri lacrimas, pauli litteras coruscare, concede huic familiae tuae felicia dona suis indefessis petitionibus obtinere. AMEN.
Atque eam de supernis sedibus placatus inspice, qui caelos fecisti aperire, petro in claue, paulo in dogmate. AMEN.
Vt praeuiantibus dulcibus illuc grex possit accedere, quo peruenerunt ipsi pariter, tam ille pastor per suspendium, quam iste doctor per gladium. AMEN.
Quod ipse.

f. 187r

1505 AD COMPLENDVM. Perceptis domine sacramentis, beatis apostolis interuenientibus depraecamur, ut quae pro illorum caelebrata sunt gloria, nobis proficiant ad medelam. Per.

CCXLVI
DOMINICA VII POST PENTECOSTEN

1506 Deus qui diligentibus te bona inuisibilia praeparasti, infunde cordibus nostris tui amoris affectum, ut te in omnibus et super omnia diligentes, promissiones tuas quae omne desiderium superant consequamur. Per.

1507 SVPER OBLATA. Propitiare domine supplicationibus nostris, et has oblationes famulorum famularumque tuarum benignus assume, ut quod singuli obtulerunt, ad honorem nominis tui cunctis proficat ad salutem. Per.

1508 PRAEFATIO. VD aeterne[1] deus. Maiestatem tuam suppliciter
/f. 187v depraecantes, ut opem tuam / petentibus dignanter impendas, et
desiderantibus benignus tribuas profuturam. Per christum.

1509 BENEDICTIO. Amoueat a uobis dominus totius maculas
simultatis, et imbuat uos muneribus pure dilectionis. AMEN.
Subiuget in uobis reluctationem carnis et sanguinis, et opem
conferat perpetuae castitatis. AMEN.
Atque uos in praesenti saeculo diligere, faciat quod a caelestis
paradysi hereditate non diuidat. AMEN.
Quod ipse praestare.

1510 AD COMPLENDVM. Quos caelesti domine dono[2] satiasti,
praesta quaesumus ut a nostris mundemur ocultis, et ab hostium
liberemur insidiis. Per.

CCXLVII

VI NON. IVL. NATALE SANCTORVM PROCESSI
ET MARTINIANI

1511 Deus qui nos sanctorum tuorum processi et martiniani
confessionibus gloriosis circumdas et protegis, da nobis et
eorum imitatione proficere, et intercessione gaudere. Per.

1512 SVPER OBLATA. Suscipe domine praeces et munera, quae ut
tuo sint digna conspectui, sanctorum tuorum praecibus
adiuuentur. Per.

1513 BENEDICTIO. Respice domine hanc familiam tuam serenis
obtutibus, et largis eam infunde benedictionibus, ut in uiam recti
/f. 188r itineris gressus suos dirigant, et fidei / suae stabilem firmitatem
teneant. AMEN.
Ac sanctis suffragantibus meritis, beatorum tuorum processi et
martiniani quorum annuam festiuitatem deuotis mentibus
exercent perseuerantiam boni operis usque in finem habere
ualeant. AMEN.
Vt proemia destinata sanctis in aeterna beatitudine possideant

---

[1] *aeternae* before correction.
[2] Final *o* over an erasure.

sine fine, et cum eis sicuti est deum facie ad faciem uiso indefectiuo mereantur uidere. AMEN.
Quod ipse praestare.

1514 AD COMPLENDVM. Corporis sacri et praetiosi sanguinis repleti libamine quaesumus domine deus noster, ut quod pia deuotione gerimus, certa redemptione capiamus. Per dominum.

CCXLVIII
IIII NON. IVL. TRANSLATIO SANCTI MARTINI

1515 Deus qui sanctam nobis diei huius sollemnitatem in honore sancti martini confessoris tui atque pontificis consecrasti, adesto familiae tuae praecibus, et dona ut cuius festa colimus, eius meritis auxilio subleuemur. Per.

1516 SVPER OBLATA. Respice domine populum tuum ad uiam sacramenta currentem, in praesenti festiuitate sancti confessoris tui atque pontificis martini, quod in honore nominis tui detulerunt, cunctis prosit ad ueniam. Per dominum.

1517 PRAEFATIO. VD aeterne[1] deus. Qui beatum martinum confessorem tuum atque pontificem laetificas / in regeneratione, in beatitudine sempiterno fine. Vt omnia possit uidere in tua claritate cum omnibus sanctis, ubi temperantia spiritalis, et suauitas mirabilis, ubi refrigerium mirabile, et laetitia inenarrabilis, ubi praesentia salutaris filii tui domini nostri in quo semper laetantes, proficere desiderant angeli. Adorant.

f. 188v

1518 AD COMPLENDVM. Gratias agimus tibi domine sanctae pater omnipotens, qui nos caelesti medela reparare dignatus es, da peccatis nostris ueniam, sicut beati martini confessoris tui, dedisti sedem pontificatus. Per.

CCXLVIIII
IN OCTAVAS APOSTOLORVM

1519 Deus cuius dextera beatum petrum ambulantem in fluctibus ne mergeretur erexit, et coapostolum eius paulum tertio naufragantem, de profundo pelagi liberauit, exaudi nos propitius

---

[1] *aeternae* before correction.

et concede ut amborum meritis aeternitatis gloriam consequamur. Per.

1520 SVPER OBLATA. Offerimus tibi domine praeces et munera, quae ut tuo sint digna conspectui, apostolorum tuorum quaesumus praecibus adiuuemur. Per.

1521 AD COMPLENDVM. Protege domine populum tuum, et apostolorum tuorum patrocinio confidentem, perpetua defensione conserua. Per dominum.

CCL

DOMINICA VIII POST PENTECOSTEN

/f. 189r **1522** / Deus uirtutum cuius est totum quod est optimum, insere pectoribus nostris amorem tui nominis, et praesta in nobis religionis augmentum, ut quae sunt bona nutrias, ac pietatis studio quę sunt nutrita custodias. Per.

1523 SVPER OBLATA. Propitiare domine supplicationibus nostris, et has populi tui oblationes benignus assume, et ut nullius sit irritum uotum, et nullius uacua postulatio, praesta ut quod fideliter petimus, efficaciter consequamur. Per dominum.

1524 PRAEFATIO. VD per christum dominum nostrum. Verum aeternumque pontificem, et solum sine peccati macula sacerdotem. Cuius sanguine fidelium corda mundantur, cuius institutione placationis tibi hostias, non solum pro delictis populi, sed etiam pro nostris offensionibus immolamus. Tuam poscentes clementiam, ut omne peccatum quod carnis fragilitate contraximus, ipso summo pro nobis antistite, interueniente soluatur. Per quem.

1525 BENEDICTIO. Benedicat uos omnipotens dominus, et per habundantiam misaericordiae suae, cor uestrum corroboret. AMEN.
Mentem sanctificet, uitam amplificet, castimoniam decoret, atque sensus uestros in bonis operibus semper aedificet, prospera tribuat, pacem concedat, salutem conferat, quietem
/f. 189v nutriat, caritate / muniat, et ab omnibus diabolicis et humanis insidiis, sua semper uos protectione et uirtute defendat. AMEN.

Et ita deuotionem uestram placatus semper suscipiat, ut quaeque ab eo postulaueritis clementer concedat, auferatque mala omnia quae gessistis, et tribuat gratiam quam semper rogatis. AMEN. Quod ipse.

1526 AD COMPLENDVM. Repleti sumus domine muneribus tuis, tribue quaesumus ut eorum et mundemur effectu, et muniamur auxilio. Per dominum.

CCLI
VI IDVS IVL. NATALE SEPTEM FRATRVM

1527 Praesta quaesumus omnipotens deus, ut qui gloriosos martyres fortes in sua confessione cognouimus, pios apud te in nostra intercessione sentiamus. Per.

1528 SVPER OBLATA. Sacrificiis praesentibus domine quaesumus intende placatus, et intercedentibus sanctis tuis, deuotioni nostrae proficiant et saluti. Per.

1529 PRAEFATIO. VD aeterne[1] deus. Donari nobis suppliciter exorantes, ut sicut sancti tui mundum in tua uirtute uicerunt, ita nos a mundanis erroribus postulant expediri. Per christum dominum nostrum.

1530 AD COMPLENDVM. Quaesumus omnipotens deus, ut illius salutaris capiamus effectum, cuius per haec mysteria pignus accepimus. Per dominum nostrum.

CCLII
EODEM DIE VIGILIA SANCTI BENEDICTI ABBATIS

f. 190r **1531** / Concede quaesumus domine alacribus animis beati confessoris tui benedicti sollemnia caelebrare, cuius diuersis decorata uirtutibus, tibi uita complacuit. Per.

1532 SVPER OBLATA. Oblatio confessoris tui benedicti honore sint tibi domine nostra grata libamina, ut nostrarum apud te supplicationum effectum obtineant. Per dominum nostrum.

---

[1] *aeternae* before correction.

1533 AD COMPLENDVM. Quos caelestibus domine recreas alimentis, interueniente beato confessore tuo benedicto, ab uniuersis tuere periculis. Per dominum.

CCLIII
V IDVS IVL. NATALE SANCTI BENEDICTI ABBATIS

1534 Omnipotens sempiterne deus qui hodierna luce carnis eductum[1] ergastulo, beatissimum confessorem tuum benedictum subleuasti ad caelum, concede quaesumus haec festa tuis famulis caelebrantibus cunctorum ueniam delictorum, ut qui exultantibus animis eius claritati congaudent, ipso apud te interueniente, consocientur et meritis. Per dominum.

1535 ALIA. Omnipotens sempiterne deus, qui radiantibus beati benedicti confessoris tui exemplis, arduum tuis imitabile famulis iter fecisti, da nobis inoffensis per eius instituta gressibus pergere, ut eiusdem in regione uiuentium, mereamur gaudiis admisceri. Per.

1536 SVPER OBLATA. Oblatis domine ob honorem beati benedicti
/f. 190v   confessoris tui placare mune/ribus, et ipsius tuis famulis interuentu cunctorum tribue indulgentiam peccatorum. Per.

1537 PRAEFATIO. VD aeterne[2] deus. Et gloriam tuam profusis praecibus exorare, ut qui beati benedicti confessoris tui ueneramur festa, te opitulante eius sanctitatis imitari ualeamus exempla, et cuius meritis nequaquam possumus coaequari, eius praecibus mereamur adiuuari. Per christum.

1538 AD COMPLENDVM. Fidelium tuorum quaesumus domine uota serenus intende, et interuentu beati benedicti cuius depositionis caelebramus diem, a cunctis nos absolutos reatibus festis interesse perpetuis. Per dominum nostrum.

---

[1]   *edoctum* before correction.
[2]   *aeternae* before correction.

CCLIIII
DOMINICA VIIII POST PENTECOSTEN

1539 Deus cuius prouidentia in sui dispositione non fallitur, te supplices exoramus, ut noxia cuncta submoueas, et omnia nobis profutura concedas. Per.

1540 SVPER OBLATA. Deus qui legalium differentiam hostiarum unius sacrificii perfectione sanxisti, accipe sacrificium a deuotis tibi famulis, et pari benedictione sicut munera abel sanctifica, ut quod singuli obtulerunt ad maiestatis tuae honorem, cunctis proficiat ad salutem. Per.

1541 PREAFATIO. [1]VD aeterne[2] deus. Et tibi uouere contriti sacrificium cordis, tibi litare humiliati uicti/mam pectoris. A quo omne bonum ut simus[3] sumimus, omnem iocunditatem ut bibamus[4] haurimus. Praecamur itaque ut tibi conscientia nostra famuletur, et ut in te de die in diem meliorata proficiat, tuae gratiae intemerata subdatur. Nostris nos domine quaesumus aeuacua malis, tuisque reple per omnia bonis. Vt percepta gratia quam nostra non exigunt merita, a cunctis aduersitatibus liberati, in bonis omnibus confirmati, supernis ciuibus mereamur coniungi. Per christum.

1542 BENEDICTIO. Sanctificet uos domini gratia, et ab omni malo custodiat. AMEN.
Arceat a uobis omne quod malum est, et spiritus uestros corporaque purificet. AMEN.
Alliget uos sibi uinculo caritatis, et pax eius habundet in cordibus uestris. AMEN.
Quod ipse.

1543 AD COMPLENDVM. Tua nos domine medicinalis operatio, et a nostris peruersitatibus clementer expediat, et ad ea quae sunt recta perducat. Per dominum.

---

[1] Partly neumed later.
[2] *aeternae* before correction.
[3] Supplied interlinearly by a later scribe.
[4] Supplied in the margin by a later scribe.

f. 191r

307

CCLV
IN OCTAVAS SANCTI BENEDICTI ABBATIS

1544 Intercessio nos quaesumus domine beati benedicti abbatis tibi[1] commendet, ut quod nostris meritis non ualemus, eius patrocinio assequamur. Per.

1545 SVPER OBLATA. Sacris altaribus domine hostias superpositas, sanctus benedictus in salutem nobis quaesumus prouenire deposcat. Per.

/f. 191v **1546** / AD COMPLENDVM. Protegat nos domine cum tui perceptione sacramenti, beatus benedictus abba pro nobis intercedendo, ut conuersationis eius experiamur insignia. Per dominum nostrum.

CCLVI
XII KL. AVG. NATALE SANCTAE PRAXEDIS

1547 Da quaesumus omnipotens deus, ut qui beatae praxedis martyris tuae natalicia colimus, et annua sollemnitate laetemur, et tantę fidei proficiamus exemplo. Per dominum nostrum.

1548 SVPER OBLATA. Hostia domine quaesumus quam in sanctorum tuorum natalicia recensentes offerimus, et uincula nostrae prauitatis absoluat, et tuae nobis misaericordia dona conciliet. Per dominum.

1549 AD COMPLENDVM. Quaesumus domine salutaribus repleti mysteriis, ut cuius sollemnia celebramus, eius orationibus adiuuemur. Per dominum.

CCLVII
X KL. AVG. NATALE SANCTI APOLLONARIS

1550 Sancti apollonaris domine confessio recensita, conferat nobis piae deuotionis augmentum, qui in tuo nomine perseuerans meruit honorari. Per.

---

[1] Supplied in the margin.

1551 SVPER OBLATA. Hostias tibi domine pro commemoratione sancti apollonaris offerimus, quem a tui corporis unitate, nulla temptatio separauit[1]. Per dominum nostrum iesum christum.

f. 192r **1552** AD COMPLENDVM. / [2]Repleti cibu putuque caelesti deus noster, te supplices exoramus, ut in cuius haec commemoratione percepimus, eius muniamur et praecibus. Per.

CCLVIII
VIII KL. <AVG.> NATALE SANCTI IACOBI APOSTOLI FRATRIS SANCTI IOHANNIS

1553 Esto domine plebi tuae sanctificator et custos, ut apostoli tui iacobi munita praesidiis, et conuersatione tibi placeat, et secura mente deseruiat. Per.

1554 SVPER OBLATA. Oblationes populi tui domine quaesumus beati apostoli tui iacobi passio beata conciliet, et quae nostris non apta sunt meritis, fiant tibi placita eius depraecatione. Per.

1555 PRAEFATIO. VD aeterne[3] deus. Quia licet nobis semper salutem operetur diuini caelebratio sacramenti, propensius tamen nobis confidimus profuturam, si beati apostoli tui iacobi intercessionibus adiuuemur. Per christum.

---

[1] *seperauit* before correction.
[2] Added in the right margin by a Corbie scribe:

XI KL. AVG. SANCTE MARIE MAGDALENE
3* Deus qui beatę marię magdalenę penitentiam ita tibi placitam gratamque fecisti, ut non solum ei peccata dimitteres, uerum etiam singulariter tui amoris intima gratia perlustrares, da nobis tuę propitiationis habundantiam, ut cuius gloria letamur, eius apud tuam misericordiam praecibus adiuuemur. Per.
4* SECRETA. Accepta domine maiestati tuę fidelis populi reddatur oblatio, optentu beatę marię magdalenę, quę se tibi hostiam sanctam et beneplacitam semper exhibuit. Per.
5* POSTCOMMVNIO. Auxilientur nobis domine sacrosancta mysteria beatę marię magdalenę ueneratione celebrata, quę spretis mundanę uanitatis illecebris te solum diligere, tibique deo uiuo et uero elegit iugiter inherere. Per.

[3] *aeternae* before correction.

309

1556 AD COMPLENDVM. Beati apostoli tui iacobi cuius hodie festiuitate, corpore et sanguine tuo nos refecisti, quaesumus domine intercessione nos adiuua, pro cuius sollemnitate percepimus, tua sancta laetantes. Per.

1557 ALIA ORATIO. Sollemnitatis apostolicae multiplicatione gaudentes, clementiam tuam depraecamur omnipotens deus, ut tribuas iugiter nos eorum et confessione benedici, et patrociniis confoueri. Per dominum nostrum.

/f. 192v

/ CCLVIIII
EODEM DIE NATALE SANCTI CVCVPHATI MARTYRIS
1558 Deus per quem fides ignem non sentit, et infidelitas sine igne exuritur, qui beato cucuphati martyri tuo flamma tui spiritus succenso superare tribuisti incendia[1] tormentorum, concede propitius praetiosam intercessionem, ut nos famulos tuos non exurat flamma uitiorum, sed dilectionis tuae amor ingenitus, nostrorum excoquat[2] rubiginem peccatorum. Per.

1559 SVPER OBLATA. Sacrificium laudis in honore et gloria tui sancti nominis praeclarae domine tuae offerimus maiestati, pro commemoratione et reuerentia sancti cucuphatis martyris tui, qui nulli inlecaebris corporalium uoluptatum, nullis promissis blandimentorum fallacium, nullo genere tormentorum, a tua potuisse separari dilectione. Quapropter te amando, effici tibi meruit sacrificium laudis, cuius praetiosa oratio quaesumus per haec sacrosancta nostrae redemptionis commertia, nobis peccatorum omnium ueniam tribuat, et proficiat ad fidei profectum, ad munditiam cordium, ad bonorum operum fructum, ad prosperitatis bonum, ad salubritatis commodum, ad religionis cultum, ad timoris tui et amoris augmentum, ad

/f. 193r perseuerantiae sanctae / triumphum, et sempiternae gloriae praemium assequendum. Per dominum nostrum.

1560 POSTCOMMVNIO. Sit nobis domine intercedente beato cucuphate[3] martyre tuo reparatio mentis et corporis, quod sancti

---
[1] *incendio* before correction.
[2] *exquoquad* before correction.
[3] *cucuphatae* before correction.

altaris tui benedictione percepimus, ut uitia nostra haec medicina expurget, nosque desiderio tuo inflammet, atque totius prauitatis incursibus muniat, sanctorum tuorum faciat esse consortes, qui infirmitatis nostrae uenisti sanare languores. Qui uiuis.

CCLX
DOMINICA X POST PENTECOSTEN

1561 Largire nobis domine quaesumus semper spiritum cogitandi quae recta sunt propitius et agendi, ut qui sine te esse non possumus, secundum te uiuere ualeamus. Per dominum nostrum.

1562 SVPER OBLATA. Suscipe munera quaesumus domine quae tibi de tua largitate deferimus, ut haec sacrosancta mysteria gratiae tuae operante uirtute, praesentis uitae nos conuersatione sanctificent, et ad[1] gaudia sempiterna perducant. Per dominum.

1563 PRAEFATIO. VD aeterne[2] deus. Et tuam misericordiam totis nisibus exorare, ne pro nostra nos iniquitate condempnes, sed pro tua piaetate in uia recta semper disponas. Nec sicut meremur delinquentibus irascaris, sed fragilitati nostrae inuicta bonitate subuenias. Per christum.

f. 193v **1564** BENEDICTIO. / Populi tui quaesumus domine postulationes exaudi, et calamitatibus constitutis, uelociter subueniet. AMEN. De sua fac liberatione gaudere, quos cernis sub pondere omnium laborare, exultent et laetentur in te, dum se uiderint saluari per te. AMEN.
Mitte eis domine defensionis tuae semper arma inuictricia, quibus faciant uniuersa bella prostrata, et auxilio tuo mentes omnium uisitentur, ut superatis inimicorum uiribus roborentur. AMEN.
Quod ipse praestare.

1565 AD COMPLENDVM. Sit nobis domine reparatio mentis et corporis caeleste mysterium, ut cuius exequimur actionem, sentiamus effectum. Per.

---

[1] Supplied interlinearly.
[2] *aeternae* before correction.

CCLXI
V KL. AVG. NATALE SANCTI SAMSONIS

1566 Exaudi domine praeces nostras quas in sanctorum samsonis ac paterni confessorum tuorum atque pontificum commemoratione deferimus, ut qui tibi digne meruerunt famulari, eorum intercedentibus meritis, ab omnibus nos absolue peccatis. Per.

1567 SVPER OBLATA. Accepta sit in conspectu tuo domine nostra deuotio, et eorum nobis supplicatione sit salutaris, pro quorum commemoratione defertur. Per.

1568 AD COMMVNIONEM. Sumentes domine gaudia sempiterna participatione sacramenti, praesta quaesumus ut beatorum samsonis atque paterni confessorum tuorum praecibus adiuuemur. Per dominum nostrum.

/f. 194r / ITEM PROPRIA MISSA SANCTI SAMSONIS

1569 Omnipotens sempiterne deus, qui in sanctis praecipuae laudaris, et mirabiliter praedicaris, tribue nobis quaesumus hodiernam diem in honore sancti samsonis confessoris tui atque pontificis, dignae caelebrare, qua membris exutus, corporeis caelestibus meruit exultare sacramentis. Per.

1570 SECRETA. Haec hostia quesumus domine deus noster quam tibi ad honorem sancti samsonis confessoris tui atque pontificis, immolandam deferimur, tuorum nobis tribuat sociaetate gaudere. Per.

1571 PRAEFATIO. VD aeterne[1] deus. Sursum cordibus erectis hanc sanctam caelebrare diem, in qua beatus samson confessor tuus, carnis solutus uinculis, carnalem finiuit pugnam, lętusque cum angelis perpetuam, translatus est ad gloriam. Cui tanta concessa est a deo potentia, ut omne quod per se deum uellet operari, caelerrimo impetraret effectu. Qui patrem relinquens solum, oceano transnato nostram delatus est in patriam, in qua multis claruit miraculis. Qui per totam absque ullo corporali alimento ebdomadam angelico sustentabatur alloquio, qui baculo in terram deposito, nulloque alio sustentaculo recepto, in natalis

---

[1] *aeternae* before correction.

312

domini nostri iesu christi, nocte sacrosancta et dominici paschae pernox orationi instabat. Qui tres mortiferos dei nutu interemit serpentes, et totidem / de morte ad uitam, deo adiuuante reduxit homines. Adhuc etiam et hi qui duce fide ad eius limina fuerint allati, quolibet morbo capti pristinae restituuntur sanitati. Per christum.

f. 194v

1572 POSTCOMMVNIO. Deus qui nos hanc diem in honore sancti samsonis confessoris tui atque pontificis uenerabilem excolere fecisti, praesta quaesumus ut quem lętis ueneramur obsequiis, eius orationibus muniamur et precibus. Per.

CCLXII
IIII KL. AVG. NATALE SANCTORVM FELICIS, SIMPLICIS, FAVSTINI, ET BEATRICIS

1573 Praesta quaesumus domine deus noster, ut sicut populus christianus martyrum tuorum felicis, simplicii, faustini et beatricis, temporali sollemnitate congaudet, ita perfruatur aeterna, et quod uotis celebrat, compręhendat effectu. Per.

1574 SVPER OBLATA. Hostias tibi domine pro sanctorum martyrum felicis, simplicii, faustini et beatricis, commemoratione deferimus, suppliciter exorantes, ut et indulgentiam pariter conferant et salutem. Per.

1575 AD COMPLENDVM. Praesta quaesumus omnipotens deus, ut sanctorum tuorum felicis, simplicii, faustini, et beatricis, caelestibus mysteriis caelebrata sollemnitas, indulgentiam nobis tuae propitiationis adquirat. Per.

CCLXIII
ITEM PROPRIA MISSA SANCTI FELICIS

/f. 195r **1576** / Infirmitatem nostram respice omnipotens deus, et quia pondus propriae actionis grauat, beati felicis martyris tui atque pontificis, intercessio gloriosa nos protegat. Per dominum nostrum.

1577 SVPER OBLATA. Accepta sit in conspectu tuo domine nostra deuotio, et eius nobis fiat supplicatione salutaris, pro cuius sollemnitate defertur. Per.

1578 AD COMPLENDVM. Spiritum nobis domine tuae caritatis infunde, ut quos uno caelesti pane satiasti, intercedente beato felice martyre tuo, tua facias pietate concordes. Per dominum.

CCLXIIII
III KL. AVG. NATALE SANCTORVM ABDON ET SENNEN

1579 Deus qui sanctis tuis abdon et sennen ad hanc gloriam ueniendi copiosum munus gratiae contulisti, da famulis tuis suorum ueniam peccatorum, ut sanctorum tuorum intercedentibus meritis, ab omnibus mereamur aduersitatibus liberari. Per.

1580 SVPER OBLATA. Hostia quaesumus haec domine quam in sanctorum tuorum nataliciis recensentes offerimus, et uincula nostrae prauitatis absoluat, et tuę nobis misericordiae dona conciliet. Per.

1581 PRAEFATIO. VD aeterne deus. Et te laudare mirabilem deum in sanctis tuis, quos ante constitutionem mundi in aeternam tibi gloriam praeparasti, ut per eos huic mundo uerita/tis tuae lumen ostenderes. Quos ita spiritu ueritatis armasti, ut formidinem mortis per infirmitatem carnis euincerent. De quorum collegio sunt martyres tui abdon, et sennis, qui in ecclesiae tuae sicut rosae et lilia floruerunt. Quos unigeniti tui sanguis in proelio confessionis, roseo colore perfudit, et ob praemium passionis, niueo[1] liliorum splendore uestiuit. Per christum.

/f. 195v

1582 AD COMPLENDVM. Per huius domine operationem mysterii, et uitia nostra purgentur, et intercedentibus sanctis tuis iusta desideria compleantur. Per dominum.

CCLXV
II KL. AVG. NATALE SANCTI GERMANI

1583 Quia nostrae uoces domine non merentur audire sancti germani confessoris tui atque pontificis, interuentio quaesumus sit accepta pro nobis. Per.

1584 SVPER OBLATA. Altaribus tuis domine munera terrena gratanter, pro commemoratione sancti germani confessoris tui

---

[1] *niuio* before correction.

314

atque pontificis offerimus, ut caelestia consequamur, damus temporalia, ut sumamus aeterna. Per.

1585 PRAEFATIO. VD aeterne[1] deus. Beati confessoris tui atque pontificis germani sollemnia domine caelebramus, quibus tanto nos credimus adiuuari, quanto[2] ad honorem tui nominis[3] patrocinia ueneramur. Per christum.

f. 196r **1586** / AD COMPLENDVM. Repleti eucharistia sancti germani confessoris tui atque pontificis, piis nos intercessionibus domine prosequamur, ut cuius sollemnia recensemus, tua ferięmur oblata praesidia. Per.

CCLXVI
DOMINICA XI POST PENTECOSTEN

1587 Pateant aures misęricordia tuae domine praecibus supplicantum, et ut petentibus desiderata concedas, fac tibi eos quaesumus placita postulare. Per.

1588 SVPER OBLATA. Concede nobis haec quaesumus domine, digne[4] frequentare mysteria, quia quotiens huius hostiae commemoratio celebratur, opus nostrae redemptionis exercetur. Per.

1589 PRAEFATIO. VD aeterne[5] deus. Et tuam misericordiam exorare, ut te annuente ualeamus quae mala sunt declinare, et quae bona sunt consequenter explere. Et quia nos fecisti ad tua sacramenta pertinere, tu clementer in nobis eorum munus operare. Per christum.

1590 BENEDICTIO. Deus qui est uita mortalium, salusque peccatorum, auferat a uobis omnes maculas delictorum. AMEN. Induat uos decore uirtutum, sanctificet mentes, purificet uoluntates, et donet uobis sanctorum consortium angelorum. AMEN.

---

[1] *aeternae* before correction.
[2] A small erasure follows.
[3] s supplied later.
[4] Supplied later.
[5] *aeternae* before correction.

Vt probabiles fide et opere inmaculati, perueniatis ad aeternam gaudiorum caelestium hereditatem. AMEN.

/f. 196v / <Q>uod ipse praestare dignetur.

1591 AD COMPLENDVM. Tui nobis domine communio sacramenti, et purificationem conferat, et tribuat unitatem. Per.

CCLXVII
KL. AVG. AD SANCTVM PETRVM AD VINCVLA

1592 Deus qui beatum petrum apostolum a uinculis absolutum inlaesum abire fecisti, nostrorum quaesumus absolue uincula peccatorum, et omnia mala a nobis propitiatus exclude. Per.

1593 SVPER OBLATA. Oblatum tibi domine sacrificium, uiuificet nos semper et muniat. Per.

1594 AD COMPLENDVM. Corporis sacri et preҭiosi sanguinis repleti libamine quaesumus domine deus noster, ut quod pia deuotione gerimus, certa redemptione capiamus. Per dominum nostrum.

CCLXVIII
EODEM DIE NATALE MACHABEORVM

1595 Fraterna nos domine martyrum tuorum corona laetificet, quae et fidei nostrae praebeat incitamenta uirtutum, et multiplici nos suffragio consoletur. Per.

1596 SVPER OBLATA. Iterata mysteria domine pro sanctorum martyrum deuota mente tractamus, quibus nobis et praesidium crescit, et gaudium. Per dominum nostrum.

1597 PRAEFATIO. VD aeterne[1] deus. Quia licet in omnium
/f. 197r sanctorum tuorum tu sis[2] domine protectione mirabilis, / in his tamen speciale tuum munus agnouimus, quos et fratres sorte nascendi, et magnifica praestitisti passione germanos. Vt simul esset et ueneranda gloria genitricis, et florentissima proles ecclesiae. Et ideo.

---

[1] *aeternae* before correction.
[2] *scis* before correction.

1598 AD COMPLENDVM. Praesta quaesumus omnipotens deus, ut quorum memoriam sacramenti participatione recolimus, fidem quoque proficiendo sectemur. Per.

CCLXVIIII

IIII NON. AVG. NATALE SANCTI STEPHANI EPISCOPI
ET MARTYRIS

1599 Deus qui nos beati stephani martyris tui atque pontificis annua sollemnitate laetificas, concede propitius ut cuius natalicia colimus, de eius etiam protectione gaudeamus. Per.

1600 SVPER OBLATA. Munera tibi domine dicata sanctifica, et intercedente beato stephano martyre tuo atque pontifice, per eadem nos placatus intende. Per.

1601 AD COMMVNIONEM. Haec nos communio domine purget a crimine, et intercedente beato stephano martyre tuo atque pontifice, caelestis remedii faciat esse consortes. Per.

CCLXX

VIII ID. AVG. NATALE SANCTI SIXTI EPISCOPI
ET MARTYRIS

1602 Deus qui conspicis quia ex nulla nostra uirtute substitimus, concede propitius, ut intercessione beati sixti martyris tui / atque pontificis, contra omnia aduersa muniamur. Per.

/f. 197v

1603 SVPER OBLATA. Sacrificiis praesentibus domine quaesumus intende placatus, ut et deuotioni nostrae proficiant et saluti. Per dominum.

1604 PRAEFATIO. VD aeterne[1] deus. Et in die festiuitatis hodiernae, qua beatus syxtus pariter sacerdos et martyr, deuotum tibi sanguinem exultanter effudit, qui ad eandem gloriam promerendam doctrinae suae filios incitauit, et quos erudiebat hortatu, praeueniebat exemplo. Per christum.

1605 Intra quorum nos consortium non aestimator meriti, sed ueniae quaesumus largitor admitte. Per christum.

---

[1] *aeternae* before correction.

CCLXXI

1606 BENEDICTIO VVAE SIVE FABAE. [1]Benedic domine et hos fructus nouos quos tu domine rore caeli et inundantia pluuiarum et temporum serenitate atque tranquillitate ad maturitatem perducere dignatus es, et dedisti ea ad usus nostros cum gratiarum actione percipere, in nomine domini nostri iesu christi. Per quem.

1607 AD COMPLENDVM. Praesta quaesumus domine deus noster, ut cuius nobis festiuitate uotiua sunt sacramenta, eius salutaria nobis intercessione reddantur. Per dominum.

CCLXXII
EODEM DIE NATALE SANCTORVM FELICISSIMI ET AGAPITI

1608 Deus qui nos concedis sanctorum martyrum tuorum felicissimi et agapiti natalicia colere, / da nobis in aeterna laetitia de eorum societate gaudere. Per dominum.

/f. 198r

1609 SVPER OBLATA. Munera tibi domine nostrae deuotionis offerimus, quae et pro tuorum tibi grata sint honore iustorum, et nobis salutaria te miserante reddantur. Per dominum nostrum.

1610 AD COMPLENDVM. Praesta nobis domine quaesumus intercedentibus sanctis tuis, felicissimo et agapito, ut quae ore contingimus, pura mente capiamus. Per dominum nostrum.

CCLXXIII
DOMINICA XII POST PENTECOSTEN

1611 Deus qui omnipotentiam tuam parcendo maxime et miserando manifestas, multiplica super nos gratiam tuam, ut ad tua promissa currentes, caelestium bonorum facias esse consortes. Per.

1612 SVPER OBLATA. Tibi domine sacrificia dicata reddantur, quae sic ad honorem nominis tui deferenda tribuisti, ut eadem remedia fieri nostra praestares. Per.

[1] Crosses supplied later.

1613 PRAEFATIO. VD aeterne[1] deus. Et tibi debitam seruitutem, per mynisterii huius impletionem persoluere. Quia non solum peccantibus ueniam tribuis, sed etiam praemia poetentibus impertiris. Et quod perpeti malis operibus promeremur, magnifica pietate depellis, ut nos ad tuae reuerentiae cultum, / et terrore cogas, et amore perducas. Per christum.

/f. 198v

1614 BENEDICTIO. Tribuat uobis dominus caritatis donum, indulgentiae fructum, et uitae aeternae consortium. AMEN.
Abstergat a uobis omnes maculas peccatorum, ut eum uigilanter meramini agnoscere fideliter colere, et desiderabiliter expectare. AMEN.
Inluminet gratiam suam super uos, et misereatur uestri, sicut illuminauit moysen et filios israel in columna ignis et nubis, donet uobis gratiae perpetuae donum, et conferat gaudium angelorum. AMEN.
Quod ipse.

1615 AD COMPLENDVM. Quaesumus domine deus noster, ut quos diuinis reparare non desinis sacramentis, tuis non destituas benignus auxiliis. Per dominum nostrum.

CCLXXIIII
VI IDVS AVG. NATALE SANCTI CYRIACI MARTYRIS
1616 Deus qui nos annua beati cyriaci martyris tui sollemnitate laetificas, concede propitius, ut cuius natalicia colimus, uirtutem quoque passionis imitemur. Per.

1617 SVPER OBLATA. Accepta sit in conspectu tuo domine nostra deuotio, et eius nobis fiat supplicatione salutaris, pro cuius sollemnitate defertur. Per.

1618 AD COMPLENDVM. Refecti participatione muneris sacri quaesumus domine deus noster, ut cuius exequimur cultum, sentiamus / effectum. Per dominum.

/f. 199r

---

[1] *aeternae* before correction.

319

CCLXXV
V IDVS AVG. VIGILIA SANCTI LAVRENTII MARTYRIS

1619 Adesto domine supplicationibus nostris, et intercessione beati laurentii martyris tui, perpetuam nobis misericordiam benignus impende. Per dominum.

1620 SVPER OBLATA. Hostias domine quas tibi offerimus propitius suscipe, et intercedente beato laurentio martyre tuo, uincula peccatorum nostrorum absolue. Per dominum.

1621 PRAEFATIO. VD aeterne[1] deus. Et te deuotis mentibus, natale beati laurentii martyris tui praeuenire. Qui leuita simul martyrque uenerandus, et proprio claruit gloriosus officio, et memorandę passionis refulsit martyrio. Per christum dominum nostrum.

1622 AD COMPLENDVM. Da quaesumus domine deus noster, ut sicut beati laurentii martyris tui commemoratione temporali gratulamur officio, ita perpetuo laetemur aspectu. Per dominum.

CCLXXVI
IIII ID. AVG. NATALE SANCTI LAVRENTII.
IN PRIMA MISSA

1623 Excita domine in ęcclesia tua spiritum cui beatus laurentius leuita seruiuit, ut eodem[2] nos replente studeamus amare quod amauit, et opere exercere quod docuit. Per.

/f. 199v **1624** SVPER OBLATA. / Sacrificium nostrum tibi domine quaesumus beati laurentii praecatio sancta conciliet, ut cuius honore sollemniter exhibetur, meritis efficiatur acceptum. Per.

1625 PRAEFATIO. VD aeterne[3] deus. Et in die sollempnitatis hodiernae, qua beatus laurentius hostia sancta, uiua, tibi placens oblatus est. Qui igne accensus tui amoris, constanter ignem sustinuit passionis. Et per inmanitatem tormentorum,

---

[1] *aeternae* before correction.
[2] *eadem* before correction.
[3] *aeternae* before correction.

peruenit ad societatem ciuium supernorum. Per christum dominum nostrum.

1626 AD COMPLENDVM. Supplices te rogamus omnipotens deus, ut quos donis caelestibus satiasti, intercedente beato laurentio martyre tuo, perpetua protectione custodias. Per dominum.

CCLXXVII
IN DIE AD MISSAM

1627 Da nobis quaesumus omnipotens deus, uitiorum nostrorum flammas extinguere, qui beato laurentio tribuisti tormentorum suorum incendia superare. Per.

1628 SVPER OBLATA. Accipe quaesumus domine munera dignanter oblata, et beati laurentii suffragantibus meritis, ad nostrae salutis auxilium prouenire concede. Per.

1629 BENEDICTIO. Corrobora gregem tuum, turris fortitudinis, qui beatum laurentium prius armasti pectore post sermonem, ante decorasti professione quam funere. AMEN.

/f. 200r

/ Infunde circumstantibus credulitatis spiritum, qui confitenti aderas, ne facerent plage trepidum, pene fessum, flamma deuictum. AMEN.

Vt ipso interueniente, ac te remunerante, illa luce plebs radiet, qua leuita fulsit in carcere, illa fide micet, qua caelos uictor martyr intrauit hodierna die. AMEN.

Quod ipse.

1630 AD COMPLENDVM. Sacro munere satiati supplices te domine depraecamur, ut quod debitae seruitutis caelebramus officio, intercedente beato laurentio saluationis tuae sentiamus augmentum. Per.

1631 ALIA. Deus cuius claritatis ardore beatus laurentius edaces incendii flammas contempto persecutore deuicit, concede ut omnes qui martyrii eius merita ueneramur, protectionis tuae auxilio muniamur. Per dominum.

CCLXXVIII
III IDVS AVG. NATALE SANCTI TYBVRTII MARTYRIS

1632 Beati tyburtii nos domine foueant continuata praesidia, quia non desinis propitius intueri, quos talibus auxiliis concesseris adiuuari. Per dominum nostrum.

1633 SVPER OBLATA. Adesto domine praecibus populi tui adesto muneribus, ut quae sacris sunt oblata mysteriis, tuorum tibi placeant intercessione sanctorum. Per dominum nostrum.

/f. 200v **1634** PRAEFATIO. / VD aeterne[1] deus. Qui dum beati tyburtii martyris, merita gloriosa ueneramur, auxilium nobis tuae propitiationis adfore depraecamur. Quoniam credimus nos per eorum intercessionem quam tibi placuere peccatorum nostrorum ueniam impetrare. Per christum.

1635 AD COMPLENDVM. Sumpsimus domine pignus redemptionis aeternae, sit nobis quaesumus interueniente beato tyburtio martyre tuo, uitae praesentis auxilium pariter et futurae. Per dominum nostrum.

CCLXXVIIII
DOMINICA XIII POST PENTECOSTEN

1636 Omnipotens sempiterne deus, qui abundantia[2] pietatis tuae et merita supplicum excedis et uota, effunde super nos misericordiam tuam, ut dimittas quae conscientia[3] metuit, et adicias quod oratio non praesumit. Per.

1637 SVPER OBLATA. Respice domine quaesumus nostram propitius seruitutem, ut quod offerimus sit tibi munus acceptum, sit nostrae fragilitati[4] subsidium. Per.

1638 PRAEFATIO. VD aeterne[5] deus. Cuius primum tuae pietatis indicium est, si tibi nos facias toto corde subiectos. Et spiritum

---

[1] *aeternae* before correction.
[2] *abundantiam* before correction.
[3] *conscientiam* before correction.
[4] *fragilitatis* before correction.
[5] *aeternae* before correction.

in nobis tantae deuotionis infundas, ut propitius largiaris consequenter auxilium. Per christum dominum nostrum.

f. 201r **1639** BENEDICTIO. / Gratiae suae dono uos dominus locupletet, et caelesti benedictione sanctificet. AMEN.

Ab omni uos aduersitate defendat, et pia semper miseratione custodiat. AMEN.

Petitiones uestras placatus intendat, et culparum omnium uobis ueniam clementer attribuat. AMEN.

Quod ipse.

1640 AD COMPLENDVM. Sentiamus domine quaesumus tui perceptione sacramenti subsidium mentis et corporis, ut in utroque saluati, caelestis remedii plenitudine gloriemur. Per.

CCLXXX
ID. AVG. NATALE SANCTI YPPOLITI MARTYRIS

1641 Da nobis omnipotens deus, ut beati yppoliti martyris tui ueneranda sollemnitas, et deuotionem nobis augeat et salutem. Per.

1642 SVPER OBLATA. Respice domine munera populi tui, sanctorum festiuitate uotiua, et tuae testificatio ueritatis, nobis proficiat ad salutem. Per.

1643 PRAEFATIO. VD aeterne[1] deus. Et tuam clementiam uoci supplici implorare, ut beati yppoliti intercessio peccatorum nostrorum obtineat ueniam, qui per tormenta passionis aeternam peruenit ad gloriam. Per christum.

1644 AD COMPLENDVM. Sacramentorum tuorum domine communio sumpta nos saluet, et in tuae ueritatis luce confirmet. Per dominum.

---

[1] *aeternae* before correction.

CCLXXXI
XVIIII KL. SEPBR. / NATALE SANCTI EVSEBII CONFESSORIS

1645 Deus qui nos beati eusebii confessoris tui annua sollemnitate laetificas, concede propitius ut cuius natalicia colimus, per eius ad te exempla gradiamur. Per.

1646 SVPER OBLATA. Laudis tuae domine hostias immolamus, in tuorum commemoratione sanctorum, quibus nos praesentibus exui malis confidimus et futuris. Per.

1647 PRAEFATIO. VD aeterne[1] deus. Et clementiam tuam pronis mentibus implorare, ut beati eusebii confessoris intercessionem salutiferam in nostris mentibus firmes deuotionem. Concedasque ut sicut te solum credimus auctorem et ueneramus saluatorem, sic in perpetuum eius interuentu habeamus adiutorem. Per christum.

1648 AD COMPLENDVM. Refecti cibu potuque caelesti deus noster, te supplices exoramus, ut in cuius haec commemoratione percepimus, eius muniamur et praecibus. Per.

CCLXXXII
EODEM DIE VIGILIA ASSVMPTIONIS SANCTAE MARIAE

1649 Deus qui[2] uirginalem aulam beatae mariae in qua habitares eligere dignatus es, da quaesumus ut sua nos defensione munitos, iocundos faciat suae interesse festiuitati. Per dominum nostrum iesum christum.

1650 SVPER OBLATA. / Magna est domine apud clementiam tuam dei genetricis oratio, quam idcirco de praesenti saeculo transtulisti, ut pro peccatis nostris apud te fiducialiter intercedat. Per.

1651 PRAEFATIO. VD aeterne[3] deus. Humiliter depraecantes ut intercedente beata maria semper uirgine, nos ab omnibus

---

[1] *aeternae* before correction.
[2] *qui in* before correction.
[3] *aeternae* before correction.

peccatis clementer eripias, et a cunctis inimicis misericorditer protegas, et ad gaudia aeterna perducas. Per christum.

1652 AD COMMVNIONEM. Concede misericors deus, fragilitatis nostrae praesidium, ut qui sanctae dei genetricis requiem celebramus, intercessionis eius auxilio, a nostris iniquitatibus resurgamus. Per dominum.

CCLXXXIII
XVIII KL. SEPB. ASSVMPTIO SANCTAE MARIAE

1653 Veneranda nobis domine huius est diei festiuitas, in qua sancta dei genetrix mortem subiit temporalem, nec tamen mortis nexibus deprimi potuit, quae filium tuum dominum nostrum de se genuit incarnatum. Qui tecum.

1654 AD MISSAM. Famulorum tuorum domine delictis ignosce, ut[1] qui tibi placere de actibus nostris non ualemus, genetricis filii tui domini dei nostri intercessione saluemur. Per eundem.

1655 SVPER OBLATA. Subueniat quaesumus domine plebi tuae dei genetricis oratio, quam etsi pro conditione carnis migrasse cognoscimus, in caelesti / gloria apud te pro nobis quaesumus orare sentiamus. Per.

/f. 202v

1656 PRAEFATIO. VD aeterne[2] deus. Et te in ueneratione sacrarum uirginum, exultantibus animis laudare, benedicere, et praedicare. Inter quas intemerata dei genetrix uirgo maria, cuius assumptionis diem caelebramus gloriosa effulsit. Quae et unigenitum tuum sancti spiritus obumbratione concepit, et uirginitatis gloria permanente, huic mundo lumen aeternum effudit iesum christum dominum.

1657 BENEDICTIO. Deus qui beatae mariae partum genus humanum dignatus est redimere, sua uos dignetur benedictione locupletare. AMEN.
Eiusque semper et ubique patrocinia sentiatis, ex cuius intemerato utero, auctorem uitae suscipere meruistis. AMEN.

---

[1] *et* before correction.
[2] *aeternae* before correction.

Et qui ad eius caelebrandam festiuitatem hodierna die deuotis mentibus conuenistis, spiritualem[1] gaudiorum aeternorum praemiorum, uobiscum munera reportetis. AMEN.
Et qui hodie sacratissimam genetricem suam supra choros angelorum paradysi sedibus collocauit, eiusdem suffragantibus meritis, non post abiectam carnis sarcinam ad aeternam iubeat perducere patriam regni caelestis in aulam. / AMEN.
Quod ipse.

/f. 203r

1658 AD COMPLENDVM. Mensae caelestis participes effecti imploramus clementiam tuam domine deus noster, ut qui festa dei genetricis colimus, a malis imminentibus eius intercessionibus liberemur. Per.

CCLXXXIIII
IN OCTAVAS SANCTI LAVRENTII

1659 Iterata festiuitate beati laurentii natalicia ueneremur[2], quę[3] in caelesti beatitudine fulgere nouimus sempiterna. Per.

1660 SVPER OBLATA. Beati laurentii martyris tui honorabilem passionem, muneribus domine geminatis exequimur, quae licet propriis sit memoranda principibus, indesinenter tamen permanet gloriosa. Per.

1661 PRAEFATIO. VD aeterne[4] deus. Beati laurentii natalicia repetentes, cui fidem confessionemque[5] non abstulit ignis ingestus, sed ut luceret magis accendit. Nam sicut aurum flammis non uritur sed probatur, sic beati martyris sancta substantia non consumitur incendiis, sed aptatur caelestibus ornamentis. Per christum.

1662 AD COMPLENDVM. Sollemne nobis intercessio beati laurentii martyris quaesumus domine pręstet auxilium, ut caelestis mensae participatio quam sumpsimus, tribuat ecclesiae tuae recensitam laetitiam. Per dominum nostrum.

---

[1] *u* supplied interlinearly.
[2] *ueneramur* before correction.
[3] *quem* before correction.
[4] *aeternae* before correction.
[5] *quae* before correction.

/ CCLXXXV
DOMINICA XIIII POST PENTECOSTEN

1663 Omnipotens et misęricors deus de cuius munere uenit, ut tibi a fidelibus tuis digne et laudabiliter[1] seruiatur, tribue quaesumus nobis, ut ad promissiones tuas sine offensione curramus. Per.

1664 SVPER OBLATA. Hostias quaesumus domine propitius intende, quas sacris altaribus exhibemus, ut nobis indulgentiam largiendo, tuo nomini dent honorem. Per.

1665 PRAEFATIO. VD aeterne[2] deus. Qui nos castigando sanas, et refouendo benignus erudis, dum magis uis saluos esse correctos, quam perire deiectos. Per christum.

1666 BENEDICTIO. Benedicat uobis caelorum rector et conditor, et det uobis tranquillitatem temporum, salubritatem corporum, salutemque animarum. AMEN.
Fragilitatis gaudium, aeternitatis praemium, lumen clarissimum sempiternum. AMEN.
Et concedat uobis suae pietatis auxilium, ut eum cogitatione mens uideat, lingua uoce proferat, actio non offendat. AMEN.
Quod ipse.

1667 AD COMPLENDVM. Viuificet nos quaesumus domine huius participatio sancta mysterii, et pariter nobis expiationem tribuat et munimen. Per dominum nostrum iesum christum filium tuum.

CCLXXXVI
XV KL. SEPBR. NATALE SANCTI AGAPITI MARTYRIS

1668 / Laetetur ecclesia tua deus, beati agapiti martyris tui confisa suffragiis, atque eius praecibus gloriosis, et deuota permaneat et secura consistat. Per.

1669 SVPER OBLATA. Suscipe domine munera quae in eius tibi sollemnitate deferimus, cuius nos confidimus patrocinio liberari. Per.

---

[1] *a fidelibus tuis digne et laudabiliter* written over an erasure.
[2] *aeternae* before correction.

1670 AD COMPLENDVM. Satiasti domine familiam tuam muneribus sacris, eius quaesumus semper interuentione nos refoue, cuius sollemnia celebramus. Per dominum.

CCLXXXVII
XIIII KL. SEPB. NATALE SANCTI MAGNI[1]

1671 Adesto domine supplicationibus nostris, et intercedente beato martyre tuo magno, ab hostium nos defende propitiatus incursu. Per.

1672 SVPER OBLATA. Praesta nobis quaesumus omnipotens deus, ut nostra humilitatis oblatio, et pro tuorum grata sit honore sanctorum, et no<s>[2] corpore pariter et mente purificet. Per.

1673 PRAEFATIO. VD aeterne[3] deus. Qui humanum genus de profundo mortis eripiens, captiuitatem nostram iesu christi filii tui domini dei passione soluisti. Per quem ita uirtus antiqui hostis elisa est, ut eius quem ipse superauerat, etiam beatum martyrem suum magnum faceret esse uictorem. Cuius triumphum in die quo sanguine suo signauit, colentes in tua gloria exultamus. Et ideo.

/f. 204v **1674** AD COMPLENDVM. / Tua sancta sumentes quaesumus domine, ut beati magni nos foueant continuata praesidia. Per dominum.

CCLXXXVIII
XI KL. SEPB. NATALE SANCTI TYMOTHEI

1675 Auxilium tuum nobis domine quaesumus placatus inpende, et intercedente beato tymotheo martyre tuo, dexteram super nos tuae propitiationis extende. Per.

1676 SVPER OBLATA. Accepta tibi sit domine sacratae plebis oblatio, pro tuorum honore sanctorum, quorum se meritis percepisse de tribulatione cognoscit auxilium. Per dominum nostrum.

---

[1] *SANCTAE MAGNAE* before correction.
[2] *nobis* before correction.
[3] *aeternae* before correction.

1677 AD COMPLENDVM. Diuini muneris largitate satiati quaesumus domine deus noster, ut intercedente beato tymotheo martyre tuo, eius semper participatione uiuamus. Per.

CCLXXXVIIII
EODEM DIE SANCTI SYMPHORIANI[1]

1678 Peculiari patroni festiuitatem annua recolentes, symphoriani martyris ornamenta piae mentes intuitus sanctificationem locum ingressi, ueneratione debita fratres karissimi, deum omnipotentem depraecamur, ut qui illi pro sui certaminis merito coronam inmarcescibilem largire dignatus es, nobis quoque famulis tuis concessa uenia peccatorum nostrorum, eo intercedente pacem largire dignetur. Per dominum nostrum iesum christum filium tuum.

f. 205r **1679** SVPER OBLATA. / Suscipe domine propitius orationem nostram, cum oblationibus hostiarum super impositis, et martyris tui symphoriani benignus acceptam, ut illa quae in eo flagrauit fortis dilectio, in nobis aspira benignus, ut in tua dilectione permanentes, in fide inueniantur stabiles, et in opere efficaces. Per.

1680 AD COMPLENDVM. Interueniat pro nobis domine petimus sanctus tuus martyr symphorianus, qui sanguinem suum pro tuo nomine glorioso fudit, ut ipso intercedente nomina carorum nostrorum quae recitata sunt, in caelesti pagina iubeas intimare. Per.

CCXC
VIII KL SEPB. NATALE SANCTI BARTHOLOMEI
APOSTOLI

1681 Omnipotens sempiterne deus qui huius diei uenerandam sanctamque laetitiam, beati apostoli tui bartholomei festiuitate tribuisti, da ecclesiae tuę quaesumus, et amare quod credidit, et praedicare quod docuit. Per.

---

[1] *SIMPHORIANI* before correction.

1682 SVPER OBLATA. Beati apostoli tui bartholomei cuius sollemnia recensemus, quaesumus domine, ut auxilio eius tua beneficia capiamus, pro quo tibi hostias laudis offerimus. Per.

1683 PRAEFATIO. VD aeterne[1] deus. Qui ecclesiam tuam sempiterna pietate non deseris, sed per apostolos tuos iugiter erudis, et sine fine custodis. Per christum.

/f. 205v **1684** BENEDICTIO. / Deus qui ecclesiam tuam in apostolicis tribuisti consistere fundamentis, quaesumus ut beatus bartholomeus pro nobis imploret apostolus, ut a nostris reatibus absoluti, a cunctis etiam periculis exuamur. AMEN.
Infunde sensibus nostris apostolica retinere dogmata quibus te contemplemur mente serena. AMEN.
Concede propitius circumstanti plebi ut in illo tremendo discusionis tempore eorum defensetur praesidio, quorum est edocta praecepto. AMEN.
Quod ipse.

1685 AD COMPLENDVM. Sumpsimus domine pignus salutis aeternae, celebrantes beati bartholomei apostoli tui uotiua sollemnia, cuius nos quaesumus perpetua defensione conserua[2]. Per dominum.

CCXCI
DOMINICA XV POST PENTECOSTEN

1686 Omnipotens sempiterne deus, da nobis fidei, spei et caritatis augmentum, et ut mereamur assequi quod promittis, fac nos amare quod praecipis. Per dominum.

1687 SVPER OBLATA. Propitiare domine populo tuo, propitiare muneribus, ut hac oblatione placatus, et indulgentiam nobis tribuas et postulata concedas. Per.

1688 PRAEFATIO. VD aeterne deus. Quia in nostra semper faciens infirmitate uirtutem, ecclesiam tuam inter aduersa crescere
/f. 206r tribuisti ut cumputaretur obpressa, / tunc potius praeualeret

---

[1] *aeternae* before correction.
[2] *cuius nos quaesumus perpetua defensione conserua* supplied later over an erasure.

exaltata. Dum simul et experientiam fidei declarat officio, et uictoriosissima semper perseuerat, te adiuuante deuotio. Per christum.

1689 BENEDICTIO. Benedictio uos domini comitetur, ubique sibique uos semper faciat adherere. AMEN.
Ipse uos sua benedictione saluificet, qui dignatus est plasmare potenter. AMEN.
Atque ita uos praestet feliciter uiuire, ut caelestis beatitudinis efficiat coheredes. AMEN.
Quod ipse.

1690 AD COMPLENDVM. Sumptis domine caelestibus sacramentis, ad redemptionis aeternae, quaesumus proficiamus augmentum. Per.

CCXCII
VI KL SEPB. NATALE SANCTI RVFI

1691 Adesto domine supplicationibus nostris, et beati rufi intercessionibus confidentes[1], nec minis aduersantium, nec ullo conturbemur incursu. Per dominum.

1692 SVPER OBLATA. Oblatis quaesumus domine placare muneribus, et intercedente beato rufo martyre tuo, a cunctis nos defende periculis. Per.

1693 PRAEFATIO. VD aeterne[2] deus. Quoniam supplicationibus nostris misericordiam tuam confidimus affuturam[3], quam beati rufi poscimus interuentu nobis, et confessione praestari. Per christum dominum nostrum.

206v **1694** AD COMPLENDVM. / Caelestibus refecti sacramentis et gaudiis supplices te rogamus domine, ut quorum gloriamur triumphis, protegamur auxiliis. Per.

---

[1] A small erasure follows.
[2] *aeternae* before correction.
[3] After correction.

CCXCIII
V KL SEPB. NATALE SANCTI HERMETIS

1695 Deus qui beatum hermen martyrem tuum uirtute constantiae in passione roborasti, ex eius nobis imitatione tribue pro amore tuo prospera mundi despicere, et nulla eius aduersa formidare. Per.

1696 SVPER OBLATA. Sacrificium tibi domine laudis offerimus in tuorum commemoratione sanctorum, da quaesumus ut quod illis contulit gloriam, nobis prosit ad salutem. Per.

1697 AD COMPLENDVM. Repleti domine benedictione caelesti, quaesumus clementiam tuam, ut intercedente beato hermen martyre tuo, quae humiliter gerimus, salubriter sentiamus. Per dominum.

CCXCIIII
EODEM DIE NATALE SANCTI AVGVSTINI EPISCOPI ET CONFESSORIS

1698 Adesto supplicationibus nostris omnipotens deus, ut quibus fiduciam sperandę pietatis indulges, intercedente beato augustino confessore atque pontifice, consuetae misaericordiae tribue[1] benignus effectum. Per.

1699 SVPER OBLATA. Sancti confessoris tui augustini nobis domine pia non desit oratio, quae / et munera nostra conciliet, et tuam nobis indulgentiam semper obtineat. Per.

/f. 207r

1700 PRAEFATIO. VD aeterne[2] deus. Qui beatum augustinum confessorem tuum, et scientiae documentis replesti, et uirtutum ornamentis ditasti. Quem ita multimodo genere pietatis inbuisti, ut ipse tibi, et ara, et sacrificium, et sacerdos esset, et templum. Per christum.

1701 AD COMPLENDVM. Vt nobis domine tua sacrificia dent salutem, beatus confessor tuus augustinus pontifex, quaesumus pro nobis praecator accedat. Per dominum.

---

[1] *tribuae* before correction.
[2] *aeternae* before correction.

CCXCV
IIII KL SEPB. NATALE SANCTAE SABINAE VIRGINIS

1702 Deus qui inter caetera potentiae tuae miracula etiam in sexu fragili uictoriam martyrii contulisti, concede propitius ut cuius natalicia colimus, per eius ad te exempla gradiamur. Per dominum nostrum.

1703 SVPER OBLATA. Hostias tibi domine beatae sabinae martyris tuae dicatas meritis benignus assume, et ad perpetuum nobis tribue prouenire subsidium. Per.

1704 AD COMPLENDVM. Diuini muneris largitate satiati quaesumus domine deus noster, ut intercedente beata sabina martyre tua, in huius semper participatione uiuamus. Per dominum.

CCXCVI
EODEM DIE DECOLLATIO SANCTI IOHANNIS BABTISTAE

207v **1705** / Sancti iohannis baptistae et martyris tui domine quaesumus ueneranda festiuitas, salutaris auxilii nobis praestet effectum. Per dominum.

1706 SVPER OBLATA. Munera tibi domine pro sancti martyris iohannis baptistae passione deferimus, quia dum finitur tur in terris, factus est caelesti sede perpetuus, quaesumus ut eius obtentu nobis proficiant ad salutem. Per.

1707 PRAEFATIO. [1]VD aeterne[2] deus. Qui praecursorem filii tui tanto munere ditasti, ut pro ueritatis praeconio, capite plecteretur. Et qui christum aqua baptizauerat, ab ipso spiritu baptizatus, pro eodem proprio sanguine tingueretur. Praeco quippe ueritatis quae christus est, herodem a fraternis thalamis prohibendo, carceris obscuritate detruditur, ubi solo[3] diuinitatis tuae lumine frueretur. Deinde capitalem sententiam subiit, et ad inferna dominum praecursurus descendit. Et quem in mundo

---

[1] Partly neumed later.
[2] *aeternae* before correction.
[3] After correction.

333

digito demonstrauit, ad inferos praetiosa morte precessit. Et ideo.

1708 BENEDICTIO. Deus qui uos beati iohannis baptistae concedit sollemnia frequentare, tribuat uobis et eadem deuotis mentibus caelebrare, et suae benedictionis dona percipere. AMEN.

/f. 208r

Et qui pro legis eius praeconio carceribus est retrusus in tenebris, intercessione sua ab tenebrosorum / operum uos liberet incentiuis. AMEN.

Et qui pro ueritate deus est caput non cunctatus amittere, suo interuentu ad caput uestrum quod christus est uos faciat peruenire. AMEN.

<Q>uod ipse praestare dignetur.

1709 AD COMPLENDVM. Conferat nobis domine sancti iohannis utrumque sollemnitas, ut magnifica sacramenta quae sumpsimus significata ueneremur, et in nobis potius edita gaudeamus. Per.

1710 SVPER POPVLVM. Perpetuis nobis domine sancti iohannis baptistae tuere praesidiis, et quanto fragiliores sumus, tanto magis necessariis attolle suffragiis. Per.

CCXCVII

III KL SEPB. NATALE SANCTORVM FELICIS ET ADAVCTI

1711 Maiestatem tuam domine supplices depraecamur, ut sicut nos iugiter sanctorum tuorum commemoratione laetificas, ita semper supplicatione defendas. Per.

1712 SVPER OBLATA. Hostias domine tuae plebis intende, et quas in honore sanctorum tuorum deuota mente celebrat, proficere sibi sentiat ad salutem. Per.

1713 AD COMPLENDVM. Repleti domine muneribus sacris, quaesumus ut intercedentibus sanctis tuis, in gratiarum tuarum, semper actione maneamus. Per dominum nostrum.

CCXCVIII
KL SEPB. NATALE SANCTI PRISCI

208v **1714** / Omnipotens sempiterne deus, fortitudo certantium, et martyrum palma sollemnitatem hodiernae[1] diei propitius intuere, et ecclesiam tuam continua fac caelebritate laetari, et intercessione beati prisci, omnium in te credentium uota perficias. Per.

1715 SVPER OBLATA. Eius tibi praecibus domine quaesumus grata reddatur oblatio, pro cuius est festiuitate immolanda. Per dominum nostrum.

1716 PRAEFATIO. VD aeterne[2] deus. Qui sic tribuis ecclesiam tuam sanctorum commemoratione proficere, ut eam semper illorum et festiuitate laetificas, et exemplo piae conuersationis exerceas, grataque tibi supplicatione tuearis. Per christum.

1717 AD COMPLENDVM. Praesta quaesumus domine ut sacramenti tui participatione uegetati, sancti quoque martyris tui prisci praecibus adiuuemur. Per.

CCXCVIIII
VI ID SEPB. NATIVITAS SANCTAE MARIAE

1718 Supplicationem seruorum tuorum deus miserator exaudi, ut qui in natiuitate dei genetricis et uirginis congregamur, eius intercessionibus conplacatus, a te de instantibus periculis eruamur. Per dominum.

1719 ALIA. Famulis tuis domine caelestis gratiae munus impertire, ut
209r quibus beatę uirginis partus / extitit salutis[3] exordium, natiuitatis eius uotiua sollemnitas, pacis tribuat incrementum. Per.

1720 SVPER OBLATA. Vnigeniti tui domine nobis succurrat humanitas, ut qui natus de uirgine, matris integritatem non minuit sed sacrauit, in natiuitatis sollemniis a nostris nos

---

[1] *hodierna* before correction.
[2] *aeternae* before correction.
[3] A small erasure follows.

piaculis exuens, oblationem nostram sibi faciat acceptam. Qui tecum.

1721 PRAEFATIO. VD aequum et salutare. Nos tibi in omnium sanctorum tuorum prouectu gratias agere, domine sanctae pater omnipotens aeternae deus. Et praecipue[1] pro meritis beatae dei genetricis, et perpetuae uirginis mariae gratia plenae, tuam omnipotentiam laudare, benedicere et praedicare. Per christum[2].

1722 BENEDICTIO. Omnipotens deus sua uos dignetur protectione benedicere, qui hunc diem per natiuitatem beatae mariae fecit clarescere. AMEN.
Et qui per eam filium suum uoluit nasci, eius intercessione ab omni uos aduersitate faciat defendi. AMEN.
Quo in praesenti ęuo eius meritis et praecibus adiuti, sempiterna ualeatis gratanter felicitate perfrui. AMEN.
Quod ipse.

1723 AD COMPLENDVM. Sumpsimus domine caelebritatis annuae uotiua sacramenta, praesta quaesumus ut et temporalis nobis uitae remedia praebeant et aeternae. Per.

/ CCC
DOMINICA XVI POST PENTECOSTEN
1724 Custodi domine quaesumus ecclesiam tuam propitiatione perpetua, et quia sine te labitur humana mortalitas, tuis semper auxiliis et abstrahatur a noxiis, et ad salutaria dirigatur. Per.

1725 SVPER OBLATA. Concede nobis domine quaesumus, ut haec hostia salutaris et nostrorum fiat purgatio delictorum, et tuae propitiatio potestatis. Per.

1726 PRAEFATIO. VD aeterne[3] deus. Qui nos de donis bonorum temporalium, ad perceptionem prouegis[4] aeternorum. Et haec tribuis, et illa largiris. Vt et mansuris iam incipiamus inferi, et praetereuntibus non teneri. Tuum est enim quod uiuimus, quia

[1] *praecipuae* before correction.
[2] *christum* supplied later over an erasure.
[3] *aeternae* before correction.
[4] *provehis* before correction.

licet peccati uulnere, natura nostra sit uitiata, tui tamen est operis ut terreni generati ad caelestia renascamus. Per christum.

1727 BENEDICTIO. Benedic domine hanc plebem tuam atque hos omnes concordes, quietos, pacificos, et sospites serua. AMEN. Tribuę eis ut sectentur non interitum sed uitam, non carnem, sed spiritum, non temporalia sed aeterna. AMEN. Et operis suis non solum absoluti, uerum etiam iustificati, digni sint[1] uitam et gloriam promereri. AMEN. Quod ipse.

1728 AD COMPLENDVM. Purificent semper et muniant tua sacramenta nos deus, et ad per/petuae ducant saluationis effectum. Per.

210r

CCCI

V IDVS SEPB. NATALE SANCTI GORGONII MARTYRIS

1729 Sanctus domine gorgonius sua nos intercessione laetificet, et pia faciat sollemnitate gaudere. Per.

1730 SVPER OBLATA. Grata tibi sit domine nostrae seruitutis oblatio, pro qua sanctus gorgonius martyr interuenit. Per dominum.

1731 PRAEFATIO. VD aeterne[2] deus. Teque in sanctorum tuorum confessionibus laudare, in cuius facta sunt uirtute uictores. Quando enim humana fragilitas, uel passionem aequanimiter ferre sufficeret, uel hostis aerei nequitias uinceret, nisi tuae firmitatis subsidium minstrares, et seua furentis inimici potenter arma conteres. Per christum.

1732 AD COMPLENDVM. Familiam tuam deus suauitas, illa contingat et uegetet, qua in martyre tuo gorgonio christi tui bono odore pascatur. Per.

---

[1] *sunt* before correction.
[2] *aeternae* before correction.

CCCII
III ID SEPB. NATALE SANCTORVM PROTI ET IACINTI

1733 Beati proti nos domine et iacinti foueat praetiosa confessio, et pia iugiter intercessione tueatur. Per.

1734 SVPER OBLATA. Pro sanctorum proti et iacinti foueat munera tibi domine commemoratione quae debemus exsoluimus, praesta quaesumus ut remedium nobis perpetuae salutis operentur. Per.

/f. 210v **1735** BENEDICTIO. / Respice domine hanc familiam tuam serenis obtutibus, et largis eam infunde benedictionibus. AMEN.
Vt in uiam recti itineris gressus suos dirigant, et fidei suae stabilem firmitatem teneant. AMEN.
Ac sanctis suffragantibus meritis beatorum martyrum tuorum proti et iacinti, quorum annuam festiuitatem deuotis mentibus exercent, perseuerantiam boni operis usque in finem habere ualeant. AMEN.
Et praemia destinata sanctis in aeterna beatitudine possideant sine fine, et cum eis est deum facie ad faciem uisu indefectiuo mereantur uidere. AMEN.
Quod ipse.

1736 AD COMPLENDVM. Vt percepta nos domine tua sancta purificent, beati proti et iacinti quaesumus imploret oratio. Per dominum nostrum.

CCCIII
XVIII KL OCTB. NATALE SANCTORVM CORNELII ET CYPRIANI

1737 Infirmitatem nostram quaesumus domine propitius respice, et mala omnia quae iuste meremur sanctorum tuorum intercessione auerte. Per.

1738 SVPER OBLATA. Adesto domine supplicationibus nostris, quas in sanctorum tuorum commemoratione deferimus, ut qui nostrae iustitiae fiduciam non habemus, eorum qui tibi placuerunt meritis adiuuemur. Per dominum.

211r 1739 PRAEFATIO. / VD aeterne[1] deus. Tuamque in sanctorum tuorum cornelii simul et cypriani festiuitate praedicare uirtutem, quod diuersis terrarum partibus greges sacros diuino pane pascentes, una fide eademque die pari nominis tui confessione coronasti. Per christum.

1740 ITEM ALIA PROPRIA SANCTI CYPRIANI. VD aeternae deus. Beati cypriani natalicia recensentes, ut qui in conspectu tuo clarus extitit dignitate sacerdotii, et palma martyrii, et in praesenti saeculo sua nos intercessione foueat, et ad misericordiam sempiternam pius interuentor perducat. Per christum.

1741 AD COMPLENDVM. Quaesumus domine salutaribus repleti mysteriis, ut quorum sollemnia celebramus, orationibus adiuuemur. Per dominum.

CCCIIII
EODEM DIE EXALTATIO SANCTAE CRVCIS

1742 Deus qui unigeniti tui domini nostri iesu christi praetioso sanguine humanum genus redimere dignatus est, concede propitius, ut qui ad adorandam uiuificam crucem adueniunt, a peccatorum suorum nexibus liberentur. Per eundem.

1743 PRAEFATIO. VD per christum dominum nostrum. Qui per passionem crucis mundum redemit. Require superius <in> inuentione sanctae crucis.

211v 1744 BENEDICTIO. / Deus qui redemisti genus humanum per beatae crucis patibulum, ut quod prius erat sceleste ad penam, sit conuersis redemptio ad uitam, concede plebi tuae eius saluari praesidio, cuius est armata uexillo. AMEN.
Sit ei crux fidei fundamentum, spei suffragium, in aduersis defensio, in prosperis iuuamentum. AMEN.
Perseueretque in hoste uictoria, in ciuitate concordia, in campo custodia, in domo fultura, ut gregem in futuro conseruet incolumen quae nobis agno uincente uersa est in salutem. AMEN.
Quod ipse praestare dignetur.

---

[1] *aeternae* before correction.

1745 AD COMPLENDVM. Quaesumus omnipotens deus ut quos diuina tribuis participatione gaudere, humanis non sinas subiacere periculis. Per dominum nostrum.

CCCV
DOMINICA XVII POST PENTECOSTEN

1746 Ecclesiam tuam domine miseratio continuata mundet et muniat, et quia sine te non potest salua consistere, tuo semper munere gubernetur. Per dominum.

1747 SVPER OBLATA. Tua nos domine sacramenta custodiant, et contra diabolicos tueantur semper incursus. Per.

1748 PRAEFATIO. VD per christum dominum nostrum. Quia aeternitate sacerdotii sui omnes tibi seruientes sanctificat sacerdotes. Quoniam mor/tali carne circumdati, ita cotidianis peccatorum remissionibus indigemus, ut non solum pro populo, sed etiam pro nobis eiusdem te pontificis sanguis exoret. Per quem.

/f. 212r

1749 BENEDICTIO. Omnipotens deus peccatorum uestrorum maculas purget, et sua uos benedictione illustret. AMEN.
Repleat uos spiritualium donis uirtutum, et perseuerare faciat in bonis propositum uestrum. AMEN.
Sicque humilitatem uestram benignus acceptet, ut suae nos pietatis remuneratione locupletet. AMEN.
Quod ipse praestare.

1750 AD COMPLENDVM. Mentes nostras et corpora possideat quaesumus domine doni caelestis operatio, ut non noster sensus in nobis, sed iugiter eius[1] preueniat effectus. Per.

CCCVI
XVII KL OCT. NATALE SANCTI NICOMEDIS MARTYRIS

1751 Adesto domine populo tuo, ut beati nicomedis martyris tui merita praeclara suscipiens, ad impetrandam misaericordiam tuam semper eius patrociniis adiuuemur. Per.

---

[1] Supplied interlinearly.

1752 SVPER OBLATA. Suscipe domine munera propitius oblata, quae maiestati tuae beati nicomedis martyris commendet oratio. Per dominum.

1753 AD COMPLENDVM. Purificent nos domine sacramenta quae sumpsimus, et intercedente beato nicomede martyre tuo a cunctis efficiant uitiis absolutos. Per.

/ CCCVII
XVI KL OCT. NATALE SANCTAE EVPHAEMIAE

1754 Omnipotens sempiterne deus qui infirma mundi eligis ut fortia quaeque confundas, concede propitius ut qui beatae euphemiae martyris tuae sollemnia colimus, eius aput te patrocinia sentiamus. Per dominum nostrum.

1755 SVPER OBLATA. Praesta quaesumus domine deus noster, ut sicut in tuo conspectu mors est praetiosa sanctorum, ita eorum merita uenerantium, accepta tibi reddatur oblatio. Per dominum.

1756 AD COMPLENDVM. Sanctificet nos domine quaesumus tui perceptio sacramenti, et intercessio beatae martyris tuae eufemiae tibi reddat acceptos. Per dominum.

CCCVIII
EODEM DIE NATALE SANCTORVM LVCI, ET GEMINIANI

1757 Praesta quaesumus domine praecibus nostris cum exultatione prouectum, ut quorum diem passionis annua deuotione recolimus, etiam fidei constantia subsequamur. Per dominum.

1758 SVPER OBLATA. Vota populi tui domine propitiatus intende, et quorum nos tribuis sollemnia caelebrare, fac gaudere suffragiis. Per.

1759 AD COMPLENDVM. Exaudi domine praeces nostras, et sanctorum tuorum quorum festa sollemniter celebramus, continuis foueamur auxiliis. Per dominum.

CCCVIIII
DOMINICA XVIII POST PENTECOSTEN

/f. 213r **1760** / Absolue quaesumus domine tuorum delicta populorum, et peccatorum nostrorum nexibus quae pro nostra fragilitate contraximus, tua benignitate liberemur. Per.

1761 SVPER OBLATA. Pro nostrae seruitutis augmento sacrificium tibi domine laudis offerimus, ut quod immeritis contulisti, propitius exequaris. Per.

1762 PRAEFATIO. VD aeterne deus. Et te incessanter praecari, ut qui te auctore subsistimus, te dispensante dirigamur. Non ut[1] nostris sensibus relinquamur, sed ad tuae reducti semper tramitem ueritatis, haec studeamus exercere quae praecipis, ut possimus dona percipere quae promittis. Per christum.

1763 BENEDICTIO. Benedicat uos pater domini nostri iesu christi, et respectu misericordiae caelestis, protegat uos sub umbra uirtutis. AMEN.
Detque uobis animarum compunctionem, immaculatam fidem, conscientiae puritatem, sensus uestros dirigat, corda compungat, in prosperis assistat, manum porrigat, in laboribus solatium ferat. AMEN.
Virtutum suarum merita multiplicet, recta consilia aduocet, terrenarum rerum a uobis pondera auferat. AMEN.
Repleat corda uestra spiritalibus donis, et abundare faciat semper perfectae incrementis. AMEN.
Quod ipse praestare.

/f. 213v **1764** / POSTCOMMVNIO. Quaesumus omnipotens deus, ut quos diuina tribuis participatione gaudere, humanis non sinas subiacere periculis. Per.

MENSIS SEPTIMI FERIA IIII. STATIO AD SANCTAM MARIAM MAIOREM

1765 Misericordiae tuae remediis quaesumus domine fragilitas nostra subsistat, ut quae sua conditione[2] atteritur, tua clementia reparetur. Per dominum.

[1] Supplied interlinearly.
[2] Partly rewritten.

342

1766 ALIA. Praesta quaesumus domine familiae supplicanti, ut dum a cibis corporalibus se abstinent, a uitiis mente ieiunent. Per.

1767 <SECRETA.> Haec hostia domine quaesumus emundet nostra delicta, et sacrificium caelebrandum, subditorum tibi corpora mentesque sanctificet. Per.

1768 PRAEFATIO. VD aeterne deus. Qui nos collectis terrae frugibus per abstinentiam tibi gratias agere uoluisti, ut ex ipso die deuotionis genere nosceremus, non haec ad exuberantiam corporalem, sed a fragilitatis sustentationem nos percoepisse, ut quod ex his sumeremus partius sumeremus, egentium proficeret alimentis, et ut salutaris castigatio mortalitatis insolentia mitigaret, et pietas largitoris, nos tuae benignitati commendatos efficeret. Sicque donis uteremur transitoriis, ut disceremus iniare perpetuis. Per christum.

1769 AD COMPLENDVM. Sumentes domine caelestia sacramenta suppliciter depraecamur, ut quae sedula seruitute donante / te gerimus, dignis sensibus tuo munere capiamus. Per.

f. 214r

CCCXI
FERIA VI AD SANCTOS APOSTOLOS

1770 Praesta quaesumus omnipotens deus, ut obseruationes sacras annua deuotione recolentes, et corpore tibi placeamus et mente. Per.

1771 SECRETA. Accepta tibi sint quaesumus domine nostri dona ieiunii, quae et expiando nos tua gratia dignos efficiant, et ad sempiterna promissa perducant. Per.

1772 PRAEFATIO. VD aeterne deus. Qui iusto pioque moderamine, et pro peccatis flagella inrogas, et post flagella ueniam propitiatus concedas, et peccatorum uitam potius uolens quam mortem. Non eos ad interitum condemnas, sed ut corrigantur miseratus expectas. Per christum.

1773 AD COMPLENDVM. Quaesumus omnipotens deus, ut de perceptis muneribus exhibentes, beneficia potiora sumamus. Per.

343

CCCXII
SABBATO AD SANCTVM PETRVM IN XII^{CIM}
LECTIONIBVS. REQVIRE IN ORDINATIONEM
CLERICORVM IN SABBATO MENSIS I

1774 Omnipotens sempiterne deus, qui per continentiam salutarem et corporibus mederis et mentibus, maiestatem tuam supplices exoramus, ut pia ieiunantium depraecatione placatus, et praesentia nobis subsidia praebeas et futura. Per dominum.

1775 ALIA. Da nobis quaesumus omnipotens deus, ut ieiunando tua /f. 214v gratia satiemur, et abstinendo cunctis efficiamur hos/tibus fortiores. per dominum.

1776 ALIA. Tuere quaesumus domine familiam tuam, ut salutis aeternae remedia quae te aspirante requirimus, te largiente consequamur. Per.

1777 ALIA. Praesta quaesumus domine sic nos ab aepulis abstinere carnalibus, ut a uitiis inruentibus partier ieiuniemus. Per dominum.

1778 ITEM ALIA. Vt nos domine tribuis sollemne tibi deferre ieiunium, sic nobis quaesumus indulgentiae praesta subsidium. Per dominum.

1779 ITEM ALIA AD MISSAM. Deus qui tribus pueris mitigasti flammas. REQVIRE RETRO IN SABBATO MENSIS PRIMI.

1780 SVPER OBLATA. Concede quaesumus omnipotens deus, ut oculis tuae maiestatis munus oblatum, et gratiam nobis deuotionis obtineat, et effectum beatae perennitatis adquirat. Per.

1781 PRAEFATIO. VD aeterne deus. Et tibi sacrificare ieiunium, quod nos ob aedificationem animarum, et castigationem corporum seruire docuisti, quia restrinctis corporibus animae saginantur. In quo homo noster affligitur exterior, dilatatur interior. Memento quaesumus domine ieiuniorum nostrorum, et misericordiarum tuarum, quas peccatoribus piae semper /f. 215r ieiunantibus contulisti. Et praesta ut non solum a cybis / sed a

peccatis omnibus abstinentes, deuotionis tibi ieiunio placeamus.
Per christum.

1782 BENEDICTIO. Benedictionum suarum super uos dominus
ymbrem infundat, et orationes uestras exaudiat. AMEN.
Thesauros misericordiae uobis aperiat, et desideriorum
uestrorum uota suscipiat, quod perit requirat, et uobis quod
bonum est tribuat. AMEN.
Dignosque uos in bonis operibus faciat, quibus uirtutum secreta
commisit ubique uos a malo eruat induci in temptationem
numquam permittat. AMEN.
Quod ipse.

1783 AD COMPLENDVM. Perficiant in nobis domine quaesumus
tua sacramenta quod continent, ut quae nunc specie gerimus,
rerum ueritate capiamus. Per dominum.

CCCXIII
DIE DOMINICO VACAT

1784 Omnipotens sempiterne deus misaericordiam tuam ostende
supplicibus, ut qui de meritorum qualitate diffidimus, non in
iudicium tuum, sed indulgentiam sentiamus. Per.

1785 SVPER OBLATA. Sacrificiis praesentibus quaesumus domine
intende placatus, ut et deuotioni nostrae proficiant et saluti. Per
dominum.

1786 PRAEFATIO. VD aeterne deus. Quia cum laude nostra non
egeas, grata tibi tamen est tuorum deuotio famulorum. Nec te
f. 215v augent nostra / preconia, sed nobis proficiunt ad salutem.
Quoniam sicut fontem uitae praeterire causa moriendi est, sic
eodem iugiter redundare affectus est sine fine uiuendi. Et ideo.

1787 BENEDICTIO. Benedicat uos omnipotens deus, et mentes
uestras omni reatu malitiae separet, et praestet uobis uelle quod
praecepit, tribuatque quod oportet, et omni uos bono
spiritualium uirtutum locupletet. AMEN.
Vt uos in fide firmet, in temptatione adiuuet, in conuersatione
castiget, in anxietate letificet, in prosperitate praeparet, omni

iniquitate emundet, in tranquillitate sublimet, et ad uitam aeternam perducat. AMEN.

Gratiam suam uobis infundet, offensa indulgeat, crimina dimittat, disciplinam ingerat, mansuetudinem tribuat, correctionem confirmet, et uitam perfectam conseruet. AMEN. Quod ipse.

1788 AD COMPLENDVM. Quaesumus omnipotens deus, ut illius salutaris capiamus effectum, cuius per haec mysteria pignus accepimus. Per dominum.

CCCXIIII
XII KL OCTB. VIGILIA SANCTI MATHEI EVANGELISTAE

1789 Da nobis omnipotens deus, ut beati mathei apostoli tui et euangelistae quam praeuenimus ueneranda sollemnitas, et /f. 216r deuotionem nobis augeat / et salutem. Per dominum.

1790 SVPER OBLATA. Apostolicae reuerentiae culmen offerimus sacris mysteriis[1] imbuendum, praesta domine quaesumus ut beati mathei euangelistę suffragiis, cuius natalicia praehimus, hic plebs tua semper et sua uota depromat, et desiderata percipiat. per.

1791 AD COMPLENDVM. Beati mathei euangelistae quaesumus domine supplicatione placatus, et ueniam nobis tribue, et remedia sempiterna concede. Per.

CCCXV
XI KL OCTB. NATALE EIVSDEM

1792 Beati euangelistae mathei domine praecibus adiuuemur, ut quod possibilitas nostra non obtinet, eius nobis intercessione donetur. Per.

1793 SVPER OBLATA. Supplicationibus apostolicis beati mathei euangelistae quaesumus ecclesiae tuae domine commendetur oblatio, cuius magnificis praedicationibus eruditur. Per dominum.

---

[1] *mysterias* before correction.

346

1794 PRAEFATIO. VD aeterne deus. Qui ecclesiam tuam in tuis fidelibus ubique pollentem, apostolicis facis constare doctrinis. Praesta quaesumus ut per quos initium diuinae cognitionis accepit, per eos usque in finem saeculi, capiat regni caelestis augmentum. Per christum.

1795 BENEDICTIO. Benedic domine populum tuum interueniente matheo apostolo et deuotum respice, humilitatem / uide, gemitus suscipe, dolentes paterna pietate iube consolari. AMEN.
Prostratum alleua, dispersum congrega, adunatumque conserua, esurientem cyba, sitientem pota, omnesque simul caelestibus donis irriga, dele in eis omnem peccati maculam, ut te gubernante ad gloriam perueniant sempiternam. AMEN.
Humiliata tibi omnium capita, dexterae tuae benedictione sanctifica, ac benedicendo peccata relaxa, sanctique spiritus infunde carismata, ut sine ulla offensione maiestatis tuae praecepta adimpleant, et ad uitam aeternam te auxiliante perueniant. AMEN.
Quod ipse.

f. 216r

1796 AD COMPLENDVM. Perceptis domine sacramentis beato matheo apostolo tuo et euangelista interueniente depraecamur, ut quae pro eius celebrata sunt gloria, nobis proficiant ad medelam. Per.

1797 ALIA. Sit nobis domine beatus matheus euangelista nostrae fragilitatis adiutor, ut pro nobis tibi supplicans copiosus audiatur. Per.

1798 ALIA. Praesta quaesumus omnipotens deus, ut qui iugiter apostolica defensione munimur, nec succumbamus uitiis, nec obprimamur aduersis. Per dominum.

CCCXVI

X KL OCTB. NATALE SANCTORVM MAVRICII CVM
SOCIIS SVIS

f. 217r **1799** / Annue quaesumus omnipotens deus, ut nos sanctorum tuorum mauricii, exsuperii, candidi, uictoris, innocentis, et uitalis, ac sociorum eorundem laetificet festiua sollemnitas, ut quorum suffragiis nitimur, nataliciis gloriemur. Per.

1800 SVPER OBLATA. Respice domine munera quae in sanctorum martyrum tuorum, mauricii, exsuperii, candidi, uictoris, innocentis, et uitalis, ac sociorum eorundem, commemoratione deferimus, et praesta ut quorum honore sunt grata, eorum nobis fiant intercessione perpetua. Per.

1801 PRAEFATIO. VD <aeterne deus.> Quoniam cognoscimus quantum apud te sit praeclara uita sanctorum, quorum nos etiam mors praetiosa laetificet et tuetur, quapropter martyrum tuorum mauricii, exsuperii, et candidi, uictoris, innocentis, et uitalis, cum sociis eorum gloriosa recensentes natalicia, laudes tibi domine referimus, supplici confessione dicentes.

1802 AD COMPLENDVM. Caelestibus refecti sacramentis et gaudiis, supplices te rogamus domine, ut quorum gloriamur triumphis, protegamur auxiliis. Per.

CCCXVII
ITEM MISSA SANCTORVM MAVRICII

1803 Omnipotens et misericors deus, qui sanctis martyribus tuis mauricio, exsuperio, candido, / et uictori, cum sociis eorum coronam martyrii praestitisti, concede quaesumus ut eorum intercessione saluemur. Per.

/f. 217v

1804 SVPER OBLATA. Hostias quaesumus domine sollemniter immolandas pro tuo commemoratione, sanctorum clementer suscipe, ut eorum intercessionibus ueniam delictorum consequi mereamur. Per.

1805 AD COMPLENDVM. Sumptis domine caelestibus sacramentis, et praemiorum gaudiis, concede quaesumus ut intercessione sanctorum martyrum thebeorum consequi mereamur ueniam delictorum. Per dominum nostrum.

CCCXVIII
DOMINICA XX POST PENTECOSTEN

1806 Tua nos quaesumus domine gratia semper et preueniat, et sequatur, ac bonis operibus iugiter praestet esse intentos. Per.

1807 SVPER OBLATA. Munda nos domine sacrificii praesentis effectu, et perfice miseratus in nobis, ut eius mereamur esse participes. Per.

1808 PRAEFATIO. VD aeterne[1] deus. Qui uicit diabolum et mundum, hominemque paradyso restituit, et uitae ianuas credentibus patefecit. Per quem.

1809 BENEDICTIO. Adesto domine propitius plebi tuae, et eam non deseras temporali consolatione, quamuis ad aeterna conscendere, et gaudia indefectiua recipere. AMEN.

f. 218r / Actus uestros dirigat, corda uestra illuminet, pedes uestros in uiam pacis dirigat, oculos spiritali gratia illuminet, et ad uidendum quae bona sunt aperiat. AMEN.

Numquam uobis facere contingat malum quod a deo separet, sed uos facere delectet, quod deo semper placeat. AMEN.

Quod ipse praestare.

1810 AD COMPLENDVM. Purifica domine quaesumus mentes nostras benignus et renoua caelestibus sacramentis, ut consequenter et corporum praesens pariter, et futurum capiamus auxilium. Per.

CCCXVIIII
V KL OCTB. NATALE SANCTORVM COSMAE ET DAMIANI

1811 Praesta quaesumus omnipotens deus, ut qui sanctorum tuorum cosmae et damiani natalicia colimus, a cunctis malis imminentibus eorum intercessionibus liberemur. Per.

1812 SVPER OBLATA. Sanctorum tuorum nobis domine pia non desit oratio, quae et munera nostra conciliet, et tuam nobis indulgentiam semper obtineat. Per.

1813 PRAEFATIO. VD aeterne[2] deus. Et clementiam tuam suppliciter obsecrare, ut cum exultantibus sanctis, in caelestis regni cubilibus gaudia nostra subiungas, et quos uirtutis imitatione

---

[1] *aeternae* before correction.
[2] *aeternae* before correction.

349

non possumus sequi, debitae uenerationis contingamus effectu. Per christum dominum nostrum.

/f. 218v **1814** AD COMPLENDVM. / Protegat domine quaesumus populum tuum et participatio caelestis indulta conuiuii, et depraecatio collata sanctorum. Per dominum.

CCCXX
III KL OCTB. DEDICATIO BASILICAE SANCTI MICHAEHELIS ARCHANGELI

1815 Deus qui miro ordine angelorum ministeria hominumque dispensas, concede propitius ut quibus tibi ministrantibus in caelo semper adsistitur, ab his in terra nostra uita muniatur. Per.

1816 SVPER OBLATA. Hostias tibi domine laudis offerimus, suppliciter depraecantes, ut eodem angelico pro nobis interueniente suffragio, et placatus accipias, et ad salutem nostrum prouenire concedas. Per dominum.

1817 PRAEFATIO. VD aeterne deus. Sancti michahelis archangeli, merita praedicantes. Quamuis enim nobis sit omnis angelica ueneranda sublimitas, quae in maiestatis tuae consistit conspectu, illa tamen est propensius honoranda, quae in eius ordinis dignitate, caelestis militię meruit principatum. Per christum.

1818 BENEDICTIO. Adesto plebi tuae misericors deus ad hodiernam sollemnitatem deuotissime confluenti, et ut gratiae tuae beneficia potiora percipiat, beati michahelis archangeli cuius
/f. 219r sollemnia celebrantur, fac supplicem depraecatio/nibus subleuari. AMEN.
Ab omni eos labe peccatorum defensa, et ad tua aeterna deduc promissa, amoue ab eis pestifera serpentis blandimenta, et inserae semper cordibus eorum praecepti tui salubria mandata. AMEN.
Actus eorum in tua dirige uoluntate, quo possint te auxiliante attingere praemia aeternae uitae, postremo tu sis eis lux, tu salus, tu pius, semper in omni aduersitate protector esse dignare, et ad haec omnia inpetranda, beatus michahel archangelus, cuius

350

frequentamus sollemnia, tibi domine praecator accedat in saecula. AMEN.
Quod ipse.

1819 AD COMPLENDVM. Beati archangeli tui michahelis intercessione suffulti, supplices te domine depraecamur, ut quod honore prosequimur, contingamus et mente. Per dominum nostrum.

CCCXXI
ALIAE ORATIONES

1820 Adesto plebi tuae misaericors deus, et gratiae tuae beneficia potiora percipiat, beati michahelis fac supplicem depraecationibus subleuari. Per dominum nostrum.

1821 ALIA. Perpetuum nobis domine tuae miserationis praesta subsidium, quibus et angelica praestitisti suffragia non deesse. Per dominum nostrum iesum christum.

f. 219v **1822** ITEM ALIA. / Da nobis omnipotens deus, beati archangeli michahelis eotenus honore proficere, ut cuius in terris gloriam praedicamus, eius praecibus adiuuemur in caelis. Per dominum nostrum.

CCCXXII
II KL OCTB. NATALE SANCTI HIERONIMI[1]

1823 Sancti tui hieronimi[2] nos domine quaesumus interuentio gloriosa commendet, ut quod nostris actibus non meremur, eius intercessionibus adiuuemur. Per.

1824 SVPER OBLATA. Suscipe domine propitius orationem nostram, cum oblationibus hostiarum superinpositis, et sancti tui hieronimi depraecatione pietati tuae perfice benignus acceptas, et illam[3] quae in eo flagrauit, fortem dilectionem in nobis aspira benignus. Per.

---

[1] First letters rewritten by a later scribe.
[2] *h* supplied interlinearly.
[3] Over an erasure.

1825 PRAEFATIO. VD aeterne deus. Et tuam misaericordiam depraecari, ut mentibus nostris beati hieronimi presbiteri repetita sollemnitate, spiritalis laetitiae tribuas iugiter suauitatem. Concedasque nobis ut uenerando depositionis eius triumphum, optentu illius et peccatorum remissionem, et sanctorum mereamur adipisci consortium. Per christum.

1826 AD COMPLENDVM. Votiua domine beati hieronimi prẹsbiteri dona percepimus, quaesumus ut eius praecibus et praesentis uitae nobis pariter et aeternae tribuas conferre praesidium. Per dominum nostrum.

/f. 220r / KL OCTB. NATALE SANCTI VEDASTI EPISCOPI

1827 Deus qui nos deuota beati uedasti[1] confessoris tui atque pontificis instantia ad agnitionem tui sancti nominis uocare dignatus es, concede propitius, ut cuius sollemnia colimus, etiam patrocinia sentiamus. Per.

1828 SVPER OBLATA. Hostias domine laudis tuis altaribus adhibemus, quas eius tibi patrocinio credimus commendandas, cuius nos uoluisti uotis ad tuae pietatis peruenire notitiam. Per dominum.

1829 PRAEFATIO. [2]VD aeterne deus. Diemque natalitium beati uedasti summa cum deuotione uenerari. Suppliciter obsecrantes, ut ipsum apud tuam misericordiam sentiamus habere patronum, quem aeternae uitae meruimus suscipere ministrum. Per christum.

1830 AD COMPLENDVM. Beati uedasti confessoris tui atque pontificis domine praecibus confidentes, quaesumus clementiam tuam, ut per ea quae sumpsimus, aeterna remedia capiamus. Per dominum.

1831 ALIA. Deus qui nos sanctorum tuorum temporali tribuis commemoratione gaudere, praesta quaesumus ut beato uedasto

---

[1] *uedasti* written over an erasure by the original scribe.
[2] Partly neumed.

interueniente, in ea non meremur sorte salutis, in qua illi sunt gratia tua gloriosi. Per dominum nostrum iesum christum.

CCCXXIII
DOMINICA XXI POST PENTECOSTEN

f. 220v **1832** / Da quaesumus domine populo tuo diabolica uitare contagia, et te solum dominum pura mente sectari. Per dominum nostrum.

1833 SVPER OBLATA. Maiestatem tuam domine suppliciter depraecamur, ut haec sancta quae gerimus, et a preteritis nos delictis, exuant et futuris. Per dominum.

1834 PRAEFATIO. VD aeternae deus. Et tuam maiestatem humiliter implorare, ut iesus christus filius tuus dominus noster sua nos gratia protegat et conseruet. Et quia sine ipso nihil recte ualemus efficere, ipsius munera capiamus, ut tibi semper placere possimus. Per quem.

1835 BENEDICTIO. Plebs tua domine quaesumus nostram benedictionem accipiat, per quam cuncta noxia declinet, et optata reperiat. AMEN.
Circumcinge eam spiritali muro tuo, praesta ei continuam sanitatem, da ei tempora tranquilla, da quieta secura et pacifica, ut possint peruenire ad gaudia aeterna. AMEN.
Mentes regat, uias dirigat, cogitationes instruat, et lacrimas ab omni facie tergat. AMEN.
Quod ipse.

1836 AD COMPLENDVM. Sanctificationibus tuis omnipotens deus, et uitia nostra curentur, et remedia nobis aeterna proueniant. Per.

CCCXXIIII
NON OCTB. NATALE SANCTI MARCI PAPAE

f. 221r **1837** / Exaudi domine quaesumus praeces nostras, et interueniente beato marco confessore tuo atque pontifice, supplicationes nostras placatus intende. Per.

1838 SVPER OBLATA. Accepta tibi sit domine sacrae plebis oblatio pro tuorum honore sanctorum, quorum se meritis percepisse, de tribulatione cognoscit auxilium. Per.

1839 AD COMPLENDVM. Da quaesumus domine fidelibus populis sanctorum tuorum semper ueneratione laetari, et eorum perpetua supplicatione muniri. Per.

CCCXXV
VIII ID OCT. VIGILIA SANCTORVM MARTYRVM
DIONISII, RVSTICI ET ELEVTHERII

1840 Concede nobis quaesumus omnipotens deus, uenturum beatorum martyrum tuorum dyonisii, rustici, et eleutherii, sollemnitatem congruo praeuenire honore, et uenientem digna celebrare deuotione. Per dominum.

1841 SVPER OBLATA. Accepta tibi sit domine nostrae deuotionis oblatio, et ad martyrum tuorum, dyonisii, rustici et eleutherii, puriores faciat nos uenire festiuitatem. Per dominum.

1842 PRAEFATIO. VD <aeterne deus.> Venientem natalem beatorum martyrum tuorum dyonisii, rustici et eleutherii, debita seruitute praeueniri, suppliciter obsecrantes, ut ipsos nos apud tuam clementiam sentiamus habere patronos, / quos tua gratia largiente meruimus, aeternae salutis suscipere ministros. Per christum.

/f. 221v

1843 AD COMPLENDVM. Praesta nobis aeternae largitor eorum ubique pia protegi oratione, quorum natalicia per hęc sancta quae sumpsimus, uotiuo praeuenimus obsequio. Per dominum.

1844 SVPER POPVLVM. Benedictionis tuae domine gratiam intercedentibus sanctis martyribus tuis dionisio, rustico, et eleutherio suscipiamus, ut quorum praeueniendo gloriam celebramus, eorum supplicando auxilium sentiamus. Per.

CCCXXVI
VII IDVS OCT. NATALE SANCTORVM DYONISII, RVSTICI
ET ELEVTHERII

1845 Deus qui hodierna die beatum dyonisium uirtute constantiae in passione roborasti, quique illi ad praedicandam gentibus gloriam tuam, rusticum et eleutherium sociare dignatus es, tribue nobis quaesumus ex eorum imitatione, pro amore tuo prospera mundi despicere, et nulla eius aduersa formidare. Per dominum.

1846 SVPER OBLATA. Hostia domine quaesumus quam in sanctorum tuorum .N. natalicia recensentes offerimus, et uincula nostrae prauitatis absoluat, et tuae nobis misericordiae dona conciliet. Per.

1847 PRAEFATIO. VD <aeterne deus.> Qui sanctorum martyrum tuorum dionisii, rustici, et eleutherii, pia certamina /ad copiosam perducis uictoriam, atque perpetuum eis largiris triumphum, ut in exemplum ecclesiae tuae per innumerosa proficiant saecula. Praesta nobis quaesumus ut per eorum intercessionem, quorum festa caelebramus, tuae pietatis aeterno perfrui auxilio. Per christum.

f. 222r

1848 BENEDICTIO. Exaudi domine praeces supplicum remuneratio gentium, recuperatio confitentium. AMEN.
Sint huic familiae tuae dona salutis adquirere, tuae maiestatis uota uotis offerre. AMEN.
Vt intercessione beatorum dyonisii, rustici et eleutherii martyrum illuc plebs occurrat deuota per ueniam, quo idem martyres meruerunt accedere per tormenta. AMEN.
Quod ipse.

1849 <AD COMPLENDVM>. Quaesumus omnipotens deus ut qui caelestia alimenta percepimus, intercedentibus sanctis tuis dyonisio, rustico et eleutherio, per haec contra omnia aduersa muniamur. Per dominum.

CCCXXVII
DOMINICA XXII POST PENTECOSTEN

1850 Dirigat corda nostra domine quaesumus tuae miserationis operatio, quia tibi sine te placere non possumus. Per dominum.

1851 SVPER OBLATA. Deus qui nos per huius sacrificii ueneranda commertia unius summeque diuinitatis participes efficis, praesta quaesumus ut sicut tuam / cognouimus ueritatem, sic eam dignis mentibus et moribus assequamur. Per.

f. 222v

1852 PRAEFATIO. VD aeterne deus. Et te suppliciter exorare, ut sic nos bonis tuis instruis sempiternis, ut temporabus quoque consolare digneris, sic praesentibus refouere, ut ad gaudia nos mansura perducas. Per.

355

1853 BENEDICTIO. Aspiciat uos rector deus aeternus, atque conseruet in uobis gratiam quam profudit largus. AMEN.

Actus probet, opera confirmet, praeterita indulgeat, praesentia emendet, futura bona praeparet. AMEN.

Sit domini manus auxiliatrix uestri, et brachium eius opituletur uobis sit super uos misaericordia illius, et subsequatur uos omnibus diebus uitae uestrae pietas eius. AMEN.

Christus uos benedicat de caelis, qui suo sancto sanguine uos dignatus est redimere in terris.

Quod ipse praestare.

1854 AD COMPLENDVM. Gratias tibi referimus domine sacro munere uegetati, tuam misaericordiam depraecantes, ut dignos nos eius participatione perficias[1]. Per.

CCCXXVIII
II ID OCTB. NATALE SANCTI CALISTI PAPAE

1855 Deus qui nos conspicis ex nostra infirmitate deficere, ad amorem tuum nos misericorditer pro sanctorum tuorum exempla restaura. Per dominum nostrum.

/f. 223r **1856** SVPER OBLATA. / Mystica nobis domine prosit oblatio, quae nos et a reatibus nostris expediat, et perpetua saluatione confirmet. Per dominum.

1857 AD COMPLENDVM. Quaesumus omnipotens deus, ut et reatum nostrum munera sacra purificent, et recte uiuendi nobis operentur effectum. Per.

CCCXXVIIII
XVII KL NOVB. OCTAVAS SANCTORVM MARTYRVM DYONISII, RVSTICI ET ELEVTHERII

1858 Protegat nos domine saepius beatorum martyrum dyonisii, rustici, et eleutherii, repetita solemnitas, ut quorum patrocinia sine intermissione recolimus, perpetua defensione sentiamus. Per.

---

[1] *peraficias* before correction.

1859 SVPER OBLATA. Hostias tibi domine pro sanctorum martyrum tuorum dyonisii, rusticii et eleutherii, commemoratione deferimus, suppliciter obsecrantes, ut et indulgentiam nobis pariter conferant et salutem. Per.

1860 AD COMPLENDVM. Sumpsimus domine pignus redemptionis aeternae, sit nobis quaesumus interuenientibus martyribus tuis dyonisio, rustico et eleutherio, uitae praesentis auxilium pariter et futurae. Per.

CCCXXX
XV KL NOV. NATALE SANCTI LVCAE EVANGELISTAE

1861 Interueniat pro nobis domine quaesumus sanctus tuus lucas euangelista, qui crucis mortificationem iugiter in suo corpore, pro tui nominis honore portauit. Per dominum.

f. 223v **1862** SVPER OBLATA. / Donis caelestibus da nobis quaesumus domine libera mente seruire, ut munera quae deferimus, interueniente euangelista tuo luca, et medelam nobis operentur et gloriam. Per.

1863 PRAEFATIO. VD aeterne deus. Et te in sanctorum tuorum meritis gloriosis, conlaudare, benedicere, et praedicare. Qui eos dimicantes contra antiqui serpentis machinamenta, et proprii corporis blandimenta, inexpugnabili uirtute rex gloriae roborasti. Ex quibus beatus lucas euangelista tuus, adsumptus scuto fidei et galea salutis et gladio spiritus sancti, et uiriliter contra uitiorum hostes pugnauit, et euangelicae nobis dulcedinis fluenta manauit. Vnde petimus domine inmensam pietatem tuam, ut qui eum tot meritorum donasti prorogatiuis, nos eius et informes exemplis, et adiuues meritis. Per christum.

1864 AD COMPLENDVM. Praesta quaesumus omnipotens aeterne deus, ut id quod de sancto altari tuo accepimus, praecibus beati euangelistae tui lucae sanctificet animas nostras, per quod tuti esse possimus. Per.

CCCXXXI
DOMINICA XXIII POST PENTECOSTEN

1865 Omnipotens et misaericors deus, uniuersa nobis aduersantia propitiatus exclude, ut mente et corpore pariter expediti, quae tua sunt liberis mentibus exequamur. Per.

/f. 224r **1866** SVPER OBLATA. / Haec munera quaesumus domine quae oculis tuae maiestatis offerimus, salutaria nobis esse concede. Per.

1867 PRAEFATIO. VD aeterne deus. Qui propterea iure punis errantes, et clementer refoues castigatos, ut nos a malis operibus abstrahas, et ad bona facienda conuertas. Quia non uis inuenire quod dampnes, sed esse potius quod corones. Qui cum pro nostris meritis, iugiter mereamur affligi, tu tamen iudicium ad correctionem temperas, non perpetuam exerces ad poenam. Iuste enim corrigis, et clementer ignoscis. In utroque uerax, in utroque misaericors. Qui nos ea lege disponis, ut cohercendo in aeternum perire non sinas, et parcendo spatium tribuas corrigendi. Qui ideo malis praesentibus nos flagellas, ut ad bona futura perducas. Ideo bonis temporalibus consolaris, ut de sempiternis facias certiores. Quo te et in prosperis et in aduersis, pia semper confessione laudemus. Per christum.

1868 BENEDICTIO. Dirigat uos dominus in omni opere bono, et pax christi quae praecellit omnem sensum, corpora uestra pariter custodire dignetur et corda. AMEN.

Illuminet oculos uestros ad agnitionem ueritatis suae, et in quacumque die inuocaueritis eum, propitius uobis adesse dignetur, et omnia quaecumque ab eo petieritis impetretis. AMEN.

/f. 224v / Omnes uos spiritalium uirtutum munere locupletet, uosque in fide firmet, in temptatione erigat, in conuersatione custodiat, in uirtute multiplicet. AMEN.

Quod ipse.

1869 AD COMPLENDVM. Tua nos domine medicinalis operatio, et a nostris peruersitatibus clementer expediat, et tuis faciat semper inhęrere mandatis. per.

358

CCCXXXII
VI KL NOV. VIGILIA APOSTOLORVM SYMONIS ET IVDAE

1870 Concede quaesumus omnipotens deus, ut sicut apostolorum tuorum symonis et iudae gloriosa natalicia praeuenimus, sic ad tua beneficia promerenda, maiestatem tuam nobis ipsi proueniant. Per.

1871 SVPER OBLATA. Muneribus nostris domine apostolorum symonis et iudae festa praecedimus, ut quae conscientiae nostrae praepediuntur obstaculis, illorum meritis tibi[1] grata reddantur. per.

1872 PRAEFATIO. VD aeterne deus. Quia tu es mirabilis in omnibus sanctis tuis, quos et nominis tui confessione praeclaros, et suscepta pro te fecisti passione gloriosos. Vnde quas ut sicut illi ieiunando, orandoque certauerunt, ut hanc possent obtinere uictoriam, ita nos eorum exemplis informemur, ut ad caelebranda praesentia festa idonei inueniamur, et ad aeterna percipienda eorum interuentu digni iudicemur. Per christum.

1873 AD COMPLENDVM. Sumpto domine sacramento suppliciter depraecamur, / ut intercedentibus beatis apostolis symone et iuda[2], quod temporaliter gerimus, ad uitam capiamus aeternam. Per dominum.

f. 225r

CCCXXXIII
V KL NOV. NATALE IPSORVM

1874 Deus qui nos per beatos apostolos tuos symonem et iudam[3], ad cognitionem tui nominis uenire tribuisti, da nobis eorum gloriam sempiternam, et proficiendo caelebrare, et caelebrando proficere. Per.

1875 SVPER OBLATA. Gloriam domine sanctorum apostolorum perpetuam praecurrentes, quaesumus ut eandem[4] sacris mysteriis expiati, dignius celebremus. Per.

---

[1] Supplied interlinearly.
[2] *symone et iuda* supplied interlinearly.
[3] Supplied interlinearly.
[4] *eadem* before correction.

1876 PRAEFATIO. VD aeterne deus. Te in tuorum apostolorum glorificantes honore, qui et illis tribuisti beatitudinem sempiternam, et infirmitati nostrae talia praestitisti suffragia, per quę tua possimus adipisci subsidia, et peruenire ad praemia repromissa. Per christum.

1877 AD COMPLENDVM. Perceptis domine sacramentis suppliciter te rogamus, ut intercedentibus beatis apostolis tuis, quae pro illorum ueneranda gerimus passione, nobis proficiant ad medelam. per.

1878 ALIAE ORATIONES. Exaudi nos deus salutaris noster, et apostolorum tuorum tuere praesidiis, quorum donasti fideles esse doctrinis. Per.

1879 ALIA. Omnipotens sempiterne deus mundi creator et rector, qui beatos apostolos nominis tui[1] gloria consecrasti, exaudi populum tuum cum sanctorum tuorum tibi patro/cinio supplicantem, ut pacis dono[2] proficiat ad fidei et caritatis augmentum. Per dominum.

/f. 225v

CCCXXXIIII
II KL NOVB. VIGILIA OMNIVM SANCTORVM

1880 Domine deus noster multiplica super nos gratiam tuam, et quorum praeuenimus gloriosa sollemnia, tribuae subsequi in sancta professione laetitiam. Per.

1881 SVPER OBLATA. Altare tuum domine deus muneribus cumulamus oblatis, da quaesumus ut ad salutem nostram omnium sanctorum tuorum praecatione proficiant, quorum sollemnia uentura praecurrimus. Per.

1882 PRAEFATIO. VD aeterne deus. Reuerentia tuae dicato ieiunio gratulantes. Quia ueneranda omnium sanctorum sollemnia desideratis praeuenimus officiis, ut ad eadem[3] caelebranda sollemniter praeparemur. Per christum.

---

[1] Supplied interlinearly.
[2] After correction.
[3] *eandem* before correction.

1883 AD COMPLENDVM. Sacramentis domine et gaudiis optata celebritate expletis, quaesumus ut eorum precibus adiuuemur, quorum recordationibus exhibentur. Per.

1884 SVPER POPVLVM. Erudi quaesumus domine populum tuum spiritalibus instrumentis, et quorum praestas sollemnia praeuenire, fac eos et consideratione deuotum, et defensione securum. Per dominum.

CCCXXXV
KL NOVBR. NATALE OMNIVM SANCTORVM

1885 Omnipotens sempiterne deus qui nos omnium sanctorum merita sub una tribuisti celebritate uenerari, quaesumus ut desideratam nobis tuae propitiationis / abundantiam, multiplicatis intercessoribus[1] largiaris. Per dominum.

226r

1886 SVPER OBLATA. Munera tibi domine nostrae deuotionis offerimus, quae et pro cunctorum tibi grata sint honore iustorum, et nobis salutaria te miserante reddantur. Per.

1887 PRAEFATIO. [2]VD aeterne deus. Clementiam tuam suppliciter obsecrantes, ut cum exultantibus sanctis tuis[3], in caelestis regni cubilibus gaudia nostra coniungas. Et quos uirtutis imitatione non possumus sequi, debitae uenerationis contigamus affectu. Per christum.

1888 BENEDICTIO. Respice domine quaesumus de alto throno magnitudinis tuę, qui uulnere propriae passionis congregasti ęcclesiam de redemptis, protege eam sub tui nominis gubernaculo, ut possit[4] beatae uitae meritis adquirere populum. AMEN.

Dilatetur cruce tua, ut coram te pulcherrima niteat praeclara, et quae de hodierna omnium sanctorum tuorum sollempnitate persultat, ab huius sęculi temptamentis impressa non obruat. AMEN.

---

[1] After correction.
[2] Partly neumed.
[3] Supplied interlinearly.
[4] *possis* after correction.

Praesta ergo domine ut omnes hi[1] qui sub oris nostri benedictione curuantur, te protegente a malis omnibus liberentur, et sint in tuis praeceptis strenui, in aduersis firmi, in prosperis moderati, ut sanctorum omnium quorum hodie sollemnia festa celebramus effecti participes, / gloriam consequantur regni caelestis heredes. AMEN.
Quod ipse praestare.

/f. 226v

1889 AD COMPLENDVM. Da quaesumus domine fidelibus populis omnium sanctorum, semper ueneratione laetari, et eorum perpetua supplicatione muniri. Per.

1890 ALIAE ORATIONES. Omnipotens sempiterne deus qui nos omnium sanctorum tuorum multiplici facis celebritate gaudere, concede quaesumus ut sicut illorum commemoratione temporali gratulamur officio, ita perpetuo laetemur aspectu. Per.

CCCXXXVI
EODEM DIE NATALE SANCTI CAESARII MARTYRIS
1891 COLLECTA AD SANCTOS COSMAM ET DAMIANVM. Adesto domine martyrum depraectione sanctorum, et quos pati pro tuo nomine tribuisti, fac tuis fidelibus suffragari. Per.

1892 AD MISSAM. Deus qui nos beati martyris tui caesarii annua sollemnitate laetificas, concede propitius ut cuius natalicia colimus, etiam actiones imitemur. Per.

1893 SVPER OBLATA. Hostias tibi domine beati caesarii martyris tui dicatas meritis benignus adsume, et ad perpetuum nobis tribue prouenire subsidium. Per.

1894 AD COMPLENDVM. Quaesumus omnipotens deus ut qui caelestia alimenta percepimus, intercedente beato[2] caesario martyre tuo, per haec contra omnia aduersa muniamur. Per dominum.

---

[1] *his* before correction.
[2] Rewritten.

362

CCCXXXVII
DOMINICA XXIIII POST PENTECOSTEN

227r **1895** / Largire quaesumus domine fidelibus tuis indulgentiam placatus et pacem, ut pariter ab omnibus mundentur offensis, et secura tibi mente deseruiant. Per.

1896 SVPER OBLATA. Caelestem nobis praebeant haec mysteria quaesumus domine medicinam, et uitia nostri cordis expurgent. Per.

1897 PRAEFATIO. VD aeterne deus. Et nos clementiam tuam suppliciter exorare, ut filius tuus iesus christus dominus noster, qui se usque in finem sęculi suis promisit fidelibus adfuturum, et praesentiae corporalis mysteriis non deserat quos redemit, et maiestatis tuae beneficiis non relinquat[1]. Per quem.

1898 BENEDICTIO. Benedicat uos dominus caelorum, rector humani generis conditor, et det uobis tranquillitatem temporum, sobrietatem actuum, salutemque animarum. AMEN.
Det uobis fragilitate gaudium, aeternitatis praemium, lumen clarissimum sempiternum. AMEN.
Benedic domine huic familiae christi sanguine comparatę, et gratiam benedictionis tuae consequi mereatur in corde. AMEN.
Sine ulla offensione maiestati tuae dignum exhibeant famulatum, sine ullis maculis impleant uitae suae cursum, et superent in bonis actibus inimicum. AMEN.
Quod ipse praestare.

227v **1899** AD COMPLENDVM. / Vt sacris domine reddamur digni muneribus, fac nos quaesumus tuis oboedire mandatis. Per.

CCCXXXVIII
VI ID NOV. NATALE SANCTORVM QVATTVOR CORONATORVM

1900 Praesta quaesumus omnipotens deus, ut qui gloriosos martyres claudium, nicostratum, simphorianum, castorium atque

---

[1] *reliquit* before correction.

363

symplicium[1], fortes in sua confessione cognouimus, pios apud te in nostra intercessione sentiamus. Per.

1901 SVPER OBLATA. Benedictio domine tua larga descendat, quae et munera nostra depraecantibus sanctis tuis tibi reddat accepta, et nobis sacramentum redemptionis efficiat. Per dominum.

1902 PRAEFATIO. VD aeterne deus. Celebrantes sanctorum natalicia coronatorum, quia dum tui nominis per eos gloriam frequentamus, in nostrae fidei augmentum succrescimus. Per.

1903 AD COMPLENDVM. Caelestibus refecti sacramentis et gaudiis, supplices te domine depraecamur, ut quorum gloriamur triumphis, protegamur auxiliis. Per dominum.

CCCXXXVIIII
V IDVS NOV. NATALE SANCTI THEODORI MARTYRIS

1904 Deus qui nos beati theodori martyris tui confessione gloriosa circumdas et protegis, praesta nobis eius imitatione proficere, et oratione fulciri. Per dominum.

1905 SVPER OBLATA. Suscipe domine fidelium praeces cum
/f. 228r   oblationibus / hostiarum, et intercedente beato theodoro martyre tuo, per haec piae deuotionis officia, ad caelestem gloriam transeamus. Per.

1906 AD COMPLENDVM. Praesta nobis domine quaesumus intercedente beato theodoro martyre tuo, ut quae ore contigimus, pura mente capiamus. Per dominum nostrum.

CCCXL
DOMINICA XXV POST PENTECOSTEN

1907 Familiam tuam quaesumus domine continua pietate custodi, ut a cunctis aduersitatibus te protegente sit libera, et in bonis actibus tuo nomini sit deuota. Per.

1908 SVPER OBLATA. Suscipe domine propitius hostias, quibus et te placari uoluisti, et nobis salutem potenti pietate restitui. Per.

---

[1] The names *seuerianum, seuerianum, carpophorum, uictorinum* supplied interlinearly.

1909 PRAEFATIO. VD aeterne deus. Maiestatem tuam suppliciter depraecantes, ut expulsis azimis uetustatis, illius agni cibo[1] satiemur et poculo, qui et nostram im[2] imaginem reparauit, et suam nobis gratiam repromisit, iesus christus dominus noster. Per quem.

1910 BENEDICTIO. Benedic domine populum tuum, et deuotum respice, humilitatem uide, gemitus suscipe, dolentes paterna pietate iube consolari. AMEN.
Prostratum alleua, dispersum congrega, adunatum conserua, esurientem cyba, sitientem pota, omnesque simul caelestibus donis irriga, dele in eis omnem peccati maculam, ut te gubernante / ad gloriam peruentiant sempiternam. AMEN.
Humiliata tibi omnium capita, dexterae tuae benedictione sanctifica, ac benedicendo peccata relaxa, sanctique spiritus infunde carismata, ut sine ulla offensione maiestatis tuae praecepta adimpleant, et ad uitam aeternam te auxiliante peruentiant. AMEN.
Quod ipse praestare.

228v

1911 AD COMPLENDVM. Inmortalitatis alimoniam consecuti quaesumus domine, ut quod ore percepimus, mente sectemur. Per.

CCCXLI
III IDVS NOV. NATALE SANCTI MENE MARTYRIS

1912 Praesta quaesumus omnipotens deus, ut qui beati menę[3] martyris tui natalicia colimus, intercessione eius in tui nominis amore roboremur. Per.

1913 SVPER OBLATA. Muneribus nostris quaesumus domine praecibusque susceptis, et caelestibus nos munda mysteriis, et clementer exaudi. Per dominum.

1914 AD COMPLENDVM. Da quaesumus domine deus noster, ut sicut tuorum commemoratione sanctorum, temporali gratulamur officio, ita perpetuo laetemur aspectu. Per dominum.

---

[1] *cibi* before correction.
[2] Marked for omission.
[3] Rewritten.

CCCXLII
EODEM DIE NATALE SANCTI MARTINI EPISCOPI ET CONFESSORIS

1915 Deus qui conspicis quia ex nulla nostra uirtute substitimus, concede propitius, ut intercessione beati martini confessoris tui contra omnia aduersa muniamur. Per dominum nostrum iesum christum.

/f. 229r **1916** SVPER OBLATA. / Da misęricors deus, ut haec nos salutaris oblatio, et propriis reatibus indesinenter expediat, et ab omnibus tueatur aduersis. Per.

1917 PRAEFATIO. VD aeterne deus. Cuius munere beatus martinus confessor pariter et sacerdos, et bonorum operum incrementis excreuit, et uariis uirtutum donis exuberauit, et miraculis choruscauit. Qui quod uerbis edocuit, operum exhibitione compleuit. Et documento simul et exemplo, subditis ad caelestia regna pergendi ducatum praebuit. Vnde tuam clementiam petimus, ut eius qui tibi placuit exemplis ad bene agendum informemur, meritis muniamur, intercessionibus adiuuemur, qualiter ad caeleste regnum illo interueniente, ac[1] te opitulante peruenire mereamur. Per christum dominum nostrum.

1918 BENEDICTIO. Omnipotens deus, qui beatum martinum praesulem tuum ita praedestinasti, ut gratiae tuae perenniter iuberes adstringi, erige uota populi tui praestitisti gloriosa merita tuo confessori. AMEN.
Proficiat his ad fructum, quicquid in sacerdote pro laude tui nominis amplectuntur, et haec plebs eius intercessione consequatur ueniam, qui te remunerante felici seruitio peruenit ad gloriam. AMEN.
/f. 229v Sit ipse confessor huius / populi assiduus custos, qui te uocante hodie penetrauit caelos. AMEN.
Quod ipse.

1919 AD COMPLENDVM. Praesta quaesumus domine deus noster, ut quorum festiuitate uotiua sunt sacramenta, eorum salutaria nobis intercessione reddantur. Per dominum.

---

[1] Supplied interlinearly.

1920 ALIA. Exaudi domine populum tuum tota tibi mente subiectum, et beati martini pontificis supplicatione custodi, ut corde et corpore protectus, quod pie credit appetat, et quod iuste sperat obtineat. Per.

1921 ALIA. Praesta quaesumus omnipotens deus, ut sicut diuina laudamus in sancti martini confessoris tui atque pontificis sollemnitate magnalia, sic indulgentiam tuam piis eius praecibus assequamur. Per dominum.

CCCXLIII
DOMINICA XXVI POST PENTECOSTEN

1922 Deus refugium nostrum et uirtus, adesto piis ecclesiae tuae praecibus auctor ipse pietatis, et praesta ut quod fideliter petimus, efficaciter consequamur. Per dominum.

1923 SVPER OBLATA. Da misaericors deus, ut haec salutaris oblatio, et a propriis nos reatibus indesinenter expediat, et ab omnibus tueatur aduersis. Per.

1924 PRAEFATIO. VD per christum dominum nostrum. Per quem sanctum et benedictum nomen tuum maiestatis tuae ubique ueneratur, adoratur, praedicatur et colitur. Qui est origo salutis, uia uirtutis, et tuae pro/pitiatio maiestatis. Per quem.

1925 BENEDICTIO. Benedicat uos pater domini nostri iesu christi, et respectu misaericordiae caelestis, protegat uos sub umbra uirtutis. AMEN.
Detque uobis animarum compunctionem, immaculatam fidem, conscientię puritatem, sensus uestros dirigat, corda compungat, in prosperis assistat, in aduersis manum porrigat, in laboribus solatium ferat. AMEN.
Virtutum suarum merita multiplicet, recta consilia aduocet, terrenarum rerum a uobis pondera auferat. AMEN.
Repleat corda uestra spiritalibus donis, et abundare faciat semper perfectę incrementis. AMEN.
Quod ipse praestare.

1926 AD COMPLENDVM. Sumpsimus domine sacri dona mysterii humiliter depraecantes, ut quae in tui commemoratione nos facere praecepisti, in nostrae proficiant infirmitatis auxilium. Per dominum.

CCCXLIIII
XI KL DECBR. VIGILIA SANCTAE CAECILIAE VIRGINIS

1927 Sanctae martyris tuae caeciliae quaesumus domine supplicationibus tribue nos fouere, ut cuius uenerabilem sollemnitatem praeuenimus obsequio, eius intercessionibus commendetur et meritis. Per.

1928 SVPER OBLATA. Muneribus nostris domine sanctae caeciliae martyris tuae festa praecedimus, ut qui conscientiae nostrae praepedimur obstaculis, illius meritis reddantur / accepta. Per dominum nostrum.

/f. 230v

1929 PRAEFATIO. VD aeterne deus. Et beatae caeciliae natalitia praeueniendo, laudare, praedicare, et benedicere. Quam tanto munere sublimasti, ut ei conferres et uirginitatis coronam, et martyrii palmam. Sicque uirtute fidei, et decore pudicitiae polleret, ut caelestia regna uirgo pariter et martyr intraret. Per christum.

1930 AD COMPLENDVM. Quaesumus omnipotens deus, ut quorum nos tribuis communicare memoriis, eorum facias imitatores. Per.

CCCXLV
X KL DECBR. NATALE SANCTAE CAECILIAE

1931 Deus qui nos annua beatae caeciliae martyris tuae sollemnitate laetificas, da ut quam ueneramur officio, etiam pię conuersationis sequamur exemplo. Per.

1932 SVPER OBLATA. Haec hostia domine placationis et laudis, quaesumus ut interueniente beata caecilia martyre tua, propitiatione dignos semper efficiat. Per.

1933 PRAEFATIO. VD aeterne deus. Qui infirmitate uirtutum perficis, et humani generis inimicum, non solum per uiros, sed etiam per feminas uincis. Cuius munerae beata caecilia, et uirginitatis proposito et confessione fidei roboratur, ut nec aetatis lubrico ab intentione mutetur. Nec blandimentis

368

213r carnalibus demulceatur, / nec sexus fragilitate deterreatur, nec tormentorum inmanitate uincatur. Sed seruando corporis ac mentis integritatem, cum uirginitatis et martyrii palma aeternam mereretur adipisci beatitudinem. Per christum.

1934 BENEDICTIO. Sanctae trinitatis super uos descendat benedictio gratissima, qui beatae caeciliae uirginis martyrisque suae festum caelebritatis mente deuotiossima. AMEN.

Illius mereamini suffragiis fulciri, eiusque auxilio roborari, quae nec saeuitia torquentium frangi, nec inmanissima tormentorum crudelitate a gloriosissima christi confessione potuit auerti. AMEN.

Et qui eam superato diuersorum tormentorum genere caelestem ad gloriam fecit cum triumpho scandere, ipse uobis concedat uigore fidei uitiorum contagia pellere, et cum electis omnibus indui inmarcessibilis corona gloriae. AMEN.

Quod ipse.

1935 AD COMPLENDVM. Satiasti domine familiam tuam muneribus sacris, eius quaesumus semper intercessione nos refoue, cuius sollemnia caelebramus. Per.

1936 ALIA. Deus cui beata caecilia ita castitatis deuotione compleuit, ut coniugem suum ualerianum, ad finemque suum tyburtium tibi 231v faceret consecrare. Nam et angelo deferente / micantium odiferas florum coronas, palmamque martyrii perceperunt, quaesumus ut ea intercedente pro nobis, beneficia tui muneris percipere mereamur. Per.

CCCXLVI

VIII KL DECB. NATALE SANCTI CLEMENTIS

1937 Deus qui nos annua beati clementis martyris tui atque pontificis sollemnitate laetificas, concede propitius ut cuius natalicia colimus, uirtutem quoque passionis imitemur. Per.

1938 SVPER OBLATA. Munera domine oblata sanctifica, et intercedente beato clemente martyre tuo, per haec nos a peccatorum nostrorum maculis emunda. Per.

1939 PRAEFATIO. VD aeterne deus. Et in hac die quam beati clementis passio consecrauit, et nobis uenerabilem exhibuit. Qui apostolica praedicatione inbutus, doctrinis caelestibus aeducatus, successionis dignitate conspicuus, et martyr insignis, et sacerdos refulsit egregius. Per christum.

1940 BENEDICTIO. Omnipotens deus uestrorum cordium archana purificet, et benedictionis suae uobis tribuat incrementa, qui hodierna die sancti clementis festiuitatem deuotae uobis concedit celebrare. AMEN.
Ab omnibus eius intercessionibus uitae praesentis periculis exuamini, et uirtutum spiritalium ornamentis induamini. AMEN.
Quo illius adiutorio fulti, sic domino seruiatis in terris, ut ei
/f. 232r   coniungi / ualeatis in caelis. AMEN.
Quod ipse.

1941 AD COMPLENDVM. Corporis sacri et praetiosi sanguinis repleti libamine quaesumus domine deus noster, ut quod pia deuotione gerimus, certa redemptione capiamus. Per dominum.

CCCXLVII
EODEM DIE NATALE SANCTAE FELICITATIS

1942 Praesta quaesumus omnipotens deus, ut beatae felicitatis martyris tuae sollemnia recensentes, meritis ipsius protegamur et praecibus. Per.

1943 SVPER OBLATA. Vota populi tui domine propitiatus intende, et quorum nos tribuis sollemnia celebrare, fac gaudere suffragiis. Per dominum.

1944 AD COMPLENDVM. Supplices te rogamus omnipotens deus, ut interuenientibus sanctis tuis, et tua in nobis dona multiplices, et tempora nostra disponas. Per dominum.

CCCXLVIII
VIII KL DECB. NATALE SANCTI GHRISOGONI[1]
MARTYRIS

1945 Adesto domine supplicationibus nostris, ut qui ex iniquitate nostra reos nos esse cognoscimus, beati chrisogoni martyris tui intercessione liberemur. Per dominum.

1946 SVPER OBLATA. Oblatis domine placare muneribus, et intercedente beato chrisogono martyre tuo, a cunctis nos defende periculis. Per.

1947 PRAEFATIO. VD aeterne deus. Qui nos assiduis martyrum passionibus consolaris, et eorum sanguinem triumphalem, quem professione nominis tui infi/delibus praebuere fundendum, ad tuorum facis auxilium transire fidelium. Per christum.

. 232v

1948 BENEDICTIO. Omnipotens deus deuotionem uestram placatus semper accipiat, et interueniente beato chrisogono martyre suo[2] quaecumque ab eo postulaueritis clementer concedat, et praemia aeterna non deneget. AMEN.
Auferat a uobis omnia mala quae gessistis, eiusque intercessione tribuat omnia bona quae ab eo deposcitis. AMEN.
Sitis semper in hoc saeculo benedicti, et ab omni malo maneatis illesi, ut ab ipso in iudicio mereamini benedici. AMEN.
Quod ipse.

1949 AD COMPLENDVM. Tui domine perceptione sacramenti, et a nostris mundemur occultis, et ab hostium liberemur insidiis. Per.

CCCXLVIIIII
DOMINICA XXVII POST PENTECOSTEN

1950 Excita domine quaesumus tuorum fidelium uoluntates, ut diuini operis fructum propensius exequentes, pietatis tuae remedia maiora percipiant. Per.

1951 SVPER OBLATA. Propitius esto domine supplicationibus nostris, et populi tui oblationibus praecibusque susceptis,

---

[1]   *H* supplied interlinearly.
[2]   *tuo* before correction.

omnium nostrorum ad te corda conuerte, ut a terrenis cupiditatibus liberi, ad caelestia desideria transeamus. Per dominum.

1952 PRAEFATIO. VD aeterne deus. Et tibi debitas laudes pio honore deferre, et mirabilium tuorum inaennarrabilia praeconia deuotę /f. 233r mentis ueneratione cae/lebrare. Teque ineffabilem, atque inuisibilem deum laudare, benedicere, adorare. Per christum.

1953 BENEDICTIO. Deus inuisibilis inaestimabilis, infinite perennis, immense auctor noster, redemptor noster, et principii in natura, alienus exterminii, tu celebrem populi huius conuentum, tamquam proprii sanguinis pignus illustra. AMEN.
Rege sensus canos uiduarum, sollicitudines uirginum, uota nuptiarum, desideria pupillorum, necessitates puerorum, lapsus infantium paruulorum. AMEN.
Quoniam tu es bonorum sensuum requies, felicium iuuenum custos, sanctarum uirginum sponsus, fidelium uiduarum defensor, honestorum coniugum fides, pupillorum laborantium, pater puerorum, proficientium doctor, infantium et susceptor pariter et nutritor. AMEN.
In te senecta aetas initiet, adulta corroboret, longeua consummet, per te gaudeat integritas non corrumpi, per te sciat castitas reparari, fides pura non destrui, uita displicens emendari, misaericordia fieri, continentia seruari, innocentia non aeuinci. AMEN.
Quod ipse praestare.

1954 AD COMPLENDVM. Concede nobis domine quaesumus ut sacramenta quae sumpsimus, quicquid in nostra mente uitiosum est, ipsius medicationis dono curetur. Per dominum.

/f. 233v <center>/ CCCL</center>
III KL DECB. NATALE SANCTI SATVRNINI MARTYRIS
1955 Deus qui nos beati saturnini martyris tui concedis natalicio perfrui, eius nos tribue meritis adiuuari. Per dominum.

1956 SVPER OBLATA. Munera domine tibi dicata sanctificata, et intercedente beato saturnino martyre tuo, per eadem nos placatus intende. Per dominum.

372

1957 PRAEFATIO. VD per christum dominum nostrum. Cuius gratia beatum saturninum in sacerdotium elegit doctrina ad praedicandum erudiit potentia, ad perseuerandum confirmauit, ut per sacerdotalem insulam, perueniret ad martyrii palmam. Docensque subditos praedicando, instruens uiuendi exemplo, confirmans patiendo, ut ad te coronandus perueniret, qui persecutorum minas intrepidus superasset. Cuius interuentus nos quaesumus a nostris mundet delictis, qui tibi placuit tot donorum praerogatiuis. Per quem.

1958 AD COMPLENDVM. Sanctificet nos domine quaesumus tui perceptio sacramenti, et intercessione sanctorum tibi reddat acceptos. Per.

CCCLI

EODEM DIE VIGILIA SANCTI ANDREAE APOSTOLI

1959 Quaesumus omnipotens deus, ut beatus andreas apostolus tuum pro nobis imploret auxilium, ut a nostris reatibus absoluti, a cunctis etiam periculis exuamur. Per dominum.

234r **1960** SVPER OBLATA. / Sacrificandum tibi domine munus offerimus, quo beati andreae sollemnia recolentes, purificationem quoque nostris mentibus imploramus. Per dominum.

1961 PRAEFATIO. VD aeterne deus. Et maiestatem tuam suppliciter exorare, ut qui beati andreae apostoli festum sollemnibus ieiuniis, et deuotis praeuenimus officiis, illius apud maiestatem tuam, et adiuuemur meritis et instruamur exemplis. Per christum dominum nostrum.

1962 BENEDICTIO. Omnipotens deus sua uos locupletet benedictione, qui beatum andream sublimauit praeconio dignitatis apostolice. AMEN.
Concedatque uobis ipsum habere intercessorem in caelis, cuius deuote praeuenitis in terra diem sollemnitatis. AMEN.
Ipsius quoque interuentu quaeatis scandere alta caelorum, quo praecessit idem per crucis passionem sequendo, dominum ac magistrum. AMEN.
Quod ipse.

1963 AD COMPLENDVM. Perceptis domine sacramentis suppliciter exoramus, ut intercedente beato andrea apostolo tuo, quae pro illius ueneranda gerimus passione, nobis proficiant ad medelam. Per.

CCCLII
II KL DECB. NATALE SANCTI ANDREAE

1964 Maiestatem tuam domine suppliciter exoramus, ut sicut ecclesiae tuae beatus andreas apostolus, / extitit praedicator et rector, ita apud te sit pro nobis perpetuus intercessor. Per.

/f. 234v

1965 SVPER OBLATA. Sacrificium nostrum tibi domine quaesumus beati andreae precatio sancta conciliet, ut cuius honore sollemniter exhibetur, meritis efficiatur acceptum. Per.

1966 PRAEFATIO. [1]VD aeterne deus. Quoniam adest nobis dies magnifici uotiua mysterii, qua uenerandus andreas apostolus germanum se gloriosi apostoli tui petri, tam praedicatione christi tui, quam conuersatione monstrauit. Vt id quod libera praedicauerat uoce, nec pendens taceret in cruce. Auctoremque uitae perennis, tam in hac uita sequi, quam in mortis genere meruit imitari. Vt cuius praecepto terrena in semetipso crucifixerat desideria, eius exemplo ipse patibulo figeretur. Vtrique igitur germani piscatores, ambo cruce eleuantur ad caelum. Vt quos in huius uitae cursum gratia tua, tot uinculis pietatis obstrinxerat, hos inmarcessibilis[2] in regno caelorum necteret et corona. Et quibus erat una causa certaminis, una retributio esset et praemii. Per christum.

1967 BENEDICTIO. Deus qui beatum andream apostolum per passionem crucis ad etherias euexit sedes, ipse uobis tribuat eiusdem uestigia sequi per sanctas / uirtutes. AMEN.
Vt quem peculiarem meruistis obtinere patronum, ad caelestem ipso intercedente ualeatis feliciter pertingere regnum. AMEN.
Eundemque mereamini uidere in caelis regnante, cuius gratulantes caelebratis sollemnissimum diem. AMEN.
Quod ipse.

/f. 235r

[1] Partly neumed.
[2] *inmarcessibiles* before correction.

374

1968 ¹AD COMPLENDVM. Sumpsimus domine diuina mysteria beati andreae festiuitate laetantes, quae sicut tuis sanctis ad gloriam, ita nobis quaesumus ad ueniam prodesse perficias. Per.

1969 AD VESPERAS. Da nobis quaesumus domine deus noster beati apostoli tui andreae intercessionibus subleuari, ut per quos ecclesiae tuae superni muneris rudimenta donasti, per eos subsidia perpetuae salutis impendas. Per dominum nostrum.

1970 ALIA. Aduiuet ecclesiam tuam tibi domine supplicando beatus andreas apostolus, et pius interuentor efficiatur, qui tui nominis extitit praedicator. Per dominum nostrum.

1971 ALIA. Deus qui es sanctorum tuorum splendor mirabilis, qui hunc diem beati andreae martyrio consecrasti, da ecclesiae tuae de eius natalicia semper gaudere, ut apud misaericordiam tuam exemplis eius protegamur et meritis. Per dominum nostrum.

f. 235v **1972** ALIA. / Exaudi domine populum tuum cum sancti apostoli tui andreae patrocinio supplicantem, ut tuo semper auxilio secura tibi possit deuotione seruire. Per.

---

¹ Added in the upper right margin by a Corbie scribe:

VIIII IDVS DEC. NATALE SANCTI NICHOLAI
6* Deus qui beatum nicholaum pontificem tuum innumeris decorasti miraculis, tribue nobis ut eius meritis et praecibus, a gehennę incendiis liberemur. Per.
7* SECRETA. Sanctifica quaesumus domine oblata munera quę in ueneratione sancti antistitis nicholai offeruntur, ut per ea uita nostra inter aduersa ubique dirigatur et prospera. Per.
8* POSTCOMMVNIO. Sacrifica quę sumpsimus domine pro sollempnitate sancti pontificis tui nicholai, sempiterna nos protectione confirment. Per dominum.

CCCLIII
MENSIS DECB. ORATIONES DE ADVENTV DOMINI.
DOMINICA I

1973 [1]Excita domine quaesumus potentiam tuam et ueni, ut ab imminentibus peccatorum nostrorum periculis, te mereamur protegente eripi, te liberante saluari. Qui uiuis.

1974 SVPER OBLATA. Haec sacra nos domine potenti uirtute mundatos, ad suum faciant puriores uenire principium. Per dominum.

1975 PRAEFATIO. VD per christum dominum nostrum. [2]Cuius primi aduentus mysterium, ita nos facias dignis laudibus et officiis caelebrare, praesentemque uitam inculpabilem ducere, ut secundum ualeamus interriti expectare. Per quem.

1976 BENEDICTIO. Omnipotens deus. Cuius unigeniti aduentum et praeteritum creditis, et futurum expectatis, eiusdem aduentus uos inlustratione sua sanctificet, et sua benedictione locupletet. AMEN.

In praesentis uitae stadio uos ab omni aduersitate defendat, et se uobis in iudicio placabilem ostendat. AMEN.

Quo a cunctis peccatorum contagiis liberati, in praesentis uitae curriculo cum sanctis animalibus tanto sessore inueniamini

---

[1] Added in the left margin by a Corbie scribe:

DOMINICA V ANTE NATALE DOMINI
9* Excita domine potentiam tuam et ueni, et quod ecclesiae tuae promisisti, usque in finem sęculi clementer operare. Qui uiuis et regnas.
10* SVPER OBLATA. Sacrificium tibi domine celebrandum placatus intende, quod et nos a uitiis nostrae conditionis emundet, et tuo nomini reddat acceptos. Per.
11* PREFATIO. VD per christum dominum nostrum. Cuius petimus primi aduentus mysterium. Ita nos facias dignis laudibus et officiis celebrare, praesentemque uitam inculpabilem ducere ut secundum ualeamus interriti expectare. Per quem maiestatem.
12* POSTCOMMVNIO. Animę nostrae diuino munere satiatae quaesumus omnipotens deus hoc potiantur desiderio et a tuo spiritu inflammentur, ut ante conspectum uenientis christi filii tui uelut clara luminaria fulgeamur. Per eundem dominum nostrum.

[2] **13*** The cue *Cui proprium est* supplied interlinearly by a Corbie scribe.

digni, et illius tremendi examinis diem / expectetis interriti. AMEN.
Quod ipse.

1977 AD COMPLENDVM. Suscipiamus domine misericordiam tuam in medio templi tui, et reparationis nostrae uentura sollemnia, congruis honoribus praecedamus. Per dominum.

CCCLIIII
IN OCTAVAS SANCTI ANDREAE

1978 Protegat nos domine sepius beati andreae apostoli repetita sollemnitas, ut cuius patrocinia sine intermissione recolimus, perpetuam defensionem sentiamus. Per.

1979 SVPER OBLATA. Indulgentiam tuam nobis praebeant haec munera quaesumus domine largiorem, quae uenerabilis andreae suffragiis offeruntur. Per.

1980 AD COMPLENDVM. Adiuuet familiam tuam tibi domine supplicando uenerandus andreas apostolus, et pius interuentor efficiat, qui tui nominis extitit praedicator. Per.

CCCLV
DOMINICA II DE ADVENTV DOMINI

1981 Excita domine corda nostra ad praeparandas unigeniti tui uias, ut per eius aduentum purificatis tibi mentibus seruire mereamur. Qui tecum.

1982 SVPER OBLATA. Placare quaesumus domine humilitatis nostrae praecibus et hostiis, et ubi nulla suppetunt suffragia meritorum, tuis nobis succurre praesidiis. Per.

1983 PRAEFATIO. VD aeterne deus. [1]Cui proprium est ac singulare quod bonus est, et nulla umquam a te es commutatione diuersus.
Propitiare quaesumus supplica/tionibus nostris, et ecclesiae tuae misericordiam tuam quam depraecatur ostende. Manifestans plebi tuę unigeniti tui et incarnationis mysterium, et aduentus

---

[1] **14*** The cue *Cuius primi aduentus* supplied interlinearly by a Corbie scribe.

mirabile sacramentum. Vt in[1] uniuersitate nationum constet esse perfectum, quod uatum oraculis fuit ante promissum. Percipiantque dignitatem adoptionis, quos exornet confessio ueritatis. Per quem.

1984 BENEDICTIO. Ccuius[2] aduentus incarnationis praeteritus creditur, et iudicii uenturus expectetur, uos antequam ueniat expiet ab omni contagione delicti. AMEN.
Prius in uobis deluat omne quod illa futura examinatione puniturus est, ut cum iustus aduenerit iudex, non in uobis inueniat quod condempnet. AMEN.
Quo ueniente non incurratis supplicium aeternum, sed remuneramini donariis sempiternis. AMEN.
Quod ipse praestare.

1985 AD COMPLENDVM. Repleti cybo spiritalis alimoniae supplices te domine depraecamur, ut huius participatione mysterii, doceas nos terrena despicere, et amare caelestia. Per.

CCCLVI
III ID DECB. NATALE SANCTI DAMASI PAPAE

1986 Misericordiam tuam domine nobis quaesumus interueniente beato confessore tuo damaso clementer impende, et nobis / peccatoribus ipsius, propitiare suffragiis. Per.

/f. 237r

1987 SVPER OBLATA. Da nobis quaesumus domine semper haec tibi uota gratanter persoluere, quibus sancti confessoris tui damasi, depositione recolimus, et praesta ut in eius semper laude tuam gloriam praedicemus. Per.

1988 AD COMPLENDVM. Sumptum domine caelestibus remedii sacramentum, ad perpetuam nobis peruenire gratiam beatus damasus pontifex obtineat. Per.

---

[1] Supplied interlinearly.
[2] Capital and minuscule *c* together.

CCCLVII
IDVS DECB. NATALE SANCTAE LVCIAE VIRGINIS

1989 Exaudi nos deus salutaris noster, ut sicut de beatae luciae festiuitate gaudemus, ita piae deuotionis erudiamur affectu. Per dominum.

1990 SVPER OBLATA. Accepta tibi sit domine sacratae plebis oblatio, pro tuorum honore sanctorum, quorum se meritis percepisse, de tribulatione cognoscit auxilium. Per.

1991 BENEDICTIO. Benedicat uos omnipotens deus, et ad omnem rectę obseruantiae plenitudinem, ut[1] intercedente beatae luciae uirginis, totius honestatis instituat uobis. AMEN.
Sit in uobis castitatis studium, modestia morum, innocentis uitae ingenium, fidei augmentum, concordiae fundamentum, continentia uirtutum, benignitas affectum. AMEN.
Vt consequi cum sanctae luciae martyris premia possitis, et ante deum apparere cum iustitiae palma, et cum illo ualeatis permanere, in / gloria sempiterna. AMEN.
Quod ipse.

f. 237v

1992 AD COMPLENDVM. Satiasti domine familiam tuam muneribus sacris, eius quaesumus semper interuentione nos refoue, cuius sollemnia celebramus. Per dominum nostrum.

CCCLVIII
XII KL IAN. NATALE SANCTI THOMAE APOSTOLI

1993 Da nobis quaesumus domine beati apostoli tui thomae sollemnitatibus gloriari, ut eius semper et patrociniis subleuemur, et fidem congrua deuotione laetemur. Per dominum.

1994 SVPER OBLATA. Debitum domine nostrae reddimus seruitutis, suppliciter exorantes, ut suffragiis beati thomę apostoli, in nobis tua munera tuearis, cuius honoranda confessione laudis tibi hostias immolamus. Per.

---

[1] Marked for omission.

1995 PRAEFATIO. VD aeterne deus. Qui ecclesiam tuam in apostolicis tribuisti consistere fundamentis. De quorum collegio beati thomae apostoli tui sollemnia caelebrantes, tua domine praeconia non tacemus. Et ideo.

1996 BENEDICTIO. Aperi domine ianuas caeli, et uisita plebem tuam in pace, emitte spiritum tuum de alto, et irriga terram nostram, ut germinet nobis spiritualem fructum. AMEN.
Sanctifica domine plebem tuam qui datus es nobis ex uirgine, et benedic hereditatem tuam in pace. AMEN.
Praesta eis semper tempora salutis, quae ante tuum aduentum
/f. 238r   prę/dixit sanctus propheta iohannes, ut hic fideliter accipiant, et in futuro cum sanctis et electis tuis uitam et regnum consequantur aeternum. AMEN.
Quod ipse praestare dignetur.

1997 AD COMPLENDVM. Conserua domine populum tuum et quem sanctorum tuorum praesidiis non desinis adiuuare, perpetuis tribue gaudere remediis. Per.

CCCLVIIII
DOMINICA III AD SANCTVM PETRVM

1998 Aurem tuam quaesumus domine pręcibus nostris accommoda, et mentis nostrae tenebras gratia tuae uisitationis inlustra. Qui uiuis.

1999 SVPER OBLATA. Deuotionis nostrae tibi quaesumus domine hostia iugiter immoletur, quae et sacri peragat instituta mysterii, et salutare tuum nobis mirabiliter operetur. Per.

2000 PRAEFATIO. VD aeterne deus. Qui tuo inenarrabili munerę praestitisti, ut natura humana ad similitudinem tui condita, dissimilis per peccatum et mortem effecta, nequaquam in aeterna dampnatione periret. Sed unde peccatum mortem contraxerat. Inde uitam tua[1] pietas inmensa repararet. Et antique uirginis facinus, noua et intemerata uirgo maria piaret. Quae ab angelo salutata, ab spiritu sancto obumbrata, illum gignere
/f. 238v   meruit, qui / cuncta nasci suo nutu concessit. Quae mirabatur et

---

[1]   *tuam* before correction.

corporis integritatem, et conceptus fecunditatem. Gaudebatque suum paritura parentem, iesum christum dominum nostrum. Per quem.

2001 BENEDICTIO. Omnipotens deus uos placito uultu respiciat, et in uos suae benedictionis donum infundat. AMEN.
Et qui hos dies incarnationis unigeniti sui fecit sollemnes, a cunctis praesentis et futurae uitae aduersitatibus uos reddat indempnes. AMEN.
Vt qui de aduentu redemptoris nostri secundum carnem deuota mente laetamini, in saeculo cum maiestate sua uenerit, praemiis uitae aeternae ditemini. AMEN.
Quod ipse praestare.

2002 AD COMPLENDVM. Imploramus domine clementiam tuam, ut haec diuina subsidia a uitiis expiatos, ad festa uentura nos praeparent. Per dominum nostrum.

CCCLX
FERIA IIII AD SANCTAM MARIAM MAIOREM

2003 Praesta quaesumus omnipotens deus, ut redemptionis nostrae uentura sollemnitas, et praesentis nobis uitae subsidia conferat, et aeternae beatitudinis praemia largiatur. Per dominum nostrum.

2004 ALIA. Festina quaesumus domine ne tardaueris, et auxilium nobis supernae uirtutis impende, ut aduentus tui consolationibus subleuentur, qui in tua pietate confidunt. Qui uiuis.

f. 239r **2005** SVPER OBLATA. / Accepta tibi sint domine quaesumus nostra ieiunia, quae et expiando nos tua gratia dignos efficiant, et ad sempiterna promissa perducant. Per.

2006 PRAEFATIO. VD per christum dominum nostrum. Quem pro salute hominum nasciturum gabrihel archangelus nuntiauit, uirgo maria spiritus sancti cooperatione concepit. Vt quod angelica nuntiauit sublimitas, uirginea crederet puritas, ineffabilis perficeret deitatis. Illius itaque obtamus te opitulante cernere faciem sine confusione, cuius incarnationis gaudemus sollemnitate. Quatinus purificati ieiuniis, cuncti purgati a uitiis natalis eius interesse mereamur sollemnibus festis. Per quem.

2007 BENEDICTIO. Deus qui es custos animarum et corporum, hanc familiam dignare brachii tui defensione protegere. AMEN.
Vt nullis antiqui hostis insidiis, corpora nostra fraude sua patiatur inludi, sed semper cum domino nostro iesu christo filio tuo maneamus inlaesi. AMEN.
Da huic familiae tuae fidei calorem, continentiae rigorem, fraternitatis amorem, abstinentiae uirtutem. AMEN.
Quod ipse.

2008 AD COMPLENDVM. Salutaris tui domine munere satiati supplices depraecamur, ut cuius laetamur gustu, reno/uemur effectu. Per dominum nostrum.

/f. 239v

CCCLXI
FERIA VI AD APOSTOLOS

2009 Excita quaesumus domine potentiam tuam et ueni, ut hi qui in tua pietate confidunt, ab omni citius aduersitate liberentur. Qui uiuis.

2010 SVPER OBLATA. Muneribus nostris quaesumus domine praecibusque susceptis, et caelestibus nos munda mysteriis, et clementer exaudi. Per dominum.

2011 PRAEFATIO. VD aeterne deus. Qui sanctificator et institutor es abstinentiae, cuius nullus finis, nullusque est numerus. Effunde quaesumus super nos in diebus ieiuniorum nostrorum, spiritum gratiae salutaris, et ab omnibus nos perturbationibus saeculi huius, tua defensione conserua, ut qui unigeniti caelebramus aduentum, continuum eius sentiamus auxilium. Per quem.

2012 BENEDICTIO. Dominus iesus christus qui sacratissimo aduentus[1] suo subuenire dignatus est mundo, animas nostras corporaque purificet a delicto. AMEN.
Det uobis crucis suae praecepta uirtute, spiritus sancti

---

[1] *s* marked for omission.

adpraehendere, ut possitis aduentum eius interriti praestolare.
AMEN.
Sicque uos ab omni reatu immunes efficiat, ut cum aduenerit
non in terrore discutiat, sed in gloria remunerandos assumat.
AMEN.
Quod ipse.

240r **2013** AD COMPLENDVM. / Tui nos domine sacramenti libatio
sancta restauret, et a uetustate purgatos, in mysterii salutaris
faciat transire consortium. Per dominum.

CCCLXII
SABBATO AD SANCTVM PETRVM IN XII LECTIONIBVS

2014 Deus qui conspicis quia ex nostra prauitate affligimur, concede
propitius, ut ex tua uisitatione consolemur[1]. Qui uiuis.

2015 ALIA. Concede quaesumus omnipotens deus, ut quia sub
peccati iugo ex uetusta seruitute deprimimur, expectata unigeniti
filii tui noua natiuitate liberemur. Qui tecum.

2016 ITEM ALIA. Indignos nos quaesumus domine famulos tuos
quos actionis propriae culpa contristat, unigeniti filii tui nos
aduentu laetifica. Qui tecum.

2017 ITEM ALIA. Praesta quaesumus omnipotens deus, ut filii tui
uentura sollemnitas, et praesentis nobis uitae remedia conferat,
et praemia aeterna concedat. Per eundem.

2018 ALIA. Pręces populi tui quaesumus domine clementer exaudi, ut
qui iuste pro peccatis nostris affligimur, pietatis tuae uisitatione
consolemur. Qui uiuis.

2019 ALIA. Deus qui tribus pueris mitigasti. REQVIRE RETRO IN
PRIMA SABBATO MENSIS PRIMI, ET ORDINEM
CLERICORVM.

2020 SVPER OBLATA. Sacrificiis praesentibus domine placatus
intende, ut et deuotioni nostrae proficiant et saluti. Per.

---

[1] *consoletur* before correction.

/f. 240v **2021** / VD aeterne deus. Qui non solum peccata dimittis, sed ipsos etiam iustificas peccatores. Et reis non tantum poenas relaxas, sed dona largiris et praemia. Cuius nos pietatem supplices exoramus, ut qui ieiuniis et uotis sollemnibus natiuitatem unigeniti tui praeuenimus, illius dono et praesentis uitae perturbationibus careamus, et aeterna munera capiamus. Per quem.

2022 BENEDICTIO. Deus qui per tuum angelum nuntiasti, christi uenturum in saeculo praesta quaesumus ut uenienti occurrere populus mereatur cum gaudio. AMEN.
Idem nos benedicat ante natiuitatem, qui suos benedixit apostolos post passionem. AMEN.
Tribuatque ipse uobis ueniam peccatorum, qui pro salute humana fudit in cruce sanguinem proprium. AMEN.
Quod ipse.

2023 AD COMPLENDVM. Quaesumus domine deus noster, ut sacrosancta mysteria, quae pro reparationis nostrae munimine contulisti, et praesens nobis remedium esse, facias et futurum. Per.

CCCLXIII
DOMINICA VACAT

2024 Excita domine potentiam tuam et ueni, et magna nobis uirtute succurre, ut[1] auxilium gratiae tuae quod nostra peccata praepediunt, indulgentia tuae propitiationis acceleret. Qui uiuis.

/f. 241r **2025** SVPER OBLATA. / Sacrificiis praesentibus domine placatus intende, ut et deuotioni nostrae proficiant et saluti. Per.

2026 PRAEFATIO. VD per christum dominum nostrum. Quem iohannes praecessit nascendo, et in desertis haeremi praedicando, et in fluentis iordanicis baptizando, et ad inferna descendendo. Cuius uenerandae natiuitatis proximae uentura sollemnitas, ita nos quaesumus tibi placitos reddat, ut cum fructu bonorum operum ad regna caelestia introducat. Vt parando in cordibus nostris uiam domino fructusque dignos

---

[1] A short erasure follows.

poenitentiae faciendo, per praedicationem iohannis obtemperemus[1] monitis nostri saluatoris. Sicque perueniamus per filium sterilis, ad filium uirginis. Per iohannem hominem magnum, ad eundem dominum nostrum hominem deum. Qui sicut uenit ad nos redimendum occultus, ita iustificet cum ad iudicandum uenerit manifestus. Per quem.

2027 BENEDICTIO. Deus qui uos et prioris aduentus gratia reparauit, et in secundo daturum se uobis regnum cum sanctis angelis repromisit, aduentus sui uos inlustratione sanctificet. AMEN.
Vincula uestra dissoluat antequam ueniat, ut liberati a uinculis peccatorum interriti tremendum eius expectetis aduentum. AMEN.

/ Et quem uenisse in terris pro uestra salute creditis, uenturumque ad iudicium sustinetis, eius aduentum inpauidi, mereamini contueri. AMEN.
Quod ipse.

2028 AD COMPLENDVM. Sumptis muneribus domine quaesumus, ut cum frequentatione mysterii, crescat nostrae salutis effectus. Per.

CCCLXIIII
ALIAE ORATIONES DE ADVENTV DOMINI
2029 Excita domine potentiam tuam et ueni, et quod ecclesiae tuae promisisti, usque in finem saeculi clementer operare. Qui uiuis.

2030 ALIA. Conscientias nostras quaesumus domine uisitando purifica, ut ueniens iesus christus filius tuus dominus noster, paratam sibi in nobis inueniat mansionem. Qui tecum.

2031 ALIA. Prope esto domine omnibus expectantibus te in ueritate, ut in aduentu filii tui domini nostri, plicitis tibi actibus praesentemur. Per eundem.

2032 ALIA. Concede quaesumus omnipotens deus, ut magnae festiuitatis uentura sollemnia, prospero celebremus effectu,

---

[1] *obtemperamus* before correction.

pariterque reddamur et intenti caelestibus disciplinis, et de nostris temporibus laetiores. Per dominum.

2033 ITEM ALIA. Mentes nostras quaesumus domine lumine tuae uisitationis inlustra, ut esse te largiente mereamur, et inter prospera humiles, et inter aduersa securi. Qui uiuis.

/f. 242r **2034** ALIA. / Prĕces populi tui quaesumus domine clementer exaudi, ut qui de aduentu unigeniti filii tui secundum carnem laetantur, in secundo cum uenerit in maiestate sua, praemium aeternae uitae percipiant. Per.

CCCLXV
MISSA DE SANCTA TRINITATE

2035 Omnipotens sempiterne deus, qui dedisti famulis tuis in confessione uerĕ fidei aeternae trinitatis gloriam agnoscere, et in potentia maiestatis adorare unitatem, quaesumus ut eiusdem fidei firmitate ab omnibus semper muniamur aduersis. Per.

2036 SVPER OBLATA. Sanctifica quaesumus domine deus per tui sancti nominis inuocationem huius oblationis hostiam, et per eam nosmetipsos tibi perfice munus aeternum. Per.

2037 PRAEFATIO. VD aeterne deus. Cuius est operis quod conditi sumus muneris quod uiuimus, pietatis quod tua erga nos dona cognoscimus. Quamuis enim natura nostra peccati uitiata sit uulnerae a terrenis, tamen ad caelestia prouehitur, tuo inenarrabili munere. Per christum.

2038 ITEM PRAEFATIO. VD <aeterne deus.> Qui cum unigenito tuo et spiritu[1] sancto. Require in octabas pentecosten.

2039 BENEDICTIO. Omnipotens trinitas, unus et uerus deus, pater et filius et spiritus sanctus, det uobis se desiderare fideliter agnoscere ueraciter, diligere sinceriter. AMEN.

/f. 242v Aequalitatem atque incommutabilem suae / essentiae, ita uestris mentibus infigat ut ab ea numquam uos quibuscumque fantasiis aberrare permittat. AMEN.

---

[1] *spirito* before correction.

Sicque uos in sua fide et caritate perseuerare concedat, ut per eam postmodum ad suam manifestationem uisionemque interminabilem introducat. AMEN.
Quod ipse.

2040 AD COMPLENDVM. Proficiat nobis ad salutem corporis et animae domine deus huius sacramenti perceptio, et sempiterna sanctae trinitatis eiusdem indiuiduę unitatis confessio. Per dominum.

2041 SVPER POPVLVM. Domine deus pater omnipotens famulos tuae maiestati subiectos, per unicum filium tuum in uirtute sancti spiritus benedic et protege, ut ab omni hoste securi, in tua iugiter laude lętentur. Per dominum.

CCCLXVI
MISSA AD POSCENDA SVFFRAGIA SANCTORVM

2042 Concede quaesumus omnipotens deus, ut intercessio nos sanctae dei genetricis mariae, sanctorumque omnium apostolorum, martyrum, confessorum, atque uirginum, et omnium electorum tuorum ubique laetificet, ut dum eorum merita recolimus, patrocinia sentiamus. Per.

2043 SVPER OBLATA. Oblatis domine placare muneribus, et intercedentibus sanctis tuis, a cunctis nos defende periculis. Per dominum.

2044 PRAEFATIO. VD aeterne deus. Debitae piaetatis obsequium omnium sanctorum exibentes, quia poten/tiam tuam domine de quorum merita extiterunt, in eorum sollemnitatibus praedicamus. Per christum.

f. 243r

2045 ¹BENEDICTIO. Omnipotens deus qui per incarnatum uerbum unigenitum tuum dedisti lumen in saeculum, eius misericordiam suppliciter exoramus, ut qui ex gentibus sanctam ecclesiam fecundauit in grege, ab omni eam gentilitatis absoluat errore. AMEN.
Custodi eam a diri serpentis incursu pietate solita, ut tuo famula tui semper possit esse continua. AMEN.
Et qui hac die natiuitatem sacratissimae uirginitatis tuae genitricis mariae celebramus deuoti, eiusdem nos atque omnium sanctorum suffragiis, post abiectam carnis sarcinam, ad aeterna iubeas regna perduci. AMEN.
Quod ipse.

2046 AD COMPLENDVM. Sumpsimus domine sanctorum tuorum sollemnia celebrantes, sacramenta caelestia, praesta quaesumus ut quod temporaliter gerimus, aeternis gaudiis consequamur. Per.

CCCLXVII
MISSA AD SVFFRAGIA ANGELORVM
2047 Perpetuum nobis domine tuae miserationis praesta subsidium, quibus et angelica praestitisti, suffragia non deesse. per.

2048 SVPER OBLATA. Hostias tibi domine laudis offerimus, suppliciter depraecantes, ut easdem angelico pro nobis interueniente suffragio, et placatus accipias, et ad salutem nostram prouenire concedas. Per.

---

¹ Added in the right margin by a Corbie scribe:
MISSA IN ECLESIA PRO VENERATIONE SANCTORVM QVORVM RELIQVIE IBIDEM CONTINENTVR
15* Concede quaesumus omnipotens deus, ut sancta dei genetrix maria, sanctique tui apostoli, martyres, confessores, uirgines, atque omnes sancti quorum in ista continentur ecclesia patrocinia nos ubique adiuuent, quatinus hic in illorum praesenti suffragio, tranquilla pace in tua lauda letemur. Per.
16* SECRETA. Munera tue misericors deus maiestati oblata benigno quaesumus suscipe intuitu, ut eorum nobis praecibus fiant salutaria, quorum sacratissime in hac basilica reliquie reconduntur. Per.
17* POSTCOMMVNIO. Diuina libantes mysteria quaesumus domine, ut eorum nos ubique intercessio protegat, quorum hic sacra gaudemus habere patrocinia. Per.

243v **2049** PRAEFATIO. / VD aeterne deus. Quamuis enim illius sublimis angelicae substantiae sit habitatio semper in caelis. Tuorum tamen fidelium praesumit affectus, pro tuae reuerentiae potestatis. Per haec piae deuotionis officia quoddam retinere pignus in terris adstantium, in conspectu tuo iugiter ministrorum. Per christum.

2050 BENEDICTIO. Deus qui ad salutem nostram angelorum suorum utitur ministerio, eorum uos munimine custodiat, custodiatque communiat. AMEN.
Det uobis mentium puritatem, et iugem corporum castitatem, qui eorum electis omnibus repromisit aequalitatem. AMEN.
Quique illis certissimam suae permansionis tribuat fiduciam, ipse uos fidei, spei caritatisque perseuerabili uirtute confirmet, adque ad eorum beatitudinis societatem perducat. AMEN.
Quod ipse.

2051 AD COMPLENDVM. Repleti domine benedictione caelesti, suppliciter imploramus, ut quod fragili caelebramus officio, sanctorum archangelorum nobis prodesse sentiamus auxilio. Per dominum.

2052 SVPER POPVLVM. Plebem tuam quaesumus domine perpetua pietate custodi, ut secura semper et necessariis ad uitam subsidiis spirituum tibimet placitorum, pia semper ueneratione laetetur. Per dominum.

f. 244r

/ CCCLXVIII
MISSA DE SAPIENTIA

2053 Deus qui per coaeternam tibi sapientiam hominem cum non esset condidisti, perditumque misericorditer reformasti, praesta quaesumus ut eadem pectora nostra te inspirante tota[1] mente amemus, et ad te toto corde curramus. Per.

2054 SVPER OBLATA. Sanctificetur quaesumus domine deus huius nostrae oblationis munus tua cooperante sapientiam, ut tibi placere possit ad laudem, et nobis proficere ad salutem. Per dominum.

---

[1] *toto* before correction.

2055 PRAEFATIO. VD aeterne deus. Qui tui nominis agnitione et tuae potentiae tibi sapientiam reuelare uoluisti, ut tuam confitentes maiestatem, et tuis inherentes mandatis tecum uitam habeamus aeternam. Per christum.

2056 BENEDICTIO. Omnipotens deus sua nos clementia benedicat, et sensum in nobis sapientiae salutaris infundat. AMEN.
Catholicę fidei nos documentis enutriat, et in sanctis operibus perseuerabiles reddat. AMEN.
Gressus nostros ab errore conuertat, et uiam pacis et caritatis sapientiamque ostendat. AMEN.
Quod ipse.

2057 AD COMPLENDVM. Infunde quaesumus domine deus per haec sancta quae sumpsimus tuae cordibus nostris lumen sapientiae, ut te ueraciter agnoscamus, ut fideliter dilagamus. Per.

/f. 244v **2058** SVPER POPVLVM. Deus qui misisti filium tuum et ostendisti creature creatorem, respice propitius super nos famulos tuos, et praepara agiae sophiae dignam in cordibus nostris habitationem. Per dominum nostrum.

CCCLXVIIII
MISSA DE CARITATE. FERIA V

2059 Omnipotens sempiterne deus, qui iustitiam tuae legis in cordibus credentium digito tuo scribis, da nobis fidei, spei, et caritatis augmentum, et ut mereamur assequi quod promittis, fac nos amare quod praecipis. Per.

2060 SVPER OBLATA. Mitte domine quaesumus spiritum sanctum qui et haec munera praesentia nostra tuum nobis efficiat sacramentum, et ad hoc percipiendum nostra corda purificet. Per.

2061 POSTCOMMVNIO. Spiritum in nobis domine tuae caritatis infunde, ut quos uno caelesti pane satiasti, tua facias pietate concordes. Per.

2062 SVPER POPVLVM. Sancti spiritus corda nostra inluminet, et perfectae caritatis tuae dulcedinem, habundanter recipiat. Per.

CCCLXX
MISSA DE SANCTA CRVCE. FERIA VI

2063 Deus qui unigeniti filii tui domini nostri iesu christi praetioso sanguine uiuifice crucis uexillum sanctificare uoluisti, concede quaesumus eos qui eiusdem sanctae crucis gaudent honore, tua / quoque ubique protectione gaudere. Per.

. 245r

2064 LECTIO AD PHILIPENSES. FRATRES. Christus factus est pro nobis oboediens patri usque ad mortem, mortem autem crucis. Propter quod et deus illum exaltauit, et donauit illi nomen quod est super omne nomen, ut in nomine iesu omne genu flectatur. Caelestium, terrestrium, et infernorum. Et omnis lingua confiteatur, quia dominus iesus christus, in gloria est dei patris.

2065 SEQVENTIA SANCTI EVANGELII SECVNDVM MATHEVM. IN ILLO TEMPORE. Ascendens iesus hiersolimam, assumpsit .xii. discipulos suos secreto et ait illis. Ecce ascendimus hierosolimam, et filius hominis tradetur principibus sacerdotum et scribis, et condempnabunt eum morte. Et tradent eum gentibus ad deludendum, et flagellandum, et crucifigendum. Et tertia die, resurget.

2066 SVPER OBLATA. Haec oblatio domine ab omnibus nos purget offensis, quae in hara crucis etiam totius mundi tulit offensa. Per.

2067 PRAEFATIO. VD aeterne deus. Qui salutem humani generis in ligno crucis constituisti, ut unde mors oriebatur, inde uita resurgeret. Et qui in ligno uincebat, in ligno quoque uinceretur. Per christum.

2068 BENEDICTIONEM REQVIRE IN EXALTATIONE SANCTAE CRVCIS.

f. 245v **2069** POSTCOMMVNIO. / Adesto domine deus noster, et quos sanctae crucis laetari fecisti honore, eius quoque perpetuis defende subsidiis. Per.

CCCLXXI
MISSA AD LAVDEM SANCTAE MARIAE. FERIA VI

2070 Concede nos famulos tuos quaesumus domine deus, perpetuae mentis et corporis sanitate gaudere, et gloriosae beatae mariae semper uirginis intercessione, a praesenti liberare tristitia, et futura perfrui laetitia. Per dominum.

2071 SVPER OBLATA. Tua domine propitiatione et beatae mariae semper uirginis intercessione, ad perpetuam atque praesentem haec oblatio nobis proficiat prosperitatem. Per dominum.

2072 PRAEFATIO. VD aeterne deus. Nos te in tuis sacratissimis uirginibus exultantibus animis, laudare, benedicere, et praedicare. Inter quas beata dei genetrix uirgo maria, intemerata gloriosissima effulsit. Per christum.

2073 AD COMPLENDVM. Sumptis domine salutis nostrae subsidiis, da quaesumus eius nos patrociniis ubique protegi, in cuius ueneratione haec tuae obtulimus maiestati. Per.

2074 SVPER POPVLVM. Omnipotens deus famulos tuos dextera potentiae tuae a cunctis protege periculis, et beata maria semper uirgine intercedente, fac eos praesenti gaudere prosperitate et futura. Per dominum.

CCCLXXII
MISSA PRO PECCATIS. FERIA II

/f. 246r **2075** / Exaudi quaesumus domine supplicum praeces, et confitentium tibi parce peccatis, ut pariter nobis indulgentiam tribuas benignus et pacem. Per.

2076 SVPER OBLATA. Hostias tibi domine placationis offerimus, ut et delicta nostra miseratus absoluas, et nutantia corda dirigas. Per dominum.

2077 IN FRACTIONE. Hanc igitur oblationem domine quam tibi offerimus, pro peccatis atque offensionibus nostris, ut omnium delictorum nostrorum ueniam consequi mereamur, quaesumus domine ut placatus accipias.

392

2078 POSTCOMMVNIO. Praesta nobis aeterne saluator, ut percipientes hoc munere ueniam peccatorum, deinceps peccata uitemus. Per.

2079 SVPER POPVLVM. Deus cui proprium est semper misereri et parcere, suscipe depraecationem nostram, et quos delictorum catena constringit, miseratio tuae pietatis absoluat. Per.

CCCLXXIII
MISSA PRO TEMPTATIONE CARNIS

2080 Vre igne sancti spiritus renes nostros et cor nostrum domine, ut tibi caste et corde seruiamus, et corpore placeamus. Per dominum.

2081 SVPER OBLATA. Disrumpe domine uincula peccatorum nostrorum, ut sacrificare tibi hostiam laudis absoluta libertate possimus, et[1] retribuere quae[2] ante tribuisti, et salua nos per indulgentiam, quos dignatus es saluare per gratiam. Per.

f. 246v **2082** POSTCOMMVNIO. / Domine adiutor et protector noster refloreat caro nostra uigore pudicitiae, uel sanctimoniae nouitate, ereptamque de manu tartari, in resurrectionis gaudium iubeas praesentari. Per.

CCCLXXIIII
MISSA PRO PETITIONE LACRIMARVM

2083 Omnipotens aeterne deus da capiti nostro habundantiam aquae, et oculis nostris fontem lacrimarum, ut peccati macula abluti, ultrices poenarum flammas fletus ubertate uincamus. Per.

2084 SVPER OBLATA. Per has oblationes quaesumus domine ut non tantum oculis nostris infundas, sed et corda nostra nimium peccatorum luctum tribuas. Per.

2085 POSTCOMMVNIONEM. Corpore et sanguine tuo domine satiati quaesumus ut pro nostris semper peccatis nobis conpunctionem cordis et luctum, fluminaque lacrimarum

---

[1] Supplied interlinearly.
[2] Rewritten.

largiaris, quatenus caelestem in futuro consolationem mereamur. Per dominum.

MISSAM SPETIALEM PRO SACERDOTE

2086 Omnipotens aeterne deus tuae gratiae pietatem, supplici deuotione deposco, ut omnium malorum meorum uincula soluas, cunctisque meis criminibus et peccatis[1] clementer ignoscas, et quia me indignum et peccatorem ad ministerium tuum uocare dignatus es, sic me idoneum tibi ministrum efficias, /f. 247r ut sacrificium de manibus meis placide / ac benigne suscipias, electorumque sacerdotum me participem facias, et de praeceptis tuis in nullo me oberrare permittas. Per dominum.

2087 [2]ALIA. Fac me quęso omnipotens deus ita iustitia indui, ut in sanctorum tuorum merear exultatione laetari, quatinus emundatus ab omnibus sordibus peccatorum, consortium adipiscar tibi placentium sacerdotum, meque tua misericordia a uitiis omnibus exuat, quem reatus propriae conscientiae grauat. Per.

2088 SVPER OBLATA. Deus qui praecipis a peccatoribus exorari, tibique sacrificium contriti cordis offerri, hoc sacrificium quod indignis manibus meis offero acceptare dignare, et ut ipse tibi hostia et sacrificium esse merear, miseratus concede, quo per mysterii huius exhibitionem, peccatorum omnium percipiam remissionem. Per.

---

[1] Supplied in the left margin by a later scribe.
[2] Added in the right margin by a Corbie scribe:
    <MISSA AD POSTVLANDAM GRATIAM SPIRITVS SANCTI>
18* Omnipotens mitissime deus respice propicius ad praeces nostras, et libera corda nostra de malarum temptatione cogitationum, ut sancti spiritus dignum fieri habitaculum inueniamur. Per.
19* <SECRETA.> Has tibi domine offero oblationes, quatinus animas nostras ab omni temptatione et cogitatione mala liberare, et sancti spiritus gratia inluminare digneris. Per.
20* <AD COMPLENDVM>. Per hoc quaeso domine sacrificium quod tuę optulimus maiestati, ab omnibus corda nostra emunda temptationibus et illumina gratię tuę splendore ut digna maiestati tuę cogitare et diligere ualeamus. Per.

2089 PRAEFATIO. VD aeterne deus. Qui dissimulatis humanae fragilitatis peccatis, sacerdotii dignitatem concedis igdignis[1]. Et non solum peccata dimittis, uerum etiam ipsos peccatores iustificare dignaris. Cuius est muneris ut non existentia sumant exordia, exorta nutrimentum, nutrita fructum, fructuosa perseuerandi auxilium. Qui me non existentem creasti, creatum fidei firmitate ditasti, fidelem / quamuis peccatis squalentem sacerdotii dignitate donasti. Tuam igitur omnipotentiam supplex exposco, ut me a praeteritis peccatis emacules, in mundi huius cursu, in bonis operibus corrobores, in perseuerantiae soliditate confirmes. Sicque me facias tuis altaribus deseruire, ut ad eorum qui tibi placuerunt sacerdotum consortium ualeam peruenire. Et per eum tibi sit meum acceptabile uotum, qui se tibi obtuli in sacrificium, qui est omnium opifex, et solus sine peccati macula pontifex, iesus christus dominus noster. Per quem.

247v

2090 POS<T>COMMVNIO. Huius mihi domine sacramenti perceptio sit peccatorum remissio, et tuae pietatis optata propitiatio, ut per haec te opitulante efficiar sacris mysteriis dignus, quae de tua pietate confisus, frequentare praesumo indignus. Per.

CCCLXXVI
ITEM ALIA MISSA PRO SACERDOTE

2091 Deus fons bonitatis et pietatis origo, qui peccantem non statim iudicas, sed ad paenitentiam miseratus expectas, te quaeso ut facinorum meorum squalores abstergas, et me ad peragendum iniunctum officium dignum efficias, et qui altaris tui ministerium suscepi indignus, perago trepidus, ad id peragendum / reddar strenuus, et inter eos qui tibi placuerunt inueniar iustificatus. Per.

248r

2092 SVPER OBLATA. Sacrificii praesentis quaeso domine, oblatio mea expurget facinora, per quod totius mundi uoluisti relaxari peccata. Illiusque frequentatione efficiar dignus, quod ut frequentarem suscepi indignus. Per dominum nostrum.

[1] For *indignis*.

2093 PRAEFATIO. VD aeterne deus. Qui dum libenter nostrae paenitudinis satisfactionem suscipis, ipse tuo iudicio quod erramus abscondis, et praeterita peccata nostra dissimulas, ut nobis sacerdotii dignitatem concedas. Tuum est enim me ad ministrandum altari tuo dignum efficere, quem peragendum id officii indignum dignatus es promouere. Vt praeteritorum actuum meorum mala obliuiscens, praesentium ordinem in tua uoluntate disponens. Futuris custodiam imponens, per eum uitiorum squaloribus expurger[1], uirtutum nutrimentis exorner, eorum sacerdotum consortio qui tibi placuerunt aduner, quem constat esse uerum summumque pontificem, solumque sine peccati contagio sacerdotem, iesum christum dominum nostrum. Quem laudant.

2094 AD COMPLENDVM. Huius domine perceptio sacramenti, peccatorum meorum maculas tergat, et ad peragendum /
/f. 248v   iniunctum officium me idoneum reddat. Per.

CCCLXXVII
MISSA VOTIVA

2095 Deus qui iustificas impium, et non uis mortem peccatorum, maiestatem tuam suppliciter depraecamur, ut famulum tuum .ill. de tua misericordia confidentem, caelesti protegas benignus auxilio, et assidua protectione conserues, ut tibi iugiter famuletur, et nullis temptationibus a te separetur. Per.

2096 SVPER OBLATA. Huius domine quaesumus uirtute mysterii, et a propriis nos munda delictis, et famulum tuum .ill. ab omnibus absolue peccatis. Per.

2097 AD COMPLENDVM. Purificent nos domine quaesumus sacramenta quae sumpsimus, et famulum tuum .ill. ab omni culpa liberum esse concede, ut qui conscientiae reatu constringitur, caelestis remedii plenitudine glorietur. Per.

---

[1] *expurget* before correction..

396

CCCLXXVIII
ALIA MISSA

2098 Omnipotens sempiternae deus miserere famulo tuo, et dirige eum secundum tuam clementiam in uiam salutis aeternę, ut te donante tibi placita cupiat, et tota uirtute perficiat. Per.

2099 SVPER OBLATA. Proficiat quaesumus domine haec oblatio, quam tuae supplices offerimus maiestati ad salutem famuli tui .ill. ut tua prouidentia eius uita inter aduersa et prospera ubique dirigatur. Per.

2100 AD COMPLENDVM. Sumentes domine perpetuae sacramenta salutis tuam depraecamur clementiam, / ut per ea famulum tuum ab omni aduersitate protegas. Per.

249r

CCCLXXVIIII
MISSA PRO SALVTE VIVORVM

2101 Praetende domine famulis et famulabus tuis .ill. et .ill. dexteram caelestis auxilii, ut te toto corde perquirant, et quae digne postulant adsequantur. Per.

2102 SVPER OBLATA. Propitiare domine supplicationibus nostris, et has oblationes famulorum famularumque tuarum, quas tibi pro incolumitate eorum offerimus benignus assume, et ut nullius sit irritum uotum, nullius uacua postulatio, praesta quaesumus ut quod fideliter petimus, efficaciter consequamur. Per dominum.

2103 AD COMPLENDVM. Da famulis et famulabus tuis quaesumus domine in tua fide et sinceritate constantiam, ut in caritate diuina firmati, nullis temptationibus ab eius integritate uellantur. Per dominum nostrum.

CCCLXXX
ITEM ALIA MISSA PRO FAMILIARIBVS

2104 Deus qui caritatis dona per gratiam sancti spiritus tuorum cordibus fidelibus infudisti, da famulis et famulabus tuis pro quibus tuam depraecamur clementiam, salutem mentis et corporis, ut te tota uirtute diligant, et quae tibi placita sunt tota dilectione perficiant. Per.

2105 SVPER OBLATA. Miserere quaesumus domine deus[1] famulis et
/f. 249v   famulabus tuis pro quibus hoc sacrificium laudis tuae offe/rimus
maiestati, ut per haec sancta supernae beatitudinis gratiam
optineant[2], et gloriam aeternae beatitudinis adquirant. Per.

2106 AD COMPLENDVM. Diuina libantes mysteria quaesumus
domine, ut haec salutaria sacramenta, illis proficiant ad
prosperitatem et pacem, pro quorum dilectione haec tuae
obtulimus maiestati. Per dominum nostrum.

2107 ALIA. Deus qui supplicum tuorum uota per caritatis officia
suscipere dignaris, da famulis et famulabus tuis in tua proficere
dilectione, et in tua laetari protectione, ut tibi secura mente
deseruiant, et in tua pace semper adsistere mereantur. Per.

CCCLXXXI
MISSA PRO ABBATE VEL CONGREGATIONE

2108 Omnipotens sempiterne deus, qui facis mirabilia magna solus,
praetende super famulum tuum .ill. abbatem, et super
congregationem illi commissam spiritum gratiae salutaris, et ut
in ueritate tibi complaceant, perpetuum eis rorem tuae
benedictionis infunde. Per dominum.

2109 SVPER OBLATA. Hostias domine famulorum tuorum placatus
intende, et quas in honorem nominis tui deuota mente pro eis
celebramus, proficere sibi sentiant ad medelam. Per dominum
nostrum.

2110 AD COMPLENDVM. Quos caelesti recreas munere perpetuo
/f. 250r   domine comitare praesidio, et quos fouere non desinis, / dignos
fieri sempiterna redemptione concede. Per.

CCCLXXXII
ORATIONES PRO FRATRIBVS IN VIA DIRIGENDIS

2111 Deus qui diligentibus te misericordiam tuam semper impendis,
et a seruientibus tibi in nulla es regione longinquus[3], dirige uiam

---

[1] Supplied interlinearly.
[2] *obtineant* before correction.
[3] First *n* supplied interlinearly.

398

famuli tui ill. in uoluntate tua, ut te protectore, et te praeduce, per iustitiae semitas, sine offensione gradiatur. Per.

2112 ALIA. Exaudi domine praeces nostras, et iter famuli tui .N. propitius commitare atque misericordiam tuam sicut ubique es, ita ubique largire, quatinus ab omnibus aduersitatibus tua opitulatione defensus, iustorum desideriorum potiatur effectibus. Per.

CCCLXXXIII
ORATIO PRO REDEVNTIBVS DE ITENERE

2113 Omnipotens sempiterne deus nostrorum temporum uiteque dispositor, famulo tuo .ill. continuae tranquillitatis largire subsidium, ut quem incolumem propriis laribus reddidisti, tua facias protectione securum. Per.

CCCLXXXIIII
ORATIO IN ADVENTVM FRATRVM SVPERVENIENTIVM

2114 Deus humilium uisitator qui nos fraterna dilectione consolaris, praetende societati nostrae gratiam tuam, ut per eos in quibus habitas tuum in nobis sentiamus aduentum. Per dominum.

CCCLXXXV
MISSA PRO ITER AGENTIBVS

2115 Adesto domine supplicationibus nostris, et uiam famuli tui .ill. in salutis tuae prosperitate dis/pone, ut inter omnes uiae et uitae huius uarietates, tuo semper protegamur auxilio. Per.

2116 SVPER OBLATA. Propitiare domine supplicationibus nostris, et has oblationes quas tibi offerimus pro famulo tuo ill. benignus assume, ut uiam illius et praecedente gratia tua dirigas, et subsequente comitare digneris, ut de actu atque incolomitate eius, secundum misericordiae tuae praesidia gaudeamus. Per.

2117 PRAEFATIO. VD aeterne deus. A quo deuiare mori, praesta[1] quo ambulare uiuere est, qui fideles tuos in tua uia deducis, et miseratione gratissima in ueritatem inducis, qui abrahę isaac et iacob, in praesentis uiae et uitae curriculo, custos dux et comes

---

[1] Over an erasure.

esse uoluisti, et famulo tuo tobi, angelum praeuium prestitisti. Cuius inmensam misericordiam humillimis praecibus imploramus, ut iter famuli tui .ill. cum suis in prosperitate dirigere, eumque inter uiae et uitae huius uarietates digneris custodire. Quatinus angelorum tuorum praesidio fultus, intercessione quoque sanctorum munitus a cunctis aduersitatibus tua miseratione defensus, profectionis et reuersionis suae felicitate potitus, et compos reddatur iustorum uotorum, et de suorum laetetur remissione peccatorum. Per christum.

/f. 251r **2118** AD COMPLENDVM. / Deus infinitae misericordiae et maiestatis inmensae, quam nec spatia locorum nec interualla temporum, ab his quos tueris adiungunt, adesto famulis tuis .ill. in te ubique fidentibus, et per omnem quam ituri sunt uiam, dux eis et comes esse dignare, nihil illis aduersitatibus noceat, nihil difficultatis obsistat, cuncta eis salubria, cuncta sint prospera, et sub ope dexterae tuae, quicquid iusto expetierint desiderio, celeri consequantur effectu. Per.

CCCLXXXVI
MISSA PRO NAVIGANTIBVS

2119 Deus qui transtulisti patres nostros per mare rubrum[1], et transuexisti per aquam nimiam laudem tui nominis decantantes, supplices depraecamur, ut in hac naui famulos tuos, repulsis aduersitatibus portu semper obtabili, cursuque tranquillo tuearis. Per.

2120 SVPER OBLATA. Suscipe quaesumus domine praeces famulorum tuorum cum oblationibus hostiarum, et tua mysteria celebrantes, ab omnibus defende periculis. Per.

2121 AD COMPLENDVM. Sanctificati diuino mysterio maiestatem tuam domine suppliciter depraecamur et petimus, ut quos donis facias caelestibus interesse, per lignum sanctae crucis, et a peccatis abstrahas, et a periculis cunctis miseratus eripias. Per.

---

[1] *robrum* before correction.

CCCLXXXVII
MISSA PRO PACE

251v **2122** / Deus a quo sancta desideria recta consilia et iusta sunt opera, da seruis tuis illam quam mundus dare non potest pacem, ut et corda nostra mandatis tuis dedita, et hostium sublata formidine, tempora sint tua protectione tranquilla. Per.

2123 SVPER OBLATA. Deus qui credentes in te populos nullis sinis concuti terroribus, dignare praeces et hostias dicatae tibi plebis suscipere, ut pax tua pietate concessa, christianorum fines ab omni hoste faciat esse securos. per.

2124 AD COMPLENDVM. Deus auctor pacis et amator, quem nosse uiuere, cui seruire regnare est, protege ab omnibus inpugnationibus supplices tuos, ut qui in defensione tua confidimus, nullius hostilitatis arma timeamus. Per dominum nostrum.

CCCLXXXVIII
MISSA DE QVACVMQVE TRIBVLATIONE

2125 Ineffabilem misericordiam tuam domine nobis clementer ostende, ut simul nos et a peccatis exuas, et a poenis quas pro his meremur eripias. Per dominum.

2126 SVPER OBLATA. Purificet nos domine quaesumus muneris praesentis oblatio, et dignos sacra participatione perficiat. Per dominum.

2127 AD COMPLENDVM. Praesta domine quaesumus, ut terrenis affectibus expiati, ad superni plenitudinem sacramenti, cuius libauimus sancta tendamus. Per dominum nostrum iesum.

CCCLXXXVIIII
MISSA PRO PESTE ANIMALIVM

2128 Deus qui laboribus hominum, etiam de mutis animalibus solacia subrogasti, supplices te rogamus, ut sine quibus non alitur humana conditio, nostris facias usibus non perire. Per.

2129 SVPER OBLATA. Sacrificiis domine placatus oblatis, opem tuam nostris temporibus clementer impende. Per.

2130 AD COMPLENDVM. Benedictionem tuam domine populus

fidelis accipiat, qua corpore saluatus ac mente, et congruam tibi exhibeat seruitutem, et propitiationis tuae beneficia semper inueniat. Per.

2131 ALIA. Auerte domine quaesumus a fidelibus tuis cunctos miseratus errores, et sęuientium morborum depelle perniciem, ut quos merito flagellas deuios, foueas tua miseratione correctos. Per dominum.

CCCXC
MISSA IN CONTENTIONE

2132 Omnipotens sempiterne deus, qui superbis resistis et gratiam praestas humilibus, tribue quaesumus ut non indignationem tuam prouocemus elati, sed propitiationis tuae capiamus dona subiecti. Per dominum.

2133 SVPER OBLATA. Ab omni reatu nos domine sancta quae tractamus absoluant, et eadem muniant a totius prauitatis incursu.

2134 AD COMPLENDVM. Quos caelesti domine mysterio refecisti, /f. 252v propriis et alienis, quaesumus propitiatus absolue delictis / ut diuino munere purificatis mentibus perfruamur. Per dominum nostrum.

2135 ALIA. Praesta quaesumus omnipotens deus, ut semper rationabilia meditantes, quae tibi sunt placita, et dictis exequamur et factis. Per dominum nostrum.

CCCXCI
MISSA CONTRA IVDICES MALE AGENTES

2136 Ecclesiae tuae domine praeces placitus admitte, ut destitutis aduersitatibus uniuersis, secura tibi seruiat libertate. Per dominum.

2137 SVPER OBLATA. Protege nos domine quaesumus tuis mysteriis seruientes, ut diuinis rebus et corpore famulemur et mente. Per.

2138 AD COMPLENDVM. Quaesumus domine deus noster, ut quos diuina tribuis participatione gaudere, humanis non sinas subiacere periculis. Per dominum.

CCCXCII
MISSA CONTRA OBLOQVENTES

2139 Praesta domine quaesumus ut mentium reproborum non curemus obloquium, sed eadem prauitate calcata exoramus[1], ut nec terreri nos lacerationibus patiaris iniustis, nec captiosis adulationibus implicari, sed potius amare quae praecipis. Per.

2140 SVPER OBLATA. Oblatio domine tuis aspectibus immolanda, quaesumus ut haec nos ab omnibus uitiis potenter absoluat, et a cunctis defendat inimicis. Per.

2141 AD COMPLENDVM. Praesta domine quaesumus, ut per haec sancta quae sumpsimus, dissimulatis lacerationibus impro/borum, eadem te gubernante quae recta sunt cautius exequamur. Per dominum nostrum.

f. 253r

CCCXCIII
ORATIO AD PLVVIAM POSTVLANDAM

2142 Terram tuam domine quam uidemus nostris iniquitatibus tabescentem, caelestibus aquis infunde atque irriga beneficiis gratiae sempiternę. Per.

2143 ALIA. Omnipotens sempiterne deus qui saluas omnes et neminem uis perire, aperi fontem benignitatis tuę, et terram aridam aquis fluenti caelestis dignanter infunde. Per dominum nostrum.

CCCXCIIII
MISSA AD PLVVIAM POSTVLANDAM

2144 Deus in quo uiuimus mouemur et sumus, pluuiam nobis tribue congruentem, ut praesentibus subsidiis sufficienter adiuti, sempiterna fiducialius appetamus. Per.

2145 ALIA. Delicta fragilitatis nostrae domine quaesumus miseratus absolue, et aquarum subsidia praebae caelestium, quibus terrena conditio uegetata subsistat. Per dominum nostrum.

---

[1] *exoremus* before correction.

2146 SVPER OBLATA. Oblatis domine placare muneribus et oportunum nobis tribue pluuiae sufficientis auxilium. Per.

2147 <AD COMPLENDVM.> Tuere nos domine quaesumus tua sancta sumentes, et ab omnibus propitius absolue peccatis. Per.

CCCXCV
ORATIO AD POSCENDAM SERENITATEM

2148 Domine deus qui in mynisterio[1] aquarum salutis tuae nobis sacra/menta sanxisti, exaudi orationem populi tui, et iube terrores inundantium cessare pluuiarum, flagellumque huius elementi, ad effectum tui conuerte mysterii, ut qui se regenerantibus aquis gaudent renatos, gaudeant his castigantibus esse correctos. Per dominum nostrum.

/f. 253v

2149 ALIA. Quaesumus omnipotens deus clementiam tuam, ut inundantiam coherceas ymbrium, et hylaritatem tui uultus nobis impertiti digneris. Per dominum nostrum.

CCCXCVI
MISSA AD POSCENDAM SERENITATEM

2150 Ad te nos domine clamantes exaudi, et aeris serenitatem nobis tribue supplicantibus, ut qui pro peccatis nostris iustae affligimur, misericordia tua praeueniente clementiam sentiamus. Per dominum.

2151 SVPER OBLATA. Praeueniat nos quaesumus domine gratia tua semper et subsequatur, et has oblationes quas pro peccatis nostris nomini tuo consecrandas deferimus benignus assume, ut per intercessionem sanctorum tuorum, cunctis nobis proficiant ad salutem. Per dominum.

2152 AD COMPLENDVM. Plebs tua domine capiat sacrae benedictionis augmentum, et copiosis beneficiorum tuorum subleuetur auxiliis, quae tantis intercessionum depraecationibus adiuuatur. Per dominum nostrum.

---

[1] *mysterio* before correction.

CCCXCVII
MISSA AD REPELLANDAM TEMPESTATEM

254r **2153** / Deus qui omnium rerum tibi seruientium naturam per ipsos motus aeris, ad cultum tuae maiestatis institutis, tranquillitatem nobis misericordiae tuae remotis largire terroribus, ut cuius iram expauimus, clementiam tuam sentiamus. Per.

2154 ¹ALIA. A domo tua quaesumus domine spiritales nequitiae repellantur, et aeriarum discedat malignitas tempestatum. Per.

2155 SVPER OBLATA. Offerimus domine laudes et munera, pro concessis² beneficiis gratias referentes, et pro concedendis semper suppliciter depraecantes. Per.

2156 AD COMPLENDVM. Omnipotens sempiterne deus, qui nos et castigando sanas, et ignoscendo conseruas, praesta supplicibus tuis, ut et tranquillitatibus huius optatę³ consolationis laetemur, et dono tuae pietatis semper utamur. Per.

CCCXCVIII
ORATIONES MATVTINALES

2157 Matutina supplicum uota domine propitius intuere, et occulta cordis nostri remedio tuae clarifica pietatis, ut desideria tenebrosa non teneant, quos lux caelestis gratiae reparauit.

---

¹ Added in the right margin by a Corbie scribe:

MISSA PRO INFIRMO
21* Omnipotens sempiterne deus salus ęterna credentium, exaudi nos pro famulo tuo .N. pro quo misericordię tuę imploramus auxilium, ut reddita sibi sanitate, gratiarum tibi in ecclesia tua referat actiones. Per.
22* SECRETA. Deus cuius nutibus uitę nostrę momenta decurrunt, suscipe praeces et hostias famuli tui .N. pro quo misericordiam tuam egrotante imploramus, ut de cuius periculo metuimus, de eiusdem salute lętemur. Per.
23* POSTCOMMVNIO. Deus infirmitatis humanę singulare praesidium, auxilii tui super infirmum nostrum .N. ostende uirtutem, ut ope misericordię tuę adiutus, ęcclesię tuę sanctę repraesentari mereatur. Per.

² *con* supplied interlinearly.
³ *obtatę* before correction.

2158 ALIA. Mmitte[1] quaesumus domine lucem tuam in cordibus nostris, ut mandatorum tuorum lege percepta, in uia tua ambulantes, nihil patiamur erroris. Per dominum.

2159 ALIA. Omnipotens sempiterne deus, apud quem nihil obscurum est, nihil tenebrosum, emitte lucem tuam in cordibus nostris, ut mandatorum tuorum lege percepta, in / uia tua ambulantes, nihil patiamur erroris. Per.

/f. 254v

2160 ALIA. Deus qui uigilantes in laudibus tuis caelesti mercede remuneras, tenebras de cordibus nostris auferre digneris, ut splendore luminis tui semper gaudeamus. Per.

2161 ALIA. Gratias tibi agimus domine sanctae pater omnipotens aeterne deus, qui nos de transacto noctis spatio ad matutinas horas perducere dignatus es, quaesumus ut dones nobis diem hunc sine peccato transire, quatinus ad uesperum et semper tibi deo gratias referamus. Per.

2162 ALIA. Exurgentes de cubilibus nostris, auxilium gratiae tuae matutinis domine praecibus imploramus, ut discussis tenebris uitiorum, ambulare mereamur in luce uirtutum. Per.

2163 ALIA. Te lucem ueram et lucis auctorem domine depraecamur, ut digneris a nobis tenebras depellere uitiorum, et clarificare nos luce uirtutum. Per.

2164 ALIA. Auge in nobis domine quaesumus fidem tuam, et spiritus sancti lucem in nobis semper accende. Per.

2165 ALIA. Gratias agimus inenerrabili pietate omnipotens deus, qui nos depulsa noctis caligine, ad diei huius principium perduxisti, et abiecta ignorantiae cecitate, ad cultum tui nominis atque scientiam reuocasti, ut labere sensibus nostris omnipotens pater, ut in praeceptorum lumine gradientes, te ducem / sequamur et principem. Per dominum.

/f. 255r

---

[1] Capital and miniscule *m* together.

2166 ALIA. Deus qui tenebras ignorantiae uerbi tui luce depellis, auge in cordibus nostris uirtutem fidei quam dedisti, ut ignis quem gratia tua fecit accendi, nullis temptationibus possit extingui. Per.

2167 ALIA. Auribus percipe quaesumus domine uerba oris nostri, clamoremque matutinum pius scrutator intellige, ut orandi ad te nobis sit fida deuotio, tuaque donetur nobis diluculo contemplatio, et peccatorum omnium exoptata remissio. Per.

2168 ALIA. Veritas tua quaesumus domine luceat in cordibus nostris, et omnis falsitas destruatur inimici. Per.

2169 ALIA. Sensibus nostris quaesumus domine lumen sanctum tuum benignus infunde, ut tibi semper simus deuoti, cuius sapientia creati sumus, et prouidentia gubernamur. Per dominum.

CCCXCVIIII
ORATIONES VESPERTINALES SEV MATVTINALES

2170 Oriatur domine nascentibus tenebris aurora iustitiae, ut peracto[1] diei[2] spatio tibi suppliciter gratias agentes, etiam mane dignanter respicias uota soluentes. Per.

2171 ALIA. Tuus est dies domine et tua est nox, concede solem iustitiae permanere in cordibus nostris, ad repellandas tenebras cogitationum iniquiarum. Per dominum nostrum.

f. 255v **2172** ALIA. / Gratias tibi agimus domine custoditi per diem, grates tibi exsoluimus custodiendi per noctem, repraesenta nos quaesumus domine matutinis horis incolumes, ut nos omni tempore habeas laudatores. Per.

2173 ALIA. Omnipotens sempiterne deus, uespere et mane et meridiae, maiestatem tuam suppliciter depraecamur, ut expulsis de cordibus nostris peccatorum tenebris, ad ueram lucem quae christus est, nos facias peruenire. Per eundem.

---

[1] Final letters over an erasure.
[2] *dei* before correction.

2174 ALIA. Deus qui inluminas noctem et lucem post tenebras facis, concede nobis ut hanc noctem sine impedimento satanae transeamus, atque matutinis horis ad altare tuum recurrentes, tibi deo gratias referamus. Per dominum nostrum.

2175 ALIA. Vespertinae laudis officia persoluentes, clementiam tuam domine humili praece deposcimus, ut nocturni insidiatoris fraudes, te protegente uincamus. Per dominum nostrum.

2176 ITEM ALIA. Propitiare domine uespertinis supplicationibus nostris, et fac nos sine ullo reatu matutinis tibi laudibus praesentari. Per dominum nostrum.

2177 ALIA. Quesumus domine deus noster, diei molestias, noctis quietae sustenta, ut necessaria temporum uicissitudine succedente, nostra reficiatur infirmitas. Per.

2178 ALIA. Exaudi domine famulos tuos uespertina nomini tuo uota
/f. 256r   reddentes, et quos per singula diei momenta / seruasti, per noctis quietem custodire dignare. Per.

CCCC

ORATIONES IN MONASTERIO MONACHORVM

2179 Deus qui renuntiantibus saeculo, mansionem paras in caelo, dilata quaesumus huius sanctae congregationis temporale habitaculum caelestibus bonis, ut fraternae teneantur compagine caritatis, unanimes continentiae praecepta custodiant, sobrii, simplices, et quieti, gratis nobis datam, gratiam fuisse cognoscamus, concordet illorum uita cum nomine[1], professio sentiatur in opere. Per dominum.

2180 ALIA. Suscipe domine praeces nostras, et muro custodiae tuae hoc sanctum ouile circumda, ut omni aduersitate depulsa, sit hoc semper domicilium incolomitatis et pacis. Per dominum nostrum.

2181 <ALIA.> Deus qui famulantibus tibi mentis et corporis subsidia misericorditer largiaris, praesta quaesumus ut quae hic pietas tua

---

[1]   *cognomine* before correction.

in usus et necessaria corporum famulorum tuorum clementer abundare et conseruare facias, ut his exterius utentes, interius indumento amicti iustitiae, deuoti semper tibi existi mereantur. Per.

CCCCI
ORATIO IN REFECTORIO

2182 Omnipotens et misericors deus qui famulos tuos in hac domo alis refectione carnali, cybum uel potum te benedicente cum gratiarum actione percipiant, et hic et in aeternum per te semper salui esse me/reantur. Per.

f. 256v

CCCCII
ORATIO IN DORMITORIO

2183 Benedic domine hoc famulorum tuorum dormitorium, qui non dormis neque dormitas, qui custodis israhel famulos tuos in hac domo quiescentes post laborem, custodi ab inlusionibus fantastimicis satanae, uigilantes in praeceptis tuis meditentur, dormientes te per soporem sentiant, et hic et ubique defensionis tuae auxilio muniantur. Per.

CCCCIII
ORATIO IN CELLARIO

2184 Omnipotens et misericors deus, qui ubique praesens es, maiestatem tuam suppliciter depraecamur, ut huic promptuario gratia tua adesse dignetur, quae cuncta aduersa ab eo repellat, et abundantiam benedictionis tuae la<r>giter infundat. Per.

CCCCIIII
ORATIO IN SCRIPTORIO

2185 Benedicere digneris domine hoc scriptorium famulorum tuorum, et omnes habitantes in eo, ut quicquid hic diuinarum scripturarum ab eis lectum uel scriptum fuerit, sensu capiant, opere perficiant. Per dominum.

CCCCV
ORATIO IN HOSPITALE

2186 Omnipotens et misericors deus, qui es doctor cordium humanorum, et magister angelorum, te humiliter quaesumus, ut cordibus famulorum tuorum, ob gratiam salutationis locum hunc

/f. 257r

frequentantium, semper adesse digneris, sit eorum sermo in timore tuo ignitus, atque sale conditus, utilitate proxi/mi plenus, ut cum hinc aduenientes recesserint, de exemplo eorum gloriam tui nominis praedicent. Per.

CCCCVI
ORATIO IN DOMO INFIRMORVM

2187 Omnipotens et misericors deus, quaesumus inmensam pietatem tuam, ut ad introitum humilitatis nostrae, hos famulos tuos in hoc loco habitaculo fessos iacentes, salutifere uisitare digneris, ut sicut uisitasti domine tobiam et sarram, socrum petri, puerumque centurionis, ita et isti pristina sanitate animae corporisque recepta, gratiarum tibi in ecclesia tua referant actionem. Per.

CCCCVII
ORATIO IN AREA

2188 Multiplica domine super nos misericordiam tuam, et preces nostras propitius exaudire dignare, et sicut exaudisti famulum tuum regem dauid, qui te in area hostias offerendo placauit, iram auertit, indulgentiam impetrauit, ita ueniat quaesumus super hanc aream speratae benedictionis ubertas, ut repleti fructibus tuis, de tua semper misericordia glorientur. Per.

CCCCVIII
ORATIO IN GRANARIO

2189 Omnipotens et misericors deus qui benedixisti horrea ioseph, aream gedeonis, et adhuc quod maius est iacta terrae semina surgere facis, cum fenore messis, te humiliter quaesumus ut sicut ad petitionem famuli tui helyae non defuit uiduae farina, ita ad nostrae prauitatis suffragia, huic horreo famulorum tuorum non desit benedictionis / tuae abundantia. Per.

/f. 257v

CCCCVIIII
ORATIO IN PISTRINO

2190 Sanctificetur istius officinae locus domine, et fugetur ab eo omnis spiritus inmundus per uirtutem domini nostri iesu christi, deturque omnibus in eo commorantibus sanitas, claritas, hylaritas, protegente ac conseruante maiestate tua omnipotens deus, qui uiuis et regnas in saecula saeculorum. Amen.

CCCCX
ORATIO IN COQVINA

2191 Deus aeterne[1] ante cuius conspectum adsistunt angeli, et cuius nutu reguntur uniuersa, qui etiam necessariis humanę fragilitatis, tua pietate consulere non desinis, te humiliter imploramus, ut habitaculum istius officinae illa benedictione perfundas, qui per manus haelysaei prophetae in olla heremetica gustus amarissimos dulcorasti, et semper hic tuae benedictionis copia redundante, laudes tibi referant serui tui, qui das aescam omni carni, et reples omne animal benedictione, saluator mundi qui uiuis et regnas.

CCCCXI
ORATIO IN LARDARIO

2192 Omnipotens et misericors deus, qui necessitatem humani generis clementer praeuidens, adminicula temporalia contulisti, humiliter imploramus, ut benedicere digneris hoc lardarium famulorum tuorum, ut quod hic tua misericordia pie contulit, nostro merito non depereat. Per dominum.

CCCCXII
ORATIO IN CAMINATA

f. 258r **2193** / Omnipotens sempiterne deus, cuius sapientia hominem docuit, ut domus haec careret aliquando frigore, a uicinitate ignis, te quaesumus ut omnes habitantes uel conuenientes in ea, careant in corde infidelitatis frigore, ac feruore ignis spiritus sancti. Per.

CCCCXVII
Incipit ordo unctionis infirmi

2194 *Hic dicatur sacerdos ad infirmum. Quid me aduocasti frater? Ille ait, ut mihi unctionem tradas. Dicit sacerdos ad eum: Donet tibi dominus noster iesus christus ueram facilemque unctionem, tam si te respexerit et sanauerit te deus, custodies illam? Respondet: Custodiam.*

2195 *Tunc sacerdos faciet crucem ex cinere cum aqua super pectus eius, et inponit cilicium desuper dicens: Si quis infirmatur, agat paenitentiam etiam ex necessitate, quia misericors deus, quia*

---

[1] *aeternae* before correction.

411

misericordia dei nec mensuras, nec tempora habet, dicente dei spiritu prophętam, cum conuersus ingemueris, tunc saluus eris. Et alibi, dic iniquitates tuas prior ut iustificeris. AN. Succurre domine infirmo huic et medica eum spiritali medicamine, ut in pristina sanitate restitutus, gratiarum tibi referat actiones. PS. Domine ne in furore tuo. Cum gloria. ALIA. Quia apud deum misericordia et copiosa apud eum redemptio, et multiplex dei misericordia ita et lapsis subuenit humanis, ut non solum per baptismi et consummationis gratiam, sed etiam per paenitentiae atque unctionis medicinam spes uitae reparetur humanae. A.

/f. 258v Cor contritum / et humiliatum deus non spernit. PS. Miserere mei deus, totum gloria, et repleantur antiphona.

2196 Collecta require. A. Opem ferat huic infirmo deus super lectum doloris eius, et ipse confirmet eum et uiuificet. PS. Beatus qui intelligit.

2197 Collecta require. A. Dominus locutus est discipulis suis in nomine meo demonia eiecient super infirmos manus uestras inponite, et bene habebunt. PS. Deus deorum. A. Saluum fac seruum tuum deus meus sperantem custodi animam eius quoniam in te speraui. Ps. Inclina domine. A. Cadent a latere tuo mille et decem milia a dextris tuis tibi autem nullum adpropinquat malum. PS. Qui habitat. A. Propitietur deus iniquitatibus tuis et sanet omnes egritudines tuas et renouetur ut aquile iuuentus tua. PS. Benedic .i. A. Domine libera animam meam a labiis iniquis et a lingua dolosa. PS. Ad dominum cum tribularer.

2198 ORATIO. Omnipotens sempiterne deus qui per iacobum apostolum tuum introducere presbiteros ecclesiae, et ungere oleo infirmos praecepisti, praesta quaesumus ut digneris per manus nostras hunc famulum tuum .ill. infirmum, de oleo sanctificato ungere et benedicere, hoc autem quod nos exterius tua carismata fideliter complectimur, hoc interius spiritaliter diuina uirtus ac mirabiliter tuae magnanimitatis[1] operaretur uirtutem. Per dominum nostrum.

2199 Vngo oculos tuos de oleo sanctificato, ut quidquid inlicito uisu deliquisti huius olei unctione expietur. Per dominum nostrum iesum christum.

---

[1] *magni nimitas* before correction.

2200 *f. 259r* ALIA. Vngo aures has sacrati olei liquore, ut quid delec/tatione nocua auditus admissum est, medicina spiritalis euacuet. Per dominum nostrum.

2201 ALIA. Vngo has nares de oleo sacrato, ut quicquid noxię contractum est, odoratus superfluo iste mundet medicatio. Per dominum nostrum.

2202 ALIA. Vngo labia ista consecrati oleo medicamento, ut quidquid otiosa uel criminosa peccasti locutione diuina, clementia miserante expietur hac unctione. Per.

2203 ALIA. Vngo pectus tuum de oleo sancto, ut hac unctione protectus, fortiter praestare ualeas aduersus ae<t>hereas cateruas. Per dominum.

2204 ALIA. Vngo has scapulas siue medium scapularum de oleo sacro, ut ex omni parte spiritali protectione munitus, iacula diabolici impetus uiriliter contempnere ac procul possis cum robore, iuuaminis repellere. Per dominum.

2205 ALIA. Vngo has manus de oleo consecrato, ut quicquid inlicito uel noxio opere egerunt, per hanc unctionem euacuetur. Per dominum.

2206 ALIA. Vngo hos pedes de oleo benedicto, ut quicquid superfluo uel noctio incessu, commiserunt ista abdeleat perunctio. Per dominum.

2207 ALIA. Vngo te oleo sanctificato in nomine patris et filii et spiritus sancti, ut more militis uncti praeparatus ad luctum possis aereas superare cateruas. Per.

2208 *f. 259v* ALIA. / Vngo te oleo sanctificato in nomine patris, et filii, et spiritus sancti, sicut unxit samuhel dauid regem et prophętam, ut non lateat in te spiritus inmundus, neque in membris, neque in medullis, neque in ulla compagine membrorum, sed te inhabitet uirtus christi altissimi et spiritus sancti, quatinus per huius operationem mysterii, et per hanc sacri olei unctionem atque nostram depraecationem uirtute sanctae trinitatis medicatus siue

413

lotus pristinam et melioratam recipere merearis sanitatem. Per eum eiusdem.

2209 ALIA. Vngo te de oleo sancto inuocata magna creatoris maiestate, qui iussit samuhelem prophetam ungere dauid regem operare creaturam.

2210 ALIA. In nomine patris et filii et spiritus sancti, sit tibi haec unctio olei sanctificati, ad purificationem mentis et corporis, et ad munimen et defensionem contra iacula inmundorum spirituum. Amen.

2211 HIC COMMVNICET. Corpus et sanguis domini nostri iesu christi, ad uitam aeternam te perducat, et in die iudicii ad sanctam requiem te resuscitet.

2212 ALIA. Vnum deum patrem et filium et spiritum sanctum unanimiter confitentes, horamus ut uoluntas eius auxiliante gratia perficiatur uite in uobis. Per.

2213 ALIA. Dominus iesus christus aput te sit ut te defendat, intra te
/f. 260r sit, ut te reficiat, circa te sit, / ut te conseruet, ante te sit ut te deducat, post te sit ut te iustificet, super te sit ut te benedicat. Qui cum.

2214 AN. Virtutum omnium deus qui ab humanis corporibus infirmitates expelle, miserere seruo tuo et uisita in salutari tuo, et caelestis gratiae tribue medicinam. PS. Beatus qui intelligit.

CCCCXVIII
MISSA PRO INFIRMO IN DOMO

2215 Omnipotens sempiterne deus qui subuenis in periculis et necessitatibus laborantibus maiestatem tuam suppliciter exoramus, ut miserere digneris sanctum angelum tuum, qui famulum tuum .ill. in hac domo consistente in angustiis et necessitatibus suis laborantem, consolationibus tuis attollat, quibus et de praesenti consequatur auxilium, et aeterna remedia compraehendat. Per.

2216 ALIA. Deus in cuius libros uocabula notata mortalium[1], concede nobis omnibus ueniam delictorum, et praesta quaesumus, ut famulum tuum .ill. infirmum, quem inmensus languor excrutiat, tua miseratio reparet ad medelam, si ei ambitio piaculi adduxit dolorem, adducat etiam confessio salutis obtabilem sanitatem. Per.

2217 LECTIO EPISTOLAE BEATI IACOBI APOSTOLI. FRATRES. Tristatur aliquis uestrum.

2218 R. Exurge domine succurre huic infirmo, et libera eum et sana eius languorem. V. Adiutor in oportunitatibus in tribulatione opem tuam tribue benignus infirmum. ALL. Mitte ei auxilium de sancto et de syon tuere eum.

2219 SECVNDVM LVCAM. In illo tempore. Intrauit iesus in capharnaum.

2220 <OF.> Domine qui publicani precibus et oratione placatus es, qui socrum petri a febre ualida liberasti et nobis pro infirmos suppli/cantibus adesto domine.

f. 260v

2221 SECRETA. Sana quaesumus domine uulnera famuli tui .ill. egritudines eius perime, peccata dimitte, et hanc oblationem quam tibi pro eo offerimus benignus suscipe, et sic cum flagella in hoc seculo, ut post transitum sanctorum mereatur adunari consortio. Per.

2222 PRAEFATIO. VD aeterne deus. Qui famulos tuos ideo corporaliter uerberas, ut mente proficiant potenter ostendens, quod sit pietas tuae praeclara saluatio, dum praestas ut operetur nobis etiam ipsam firmitas salutem. Per christum.

2223 BENEDICTIO. Omnipotens deus hunc infirmum uisita, egrotum sana, inualidum confirma, ualidumque corrobora, ad regna erige caelestia. AMEN.
Exaudi orantem, trahe ruentem, erue errantem, dirige negligentem, infirmo huic concede caritatem. AMEN.

---

[1] *martalium* before correction.

415

Liberes eum de uariis languoribus, de terrenis cupiditatibus de diaboli atque inferni faucibus. AMEN.

Sana domine omnium medicator eius febrium, et cunctorum languorum cruciatus, egritudineque et dolorum omnium dissolue tormenta. AMEN.

Visceraque eius in terra sana medicina putridines, te uacua cicatrices sana, carnis et sanguinis materiem reforma. AMEN. Quod ipse.

2224 COMMVNIO. Succurre domine infirmum hunc.

2225 AD COMPLENDVM. Muneribus diuinis perceptis quaesumus
/f. 261r   domine deuotionem famuli tui .ill. confirmes / in bono, et mittas ei auxilium de sancto, et de sion tuearis eum. Per dominum nostrum iesum christum.

CCCCXVIIII
INPOSITIO MANVS SVPER ENERGVMINVM

2226 Omnipotens sempiterne deus, a cuius fiducie caeli distillant, montes sicut caera liquescunt, terra tremit, cui patent abyssi, quem infernus pauescit, quem omnis irarum motus, aspitiens humiliatur, te supplex depraecor dominator domine, ut inuocatione nominis tui, ab huius famuli tui[1] uexatione, inimicus confusus abscedat, et ab huius possessione anima liberata, ad auctorem suae salutis recurrat, liberatoremque suum diabolico fetore depulso, et odore suauissimo spiritus sancti praecepto sequatur. Per.

2227 ITEM ALIA PRO PARVVLO ENERGVMINO. Domine sanctae pater, omnipotens sempiterne deus, uirtutem tuam totis exoro gemitibus pro huius famuli tui, diabolo obpraesso infantia, qui etiam indignis inter pressuras donas praesidium, exurge pro huius infantia debellata, et noli diu retinere uindictam, nec ante conspectum tuum uenient parentum delicta, qui nec pro filio patrem, nec pro patre promi<si>sti filium iudicari, auxiliare quaesumus inimici furore uexato, ne sine baptismate fatias eius animam a diabolo possideri, sed potius tenera aetas maligni oppressionibus liberata, tibi sempiternas gratias referat. Per.

---

[1] Supplied interlinearly.

.261v **2228** / ITEM ALIA SVPER ENERGVMINO BABTIZATO. Deus angelorum, deus archangelorum, deus prophętarum, deus apostolorum, deus martyrum, deus uirginum, deus pater domini nostri iesu christi, inuoco nomen sanctum tuum, ac praeclara maiestatis tuae, clementiam supplex exposco, ut mihi auxilium praestare digneris, aduersus hunc nequissimum spiritum, ut ubicumque latet, audito nomine tuo, uelociter exeat uel recedat. Ipse tibi imperat diabole, qui uentis et mari uel tempestatibus imperauit. Ipse tibi imperat, qui te de supernis caelorum, in inferiora terrae, demergi praecepit. Ipse tibi imperat, qui te retrorsum redire praecepit. Audi ergo et time satana uictus, et prostratus, abscede in nomine domini nostri iesu christi. Tu ergo nequissimae satana, inimicus fidei, generis humani mortis raptor, iustitiae declinator, malorum radix, fomes uitiorum, seductor hominum, perditor gentium, incitator inuidiae, origo auaritiae, causa discordiae, excitator dolorum, daemonum magister, quid stas et resistis, cum scis eum tuas perdere uires, illum metuae qui in isaac immolatus est, in ioseph uenundatus, in agno occisus, in homine crucifixus, deinde triumphator, recede in nomine patris et filii, et spiritus sancti, et da locum spiritui sancto, per hoc signum crucis christi domini nostri, qui cum patre et spiritu sancto uiuit et regnat deus, per omnia saecula saeculorum. AMEN.

f. 262r **2229** ITEM ALIA ORATIO. / Cconditor[1] et defensor generis humani, qui hominem ad imaginem et similitudinem tuam formasti, respice super famulum tuum hunc qui dolis inuidi serpentis appetitur, quem uetus aduersarius, et hostis antiquus, atrae formidinis horrore circumuolat, et sensum mentis humanae stupore deficit, terrore conturbat, et metu trepidi tremoris exagitat. Repelle domine uirtutem diaboli, fallacesque eius insidias amoue procul impius, temptator effugiat, sit nominis tui signo famulus tuus, et animo[2] totus et corpore, tu pectoris huius in terra custodias, tu uiscera regas, tu corda confirmes, in anima aduersarie potestatis temptamenta uanescant. Da ad hanc inuocationem nominis tui gratiam, ut qui hucusque terrebat, territus abeat, et uictus abscedat. Tibique possit hic seruus tuus

[1] Capital and minuscule *c* together.
[2] *anomo* before correction.

417

corde firmato, et mente sincera, debitum praebere famulatum. Per.

2230 ALIA. Domine sanctae pater omnipotens aeterne deus, osanna in excelsis, pater domini nostri iesu christi, qui illum refugam tyrannum gehennae deputasti, qui unigenitum tuum in hunc mundum misisti, ut illum rugiente in leonem contereret, uelociter attende, accelera ut eripias hominem ad imaginem et similitudinem tuam creatum, a ruina et demonio meridiano, da domine terrorem tuum super bestiam, quae exterminauit

/f. 262v
uineam[1] tuam, / da fidutiam seruis tuis, contra nequissimum draconem fortiter stare, ne contempnat sperantes in te, et dicat, sicut in pharaone iam dixit. Deum non noui, nec israhel dimitto, urgeat illum domine dextera tua potens, discederet a famulo tuo, ne diutius praesumat captiuum, tenere hominem, quem tu ad imaginem tuam facere dignatus es. Adiuro te ergo serpens antiquae per iudicem uiuorum et mortuorum, per factorem mundi, per eum qui habet potestatem mittere in gehennam, ut ab hoc famulo dei, qui ad ecclesiae praesepia concurrit, cum metu et exercitu furoris tui festinus discedas, adiuro te non mea infirmitate sed in uirtute spiritus sancti, ut desinas ab hoc famulo deo, quem omnipotens deus ad imaginem suam fecit, cede, cede, non mihi, sed mysteriis christi. Illius enim te perurget potestas, qui te affligens crucis suae subiugauit. Illius brachium contremesce, qui deuictis gemitibus inferni, animas ad lucem perduxit. Sit tibi terror corpus hominis, sit tibi formido imago dei, nec resistas, nec meroris discedere ab homine, quoniam complacuit christo, ut in homine habitaret, et ne me infirmum contempnendum putes, dum me peccatorem nimis esse cognoscis. Imperat tibi dominus. Imperat tibi maiestas christi. Imperat tibi deus pater. Imperat tibi filius et spiritus

/f. 263r
sanctus. / Imperat tibi apostolorum fides, sancti petri, et sancti pauli, et caeterorum apostolorum. Imperat tibi martyrum sanguis. Imperat tibi indulgentia confessorum. Imperat tibi sacramentum crucis. Imperat tibi mysteriorum uirtutis, exi transgressor, exi seductor, plene omni dolo et fallacia, ueritatis inimice, innocentium persecutor, da locum durissime, da locum christo, da locum impiissime, in quo nihil inuenisti de operibus

---

[1]   *ueneam* before correction.

tuis, qui te expoliauit, qui regnum tuum destruxit, qui te uictum ligauit, et uasa tua disrupit, qui te proiecit in tenebras exteriores, ubi tibi cum ministris tuis erit praeparatus interitus, sed quid nunc truculente recogitas[1], quid temerarię retractas? reus omnipotenti deo cuius statuta transgressus es, reus filio eius iesu christo, qui temptare ausus es, et crucifigere praesumisti, reus humano generi cui mortuis persuasionibus uenit. Adiuro ergo te draco nequissime in nomine agni inmaculati, qui ambulauit super aspidem et basiliscum, qui conculcauit leonem, et draconem, ut discedas ab homine, discedas ab ecclesia dei, contremesce et effuge, inuocato nomine domine, illius quem inferi tremunt, cui uirtutes caelorum, et potestates, et dominationes subiectae sunt, quem cherubin et seraphin indefessis uocibus laudant. Imperat tibi uerbum caro factum.

Imperat tibi natus ex uirgine. Imperat / tibi iesus nazarenus, qui tecum discipulo eius contemneris, elisum et prostratum exire iussit ab homine, quo praesente cum te ab homine separasset, nec porcorum gregem praesumebas contingere. Recede ergo nunc adiuratus, in nomine eius, ab homine quem ipse plasmauit, durum tibi est christo uelle resistere, durum tibi est contra stimulum calcitrare, quia quanto tardius exis, tanto tibi supplicium maius crescit, quoniam non hominem contemnis, sed illum qui dominator uiuorum et mortuorum, qui uenturus est.

2231 ALIA. Domine sanctae pater omnipotens aeterne deus, per inpositionem scripturę huius, et gustu aquae, expelle diabolum ab homine isto, de capite, de capillis, de uertice, de cerebro, de fronte, de oculis, dae auribus, de naribus, de ore, de lingua, de sublingua, de gutture, de collo, de corpore toto, de omnibus membris, de compaginibus membrorum suorum, intus et foris, de ossibus, de uenis, de neruis, de sanguine, de sensu, de cogitationibus, de omni conuersatione, et operetur in te uirtus christi in eo, qui pro te passus ut ad uitam aeternam merearis. Per.

---

[1] Some letters rewritten.

CCCCXX
ORATIONES AD VISITANDVM INFIRMVM

2232 Deus qui famulo tuo ezechiae ter quinos annos ad uitam donasti, ita et famulum tuum a lecto aegritudinis tua potentia erigat ad salutem. Per dominum nostrum iesum christum.

/f. 264r **2233** ALIA. / Respice domine famulum tuum .ill. in infirmitate sui corporis laborantem, et animam refoue quam creasti, ut castigationibus emendata, continuo se sentiat tua medicina saluatum. Per.

2234 ALIA. Deus qui facturae tuae pio semper dominaris affectu, inclina aurem tuam supplicationibus nostris, et famulum tuum .ill. ex aduersa ualitudine corporis laborantem placatus respice, et uisita in salutari tuo, ac caelestis gratiae praesta medicinam. Per.

2235 ALIA. Deus qui humano generi et salutis remedium, et uitae aeternae munera contulisti, conserua famulo tuo .ill. tuarum dona uirtutum, et concede ut medelam tuam non solum in corpore, sed etiam in anima sentiat. Per.

2236 ALIA. Virtutum caelestium deus qui ab humanis corporibus omnem languorem, et omnem infirmitatem praecepti tui pietate depellis, adesto propitius huic famulo tuo .ill. ut fugatis infirmitatibus et uiribus receptis, nomen sanctum tuum instaurata protinus sanitate benedicat. Per dominum.

2237 ALIA. Domine sanctae pater omnipotens aeternę deus, qui fragilitatem conditionis nostrae infusa uirtutis tuae dignatione confirmas, ut salutaribus remediis pietatis tuae corpora nostra et membra uegetentur, super hunc famulum tuum .ill. propitiatus
/f. 264v intende, ut omni / necessitate corporeae infirmitatis exclusa, gratia in eo pristinę sanitatis perfecta reparetur. Per.

ORATIO PRO REDDITA SANITATE

2238 Domine santae pater omnipotens aeternae deus, qui benedictionis tuae gratiam aegris infundendo corporibus, facturam tuam multiplici pietate custodis, ad inuocationem nominis tui benignus adsiste, et hunc famulum tuum ill.

420

liberatum aegritudine, et sanitate donatum, dextera tua erigas, uirtute confirmes, potestatae tuearis, ecclesiae tuae sanctisque altaribus tuis cum omni desiderata prosperitate restitutas. Per dominum nostrum.

CCCCXXI

Incipiunt orationes in agenda mortuorum

2239 *Cum anima in agone sui exitus dissolutione corporis uisa fuerit laborare, conuenire studebunt fratres, uel caeteri quique fideles, et canendi sunt, .vii^{tem}. poenitentiae psalmi, id est duo.* Domine ne in furore tuo, et duo, Domine exaudi. Beati quorum. Et de profundis. Et miserere mei deus.

2240 *Atque agenda est laetania prout permiserit ratio temporis, et secundum quod in causa egressuri perspici poterit uel aestimari. Finitis autem sanctorum nominibus mox incipiatur ab omnibus responsus:* Subuenite sancti dei. *Quo finito dicat sacerdos hanc orationem siue commendationem pro eo.*

f. 265r **2241** ORATIO. / Tibi domine commendamus animam famuli tui .ill. ut defunctus saeculo tibi uiuat, et quae per fragilitatem mundanae conuersationis peccata admisit, tu uenia misericordissimae pietatis absterge. Per dominum.

2242 ORATIO. Misericordiam tuam domine sanctae pater omnipotens aeternae deus, pietatis affectu rogare pro aliis cogimur, qui pro nostris supplicare peccatis nequam sufficimus. Tamen de tua confisi gratuita pietate, et inolita benignitate, clementiam tuam deposcimus, ut animam serui tui ad te reuertentem, cum pietate suscipias. Adsit ei angelus testamenti tui michahel, et per manus sanctorum angelorum tuorum, inter sanctos et electos tuos, in sinibus abrahę, isaac, et iacob patriarcharum tuorum, eam collocare digneris, quatinus liberata de principibus tenebrarum et de locis poenarum, nullis iam primae natiuitatis uel ignorantiae, aut propriae iniquitatis seu fragilitatis confundatur erroribus, sed potius agnoscatur a tuis, et sanctae beatitudinis requiae perfruatur, ut quae cum magni iudicii dies aduenerit, inter sanctos et electos tuos resuscitatus, gloria manifestę contemplationis tuae perpetuo satietur. Per dominum.

2243 *Si autem quidem superuixerit, canantur alii psalmi, uel agatur laetania usquequo anima corpore corruptionis absoluatur. In*
/f. 265v *cuius egressu dicatur / antiphona.* Suscipiat te christus qui uocauit te, et in sinum abrahę angeli deducant te. PSAL. In exitu israhel.

2244 SEQVITVR ORATIO. Omnipotens sempiterne deus qui humano corpori animam ad similitudinem tuam inspirare dignatus es, dum te iubente puluis in puluerem reuertitur, tu imaginem tuam cum sanctis et electis tuis, aeternis sedibus praecipias sociari, eamque ad te reuertentem de aegypti partibus blande leniterque suscipias, et angelos tuos sanctos ei obuiam mittas, uiamque illi iustitiae demonstra, et portas gloriae tuae aperi. Repelle quaesumus ab ea omnes principes tenebrarum, et agnosce depositum fidele quod tuum est. Suscipe domine creaturam tuam, non a diis alienis creatam, sed a te solo deo uiuo et uero, quia non est alius praeter te domine, et non est secundum[1] opera tua. Laetifica clementissime deus animam serui tui .ill. et clarifica eam in multitudine misaericordiae tuae, ne memineris quaesumus iniquitatum eius antiquarum, et ebrietatum quas suscitauit furor mali desiderii. Licet enim peccauerit, tamen te non negauit, sed signo fidei insignitus, te qui omnia et eum inter omnia fecisti, fideliter adorauit. Qui uiuis.

2245 ITEM ANTIPHONA. Chorus angelorum te suscipiat, et in sinu abrahae te collocet, ut cum lazaro quondam paupere aeternam habeas requiem. PSAL. Dilexi quoniam, usque ad dominum cum tribularer.

/f. 266r **2246** SEQVITVR ORATIO. / Diri uulneris nouitate perculsi, et quoddammodo cordibus sauciati, misericordiam tuam mundi redemptor flebilibus uocibus imploramus, ut cari nostri .N. animam ad tuam clementiam, qui fons pietatis es reuertentem, blande leniterque suscipias, et quas illa ex carnali commoratione contraxit maculas, tu deus inolita bonitate clementer deleas, pie indulgeas, obliuioni in perpetuum tradas, atque hanc laudem tibi cum caeteris reddituram, et corpus quandoque reuersuram, sanctorum tuorum coetibus aggreri praecipias. Qui cum deo

---

[1] Some letters rewritten.

patre in unitate spiritus sancti deus uiuis et regnas deus, per omnia saecula saeculorum. Amen.

2247 TVNC ROGAT PRO EO SACERDOS ORARE. Et ne nos inducas in tentationem. Requiem aeternam. Anima eius in bonis demorabitur. Et non intres in iudicium. A porta inferi.

2248 Partem beate resurrectionis obtineat, uitamque aeternam habere mereatur in caelis, per te christe iesu, qui uiuis et regnas deus, per omnia saecula saeculorum.

2249 ALIA. Deus cui soli competit medicinam praestare post mortem, praesta quaesumus ut animam famuli tui .ill. terrenis exuta contagiis, in tuae redemptionis parte numeretur. Per.

2250 *Tunc lauatur corpus defuncti. Oratio post lauationem corporis antequam de domo efferatur.*

2251 ORATIO. Suscipe domine animam serui tui .N. quam de ergastulo / huius saeculi uocare dignatus es, et libera eam de principibus tenebrarum et de locis poenarum, ut absoluta omnium peccatorum, quietis ac lucis aeternae beatitudine perfruatur, et inter sanctos et electos tuos in resurrectionis gloria, resuscitari mereatur. Per.

2252 ALIA. Suscipe[1] domine animam serui tui .N. ad te reuertentem uestem caelestem indue eam et laua eam sancto fonte uitae aeternae, et inter gaudentes gaudeat, et inter sapientes sapiat, et inter martyres consedeat, et inter patriarchas proficiat, et inter prophetas et apostolos christum sequi studeat. Et inter angelos et archangelos claritatem dei praeuideat. Et inter paradysi rutilos lapides gaudium possideat, et noticiam ministeriorum dei agnoscat. Et inter cherubin et seraphin claritatem dei inueniat. Et inter uiginti quattuor seniores, cantica canticorum audiat. Et inter lauantes stolas in fonte luminis lauet, et inter pulsantes depulset, et portas apertas caelestis hierusalem reperiat, et inter uidentes deum, facie ad faciem uideat. Et inter cantantes

[1] *S* supplied in crimson.

canticum nouum cantet. Et inter audientes auditum caelesti sono exaudiat. Per.

2253 TVNC CVM RESPONSO. Subuenite sancti dei. *Et aliis responsis defunctorum deportatur, et cum adpropinquatum fuerit ecclesiae, canitur psalmus.* Miserere mei deus, *cum antiphona*: / Requiem aeternam. *In ecclesia autem requiescet corpus defuncti quoadusque pro eius anima missa canatur, et offeratur ab omnibus quibus fuerit uisum.*

/f. 267r

CCCCXXII
INCIPIVNT MISSAE ORATIONES

2254 Quaesumus domine pro tua pietate miserere animae famuli tui ill. et a contagiis mortalitatis exutam, in aeternae saluationis partem restituae. Per.

2255 LECTIO EPISTOLAE BEATI PAVLI APOSTOLI AD THESALONICENSES. FRATRES. Nolumus autem uos ignorare de dormientibus, ut non contristemini sicut et cęteri qui spem non habent. Si enim credimus quod iesus mortuus est et resurrexit, ita et deus eos qui dormierunt per iesum adducet cum eo. Hoc enim uobis dicimus in uerbo domini, qui nos qui uiuimus qui residui sumus, in aduentum domini, non praeueniemus eos qui dormierunt. Quoniam ipse dominus in iussu et in uoce archangeli, et in tuba dei descendet de caelo, et mortui qui in christo sunt resurgent primi. Deinde nos qui uiuimus qui relinquimur, simul rapiemur cum illis in nubibus, obuiam christo in aera, et sic semper cum domino erimus. Itaque consolamini inuicem, in uerbis istis.

2256 SEQVENTIA SECVNDVM IOHANNEM. In illo tempore. Dixit martha ad iesum. Domine, si fuisses hic, frater meus non fuisset mortuus. Sed et nunc scio, quia quęcumque poposceris a deo, dabit tibi deus. Dicit illi iesus. Resurget frater tuus. Dicit ei martha. Scio, quia resurget in resurrectione in nouissimo die. Dicit ei iesus. Ego sum resurrectio et uita, qui credit in me etiam si mortuus fuerit uiuet. Et omnis qui / uiuit et credit in me, non morietur in aeternum. Credis hoc? Ait illi. Vtique domine. Ego credidi quia tu es christus filius dei, qui in hunc mundum uenisti.

/f. 267v

424

2257 SVPER OBLATA. Animam famuli tui .ill. domine ab omnibus uitiis et peccatis conditionis humanae haec absoluat oblatio, quae totius mundi tulit immolata peccatum. Per dominum.

2258 PRAEFATIO. VD aeterne[1] deus. Quoniam quamuis humano generi mortis inlata conditio peccata nostra contristet, tamen clementiae tuae[2] dono spe futurae inmortalitatis erigimur, ac memores salutis aeternae, non timemus lucis huius sustinere iacturam. Quoniam beneficio gratiae tuae, fidelibus uita non tollitur, sed mutatur. Atque animae corporeo ergastulo liberate, horrent mortalia, dum inmortalia consequuntur. Vnde quaesumus ut famulus tuus .ill. beatorum tabernaculis constitutus, euasisse se carnales glorietur angustias, diemque iudicii, cum fiducia uoto glorificationis exspectet.

2259 INFRA ACTIONEM. Hanc igitur oblationem quam tibi pro anima famuli tui .ill. offerimus, quem hodie carnali corruptione liberasti quaesumus domine placatus accipias, et quicquid humanae conditionis obreptione contraxit expedias, ut tuis purificata remediis, ad gaudium sempiternum perueniat. Per dominum nostrum iesum christum.

.268r **2260** AD COMPLENDVM. / Prosit domine quaesumus animae famuli tui .ill. diuini caelebratio sacramenti, ut eius in quo sperauit et credidit, aeternum capiat te miserante consortium. Per.

CCCCXXIII

2261 *Post celebrationem denique missae stat sacerdos iuxta feretrum et dicit hanc orationem*: Non intres in iudicium cum seruo tuo domine .ill. quoniam nullus apud te iustificabitur homo nisi per te omnium peccatorum tribuatur remissio, non ergo eum tua quaesumus iudicialis sententia premat, quem tibi uera supplicatio fidei christianae commendat, sed gratia tua illi succurrente, mereatur euadere iudicium ultionis, qui dum uiueret insignitus est signaculo trinitatis. Per.

---

[1] *aeternae* before correction
[2] *u* supplied interlinearly.

425

2262 SEQVITVR RESPONSORIVM. Subuenite sancti dei. V. Chorus angelorum eam suscipiat, et in sinu abrahae eam collocet. ET TER Kyrrie eleison.

2263 ITEM ORATIO. Deus cui omnia uiuunt, et cui non pereunt moriendo corpora nostra sed mutantur in melius, te supplices depraecamur, ut quicquid anima famuli tui .ill. uitiorum tuaeque uoluntati contrarium fallente diabolo et propria iniquitate atque fragilitate contraxit, tu pius et misericors ablue indulgendo. Eamque suscipi iubeas per manus angelorum tuorum, deducendam in sinum patriarcharum tuorum, abraham scilicet amici tui, et isaac electi tui, atque iacob dilecti tui, quo aufugit /f. 268v dolor et tristitia, atque sus/pirium, fidelium quoque animae, felici iocunditate laetantur. Et in nouissimo magni iudicii die, inter sanctos et electos tuos eam facias perpetuae gloriae percipere portionem, quam oculus non uidit, et auris non audiuit, et in cor hominis non ascendit, quae praeparasti diligentibus te. Per.

2264 SEQVITVR RESPONSORIVM. Antequam nascerer nouisti me. V. Comissa mea pauesco. ET TER Kyrrie eleison.

2265 ITEM ORATIO. Fac quaesumus domine hanc cum seruo tuo defuncto .ill. misericordiam, ut factorum suorum in poenis non recipiat uicem, qui tuam in uotis tenuit uoluntatem. Et quia hic illum uera fides iunxit fidelium turmis, illic cum tua miseratio societ angelicis choris. Per.

2266 TVNC ROGAT PRO EO ORARE SACERDOS. Et ne nos inducas. Requiem aeternam. A porta inferi.

2267 ORATIO. Inclina domine aurem tuam ad praeces nostras quibus misericordiam tuam supplices depraecamur, ut animam famuli tui ill. quam de hoc saeculo migrare iussisti, in pacis ac lucis regione constituas, et sanctorum tuorum iubeas esse consortem. Per.

2268 ET SIC LEVATVR DE ECCLESIA CVM ANTIPHONA. Aperite mihi[1] portas iustitiae. ET PSALMVS .CXVII. ID EST Confitemini domino quam bonus. ET DEPORTATVR VSQVE AD SEPVLCHRVM.

CCCCXXIIII

2269 ORATIO ANTE SEPVLCHRVM. Piae recordationis affectu fratres carissimi commemorationem faciamus cari nostri .ill. / quem dominus de temptationibus huius saeculi assumpsit, obsecrantes misericordiam dei nostri, ut ipse ei tribuere dignetur placidam et quietam mansionem, et remittat omnes lubricae temeritatis offensas, ut concessa uenia plenae indulgentiae quicquid in hoc saeculo proprio uel alieno reatu deliquid, totum ineffabili pietate ac benignitate sua deleat et abstergat. Quod ipse praestare dignetur, qui cum patre et spiritu sancto uiuit et regnat deus. Per omnia.

2270 SEQVITVR ANTIPHONA. Ingrediar in locum tabernaculi. PS. Quemadmodum desiderat.

2271 ORATIO. Obsecramus misericordiam tuam omnipotens aeternae deus, qui hominem ad imaginem tuam creare dignatus es, ut spiritum famuli tui .ill. quem hodierna rebus humanis eximi, et[2] ad te accersiri iussisti, blande et misericorditer suscipias, non ei dominentur umbrae mortis, nec tegat eum chaos et caligo tenebrarum, sed exutus omnium criminum labe, in sinu abrahę patriarchae collocatus, locum lucis et refrigerii se adeptum esse gaudeat, et cum dies iudicii aduenerit, cum sanctis et electis tuis eum resuscitari iubeas. Per.

2272 SEQVITVR ANTIPHONA. Haec requies mea in saeculum saeculi. PS. Memento domine dauid.

2273 ORATIO. Deus apud quem mortuorum spiritus uiuunt, et in quo electorum animae deposito carnis onere plena felicitate laetantur, praesta supplican/tibus nobis ut anima famuli tui .ill.

---

[1] *illi* before correction.
[2] Over an erasure.

quae temporali per corpus uisionis, huius luminis caruit uisu, aeternae illius lucis solatio potiatur, non eum tormentum mortis attingat, non dolor horrendę uisionis afficiat, non poenalis timor excruciet, non reorum proxima catena constringat. Sed concessa sibi uenia delictorum omnium optatę quietis consequatur gaudia repromissa. Per.

2274 SEQVITVR ANTIPHONA. De terra plasmasti me. Ps. Domine probasti me. ET PONITVR IN SEPVLCHRO CORPVS DEFVNCTI.

CCCCXXV

2275 ORATIONES POST SEPVLTVM CORPVS. Oremus fratres carissimi pro spiritu cari nostri .ill. quem dominus de laqueo huius saeculi liberare dignatus est, cuius corpusculum hodie sepulturae traditur, ut eum pietas domini in sinu abrahae, isaac et iacob collocare dignetur, ut cum dies iudicii aduenerit, inter sanctos et electos suos, eum in parte dextera collocandum resuscitari faciat, praestante domino nostro iesu christo, qui cum eo in unitate spiritus sancti uiuit et regnat deus. Per omnia saecula saeculorum. Amen.

2276 ALIA. Deus qui iustis supplicationibus semper pręsto es, qui pia uota dignaris intueri, da famulo tuo .ill. cuius depositioni hodie officia humanitatis exhibemus, cum sanctis et fidelibus tuis beati muneris portionem. Per dominum nostrum iesum christum filium tuum.

/f. 270r **2277** ITEM ALIA ORATIO. / Deus uitae dator et humanorum corporum reparator, qui te a peccatoribus exorari uoluisti, exaudi praeces quas spetiali deuotione pro anima famuli tui .ill. tibi lacramabiliter fundimus, ut liberare eam ab infernorum cruciatibus, et collocare inter agmina sanctorum tuorum digneris. Veste quoque caelesti et stola inmortalitatis indui, et paradysi amoenitate confoueri iubeas. Per.

2278 ITEM ALIA. Deus qui humanarum animarum aeternus amator es, animam famuli tui .ill. quam[1] uera dum in corpore maneret

---

[1] *quo* before correction.

428

tenuit fides, ab omni cruciatu inferorum redde extorrem, ut segregata ab infernalibus claustris, sanctorum mereatur adunari consortiis. Per.

2279 ALIA. Deus qui iustis supplicationibus semper praesto es, qui pia uota digneris intueri, qui uniuersorum es conditor et redemptor, misericordia quoque peccatorum, et tuorum beatitudo sanctorum, da famulo tuo .ill. cuius depositioni hodie officium humanitatis[1] exibemus, cum sanctis et electis tuis beati muneris portionem. Eumque a corporibus nexibus absolutum, in resurrectione electorum tuorum facias praesentari. Per dominum.

2280 ITEM ALIA. Temeritatis quidem est domine, ut homo hominem mortalis mortuum[2], cinis cinerem, tibi domino deo nostro audeat commendare. Sed qui terra / suscipit terram, et puluis conuertitur in puluerem, donec omnis caro in suam redigatur originem. Tuam piissime pater lacrimabiliter quaesumus pietatem, ut huius famuli tui .ill. animam, quam de huius mundi uoragine coenulenta ducis ad patriam, abrahae amici tui sinu recipias, et refrigerii rore perfundas. Sit ab aestuentis gehennae truci incendio segregata, et beatae requiei te donante coniuncta. Et quae illi sunt domine digne cruciatibus culpę, tu eas gratiae mitissima laenitate indulge, nec peccati recipiat uicem, sed indulgentiae tuae piam sentiat bonitatem, cumque finito mundi termino, supernum cunctis inluxerit regnum, nouus homo sanctorum omnium coetibus aggregatus, cum electis tuis resurgat in parte dextera coronandus. Per dominum nostrum.

2281 ALIA. Debitum humani corporis sepeliendi officium, fidelium more complentes, deum cui omnia uiuunt fideliter depraecemur, ut hoc corpus cari nostri .ill. a nobis in infirmitate sepultum, in ordine sanctorum suorum resuscitet, et eius spiritum, sanctis ac fidelibus aggregari iubeat. Cum quibus inenarrabili gloria, et perenni felicitate perfrui mereatur, praestante domino nostro iesu christo, qui cum eo et spiritu sancto uiuit et regnat deus. Per omnia saecula saeculorum. Amen.

---

[1]   *huminitatis* before correction.
[2]   *mortalem* before correction.

270v

429

/f. 271r **2282** / TVNC ROGAT PRO EO ORARE SACERDOS, ET DICIT CAPITVLA SICVT SVPERIVS.

2283 Et partem beatae resurrectionis obtineat, uitamque aeternam habere mereatur in caelis, per te christe iesu qui cum deo patre in unitate spiritus sancti uiuis et regnas deus. Per omnia saecula saeculorum. Amen.

2284 PS. Miserere mei deus secundum magnam. Requiem aeternam.

2285 SEQVITVR ORATIO. Absolue domine animam famuli tui .ill. ab omni uinculo delictorum, ut in resurrectionis gloria, inter sanctos tuos resuscitatus respiret. Per dominum nostrum iesum christum filium tuum, qui tecum uiuit et regnat deus in unitate sancti, per omnia saecula saeculorum. Amen. Requiescat in pace. Amen.

CCCCXXVI

MISSA VNIVS DEFVNCTI

2286 Omnipotens sempiterne deus, cui numquam sine spe misericordiae supplicatur, propitiare animae famuli tui .ill. ut qui de hac uita in tui nominis confessione discessit, sanctorum tuorum numero facias aggregari. Per.

2287 SVPER OBLATA. Propitiare domine quaesumus animae famuli tui .ill. pro qua tibi hostias placationis offerimus, et quia in hac luce in fide mansit catholica, in futura uita ei retributio condonetur. Per.

2288 PRAEFATIO. VD per christum dominum nostrum. Per quem salus mundi, per quem uita hominum, per quem resurrectio
/f. 271v mortuorum. Per ipsum te domine suppliciter depraecamur, / ut animae famuli tui .ill. cuius diem .ill. caelebramus indulgentiam largiri digneris perpetuam, atque contagiis mortalitatis exutam, in aeternae saluationis parte restituas. Per quem.

2289 INFRA ACTIONEM. Hanc igitur oblationem quam tibi pro requie animae famuli tui .ill. offerimus, quaesumus domine placatus accipias, et tua pietate concedas, ut mortalitatis nexibus absoluta, inter fideles meatur habere portionem. Per.

430

2290 AD COMPLENDVM. Praesta quaesumus omnipotens deus, ut animam famuli tui .ill. ab angelis lucis susceptam, in praeparatis habitaculis deduci facias beatorum. Per.

CCCCCXXVII
MISSA IN ANNIVERSARIO VNIVS DEFVNCTI

2291 Praesta domine quaesumus ut anima famuli tui .ill. cuius anniuersarium depositionis diem caelebramus, his purgata sacrificiis indulgentiam pariter et requiem capiat sempiternam. Per.

2292 SVPER OBLATA. Propitiare[1] domine supplicationibus nostris, pro anima et spiritu famuli tui .ill. cuius hodie annua dies agitur, pro qua tibi offerimus sacrificium laudis, ut eam sanctorum tuorum consortio sociare digneris. Per.

2293 INFRA ACTIONEM. Hanc igitur oblationem domine quam tibi offerimus pro anima famuli tui .ill. cuius hodie annua dies agitur, quaesumus domine placatus intende, eamque mortalitatis nexibus absolutam, inter tuos fideles ministros habere perpetuam iubeas portionem. Quam oblationem.

f. 272r **2294** AD COMPLENDVM. / Suscipe domine praeces nostras, pro anima famuli tui .ill. ut si quae ei maculae de terrenis contagiis adheserunt, remissionis tuae misericordia deleantur. Per.

CCCCCXXVIII
MISSA PRO DEFVNCTO NVPER BABTIZATO

2295 Deus qui ad caeleste regnum, nonnisi renatis per aquam et spiritum sanctum pandis introitum, multiplica super animam famuli tui .ill. misericordiam tuam, et cui donasti caelestem et incontaminatum transitum post baptismi sacramentum, da ei aeternorum plenitudinem gaudiorum. Per dominum nostrum.

2296 SVPER OBLATA. Propitiare domine supplicationibus nostris, pro anima famuli tui .ill. pro qua tibi offerimus sacrificium laudis, ut eam sanctorum tuorum consortio sociare digneris. Per.

---

[1] *ti* supplied interlinearly.

2297 INFRA ACTIONEM. Hanc igitur oblationem quam tibi offerimus domine pro anima famuli tui .ill. benignus assume, eumque regenerationis fonte purgatum, et periculis uitae huius exutum beatorum numero digneris inserere spirituum. Per dominum.

2298 AD COMPLENDVM. Propitiare domine animae famuli tui .ill. ut quem in fine istius uitae regenerationis fonte mundasti, ad caelestis regni beatitudinem facias peruenire. Per.

CCCCXXVIIII
MISSA PRO DEFVNCTIS DESIDERANTIBVS
PAENITENTIAM, ET MINIMAE CONSEQVENTIBVS

2299 Si quis paenitentiam petens dum sacerdos uenit fuerit officio /f. 272v linguae priuatus, constitutum est ut si idonea / testimonia hoc dixerint, et ipse per motus aliquos satisfacit, sacerdos impleat omnia circa petentem ut mos est.

2300 AD MISSAM. Omnipotens et misericors deus, ut cuius humana conditio potestate consistit, animam famuli tui .ill. quaesumus ab omnibus absolue peccatis, et paenitentiae fructum quem uoluntas eius optauit, praeuentus mortalitatis non perdat. Per.

2301 SVPER OBLATA. Satisfaciat tibi domine quaesumus pro anima famuli tui .ill. sacrificii praesentis oblatio, et peccatorum ueniam quam quaesiuit inueniat, et quod officio linguae implere non potuit, desideratae paenitentiae compensatione percipiat. Per dominum.

2302 INFRA ACTIONEM. Hanc igitur oblationem quam tibi offerimus pro anima famuli tui .ill. cuius depositionis diem illum celebramus, quaesumus ut placatus accipias, et ineffabili pietate concedas, ut quod exequi praeuentus conditione mortali ministerio linguae non potuit, mereatur indulgentia sempiterna. Per. Diesque nostros.

2303 AD COMPLENDVM. Deus a quo speratur humani corporis omne quod bonum est, tribuę per haec sancta quaesumus, ut sicut animae famuli tui .ill. paenitentiae uelle donasti, sic indulgentiam tribue miseratus obtatam. Per dominum nostrum iesum christum.

CCCCXXX
MISSA PLVRIMORVM DEFVNCTORVM

273r **2304** / Propitiare domine quaesumus animabus famulorum famularumque tuarum, misericordia sempiterna, ut mortalibus nexibus expeditas, lux eas aeterna possideat. Per.

2305 SVPER OBLATA. Hostias tibi domine humili placatione deferimus, ut animae famulorum famularumque tuarum, per haec placationis officia, tuam misericordiam consequantur. Per.

2306 INFRA ACTIONEM. Hanc igitur oblationem quam tibi pro requiae animarum famulorum famularumque tuarum offerimus, quaesumus domine propitiatus intuere, et concede ut mortuis prosit ad ueniam, quod cunctis uiuentibus praeparare dignatus es ad medelam. Diesque nostros in tua pace.

2307 AD COMPLENDVM. Inueniant quaesumus domine animae famulorum famularumque tuarum .ill. et illa. omniumque in christo quiescentium lucis aeternae consortium, qui in hac luce positi, tuum consecuti sunt sacramentum. Per.

CCCCXXXI
ALIA MISSA

2308 Fidelium deus omnium conditor et redemptor, animabus famulorum famularumque tuarum, remissionem cunctorum tribue peccatorum, ut indulgentiam quam semper optauerunt, piis supplicationibus consequantur. Per.

2309 SVPER OBLATA. Hostias quaesumus domine, quas tibi pro animabus famulorum famularumque tuarum offerimus propitius intende, ut quibus fidei christianae meritum contulisti, dones et praemium. Per.

273v **2310** PRAEFATIO. / VD aeterne deus. Qui es redemptor animarum sanctarum. Quamuis enim mortis humano generi inlata conditio, pectora humana mentesque contristet, et tamen clementiae tuae dono spe futurae inmortalitatis erigimur. Et memores salutis nostrae, non timemus lucis huius subire dispensum, quia misericordiae tuae munere fidelibus uita mutatur non tollitur, et in timoris tui obseruatione defunctis domicilium perpetuae

433

felicitatis adquiritur. Tibi igitur clementissime pater praeces supplices fundimus, et maiestatem tuam deuotis mentibus exoramus, ut animae famulorum famularumque tuarum, quorum diem commemorationis caelebramus, mortis uinculis absolutae transitum mereantur ad uitam, et in obuium tibi placitarum benedictione aeternum numerentur ad regnum. Per christum.

2311 INFRA ACTIONEM. Hanc igitur oblationem quam tibi pro commemoratione animarum in pace dormientium suppliciter immolamus, quaesumus domine benignus accipias, et tua pietate concedas, ut et nobis proficiat huius pietatis affectus, et illis impetret beatitudinem sempiternam. Quam oblationem.

2312 AD COMPLENDVM. Animabus quaesumus domine famulorum famularumque tuarum .ill. et .illa. oratio proficiat supplicantium, ut eas et ap[1] peccatis exuas, et tuae redemptionis facias / esse participes. Per.

/f. 274r

CCCCXXXII
ITEM ALIA MISSA

2313 Animabus quaesumus domine famulorum famularumque tuarum, misericordiam concede perpetuam, ut eis proficiat in aeternum, quod in te sperauerunt et crediderunt. Per.

2314 SVPER OBLATA. His quaesumus domine placatus intende muneribus, et quod ad laudem tui nominis supplicantes offerimus, ad indulgentiam proficiat[2] defunctorum. Per.

2315 AD COMPLENDVM. Supplices quaesumus domine pro animabus famulorum famularumque tuarum praeces effundimus sperantes, ut quicquid conuersatione contraxerunt humanae, et clementer indulgeas, et in tuorum sede laetantium constituas redemptorem. Per dominum.

---

[1]   For *ab*.
[2]   Second *i* supplied interlinearly.

CCCCCXXIII
MISSA IN CYMITERIIS

2316 Deus cuius miseratione animae fidelium requiescunt, famulis tuis .ill. et .illa. uel omnibus, hic in christo quiescentibus da propitius ueniam peccatorum, ut a cunctis reatibus absoluti, sine fine laetentur. Per.

2317 SVPER OBLATA. Pro animabus famulorum famularumque tuarum .ill. et .illar. et hic omnium catholicorum dormientium, hostiam domine suscipe benignus oblatam, ut hoc sacrificio singulari, uinculis horrendae mortis exuti, uitam mereantur aeternam. Per.

2318 INFRA ACTIONEM. Hanc igitur oblationem quam tibi offerimus domine pro tuorum requie famulorum famularumque tuarum .illor. et .illar. et omnium fidelium catholi/corum ortodoxorum in hac basilica in christo quiescentium, et qui in circuitu huius ecclesiae requiescunt, quaesumus domine placatus accipias, ut per haec salutis humanae subsidia, in tuorum numero redemptorum, sorte perpetua censeantur. Per.

2319 AD COMPLENDVM. Deus fidelium lumen animarum, adesto supplicationibus nostris, et da famulis et famulabus tuis .ill. et .ill. uel quorum corpora hic requiescunt, refrigerii sedem, quietis beatitudinem luminis claritatem. Per dominum.

CCCCXXXIIII
MISSA PRO SALVTE VIVORVM VEL IN AGENDA
MORTVORVM

2320 Sanctorum tuorum intercessionibus quaesumus domine, et nos protege famulis et famulabus tuis, quorum commemorationem agimus, et quorum elemosinas recepimus, seu etiam his qui nobis familiaritate iuncti sunt, misericordiam tuam ubique praetende, ut ab omnibus inpugnationibus defensi, tua opitulatione saluentur. Et animas famulorum famularumque tuarum, omnium uidelicet fidelium catholicorum orthodoxorum, quorum commemorationem agimus, et quorum corpora in hoc monasterio requiescunt, uel quorum nomina ante sanctum altare tuum scripta adesse uidentur, electorum tuorum iungere digneris consor/tio. Per dominum nostrum.

274v

f. 275r

2321 SVPER OBLATA. Propitiare domine supplicationibus nostris, et has oblationes quas pro incolumitate famulorum famularumque tuarum, et pro animabus omnium fidelium catholicorum orthodoxorum, quorum nomina ante sanctum altare tuum scripta adesse uidentur, nomini tuo consecrandas deferimus, benignus assume, ut sacrificii praesentis oblatio, ad refrigerium animarum eorum te miserante perueniat. Per dominum nostrum.

2322 AD COMPLENDVM. Purificent nos quaesumus domine, et diuini sacramenti perceptio, et gloriosa sanctorum tuorum oratio, et animabus famulorum famularumque tuarum, quorum commemorationem agimus, remissionem cunctorum tribue peccatorum. Per dominum nostrum.

[1]MISSA PRO SACERDOTE VEL ABBATE

2323 Deus qui famulum tuum .ill. sacerdotem atque abbatem sanctificasti uocatione misericordię et assumpsisti consummatione felici, suscipe propicius praeces nostras, et presta quaesumus ut sicut ille tecum est meritis, ita a nobis non ręcedat exemplis. Per.

2324 ALIA. Omnipotens sempiterne deus maiestatem tuam suppliciter exoramus ut famulo tuo .ill.

/f. 275v abbati atque sacerdoti / quem in requiem tuam uocare dignatus es dones sedem honorificatam et fructum beatitudinis sempiternę, ut ea quę oculis nostris docuit et gessit, non iuditium nobis pariant sed profectum attribuant ut pro quo nunc in te gaudemus in terris, cum eodem apud te exultare mereamur in cęlis. Per.

2325 LECTIO LIBRI APOCALYPSIS IOHANNIS APOSTOLI. IN DIEBVS ILLIS. Audiui uocem, de cęlo dicentem. Beati mortui, qui in domino moriuntur. Amodo enim iam dicit spiritus ut requiescant a laboribus suis. Opera enim illorum, secuntur illos.

---

[1] Nos 232338 added at Corbie.

2326 SECVNDVM IOHANNEM. IN ILLO TEMPORE. Dixit iesus discipulis suis et turbis iudeorum. Sicut pater suscitat mortuos et uiuificat, sic et filius quos uult[1] uiuificat. Neque enim pater iudicat quemquam[2], sed iudicium omne dedit filio, ut omnes honorificent filium sicut honorificant patrem. Qui non honorificat filium, non honorificat patrem qui misit illum. Amen amen dico uobis, quia qui uerbum meum audit, et credit ei qui misit me habet uitam ęternam. Et in iudicium non uenit, sed transit a morte in uitam.

2327 ORATIO. Suscipe sancta trinitas deus hanc oblationem quam tibi offero pro anima famuli tui .ill. ut requiem ęternam dones ei inter sanctos et electos tuos ut in illorum consortio / uita perfruatur ęterna. Per.

276r

2328 SVPER OBLATA. Concede quaesumus omnipotens deus ut anima famuli tui .ill. abbatis atque sacerdotis, per hęc sancta mysteria in tuo conspectu semper clara consistat, que fideliter ministrauit. Per.

2329 INFRA ACTIONEM. Hanc igitur oblationem quam tibi pro anima famuli tui .ill. abbatis atque sacerdotis offerimus, quaesumus domine placatus intende, pro qua maiestati tuę supplices fundimus preces, ut eam in numero sanctorum tuorum placentium facias dignanter adscribi. Diesque nostros.

2330 AD COMPLENDVM. Prosit quaesumus domine animę famuli tui .ill. abbatis atque sacerdotis misericordię tuę implorata clementia, ut eius

---

[1] *quos uult* over an erasure.
[2] originally *quenquam*.

in quem sperauit et credidit, ęternum capiat te miserante consortium. Per dominum.

MISSA PRO VIVIS VEL DEFVNCTIS SANCTI AVGVSTINI

2331 Omnipotens sempiterne deus, qui uiuorum dominaris, simul et mortuorum, omniumque misereris quos tuos fide et opere futuros esse pręnoscis, te suppliciter exoro, ut pro quibus effundere praeces decreui, quosque adhuc uel pręsens sęculum in carne retinet, uel futurum iam exutos corpore suscepit, pietatis tuę clementia delictorum suorum ueniam consequantur. Per.

2332 SECRETA. Deus cui soli cognitus est numerus electorum in superna felicitate locandus, tribue quęso ut uniuersorum quos in oratione com/mendatos suscepi, uel omnium fidelium nomina beatę prędestinationis liber, ascripta retineat. Per.

/f. 276v

2333 POSTCOMMVNIONEM. Purificent nos quaesumus omnipotens et misericors deus sacramenta quę sumpsimus, et presta ut hoc sacramentum[1] non sit nobis reatus ad poenam, sed intercessio salutaris ad ueniam, sit ablutio[2] scelerum, sit fortitudo fragilium, sit contra mundi pericula firmamentum, sit uiuorum atque mortuorum remissio omnium delictorum. Per.

MISSA VNIVS DEFVNCTI

2334 Omnipotens sempiterne deus cui numquam sine spe misericordię supplicatur, propitiare animę famuli tui .ill. ut qui de hac uita in tui nominis confessione discessit, sanctorum tuorum numero facias aggregari. Per.

---

[1] *cra* supplied interlinearly.
[2] *l* supplied interlinearly.

2335 SVPER OBLATA. Propitiare domine quaesumus animę famuli tui .ill. pro qua tibi hostias placationis offerimus, et quia in hac luce in fide mansit catholica, in futuro ei uita tribuatur ęterna. Per.

2336 INFRA ACTIONEM. Hanc igitur oblationem quam tibi pro requie animę famuli tui .ill. offerimus, quaesumus domine placatus accipias et tua pietate concedas ut mortalitatis nexibus absoluta, inter sanctos tuos mereatur habere portionem. Diesque.

2337 AD COMPLETA. Presta quaesumus omnipotens deus ut animam famuli tui ill. ab angelis lucis susceptam in preparata habitacula deduci facias beatorum. Per.

277r / [1]SERMO BEATI FVLGENTII DE NATALE DOMINI

2338 Cupientes aliquid de huius diei sollempnitate narrare, simulque considerantes illud unum uerbum de quo dicere uolumus, nulla inuenimus uerba, quibus sufficienter aliquid dicere ualeamus. Est enim hoc uerbum, non quod desinit prolatum, sed quod permanet natum. Non transitorium, sed ęternum. Non factum a deo patre, sed genitum. Non solum genitum, sed etiam unigenitum. Vnum quippe uerbum, deus pater genuit de seipso, per quem omnia creauit ex nichilo. In principio enim erat uerbum, et uerbum erat apud deum, et deus erat uerbum. Hoc erat in principio apud deum. Omnia per ipsum facta sunt, et sine ipso factum est nichil. In hoc autem quod per illud uerbum deus pater omnia fecit, ostenditur quia hoc uerbum genuit, ipse non fecit. Illud igitur uerbum, de deo deus est, de creatore creator est, unde hoc in se

---

[1] No. 2338 by another scribe.

naturaliter habet esse quod pater est. Natus
est itaque de patre deo, deus solus, alter in
persona, non alius in natura. Semper apud
patrem. Semper cum patre. Semper de patre.
Semper in patre. Semper apud patrem, cum quo
illi una est naturalis inmensitas. Semper cum
patre, cum quo illi una est naturalis
ęternitas. Semper de patre, de quo illi est
naturaliter aeterna natiuitas. Semper in
patre, cum quo illi est una naturaliter
ęqualisque diuinitas. Et alter quidem ille
/f. 277v   quod pater es, alter ille quod filius est. /
Neuter tamen alter deus, quia pater et filius
unus est deus. Quapropter quando de patre deo
nascitur sermo, digne dicimus alterum esse
patrem, et alterum filium, et nichilhominus[1]
digne dicimus, unum deum esse patrem, et
filium. Cum enim dicimus alterum esse patrem,
atque alterum filium, discretas personas
genitoris genitique monstramus. Cum uero
dicimus unum deum esse patrem et filium,
ipsam naturam indiscretae diuinitatis
ostendimus. Altera ergo persona est genitoris
et geniti. Quando uero sufficienter aut digne
loqui poterit. Quis de quo? Homo de deo,
mortalis de imortali? Visibilis de
inuisibili? Mutabilis de incommutabili? Opus
de opifice? De factore factura? Paruus de
inmenso? Humilis de altissimo? Plasmatus e
limo, de illo qui omnia creabit ex nichilo?
Cuius inenarrabilis omnipotencia, gratuita
bonitate fecit, nec minus tamen inenarrabilis
gratia, quia nos omnipotentissima miseratione
saluauit. Qui et opus creatricis omnipotentię
gratis fecit, et opus gratię saluatricis
omnipotenter impleuit, illic habens

---

[1]   *h* supplied interlinearly.

potestatem condendi et regendi creaturam suam, hic habens potestatem ponendi et sumendi pro nobis animam suam. Omnipotenciam uero hanc dicimus quia uerbum /

COLLATION TABLES

MANUSCRIPTS CITED

Add.: A series of interpolations appearing in the texts of the earliest copies of the Hadrianic Gregorian sacramentary, ed. J. Deshusses, *Le sacramentaire grégorien*, 3 vols, Spicilegium Friburgense 16, 24 and 28, 2nd ed. (Fribourg, 1979–85) I, 687–715, nos 1*–416*.

Amiens: the order of mass preserved in Paris, Bibliothèque nationale de France, lat. 9432, an early-tenth-century sacramentary probably from Amiens, ed. V. Leroquais, 'L'Ordo Missae du sacramentaire d'Amiens. Paris, Bibliothèque nationale, ms. lat. 9432 (IXe s.)', *EL* 41 (1927), 435–46.

Angoulême: Paris, Bibliothèque nationale de France, lat. 816, a late-eighth- or early-ninth-century 'Eighth-Century Gelasian' sacramentary from Angoulême, ed. P. Saint-Roch, *Liber Sacramentorum Engolismensis*, CCSL 159C (Turnhout, 1987).

Arras: Arras, Bibliothèque municipale 444, a thirteenth-century sacramentary from Arras, ed. (in synopsis), L. Brou, *The Monastic Ordinal of St Vedast's Abbey, Arras*, 2 vols, HBS 86–7 (1955–6) I, 73–89.

Cambrai: The order for the visitation of the sick preserved in Cambrai, Mediathèque municipale, 223, a thirteenth-century pontifical from Cambrai, ed. Martène, *AER*, Bk II, cap. vii, art iv, ordo 19.

CBP: *Corpus Benedictionum Pontificalium*, ed. E. Moeller, CCSL 162, 162A–C (Turnhout, 1980–81).

Claudius: London, British Library, Cotton Claudius III (fols 31–8, 106–36, 39–86, 137–50), ed. D. H. Turner, *The Claudius Pontificals*, HBS 97 (London, 1971). Cited by page number, then formula.

Cologne: the mass ordinary added to Cologne, Dombibliothek 88, an early- to mid-tenth-century sacramentary from Cologne, by one of the book's principal scribes, ed. A. Odenthal, 'Zwei Formulare des Apologientyps der Messe vor dem Jahre 1000', *Archiv für Liturgiewissenschaft* 37 (1995), 25–45, at 29–36.

Corpus 44: Cambridge, Corpus Christi College 44, a pontifical written at St Augustine's Abbey, Canterbury, probably prospectively, for Archbishop Lanfranc (1070–89). Cited by page number.

DC: Durham Cathedral Library A. iv. 19, an early-tenth-century collectar written in southern England and acquired by the refugee community of Chester-le-Street, ed. A. Corrêa, *The Durham Collectar*, HBS 107 (London, 1992).

Dol: Paris, Bibliothèque nationale de France, lat. 2297, an early-eleventh-century sacramentary, probably from a house in the diocese of Dol. Cited by folio number.

Dunstan: Paris, Bibliothèque nationale de France, lat. 943, the pontifical written for Archbishop Dunstan (d. 988) at some point in the 970s. Text calendared by N. K. Rasmussen and M. Haverals, *Les pontificaux manuscrits du haut moyen âge, genèse du livre de l'évêque*, Spicilegium Sacrum Lovaniense 49 (Paris, 1998).

Echternach: Paris, Bibliothèque nationale de France, lat. 9433, the late-ninth- or early-tenth-century sacramentary of Echternach, ed. Y. Hen, *The Sacramentary of Echternach*, HBS 110 (London, 1997).

Egbert: Paris, Bibliothèque nationale de France, lat. 10575, a pontifical written in southern England in the late tenth century, ed. H. M. J. Banting, *Two Anglo-Saxon Pontificals*, HBS 104 (London, 1989), pp. 3–153.

Eleven Forms: The coronation order generally known as the 'Order of Eleven Forms', ed. R. A. Jackson, *Ordines coronationis Franciae. Texts and ordines for the coronation of Frankish and French Kings and Queens in the Middle Ages*, 2 vols (Philadelphia, 1995–2000) I, 159–67.

Eligius: Paris, Bibliothèque nationale de France, lat. 12050, the so-called 'Missale sancti Eligii', a mid-ninth-century written at Corbie probably for Odo, bishop of Beauvais (861–81). Its text is ed. PL 78, cols 25–240. Cited by column number, then formula.

Erdmann: The coronation order generally known as the 'Erdmann Order', ed. Jackson, *Ordines coronationis Franciae*, I, 147–53.

F: Göttingen, Universitätsbibliothek, theol. 231, a late-tenth-century sacramentary from Fulda, ed. G. Richter and A. Schonfelder, *Sacramentarium Fuldense saeculi X* (Fulda, 1912), repr. HBS 101 (London, 1977).

Gellone: Paris, Bibliothèque nationale de France, lat. 12048, an 'Eighth-Century Gelasian' sacramentary-cum-pontifical prepared for Hildoard, bishop of Cambrai, but soon after at Gellone, ed. A. Dumas and J. Deshusses, *Liber Sacramentorum Gellonensis*, 2 vols, CCSL 159 and 159A (Turnhout, 1981).

Ha. & Sp.: The Hadrianic Gregorian Sacramentary and the Supplement probably compiled by Benedict of Aniane, ed. Deshusses, *Le sacramentaire grégorien*, I.

Illyricus: The order for mass preserved in Wolfenbüttel, Herzog August-Bibliothek, Helmst 1151, a sacramentary drawn up for Sigebert, bishop of Minden (1022–36), ed. PL 138, cols 1305–36. Cited by column number, then formula.

Lanalet: Rouen, Bibliothèque municipale 369, an early-eleventh-century pontifical from Crediton or Cornwall, ed. G. H. Doble, *Pontificale Lanaletense*, HBS 74 (London, 1937). Cited by page number, then formula.

Leofric: Oxford, Bodleian Library, Bodley 579, the so-called 'Leofric Missal', a sacramentary-cum-pontifical written by a scribe from Arras probably for Plegmund, archbishop of Canterbury, that later found its way into the hands of Leofric, bishop of Exeter (1050–72), ed. N. A. Orchard, *The Leofric Missal,* 2 vols, HBS 113–114 (London, 2002).

OR: *Les ordines romani*, ed. M. Andrieu, 5 vols, Spicilegium Sacrum Lovanense 11, 23, 24, 28 and 29 (Louvain, 1931–61).

Pad: Padua, Biblioteca Capitolare, D. 47, an early-ninth-century copy of a pre-Hadrianic Gregorian sacramentary probably from Pavia, ed. Deshusses, *Le sacramentaire grégorien*, I, 609–84, nos *1–959*.

Pam: J. Pamelius, *Liturgica Latinorum*, 2 vols (Cologne, 1571).

Paris: Paris, Bibliothèque nationale de France, lat. 2290, the late-ninth-century sacramentary of Saint-Denis, ed. Deshusses, *Le sacramentaire grégorien*, under the siglum 'R'.

Regularis: *Regularis Concordia Anglice Nationis Monachorum Sanctimonialiumque. The Monastic Agreement of the Monks and Nuns of the English Nation*, ed. T. Symons (Edinburgh, 1953). Cited by page number.

Reims: A species of 'Eighth-Century Gelasian' sacramentary written *c.* 800 by the monk Lanbert to the order of Godelgaudus, dean of the abbey of Saint-Remi at Reims. The book was lost in the conflagration of 1774, but a partial transcription of its text was made by Jean de Voisin in the early seventeenth century, ed. U. Chevalier, *Sacramentaire et martyrologe de l'abbaye de Saint-Remy*, Bibliothèque liturgique 7 (Paris, 1900).

RGP: The Romano-German Pontifical, ed. C. Vogel and R. Elze, *Le pontificale Romano-Germanique du dixième siècle*, 3 vols, Studi e Testi 226, 227 and 269 (Vatican City, 1963–72).

Richter: M. Richter, *Canterbury Professions*, Canterbury and York Society 67 (London, 1973).

Robert: Rouen, Bibliothèque municipale 368, the so-called 'Benedictional of Archbishop Robert', a late-tenth-century pontifical probably prepared at the New Minster, Winchester, for Æthelgar, bishop of Selsey, ed. H. A. Wilson, *The Benedictional of Archbishop Robert*, HBS 24 (London, 1903).

SidSx: Cambridge, Sidney Sussex College 100, a pontifical written late in the tenth century for Oswald, bishop of Worcester, ed. Banting, *Two Anglo-Saxon Pontificals*, pp. 157–170.

Stavelot: The *ordo missae* preserved in Brussels, Bibliothèque royale, 2031–2032 (fols 1–18v), an eleventh-century liturgical miscellany from Liège. The text is ed. Martène, *AER*, Bk I, cap. iv, art. xii, ordo 15.

TC: *Textes complémentaires*, a series of texts accompanying the earliest copies of the Gregorian sacramentary, ed. Deshusses, *Le sacramentaire grégorien*, II and III.

VGel: Vatican City, Biblioteca Apostolica Vaticana, lat. 316, the so-called 'Old or Vatican Gelasian' sacramentary, a sacramentary-cum-pontifical copied at some point in the mid eighth century either at Chelles or Jouarre for use at Paris, ed. L. C. Mohlberg, *Liber Sacramentorum Romani aecclesiae ordinis anni circuli*, Rerum ecclesiasticarum Documenta, Series maior, Fontes 4 (Rome, 1960).

Winch: Orléans, Bibliothèque municipale, 105, a late-tenth-century sacramentary from Winchcombe, ed. A. Davril, *The Winchcombe Sacramentary*, HBS 109 (London, 1995).

COLLATION TABLES

Ratoldus	Ha. & Sp.	Pad.	Gellone	Angoulême	Winch.	Others
i						
ii						TC 4392
iii						Winch. 1535 (Tc 3074)
iv						Winch. 1564 (Tc 3075)
v						Winch. 1600 (Tc 3077)
vi						
vii						Cologne 13
viii						Cologne 17
ix						Cologne 16
x						Cologne 15

TABLE OF CONTENTS

1						

ORDER FOR THE DEDICATION OF A CHURCH

Ratoldus	Gellone	OR 41	RGP	Paris	Claudius	Others
2				200		
3				201		Ha. 198, TC 4119
4				201		
5				201		
6		(2)				Lanalet 5
7		3–4		201		
8		4		201		
9		5		(201)		
10		6		201		
11		7	XL, 8		44	Sp. 1454, TC 4087
12	2417	8	XL, 31		45	(TC 4088)
13			XL, 6		45	Sp. 1452, TC 4114
14			XL, 33		45	Sp. 1451, TC 4113
15			XL, 36		45	
16		9	XL, 38	(201)	46	Sp. 1455, TC 4115
17	2424	(10)	(XL, 41)	201	46	(TC 4089)
18		OR 42, 6			46	
19		(11)		(202)	46	
20		12			46	
21		(14)	(XL, 44)		(46)	
22						Lanalet 9–10
23						

COLLATION TABLES

Ratoldus	Gellone	OR 41	RGP	Paris	Claudius	Others
24						
25	2425	(15)	XL, 46	202	47	TC 4090
26		(14)		202		
27	2426	16	XL, 47	202	47	TC 4091
28			XL, 48		47	
29		(17)	(XL, 49)	202	48	
30	2436			202	48	TC 4102
31	2437				48	TC 4103
32		18	(XL, 52)	202	49	
33		(19)		203		
34		(20, 22)	(XL, 57)		(49)	
35						
36						
37	2427	(23, 24)	XL, 59	203	49	Sp. 1255, TC 4092
38	2428	(25)	XL, 60	203	49	Sp. 1256, TC 4093
39			XL, 61		50	
40			XL, 63		50	
41		(26)	(XL, 64)	203	(50)	
42			XL, 78		51	TC 4116
43	2429		XL, 74			TC 4094
44	(2430)		(XL, 77)		51	(TC 4095)
45	2431		XL, 88		58	TC 4096
46	2431		XL, 91		58	TC 4097
47	2432		XL, 92		59	TC 4098
48	2433		XL, 93		59	TC 4099
49	2435		XL, 94			TC 4101
50			XL, 85		59	TC 4147
51					59	
52			XL, 76		60	
53			XL, 79		62	
54			XL, 80		62	
55	2447		(XL, 97)		58	TC 4106
56	2448		XL, 98		58	TC 4107
57						
58					58	

CONSECRATION OF A CEMETERY

Ratoldus	Gellone	OR 41	RGP	Paris	Claudius	Others
59			LIV, 1–2		60, 3	
60			LIV, 3		60, 4	
61			LIV, 4		61, 1	

COLLATION TABLES

CONSECRATION OF A SEPULCHRE

Ratoldus	Gellone	OR 41	RGP	Paris	Claudius	Others
62	(2448)		LV, 1			(TC 4107)
63	(2870)		LV, 2			(TC 4299)
64	(2722)		LV, 3			(Pa 899)

CONSECRATION OF BELLS

Ratoldus	Gellone	OR 41	RGP	Paris	Claudius	Others
65	2440–1		LI, 5		56	TC 4322
66	2442		LI, 10		56	TC 4322a, 4323
67	2443		LI, 11		57	TC 4323a
68	2444		LI, 13		57	TC 4324
69	2445		LI, 14		57	TC 4324a
70	2446		LI, 15		57	TC 4325

DEPOSITION OF RELICS

Ratoldus	Gellone	OR 42	RGP	Paris	Claudius	Others
71		(1)	(XL, 123)		51–2	(OR 41, 28)
72		(3)	(XL, 126–7)		(52)	
73		8	XL, 134		(52)	
74						
75			XL, 131		52	
76					(53)	
77						
78						Lanalet 6,3
79		(10)	XL, 135		52	OR 41, 29
80		11–12	XL, 136–7		52	OR 41, 29
81		13	XL,140, 142		52	
82						
83		16	XL, 145		53	
84			XL,148		53	
85			XLI, 1		53	
86						
87					53	
88						
89					53	
90			XLII, 2		54	
91			XLI, 3		54	

COLLATION TABLES

92			XLI, 4		54	CBP 123
93					53	
94			XLII, 4		54	

CONSECRATION OF A BAPTISTERY

Ratoldus	Gellone	OR 42	RGP	Paris	Claudius	Others
95			LIII, 1		66, 3	Robert 110, 1
96			LIII, 4		66, 4	Robert 110, 2
97						(Robert 100, 5)

ORDINATION OF A BISHOP/ARCHBISHOP

Ratoldus	Ha. & Sup.	Gellone	Leofric	RGP	Lanalet	Others
98				(LVI, 1–5)		
99			2337	LXII, 2		
100			2338	LXIII, 16		
101						Richter, no. 9
102			2339	LXIII, 43		
103				LXIII, 38		
104			2340	LXIII, 39	59, 1	
105					58, 5	
106			2341	LXIII, 42		
107				LXIII, 41	58, 6	
108			2342	LXIII, 6		
109			2348	LXIII, 29	57, 2	
110			2346	LXIII, 21		
111			2342	LXIII, 22		
112				(LXIII, 19–20)		
113	21	2546	2349	LXIII, 32	57, 3	
114	22	2548	2350	LXIII, 34	57, 4	
115	23	(2549–50)	2352	LXIII, 35	57, 5	
116			2351		58, 2	
117		(2552)		(LXIII, 36)	58, 4	
118				LXIII, 35b	58, 1	
119					59, 4	
120			2347	LXIII, 51		
121			(2343)	LXIII, 52		
122	24					
123	25					
124				LXIII, 57		CBP 1081

COLLATION TABLES

125				(59)		
126			(2343)	61		
127				62		
128				LXII, 5	59, 3	

PRAYERS FOR THE CONSIGNING OF THE PALLIUM

Ratoldus	Ha. & Sp.	Gellone	Leofric	RGP	Lanalet	Others
129			2467	LXIV, 1		
130			2468	LXIV, 2		
131			2469	LXIV, 3		

CORONATION ORDER

Ratoldus	Ha. & Sp.	Leofric	Erdmann	11 Forms	Robert	Others
132			2			
133			3			
134			4		140, 2	
135		2458			141, 1	
136			6		141, 2	
137		2459			141, 3	
138			7		142, 1	
139					142, 2	
140					(143, 1)	
141		2460		2	143, 2	
142				3	143, 3	
143			8		144, 1	
144			9		144, 2	
145			10		144, 4	
146					144, 5	
147			11		144, 6	
148		2465			145, 1	
149			13		145, 2	
150			12		145, 3	
151				5	145, 4	
152			(17–19)		146, 1	
153		(2461)			146, 2	
154				8	147, 1	
155		2466			140, 5	
156						
157			24			

Ratoldus	Ha. & Sp.	Leofric	Erdmann	11 Forms	Robert	Others
158			26		148, 1	
159			27		148, 2	
160			28		148, 3	
161			29		148, 4	
162			30		148, 5	
163			31		148, 6	
164	1266	1965				Angoulême 2624
165	1267	1966				Angoulême 2626
166	1719					
167	1268	1967				Angoulême 2314
168						
169	1269	1968				Angoulême 2315
170	1270		15			
171	1271		16			
172	1723					
173						
174	1272		20			
175						

OCCASIONAL BLESSINGS

Ratoldus	Ha. & Sp.	TC	Gellone	Egbert	Lanalet	Others
176	1451	4206		39, 2	7, 8	
177	1452	4267		39, 3	7, 9	
178	1453	4268		(39, 4)	(7, 10)	
179	1454	4269	2416	40, 1	8, 1	
180	1455	4270		41, 1	8, 3	
181	1456	4271	2418			
182	1457	4317	2818	124, 5		
183					108, 2	(RGP CCXLVII, 16)
184		4499	3024		108, 3	
185						
186				139, 5		
187		4343	2839	137, 2		
188						Claudius 72, 1
189					2, 3	Add. 304*
190				134, 5		DC 638
191		4366	2850			
192		4368				

COLLATION TABLES

Corbie Additions

Ratoldus	Ha. & Sp.	Pad.	Gellone	Angoulême	Winch.	Others
193	1262		2483			
194	1263		2484			
195			2485			
196	1264		2486			
197	1265		2487			
198	(776)		(931)			
199	(634)		(1291)			
200						
201	(585)		(1048)			

CALENDAR

202						

Corbie Additions

Ratoldus	Ha. & Sp.	Pad.	Gellone	Angoulême	Winch,.	Others
203						Ech 1505
204						Ech 1506
205						Ech 1507
206						Ech 1508
207						Claudius 72,2
208						
209						Claudius 73,2
210						Claudius 72,5
211						

CANON OF THE MASS

Ratoldus	Ha. & Sp.	Pad.	Gellone	Angoulême	Winch.	Others
212	2					
213	3a	(875)	1930			
214	3b	(875)	1931			
215	(4)	(875)	(1932)			Add. 1*
216	3a	(875)	1930			
217	3b	(875)	1931			
218	(4)	(875)	(1932)		27b	Add. 1*

COLLATION TABLES

Ratoldus	Ha. & Sp.	Pad.	Gellone	Angoulême	Winch.	Others
219	5	876	1933			
220	6	877	1934			
221	7	878	1935		(10)	
222	8	879	1936		11	
223	9–10	880–81	1937–8		12–13	
224	11–13	882–4	1939–41		14–16	
225	13bis	885	1942		18	
226	14	887	1943		19	
227	15–16	888–9	1944–5		20–21	
228	17	890	1946		22	
229	18	891	1947		23	
230	19	892	1948		24	
231	20	(893)	1949		25–26	

TEMPORAL

Ratoldus	Ha. & Sp.	Pad.	Gellone	Angoulême	Winch.	Others
232	33	1	1		28	
233	34	2	2		29	
234	1516		5		30	
235	1738					CBP 1643
236	35	3	6	26	31	
237	36	4	8		32	
238	37	5			33	
239	38					
240	39		12	5	35	
241						CBP 1857
242	40	8	14	6	36	
243	42	10	20	12	37	
244	41	9			38	
245	44	12	10	2	39	
246	43	11	17	8	40	
247	46	14	22	15	41	
248					42	
249						CBP 1021
250	48	16	23	17	43	
251	47	15	19	10	44	
252	58	24	25	19	45	
253	49	17	26	21	46	
254	50	18	28		47	

COLLATION TABLES

Ratoldus	Ha. & Sp.	Pad.	Gellone	Angoulême	Winch.	Others
255	51	6			48	
256	52		30	25	49	
257	1739					CBP 321
258	53	19			50	
259						CBP 931
260	53*					
261	54	20	9	1	51	
262	55	21	32	31	52	
263	56	22	15	11	53	
264	57	23	38	37	54	
265	59		39	33	55	
266	60		40	38	56	
267	61		41	39	57	
268	62	25	42	42	831	
269	63	26			832	
270	1518		45	44	833	
271	1740					CBP 854
272	64	28			834	
273	65	30	43	40	835	
274					836	
275						
276			46	46		
277	(73)		50	50		Pamelius II, 190
278						Pamelius II, 190
279						Pamelius II, 190
280	67	32	51	51	837	
281	68	33	52	53	838	
282	1519	34	53	54	839	
283	1741					CBP 1566
284	69	35	54	56	840	
285	70	36			841	
286	71	37			842	
287	72	38			843	
288	74				845	
289	75	39	58	60	846	
290	76	40			847	
291	1520	41	61	63	849	
292	1742					CBP 1600
293	77	42	62	64	850	
294	78		64	66	851	
295			63	65		
296						Add. 324*

Ratoldus	Ha. & Sp.	Pad.	Gellone	Angoulême	Winch.	Others
297						CBP 579
298	82	49	67	69	63	
299	83	50	69	70	64	
300	1521		70	72	65	
301						CBP 1523
302	40	51	71	73	66	
303	79	46	73	75	852	
304	80	47	74	78	853	
305	1714					
306						CBP 1797
307						
308	81	48	75	77	854	
309			76	82	58	Add. 13*
310			78	84	59	Add. 14*
311	1522		79	85	60	Add. 15*
312	1743					CBP 1545
313			86		61	
314			80	86	62	Add. 16*
315					855	TC 3437
316					856	TC 3438
317					857	TC 3439
318					858	TC 3440
319	85		91	91	67	CBP 1168
320			93	93	68	Add. 17*
321	1523		94	94	69	Add. 18*
322						CBP 1168
323			95	95	70	Add. 19*
324			97	97	71	Add. 20*
325			98	98	72	Add. 21*
326	1524		99	99	73	Add. 22*
327			100	100	74	Add. 23*
328	87	58	101	101	75	
329	88	59	103	105	76	
330	1525		104	106	77	
331	1774					CBP 732
332	90	61	105	107	78	
333	91	62	106	108	79	
334	92	63	108	110	80	
335	93	64			89	
336	94		111	111	81	
337	95				82	
338	96		109	112	83	

Ratoldus	Ha. & Sp.	Pad.	Gellone	Angoulême	Winch.	Others
339	97		110	113	84	
340	98		112			Add. 23*
341	1096	66	113	114	85	
342	1097	67	116	116	86	
343	1526		117	117	87	
344						CBP 926
345	1098	68	118	118	88	
346			121	120	89	Add. 25*
347					859	TC 3441
348					860	TC 3442
349			115	121	90	Add. 26*
350					861	TC 3443
351						CBP 1086
352			124	122	91	Add. 27*
353					862	TC 3444
354	99	69	127	124	863	
355	100				864	
356	1527		129	127	865	
357	101		132		866	
358	102	75			867	
359	103	76			868	
360	1529		143	138	869	
361	104	77	145	139	870	
362	105	78	149	144	871	
363	106	79	150	145	872	
364	1717					
365	107	80	151	146	873	
366			152	148		
367			153	149		
368			154	150		
369	1099		134	129	92	Add. 32*
370	1100		136	131	93	Add. 33*
371	1528		137	132	94	Add. 34*
372						CBP 1143
373	1101		138	133	95	Add. 35*
374	111	84	161	156	877	
375	108	81	156	151	874	
376	112	85			848	
377	109	82			875	
378	1530		165	159	879	
379						CBP 1160
380	113	86	166	160	880	

Ratoldus	Ha. & Sp.	Pad.	Gellone	Angoulême	Winch.	Others
381	110	83	160	155	876	
382						
383	114	87	169		881	
384	115	88			882	
385	1531				883	
386						CBP 175
387	116	90			884	
388						
389			168	163		
390	117	91	167	162	885	
391	118	92	173	167	886	
392	1532				887	
393						CBP 156
394	119	93			888	
395	1102		175	169	96	Add. 36*
396	1103		176	171	97	Add. 37*
397	1533		178	173	98	Add. 38*
398						CBP 1711
399	1104		180	175	99	Add. 39*
400				181	889	Add. 40*
401				182	890	Add. 41*
402	1535				891	
403						CBP 940
404					892	Add. 42*
405					893	
406	120	97	190	190	898	
407	121	98			899	
408	122	99			901	
409					902	Claudius 67, 1
410	123	103	195	201	903	
411	124	104	196	202	904	
412	125	105	197	204	905	
413			198	206	906	
414	1745					CBP 1674
415	126	106	199	207	907	
416			200			
417	1105				100	Add. 43*
418	1106				101	Add. 44*
419	1536			198	102	Add. 45*
420						CBP 2019
421	1107				103	Add. 46*
422	128	107	202		909	

Ratoldus	Ha. & Sp.	Pad.	Gellone	Angoulême	Winch.	Others
423	129	108			911	
424	1538		204	211		
425						CBP 1956
426	130	110			913	
427	131	111	201	209		
428	132				915	
429	133					
430			(1705)			Arras, 82
431			(1706)			Arras, 82
432						
433						CBP 910
434			(1707)			Arras, 82
435	1108				104	Add. 47*
436	1109		208	215	105	Add. 48*
437	1539		209	216	106	Add. 49*
438						CBP 855
439	1110		210	217	107	Add. 50*
440	134	115			920	
441	135	116			921	
442						CBP 807
443	136	117			922	
444			234	238	923	Add. 64*
445			235	239	924	Add. 65*
446	1541		236	240	925	
447						
448			237	241	926	Add. 66*
449	1111		218	225	108	Add. 51*
450	1112		220	227	109	Add. 52*
451	1540		222	228	110	Add. 53*
452						CBP 1005
453	1113		223	229	111	Add. 54*
454	137				935	
455	138				936	
456	1542				937	
457						CBP 807
458	139				938	
459						
460						
461						SidSx 169, 4
462						(CBP 1254)
463						
464						TC 3458

Ratoldus	Ha. & Sp.	Pad.	Gellone	Angoulême	Winch.	Others
465						TC 3459
466					946	TC 3460
467						(CBP 1254)
468					947	TC 3461
469						(TC 2602)
470	140				955	
471	141				956	
472	142				959	
473	1705					
474						CBP 874
475	143				961	
476						
477						
478						
479						
480	144	118	252	255	112	
481	145	119			113	
482	1543		250	253	114	
483						CBP 1584
484	146	120			115	
485	147	121	253	256	116	
486	148				117	
487	1544		256	260	118	
488						CBP 632
489	149				119	
490	150	124	259	263	120	
491	151	125			121	
492	1545				122	
493						CBP 1694
494	152	126			123	
495						Claudius 83, 3
496	1379		266	271		Claudius 83, 4
497						Claudius 83, 5
498						Claudius 84, 1
499						Claudius 84, 2
500	1380		267	272	126	Claudius 84, 3
501						Claudius 84, 4
502	1381		268	273	127	Claudius 84, 5
503						Claudius 84, 6
504	1382		269	274	128	Claudius 84, 7
505						Claudius 84, 8
506						Claudius 85, 1

Ratoldus	Ha. & Sp.	Pad.	Gellone	Angoulême	Winch.	Others
507						Claudius 85, 2
508					124	Claudius 85, 3
509	1549					
510						Claudius 85, 4
511	989					Claudius 85, 5
512						
513	153	127	274	276	129	
514	154	128	275	277	130	
515	155	129	276	278	131	
516	1546		277	279	132	
517	1746					CBP 247
518	156	130	278	280	133	
519	157	131	283	285	134	
520	158				135	
521	159				136	
522	160				137	
523	161				138	
524	162	132	285	286	139	
525	163	133			140	
526	164	134			141	
527	165	135	279	281	142	
528			290	292	143	Add. 71*
529			292	294	145	
530			293	295	146	
531	166	136	296	297	148	
532	167	137	297	300	149	
533	1547		298	301	150	
534	1746					CBP 192
535	168	139	299	303	151	
536	169	140	301	305	152	
537	170	141	305	306	153	
538	171	142	306	307	154	
539	172				155	
540	1548				156	
541						CBP 101
542	173	144	310	312	157	
543	174	145			158	
544	175	146	312	315	159	
545	176	147	314	319	160	
546	1549		315	320	161	
547	177	148			162	
548	178	149	317	322	163	

COLLATION TABLES

Ratoldus	Ha. & Sp.	Pad.	Gellone	Angoulême	Winch.	Others
549	179	150	319	323	164	
550	180	151	325	324	165	
551	181	152			166	
552	1550		321	326	167	
553						CBP 1924
554	182	153	322	327	168	
555	183	154			169	
556			318	330	170	
557	185	190	320	325	172	
558	1551		327	333	173	
559	186	191			174	
560	187	192			175	
561	188	159	331	336	176	
562	189	160	332	339	177	
563	1552				178	
564	190				179	
565	191	163			180	

ORDINATION OF CLERICS

Ratoldus	Ha. & Sp.	TC	Eligius	RGP	Lanalet	Others
566	991	4182		I, 3		
567	1246	4186	212, 3	III, 1		
568	1247	4187	212, 4	III, 2		
569	1248–9	4188–9	212, 5	III, 3		
570	1250	4189	212, 6	III, 5		
571	993	4185		IV, 1		
572				XI, 1	48, 3	

EMBER SATURDAY

Ratoldus	Ha. & Sp.	Pad.	Gellone	Angoulême	Winch.	Others
573						
574	192		336	354		

ORDINATION OF OSTIARIES

Ratoldus	Ha. & Sp.	TC	Eligius	RGP	Lanalet	Others
575	1790	4193	218, 4	XV, 9	50, 1–2	
576						Corpus 44

463

Ratoldus	Ha. & Sp.	TC	Eligius	RGP	Lanalet	Others
577	1791	4194	218, 5	XV, 10	50, 3	
578	1792	4195	218, 6	XV, 11	50, 4	

EMBER SATURDAY

Ratoldus	Ha. & Sp.	Pad.	Gellone	Angoulême	Winch.	Others
579						
580	193					

ORDINATION OF LECTORS

Ratoldus	Ha. & Sp.	TC	Eligius	RGP	Lanalet	Others
581	1793	4196	218, 7	XV, 12	50, 5	
582	1793b	4196b	218, 8	(XV, 13)	50, 6	
583	1794	4197	219, 1	XV, 16	51, 1	

EMBER SATURDAY

Ratoldus	Ha. & Sp.	Pad.	Gellone	Angoulême	Winch.	Others
584						
585	194		337	355		

ORDINATION OF EXORCISTS

Ratoldus	Ha. & Sp.	TC	Eligius	RGP	Lanalet	Others
586	1795	4198	219, 2–3	XV, 17	51, 2–3	
587	1796	4199	219, 4	XV, 18	51, 4	
588	1797	4200	219, 5	XV, 19	51, 5	

EMBER SATURDAY

Ratoldus	Ha. & Sp.	Pad.	Gellone	Angoulême	Winch.	Others
589						
590	195		338	356		

COLLATION TABLES

ORDINATION OF ACOLYTES

Ratoldus	Ha. & Sp.	TC	Eligius	RGP	Lanalet	Others
591	1798	4201	219, 6	XV, 20	51, 6	
592			219, 7			
593	1798b	4201b	219, 8	(XV, 20)	51, 6b	
594	1799	4202	219, 9	XV, 24	51, 7	
595		4203		XV, 22	51, 8	
596	1801	4207	219, 10	X, 1	52, 1	Claudius 33, 5

EMBER SATURDAY

Ratoldus	Ha. & Sp.	Pad.	Gellone	Angoulême	Winch.	Others
597						
598	196					

ORDINATION OF SUBDEACONS

Ratoldus	Ha. & Sp.	TC	Menard	RGP	Lanalet	Others
599	1802	4208	220, 1	XVI, 5	52, 3	Claudius 34, 1
600	1803	4209	220, 2a	XVI, 6	52, 4a	Claudius 34, 2
601	1803b	4209b	220, 2b		52, 4b	Claudius 34, 3
602	1804	4210	220, 3	XVI, 7	53, 1	Claudius 34, 4
603	1805	4211	220, 4	XVI, 8	53, 2	Claudius 34, 4

ORDO QUALITER

Ratoldus	Ha. & Sp.	TC	Eligius	RGP	Lanalet	Others
604	1800a	4204	220, 5	XVI, 1a	53, 3	
605			221, 1	XVI, 1b	53, 4	
606			222, 2–3	XVI, 1c–d	53, 5–6	
607	(1800b)	4212a		XVI, 1e	53, 7–8	
608	(1800c)	4212b	222, 5	XVI, 1f	54, 1	
609	(1800d)	(4213)	(222, 6)	XVI, 2	(54, 2)	
610						
611						

EMBER SATURDAY

Ratoldus	Ha. & Sp.	Pad.	Gellone	Angoulême	Winch.	Others
612						
613	197					

ORDINATION OF DEACONS

Ratoldus	Ha. & Sp.	TC	Eligius	RGP	Lanalet	Others
614		4214	(221, 6)	XVI, 9	54, 3	Claudius 35, 2
615	30	4215	221, 7	XVI, 12	54, 7	Claudius 35, 3
616	31	4216	221, 8	XVI, 13	54, 8	Claudius 35, 4
617		4220			54, 9	Claudius 35, 5
618	32	4217	221, 9	XVI, 14	54, 10	Claudius 36, 1
619				XVI, 15		Claudius 37, 1
620			222, 1			
621					54, 4	Claudius 37, 2
622		4219		XVI, 18	55, 2	Claudius 36, 3
623		4218			55, 1	Claudius 36, 2
624				XVIII, 1		Add. 399*; Claud. 37, 6
625				XVIII, 2		Add. 400*; Claud. 38, 1
626				XVIII, 3		Claudius 38, 2
627						CBP 218; Claud. 38, 3
628						Claudius 38, 4

EMBER SATURDAY

Ratoldus	Ha. & Sp.	Pad.	Gellone	Angoulême	Winch.	Others
629						
630	197					
631						
632	199					

ORDINATION OF PRIESTS

Ratoldus	Ha. & Sp.	TC	Eligius	RGP	Lanalet	Others
633		4221	222, 2		55, 4	
634	27	4222	222, 3	XVI, 27	55, 5	
635	28	4223	222, 4	XVI, 28	55, 6	
636	29	4224	222, 5	XVI, 29	55, 8	

COLLATION TABLES

Ratoldus	Ha. & Sp.	TC	Eligius	RGP	Lanalet	Others
637					56, 3	
638		4227	223, 1	XVI, 37	56, 4	Add. 8*
639		4228	223, 2	(XVI, 35)	56, 1	Add. 9*
640					56, 2	
641		4229				Add. 10*
642		4225		XVI, 33	56, 5	
643		4226		XVI, 34	56, 6	

EMBER SATURDAY

Ratoldus	Ha. & Sp.	Pad.	Gellone	Angoulême	Winch.	Others
644						
645	200		342	359		
646						
647						CBP 702
648	201					

MASS FOR THE ORDINATION OF PRIESTS

Ratoldus	Ha. & Sp.	TC	Eligius	RGP	Lanalet	Others
649				XVII, 1		Claudius 40, 4
650				XVII, 2		Claudius 40, 5
651						Claudius 40, 6
652						CBP 1803; Claud. 41, 2
653				(XVII, 6)		Add. 88*: Claud. 41, 3

TEMPORAL AND SANCTORAL

Ratoldus	Ha. & Sp.	Pad.	Gellone	Angoulême	Winch.	Others
654	202	174	352	363	193	
655	203	175			194	
656	1554		355	367	195	
657	1747					CBP 1576
658	204				196	
659	205	177	359	370	197	
660	206	178	360	373	198	
661	1555				199	
662						CBP 909
663	207	179			200	

Ratoldus	Ha. & Sp.	Pad.	Gellone	Angoulême	Winch.	Others
664	208	180			201	
665	209	181	364	377	202	
666	210	182	365	380	203	
667	1556				204	
668	211	183			205	
669	212	184	390	412	206	
670	213	185	372	388	207	
671	214	186	370	385	208	
672	1557				209	
673						CBP 218
674	215	187			210	
675	216	188			211	
676	217	217			212	
677	218	218			213	
678	1558				214	
679	219	219	371	387	215	
680	220	220	377	393	216	
681	221	193	379	394	217	
682	222	194	380	397	218	
683	1559				219	
684						CBP 169
685	223	196	381	399	220	
686	224	197	382	401	221	
687	225	198	384	403	222	
688	226	199	385	406	223	
689	1560				224	
690	227	200	386	408	225	
691	228	210			226	
692	229	202	389	411	227	
693	230	203			228	
694	1561				229	
695	1748					CBP 1577
696	231	204	393	415	230	
697	232	205	416	424	231	
698	233	206		426	232	
699	1562				233	
700	1773					CBP 1554
701	234	207			234	
702	235	208			235	
703	236	209	411	429	236	
704	237	210	418	431	237	
705	1563					

Ratoldus	Ha. & Sp.	Pad.	Gellone	Angoulême	Winch.	Others
706	238	211	419	432	239	
707	239	212			240	
708	240	213	421	434	241	
709	241	214	423	436	242	
710	1564				243	
711						CBP 1913
712	242	215	424	437	244	
713	243	216	431	443	245	
714			427	440		Add. 85*
715	244	246			246	
716	245	247			247	
717	1565				248	Add. 87*
718	246	248			249	
719	247		394	416	250	Add. 89*
720	248	221	432	444	255	
721	249	222	434	448	256	
722	1566				257	
723						
724	250	224	435	450	258	
725	251	225	455	469	259	
726	252	226			260	
727	253	227			261	
728	1567				262	
729	254	228			263	
730	255	229	448		264	
731	256		443	458	265	
732	257	231	445	460	266	
733	1568				267	
734	1749					CBP 1193
735	258		447	462	268	
736	259	230	444	459	269	
737	260	233			270	
738	261				271	
739	1569				272	
740						CBP 286
741	262				273	
742	263				274	
743	264	237	459	473	275	
744	265				276	
745	1570				277	
746	266	239			278	
747	267	240	463	478	279	

Ratoldus	Ha. & Sp.	Pad.	Gellone	Angoulême	Winch.	Others
748	268	241	464	479	280	
749	269	242	465	480	281	
750	270	243	466	481	282	
751	1571				283	
752						
753	271	244	467	483	284	
754	272	245	468	484	285	
755	273		465	480	286	
756	274		461	476	287	
757	1572				288	
758	275		462	477	289	
759	276		473	490	290	
760	277	250	474	491	291	
761	278	251			292	
762	1573				293	
763						
764	279	252	477	495	294	
765	280	253			295	
766	281	254			296	
767	282	255	481	499	297	
768	1574				298	
769	283	256	482	501	299	
770	284	257	485	505	300	
771	285	258	484	504	301	
772	286	259			302	
773	1575		487	507	303	
774	1750					CBP 8
775	287	260	488	508	304	
776	288	261	495	514	305	
777	289	262	497	518	306	
778	1576				307	
779	290	263	498	519	308	
780	291	264			309	
781	292	265	500	522	310	
782	293	266	502		311	
783	1577				312	
784	294	267	503	527	313	
785	295	268	489	509	314	
786	296	269	506	529	315	
787	297	270	507	531	316	
788	1578				317	
789						CBP 13

Ratoldus	Ha. & Sp.	Pad.	Gellone	Angoulême	Winch.	Others
790	298	271	508	533	318	
791	299	272	496	515	319	
792	300		439	453	320	
793	301		440	455	321	
794	1579				322	
795	302		442	457	323	
796	303				324	
797	304	277	516	542	325	
798	305	278			326	
799	1580				327	
800						CBP 288
801	306	279	518	545	328	
802	307				329	
803	308		454	468	330	
804	309		456	470	331	
805	1581				332	
806	310		457	471	333	
807	311		458	472	334	
808					336	Add. 95*; Claud. 64, 1
809					335	
810						Claudius, 63, 4
811						
812						
813	312	281	566	558	338	
814	313	282			339	
815	1582		568	561	340	
816	1751					CBP 180
817	314				341	
818	315	284	572	565	342	
819	316	285			343	
820	1583				344	
821	1752					CBP 1671
822	317	286			345	
823	318	287			346	
824	319	288	577	572	347	
825	320	288bis			348	
826	1584				349	
827	321				350	
828	322	290			351	
829	323	291	582	580	352	
830	324	292	583	586	353	
831	325	293			354	

COLLATION TABLES

Ratoldus	Ha. & Sp.	Pad.	Gellone	Angoulême	Winch.	Others
832	1585				355	
833						CBP 1097
834	326	294	586	584	356	
835	327	295	587	590	357	

ORDER FOR MAUNDY THURSDAY

Ratoldus	Ha. & Sp.	Gellone	RGP, XCIX	Egbert	Winch.	Others
836			(252)	147, 3		
837			(253)	148, 1		
838	328	633	254	148, 2	361	
839			255	148, 2		
840			255	147, 3		
841			255			
842				148, 2		
843			230	148, 2		TC 3963
844			235	148, 3		TC 3964
845			248	148, 4		TC 3980bis
846			(245)	150, 1		TC 3965
847				150, 3		TC 3960; Cant. 46, 1
848			(245b)			Cant. 46, 2a
849			(239)	150, 2		TC 3977; Cant. 46, 2b
850				150, 4		TC 3978; Cant. 46, 3
851				150, 5		
852			255	150, 6		
853			256	150, 6		
854	329	634		150, 6	362	
855	1586	614		150, 6	363	
856	1587	635		150, 6	364	
857	330	636		150, 6	365	
858	331	637		150, 6	366a	
859	332	638		150, 6	366b	
860				150, 7		Claudius 28, 1
861			(259)	150, 7		Claudius 28, 1
862	334	619	261	150, 8	367	Claudius 28, 2
863			(265)	150, 8		Claudius 28, 3
864			266	151		CBP 233
865			(263, 267)	151		Claudius 28, 3
866			(270, 273)	151		Claudius 29
867				151, 1		TC 4100, Claud 29, 1
868				151, 2		TC 4101, Claud 29, 2

Ratoldus	Ha. & Sp.	Gellone	RGP, XCIX	Egbert	Winch.	Others
869	335	623	275	151–152	368	Claudius 29, 3
870			(276, 277)	152, 1		
871	336	621	279	152, 2	369	Claudius 30, 1
872				152, 2		
873			(280)	152, 2		
874			284	152, 3		
875	337	639	281	152, 3	370	
876				152, 3		
877			(287)	152–153		
878						
879			289	153, 2		
880			290	153, 3		TC 4473
881						

ORDER FOR GOOD FRIDAY

Ratoldus	Ha. & Sp.	Gellone	OR 28	RGP, XCIX	Winch.	Others
882		641		(304)	(371)	
883		642	33		(372)	
884			34	(305)	(372)	
885				(305)	(372)	
886	328	644			373	Add. 118*
887				(307)	(373)	
888				(307)	(373)	
889				(307)	(373)	
890	338	646	35	309	374	
891	339	647		311	375	
892	340	648		312	376	
893	341	649		313	377	
894	342	650		314	378	
895	343	651		315	379	
896	344	652		316	380	
897	345	653		317	381	
898	346	656		318	382	
899	347	657		319	383	
900	348	658		320	384	
901	349	659		321	385	
902	350	660		322	386	
903	351	661		323	387	
904	352	662		324	388	
905	353	663		325	389	
906	354	664		326	390	

Ratoldus	Ha. & Sp.	Gellone	OR 28	RGP, XCIX	Winch.	Others
907	355	665		327	391	
908			(38)	(328–30)		(Regularis 42)
909				330		(Regularis 42)
910				(334)		(Regularis 42)
911						(Regularis 43)
912						Regularis 43-4
913						(Regularis 44)
914			41–4	(334)		(Regularis 45)
915			45–6	(335)		(Regularis 45)
916			46–8	(335)		(Regularis 45)

ORDER FOR HOLY SATURDAY
Baptismal Scrutinies

Ratoldus	VGel.	Gellone	OR 11	RGP, XCIX	Winch.	Others
917	283	2215	1	85–6		
918	284	(2216)	2	(87)		
919	285	2217	4	88		
920		2223	7-8	(92)		
921		2225	9	(93)		
922		2226a	10–11	(94)		
923		2226b	11	(94)		
924		2226c	12	(94)		
925	291	(2227–8)	12, 14	(94–5)		
926	293	2231	16	97		
927		2233				
928	295	2228	19	101		
929	296	2238	21	103		
930	297	2240	22	103		
931	298	2242	24	107		
932		2243a	26	(108)		
933		2243b	27	(108)		
934		2243c	28	(108)		
935		2246	29			
936		2246–8	29–32	(110)		
937	194	2249	33	113		
938	195	2251	34	114		
939	(195)	(2251)				
940	196	2252	(35)	115		
941	197	2252	35	116		
942	198	2253		117		
943	199	2254		118		

Ratoldus	VGel.	Gellone	OR 11	RGP, XCIX	Winch.	Others
944		2255	(36–8)	(119)		
945	225	2329		121		
946						
947	226	2330		122		
948	(226)	2331		123		
949	227	2332		123		
950	228	2333		124		
951		(2256–8)	39	(125)		
952		2258	40	(125)		
953	254	2334		127		
954		(2258–60)	(41–3)	(128)		
955	299	(2262)	(44)	(131)		
956	300	2263	45	131–2		
957	302	(2265)	(46, 48)	(134)		
958	303	2267	50	(138)		
959	(304)		(51, 53)	(139)		
960	305	2271	54	140		
961	(306)		(55–6)	(141)		
962	307	2275	57	142		
963	(308)		(58–9)	(143)		
964	309	2279	60	144		
965	310	2280	61	145		
966	(311)	(2281)	(62)	146		
967	(311)	(2281)	(63–4)	147		
968	314	2282	65	(147)	423	
969	315	2284	66–7	148		
970	(319)	(2232)	(68)	(149)		
971	319	2286	69a	150a		
972	320	2287	69b	150b		
973	321	2288	69c	150c		
974	322	2289	69d	150d		
975	323	2290	69e	150e		
976	324	2291	69f	150f		
977	325	2292	69g	150g		
978	326	2293	69h	150h		
979	327	2294	69i	150i		
980	(328)	2295	(70)	(151)		
981	328	2296	71	152		
982		2298–2300	(73–6)	(153)		
983		2301	(81)			
984		2303–4	(84)	154		
985	255	2335				

Ratoldus	VGel.	Gellone	OR 11	RGP, XCIX	Winch.	Others
986	(255)	2336				
987	256	2337		156		
988	257	2338		157		
989		2309	(87)			
990		2310				

Baptismal Order

Ratoldus	VGel.	Ha. & Sp.	Gellone	RGP, CX	Winch.	Others
991				5		TC 3928
992				6		TC 3927
993	285	1065	2217	6	408	
994	286	1066	2218	7	409	
995	287	1067	2219	8	410	
996	288	1068	2220	9	411	
997	289	1069	2221	10	412	
998	290	1070	2222	11	413	
999	291	1071	2228	13–14	414	
1000	292	1072	2229		415	
1001	293	1073	2231	15–16	416	
1002		1074	2233	25	417	
1003	294	1075	2234		418	
1004	295	1076	2236	18	419	
1005	296	1077	2238	19	420	
1006	297	1078	2240	20	421	
1007	298	358, 1079	2242	21	422	
1008	419	359, 1080	2304	23	426	
1009	420	360, 1081	2305	24	427	
1010	421	361, 1082	2306	27	430	
1011					431	TC 3938

Blessing of the Paschal Candle

Ratoldus	VGel.	Ha. & Sp.	Gellone	RGP, XCIX	Winch.	Others
1012						
1013			2848	(218)		TC 4358
1014			2849			TC 4359
1015				(344)		Lan. 17, 6: Egb. 138, 1
1016						Egbert 138, 1
1017	429		676d	219		Lanalet. 17, 7
1018		1021	677			
1019		1022	678a–c			

Baptismal Order

Ratoldus	VGel.	Ha. & Sp.	TC	Gellone	Winch.	Others
1020	(432)	1024		681	(394)	Deshusses III, 100–2
1021		1025			394	for whole
1022	(433)	1026		683	(395)	
1023	432	1027		682	395	
1024	(434)	1028		685	(396)	
1025	434	1029		686	396	
1026	(435)	1030		687	(397)	
1027	435	1031		688	397	
1028	(436)	1032			(398)	
1029		1035			398	
1030	(438)	1034			(399)	
1031		(1027)			399	
1032	(437)	1036		691	(400)	
1033	437	1037		692	400	
1034		1038			(401)	
1035	431	1023		680	393	
1036		1040		695, 697	(402)	
1037	433	1041		684	402	
1038	(439)	1042			(403)	
1039	439	1043			403	
1040	(440)	1044		697	(404)	
1041	440	1045			404	
1042	(441)	1046		699	(405)	
1043	441	1047		700	(405)	
1044	(442)	1048				
1045	442	1048		701	406	
1046		399				
1047	(443)					
1048	444	373	3939	703	428	
1049	445–8	374	3940	704	429a–e	
1050			(3942)	(705)	429f	TC 3941
1051	449	(1084)	3930	706	432	
1052					433	
1053		1085	3920	(707)	434	
1054	450	375, 1086	3921	708, 711	434-5	
1055		(1087)	3943		436	Add. 119*, TC 3943
1056						
1057	454	377			438	
1058						
1059	456	378			439	

COLLATION TABLES

Ratoldus	VGel.	Ha. & Sp.	TC	Gellone	Winch.	Others
1060	458	379			440	
1061	459	380			441	
1062	460	381			442	
1063						TC 4355
1064		1754				CBP 879
1065						
1066		382			443	

ORDER OF MASS

Ratoldus	Ha. & Sp.	TC	Amiens	Leofric	Illyricus	Others
1068						
1069		4288				
1070						
1071		4289				
1072						
1073						
1074						
1075				321a		
1076				321b		
1077				321c		
1078		4381	8		1308, 8	Echternach vii
1079				321d		
1080						
1081						
1082						
1083						
1084				321e		
1085				321f		
1086						
1087					1311, 4	Echternach i
1088						
1089		4384			1313, 3	
1090						
1091					1314, 3	
1092						
1093						
1094						
1095					(1321, 2)	
1096						
1097						
1098			16			

COLLATION TABLES

Ratoldus	Ha. & Sp.	TC	Amiens	Leofric	Illyricus	Others
1099						Stavelot
1100						
1101	384					
1102						
1103	385					
1104			30		1329, 6	Echternach xxiii
1105						
1106	386					
1107	387					
1108		4343				
1109						
1110						
1111						
1112	1775					CBP 292
1113						
1114			33		1332, 6	Echternach xxvi
1115						Echternach xxiv
1116						
1117					1333, 2	Echternach xxvii
1118			35		1333, 9	Echternach xxxi
1119			22		1333, 7	
1120						
1121						
1122	388					
1123						
1124			40		1334, 1	
1125	389					
1126	390					
1127	391					
1128						
1129	394					Gellone 730

TEMPORAL AND SANCTORAL

Ratoldus	Ha. & Sp.	Pad.	Gellone	Angoulême	Winch.	Others
1130	392	337	739	784	453	
1131	393		719	775	454	
1132	1590				455	
1133						CBP 510
1134	(395–6)		(742)	(787)	(456–7)	
1135	397		732	778	458	
1136	398	338	745	789	459	

479

Ratoldus	Ha. & Sp.	Pad.	Gellone	Angoulême	Winch.	Others
1137	399	339	744	790	460	
1138	400	340	746	791	461	
1139	401	341	748	792	462	
1140	402	342	719	775	463	
1141	1591		750	795	464	
1142	(395–6)		(751)	(795)	(465)	
1143						CBP 1207
1144	404	344	753	796	466	
1145	405	345	754	797	467	
1146	406	346	755	798	468	
1147	407	347	756	799	469	
1148	408	348		800	470	
1149	409	349	759	802	471	
1150	1592				472	
1151	(395-6)		(761)	(803)	473	
1152						CBP 1268
1153	411	350	763	804	474	
1154	412	351	764	805	475	
1155	413	352	765	806	476	
1156	414	353	766	807	477	
1157	415	354	768	808	478	
1158	416	355	770	810	479	
1159	1593				480	
1160	(395-6)		(772)	(811)	481	
1161						CBP 995
1162	419	356	774	812	482	
1163	420	357	775	813	483	
1164	421	358	776	814	484	
1165	422	359	777	815	485	
1166	423	360	779	816	486	
1167	424	361	780	818	487	
1168	1595					
1169	(395–6)		(782)	(819)	489	
1170						CBP 576
1171	426	363	784	820	490	
1172	427	364	785	821	491	
1173	428	365	786	822	492	
1174	429	366	788	823	493	
1175	430	367	789	825	494	
1176	(395–6)		(791)	(826)	496	
1177	1595				495	
1178						CBP 1076

Ratoldus	Ha. & Sp.	Pad.	Gellone	Angoulême	Winch.	Others
1179	432	368	793	827	497	
1180	433	369	794	828	498	
1181	434	370	795	829	499	
1182	435	371	797	830	500	
1183	436	372		832	501	
1184	1596			833	502	
1185	1756					CBP 679
1186	437	373			503	
1187	438	374	802	837	504	
1188	440	375	804	839	506	
1189	442	376	757	843	508	
1190	448	378		844	514	
1191	449		883	846	515	
1192	451		806	848	517	
1193	453		831	851	519	
1194	457		832	850	523	
1195	455		820		521	
1196	458				524	
1197	459				525	
1198			870	901	962	
1199			872	903	963	
1200					964	
1201			874	905	965	
1202		381	837	867	526	Add. 122*
1203		382	839	869	528	Add. 123*
1204	1597	383	840	870	529	Add. 124*
1205		384	842	872	531	Add. 125*
1206	1114	390	861	892	532	
1207	1115	391	863	894	533	
1208	1599				534	
1209						CBP 1815
1210	1116	392	865	896	535	
1211	1117	396	879	910	536	
1212	1118	397	881	912	537	
1213	1602	398			538	
1214						CBP 216
1215	1119	399	883	914	539	
1216	460	393	875	906	966	
1217	461	394			967	
1218	1601		877	(908)		
1219						CBP 153
1220	462	395			969	

Ratoldus	Ha. & Sp.	Pad.	Gellone	Angoulême	Winch.	Others
1221	463				970	
1222	464				971	
1223	1603				972	
1224						CBP 57
1225	465				973	
1226	1120	411	925	922	540	
1227	1121	412	927	924	541	
1228	1607	413			542	
1229						CBP 859
1230	1122	414	929	926	543	
1231	1123	424	949	944	544	
1232	1124	425		946	545	
1233	1610	426			546	
1234						CBP 314
1235	1125	427	954	948	547	
1236	466	400	890	959	548	
1237	467	401	891	960	549	
1238	468	402	892	961	550	
1239	469	403	893	962	551	
1240	470	404	894	963	552	
1241	471		898		553	
1242	472	405	895	965	554	
1243	473	406	896	966	555	
1244	1604			967	556	
1245						CBP 112
1246	474	407	897	968	557	
1247	475			969	558	
1248				975		Reims 332; F 920
1249				975		Reims 333: F 921
1250	1605					F 922
1251	1759					CBP 156
1252			899	978		Reims 333
1253			921	979		Reims 333; F 929
1254			913	980		Reims 333
1255				976		F 921
1256	1606				566	F 933
1257						CBP 1919
1258						Reims 333: F 923
1259				982		
1260	497	440	978		574	
1261	498	441	979		576	
1262	499	442	980		577	

Ratoldus	Ha. & Sp.	Pad.	Gellone	Angoulême	Winch.	Others
1263	500	443	981		579	Add. 142*
1264	1760					CBP 281
1265	501	444	982		580	
1266	502	446	984		581	
1267	503	447	985		582	
1268			976			
1269	476	408			978	
1270	477	409	923		980	
1271	478	410			981	
1272	1612				578	
1273	1126	448			583	
1274	1127	449			585	
1275	1613				586	
1276						CBP 380
1277						CBP 1152
1278	1128	451			587	
1279	479	415	930	927	983	
1280	480	416	932		985	
1281	1608				986	
1282						CBP 905
1283	481	417			987	
1284	482	418	941	936	994	
1285	483				995	
1286	484				996	
1287		421	944	939	989	Add. 129*
1288			946	941	991	Add. 131*
1289	1609				992	Add. 132*
1290	1775					CBP 310
1291		423	948	943		Add. 134*
1292			945	940	990	Add. 130*
1293	485	428	955	949		
1294	486	429				
1295	487	430				
1296	488	431			997	
1297	489	432			998	
1298	490	433	960	954	999	
1299	491	434	965		1000	
1300	492	435	966		1002	
1301	493	436	967		1005	
1302			961	955	1001	
1303			962	956	1003	
1304	1611		963	957	1004	

Ratoldus	Ha. & Sp.	Pad.	Gellone	Angoulême	Winch.	Others
1305						CBP 1916
1306	490	433	960	954	1006	
1307	494	437	968			
1308	495	438	969			
1309	496	439	970			
1310	504	452	993		1007	
1311	505	453			1008	
1312	506	454			1009	
1313	507	455	999			
1314	508	455	1000		588	
1315	509	456	1003		589	
1316	510	456	1008		589	
1317	511	457	1005		590	
1318	512	457			590	
1319	513	458	1007		591	
1320	514	458			591	
1321	515	459	1009			
1322	515	459				
1323	516	467			593	
1324	517	468	1035		594	
1325	518	473	1022		595	
1326	519		996			
1327	520	460	1014		597	
1328	521	461	1029		598	
1329	522	462	1016		605	
1330	523	463	1017		600	
1331	524	464	1018		601	
1332	1761					CBP 186
1333	525	465	1033		602	
1334	526	466	1027		603	
1335						
1336	1762					CBP 948
1337	531		1033		608	
1338			1036			
1339			1034			
1340	532	474	1038		609	
1341	533	475	1039		610	
1342	1615				611	
1343						CBP 1659
1344	534	476	1040		612	
1345	535	477	1041		613	
1346	536	478	1042		614	

Ratoldus	Ha. & Sp.	Pad.	Gellone	Angoulême	Winch.	Others
1347	1616				615	
1348						CBP 187
1349	537	479	1043		616	
1350	538	480	1044		617	
1351	539	481	1045		618	
1352	1617				620	
1353						CBP 1804
1354	541	483	1048		621	
1355	542	484	1049		626	
1356	543	485	1050		627	
1357	1618				624	
1358	544	486	1052		629	
1359	539	481	1045		618	
1360			1050			
1361	1619					
1362			(1022)			
1363	545	487	1053		630	
1364	546	488	1054		631	
1365	547	489	1055		632	
1366	548	490	1056		633	
1367	549	491	1057		634	
1368	550	492	1058		635	
1369	551	493	1059		636	
1370	1620				637	
1371						CBP 1258
1372	552	495	1061		638	
1373			1062		639	Add. 427*
1374			1064		641	Add. 428*
1375	1621		1065		642	
1376						CBP 350
1377			1066		643	Add. 429*
1378	556	499	1068		1010	
1379	557	500	1069		1011	
1380	558	501	1070		1012	
1381	559	502			1013	
1382	560	503			1014	
1383	1622				1015	
1384	561	504			1016	
1385	1129	505	1076		665	
1386	1130		1078		666	
1387	1623		1079		667	
1388						CBP 98

Ratoldus	Ha. & Sp.	Pad.	Gellone	Angoulême	Winch.	Others
1389	1131	507	1080		668	
1390						Add. 152*, TC 3501
1391						Add. 153*, TC 3502
1392						
1393						(CBP 1256)
1394						Add. 154*, TC 3503
1395			1082	987	1017	Add. 158*
1396			1083	988	1018	Add. 159*
1397			1084	989	1019	Add. 160*
1398	153					
1399			1096		644	
1400			1098		646	
1401	1626				647	
1402			1099		648	
1403			1100			
1404			1102		651	
1405			1103		652	
1406						(CBP 98)
1407			1104		653	
1408			1105		654	
1409			1106		655	
1410			1107		656	
1411			1108		657	
1412			1109		658	
1413			1110		659	
1414	550		(1111)		661	
1415			(1503)			
1416			1112			
1417	1674					
1418						(CBP 98)
1419					663	
1420					664	
1421	1132		1088	993	669	
1422	1133	509	1090	995	670	
1423	1624		1091	996	671	
1424						CBP 1880
1425	1134	510	1092	997	672	
1426			1085	990	1020	Add. 164*
1427			1086	991	1021	Add. 165*
1428						Claudius 76, 1
1429			1087	992	1022	Add. 166*
1430			1122	1003	1023	

Ratoldus	Ha. & Sp.	Pad.	Gellone	Angoulême	Winch.	Others
1431			1123	1004	1024	
1432			1124	1005	1025	
1433			1125	1006	1026	
1434	562	511			1027	
1435	563	512			1028	
1436	564	513	1128	1009	1029	
1437	553	496	1116	998		Sp. 1145
1438	554	497	1118	999		Sp. 1136
1439	1626					
1440						CBP 169
1441	555	498	1120	1002		Sp. 1137
1442			1129	1011		
1443			1130	1013		
1444			1131	1014		
1445	565	514			1030	
1446	566	515			1031	
1447	1627				1032	
1448						CBP 1266
1449	567	516			1033	
1450	1138	517	1137	1019	677	
1451	1139	518	1139	1021	678	
1452	1626				675	
1453						CBP 1337
1454	1140	519	1141	1023	680	
1455	568	520	1143	1024	1034	
1456	569	521		1026	1036	
1457	1629			1027	1037	
1458						CBP 835
1459	570	522	1147	1028	1038	
1460	571	523	1149	1030	1049	
1461	572	524			1036	
1462	573	525	1151	1032	1045	
1463	574	526	1152	1033	1040	
1464	575	527	1154	1035	1042	
1465	1630		1155		1043	
1466	1763					CBP 179
1467	576	528	1156	1037	1044	
1468	577	531	1160	1039	1047	
1469	578	530	1161	1040	1048	
1470	579		1162	1041	1050	
1471	580	529	1163	1042	1051	
1472	581		1164	1043	1041	

Ratoldus	Ha. & Sp.	Pad.	Gellone	Angoulême	Winch.	Others
1473	582		1158	1044	1046	
1474	583	532	1168	1049	1052	
1475	584	533	1170	1050	1053	
1476	1631				1054	
1477	585	534			1055	
1478	1141	535	1174	1054	681	
1479	1142	536	1176	1056	682	
1480	1628				679	
1481						CBP 22
1482	1143	537	1178	1058	684	
1483	586				1056	
1484	587				1057	
1485	588				1058	
1486	589	538	1181	1060	1059	
1487	590	539			1061	
1488	591	540	1192	1070	1068	
1489	592	541	1184	1063	1063	
1490	593	542	1186	1077	1064	
1491	594	543	1188	1067	1065	
1492	595	544	1190		1067	
1493	1633		1183	1062		
1494	1765					CBP 193
1495	597		1184	1063	1069	
1496	598	545			1071	
1497	599	546	1195		1070	
1498	600		1202	1084	1072	
1499	601	547	1199	1083	1073	
1500	602				1074	
1501	603				1075	
1502	604	548	1203	1073	1076	
1503	605	549			1077	
1504						CBP 981
1505	606	550	1207	1076	1079	
1506	1144	554	1211	1095	685	
1507	1145	555	1213	1097	686	
1508	1632				683	
1509						CBP 31
1510	1146	556	1215	1099	687	
1511	610	551	1208	1092	1080	
1512	611	552	1209	1093	1081	
1513						CBP 1916
1514	612	553	1210	1094	1082	

Ratoldus	Ha. & Sp.	Pad.	Gellone	Angoulême	Winch.	Others
1515						TC 3501, Dol 31r
1516						TC 3502, Dol 31v
1517						CP 841, Dol 31v
1518						TC 3503, Dol 31v
1519	607	557	1217	1106	1086	
1520	608	558	1218	1107	1088	
1521	609	560	1221	1110		
1522	1147	564	1227	1116	689	
1523	1148	565	1229	1118	690	
1524	1634		1214	1098	687	
1525						CBP 289
1526	1149	566	1231	1120	692	
1527	613	561	1223	1112	1090	
1528	614	562	1224	1113	1091	
1529	1635			1114	1092	
1530	615	563	1226	1115	1093	
1531					939	
1532					940	
1533					941	
1534					943	
1535					944	
1536					945	
1537	1637				1096	
1538					949	
1539	1150	567	1241	1125	693	
1540	1151		1242	1127	694	
1541	1636		1230	1119	691	
1542						CBP 1962
1543	1152	569	1245	1129	696	
1544				1121	1094	Add. 170*
1545				1122	1095	Add. 171*
1546				1124	1097	Add. 172*
1547	(105)					
1548	(106)					
1549	(107)					
1550						TC 3543
1551						TC 3546
1552						TC 5347
1553			1247	1135	1106	Add. 177*
1554			1248	1136	1108	Add. 178*
1555	1640		1249	1137		Add. 179*
1556			1250	1138	1110	Add. 180*

Ratoldus	Ha. & Sp.	Pad.	Gellone	Angoulême	Winch.	Others
1557			1251	1139	1117	
1558						
1559						
1560						
1561	1153	570	1252	1130	697	
1562	1154	571	1254	1132	698	
1563	1638				695	
1564						CBP 71
1565	1155	572	1256	1134	700	
1566						Add. 391*
1567						TC 3415
1568						TC 3376
1569						Dol 32v
1570						Dol 32v
1571						Dol 32v–33r
1572						Dol 33r
1573			1257	1140	1112	Add. 181*
1574			1258	1141		Add. 182*
1575			1259	1142	1115	Add. 183*
1576	616	573			1111	
1577	617	574			1113	
1578	618	575	1262		1114	
1579	619	576	1266		1116	
1580	620	577			1117	
1581	1641				1118	
1582	621	578	1268		1119	
1583						Dol 34r
1584					1121	Dol 34r
1585						Dol 34r
1586					1122	Dol 34r
1587	1156		1272	1152	701	
1588	1157	580	1273	1153	702	
1589	1639				699	
1590						CBP 921
1591	1158	581	1275	1155	704	
1592	622				1123	
1593	623				1124	
1594	624				1125	
1595			1277	1156	1126	Add. 184*
1596			1279	1158	1128	Add. 185*
1597	1643		1280		1129	
1598			1281	1160	1130	Add. 187*

Ratoldus	Ha. & Sp.	Pad.	Gellone	Angoulême	Winch.	Others
1599	625	582	1282	1164	1131	
1600	626	583	1283	1165	1132	
1601	627	584	1284	1166	1133	
1602	628	585			1134	
1603	629	586			1135	
1604	1644		1288	1170	1136	
1605	630				1137	
1606	631				1138	
1607	632	587			1139	
1608	633	588	1290	1172	1140	
1609	634	589	1291	1173	1141	
1610	635	590	1292	1174	1142	
1611	1159	591	1332	1179	705	
1612	1160	592	1334	1181	706	
1613	1642		1274		703	
1614						CBP 2024
1615	1161	593	1336	1183	708	
1616	636	594	1297	1184	1146	
1617	637	595			1147	
1618	638	596			1148	
1619	639	597	1300	1187	1149	
1620	640	598	1302	1190	1151	
1621	1646				1152	
1622	641	599	1306	1192	1153	
1623	642	600	1308	1194	1150	
1624	643	601				
1625	1647		1314		1158	
1626	644	602				
1627	645	603	1311	1199	1155	
1628	646	604			1157	
1629						CBP 597
1630	647	606			1159	
1631	648	607	1316	1204	1160	
1632	649	609	1321	1208	1161	
1633	650	610		1210	1162	
1634	1648		1323	1211	1163	
1635	651	611	1324	1212	1164	
1636	1162	615	1375	1217	709	
1637	1163	616	1377	1219	710	
1638	1645				707	
1639						CBP 1388
1640	1164		1379	1221	712	

Ratoldus	Ha. & Sp.	Pad.	Gellone	Angoulême	Winch.	Others
1641	652	617			1165	
1642	653	612	1328	1214	1166	
1643	1649	613			1167	
1644	654		1331	1216	1168	
1645	655	614	1338	1222	1169	
1646	656	618	1339	1223	1170	
1647	1651	619			1171	
1648	657				1172	
1649	658	620			1173	
1650	659				1174	
1651						
1652	660				1175	
1653	661				1176	
1654	662				1177	
1655	663				1178	
1656	1652				1179	
1657	1766					CBP 1053
1658	664				1180	
1659			1354	1241	1183	Add. 193*
1660			1355	1232	1184	Add. 194*
1661	1653		1356	1233	1185	Add. 195*
1662			1357	1234	1186	Add. 196*
1663	1165		1371	1248	713	
1664	1166		1372	1249	714	
1665	1650		1378		711	
1666						CBP 239
1667	1167		1374	1251	716	
1668	665	625			1187	
1669	666	626	1359	1236	1188	
1670	667	627			1189	
1671			1361	1238	1190	Add. 199*
1672			1362	1239		Add. 200*
1673			1364	1241		
1674			1365	1242	1192	Add. 201*
1675	668	631	1366	1243	1193	
1676	669	632			1194	
1677	670	633	1369	1246	1196	
1678					(1197)	
1679					1198	
1680					(1200)	
1681			1382	1252	1201	Add. 202*
1682			1383	1253		Add. 203*

Ratoldus	Ha. & Sp.	Pad.	Gellone	Angoulême	Winch.	Others
1683	1656		1384	1254	1203	
1684						CBP 905
1685			1385	1255	1204	Add. 204*
1686	1168	634	1402	1273	717	
1687	1169	635	1404	1275	718	
1688	1655		1373		715	
1689			1406			CBP 360
1690	1170	636	1387	1277	720	
1691			1388	1257	1206	
1692			1390	1259	1207	
1693	1657		1392	12262	1208	
1694					1209	
1695					1211	
1696					1213	
1697			1400	1271	1216	
1698			1393	1263	1210	Add. 205*
1699			1394	1264	1212	Add. 207*
1700	1659				1214	
1701			1396	1266	1215	Add. 208*
1702	674	640			1224	
1703	675	641			1225	
1704	676	642			1226	
1705		643	1411	1281	1218	Add. 209*
1706		644	1413	1283	1220	Add. 211*
1707	1661		1414	1284	1221	Add. 214*
1708	1767					CBP 1194
1709			1415	1285	1222	Add. 215*
1710				1282	1219	
1711			1416	1286	1227	
1712			1417	1287	1228	
1713			1418	1288	1229	
1714			1419	1289	1230	
1715			1420	1290	1231	
1716	1163		1421	1291	1232	
1717			1422	1292	1233	
1718	680				1234	
1719	681				1235	
1720	682				1236	
1721	1664					
1722						CBP 1697
1723	683				1238	
1724	1171		1423	1293	721	

493

COLLATION TABLES

Ratoldus	Ha. & Sp.	Pad.	Gellone	Angoulême	Winch.	Others
1725	1172	650	1425	1295	722	
1726	1660				719	
1727						CBP 77
1728	1173	651		1297	724	
1729			1435	1307	1240	Add. 221*
1730			1436	1308	1241	Add. 222*
1731	1665		1437	1309	1242	
1732			1438	1310	1243	Add. 224*
1733	684	656	1439	1311	1244	
1734	685	657	1440	1312	1245	
1735						CBP 1916
1736	686	658	1441	1313	1246	
1737	687	662			1253	
1738	688	663		1324	1254	
1739	1668			1326	1255	
1740	1669					
1741	689	664			1256	
1742	690	665		1322	1247	
1743	(1609)				992	Add. 228*
1744						CBP 792
1745	692				1251	
1746	1174		1442		725	
1747	1175	660	1444		726	
1748	1663		1426		723	
1749						CBP 1745
1750	1176	661	1446		728	
1751	693	666	1461	1332	1257	
1752	694	667			1258	
1753	695	668	1463	1334	1259	
1754	696	669	1464	1335	1263	
1755	697	670	1465	1336	1264	
1756	698	671	1466	1337	1265	
1757	699				1260	
1758	700		1468	1339	1261	
1759	701		1469	1340	1262	
1760	702	676	1470	1341	733	
1761	703	677	1472	1343	734	
1762	1666				727	
1763						CBP 220
1764	704	678	1474	1345	735	
1765	705	679	1485	1359	736	
1766	706	680	1486	1360	737	

COLLATION TABLES

Ratoldus	Ha. & Sp.	Pad.	Gellone	Angoulême	Winch.	Others
1767	707	681			738	
1768	1672		1488	1362	739	
1769	708	682	1489	1363	740	
1770	709	683	1491	1364	741	
1771	710	684	1493	1365	742	
1772	1673		1494		743	
1773	711	685	1496	1367	744	
1774	712	686			745	
1775	713	687	1499	1369	746	
1776	714	688	1509	1379	747	
1777	715	689			748	
1778	716	690	1502	1372	749	
1779	717	691			750	
1780	718	692			751	
1781	1674		1495	1375	752	
1782						CBP 380
1783	719	693	1506	1376	1753	
1784	720	694	1508	1378	754	
1785	721	695			755	
1786	1670			1344		
1787						CBP 288
1788	722	696			757	
1789			1476	1346	1266	Add. 236*
1790			1477	1347	1267	Add. 237*
1791			1478	1348	1268	Add. 238*
1792			1479	1349	1269	Add. 239*
1793			1480	1350	1271	Add. 240*
1794	1671		1481	1351	1272	Add. 241*
1795						CBP 101
1796			1482	1352	1273	Add. 242*
1797			1483	1353	1270	Add. 243*
1798			1484	1354	1274	Add. 244*
1799					1275	TC 3597
1800				1356	1276	TC 3598
1801				1357	1277	TC 3599
1802				1358	1278	TC 3600
1803						
1804						
1805						
1806	1177		1532	1396		
1807	1178	706	1533	1397	759	
1808	1675		1511	1381	756	

495

Ratoldus	Ha. & Sp.	Pad.	Gellone	Angoulême	Winch.	Others
1809						
1810	1179	707	1535	1399	761	
1811	723	697			1279	
1812	724	698			1281	
1813	1676		1516	1385	1282	
1814	725	699			1283	
1815	726	700	1518	1387	1285	
1816	727	701	1520	1390	1287	
1817	1677		1521	1392	1288	
1818						CBP 14
1819	728	702	1522	1393	1289	
1820			1523	1394	1290	
1821		704	1525	1388	1291	
1822		703	1519	1389	1286	
1823			1528			TC 3603
1824						
1825	1534					
1826						
1827						Add. 59*, Arras 81
1828						Add. 60*, Arras 81
1829						Add. 61*
1830						Add. 62*, Arras 81
1831						Add. 63*, Arras 81
1832	1180		1543	1406	762	
1833	1181	718	1545	1408	763	
1834	1678				760	
1835						CBP 1852
1836	1182	719	1547	1410	765	
1837	729	708			1307	
1838	730	709			1308	
1839	731	710			1309	
1840					1310	Add. 253*, TC 3631
1841					1311	Add. 254*, TC 3632
1842					1312	Add. 255*, TC 3633
1843					1313	Add. 256*, TC 3634
1844					1314	Add. 257*, TC 3635
1845					1315	Add. 258*, TC 3636
1846					1316	Add. 259*, TC 3637
1847					1317	Add. 260*, TC 3638
1848						CBP 1347
1849					1318	Add. 261*, TC 3639
1850	1183		1552	1414	766	

Ratoldus	Ha. & Sp.	Pad.	Gellone	Angoulême	Winch.	Others
1851	1184	712	1554	1416	767	
1852	1679		1546	1409	764	
1853						CBP 42
1854	1185	713	1556	1418	769	
1855	732	714	1548	1411	1319	
1856	733	715	1549	1412	1320	
1857	734	716	1550	1413	1321	
1858					1322	
1859					1323	
1860					1324	
1861			1558	1419	1325	Add. 271*
1862			1559	1420	1326	Add. 272*
1863	1681			1421	1327	Add. 273*
1864			1561	1422	1328	Add. 274*
1865	1186	720	1562	1423	770	
1866	1187	721	1564	1425	771	
1867	1680		1555	1417	768	
1868						
1869	1188	722	1566	1427	773	
1870			1568	1435	1329	Add. 275*
1871			1569	1436	1330	Add. 276*
1872	1683		1570	1437	1331	Add. 277*
1873			1571	1438	1332	Add. 278*
1874			1572	1439	1333	Add. 279*
1875			1574	1441	1335	Add. 281*
1876	1684		1575	1442	1336	Add. 282*
1877			1576	1443	1337	Add. 283*
1878			1578	1444	1338	
1879			1573	1440	1334	Add. 284*
1880					1339	Add. 285*, TC 3647
1881					1340	Add. 286*, TC 3648
1882					1341	Add. 287*, TC 3649
1883					1342	Add. 288*, TC 3650
1884					1343	Add. 289*, TC 3651
1885					1344	Add. 290*, TC 3652
1886					1345	Add. 291*, TC 3653
1887					1346	Add. 292*, TC 3654
1888						CBP 1923
1889					1347	Add. 293*, TC 3655
1890					1348	Add. 294*, TC 3656
1891	735	726	1585	1450	1349	
1892	736	727	1586	1451	1350	

497

Ratoldus	Ha. & Sp.	Pad.	Gellone	Angoulême	Winch.	Others
1893	737	728	1587	1452	1351	
1894	738	729			1352	
1895	1189		1579	1145	774	
1896	1190	724	1581	1147	775	
1897	1682		1565	1426	772	
1898						
1899	1191	725	1583	1449	777	
1900	739	733	1596	1463	1353	
1901	740	734			1354	
1902	1687		1599	1466	1355	
1903	741	735			1356	
1904	742	736	1602		1357	
1905	743	737	1603	1469	1358	
1906	744	738			1359	
1907	1192		1590	1459	778	
1908	1193	730	1591	1460	779	
1909	1685			1448	776	
1910						CBP 101
1911	1194	732	1594	1462	781	
1912	745	739	1605	1474	1360	
1913	746	740			1361	
1914	747	741			1362	
1915	748	742	1608		1363	
1916	749	743			1365	
1917	1688				1366	
1918						CBP 1609
1919	750	744			1367	
1920			1613	1479	1368	
1921				1480	1369	
1922	1195		1615	1481	782	
1923	1196		1617	1483	783	
1924	1686		1593		780	
1925						CBP 340
1926	1197	747	1619	1485	785	
1927			1627	1493	1370	
1928			1628	1494	1371	
1929	1691		1629	1495	1372	
1930				1496	1373	
1931	751	751			1374	
1932	752	752	1633	1499	1375	
1933	1692		1634	1500	1376	
1934						CBP 1948

Ratoldus	Ha. & Sp.	Pad.	Gellone	Angoulême	Winch.	Others
1935	753	754			1377	
1936			1631	1497		
1937	754	755			1378	
1938	755	756			1379	
1939	1693				1380	
1940						CBP 1706
1941	756	758			1381	
1942	757	759	1641	1507	1382	
1943	758	760			1383	
1944	759	761	1644		1384	
1945	760	762	1646		1385	
1946	761	763			1386	
1947	1694		1648	1513	1387	
1948						CBP 1561
1949	762	764			1388	
1950	1198	748	1621	1487	786	
1951	1199	749	1623	1489	787	
1952	1689		1618	1484	784	
1953						CBP 725
1954	1200	750	1625	1491	789	
1955	763	768			(1389)	
1956	764	769				
1957	1696				1392	
1958	765	770				
1959	766	771	1659	1523	1394	
1960	767	772	1661	1525	1395	
1961	1697				1396	
1962						CBP 1695
1963	768	773	1663	1527	1397	
1964	770	774	1664	1528	1398	
1965	771	775	1666	1531	1400	
1966	1698		1667	1533	1401	
1967						CBP 817
1968	773	777			1402	
1969	774	778	1670	1537	1405	
1970	775	780			1403	
1971	776		1671		1399	
1972	777		1672	1538	790	
1973	778	781	1674	1539	791	
1974	779	782	1676	1541	800	
1975	1695					
1976	1768					CBP 1544

Ratoldus	Ha. & Sp.	Pad.	Gellone	Angoulême	Winch.	Others
1977	780	783	1678	1543	795	
1978			1705	1571	1411	
1979			1706	1572	1412	
1980			1707	1573	1413	
1981	781	784	1711	1577	796	
1982	782	785	1713	1579	797	
1983	1695		1714		800	
1984						CBP 663
1985	783	786	1715	1581	801	
1986			1708	1574	1414	
1987			1709	1575	1415	
1988			1710	1576	1416	
1989	784	787			1417	
1990	785	788			1418	
1991						CBP 286
1992	786	789			1419	
1993			1757	1621	1420	Add. 301*
1994			1758	1622	1421	Add. 302*
1995			1759		1422	
1996	1709					CBP 37
1997			1761	1624	1423	Add. 303*
1998	787	790	1720	1586	802	
1999	788	791	1722	1588	803	
2000	1703				798	
2001	1769					CBP 1722
2002	789	792	1724	1590	805	
2003	790	793	1726	1592	806	
2004	791	794	1727	1593	807	
2005	792	795			808	
2006	1705				809	
2007						CBP 909
2008	793	796			810	
2009	794	797	1733	1598	811	
2010	795	798			812	
2011	1706				813	
2012						CBP 1307
2013	796	799			814	
2014	797	800	1740	1605	815	
2015	798	801	1696	1564	816	
2016	799	802	1743	1607	817	
2017	800	803	1695	1561	818	
2018	801	804			819	

COLLATION TABLES

Ratoldus	Ha. & Sp.	Pad.	Gellone	Angoulême	Winch.	Others
2019	802	805	1746	1610	820	
2020	803	806			821	
2021	1707				822	
2022						CBP 1072
2023	804	807	1749	1613	823	
2024	805	808	1751	1615	824	
2025	806	809	1753	1617	825	
2026	1708				826	
2027						CBP 1200
2028	807	810	1755	1620	827	
2029	808	811	1650	1515		
2030	809		1651	1516		
2031	810	813	1734	1599		
2032	811	812	1693	1558		
2033	812	814	1694	1559		
2034	813	815		1560		

VOTIVES

Ratoldus	Sp.	TC	Gellone	Angoulême	Winch.	Others
2035		1806			1507	
2036		1807			1536	
2037						
2038		1808	1065			
2039						CBP 1804
2040		1809			1565	
2041		1810				
2042	1243	1882	74			
2043	1244	1883	314			
2044						
2045						CBP 1654
2046	1245	1884	359			
2047		1856				
2048		1857				
2049		1858				
2050						CBP 779
2051		1859				
2052		1860				
2053		1814			1522	
2054		1815			1550	
2055		1816				
2056						CBP 1696

Ratoldus	Sp.	TC	Gellone	Angoulême	Winch.	Others
2057		1817			1582	
2058		1818				
2059		2302	2772		1521	
2060		2303			1549	
2061		2304	2779		1580	
2062		2306*			602, 608	
2063		1835				
2064						Deshusses II, 302, 9
2065						Deshusses II, 302, 9
2066		1836			1681	
2067		1837				
2068						(CBP 2068)
2069		1838				
2070		1841			1508	
2071		1842			1537	
2072						
2073		1843			1567	
2074		1844				
2075	1323	2681	2176		1611	
2076	1324	2682	208		1612	
2077	1325	2684	1851			
2078	1326	2685			1614	
2079	1327	2686	900		1615	
2080		2320			1524	
2081		2321			1551	
2082		2322			1583	
2083		2335				
2084		2336				
2085		2338				
2086	1280	2111			1525	
2087	1281	2112				
2088	1282	2113			1553	
2089	1283	2114				
2090	1284	2115			1584	
2091	1285	2122				
2092	1286	2123				
2093	1287	2124				
2094	1288	2125				
2095	1289	2358	1860		1601	
2096	1290	2357	1853		1602	
2097	1292	2356	1852		1603	
2098	1293	2381			1604	

Ratoldus	Sp.	TC	Gellone	Angoulême	Winch.	Others
2099	1294	2382			1605	
2100	1295	2384			1606	
2101	1300		1855		1677	
2102	1301		1856		1678	
2103	1303		1859		1679	
2104	1304	2420			1528	
2105	1305	2421			1557	
2106	1306	2423			1590	
2107	1307	2424				
2108		2242			1529	
2109	1309	2243	2590		1558	
2110	1310	2245	2593		1592	
2111	1313	2736	2791		1635	
2112	1314	2731	2798		1636	
2113	1315	4482	2804		1638	
2114	1316	4485	2809		1639	
2115	1317	2730	2790		1642	
2116	1318	2732	2792		1643	
2117	1726	2736				
2118	1319	2735	2797		1644	
2119	1320	2757	2805		1645	
2120	1321	2758	2806		1646	
2121	1322	2759	2808		1647	
2122	1343	2575	2764		1519	
2123		2576			1548	
2124	1345	2577	2766		1578	
2125	1346	2475	2681		1616	
2126	Ha 536	2476			1617	
2127	1348	2477	2685		1618	
2128	1349	2603	2711		1673	
2129	1350	2604	2713		1674	
2130	1351	2606	2715		1675	
2131	1352	2607	2716		1676	
2132	1353	2654	2738		1667	
2133	1354	2655	2740		1668	
2134	1355	2657	2742		(1669)	
2135	1356	2658	2743			
2136	1357	2651	2723		1664	
2137	1358	2652	2724		1665	
2138	1359	2653	2725		1666	
2139	1360	2660	2731		1670	
2140	1361	2661	2734		1671	

Ratoldus	Sp.	TC	Gellone	Angoulême	Winch.	Others
2141	1362	2662	2736		1672	
2142	1363	1624	2663		1649	
2143	1365	2626			1651	
2144	1366	2620	2662		1648	
2145	1367	2623	2664		1652	
2146	1368	2621	2665		1653	
2147	1369	2622	2667		1654	
2148	1370	2642			1656	
2149	1371	2644				
2150	1372	2638	2669		1655	
2151	1373	2639	2671		1658	
2152	1374	2640	2673		1659	
2153	1375	2641	2670		1660	
2154	1376	2636	2678		1661	
2155	1377	2647	2679		1662	
2156	1378	2648	2680		1663	
2157	1487	4398	2105		1754	
2158	1488		2106		1755	
2159	1489		2107		1756	
2160	1490				1757	
2161	1491		2108		1758	
2162	1492		2109		1759	
2163	1493		2110		1760	
2164	1494		2111		1761	
2165	1495		2112		1762	
2166	1496		2113		1763	
2167	1497				1764	
2168	1498				1765	
2169	1499		2114		1766	
2170	1501		2141		1768	
2171	1502		2138		1769	
2172	1503		2142		1770	
2173	1504		2134		1771	
2174	1505		2137		1772	
2175	1506		2140			
2176	1507				1774	
2177	1508		2143		1775	
2178	1509				1776	
2179	1311		2581			
2180	1312		2582			
2181		4292				
2182	1475		2864			

COLLATION TABLES

Ratoldus	Sp.	TC	Gellone	Angoulême	Winch.	Others
2183	1476		2862			
2184	1477		2865			
2185	1478		2875			
2186	1479		2876			
2187	1480		2877			
2188	1481		2873			
2189	1482		2869			
2190	1483		2870			
2191	1484		2867			
2192	1485		2868			
2193	1486		2874			

ORDER FOR THE VISITATION OF THE SICK

Ratoldus	Sp.	TC	Lanalet	Robert	Winch.	Others
2194						Cambrai 9
2195			(135)	(290–91)		Cambrai 10
2196			136	291, 1		
2197			(136-7)	(291)		(Cambrai 20)
2198		4016		290, 5	1794	
2199			135, 5	292, 2	1796	Cambrai 24
2200			136, 3	292, 6	1797	Cambrai 25
2201			136, 1	292, 7	1798	Cambrai 26
2202			136, 5	292, 8	1802	Cambrai 27
2203			137, 1	293, 2	1801	Cambrai 30
2204			136, 10	293, 1	1803	Cambrai 29
2205			137, 3	293, 3	1804	Cambrai 31
2206			137, 5	293, 4	1805	Cambrai 32
2207		4002	137, 7	293, 5	(1793)	
2208		4012	135, 3	292, 9	(1795)	Cambrai 33
2209		4010	137, 9		1791	
2210		4003		293, 6	1792	Cambrai 34
2211						
2212						(Cambrai 42)
2213		3994		294, 5	1814	
2214				295, 4		
2215		2791		295, 5	1823	
2216		2782			1828	
2217				295, 6		
2218				295, 7		
2219				295, 8		
2200				295, 9	1839	

505

Ratoldus	Sp.	TC	Lanalet	Robert	Winch.	Others
2221		2783			1829	
2222	1732				1833	
2223			110, 2			CBP 1575
2224				296, 1		
2225		2793				
2226	1510		2400			
2227	1511		2401			
2228	1512		2403			
2229	1513		2404			
2230	1514a–c		2405			
2231						Leofric 2479
2232	1386	3981			1788	
2233	1387	3982				
2234	1388	3983	2878		1808	
2235	1389	3984	2879		1809	
2236	1390	3985	2880		1810	
2237	1391	3986	2881		1811	
2238	1395		2887		1813	

ORDER OF THE DEAD

Ratoldus	Sp.	TC	Gellone	Robert	Winch.	Others
2239				297, 2		Deshusses III, 171–5
2240				297, 2		for ordo
2241	1415	4068		297, 4	1841	
2242		4071		297, 5	1842	
2243				297-8		
2244		4063		298, 2	1843	
2245				298, 3		
2246		4059	2901	298, 4	1844	
2247				(298, 5)		
2248		4072		299, 1	1845	
2249		4073		299, 2	1846	
2250				299, 3		
2251	1400	4048		299, 4	1847	
2252		4051				
2253				299, 5		
2254		2878		299, 7	1895	
2255						
2256						
2257		2879			1849	
2258					1850	

Ratoldus	Sp.	TC	Gellone	Robert	Winch.	Others
2259		2880*		300, 1	1851	
2260		2880			1852	
2261	1401	4032			1853	
2262						
2263	1399	4030			1854	
2264						
2265	1402	4033		300, 9	1855	
2266						
2267	1403	4034		300, 2	1856	
2268				300, 11		
2269	1398	4029	2899	300, 12	1857	
2270				301, 1		
2271	1409	4040			1858	
2272				301, 3		
2273	1410	4041		301, 4	1859	
2274				301, 5		
2275	1411	4042	(2915)	301, 7	1860	
2276	1412	4043	2910	301, 8	1861	
2277	1407	4038		302, 1	1862	
2278	1408	4039		302, 2	1863	
2279	1412	4043	(2910)		1864	
2280	1414	4045		302, 3	1865	
2281	1413	4044	2916	302, 4	1866	
2282				302, 5		
2283		(4072)		303, 1	1866	
2284						
2285	1404	4035		303, 2	1867	
2286	1416	2960	2968			
2287	1417	2961	2969			
2288	1735	2966		303, 5		
2289	1418	2963	2971			
2290	1419	2964	2972			
2291	1429	2895	3006	308, 3	1876	
2292	1430	2896	3007	308, 4		
2293	1431	2897	3008			
2294	1432	2898	3009			
2295	1420	2911	2953		1868	
2296	1421	2912	2955		1869	
2297	1422	2913	2956		1870	
2298	1423	2914	2957		1871	
2299	1424	2924	2963		1872	
2300	1425	2925	2964		1873	

Ratoldus	Sp.	TC	Gellone	Robert	Winch.	Others
2301	1426	2926	2965		1874	
2302	1427	2927	2966		1875	
2303	1428	2928	2967			
2304	1433	3018	2973			
2305	1434	3020	2975			
2306	1435	3022	2977			
2307	1436	3023	2978			
2308	1437	3028	2979			
2309	1438	3029	2981			
2310		3033				
2311	1439	3030	2982			
2312	1440	3031	2983			
2313	1441	3046	2984	309, 3		
2314	1442	3047	2985	309, 4		
2315	1443	3048	2987	309, 5		
2316	1444	2935	2988	310, 2		
2317	1445	2937	2990	310, 3		
2318	1446	2938	2991			
2319	1447	2939	2992	310, 4		
2320	1448	3079		311, 4		
2321	1449	3080		311, 5		
2322	1450	3081		312, 1		

Additions

Ratoldus	Sp.	TC	Gellone	Robert	Winch.	Others
2323		2837		305, 2		
2324		2841				
2325						Deshusses, III, 300
2326						Deshusses, III, 300
2327		3069				
2328		2838		305, 3		
2329		2839				
2330		2840		305, 5		
2331		3085		310, 5		
2332	1416	3086		310, 6		
2333	1417	3087		310, 7		
2334	1418	2960		306, 5		
2335	1419	2961				
2336		2963				
2337		2964				
2238						Eligius 36, 5

INDEX OF MANUSCRIPTS CITED

INDEX OF BLESSINGS, EXORCISMS
AND PRAYERS

513

Benedictionem domine nobis conferat salutarem sacra semper oblatio ut quod agit, 1207

Benedictionem tuam domine populus fidelis accipiat qua corpore saluatus ac mente et, 2130

Benedictionum suarum super nos dominus imbrem infundat et claritatis suae thesauros, 1276

Benedictionum suarum super uos dominus ymbrem infundat et orationes uestras exaudiat, 1782

Caelestem nobis praebeant haec mysteria quaesumus domine medicinam et uitia nostri, 1896

Caelesti lumine quaesumus domine semper et ubique nos praeueni ut mysterium cuius, 1197

Caelestia dona capientibus quaesumus domine non ad iudicium peruenire patiaris quod, 758

Caelestibus domine pasti deliciis quaesumus ut semper eadem per quę ueraciter uiuimus, 453

Caelestibus refecti sacramentis et gaudiis supplices te domine depraecamur ut quorum, 1903

Caelestibus refecti sacramentis et gaudiis supplices te rogamus domine ut quorum, 1694, 1802

Caelestis doni benedictione percepta supplices te deus omnipotens deprecamur ut hoc idem, 522, 790

Caelestis lumine quaesumus domine semper et ubique nos praeueni ut mysterium cuius nos, 352

Caelestis uitae munere uegetati quaesumus domine ut quod est nobis in praesenti uita, 530

Christus rex regum ex aeuo qui regnat in aeuum istum confortet regem sua iura tenentem, 173

Clementiam tuam domine suppliciter exoramus ut pachalis muneris sacramentum quod, 1203

Clementissime domine cuius inenarrabilis uirtus cuius mynisteria archani mira caelebrantur, 50

Colla iugo subdenda tuo deus alme sacrato ad cuius dignum pretiosa morte sepulchrum, 1079

Commune uotum permaneat communis oratio prosequatur ut hi totius ecclesiae prece qui, 623

Communicantes et diem sacratissimum caelebrantes quo dominus noster iesus christus pro, 857

Communicantes et diem sacratissimum caelebrantes quo unigenitus tuus in tua tecum gloria coaeternus, 332

Communicantes et diem sacratissimum celebrantes quo dominus noster unigenitus filius tuus unitam, 1263

Communicantes et diem sacratissimum pentecosten praeuenientes quos spiritus sanctus apostolis, 1330

Communicantes et memoriam uenerantes inprimis gloriosę semper uirginis marię genetricis dei et domini, 221

---

[1]   *martalium* before correction.

[1]   *cessis* before correction.

Quaesumus omnipotens deus ut qui caelestia alimenta percepimus intercedentibus sanctis,   1298, 1849

Quaesumus omnipotens deus ut qui caelestia alimenta percepimus per haec contra omnia,   494

Quaesumus omnipotens deus ut quorum nos tribuis communicare memoriis eorum facias,   1930

Quaesumus omnipotens deus ut quos diuina tribuis participatione gaudere humanis non,   1745, 1764

Quaesumus omnipotens deus ut sanctorum tuorum caelestibus mysteriis caelebrata,   1397

Quam oblationem tu deus in omnibus quaesumus benedictam adscriptam ratam,   223

Quantum humana fragilitas nosse sinit et scio et testificor ipsos dignos ad huius onus,   606

Quesumus domine deus noster diei molestias noctis quietae sustenta ut necessaria,   2177

Quesumus omnipotens deus ut famulus tuus rex noster qui tua miseratione suscepit regni,   170

Qui pridie quam pro nostra omnium salute pateretur hoc est hodie accepit panem in,   859

Qui super astra sedes qui regni sceptra tueris summus adesto deus mihimet tua iussa,   1085

Quia nostrae uoces domine non merentur audire sancti germani confessoris tui atque,   1583

Quod ore sumpsimus domine mente capiamus et de munere temporali fiat nobis remedium,   795

Quos caelesti domine alimento satiasti apostolicis intercessionibus ab omni aduersitate,   1489, 1495

Quos caelesti domine dono satiasti praesta quaesumus ut a nostris mundemur ocultis et ab,   1510

Quos caelesti domine mysterio refecisti propriis et alienis quaesumus propitiatus absolue,   2134

Quos caelesti recreas munere perpetuo domine comitare praesidio et quos fouere non,   2110

Quos caelestibus domine recreas alimentis interueniente beato confessore tuo benedicto,   1533

Quos ieiunia uotiua castigant tua domine sacramenta uiuificent ut terrenis affectibus,   1402

Quos tantis domine largiris uti mysteriis quaesumus ut effectibus eorum ueraciter aptare,   399

Rectitudo regis est nouiter ordinati et in solium sublimati haec tria praecepta populo,   155

Redemptionis nostrae munere uegetati quaesumus domine ut hoc perpetuae salutis,   1179

Refecti cibo potuque caelesti deus noster te supplices deprecamur ut in cuius haec,   284

Suscipe domine praeces nostras pro anima famuli tui .ill. ut si quae ei maculae de
terrenis,   2294
Suscipe domine propitius hostias quibus et te placari uoluisti et nobis salutem
potenti,   1908
Suscipe domine propitius orationem nostram cum oblationibus hostiarum super
impositis,   1679, 1824
Suscipe domine quaesumus praeces populi tui cum oblationibus hostiarum ut
paschalibus,   1059, 1101, 1131
Suscipe domine sacrificium cuius te uoluisti dignanter immolatione placare praesta,
529
Suscipe munera domine quae in beatę agatae martyris tuae sollempnitate deferimus
cuius,   423
Suscipe munera domine quae in eius tibi sollemnitate deferimus cuius nos
confidimus,   281
Suscipe munera quaesumus domine exultantis ecclesiae et cui causam tanti gaudii,
1183
Suscipe munera quaesumus domine quae tibi de tua largitate deferimus ut haec,
1562
Suscipe quaesumus domine hostias leuitarum tuorum quibus mentium integritates
tuo,   625
Suscipe quaesumus domine munera dignanter oblata et beati marcelli
suffragantibus,   359
Suscipe quaesumus domine munera nostris oblata seruitus et tua propitius dona
sanctifica,   562
Suscipe quaesumus domine munera populorum tuorum propitius ut confessione
tui,   1158
Suscipe quaesumus domine praeces famulorum tuorum cum oblationibus hostiarum
et tua,   2120
Suscipe quaesumus domine praeces populi tui cum oblationibus hostiarum et tua
mysteria,   709
Suscipe sancta trinitas deus hanc oblationem quam tibi offero pro anima famuli tui
ill. ut,   2327
Suscipe sancta trinitas hanc oblationem quam tibi offero in memoriam
incarnationis,   ii
Suscipiamus domine misericordiam tuam in medio templi tui et reparationis nostrae,
1977

Tabernaculum hoc ingredire quaesumus omnipotens deus sempiternae et famulos
tuos,   78
Tantis domine repleti muneribus praesta quaesumus ut et salutaria dona capiamus et
a tua,   1389
Te igitur clementissime pater per iesum christum filium tuum dominum nostrum,
219, 1105
Te inuocamus domine sanctae pater omnipotens aeternae deus ut hunc famulum
tuum .N.,   135
Te lucem ueram et lucis auctorem domine depraecamur ut digneris a nobis tenebras,
2163

INDEX OF PREFACES

586

VD aeterne deus. Et tuam inmensam clementiam supplici uoto deposcere ut nos
famulos tuos, 717

VD aeterne deus. Et tuam iugiter exorare clementiam ut mentes nostras quas
conspicis terrenis, 689

VD aeterne deus. Et tuam maiestatem humiliter implorare ut iesus christus filius
tuus dominus noster sua nos, 1834

VD aeterne deus. Et tuam misaericordiam depraecari ut mentibus nostris beati
hieronimi presbiteri repetita sollemnitate, 1825

VD aeterne deus. Et tuam misericordiam exorare ut te annuente ualeamus quae
mala sunt declinare, 1589

VD aeterne deus. Et tuam misericordiam totis nisibus exorare ne pro nostra nos
iniquitate condempnes, 1563

VD aeterne deus. Et tuam omnipotentiam deuotis praecibus implorare ut nos
spiritus tui lumen infundat, 1370

VD aeterne deus. Et tuam suppliciter misericordiam implorare ut exercitatio
ueneranda ieiunii, 739

VD aeterne deus. Et tui misericordiam muneris postulare ut tempora quibus post
resurrectionem, 1228

VD aeterne deus. Exibentes sollemne ieiunium quo beati iohannis baptistae
natalicia praeuenimus, 1457

VD aeterne deus. Honorandi patris benedicti gloriosum caelebrantes diem in quo
hoc saeculum, 466

VD aeterne deus. Honorum auctor et distributor omnium dignitatum, 636

VD aeterne deus. Humiliter depraecantes ut intercedente beata maria semper
uirgine nos ab omnibus, 1651

VD aeterne deus. In hac die migrationis ad christum sanctissimi sacerdotis cutberhti
qui in primo, 461

VD aeterne deus. Inluminator et redemptor animarum nostrarum qui nos per
primum adam abstinentiae, 646

VD aeterne deus. Maiestatem tuam propensius implorantes ut quanto magis dies
salutifere festiuitatis, 773

VD aeterne deus. Maiestatem tuam suppliciter depraecantes ut expulsis azimis
uetustatis illius agni cibo, 1909

VD aeterne deus. Maiestatem tuam suppliciter depraecantes ut opem tuam
petentibus dignanter, 1508

VD aeterne deus. Misericordiae dator et totius bonitatis auctor qui ieiuniis
orationibus et elemosinis, 768

VD aeterne deus. Nos te in tuis sacratissimis uirginibus exultantibus animis laudare
benedicere et praedicare, 2072

VD aeterne deus. Per mediatorem dei et hominum iesum christum dominum
nostrum qui mediante, 745

VD aeterne deus. Pro annua dedicatione tabernaculi huius laudes tibi gratiasque
referre cuius uirtus, 195

VD aeterne deus. Quamuis enim illius sublimis angelicae substantiae sit habitatio
semper in caelis, 2049

VD aeterne deus. Qui beatum augustinum confessorem tuum et scientiae
documentis replesti, 1700

VD aeterne deus. Qui infirmitate uirtutum perficis et humani generis inimicum non solum per uiros sed etiam, 1933

VD aeterne deus. Qui inuisibili potentia sacramentorum tuorum mirabiliter operaris effectum, 1049

VD aeterne deus. Qui iusto pioque moderamine et pro peccatis flagella inrogas et post flagella ueniam, 1772

VD aeterne deus. Qui non solum peccata dimittis sed ipsos etiam iustificas peccatores et reis non, 2021

VD aeterne deus. Qui nos assiduis martyrum passionibus consolaris et eorum sanguinem triumphalem, 1947

VD aeterne deus. Qui nos castigando sanas et refouendo benignus erudis dum magis uis saluos esse, 1665

VD aeterne deus. Qui nos collectis terrae frugibus per abstinentiam tibi gratias agere uoluisti ut ex ipso die, 1768

VD aeterne deus. Qui nos de donis bonorum temporalium ad perceptionem prouegis aeternorum, 1726

VD aeterne deus. Qui ob animarum medelam ieiunii deuotione castigari corpora praecepisti concede, 667

VD aeterne deus. Qui peccantium non uis animas perirę sed culpas et peccantes non semper continuo, 705

VD aeterne deus. Qui peccato primi parentis hominem a salutis finibus exulantem pietatis indulgentiam, 321

VD aeterne deus. Qui praecursorem filii tui tanto munere ditasti ut pro ueritatis praeconio capite plecteretur, 1707

VD aeterne deus. Qui propterea iure punis errantes et clementer refoues castigatos ut nos a malis operibus, 1867

VD aeterne deus. Qui rationabilem creaturam ne temporalibus dedita bonis ad praemia sempiterna, 487

VD aeterne deus. Qui salutem humani generis in ligno crucis constituisti ut unde mors oriebatur, 2067

VD aeterne deus. Qui sanctificator et institutor es abstinentiae cuius nullus finis nullusque est numerus, 2011

VD aeterne deus. Qui sanctorum martyrum tuorum dionisii rustici et eleutherii pia certamina ad copiosam, 1847

VD aeterne deus. Qui sic nos tribuis sollemne tibi deferre ieiunium ut indulgentiae tuae speremus, 794

VD aeterne deus. Qui sic tribuis ecclesiam tuam sanctorum commemoratione proficere ut eam semper illorum, 1716

VD aeterne deus. Qui tui nominis agnitione et tuae potentiae tibi sapientiam reuelare uoluisti ut tuam confitentes, 2055

VD aeterne deus. Qui tuo inenarrabili munerę praestitisti ut natura humana ad similitudinem tui condita dissimilis, 2000

VD aeternae deus. Qui ut de hoste generis humani maior, 248

VD aeterne deus. Qui uicit diabolum et mundum hominemque paradyso restituit et uitae ianuas credentibus patefecit, 1808

VD aeterne deus. Quia competenter atque salubriter religiosa sunt nobis instituta ieiunia ut corporeae, 558

VD aeterne deus. Te domine sancte pater omnipotens aeterne deus qui beatum
medardum, 1392
VD aeterne deus. Te in tuorum apostolorum glorificantes honore qui et illis tribuisti
beatitudinem, 1876
VD aeterne deus. Te quidem omni tempore sed in hac potissimum nocte gloriosius
conlaudare et praedicare, 1128, 1129
VD aeterne deus. Te quidem omni tempore sed in hoc potissimum die gloriosius
praedicare, 1128, 1129
VD aeterne deus. Te suppliciter exorantes ut sic nostra sanctificentur ieiunia quo
cunctorum, 778
VD aeterne deus. Teque in sanctorum tuorum confessionibus laudare in cuius facta
sunt uirtute uictores, 1731
VD aeterne deus. Tuamque in sanctorum tuorum cornelii simul et cypriani
festiuitate praedicare, 1739
VD aeterne deus. Tuamque misẹricordiam suppliciter exorare ut ieiuniorum
nostrorum sacrosancta, 710
VD aeterne deus. Venientem natalem beatorum martyrum tuorum dyonisii rustici et
eleutherii debita seruitute, 1842
VD aeterne deus. Vt propensiori cura et adtentiori famulatu tibi seruitutis officia
deferamus hoc praesertim in tempore, 39
VD aeterne deus. Vt quia tui est operis sed quod tibi placitum est aut cogitemus aut
agamus, 1256

VD gratias agere. Vota soluere munera consecrare domine sanctae pater omnipotens
aeterne deus, 350

VD per christum. Cuius hodie circumcisionis diem et natiuitatis octauum
caelebrantes tua domine, 311
VD per christum. Cuius hodie faciem in confessione praeuenimus et uoce supplici
exoramus, 234
VD per christum. Cuius nos humanitas colligit humilitas aerigit traditio obsoluit
poena redemit, 820
VD per christum. Cuius salutiferẹ passionis et gloriosẹ resurrectionis dies
adpropinquare noscuntur, 826
VD per christum. In quo ieiunantium fides additur spes prouehitur caritas roboratur
ipse, 546
VD per christum. Per quem discipulis spiritus sanctus in terra datur ob dilectionem
proximi et de caelo, 1352
VD per christum. Per quem nobis indulgentia largitur et pax per omne saeculum
praedicatur, 815
VD per christum. Per quem pietatem tuam suppliciter petimus ut spiritus sanctus
corda nostra, 1357
VD per christum. Per quem te suppliciter deprecamur ut altare hoc sanctis usibus
praeparatum, 91
VD per christum. Pro cuius nomine gloriosus leuita uincentius et miles inuictus
rabidi hostis, 392
VD per christum. Pro cuius nomine poenarum mortisque contemptum in utroque
sexu, 424

INDEX OF CHANT AND READINGS

COMMUNIONS

GRADUALS

HYMNS, CANTICLES, REPROACHES, ETC.

INTROITS

OFFERTORIES AND OFFERTORY VERSES

PSALMS AND PSALM VERSES

READINGS

RESPONSES

TRACTS AND TRACT VERSES

VERSICLES AND PRECES